Understanding International Trade Law

Understanding International Trade Law

SIMONE SCHNITZER
Assessorin
Doktor der Rechte (Dr. Jur., summa cum laude)
Senior Lecturer in Law, Northumbria University, Newcastle upon Tyne

LawMatters
PUBLISHING

Published by Law Matters Publishing
Law Matters Limited
33 Southernhay East
Exeter EX1 1NX
Tel: 01392 215577
www.lawmatterspublishing.co.uk

British Library Cataloguing-in-Publication Data

A catalogue record for this book is available from the British Library.

ISBN   1 84641 002 9

Typeset by Pantek Arts Ltd, Maidstone, Kent

Printed by Ashford Colour Press Ltd, Gosport, Hampshire

Contents

3

4   **Contracts of Affreightment**   **99**

5   **Marine Cargo Insurance**   **152**

Acknowledgements

I would like to take this opportunity to express my deep thanks to everyone who has supported me throughout my personal and professional life and particularly my parents Dr Günter and Marianne Schnitzer. There are many people who deserve gratitude. Named below are only a few who have supported me on a professional and personal level during the last months.

The support, enthusiasm and the helpful comments of my colleagues, Dr Rhona Smith, Prof Ann Kenny, Busola Akande, Jenny Adams and Ralph Tiernan and my partner, Dr John Lamont-Black were invaluable. Thank you from the depth of my heart. Without Dr Rhona Smith's enthusiasm and hands-on support, I would not have even started.

I am very grateful for all the support which I received from Northumbria School of Law and my colleagues. Many thanks also to the numerous authors of books in this subject area from which I was able to draw inspiration and understanding.

My deep appreciation and thanks also to the whole team at Law Matters Publishing for their friendly, efficient and professional support, particularly to Jeremy Stein, David Stott and Alison Morley.

This book is dedicated to my partner, John and everyone who brings love and light to this world.

'May law be used to enhance our relationships and to live together in peace and harmony, rather than to abuse the weaker or less knowledgeable party.'

Copyright acknowledgements

The GAFTA form contracts No 100 and No 119 in appendix B and C are reproduced with kind permission of the Grain and Feed Trade Association, London. I am most grateful to Kirby Johnson and Lisa Gray for their kindness.

The SITPRO forms and documents in appendices D–N are reproduced with kind permission of the Simplifying International Trade Ltd, London. I am particularly grateful to Gordon Cragge for all his efforts.

Copyright permission for the reproduction of the BIMCO forms and rules in appendices O–Z was received from the Baltic and International Maritime Council, Copenhagen. Peter Holst dealt with the request in a quick and welcoming manner for which I am deeply grateful.

I have endeavoured to state the law as it stands at 1 June 2005, but was able to include some new developments up to 1 October 2005. The web pages referred to in the text were in operation at the time of writing, but may be subject to change.

Simone Schnitzer
Newcastle
10 October 2005

List of cases

List of statutes

List of statutory instruments

International Conventions

European Instruments:

List of abbreviations

AA 1996	Arbitration Act 1996
Arrest Convention 1952	International Convention for Unification of Certain Rules relating to the Arrest of Seagoing Ships 1952
BoEA 1882	Bills of Exchange Act 1882
bol	bill of lading contract
Bolero	Bill of Lading Electronic Registration organisation
BC	Brussels Convention 1968
c & f	cost and freight
cfr	cost and freight
chp	charterparty
cif	cost, insurance, freight
CIM	International Convention concerning, the Carriage of Goods by Rail
cip	carriage and insurance paid to
CISG	UN Convention on Contracts for the International Sale of Goods 1980
CJJA 1982	Civil Jurisdiction and Judgments Act 1982
CJJO	Civil Jurisdiction and Judgments Order 2001
CMI	Comité Maritime International
CMR	Convention on International Carriage of Goods by Road
CoGSA 1992	Carriage of Goods by Sea Act 1992
COTIF 1980	Convention concerning International Carriage of Goods by Rail
cpt	carriage paid to
daf	delivered at frontier
ddp	delivered duty paid
ddu	delivered duty unpaid
deq	delivered ex quay
des	delivered ex ship
ECJ	European Court of Justice
EEO Reg	Regulation 805/2004/EC
ERPL	European Review of Private Law
fas	free alongside ship
fca	free carrier
fcl	full container load

FIATA	International Federation of Freight Forwarders Associations
fiost	free in out stowed and trimmed
fob	free on board
for	free on rail
FOSFA	Federation of Oils, Seeds and Fats Association Ltd
fot	free on truck
GAFTA	Grain and Feed Trade Association
Hague Rules	International Convention for the Unification of Certain Rules Relating to Bills of Lading 1924
Hague-Visby Rules	Hague Rules as amended by the Brussels Protocol 1968
Hamburg Rules	UN Convention on the Carriage of Goods by Sea 1978
HVR	Hague-Visby Rules
ICAO	International Civil Aviation Organisation
ICC	International Chamber of Commerce
IMO	International Maritime Organisation
Incoterms	International Commercial Terms of the International Chamber of Commerce
Intraterms	International Trade Terms
ISP 98	International Standby Practices
JBL	Journal of Business Law
JIML	Journal of International Maritime Law
LC	Lugano Convention 1988
l/c	letter of credit
lcl	less than full container load
LMCLQ	Lloyd's Maritime and Commercial Law Quarterly
MC	Montreal Convention
MIA 1906	Marine Insurance Act 1906
MSA 1995	Merchant Shipping Act 1995
OTIF	Intergovernmental Organisation for International Carriage by Rail
PILMPA 1995	Private International Law (Miscellaneous Provisions) Act 1995
ppi	policy proof of interest
RC 1980	Rome Convention on the Law applicable to Contractual Obligations 1980
Ro-Ro	roll on-roll off
SGSA 1982	Supply of Goods and Services Act 1982
SoGA 1979	Sale of Goods Act 1979
UCC 522	Uniform Rules for Collections (1995 revision)
UCP	Uniform Customs and Practices for Documentary Credits
UCTA 1977	Unfair Contract Terms Act 1977
UNCITRAL	UN Commission on International Trade Law
UNCTAD	UN Conference on Trade and Development
UNIDROIT	International Institute for the Unification of Private Law
URCG	ICC's Uniform Rules for Contract Guarantees
URDG	ICC's Uniform Rules for Demand Guarantees
Vienna Convention 1980	UN Convention on Contracts for the International Sale of Goods
WC	Warsaw Convention

1 Introduction

1.1 Aims of this book

In an increasingly global market, the growing importance of international trade law is evident. Not only law students benefit from a greater understanding of the issues and pitfalls that threaten the success of international business transactions, but businesses may want to obtain an understanding of their role, as well as their legal rights and duties.

Therefore, this book aims to introduce and clarify, in easy language, some of the many issues relating to international trade law. The book focuses mainly on the international sale transaction of goods carried by sea, and intends to introduce the reader to the relevant contractual and factual matters in this context. Brief mention will be made of other forms of carriage of goods. We will start by discussing the main issues relating to the international character of the sale contract and the financial arrangements enabling the seller and buyer to secure payment and finance regardless of the distance and borders between them. We will then look at the carriage arrangements made to get the goods from A to B, the insurance for the goods in transit, and any dispute resolution questions caused by the international aspects of trade. The last includes such diverse questions as: arbitration or litigation; which country's courts will have jurisdiction; and which law will the courts apply to the matter? General issues on domestic commercial and contract law, however, are beyond the remit of this text and are best researched by consulting a specialised textbook in the matter.

In order to help the newcomer to this subject to get a good foundation and overview, the emphasis will be on understanding the bigger picture and how the above areas interlink, rather than providing detailed and easily confusing depth at this stage. Thus a logical and structural approach has been taken, supported by many checklists and charts to provide a useful guide for the reader. Once this understanding has been achieved the reader may wish to venture into greater depth using specific textbooks and practitioner guides, which focus on a detailed analysis of individual issues and cases. There are many good books on the market. To help the reader in his initial attempt to consolidate and deepen his knowledge, a list of books is provided in **Chapter 8**. This list is by no means conclusive, but should facilitate further research. In addition there are many books, particularly in the area of commercial law and business law, which cover aspects of international trade law within their field.

1.2 How to use this book

Alongside reading this book you are strongly recommended to familiarise yourself directly with the conventions and statutes referred to in the text. Within the limits of this book only the broad sense of these materials can be conveyed. It is essential for the law student to get used to working with and researching extraneous sources of law. Therefore, law students are urged to use the following educational and practical tool: a statute book. A list of statute books for this purpose is included in Chapter 8. Whilst reading this or any other textbook, consult the relevant statute book and directly study the exact wording and context of the legislation referred to. Constantly ask yourself whether you would have come to the same conclusion as the textbook, by consulting the relevant piece of legislation. This will enable you to develop a systematic approach and to develop the relevant legal skills. These are essential for a successful life in practice. Once you have acquired these skills you will have the tools available to work out any solution you need, regardless of whether or when you had studied this area of law before.

In order to supplement the discussion of the law, a sample of forms used in international trade practice has been included. These forms have been developed by international organisations according to their research into the needs of the industry. In order to develop a clearer picture, you should try to refer to the relevant forms and rules as you study the individual chapters. Further, in **1.3** below, efforts have been made to introduce you to the skills of researching the status of conventions. Only then can you determine the application of a convention.

1.3 How to research the status of treaties and conventions

The best way to ensure up-to-date information is to research the contracting States to a convention via the depositing State or international body of the convention. All States ratifying a convention have to notify the depository for the ratification to be internationally effective. The name of the convention can be the first indicator. Thus, the United Nations is the depository for UN conventions, for example the United Nations Convention on the Carriage of Goods by Sea 1978 (the Hamburg Rules). Also, in many cases the government of the State where the convention was signed will be the depository, for example the Belgian government is the depository for the International Convention for the Unification of Certain Rules Relating to Bills of Lading of 1924 (known as the Hague Rules) and for the Brussels Protocol of 1968 (known as the Hague-Visby Rules), both done at Brussels (see its treaty website at http://www.diplomatie.be/en/treaties/default.asp). (See **Chapter 4** for further information on these carriage conventions.)

A good source of information is the internet, but the information given on sites other than those maintained by the depositories should always be regarded with caution. A country's Foreign Office usually gives information on the treaties ratified by it; for example the UK Foreign and Commonwealth Office provides a treaty enquiry service free of charge. It maintains a database of all treaties to which the UK is, or has been, party. Links to this service (use the 'enquiries service' button) and to the sites of other depository countries (use the 'useful links' button) can be found via: http://www.fco.gov.uk/treaty. The contracting States to treaties to which the UK is party can also be found in *Halsbury's Laws of England*, which is an excellent source for matters of English Law. Here you will need to access the relevant sections, for example 'Carriage of goods by sea' for sea carriage conventions (Volume 43(2), Chapter 14).

The UN Treaty site (see http://untreaty.un.org/) can only be researched by subscribers, but the full text, the status and the contracting States to UN conventions developed by the United Nations Commission on International Trade Law (UNCITRAL) can also be in found on UNCITRAL's website via http://www.uncitral.org or more directly at http://www.uncitral.org/uncitral/en/index.html. There you can find this information, for example, on the:

(a) United Nations Convention on Contracts for the International Sale of Goods (signed in 1980 in Vienna, known as the 'Vienna Convention 1980'), referred to in **Chapter 2**;

(b) United Nations Convention on International Bills of Exchange and International Promissory Notes (signed in New York in 1988) and the United Nations Convention on Independent Guarantees and Stand-by Letters of Credit (signed in New York in 1995), referred to in **Chapter 3**;

(c) United Nations Convention on the Carriage of Goods by Sea (signed in 1978 in Hamburg, known as the 'Hamburg Rules'), referred to in **Chapter 4**; and

(d) United Nations Convention on the Recognition and Enforcement of Foreign Arbitral Awards (signed in New York in 1958), referred to in **Chapter 6**.

The full text and full status report for conventions developed by the Hague Conference on Private International Law can be found at http://hcch.e-vision.nl/index_en.php?act=conventions.listing. Information on the Conventions adopted by the International Maritime Organisation can be found at http://www.imo.org/home.asp. Information on the agreements concluded between the Member States of the European Union and between the European Communities and third parties can be found by searching the agreements database of the Council of the European Union at http://ue.eu.int/cms3_fo/showPage.asp?id=252&lang=EN.

1.4 Introduction to international trade law

International trade can be described as the sale of goods with an international element. This element could be present due to the fact that the seller and buyer are established in different countries, or that the goods have to be transported from one country to another, or that the parties have chosen a jurisdiction and/or law different from their domestic one. Some pieces of legislation provide their own definitions, in which case these definitions are crucial. For example both the United Nations Convention on Contracts for the International Sale of Goods 1980 (CISG) and the Unfair Contract Terms Act (UCTA) 1977 provide their own definitions. Both pieces of legislation focus on the parties having their place of business in different countries, but also add further criteria. The CISG does so in order to clarify its field of application, as it only deals with international sale contracts (CISG, art 1). On the other hand, the UCTA 1977 does not apply to international supply contracts. Thus, s 26 of the UCTA 1977 determines when the Act is not applicable.

Due to the international character of the contract, the seller and buyer bear additional risks to those incurred in domestic sales, such as the following.

Physical risks

Physical risks can arise due to the transportation of the goods, which may be over a huge distance and conducted by various means such as ships, planes, trains or lorries. The goods will be exposed to the risks inherent in the form of transportation, and for a substantial amount of time may be totally out of the seller's and/or buyer's control. Carriage and insurance arrangements therefore become of high importance. They can be arranged so as to give the parties to the sale contract a reasonably secure position concerning their rights over the goods. They also should provide for indemnity in case the goods are damaged or lost during transit.

Financial risks

Financial risks abound regarding exchange rate fluctuations and payment systems across more than one country. Most likely the contracting parties have no knowledge of each other's integrity, solvency and creditworthiness. Thus, neither will the seller want to dispatch the goods without the buyer providing some sort of security for payment, nor will the buyer want to pay the price before he has some kind of legal right over the goods. In addition, the parties may have to be careful not to block their cash flow whilst the goods are in transit. Therefore, payment systems and credit facilities (such as letters of credit or bills of exchange) will have to be adopted to secure the position of the parties, taking into account their individual needs and business relationship.

Legal risks

The parties may be confronted with foreign jurisdictions and/or laws, or they may have to enforce a judgment or an arbitral award in a foreign country. Cross-border dealings of the parties will automatically raise questions relating to the resolution of any disputes and may adversely affect practicality, length and costs of any proceedings. The parties would therefore be well advised to include 'choice of law' and jurisdiction clauses into their contract terms. They may also wish to opt for arbitration as a means of dispute resolution instead of litigation in the courts.

Political risks

Political risks could amount to such serious situations as wars, embargoes and blockades. If trading in a politically unstable area, it might be beneficial for the parties to take out extra insurance in addition to the ordinary marine policy, such as the 'Institute War Clauses' developed by the Institute of London Underwriters or the 'Institute Strike Clauses'.

Parties to an international sales transaction should therefore carefully plan their transactions. As indicated above, many of the risks can be minimised or avoided, by taking out appropriate insurance, or by contracting on carefully selected terms. To this end, trade terms and legal rules have shifted the emphasis away from the goods towards the documents that represent them (in particular the sales invoice, the transport document and the insurance policy), to the extent that some of the documents give title to the goods, or represent at least a means to indemnity, or to pledge as security for credit purposes.

Useful trade terms have been developed largely by trade custom and assimilated into English law. In order to avoid confusion caused by different interpretations of particular developed standard trade terms, some trade associations and international bodies have attempted to standardise these rules. The International Chamber of Commerce, for example, has developed the Incoterms (International Commercial Terms, which are international rules for the interpretation of trade terms), which are widely recognised. They are updated on a regular basis to reflect the changes in trade custom, the current version being the Incoterms 2000. In some countries these terms have customary or even statutory force, but in English law these terms will only be applicable if the parties have specifically and clearly chosen their incorporation into the contract. Some trade associations have their own standard contract forms, which are tailored to the particular needs of their trade and are well tested, some of which even provide for a specific dispute resolution mechanism. These standard contracts only apply if the parties to a contract of sale adopt them. Their terms can normally be varied according to the needs and wishes of the parties. Examples are: GAFTA forms developed by the Grain and Feed Trade Association or FOSFA forms drawn up by the Federation of Oils, Seeds and Fats Associations Limited.

On a supranational level international conventions have been developed in an attempt to harmonise the rules relating to international trade law. In order to identify whether such a convention is applicable we need to discern the States that have signed and ratified it. A given convention may be applicable to the contract, if the law that is held to govern the contract is the law of a contracting State to such a treaty. Therefore, we will discuss briefly the most relevant international conventions within the individual chapters in turn. However, because our study here focuses on international trade law from an English law perspective, our detailed discussions will concentrate on the treaties ratified by the United Kingdom.

To summarise, international sales law and the rules relating to the transport of such goods are found in a variety of sources:

(a) international conventions;

(b) statutes;

(c) common law;

(d) trade terms and customs;

(e) contract terms.

As we have seen above, the international sale contract necessarily results in further contractual relationships being created, to lead the initial sale contract to fruition. Thus the parties to the sale contract become parties to further contracts, which create rights and duties for them. A seemingly single business transaction results in a multitude of interrelated contracts. (Fig 1.1)

Fig 1.1 A multitude of contracts initiated by the international sales contract

This leads us to discuss the following questions over the next few chapters of this text.

(a) Which of the parties to the sale contract will have to arrange for these successive contracts and obligations, and who will be party to them?

(b) On which terms do the successive contracts have to be concluded, in order to fulfil the obligations derived from the sale contract?

(c) Which further rights and obligations will these contracts bring to (i) the initial parties (to the sale contract) and (ii) the further parties?

(d) Will failure to fulfil obligations in one contract have a knock-on effect on the others?

(e) What happens if a dispute arises in one of the contracts? Will this have an effect on the others?

(f) How can any disputes be resolved and which challenges need to be overcome?

We will start our investigation with the root of all the above obligations, the international sale contract and its possible variants.

2 The International Sale Contract

2.1 Introduction to sale of goods

Before immersing ourselves in the specialities of the international sale contract, we first want to consider some basic sale of goods law in order to provide a foundation on which to build.

2.1.1 The Sale of Goods Act

The sale of goods law in England and Wales is governed by the Sale of Goods Act 1979 (SoGA 1979), as amended, and the Supply of Goods and Services Act 1982 (SGSA 1982). The SoGA 1979 consolidates and amends the original Sale of Goods Act 1893 which first codified the law on the sale of goods. Thus, in interpreting the meaning of provisions of the Sale of Goods Act, case law predating the 1893 Act should only be used with extreme caution.

The SoGA 1979 recognises the principle of party autonomy: the parties are free to negotiate their respective rights and duties and can vary their obligations arising from the SoGA 1979. However such variation must be clear and unambiguous in order to be upheld by the courts.

According to s 2 (1) of the SoGA 1979 a contract of sale of goods is 'a contract by which the seller transfers or agrees to transfer the property in goods to the buyer for a money consideration called price'. The contract is made by offer and acceptance.

The parties are free to choose their contract terms, but in the absence of intention to the contrary, the SoGA 1979 implies certain terms and connects particular duties to the contract. These implied terms and the consequences of their breach will be discussed later (at **2.8**), once we have identified the different international trade terms. These trade terms have been developed by the industry. Where chosen by the parties, these terms determine the parties' rights and duties in accordance with the needs of the particular trade.

The emphasis of this text is a sale of goods placed in an international context. Only some basic principles of sale of goods law will be introduced briefly, to provide some grounding. However, you should not hesitate to consolidate your knowledge in sale of goods law by consulting specialist books on the topic.

2.1.2 Different types of goods

The SoGA 1979 distinguishes between a 'sale', where under the contract of sale property in the goods is transferred from the seller to the buyer (SoGA 1979, s 2(4)) and an 'agreement to sell' where property is to pass at a future time or subject to some condition later (SoGA 1979, s 2(5)). The subject matter of the contract can either be 'existing goods' or 'future goods'. The latter are goods which are yet to be manufactured or which the seller has yet to purchase. A contract to sell future goods will be an 'agreement to sell' (see SoGA 1979, s 5(3)).

At the time the contract is made goods are either 'specific' or 'unascertained'. Specific goods are defined in s 60(1) of the SoGA 1979 as 'goods identified and agreed on at the time a contract of sale is made...'. For example a particular item, such as a particular piece of antique furniture selected by the parties before or at the time of conclusion of the sale contract, qualifies as specific; only the particular piece of furniture will conform to the contract. However if the parties agree on the sale of an item which is only described by its category and the parties decide that one item from that category will later be selected to fulfil the contract, the subject of the sale is, at the relevant time of the sale, still unascertained. If the item, for example, is a printer LaserJet 1100, the seller can fulfil that contract with any printer fitting that category.

There is no statutory definition of unascertained goods. Commodities, raw materials such as sugar, grain or oil, are most likely to be sold as unascertained goods. On the other hand, if the commodity sold is qualified to the extent that there can be no doubt as to the exact goods sold, for example 'all the rice in the seller's warehouse' or 'the whole cargo of wheat on a particular ship', then, despite the fact that commodities are sold, these goods are specific.

Unascertained goods can be ascertained later, but they can never become 'specific' goods. They become ascertained once they have been set aside and are clearly identified as being the goods intended to satisfy the particular contract. Ascertained goods can thus be defined as goods which are identified as the subject matter of the contract after the contract of sale was concluded. The seller can do this by separating the correct quantity of goods from other goods of the same kind in his warehouse or by packaging them in readiness for delivery to or collection by the buyer. To come back to our previous example concerning the printer, ascertainment takes place once the seller takes one of the printers of the agreed description, labels and/or packs it for delivery to the buyer.

Unascertained goods can either be

(a) 'generic goods' which are 'wholly unascertained', for example a 'printer LaserJet 1000' or '10 tons of sugar'; or

(b) 'quasi-specific goods' which are a portion of goods from an ascertained whole. An example here would be 'a printer out of the seller's stock at his warehouse' or goods identified as '10 tons of a cargo of 1,000 tons of sugar on board of the specific vessel, the *Ocean Pride*'. Quasi-specific goods can be ascertained in the same way as generic goods, by being set aside as the goods with which to fulfil the particular contract, but they can also be ascertained by exhaustion. The latter takes place when the identified bulk of which the goods form a part is reduced to a quantity no greater than the contracted amount (see also SoGA 1979, s 18, Rule 5(3)), for example, the sugar on board the **Ocean Pride** has all been discharged apart from the 10 tons for buyer B.

A variety of legal rules draw on the distinction between the categories of goods as described above. For example, the rules dealing with the consequences of sold goods perishing before a certain time differentiate in the following manner. If the goods are specific and they have perished without the knowledge of the seller at the time the contract is made, the contract is void (SoGA 1979, s 6). If specific goods perish before the risk passes without fault of either party (seller or buyer), the agreement is avoided (SoGA 1979, s 7).

Different rules for transfer of property between the seller and the buyer apply depending on the status of the goods in question, as we will see below.

2.1.3 Passing of property

The question of when property passes is of particular importance when determining the parties' remedies against each other or against third parties, such as the carrier. It is also crucial in case one of the parties becomes insolvent without having fulfilled all of its duties.

Property passes to the buyer when the parties intend it to but only if the goods are specific or have been ascertained (SoGA 1979, s 17). Section 16 of the SoGA 1979 clarifies that under a contract of sale of unascertained goods, no property is transferred to the buyer until the goods are ascertained. However this section is subject to the new rules contained in s 20A of the SoGA 1979, which will be discussed below.

In order to determine the parties' intention for transfer of property attention must be paid to the terms of the contract, the conduct of the parties and the circumstances of the case (SoGA 1979, s 17(2)). In the absence of the parties' intention to the contrary, s 18 of the SoGA 1979 provides several rules as to when property is intended to pass. For example in the case of the sale of specific goods in a deliverable state, property passes to the buyer when the contract is made, regardless of whether the goods are delivered or paid for at that time (SoGA 1979, s 18 Rule 1).

Where unascertained or future goods by description have been sold, property generally passes when goods of that description have been unconditionally appropriated to the contract (SoGA 1979, s 18 Rule 5). Unconditional appropriation is an act by which the goods are separated in order to fulfil the particular contract, in a way that is no longer reversible by that party. For example, the goods separated in the seller's warehouse are being loaded onto the buyer's lorry. From that time of loading, the goods are unconditionally appropriated to the contract, as the seller can no longer exchange the goods for others or choose to deliver them to another buyer.

Rule 5 is subdivided further. Where the unascertained goods are in a deliverable state, one party, with the assent of the other, must appropriate them unconditionally to the contract (Rule 5(1)). Unconditional appropriation is presumed to have happened where the seller, without reserving the right of disposal, delivers the goods to the buyer, or to a carrier or bailee for transmission to the buyer (Rule 5(2)).

However, whether the carrier is in fact taken to perform as the buyer's or the seller's agent depends on the seller's duty of delivery. Until the goods have reached the contractually designated place, the carrier is held to be acting as agent for the seller (see *Comptoir d'Achat et de Vente du Boerenbond Belge SA v Luis de Ridder Limitada (The Julia)*, HL) with the consequence that the goods are not unconditionally appropriated until they reach that destination. Thus, where the seller has contracted to deliver the goods to the buyer's warehouse, appropriation does not take place when the seller hands the goods to the carrier for delivery, but only when they arrive at that warehouse.

According to Rule 5(3) and (4) quasi-specific goods, being a portion of an ascertained bulk, are taken to be unconditionally appropriated to the contract with the consequence of passing of property either:

(a) once the bulk has been reduced to the amount or less than agreed in the contract; or

(b) once the bulk has been consolidated to the amount or less of the 'aggregate of quantities due to a single buyer under separate contracts' out of the same bulk.

In the first instance, for example, the cargo of 1,000 tons of sugar has been discharged to the extent that only 10 tons are left, which are due to the buyer. In the second case the buyer may have bought 400 tons of sugar under separate contracts and the surplus of 600 tons on board the same ship has been delivered to other recipients, leaving the 400 tons for the buyer in question. Property passes once the goods due to other buyers are unloaded. The fact that the full amount due to the buyer stems from separate contracts is irrelevant.

Even if the bulk is not reduced or consolidated, property passes in such quasi-specific goods once the buyer has paid the purchase price (see SoGA 1979, s 20A). However in such a case we still do not know which particular goods are the ones for the buyer. Thus, the buyer only becomes owner in common in respect of his proportion of goods from the whole bulk. He is deemed to have consented to any delivery to a co-owner or any dealing with goods consistent with the purpose of this co-ownership (see SoGA 1979, s 20B). Sections 20A and 20B have been added by the Sale of Goods (Amendment) Act 1995.

The above rules are only presumptions in ascertaining the parties' intentions. They can be rebutted where the parties have agreed on different terms. Regard is to be had to the specific trade terms and their general implications as to passing of property and risk. In order to avoid any doubt as to the act of appropriation, international sale contracts often require the seller to give notice of appropriation, which normally is to be given within a certain timeframe.

The seller can reserve his right of disposal by agreement in accordance with s 19(1) of the SoGA 1979. This means that property in the goods will only pass once the conditions imposed by the seller have been fulfilled. The condition is usually payment of the purchase price or acceptance of a financial document which represents payment, such as a bill of exchange. (A bill of exchange is a payment and credit mechanism by which one person orders another person to pay a sum of money to a named person or the bearer of the bill. A cheque is one example; for details see **3.2** below.)

Section 19(2) and (3) of the SoGA 1979 presume that the seller has reserved his title to the goods:

(a) if the transport document is taken out in his or his agent's name or to his order, as the seller can still change his mind and transfer the document to a person other than the buyer; or

(b) if the transport document is delivered to the buyer together with a financial document which the buyer is expected to honour. If the buyer does not do so, he will not obtain property in the goods.

2.1.4 Ownership in the goods sold

As a general rule the seller can only give property in the goods to the buyer if he is the owner of the goods or if he acts with the owner's authority. According to s 21(1) of the SoGA 1979 the buyer acquires no better title to the goods than the seller had.

However there are a number of exceptions to this rule. These can be found at common law, in the SoGA 1979 and in the Factors Act 1889. According to s 21(2) of the SoGA 1979, the rules of common law and of the Factors Act 1889 remain in force alongside the rules of the SOGA 1979 (ss 21–26 and s 48 (2)).

These exception rules commonly protect a purchaser who is in good faith and has no notice of the defect, where the purchaser obtains either the goods from a person in possession of them or of the documents of title. Documents of title are documents which represent the goods to such extent that transfer in the documents represents transfer in the goods.

The owner may be estopped from denying the seller's authority if he either:

(a) by his words or conduct towards the buyer; or

(b) by his failure to act

created the impression that the seller was the owner or at least authorised to sell (SoGA 1979, s 21(1) and common law).

Section 2 of the Factors Act 1889 provides for rules according to which a mercantile agent in possession of the goods or the documents of title representing the goods can make a valid sale to a bona fide purchaser even without consent of the owner.

A seller with violable title can nevertheless transfer a good title to a buyer in good faith before the seller's title has been avoided (SoGA 1979, s 25).

An initial seller who is still in possession of the goods or the documents of title can validly resell to a bona fide purchaser goods for which property has already passed to the first buyer. The second buyer obtains ownership to the same extent as if the first buyer had authorised the sale (SoGA 1979, s 24).

According to s 25 of the SoGA 1979 the buyer in possession after the sale can resell the goods to the same effect as if he were a mercantile agent.

Where an unpaid seller who has exercised his right of lien or stoppage in transit in accordance with ss 41–46 of the SoGA 1979 resells the goods, the buyer acquires a good title to the goods as against the original buyer (SoGA 1979, s 48(2)). The right of an unpaid seller is however defeated or limited where the documents of title have been transferred from the original buyer to a purchaser in good faith and against consideration (SoGA 1979, s 47(2)(a) and (b)).

2.1.5 Passing of risk and frustration

The rules for passing of risk divide the risk of accidental loss or damage to the goods between the parties. Whoever has the risk must bear the loss or damage and must nevertheless fulfil his duties under the contract.

A contract can only be avoided (see SoGA 1979, ss 6 and 7) with the consequence that the seller is freed from his contractual obligations, where the performance of a contract for the sale of specific goods was either impossible at the outset or at least became impossible before risk passed. Unascertained goods can usually be purchased in the market place; thus impossibility does not occur even if the goods, which the seller wanted to use, have perished. However if the goods sold were quasi-specific goods (an undivided part of an ascertained bulk), the contract can be frustrated where the whole bulk, of which the contracted goods were part, has perished, for example where the ship carrying the contracted cargo has sunk.

According to statutory presumption (SoGA 1979, s 20), the risk passes together with property. However this rule is subject to express or implied agreement of the parties to the contrary. In international sale contracts risk is often intended to pass separate from property. We will discuss the details later at **2.5.7** and **2.6.6** when explaining the different trade terms.

2.1.6 Delivery and acceptance of the goods

In order to perform the contract, the seller must deliver the goods in accordance with the contract terms. The buyer has to accept the goods and pay for them (SoGA 1979, s 27). Delivery is defined in s 61(1) of the SoGA 1979 primarily as 'voluntary transfer of possession from one person to another'. Delivery can be actual or constructive, for example in the latter case by delivery of the documents of title to the goods under a cif contract. (A cif contract is a sale contract whereby the seller undertakes to arrange for carriage and insurance of the goods free of charge – see **2.2.2.3**.) It should be noted that delivery does not mean passing of risk and/or property, even though they might sometimes coincide with delivery. All three are separate concepts and need to be identified separately.

The place of delivery depends on the contract, but in the absence of provisions to the contrary it is deemed to be the seller's place of business (SoGA 1979, s 29(1) and (2)). Sections 29–32 of the SoGA 1979 provide rules for delivery. In our context s 32 of the SoGA 1979 is particularly worth mentioning. It sets out specific rules according to which the seller, by virtue of his delivery to the carrier, is taken to have delivered to the buyer. The presumption in s 29(2) of the SoGA 1979 is rebutted in most international sale contracts; the presumption in s 32 of the SoGA 1979 to a lesser extent, depending on the contract terms chosen.

Once the goods are delivered to the buyer, he has a reasonable time to examine the goods. It is then that the buyer must decide whether to accept or reject the goods. The buyer is deemed to have accepted the goods either:

(a) after a lapse of reasonable time; or

(b) when he has intimated to the seller that he has accepted them; or

(c) where the buyer to whom the goods have been delivered undertakes any act inconsistent with the ownership of the seller (SoGA 1979, s 35(4) and (1)). This is the case where the buyer deals with the goods in a way that is inconsistent with the seller's right to have them restored, for example the wheat delivered is milled to flour. However mere delivery to another under a subsale is not deemed such an act (see SoGA 1979, s 35(6)(b)).

Unless the contract terms provide otherwise, a buyer can no longer reject the goods for breach of condition once he has accepted them. Instead, he can only sue the seller for breach of warranty (SoGA 1979, s 11(4)).

2.1.7 Exclusion clauses

The parties to a sale contract may seek to exclude or limit their liability for breach of contract. In general, such terms are valid (SoGA 1979, s 55) within the boundaries imposed by certain statutory rules.

In sale of goods law we need to observe the rules of the Unfair Contract Terms Act 1977 to that extent. The UCTA 1977 provides that a contracting party cannot limit its liability, whether by using specific contract terms, notices or standard terms of business or otherwise, unless these terms satisfy the test of reasonableness. However s 26 of the UCTA 1977 makes clear that the provisions of the UCTA 1977 are not applicable to international supply contracts as defined in s 26. Thus the UCTA 1977 is not applicable to the usual international sale contract, with the result that the parties are free to choose their exclusion clauses. For such an exclusion to be upheld by the courts it must have been validly incorporated into the contract and the exclusion clause must cover the situation expressly. The courts interpret terms, which limit the parties' liability, restrictively.

2.2 International sale of goods and international trade terms overview

2.2.1 International trade terms

Over the years, in order to cater for the particular needs of international trade, numerous trade terms have been developed by international mercantile custom, to describe the rights and duties of the contracting parties. Thus trade terms can have the same or a similar name, but a different meaning assigned to them by different jurisdictions or systems of law. Standard trade terms have been created at international level to clarify any ambiguities, for example the 'Incoterms' (International Commercial Terms sponsored by the International Chamber of Commerce based in Paris) and 'Intraterms' (International Trade Terms, a set of trade terms using plain language, to eliminate any doubts as to the meaning of the terms). In some countries such pre-designated trade terms form part of the national law and cannot be varied, in others they are equivalent to customs. In the UK they have a purely contractual character. They must be incorporated into the contract if the parties wish to apply them, and can be varied according to the needs and wishes of the contracting parties. It is therefore essential to clarify whether or not the contract is to be governed by these standard trade terms, because this will vary the parties' rights and duties. Where there is doubt, an English court will construe the trade term according to the traditional meaning under common law, unless the parties have clearly and unambiguously adopted a particular trade term from a published standard set of terms.

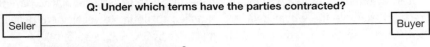

Q: Under which terms have the parties contracted?

Seller ——————————————————————————————— Buyer

1. What does the contract say?
2. Are there any other contracts, other business dealings or old established practices which influence the particular sale contract?
3. Have the parties incorporated standard trade terms? If so, which ones?
4. Have the parties agreed on particular rights and duties?
5. Have they varied any chosen trade terms? If so, are the alterations valid?
6. Are the contract terms in line with general principles of contract law?

Fig 2.1 Terms of the contract

Both under common law and the Incoterms, there are four main categories of trade terms relevant to the international sale of goods:

(a) E terms or collection contracts, where the buyer collects the goods;

(b) F terms, where the seller has to load the goods on a carriage device provided by the buyer;

(c) C terms, where the seller has to send the goods to the buyer; and

(d) D terms or arrival contracts, where the seller only fulfils his duties once the goods arrive at the agreed destination.

They can be broadly distinguished by looking at the risks and responsibilities of the parties in relation to the export, transportation and import of the goods. The risks and duties can be determined by looking at the following milestones on the goods' journey: collection/departure; export clearance; loading; transit; unloading; import clearance; delivery/arrival. Figure 2.2 gives a brief illustration of the duties from a seller's perspective. The top half of the chart indicates that the goods are to be transported from the seller's country to the country of destination by sea, air, road or rail. The bottom half shows the extent of the seller's duties with respect to each of the different groups of contract terms. Where the seller's duties end, the buyer's responsibilities begin. The black vertical lines represent the international border and thus any formalities and charges which need to be taken care of, due to the exportation and importation of the goods.

Let us now take an overview of the various trade terms and their main features.

2.2.2 Most common terms of sale, derived from common law, Incoterms 2000 and Intraterms

The list of common trade terms which follows is derived from common law, Incoterms and Intraterms. To clarify beyond doubt, which terms are part of the Incoterms 2000, these terms are set out in Appendix A at the end of this book. Please note that common law and Incoterms may use the same denomination, but impose slightly different duties on the parties. For example, a cif contract under both systems contains the same major duties on behalf of the seller (shipment of insured goods to the buyer), but the 'small print' of how these duties are to be fulfilled may differ (for example the extent to which the goods have to be insured is different under common law and Incoterms).

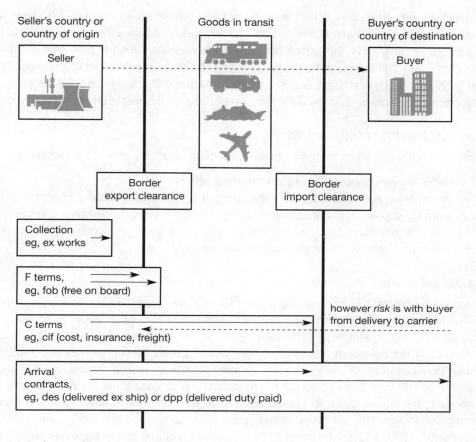

Fig 2.2 Trade terms from the seller's perspective

Thus, parties to an international sale contract should stipulate clearly if they wish to apply the Incoterms 2000 and not the common law interpretation of a trade term. The following is an example of such an express incorporation clause, where the goods were sold on 'cost, insurance and freight terms', to be shipped to Hamburg as the port of destination: 'cif (Hamburg) Incoterms 2000'. The Incoterms 2000 can be purchased from the International Chamber of Commerce directly (http://www.iccwbo.org). You can also find the fob and cif terms of the Incoterms 2000 in the appendix of the cases and materials book by Paul Todd, *Cases & Materials on International Trade Law* (2003).

Even if the seller is not at all involved in the transportation and insurance of the goods, he must still give the buyer all information and assistance necessary to enable the buyer to obtain adequate insurance cover and any export documentation. Also, the seller must pack the goods appropriately for the particular journey and chosen method of transport. What is appropriate will depend upon the custom of the particular trade or the buyer's instructions.

As a general rule, the party responsible for loading the goods is also responsible for obtaining export licences and payment of custom duties. This is because the selected transport device constitutes the imaginary customs border. A similar rule applies to import duties and unloading depending on whether the seller or buyer has to unload the goods. However, the seller might be in a much better position to complete the formalities for export and the buyer for import. Thus, the parties have often altered this position in their contract. Now, the Incoterms 2000 have been adapted to reflect this trend in practice in its fas (free along-side ship) and deq (delivered ex quay) terms respectively. If relying solely on the common law terms, it would be best to clarify the parties' duties in this respect, to avoid any doubt.

2.2.2.1 E terms or collection contracts

Here the seller minimises his risk by making the goods available only at his premises.

Ex works, ex warehouse, ex factory (named place)
The buyer or his agent has to collect the goods from the seller's factory or warehouse or other arranged place. Risk and property is transferred on delivery. The buyer is responsible for export licences and customs, but the seller has to provide any necessary information and assistance for export formalities and insurance purposes.

2.2.2.2 F terms

Under f terms the seller arranges and pays for any pre-carriage in the country of export. Whether he also has to complete all customs and export formalities depends on the point of delivery. If it is still within the country of export, then this duty falls on the buyer. However if the delivery is across the border or a fictitious border, such as the ship's rail, then the obligation for export clearance is still with the seller. The main carriage is gener-ally to be arranged by the buyer. Risk and property pass once the seller has delivered the goods at the agreed place. In case of sea transit, the seller must usually give an effective notice of shipment to the buyer to enable the latter to arrange for appropriate insurance (see SoGA 1979, s 32(3)). However this notice is not required where the buyer already has all the necessary information for insurance purposes (see Wimble, *Sons & Co Ltd v Rosenberg & Sons, CA*).

Free carrier (named place)
The seller is responsible for delivering the goods into the custody of the carrier at the named point, where the risk passes.

Fas (named port of shipment) 'free alongside ship'
This term is to be used for sea carriage only.

The seller is responsible for delivering the goods alongside the ship (where risk passes), so that the buyer or his agent can load the goods. Alongside means within reach of the ship's tackle, which might require the seller to load the goods on a lighter to get within reach. Initially, the buyer is responsible for obtaining export licences and clearing customs, whereas the seller only has to co-operate where necessary. However under fas Incoterms 2000 the seller is burdened with the export formalities.

Fob airport 'free on board airport'; fca airport 'free carrier airport'
The seller is responsible for delivering the goods into the custody of the air carrier or his agent /or other person named by the buyer, at which point the risk is transferred. Unless otherwise agreed, the buyer is responsible for obtaining export licences and clearing cus-toms, whereas the seller only has to co-operate where necessary.

The term fob airport is not to be confused with the lesser-used term fob aircraft, in which case the seller would be responsible for the goods until they have been loaded on board the aircraft. The seller would then also have to arrange for export clearance and pay the relevant duties.

Fob (named port of shipment) 'free on board'
In English practice, this term is to be used for sea carriage only.

Generally, the buyer has to nominate the vessel. The seller is responsible for loading the goods on board ship and paying all charges up to the point where the goods pass the ship's rail, including — if required — export licence. Risk and property usually pass once the goods are loaded on board.

2.2.2.3 C terms
Under c terms the seller arranges and pays for the main carriage but risk passes when the goods are either loaded on board a vessel, or given into custody of the first carrier. Property usually passes once the bill of lading or the transport documents are tendered. As the seller arranges for the carriage to the point of destination, it is up to the seller to undertake all export formalities. The import formalities are the buyer's duty. Where the seller is not obliged to procure insurance for the goods, he must give an effective notice of shipment to the buyer to enable the latter to arrange for appropriate insurance (see SoGA 1979, s 32(3)).

Cpt (named place of destination) 'carriage paid to'
The seller must arrange for carriage and deliver goods into the custody of the carrier, at which point risk passes. He has to clear the goods for export but does *not* have to arrange for insurance.

Cip (named place of destination) 'carriage and insurance paid to'
The seller must arrange for carriage and insurance and deliver the goods, which have been cleared for customs, into the custody of the carrier. With delivery into the custody of the carrier risk passes.

C & f (named port of destination) or cfr (named port of destination) 'cost and freight'
This term is to be used for sea carriage only.

The seller must arrange and pay for the contract of carriage and is responsible for loading the goods over the ship's rail and for arranging any export clearance. He must give an effective notice of shipment to the buyer to enable the latter to arrange for appropriate insurance. (This is the only difference from the ordinary cif as introduced below.) The seller then has to tender an invoice (charging the agreed price for the agreed goods) and a clean bill of lading (which is the transport document for the goods) to the buyer, as well as all other contractually required documents.

Cif (named port of destination) 'cost, insurance, freight'
This term is to be used for sea carriage only.

The seller must arrange and pay for the contract of carriage and the level of insurance of the goods that is customary in the particular trade. However under cif Incoterms 2000 he only needs to take out minimum insurance cover. The seller is responsible for loading the goods over the ship's rail and for completing all export duties. He then has to tender an invoice (charging the agreed price for the agreed goods), an insurance policy and a clean bill of lading for the goods, as well as any other contractually required documents (for example certificates of origin and of quality) to the buyer.

2.2.2.4 Arrival contracts or d terms

Under d terms, the seller must make the goods available upon arrival at the agreed destination: his cost and risk is therefore maximised. The seller must complete all formalities and pay all charges for the export of the goods. However who has to clear the goods for import and pay the respective duties depends on the point of delivery. Where the goods cross the fictitious border to the import country before delivery to the buyer, the duty is still with the seller. If the buyer accepts delivery from the vessel directly or explicitly without clearance, such as under the term 'delivered duty unpaid', it is the buyer's responsibility.

For the following terms the duty for import clearance is with the buyer:

Daf (named place) 'delivered at frontier'
This term is to be used for carriage by road or rail only.

The buyer must take delivery at the frontier, where risk passes. The buyer must clear the goods for import and pay all charges in that respect.

Ddu (named place of destination) 'delivered duty unpaid'
The buyer must take delivery of the goods from the named place of destination and is responsible for import clearance and charges.

Ex ship/arrival/des (named port of arrival) 'delivered ex ship'
This term is to be used for sea carriage only.

The seller must deliver the goods at the named port to the buyer. Risk and property passes when the goods are handed over to the buyer at the agreed port of destination. The import formalities have to be borne by the buyer, as he is responsible for taking delivery from the vessel, unless the parties have varied this in their contract.

For the following terms the responsibility for import clearance shifts to the seller.

Ex quay/port of discharge/deq (named port of destination) 'delivered ex quay'
This term is to be used for sea carriage only.

The seller must deliver the goods to the buyer from a ship that has arrived at the agreed port and in addition the seller has to pay import duties and unloading charges. The buyer must take delivery of the goods from the quay. However under Incoterms 2000 the buyer is burdened with the import formalities.

Delivered free/free delivery/franco domicile
The seller is responsible for all charges up to the delivery of the goods to the buyer's address, including import duties.

Ddp (named place of destination) 'delivered duty paid'

The buyer must take delivery of the goods from the named place of destination. All import formalities and charges are the seller's responsibility.

2.2.3 Use of terms depends on transport device

It should be noted that some of the trade terms are for sea carriage only, whereas others are only for carriage by land — road or rail. Most of the sea carriage terms use words in their title which are derived from shipping, such as 'ship', 'on board', 'freight' or 'quay', thus helping to identify their scope. Most other terms can be used for any mode of transport or multimodal transport. Multimodal transport means that the goods are carried by more than one transport device, for example by road and sea. In container trade, whether the goods are shipped as fcl 'full container load' or lcl 'less than full container load', the terms fca 'free carrier', cpt 'carriage paid to' and cip 'carriage and insurance paid to' are particularly suitable. They cater well for roll on-roll off operations, having the effect that risk is transferred at an earlier point than the ship's rail. (The term 'roll on-roll off operations', also abbreviated as 'Ro-Ro', refers to containers being transported on lorries, both together rolling on and off the ship, for the sea leg of the journey.) However if the contract is about sea carriage only, the sea terms (as illustrated in Fig 2.3) are the most specific and thus should be used accordingly.

American practice differs from the English practice. In American practice the term 'fob vessel' indicates sea carriage, whereas 'fob' as such is used for any transport type.

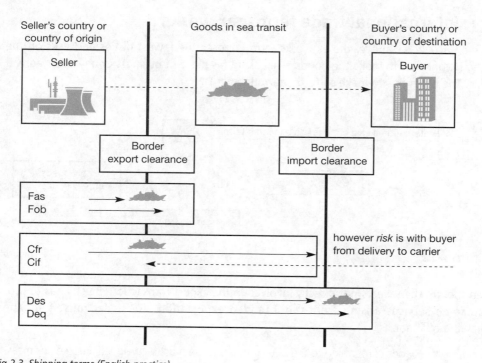

Fig 2.3 Shipping terms (English practice)

2.2.4 Use of terms depends on commercial considerations

Which of these terms would a seller select and when? A seller, inexperienced in the export trade, may want to keep his risks to the minimum by contracting on terms most akin to a domestic sale. He thus may choose the ex works contract, only charging the price for the goods without any additional services. Similarly, a buyer wanting to minimise his risk and involvement in the international transaction, may wish to pay more but receive the goods at his doorstep. In this instance he might choose ddp 'delivered duty paid' terms.

A very experienced seller with good contacts in the carriage industry and/or good bargaining power, may want to widen his profit margin by charging more in total for either a cif 'cost, insurance and freight' or even a delivery contract. In such a case he bears a higher risk, for example in price fluctuations for carriage and insurance of the goods, availability of vessels, risk of loss or damage to the goods during transit, etc. Similarly, a buyer may want to use his contacts in the industry to reduce the sale price for the goods, by making his own carriage and insurance arrangements on f terms. Some tradesmen or companies export and import so much that they employ their own vessels or charter ships on a regular basis, thus taking care of the carriage themselves.

More than 90% of the world's trade is carried by sea. It is thus unsurprising that fob and cif terms and various modifications of these classic types are the most commonly used terms. These terms will therefore be analysed in more depth, after the extremes on both sides have first been covered: ex works and delivered duty paid.

2.3 International trade terms: ex works

As seen at 2.2.2.1 above, the ex works term imposes the fewest duties and risks on the seller. He only has to make the goods available at his place of business or any other agreed place. The buyer has to make all further arrangements.

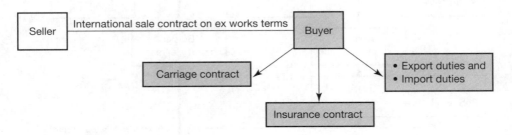

Fig 2.4 Ex works

Even though the seller is not directly involved in the export transaction, he still has to provide some services arising from the intended exportation. The seller must fulfil the following obligations.

(a) Supply the goods conforming to the sale contract. These must be weighed, checked or measured if and as agreed. The seller must supply the goods with adequate packaging. It is best practice to clarify in the contract whether this is to be export packaging or some other. The Incoterms 2000, ex works term, stipulate that the seller has to package the goods as required for the transport, which seems to indicate that the seller has to package for export and at his expense. Section 14 of the SoGA 1979 put the onus on the seller to supply goods that are fit for any purpose made known to him. From this follows that the seller has to provide the goods carefully packaged in a manner as to enable them to arrive safely at their destination.

(b) Deliver the goods by making them available at the place and time agreed, and notifying the buyer to this extent.

(c) Supply, by the agreed means, the invoice and any other documents called for under the contract, for example certificates of origin.

(d) Provide any assistance to the buyer to enable him to clear the goods for export and to insure them.

(e) Pay any costs incurred to put the goods at the buyer's disposal.

The buyer's duties are as follows.

(a) Take delivery and pay for the goods. Unless other arrangements have been made, the purchase price is due on delivery of the goods.

(b) Clear the goods for export, import and any transit, and pay all relevant charges.

(c) Arrange and pay for the transportation of the goods and, at his choice, for any insurance.

(d) Pay any other costs incidental to the exportation of the goods, for example any pre-shipment inspections, official charges and any costs incurred by the seller while assisting the buyer with the relevant formalities.

Overall, the seller fulfils his obligations in much the same way as if the goods were sold domestically. Whilst negotiating the contract terms, the parties should therefore bear in mind that any clauses excluding or limiting their liability might have to comply with the test of reasonableness in the sense of the Unfair Contract Terms Act 1977. The UCTA 1977 is applicable, unless the transaction is an international supply contract in accordance with its s 26. One of the qualifying criteria for such an international supply contract is the transportation of goods from the territory of one State to another, which is not fulfilled under an ex works contract. This means that the contract terms negotiated between the parties will have to stand up to the scrutiny of the UCTA 1977, unless other qualifying criteria of s 26(4) of the UCTA 1977 are met. The latter are either that offer and acceptance took place in different States, or that the goods were delivered to a State other than the one where offer and acceptance took place.

2.4 International trade terms: delivered duty paid

The other extreme is when the seller has to deliver the goods at his risk and on his account to the buyer at the buyer's place of business or at any other agreed place.

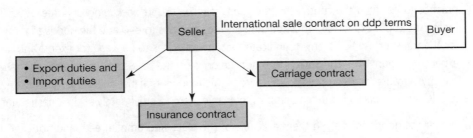

Fig 2.5 Delivered duty paid

The seller must:

(a) supply the contractual goods;

(b) deliver them at his risk and expense to the buyer at the agreed destination. This means the seller must arrange for carriage and insurance contracts and bear all costs in this respect;

(c) clear the goods for export, import and all transit, including the procurement of relevant licences and payment of all charges incurred throughout the transportation.

The buyer only has to take delivery and pay for the goods. This contract is an arrival contract with the consequence that the price only becomes due on delivery of the goods themselves.

2.5 International trade terms: cost, insurance and freight

2.5.1 General rights and duties under cif

When contracting on cif terms the seller undertakes to ship the contractual goods, insured, to the agreed destination. Alternatively, he may purchase goods afloat, which are already bound for that destination. The seller must tender the transport documents, to put the buyer in the position of being able to claim against the carrier and insurer, if need be. The seller does not undertake that the goods will arrive. The risk of damage or loss of the goods passes from the seller to the buyer on shipment, whereas property passes on tender of the documents, both regardless of whether the goods arrive. Thus the cif contract has been called a 'sale of documents relating to goods', rather than a sale of goods themselves: *Arnold Karberg & Co v Blythe, Green, Jourdain & Co*, KBD per Scrutton J.

The purchase price includes all services and charges relating to the transport and insurance arrangements. Any fluctuation in the cost of carriage and insurance after conclusion of the sale contract is at the seller's risk or benefit. He cannot pass any increase on to the buyer.

The buyer only has to arrange for import licences and pay any import duties and charges at the port of destination. He must accept correctly tendered documents and take delivery of the goods from the vessel once it has arrived. The respective duties of the seller and buyer can be illustrated as shown in Fig 2.6.

Fig 2.6 Cost, insurance and freight

Unless otherwise agreed, the general duties of the seller are as follows.

(a) Ship the contracted goods which are packaged for export, or to buy conforming goods afloat.

(b) Procure a contract of carriage with a suitable vessel for the carriage of the goods, on reasonable terms as common in the particular trade, and secure a bill of lading in relation to the goods.

(c) Clear the goods for export.

(d) Procure a contract of insurance for the goods in transit, as common in the particular trade, which can be assigned to the buyer. Assignment of the insurance policy usually takes place on tender of the documents.

(e) Produce the sales invoice and all other documents as provided for in the sales contract (for example a certificate of inspection of the goods).

(f) Tender the transport documents and any others if so agreed. The necessary transport documents are the bill of lading (evidencing the contract of carriage, being a receipt for the goods and being a document of title to the goods), the insurance policy (covering the goods for the transit) and the sales invoice corresponding with the goods as stated in the bill of lading.

The buyer's duties are as follows.

(a) Clear the goods for import: obtain the relevant licences and pay any charges.

(b) Accept the tendered transport documents if they conform with the contract.

(c) Take delivery from the ship, once it has arrived at the port of destination.

(d) Pay the contract price.

From a business point of view, the parties involved in a cif transaction have a variety of benefits, which are partially due to the role of the documents in the transaction. The advantages for the seller are that:

(a) he accommodates the buyer;

(b) he has the opportunity to increase his profits by making the carriage and insurance arrangements;

(c) he retains the right of disposal of the goods until payment is made, thus keeping some level of security; and

(d) he does not bear any risk during transit of the goods.

The buyer's advantages are that he obtains:

(a) a means to take delivery of the goods;

(b) a means to trade the goods on, or to pledge them as security for finance;

(c) rights against the carrier and insurer to recover at least the value of the goods if they are damaged or lost in transit.

Now we shall take a closer look at some of the cif issues.

2.5.2 Special features of a cif contract

Regarding the goods, the seller has two major duties under a cif contract. He must:

(a) ship the contractual goods or buy corresponding goods afloat, bound for the agreed destination; and

(b) tender the transport documents.

To ship the goods means the seller must put the goods on board ship and the transport document must reflect this. Failure to ship the goods, or to tender the documents, would result in a breach of condition in each case. It would be the same outcome for not meeting the time stipulations for shipment of goods and/or tender of documents. The House of Lords has stated in *Bunge Corporation v Tradax SA* that in mercantile contracts all time stipulations are to be treated as conditions.

The seller does not undertake that the goods will arrive. If the goods are lost in transit, the buyer still has to fulfil his contractual duties, but he can try to get redress against the carrier and insurer, using the tendered documents.

The buyer in turn has two separate and independent rights of rejection.

(a) Rejection of discrepant documents. Q: Has the seller tendered at the correct time genuine documents, which are in conformity with the sale contract? And/or

(b) Rejection of non-conforming goods. Q: Has the seller fulfilled his duty to ship at the correct time goods which are conforming to the contract requirements, in a manner that enables the safe arrival of the goods at the port of destination? Please note: the question is not whether the goods have arrived undamaged. If the goods are damaged during transit, the buyer, at whose risk they are travelling, has to get redress against the carrier or claim on the insurance for compensation.

If either the documents or the goods can be rejected on valid grounds and the seller is not able to cure the defect, the buyer can treat the contract as repudiated and claim damages for non-delivery. The right to reject the documents does not influence the right to reject the goods and vice versa (as shown in Fig 2.7), unless the particular discrepancies have been waived.

Fig 2.7 Buyer's right to reject corresponds with seller's duties

2.5.3 Notice of appropriation

If the goods sold were unascertained at the time the contract was made, the international sale contract often requires the seller to give notice of appropriation. Such appropriation is the contractual binding act of the seller, allocating certain goods to the contract, for example by putting the goods aside in his warehouse or loading the goods on board a particular ship. Acting in accordance with this meaning, the seller binds himself to deliver these particular goods and no other. For example, in many standard term contracts the seller undertakes to give the buyer notice of appropriation, which usually states the name of the vessel on which the goods are shipped and, if applicable, the approximate weight of the goods or other identifying criteria.

At which point appropriation itself takes place is to be determined either from the contract terms, whether express or implied, or by reference to the circumstances of the case. Appropriation has certain consequences.

(a) Once the seller has given notice of appropriation, for example nominated the vessel, he cannot change his mind and fulfil the contract with other goods, for example goods that have been shipped on a different vessel from that named in the notice of appropriation. Should he try to do so, the buyer can validly reject the tender of the documents relating to these other goods, see *Kleinjan and Holst NV Rotterdam v Bremer Handelsgesellschaft mbH Hamburg*, QBD. If the contract calls for such notice of appropriation, the seller must ensure he complies with the exact requirements of this obligation, particularly the timing of the notice. If he fails to give notice within the agreed timeframe, the buyer is entitled to reject the tender of the documents, see *Société Italo-Belge pour le Commerce et l'Industrie SA v Palm and Vegetable Oils (Malaysia) Snd Bhd (The Post Chaser)*, QBD (Comm). However, where time is not an issue, the seller is entitled, if the buyer rejects the first notice of appropriation as invalid, to withdraw it and issue a second one, see *Borrowman Phillips and Co v Free & Hollis*, CA.

(b) The moment of appropriation may also be the time of passing of property. In accordance with s 18 Rule 5 of the SoGA 1979, unless the parties intend otherwise, property in unascertained goods only passes once the goods have been unconditionally and irrevocably appropriated to the contract. However, under a cif contract such appropriation will seldom be unconditional, as the seller usually retains the right of disposal of the goods until payment has been effected. Also, where goods are shipped as part of a larger bulk, appropriation alone will not be sufficient to ascertain the goods and thus not be enough to pass property. Property can generally only pass once the goods are ascertained (see SoGA 1979, s 16) or where the requirements of s 20A of the SoGA 1979 are fulfilled. In the latter case, the notice of appropriation would identify the bulk of which the contractual goods are part, leaving the last requirement to be fulfilled before property can pass: the buyer has to pay for the goods (SoGA 1979, s 20A(1)).

2.5.4 Transport documents

As we have seen, the transport documents play a major part in the performance of a cif contract. In general these documents comprise:

(a) the bill of lading (usually issued in sets of three) or any other transport document as agreed in the sale contract;

(b) the insurance policy;

(c) the sales invoice;

(d) any other document as agreed between the parties. Examples include:

  (i)   quality certificates;

  (ii) superintendence certificate in case of sampling and analysis stipulations;

  (iii) weight certificate;

  (iv) certificate of origin;

  (v)   if necessary a phytosanitary certificate, which is a government document confirming to the receiving country that its regulations are met.

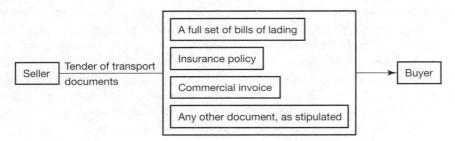

Fig 2.8 Transport documents

Each of these documents must fulfil particular requirements in order to be in conformity with the contract of sale. Failure to do so will entitle the buyer to reject the documents. These requirements are described below.

2.5.4.1 Bill of lading

The bill of lading has a number of functions in relation to the carriage contract. It is a receipt of the goods, it evidences the contract of carriage and it is a document of title to the goods. We will look at the first two functions at **4.2.2.2** below. Here we will concentrate on the qualities that the bill of lading must have in order to fulfil the cif sale contract requirements.

(a) The bill must be effective as a contract of carriage and must cover the entirety of the carriage. Thus the bill must give the buyer continuous cover from the time of shipment until the arrival at the port of destination, so that he has a possible right of suit against the carrier at all times; see *Hansson v Hamel & Horley Ltd*, HL. Unless otherwise agreed, the seller has to procure an ordinary contract of carriage to the place of destination by the usual or customary route for such transports. The carriage contract needs to be 'reasonable' having regard to the nature of the goods and any other particular circumstances of the case (see the implied duty in SoGA 1979, s 32(2)). As with the common law interpretation of the term, the Incoterms 2000 call for a contract of carriage on 'usual' terms (see Incoterms cif, seller's duties A3, A8). If the seller fails to produce a reasonable carriage contract, the risk in effect does not pass to the buyer and the seller remains responsible for any transit loss. Where the bill of lading reveals the inadequacy of the carriage contract, the buyer can reject the documents (see *SIAT di del Ferro v Tradax Overseas SA, CA* and *Soules Caf v PT Transap of Indonesia*, QBD (Comm)).

It is in the buyer's interest to include all shipping requirements in the sale contract, thus obliging the seller to tender a bill of lading explicitly mentioning all these requirements (*SIAT di del Ferro v Tradax Overseas SA*, CA). If the seller does not do so, the buyer can reject the documents for non-conformity with the sale contract, at a time before payment is effected.

(b) The bill must be clean, genuine and unaltered. A buyer only has to accept a clean bill. This is a bill which has no qualifying comments as to the quality and condition of the goods on loading. However the bill must show the facts on shipment accurately, particularly the date of shipment, see *Finley v Kwik Hoo Tong etc*, CA.

(c) The bill must state a date of shipment within the agreed shipment period or by the agreed shipping date in the sale contract.

(d) Unless otherwise agreed, a bill of lading must be tendered, not any other transport document. A sea waybill or ship's delivery order (these carriage documents are discussed in more detail at **4.2.2** below) is only sufficient on agreement of the parties. The bill must confirm that the goods have actually been shipped onboard and must state the date of loading; thus it is called a 'shipped bill of lading'. Unless the parties have so agreed or contrary trade custom applies, a 'received for shipment bill of lading' is not sufficient. The latter bill only states that the goods have been received into the custody of the carrier without yet being loaded. In container trade however, due to the trade customs and practicalities, the parties' intention is invariably that such a bill is good tender.

(e) The bill must be an effective and transferable document of title. A bill of lading represents the goods and vests rights in the lawful holder of the bill, one of which is the right to demand delivery from the carrier (see Carriage of Goods by Sea Act (CoGSA) 1992, s 2). Possession of the bill is, in many respects, equivalent to possession of the goods, and transfer of the bill acts as symbolic transfer of the possession of the goods. If the parties intend it to, and within the limits of the SoGA 1979 (see SoGA 1979, ss 16, 17), transfer of the bill of lading can also pass property in the goods.

The bill of lading can be made out to: a specific consignee (straight consigned bill); the bearer (bearer bill); or a named consignee or his order (order bill). In the first instance, only the specific consignee can demand delivery of the goods, whereas in the second any bearer of the bill can do so. In case of an order bill, the named consignee or any other person to whom the bill has been lawfully transferred, has the rights represented by the bill vested in him. Transfer of an order bill is done by indorsement (meaning the previous consignee signing it, either in blank or to a named person) and delivery. Bearer bills are transferred by delivery only and are therefore not often used in international trade due to lack of security.

A buyer who neither intends to sell the goods on nor needs trade finance from a bank, may be happy to accept a straight consigned bill. The issue is that a straight consigned bill cannot be transferred and thus is 'non-negotiable'. However, it is still a document of title as recently clarified by the decision of the Court of Appeal in *JI MacWilliam Co Inc v Mediterranean Shipping Co SA (The Rafaela S)* which was upheld by the House of Lords. As opposed to a sea waybill, a straight bill of lading either by express or implied term requires presentation to the carrier on delivery. From this it follows that, even though the bill is not freely transferable, the shipper can still transfer possession and also property to the consignee by means of the transfer of the bill. Thus, under English law, a straight bill of lading is a document of title.

Any other buyer, however, will be keen to have the option to transfer (trade or pledge) the bill to another person. So unless the sale contract stipulates otherwise, the seller will only fulfil his duty if he procures and tenders a freely transferable bill of lading, also called a 'negotiable' bill of lading. In order to fulfil this criterion of negotiability, an order bill of lading needs to have the words 'or order or assigns' added beside the name of the consignee, to indicate this fact (*Henderson & Co v The Comptoir d'Escompte de Paris,* PC (Hong Kong)). Otherwise, the bill is treated as being non-negotiable, resulting in any indorsement of the bill being ineffective (*International Air and Sea Cargo GmbH v Owners of the Chitral (The Chitral),* QBD (Comm)).

2.5.4.2 Insurance policy

The seller must tender an insurance policy which covers the goods for the entire journey, so that the buyer is able to claim against the insurer. It should provide cover against those risks which are customarily insured against in the particular trade, unless the parties have chosen to contract on Incoterms 2000, where minimum cover suffices. To avoid any uncertainty, it is advisable to agree on the nature of the policy and to stipulate any additional risks that should be covered. For example the parties should agree whether the Institute Cargo Clauses A, B or C to the Lloyd's Marine Policy are taken out and whether any additional cover provided for by the Institute War Clauses and Institute Strike Clauses should be obtained. The parties should bear in mind that either of them might need to claim against the policy, depending on the circumstances of the case. The seller's interest in appropriate insurance cover for the goods becomes particularly obvious in cases where the buyer validly rejects the goods or documents, or where the buyer is insolvent and the seller stops the goods in transit. It will then be the seller who will want to claim from the insurer, if the goods are lost or damaged in transit.

In the absence of a specific agreement or any trade custom, the seller only needs to insure the goods to a reasonable value at the place of shipment. This is the cost price of the goods including commission, shipping charges and insurance premium. It does not cover any anticipated profits of the buyer or a rise in value of the goods or even freight, which ordinarily is only due on arrival of the goods. If a buyer wants to have these interests covered he will have to make express arrangement in the sale contract to that effect. Effective insurance cover to that extent might be crucial for the buyer to obtain finance from a bank for the transaction, because the banks will want to secure a certain insurance value to ensure effective security. Usually the parties insure the goods at invoice value, plus the incidental shipping charges plus a percentage (around 10 to 15 %) for the buyer's anticipated profits.

The seller must tender the insurance policy. This raises the question: can a cif seller tender a broker's cover note or certificate of insurance? According to older English decisions (*Wilson, Holgate & Co v Belgian Grain and Produce Co*, KBD; *Diamond Alkali Export Corporation v Bourgeois*, KBD and *Donald H Scott & Co v Barclays Bank*, CA), these documents are not equivalent to the policy and thus can only be acceptable based on agreement of the parties or trade usage. The parties can agree implicitly or explicitly on a different insurance document, particularly if the document puts the holder in a similar position, either entitling him to demand the issue of a policy, or under which he can claim against the insurer. In American practice, however, a certificate of insurance issued by or on behalf of the insurance company can be tendered generally in lieu of the policy.

The requirement to obtain an effective insurance policy to cover the goods for the transit is a condition of the cif contract. It is irrelevant that the uninsured goods arrive safely at the agreed destination: the buyer is still entitled to reject the documents for lack of suitable insurance cover (*Orient Company Ltd v Brekke & Howlid*, KBD and *Diamond Alkali Export Corporation v Bourgeois*, KBD).

2.5.4.3 Sales invoice and any other documents

The invoice and any other required documents, such as certificate of origin, quality or inspection, should comply with the agreement of the parties and should all link together with the other transport documents. In other words, they should describe and cover the same goods in a manner that is consistent with the other documents. This compliance is particularly relevant if payment is made by letter of credit via banks, where the banks check on the face of the documents that they are in compliance with the letter of credit. (Letter of credit is a payment and credit facility. The buyer opens this facility with a bank, which in turn guarantees payment to the seller on tender of the correct documents, as stipulated in the letter of credit.) Unless the parties have agreed otherwise, failure to tender the additional documents in the required form will normally have the same consequences as the failure to tender the principal documents correctly. Thus the buyer is able to reject the documents.

The invoice will usually debit the buyer for the agreed price including commission charges, freight and the insurance premium, but will credit the buyer in case of 'freight collect' arrangements. In that case the buyer will have to pay the freight or parts of it on collection of the goods from the carrier.

2.5.5 Time of tender and recipient of documents

The seller must tender the documents within the agreed timeframe or at the agreed date and to the named party, as provided for in the contract of sale.

If the time is not specified, either expressly or impliedly, the seller has to tender within a timeframe after shipment that is reasonable. What is reasonable will depend on the circumstances of the case, the nature of the goods, the distance to cover and any other element.

However, uncertainty as to what is reasonable can cause problems for the parties: the time of tender is generally a condition of the sale contract (*Toepfer v Lenersan-Poortman NV*, CA). Thus, a seller who does not tender the documents in time is in breach of the sale contract, enabling the buyer to reject the late documents and to treat the contract as repudiated, even if the goods have arrived (see *Kwei Tek Chao & Others v British Traders and Shippers Ltd*, QBD). If no timescale has been agreed upon, it can be very unsatisfactory for the buyer if he does not know how long he has to wait for tender of the documents and when he can safely treat the contract as repudiated. Similarly it is unsatisfactory for the seller, if he is uncertain whether any effort in getting the correct transport documents to the buyer is worth his while or whether the buyer is just going to reject them.

The timescale issue is even more important in the case of a corrective tender. This occurs where the seller had tendered the documents to the buyer, but the buyer had validly rejected them for discrepancies. Can the seller now re-tender good documents and if so, by which deadline? It is a matter of dispute whether the seller is free to make a corrective tender of documents. It was thought that the case of *Borrowman Phillips & Co v Free & Hollis*, CA suggested that a seller could so tender; however this is controversial (for further discussion, see Ahmad H Al-Rushoud, 'The right to cure defects in goods and documents', [1999] LMCLQ 456; Antonia Apps, 'The right to cure defective performance', [1994] LMCLQ 525; and Rex J Ahdar, 'Seller cure in the sale of goods', [1990] LMCLQ 364). Nevertheless, if one accepts that the wrongful tender has breached the sale contract, but has not by itself terminated the contract, the following conclusions can be drawn: the right to make a corrective tender will depend first on whether the buyer has valid grounds to treat the contract as repudiated and secondly on whether he elects to do so. If not, the seller should be allowed to cure the fault by tendering documents, this time in conformity with the contract. This, however, is only acceptable if the second tender is within the original timeframe.

The tender must be made to the buyer, but it could also be stipulated that it is to be made to another party. This might be an agent, or a bank in case the parties have agreed on a particular payment form. If the parties have chosen for payment to be effected by letter of credit, tender of the documents must be made to the bank against payment of the contract price. The seller cannot then fulfil his duties under the sale contract by tendering to the buyer directly and thus short-circuit this payment arrangement. Where a letter of credit is in place, a tender to the buyer directly will be ineffective (see *Soproma SpA v Marine & Animal By-Products Corporation*, QBD (Comm)).

2.5.6 Relationship with the carrier and insurer

The seller takes out the carriage and insurance contract and thus becomes a party to these contracts. At this point the buyer is not involved at all. This means that he has no contractual rights, as he is not privy to the contracts. However once the risk of damage or loss of the goods has passed, even if property has not, the buyer has a strong interest in the safe arrival of the goods and thus the proper performance of the carriage contract. The Contracts (Rights of Third Parties) Act 1999, which confers enforceable rights to the beneficiaries of contracts to which they are not party, is not applicable to a contract of the carriage of goods by sea, nor to any contract of carriage by road, rail or air in so far as it is subject to an international transport convention (s 6 (5) of the Act).

In the past, according to s 1 of the Bill of Lading Act 1855, the buyer only had rights of suit against the carrier 'as if he had been party to the contract', once he had become owner of the goods by reason of the consignment or indorsement of the bill of lading. The Bill of Lading Act 1855 has now been repealed and replaced by the Carriage of Goods by Sea Act (CoGSA) 1992. Under the CoGSA 1992 property in the goods is no longer the decisive factor. According to ss 2 and 3 of the CoGSA 1992, when the buyer has become lawful holder of the bill of lading or consignee according to the transport documents, he will obtain rights and duties as if he were party to the carriage contract. Thus the buyer can sue the carrier for any breach of the carrier's contractual duties. But in return, once the buyer either makes such a claim or if he demands delivery of the goods from the carrier, the carrier can also sue the buyer for freight and damages. The transfer of the bill of lading to the buyer also results in the extinction of any rights of the seller, as an original party to the carriage contract, against the carrier (CoGSA 1992, s 2(5)).

In order for the buyer to be able to claim against the insurer, the seller has to assign the policy to him (Marine Insurance Act (MIA) 1906, s 50). The buyer then 'steps into the shoes' of the seller, meaning he can claim in his own name, but the insurer can also make any defence against the buyer as he would have done against the seller (MIA 1906, s 50(2)). Once the policy is assigned to the buyer, the seller has lost his right to claim from the insurance. Should the buyer thereafter reject the goods, and the seller then wish to claim on the insurance policy, the buyer will have to assign it back. However, this only works if the buyer still has an insurable interest at the time he agrees to do so. Thus it might be beneficial to insert a contract term to this extent into the sale contract, obliging the buyer to reassign the insurance policy.

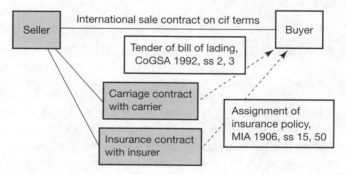

Fig 2.9 Relationship of a cif seller and buyer to the carrier and insurer

2.5.7 Risk and property

Under a cif contract the presumptions of s 20 and s 32(1) of the SoGA 1979 do not apply. Delivery of the transport documents to the buyer is deemed delivery of the goods to the buyer, instead of focusing on the delivery of the goods to the carrier as in s 32(1) of the SoGA 1979. In contrast to s 20 of the SoGA 1979, property and risk pass independently from each other. Risk passes on shipment of the goods, but property normally passes later. If the seller sells goods which were already afloat when the contract with the buyer was made, risk is still regarded as being with the buyer from time of shipment, even if this was before the contract date.

Property usually passes on tender of the bill of lading, except in the following situations.

(a) If the goods out of a bulk are not yet ascertained, the goods that are to be used to fulfil the particular contract are not yet identified. According to s 16 of the SoGA 1979, the passing of property is postponed until ascertainment. Sections 20A and 20B of the SoGA 1979, introduced by the Sale of Goods (Amendment) Act 1995, provide rules in case of shipment of goods in bulk (for more detail see **2.1.3** above).

(b) Where the parties have agreed differently. According to s 17 of the SoGA 1979 property passes when the parties intend it to and thus other arrangements can be made to this effect.

Property that passes on delivery of the bill of lading is conditional property: conditional on the acceptance on inspection of the goods by the buyer. If the buyer rejects the goods, property is to revert to the seller; see *Kwei Tek Chao & Others v British Traders and Shippers Ltd*, QBD and *Gill & Duffus SA v Berger & Co Inc*, HL.

2.5.8 Payment of price

Unless contrary arrangements have been made, payment under a cif contract will be due on valid tender of the documents. This is regardless of whether the goods arrive or are lost at sea. Any stipulation to the contrary will have to be expressed clearly. The contract price covers the goods, including export packaging, all the arrangements for carriage and insurance, and the export clearance. Where the freight is not pre-paid in full, the seller will have to discount the purchase price for the amount of freight due on arrival. Should the seller pay any charges due after arrival of the goods at the port of discharge, the buyer will have to reimburse him, as this is for his account.

2.6 International trade terms: free on board

2.6.1 Types of fob

Under fob, the seller contributes to the transportation in so far as he has to load the goods on a ship nominated by the buyer at the agreed port. The purchase price includes all costs incurred up to this point. Once the goods are loaded, the property passes to the buyer and the goods are at his risk and expense. He then is responsible for all further arrangements and charges.

The fob contract has been described as a flexible instrument by Devlin J in *Pyrene Co Ltd v Scindia Navigation Co Ltd*, QBD, which can be tailored to the parties' needs. The Court of Appeal in the case of *El Amria and El Minia*, approved the three types of variants which Devlin J had observed. These variants are set out as follows, however the names given to them seem to vary.

(a) *Simple fob, also called modern fob.* The buyer arranges the contract of carriage himself or via agents. The seller only loads the goods on the ship nominated by the buyer. The bill of lading is taken out directly by the buyer or his agent, without the seller's involvement.

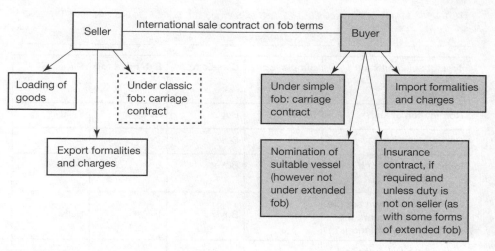

Fig 2.10 Free on board

(b) *Classic fob.* The buyer nominates the vessel and takes out insurance if required. The seller loads the goods on the vessel and takes out the bill of lading or other transport document in his name as consignor, but for the buyer's account. The seller, therefore, becomes party to the contract of carriage. The bill can be made out either directly to the buyer's order or to the seller's order. In the latter case, the seller has reserved his right of disposal in the goods until payment of the goods by the buyer. The seller has to transfer the bill of lading to the buyer.

(c) *Fob with additional services, also known as extended fob.* Here the seller makes the arrangements for carriage and also sometimes for insurance in his own name, but for the account of the buyer. Thus the risk of price fluctuations relating to these contracts is borne by the buyer — this is one of the important differences between the extended fob and the cif or the cost and freight (in case insurance is not required), where the seller has to bear this risk. The seller will usually charge commission for his services.

The differences in the duties of/and risks for the parties within these types are illustrated in Fig 2.11 and are compared with those under a cif contract.

2.6.2 General rights and duties under fob

The variations of the fob contracts contain distinctions as to which of the parties takes out the carriage contract and sometimes even the insurance contract. However, the *general* duties of the parties under fob can still be summarised as follows.

The duties of the buyer are:

(a) to nominate a suitable vessel for the goods and the voyage concerned (except in case of an extended fob). The buyer might have to provide a substitute vessel if the nominated ship fails to load the goods as agreed, but can only do so where the nomination was not 'definite' or 'final' according to the sale contract;

From left to right: the buyer's duties decrease while the seller's duties and risks increase.

Type of sale contract: - Who takes out:	Simple fob	Classic fob	Extended fob	Cif
Nomination of ship	Buyer	Buyer	Seller	Seller
Carriage contract	Buyer	Seller	Seller	Seller
Insurance contract if applicable	Buyer	Buyer	Seller	Seller
For whose account are the contracts/who bears the risk of price fluctuations?	Buyer	Buyer	Buyer	Seller
When does risk pass to buyer?	On shipment	On shipment	On shipment	On shipment
Generally, when does property pass to buyer?	On shipment	On shipment, unless other intention of parties, eg on tender of documents	On shipment, unless other intention of parties, eg on tender of documents	On tender of transport documents

Fig 2.11 Different fob types in overview and comparison with the cif contract

(b) to notify the seller of the nomination and readiness of the vessel in good time;

(c) to take out marine insurance cover, if applicable;

(d) to clear the goods for import, obtain licences, pay customs duties;

(e) to take all risk and bear all costs from the time of delivery of the goods on board ship, and if so provided, any costs for the seller's assistance;

(f) to pay for the goods.

The seller in turn must fulfil the following obligations:

(a) supply goods conforming to the sale contract, which are packaged appropriately;

(b) supply the commercial invoice and any documentation in the mode required in the sale contract, eg certificate of origin, etc;

(c) deliver the goods to the buyer by loading them on board the nominated ship at the agreed time and give the buyer notice of loading;

(d) clear the goods for export;

(e) pay any costs up to delivery of goods, including loading;

(f) to co-operate with the buyer in procuring the bill of lading or other transport documentation;

(g) to provide proof of delivery according to the sale contract and provide all information required for the buyer to insure the goods.

In the following paragraphs we will examine more closely some of these duties.

2.6.3 Arrangement of carriage and insurance; relationship with the carrier and insurer

As we have already seen, the responsibilities of who is to take out the carriage and insurance contracts differ depending on the chosen fob variant.

2.6.3.1 Simple fob

As previously explained, under a simple fob the buyer arranges for carriage and insurance himself, in his name and for his own account. Thus, under ordinary circumstances, no contractual rights and duties arising out of the carriage and the insurance contracts need to be transferred to the buyer. They are already vested in him from the beginning.

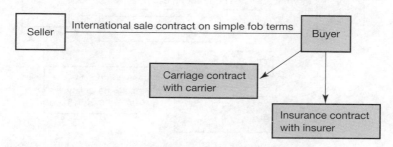

Fig 2.12 Simple fob: relationships of the seller and buyer with the carrier and insurer

Where does this leave the seller in case the goods are damaged during loading or during the voyage? In general, under a simple fob, where the buyer is the shipper, the seller is not party to the carriage contract. Thus the seller could only sue in tort if he was still the owner of the goods at the time where loss or damage occurred.

In the case of *Pyrene Co Ltd v Scindia Navigation Co Ltd*, QBD Devlin J implied a contract between the seller and the carrier. This had the effect that the Hague Rules, which were governing the contract of carriage, were applicable and the carrier could limit his liability accordingly. However the decision has been criticised and it is doubtful whether the decision can be generalised. In order to imply a contract, one must be able to infer all the different elements of offer, acceptance and consideration. This, however, might not be possible.

If the buyer takes out insurance for the cargo, the seller is not privy to the contract. Should the goods be lost or damaged during transit and the buyer able to reject the goods validly, the seller will have to bear the loss. Unless he himself took out additional insurance for his risk, he will not be covered. He might want to get the buyer to assign the marine policy to him, so that he, the seller, can claim against the insurer. However, the buyer is under no obligation to do so. Also, assignment is only possible as long as the buyer still has an insurable interest in the goods (MIA 1906, s 51). Once the buyer has finally rejected the goods, he has lost his insurable interest and thus can no longer assign any rights under the policy.

2.6.3.2 Classic and extended fob

Even if the seller had taken out the carriage contract, the buyer, once the lawful holder of the bill of lading or consignee according to the transport documents, will obtain rights and duties as if he were party to the carriage contract (CoGSA 1992, ss 2 and 3). The transfer of the bill of lading to the buyer results in the extinction of any rights of the seller (as original party to the carriage contract) against the carrier (CoGSA 1992, s 2(5)). If the seller had also taken out insurance under the extended fob, rights to claim from the insurance will transfer to the buyer with assignment of the policy (MIA 1906, s 50). As from this time the seller cannot claim against the insurance unless the buyer re-assigns the policy to him. Under the extended fob the relationship between the contract parties and the buyer is practically the same as under a cif contract.

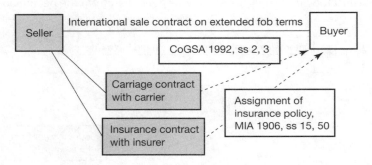

Fig 2.13 Extended fob contract: relationship of the seller and buyer to the carrier and insurer

2.6.4 Export clearance

It is normally stipulated in the contract which party is to apply for the export licence and pay the customs duties. Usually the duty falls on the seller, unless the sale is a supply transaction from a supplier to an exporter within the same country. The seller is most likely better acquainted with the licensing practices of the exporting country and also delivers the goods onto the ship, across the imaginary border.

2.6.5 Nomination of a suitable vessel

Unless there is a stipulation to the contrary, as for example under an extended fob, the duty of nominating a suitable vessel is on the buyer. The vessel has to depart from the port stipulated in the sale contract or, if a range of ports had been agreed upon, as chosen by the buyer (*Boyd & Co Ltd v Louis Louca*, QBD (Comm)). The buyer's duty to nominate a suitable ship is a condition precedent to the seller's duty to load. The port of loading is of the essence of the sale contract. It is considered to be part of the description of the goods according to s 13 of the SoGA 1979 (see *Petrograde Inc v Stinnes Handel GmbH*, QBD (Comm)).

The buyer has to notify the seller of any choice as to the port and of the shipping details in good time so that the seller can make the necessary arrangements for the delivery of the goods at the correct place and the appropriate time for loading the goods on board. Thus the duty to nominate a vessel is twofold. It comprises:

(a) the name of a suitable ship in which the goods can be carried; and

(b) the notice of probable readiness of the ship to receive the cargo. This has to be given in the timeframe as provided by the sale contract and, in the absence of such stipulation, as reasonable. This requirement is held to be a condition of the contract, because in mercantile contracts stipulations as to time are usually of the essence (see *Bunge Corporation v Tradax Export SA*, HL).

The ship is suitable if it is able, willing and ready to carry the cargo from the stipulated port within the shipping period as agreed in the sale contract. Any special requirements regarding the nature and carriage of the cargo must be met. For example goods that need to be kept cool need refrigerating equipment on board; crude oil in bulk is carried differently from a cargo of grain in bulk or from containerised goods.

Where the nomination fails (for example the nominated vessel does not arrive at all at the port of loading or not in time for shipment), the buyer is obliged to nominate a substitute vessel and to bear all additional expenses caused by this substitution. However substitution is only allowed within the contractual time or according to any trade practices (*Cargill v Continental*, QBD (Comm) and CA) and is not permissible if, according to the sale contract, the initial nomination is to be final or definite.

If the buyer is in breach of his duty to nominate a suitable ship, the seller can treat the contract as repudiated and claim damages for the failure to nominate or any delay in nominating the ship (see *Olearia Tirrena SpA v NV Algermeene Oliehandel (The Osterbek)*, QBD (Comm); affirmed by CA). However he cannot claim the contract price, because delivery has not taken place; the seller has still got the goods (*Colley v Overseas Exporters*, KBD).

2.6.6 Passing of risk and property

As a general rule, the delivery of the goods by the seller to the buyer under a 'free on board' contract is completed with shipment of the goods, thus risk and property generally pass on shipment (*Browne v Hare*, Ex Ch; *Stock v Inglis*, CA (on appeal sub nom *Inglis v Stock*, HL)). However, property in fob contracts passes on shipment only if:

(a) the goods are specific or ascertained; and where

(b) there is no stipulation to the contrary, expressed or implied (SoGA 1979, s 17) as to when property is to pass.

If the goods are not ascertained, property passes once the appropriate portions are appropriated to the various buyers or according to the rules of s 20A of the SoGA 1979 (see **2.1.3** above). However, usually under fob, the seller will have appropriated the goods out of a bulk by delivering the goods to the carrier nominated by the buyer. No other goods of the bulk other than the ones intended for the buyers will be loaded. In this context Rule 5(2) of s 18 of the SoGA 1979 clarifies the ascertaining intention of the parties: unascertained goods are held to have been unconditionally appropriated to the contract with the consequence that property passes to the buyer, when the seller delivers the goods to the carrier 'for the purpose of transmission to the buyer'. In such a case property passes unless the seller has reserved his right of disposal.

Reservation of the right of disposal is most likely to have been intended where the seller retains the documents until performance of the contractual terms of payment, for example until acceptance of a bill of exchange or payment in cash or under a letter of credit (*Owners of Cargo Lately Laden on Board the Subro Valour v Owners of the Subro Vega (The Subro Valour), (The Subro Vega)*, QBD (Admlty)). Where the seller concludes the contract of carriage in his own name and ships the goods as consignor or to his order, the presumption of s 19(2) of the SoGA 1979 states that the seller has thereby reserved his right of disposal (*Mitsui & Co Ltd v Flota Mercante Grancolombiana SA*, CA and also *Concordia Trading BV v Richco International Ltd*, QBD (Comm)). In order for property to pass the seller has to be paid first. However where the documents are taken out in the buyer's name or to his order the above presumption is not applicable and property is assumed to have passed on delivery to the carrier (SoGA 1979, s 18 Rule 5(2)).

As under fob contracts risk and, unless intended otherwise by the parties, also property passes 'on shipment', it is important to appreciate the meaning of 'shipment'. What are the duties of the seller with regard to shipment and thus loading of the goods? There are two views possible.

(a) The seller is only responsible for the stages of the loading operation until the goods pass the ship's rail and therefore it is irrelevant if the goods thereafter do not arrive safely on the ship. This understanding has been employed by the Incoterms 2000; see also *Frebold and Sturznickel (Trading as Panda OHG) v Circle Products Ltd*, CA. However Devlin J in *Pyrene Co Ltd v Scindia Navigation Co Ltd*, QBD had highlighted that the ship's rail as the passing point of responsibilities might not be the most appropriate. Where an accident happens during the loading process, it seems to be rather fortuitous whether this occurred before or after passing the ship's rail. It seems artificial to split the risk during what is, in reality, a single operation.

(b) The other view is that the seller has only discharged his duties once the goods are successfully stowed and loading is fully completed. *Colley v Overseas Exporters*, KBD and *Compagnie Commerciale Sucres et Denrees v C Czarnikow Ltd (The Naxos)*, CA seem to suggest this solution. If parties contract on terms such as 'fob stowed' or 'fob trimmed', this indicates that the seller is to pay the charges for loading the goods until stowed or trimmed. However such a term does not necessarily stipulate the passing of risk. Therefore this should be clarified in the contract, for example by stating 'goods at seller's cost and risk until fob stowed'.

2.6.7 Payment of price

If there are no stipulations to the contrary, payment is due on delivery of the goods by the seller free on board; see s 28 of the SoGA 1979. However it is most common in the trade to insert payment clauses similar to those in cif contracts, for example cash against documents, payment by letter of credit or documents against acceptance of a bill of exchange (for more detail see **Chapter 3** below). The effect of such terms is usually that passing of property is also postponed until payment has been effected accordingly.

2.6.8 Examination and acceptance of the goods

The fob buyer does not need to examine the goods on delivery on board in order to reserve his right to rejection (SoGA 1979, ss 34 and 35). Unless the parties have agreed on a pre-shipment inspection, the buyer can inspect them once they have arrived at their place of destination. Where goods are transported there is a prima facie presumption that the place and time of examination are the place and time of delivery of the goods. However this presumption can be displaced by arrangement between the parties, the circumstances of the sale or by custom of the trade. According to Bailache J in *Saunt v Belcher and Gibbons*, KBD, in order for the presumption to be displaced two conditions must be met:

(a) the seller must know, either because he was told or by necessary inference, that the goods are transported further; and

(b) the place of delivery by the seller must either be unsuitable for inspection or the nature of the packaging of the goods must make inspection at that place unreasonable.

Under export sales place and time of examination are often postponed. In cif sales and classic or extended fob sales where the seller has to deliver the bill of lading, constructive delivery of the goods will take place at the time when the bill of lading is tendered. This is completely divorced from the actual situation of the goods. Where, for example, under an ex works, strict fob or fas contract the seller is not obliged to tender a bill of lading, delivery of the goods packaged for export will take place in the seller's country, which does not seem to be a suitable place for the buyer to examine the goods. In these cases, it seems that the conditions for postponement as in *Saunt v Belcher and Gibbons*, KBD are fulfilled. Once the goods arrive at the port of destination, but are still to be transported further to the buyer's warehouse or depot, the place of examination will usually be the buyer's depot (see *B & P Wholesale Distributors v Marko*). In *Molling & Co v Dean & Sons Ltd* the goods sold were subject to a resale to an overseas destination. The seller knew about the resale and packaged the goods for the onward transport. It was held that place and time of examination contemplated by the original sale contract was postponed until the arrival at the overseas destination.

The buyer has a reasonable time in which to inspect the goods (see SoGA 1979, s 35(2), (4) and *Clegg v Andersson (t/a Nordic Marine)*, CA for what is reasonable). Once this time has lapsed without the buyer having indicated that he wishes to reject the goods, he is deemed to have accepted them (see SoGA 1979, s 35(4)). He is also deemed to have accepted the goods where he intimates to the seller that he has accepted them or if he acts in any way inconsistent with the ownership of the seller (SoGA 1979, s 35(1); see also *Tradax Export SA v European Grain & Shipping Ltd*, QBD (Comm)) with respect to the latter point). However, delivery under a subsale does not constitute such an act (see SoGA 1979, s 35(6)). (For a general introduction to delivery and acceptance of goods see **2.1.6** above.)

2.7 Standard term contracts and common contractual clauses

In order to overcome some of the difficulties presented to the parties by the facts of the case and the applicable legal system, clauses are inserted into the contract to create a level of certainty regarding the performance of particular rights and duties. This can be done by adding specific clauses or by using a particular standard form contract. The latter may be drawn up by organisations representing the interests of a particular industry or by one of the contract parties tailored to their needs. Based on the principle of party autonomy, within the limits of the mandatory rules of law, these contract clauses are valid. They thus vary the standard trade terms and the inferences otherwise made by the law in so far as these clauses are clear and precise.

Problems arise when the parties have chosen a standard trade term, but add separate undertakings of the parties, which are in conflict with that term. For example the parties choose to contract under cif terms, but agree that the goods must arrive at a specific date at the buyer's place of business. In this case the fundamental division of rights and duties between the parties under cif terms conflicts with the additional stipulations, which here point to an arrival contract. Ambiguities of such a kind should be avoided, as they can lead to long and protracted litigation, when finally the courts have to decide the meaning of these stipulations and the contract. The terms inconsistent with the overall designation of the contract may be struck out (see *Gill & Duffus SA v Berger & Co Inc*, HL) or they might be interpreted in a way that does not conflict with the designation of the contract (see *Vitol SA v Esso Australia Ltd (The Wise)*, QBD (Comm); the case was remitted to the Commercial Court on other grounds). On the other hand, the individually agreed terms might be so strong, clear and unambiguous that they override the designation of the standard trade term altogether (see *Comptoir d'Achat et de Vente du Boerenbond Belge SA v Luis de Ridder Limitada (The Julia)*, HL.

In the appendices at the end of this book some standard term contracts developed by GAFTA, the Grain and Feed Trade Association, have been included to provide an overview of possible clauses and their wording. Please take the time to read them in full. Some of the common clauses are briefly introduced below. As far as possible, reference is made to the appended 'contract for shipment of feeding stuffs in bulk, *tale quale* – cif terms', by GAFTA (Gafta No. 100). The common contract clauses include the following.

2.7.1 Allowances

The parties agree that certain minor breaches of contract are treated with a degree of lenience. If the breach is within the stated allowance, the innocent party is not entitled to terminate the contract, but receives compensation according to a pre-fixed scale. For example the buyer can reduce the contract price for a certain percentage per unit of deficiency of the warranted quality. Such a term for example is contained in the first part of clause 5 of Gafta No. 100. However once the defect is outside the allowance, the buyer can reject the goods and/or documents.

2.7.2 Notice of appropriation

The contract often stipulates how, when and with which content the seller has to give notice of appropriation. As seen in **2.5.3** above, appropriation is the binding act of the seller of selecting goods to the contract. Usually the seller has to state the vessel and the approximate weight of the goods shipped and dispatch this notice in a particular way within a certain time. For an example see clause 10 of Gafta No. 100.

2.7.3 Default clauses

Default clauses state what is to happen where a breach occurs that entitles the innocent party to terminate the contract. The clause may give details of how the damages are to be calculated and which steps the parties can take towards establishing the default price of the goods. It may also call for arbitration in case the parties cannot agree on certain parameters. Read clause 23 of Gafta No. 100 as an example.

2.7.4 Laytime and demurrage clauses

Parties to a voyage charterparty (a contract under which a trader, then called a charterer, is employing a whole ship for a particular journey – see **4.2.7.1**) usually negotiate particular rules regarding the timeframe within which the loading and unloading operations are to take place. If this time limit is exceeded then the charterer has to pay liquidated damages called demurrage to the shipowner. Depending on the trade and size of the business, the seller or the buyer may charter a ship. However, according to the sale contract, this party (the seller or buyer, as the case may be) is not responsible for all the loading and unloading operations, but only for one leg. For example, a cif seller might charter a vessel, being only responsible for the loading operation, whereas it is the buyer's duty to unload. Or a fob buyer might be the charterer of a vessel awaiting loading by the seller. Thus, the charterer (being the seller or buyer under the sale contract) has no control over one of the legs of the loading/discharge operations, but is still responsible to the shipowner under the charterparty to pay demurrage or damages for detention of the vessel once the agreed time limit for this operation is exceeded. Therefore, it is in the charterer's interest to 'encourage' the other party to the sale contract to fulfil its loading/discharge obligations under the sale contract within a reasonable time or to face charges of liquidated damages for any delay. This is achieved by inserting a laytime and demurrage clause into the sale contract. The obligation to pay laytime and demurrage under the sale contract is usually independent from any such obligation under the charterparty. So it will be irrelevant whether, under the charterparty, the charterer in fact had to pay demurrage or not; between the seller and the buyer, only the criteria of the clause in the sale contract need to be fulfilled.

2.7.5 Force majeure clauses

The law has very tight rules regarding impossibility of performance and frustration of contract, particularly in commodity sales (sale of agricultural products or raw materials, such as grain, sugar, coffee, oils, metals and ores). This is due to the fact that, even if the intended source for obtaining the goods is not available, comparable goods can normally be bought elsewhere, in order to fulfil the contract. In response to these very strict rules of law, businessmen have developed force majeure clauses. These state which events would entitle one party either to suspend its obligations, to extend time for performance of delivery, or to bring the contract to an end and free the parties from performance. Force majeure clauses usually set out the steps which must be taken by the parties in this process, for example as in clause 19 of Gafta No. 100.

2.7.6 Retention of title clause/Romalpa clause

Based on a simple retention of title clause, the seller retains property in the goods until certain conditions are met, for example payment of the purchase price. An extended retention of title clause, also called a Romalpa clause, stipulates in addition that the buyer may resell the goods only as agent of the seller, and receive the purchase price as agent for, on behalf of and on account of the seller. Such a stipulation has been upheld under English law in the case of *Aluminium Industrie Vaassen BV v Romalpa Aluminium Ltd*, CA. However, there are strict boundaries which need to be observed. If the retention of title clause can be interpreted as constituting a charge within the ambit of s 396 of the Companies Act 1985, it will only be valid if registered according to the Companies Act (see *Re Bond Worth Ltd*, ChD).

2.7.7 Certificate final clauses

These clauses make a certificate final as to the question whether the seller has performed certain duties in accordance with the contract; for example the duty to ship goods of the agreed quality (see clause 5, line 61 of Gafta No. 100). If the seller tenders the correct document, stating the goods conform to the contract, the buyer is estopped from pleading and proving breach of performance. Thus, the effect of such a clause is the conversion of the seller's duty to ship contractual goods, into a documentary duty of tendering the correct documents. In respect of any other breach of performance which is outside the ambit of the certificate, the remedies of the buyer remain unaffected.

2.7.8 Choice of law and jurisdiction clauses

The standard term contracts are drafted against the background of a particular legal system, which imposes particular rights and obligations on the parties. In order to ensure that the envisaged distribution of responsibilities is upheld, the contract needs to be understood and evaluated in the light of this particular legal system. Thus, 'choice of law' clauses determine the legal system, the applicable law (for example English law or French law) to be used to identify the parties' rights and duties. The best way to ensure that this choice is accepted and interpreted in the way intended, is to choose not only the applicable law but also the jurisdiction of the courts of a particular country in which adjudication is to take place (for example the jurisdiction of English courts or more specifically, of the High Court of England), or a particular body offering arbitration. Clause 26, of Gafta No. 100 is providing an example.

2.7.9 Arbitration clause or *Scott v Avery* clause

This is an arbitration clause, also called a *Scott v Avery* clause, that stipulates that the parties must arbitrate over any disputes initially, before they can even call on the courts to judge on the issues in question. The arbitral award is a condition precedent for any court proceedings. Should one of the parties nevertheless start proceedings in court despite this clause, the other party can apply for a stay of these proceedings until arbitration is completed. Clause 27 of Gafta No. 100 gives an example.

2.7.10 Exclusion of international conventions

The contracts are drafted with reference to either English law or another legal system. To ensure they can function within the chosen legal system, they often exclude the application of international conventions. This ensures that the responsibilities of the parties is as envisaged and not altered by the convention. For example, clause 28 of Gafta No. 100 expressly excludes the application of the Hague Conventions of 1964 on the Uniform Law on Sales and the Uniform Law on Formation of Contracts, the United Nations Convention on the International Sale of Goods of 1980, the 1974 United Nations Convention on the Prescription (Limitation) in the International Sale of Goods and the amending Protocol of 1980, and the Incoterms.

2.7.11 Contract guarantee

The contract may call on one of the parties to enter a separate guarantee to warrant satisfactory performance of the contract. This can be done via one of the following means: a performance guarantee; demand guarantee; performance bond; or standby letter of credit. Each of the aforementioned is an independent undertaking of a third party, normally a bank, to pay a certain amount of money on demand and/or on fulfilment of certain strict criteria, such as tender of specific documents (see **3.5** below for more details). As this undertaking is separate from the underlying contract of sale it is not affected by any disputes arising from the sale. Thus it provides adequate security for the beneficiary. It is often taken out for the benefit of the buyer, who can call on it if the goods do not conform to the contract. Where the buyer has already paid in full for the goods on tender of the documents, this can prove to be particularly useful. Where the buyer must pay the price on tender of the documents he has no opportunity to inspect the goods prior to payment. Thus a performance guarantee at least provides him with a reasonable security. Having access to money which represents possible damages or the contract price, as the case may be, without having to claim them from the seller in a different country, is of great benefit.

2.8 Consequences of breach of contractual obligations

2.8.1 Introduction

As we have seen in **2.1** above, the law relating to the sale of goods in England and Wales is governed mainly by the Sale of Goods Act 1979 (as amended by the Sale and Supply of Goods Act 1994 and the Sale of Goods (Amendment) Act 1995) and common law.

The Sale of Goods Act 1979 sets out rules regarding the performance of the contract. Rules about delivery, and delivery of wrongful amount, can be found in ss 29–32, with s 31 covering instalment deliveries. The rules relating to the examination, acceptance and rejection of goods are covered by ss 34, 35 and 35A of SoGA 1979. As a general principle, the buyer cannot reject the goods once he is deemed to have accepted them (see **2.6.8** above for more detail). However, he will be able to claim damages if the goods do not correspond with the contracted goods. The claim for damages is governed by the SoGA 1979 and by general legal principles.

Loss of a claim by lapse of time is generally governed by the Limitation Act 1980. It provides that after a period of six years from the breach of contract, the defendant is entitled to plead the defence of limitation. For example if the buyer wants to sue the seller for damages due to a breach of contract, the seller is entitled to use the defence of limitation if the claim is brought after six years from the date of the breach.

Where a contract is not performed to full satisfaction, the aggrieved party will want to be advised as to its rights and the appropriate cause of action. Can the goods be rejected or damages claimed? Can the seller sue for the contract price? In order to determine the available remedy we first need to ascertain the type of contract term that has been breached. This will determine the cause of action possible.

2.8.2 Different categories of contract terms: conditions and warranties, innominate terms

The terms of a contract of sale are either conditions, warranties or innominate terms. Depending on which of these categories the term belongs to, the effect of a breach of contract differs. For example, if a *condition* is breached, the aggrieved party is entitled to treat the contract as repudiated, however it can only claim damages if a *warranty* is not complied with.

A condition is a term describing the essence of the contract. A warranty is a contract term of less importance; it is collateral to the main purpose of the contract. An innominate term (also called intermediate term) is a contractual term which is neither a condition nor a warranty. The effects of a breach of an innominate term will depend on the nature and gravity of the breach. If the breach is grave, the innocent party can treat the contract as repudiated, as if the term were a condition. If it is slight, only damages can be claimed, as if it was a breach of warranty (Fig 2.14).

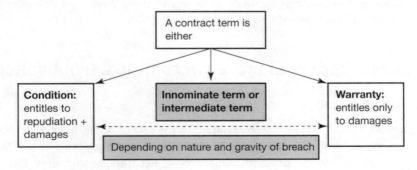

Fig 2.14 Different categories of contract terms

The parties can choose to state in their contract whether a term should be a condition, warranty or an innominate term. In addition to any express terms, further terms may be implied in a contract by statute or case law (Fig 2.15). These terms can take effect as conditions, warranties or innominate terms. In international sale contracts many terms, however, will take effect as conditions.

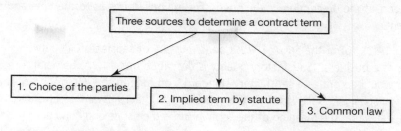

Fig 2.15 Sources for determining a contract term

We shall now take a closer look at these categories of contract terms.

2.8.2.1 Condition

This is a term of such importance to the parties making the contract that it can be classed as the essence of the contract. Breach of a contract condition gives the innocent party the right to treat the contract as repudiated and to claim damages. For example if the seller has breached a condition regarding the goods and there are no special considerations, such as trade custom or party agreement to the contrary, then the buyer can reject the goods (SoGA 1979, s 11(3)) and claim damages from the seller for non-delivery of the goods. The damages are for the difference between the market price of the goods at the time of contracted delivery and the purchase price, as well as including any consequential losses (SoGA 1979, s 51).

However the buyer may waive a breach of condition of the seller and treat it only as a breach of warranty (SoGA 1979, s 11(2)). In such a case he can only claim damages for the difference in value of the goods between the value delivered and the contracted value (SoGA 1979, s 53). This might be a good solution where the breach is minimal and the buyer is still interested in the goods regardless. In cases where the buyer has already parted with the contract price and is unsure of the financial standing of the seller, he might be better advised to keep the goods and only claim damages. This might be better than not only losing the goods and the price but also having to sue the seller in another jurisdiction.

As we have seen, certain terms implied into a contract of sale are regarded as conditions by the SoGA 1979. However, according to s 55 of the SoGA 1979, these terms can be excluded or varied by express agreement. Therefore each contract must be studied carefully. Although this right to negate or vary these implied terms is subject to the Unfair Contract Terms Act 1977, this Act does not apply to international supply contracts (see UCTA 1977, s 26). This means that generally in international sale contracts the parties are free to choose their contract terms.

Relevant examples of implied conditions under the SoGA 1979 are outlined below.

(a) Section 12 (1), (5A) of the SoGA 1979: the seller must have the right to sell the goods or, in a case of an agreement to sell, he must have acquired such a right by the time property is to pass to the buyer.

(b) Section 13 (1), (1A) of the SoGA 1979: where sold by description, the goods must comply with that description. Shipment terms in international sale contracts are often treated as being part of the description of the goods, for example terms as to the time and place of shipment.

(c) Section 14(2), (6) of the SoGA 1979: goods must be of satisfactory quality if sold 'in the course of a business'. Satisfactory quality is described in s 14(2A) as what a reasonable person would accept as a satisfactory standard, considering the description of the goods (see also *Rapalli v KL Take Ltd*, CA), their price and all other relevant circumstances. Section 14(2B) states that the meaning of this term includes their state and condition; factors, such as fitness for all purposes for which such goods are commonly supplied, appearance and finish, freedom from minor defects, safety and durability are, amongst others, taken to be aspects of the quality of the goods. Section 14(2C) excludes any matter which has been drawn to the attention of the buyer or ought to have been revealed during any pre-contract examination.

(d) Section 14(3), (6) of the SoGA 1979: if the goods are sold 'in the course of a business', the goods have to be reasonably fit for any purpose that was specifically indicated to the seller before the contract was concluded. In the absence of such specific purpose being made known to the buyer, the goods must by implication nevertheless be fit for the purpose for which these goods are commonly supplied (see SoGA 1979, s 14 (2B) (a), (3), (6)).

(e) Section 15(2), (3) of the SoGA 1979: goods bought on the basis of a sample must correspond with the sample.

Particular shipping terms in international sales have been taken to be conditions, mostly as being part of the description of the goods.

(a) Generally, any term in the sale contract stipulating a specific time for the performance of a specific act; for example the time for giving the notice of readiness under a fob contract (see *Bunge Corporation v Tradax Export SA*, HL) or the time of shipment (see *Ashmore & Son v C S Cox*, QBD (Comm)).

(b) Formal requirements of the notice of appropriation (see *Bunge Corporation v Tradax Export SA*, CA).

(c) The port of loading in a fob contract (see *Petrograde Inc v Stinnes Handel GmbH*, QBD (Comm)); the place of shipment and discharge, where the contract specifically stipulates these (see *Gill & Duffus v Société pour L'Exportation des Sucres*, QBD (Comm), affirmed by CA).

(d) The name and type of the vessel to be used for the carriage only in the unusual event that this is specifically agreed; otherwise a vessel that is usual in the trade for the carriage of such goods (see *Ashmore & Son v C S Cox*, QBD (Comm) *and Bowes v Shand*, HL); see also *Thomas Borthwick Ltd v Bunge Ltd*, QBD (Comm) for the name of the vessel that was to be used, but this is depending on the circumstances of the case and the contractual duties.

(e) The route to be used by the vessel; for example in case a direct shipment clause was breached due to the ship calling at transit and intermediate ports (*Bergerco USA v Vegoil*, QBD (Comm)).

In case of a minor breach of condition s 15A of the SoGA 1979 stipulates a new rule. This section has been inserted by the Sale and Supply of Goods Act 1994. It is only applicable in non-consumer cases. According to s 15A(1) a breach of condition of ss 13–15 of the SoGA 1979 cannot be treated as such if the breach is so slight that it would be unreasonable to do so. This rule, however, is subject to the parties' contrary intention or the implication of the contract (SoGA 1979, s 15A (2)). It is suggested that parties to an international sale contract do not intend s 15A of the SoGA 1979 to apply. In international sale contracts the strict performance of many obligations is considered to be implied in the contract. So it would seem that by using one of the trade terms, such as cif and fob, the parties intend to exclude s 15A of the SoGA 1979, even if they have not inserted an express exclusion clause to that effect.

A similar line of argument is taken in case of delivery of the wrong quantity. The quantity of the goods has been held to be a description of the goods and therefore a condition according to s 13(1), (1A) of the SoGA 1979. However, the new s 30(2A) of the SoGA 1979 does not allow for rejection on this basis if the variation is only slight. Again, it is submitted that the parties to an international sale contract do not intend these rules to apply (SoGA 1979, s 30(5)). Thus the quantity is crucial, unless the parties have provided for special allowances in their contract (which can be found in many standard term contracts).

The impact on international sales law and the application of existent case law would be significant should the courts decide otherwise and turn to apply ss 15A and 30(2A) of the SoGA 1979 in the international sale context. A decision has yet to be made.

2.8.2.2 Warranty

A warranty is a contract term of less importance. It is collateral to the main purpose of the contract. Its breach does not entitle the buyer to reject the goods (see SoGA 1979, s 11(3)) but to claim damages according to s 53 of the SoGA 1979.

2.8.2.3 Innominate terms

An innominate term is a contractual term which is neither a condition nor a warranty. It has been developed in shipping/carriage contracts in relation to stipulations as to the seaworthiness of the vessel (*Hong Kong Fir Shipping Co Ltd v Kawasaki Kisen Kaisha Ltd*, CA) and has since been extended to other types of contracts. The effects of a breach will depend on the nature and gravity of the breach:

(a) where the breach is grave: the contract can be treated as repudiated by the party not at fault;

(b) where the breach is not serious: the contract still has to be performed but the innocent party can claim damages arising from the breach.

An example of an innominate term is the stipulation of 'shipment to be made in good condition' (see *Cehave NV v Bremer Handelsgesellschaft mbH (The Hansa Nord)*, CA).

2.8.3 Calculation of damages

As a general rule damages are compensatory and the rules are designed to give the innocent party the benefit of the agreed bargain. The measure of the damages, regardless of who is claiming and on what basis, is stated as 'the estimated loss directly and naturally resulting, in the ordinary course of events', from the breach of the other party (see SoGA 1979, ss 50(2), 51(2), 53(2)). If the sale fails and there is a market price for the goods in question, the damages are generally calculated on the basis of that market price, regardless of whether or not the innocent party acted upon it, for example sold or bought goods. In detail, the damages are measured as follows.

(a) According to s 50(3) of the SoGA 1979 *damages for the seller for non-acceptance* of the goods by the buyer are 'prima facie to be ascertained by the difference between the contract price and the market or current price at the time or times when the goods ought to have been accepted or (if no time was fixed for acceptance) at the time of the refusal to accept'.

(b) *Damages for the buyer due to non-delivery* are 'prima facie to be ascertained by the difference between the contract price and the market price or current price of the goods at the time or times when they ought to have been delivered or (if no time was fixed) at the time of the refusal to deliver' (see SoGA 1979, s 51(3)).

An important question in practice might be whether the innocent party has reasonable access to an available market. The innocent party is expected to mitigate the loss, but does not have to search the world for a market. The test is whether a party has acted reasonably in the circumstances of the case.

If there is an available market the innocent party is expected to use this market to put itself in the same position as if the sale had gone ahead. This means all profits should have been recovered, leaving no scope to claim for lost profits or other consequential losses as referred to in s 54 of the SoGA 1979.

If a market is not available the court must apply the rule in section 50(2) of the SoGA 1979 (for non-acceptance), or in s 51(2) of the SoGA 1979 (for non-delivery) or in s 53(2) of the SoGA 1979 (for breach of warranty) and assess the value of the goods to the innocent party. The loss is estimated by taking into account the cost to remedy the fault or to replace the goods or any price agreed in a subsale of these particular goods. The innocent party should be able to recover any lost profits on a subsale for the specific goods and any other consequential losses according to s 54 of the SoGA 1979. These however are only recoverable if the other party knew or should have known of the circumstances giving rise to these losses (see *R & H Hall Ltd v W H Pim Junr & Co Ltd*, HL for contemplation of a resale of the particular goods).

Particularly in a rising or falling market, the date for assessment of damages under ss 51(3) and 50(3) of the SoGA 1979 is crucial. This is the date of breach, ie the time when the goods ought to have been delivered or ought to have been accepted. This will depend on the specific contract and circumstances. As a general rule, the focus is on the time when the innocent party could reasonably know that the other party is not performing the contract.

For example, the due date for delivery under a cif or fob contract will often be taken as the date when the documents ought to have been tendered (for more detail see **2.6.8** above). The due date for acceptance in cif and fob sales will depend on the circumstances of the non-acceptance and also on the contract. However, it will often relate to the due time for acceptance of the documents rather than acceptance of the goods themselves (for more detail see **2.6.8** above). Once the innocent party is aware of the other party's failure to honour the contract, it has to go out into the market immediately and make a replacement contract.

Careful examination of the detailed facts of each scenario is important. For example buyer whose seller is in repudiatory breach, might be in a very different position depending on the facts of the case:

(a) if the seller did not deliver the goods at all, the date for calculating the damages is likely to be the due date for tendering the documents or the last date for delivery of the goods on board ship or to the carrier, depending on the contract terms;

(b) if the buyer rejected the goods for non-conformity with the contract after examination, it is the time when the buyer could have reasonably examined the goods upon their arrival.

In a rising or falling market this difference in time can translate into a vast monetary difference in market price and value of the goods.

Similarly, in case of the seller's *breach of warranty*, the market rule and duty to mitigate the loss is of importance. Section 53(3) of the SoGA 1979 states that the buyer can claim damages which are 'prima facie the difference between the value of the goods at the time of delivery to the buyer and the value they would have had if they had fulfilled the warranty'. Again, if there is an available market, the buyer must fulfil any obligations under a subsale for goods of the same description by buying goods corresponding to the subsale. Lost profit due to the breach of warranty is therefore not recoverable. However, if there is no available market or if the buyer has already sold the specific goods under the original contract, he can recover the lost profits and any other consequential losses, provided the seller was aware of the possibility of a subsale (SoGA 1979, s 54).

Damages for *late delivery* are normally calculated on the basis of the difference between the market price on the date when delivery should have been made and on the date of actual delivery. This is the case where the intention was to resell the goods on the market. Special damages, such as consequential losses, which were within the contemplation of the parties when the contract was made, can be recovered according to s 54 of the SoGA 1979.

The parties might choose to estimate the likely damages and thus agree on a *liquidated damages clause* in the event of a breach. This clause will usually contain rules for remedies and the amount of damages payable in the event of failure to perform the contractual duties. The parties should make sure that the damages are a genuine pre-estimate of the loss, otherwise the court might class them as a disguised penalty, which will not be upheld.

2.9 Remedies of the buyer

There are several possible remedies which the buyer might be able to use against the seller. The remedy depends on the type of breach and, in some cases, on the choice of the buyer as to how to proceed after he took notice of the breach. In the absence of a contract clause specifying the remedies and damages, the following rules apply.

2.9.1 Rights of rejection

The buyer has two rights of rejection:

(a) rejection of the documents for a non-conformity (which is a breach of condition); or

(b) rejection of the goods if a condition is breached (for more detail see **2.5.2** above).

The right to reject the goods and the right to reject the documents are separate from each other and need to be taken into account separately (see *Finley & Co Ltd v NV Kwik Hoo Tong Handel Maatschappij*, CA and *Kwei Tek Chao v British Traders and Shippers Ltd*, QBD). Thus the acceptance of the documents and the payment of the price does not prejudice the buyer's right to reject the goods and vice versa.

The rejection must be clear, final and unequivocal. It must be noted that the definitive rejection of the documents entails the rejection of the goods as a necessary consequence.

However, if documents are accepted regardless of a discrepancy with the contractual terms, the goods cannot be rejected on the same grounds. The particular discrepancy is either deemed to be waived or treated by applying estoppel (*Panchaud Frères SA v Etablissements General Grain Co*, CA, but see also *Glencore Grain Rotterdam BV v Lebanese Organisation for International Commerce*, CA, putting the *Panchaud Frères* decision into context).

If the circumstances allow, the buyer has a right to partial rejection according to the new s 35A of the SoGA 1979. If the seller is in breach of the contract, entitling the buyer to reject the goods, the buyer can still accept that part of the goods unaffected by the breach, without losing his right to reject the other goods.

Even if a condition is breached, the buyer can still choose whether he wants to reject the documents or goods, or whether he prefers to accept performance of the contract. In the latter case, he can waive the breach of condition and claim damages for the discrepancy instead (SoGA 1979, s 11(2)). Particularly in cases where the buyer has already paid for the goods and is uncertain about the seller's solvency, he might not want to risk losing both, the purchase price and the goods. He might prefer to minimise his risk by accepting the goods, thus being able to sell them on, and claiming damages for breach of warranty. However, this intention to claim damages for the breach should be clearly communicated to the other party to make sure that this right cannot be lost by way of waiver or estoppel. If the buyer chooses to reject the goods finally (either directly or via the rejection of the documents) he can claim damages for non-delivery.

2.9.2 Seller's right to retender conforming documents?

If the buyer rejects the documents, the question arises whether the seller can cure the defect and tender documents a second time, now conforming to the contract. The issue of (re)tender of documents is controversial. (For details see Ahmad H Al-Rushoud, 'The right to cure defects in goods and documents' [1999] LMCLQ 456; Antonia Apps, 'The right to cure defective performance' [1994] LMCLQ 525; and Rex J Ahdar, 'Seller cure in the sale of goods', [1990] LMCLQ 364.) One line of argument goes in favour of a right to cure within the time limit for the tender. Another sees the tender of non-conforming documents as a breach of the sale contract which entitles the buyer to treat the contract as repudiated thus denying a right to cure.

A different way of looking at this issue is to start with looking at the consequences of the particular breach of contract (see also J Chuah, *Law of International Trade* (3rd edn, 2005, 4–48): if the seller tenders non-conforming documents the buyer can reject the documents. This in itself is *not* a repudiation of the contract. Thus, one could argue with Mance J in *Hyundai Merchant Marine Co Ltd v Karander Maritime Inc (The Nizuru)*, QBD (Comm) (at p 70) that the seller has the right to present complying documents within the contractually appointed time (similarly for a notice of appropriation in *Borrowman Phillips & Co v Free & Hollis*, CA). Only if the seller fails to do so 'may the buyer treat himself discharged from further performance and claim damages for non-delivery' (Mance J in *Hyundai Merchant Marine Co Ltd v Karander Maritime Inc (The Nizuru)*, QBD (Comm) (at p 70)). However the seller's conduct might amount to a repudiation or, alternatively, a cure might be impossible on the facts, thus in both cases relieving the buyer from having to wait for a curative tender.

2.9.3 Damages for non-delivery

In case of non-delivery of the goods, that is, either if the seller refuses to deliver or if the buyer rejects the goods for valid reasons, the buyer can claim damages for non-delivery according to s 50 of the SoGA 1979. As we have seen, the damages are normally calculated on the basis of the market price rule. Thus, any profit or loss of the buyer under a subsale of goods of the same description is generally not taken into account in assessing the damages (see *Williams Brothers v EDT Agius Limited*, HL). If however, the very same goods were subcontracted for sale before the delivery date under the first contract and this was within the contemplation of parties to the original contract, any loss on this subsale can be claimed according to s 54 of the SoGA 1979 (see *R & H Hall Ltd v W H Pim Junr & Co Ltd*, HL).

2.9.4 Damages for breach of warranty

If the seller has breached a warranty of the contract or a condition which the buyer has either elected or was compelled to treat as a warranty, the buyer can claim damages according to s 53 SoGA 1979, and if the circumstances allow, also according to s 54 of the SoGA 1979. For the measure of damages see **2.8.3** above. The buyer can off-set his loss against any action by the seller for the price (SoGA 1979, s 53(4)).

2.9.5 Damages for late delivery

Terms as to time of delivery will usually be conditions of the contract. Thus, in case of late delivery, the buyer will usually have the option to treat the contract as repudiated and claim for non-delivery or to treat it as breach of warranty and only claim damages for the delay. For the measure of damages see **2.8.3** above.

2.9.6 Remedy seeking specific performance, s 52 of the SoGA 1979

In case of the sale of specific or ascertained goods, the buyer can apply to the court to order the seller's performance (SoGA 1979, s 52). This is a discretionary power of the courts and will usually only be granted if damages are insufficient to compensate for the buyer's loss (see *Behnke v Bede Shipping Co*, KBD).

In certain situations the buyer might want to claim against parties other than the seller, as follows.

2.9.7 Action in tort

A claim in tort of negligence, for example against the carrier, will only succeed if, at the time of damage, the buyer had either possession of or property in the goods (see *Leigh and Sillivan Ltd v Aliakmon Shipping Co Ltd (The Aliakmon)*, HL).

The buyer's remedy for conversion of the goods under the Torts (Interference with Goods) Act 1977 will depend on the buyer's immediate right to possession of the goods. For example, a person withholding possession from the buyer or dispossessing him of the goods might incur liability for conversion. This could happen for example in connection with bailment. (Bailment in the context of international trade is usually a contract under which a person holds the property of another in his custody for a limited period of time, eg in contracts of carriage or warehousing.) Where a bailee sub-bails the goods without permission, where he withholds delivery to the bailor, or sells the goods on to a third party without permission of the bailor, he might be liable for conversion of the goods. For example if the carrier under a bill of lading contract delivers the goods without demanding production of the bill he runs the risk of becoming liable in tort for conversion, if he happens to deliver the goods to someone not entitled to them (see *Chabbra Corporation Pte Ltd v Jag Shakti (Owners) (The Jag Shakti)*, PC and *The Winkfield*, CA).

2.9.8 Other damages

The buyer might have claims against other third parties, namely the parties to the further contracts, which were concluded in performance of the international sale contract, for example the carriage and insurance contract. (For more information see **Chapters 4** and **5**.)

2.10 Remedies of the seller

The seller, often having to part with the possession of and property in the goods before he receives payment, is in a particularly vulnerable position. He might therefore be wise to call for a secure payment method or payment in advance, or at least to insert a contract clause reserving title in the goods until he has received the purchase price. Even if he has not included any such clauses, the law affords him some protection: the seller can claim against the buyer for the price or damages, and can also take action against the goods themselves. The seller's remedies are set out mainly in ss 38–50 of the SoGA 1979, unless the parties have chosen to include a contractual clause determining the remedies and damages differently.

2.10.1 Remedies against the goods themselves

2.10.1.1 Overview

If the seller has not been fully paid (as defined in SoGA 1979, s 38), then notwithstanding passing of property, he has the rights set out in s 39(1) of the SoGA 1979. These are:

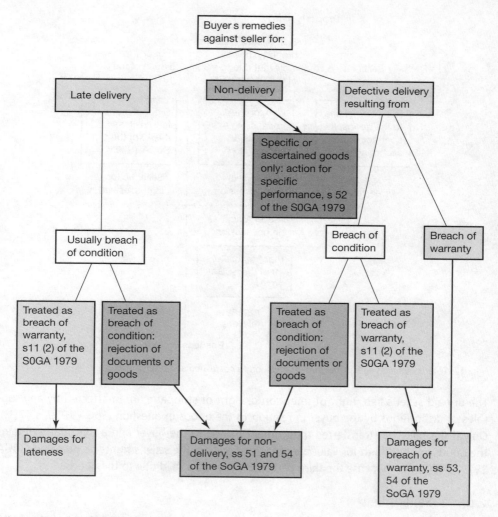

Fig 2.16 Buyer's remedies against seller

(a) a lien on the goods or right to retain them whilst he is still in possession of the goods;

(b) a right of stoppage in transit in case the buyer is insolvent, after he lost possession; and

(c) a right to resell the goods within the limits determined by the Act.

If the seller had retained the property in the goods (by means of a clause in the contract), he has a right to withhold delivery analogous to a lien or the right of stoppage in transit (SoGA 1979, s 39(2)). Thus s 39(2) of the SoGA 1979 confirms that a seller who still owns the goods is in a no less advantageous position than if property had passed. According to s 38(2) of the SoGA 1979, not only the seller, but any person 'who is in the position of a seller' may claim these rights, such as an agent of the seller for whom the bill of lading has been indorsed, or a consignor or confirming agent who has himself paid the price or is directly responsible for it. The above rights can however only be applied in relation to the price of the goods, not for other expenses such as storage charges incurred during the default of the buyer (see *Somes v British Empire Shipping Co*, HL).

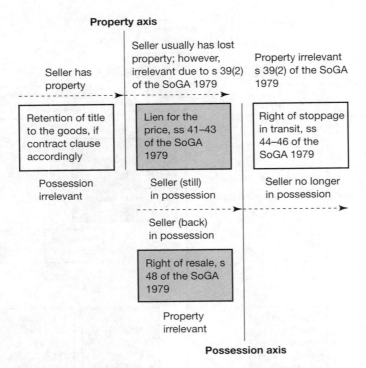

Property axis

Seller has property / Seller usually has lost property; however, irrelevant due to s 39(2) of the SoGA 1979 / Property irrelevant s 39(2) of the SoGA 1979

| Retention of title to the goods, if contract clause accordingly | Lien for the price, ss 41–43 of the SoGA 1979 | Right of stoppage in transit, ss 44–46 of the SoGA 1979 |

Possession irrelevant / Seller (still) in possession / Seller no longer in possession

Seller (back) in possession

Right of resale, s 48 of the SoGA 1979

Property irrelevant

Possession axis

Fig 2.17 Seller's remedies against the goods in relation to possession and property

The unpaid seller's lien, right of retention or right of stoppage are unaffected by any sub-sales or dispositions by the buyer in relation to the goods in question (SoGA 1979, s 47(1)). Only if the seller has transferred a document of title to the buyer and a third party obtains the goods in good faith for valuable consideration, will the seller's rights be defeated (SoGA 1979, s 47(2)). In that case the third party has acquired a valid title to the goods.

2.10.1.2 Seller's lien

A lien is a form of possessory security. The seller's lien is set out in ss 41–43 of the SoGA 1979: the seller, who has lost the property but is still in possession of the goods, can retain possession until payment of the purchase price is made (unless the seller has given credit to a solvent buyer, which has not expired). The lien is lost when the seller parts with possession, particularly when he delivers the goods to the carrier without reserving the right of disposal, or if he waives his lien (SoGA 1979, s 43(1)).

2.10.1.3 Stoppage in transit

Once the seller has parted with the possession of the goods he can exercise his right of stoppage in transit if, and only if, the buyer becomes insolvent (SoGA 1979, ss 44–46). The seller can then resume possession and withhold the goods until payment is made. The right of stoppage can only be used during the transit of the goods. This is defined in s 45(1) of the SoGA 1979 as from the time of delivery of the goods to a carrier or other bailee or custodier for the purpose of transmission to the buyer, until the buyer or his agent in that behalf takes delivery. Once the seller gives notice of stoppage to the carrier or other bailee or custodier in possession, the latter must redeliver the goods to the seller or act according to the directions of the seller. Any expenses of redelivery must be borne by the seller (SoGA 1979, s 46(4)).

Difficulties arise in international trade if the buyer or his agent is involved in the transport of the goods. If the goods are shipped on the buyer's own vessel, delivery to the carrier will be delivery to the buyer. In such a case transit ends and the right of stoppage is lost. If, however, the buyer has only chartered a vessel, we need to distinguish between the different types of charterparty.

A charterparty is the contract between the shipowner and another (here the buyer) to put the ship at the other party's disposal, in return for remuneration. If the buyer employs the vessel for a particular length of time, whilst it is still operated by the shipowner, the contract is called a time charterparty. If it is for a particular voyage or journey it is called a voyage charterparty. Under a demise charterparty (also called bareboat charterparty) the buyer takes full direction, management and control over the vessel and employs the crew directly; he therefore acts as if he were the owner of the ship.

Delivery of the goods to the master of a demise-chartered ship will therefore be delivery to the buyer; hence transit in the sense of s 45 of the SoGA 1979 ends. Delivery on board a ship under a time or voyage charter, however, is delivery to the shipowner, who is still acting as the carrier, despite the fact that the buyer employs the ship. In this case the right of stoppage in transit is not lost (*Ex parte Rosevear China Clay; Re Cock*, CA). The loss of the right to stoppage does not depend on constructive delivery, as in s 32 (1) of the SoGA 1979, but on actual delivery to the buyer or his agent who acts in that behalf.

The right of stoppage is not linked to the passing of property. The fact that the bill of lading, taken out in the seller's name, is transferred to the buyer, or even the fact that the bill is taken out in the buyer's name directly, does not interfere with the right of stoppage.

2.10.1.4 Resale by the seller

Exercising his lien, right of retention or right of stoppage in transit only gives the seller the right to keep or regain possession of the goods until he is paid. It does not give the seller an automatic right of resale, nor does it rescind the original contract (SoGA 1979, s 48(1)).

In reselling a seller must observe the criteria set out in s 48(3), (4) of the SoGA 1979 in order not to breach the sale contract himself and to become liable for damages to the buyer. The unpaid seller can safely resell the goods and claim damages for the buyer's breach:

(a) if the goods are of perishable nature, without further notice;

(b) if the seller has reserved a right of resale in the event of the buyer's default, without further notice on default of the buyer;

(c) otherwise the seller needs to give the buyer notice of his intention to resell and wait a reasonable time to enable the buyer to pay or tender the price. After that time he can resell the goods free from any liability towards the buyer.

When the unpaid seller resells the goods, the original contract is rescinded, but without prejudice to the right to claim damages. The new buyer of the goods acquires a good title to the goods ((SoGA 1979, s 48(2)).

2.10.2 Personal remedies against buyer

2.10.2.1 Action for price

The seller can sue the buyer who wrongfully neglects or refuses to pay for the price if:

(a) property has passed to the buyer (SoGA 1979, s 49(1)); or

(b) the price is payable on a certain day, irrespective of delivery (SoGA 1979, s 49(2)).

Where property has not passed to the buyer, the seller cannot sue for the price, despite the fact that it was the buyer's fault. In such a case the seller can only claim damages for non-acceptance (see *Colley v Overseas Exporters*, KBD), unless a specific date for payment was fixed.

Section 54 of the SoGA 1979 preserves any right the seller may have to recover interest on the price. Of importance in this context is the statutory entitlement to interest under the Late Payment of Commercial Debts (Interest) Act 1998 and the wide discretion of the courts to award interest in many cases under s 35A of the Supreme Court Act 1981.

2.10.2.2 Damages for non-acceptance

In the case of the buyer's wrongful non-acceptance of the goods, the seller can claim damages for non-acceptance according to s 50 of the SoGA 1979, the measure of which is generally identified on the basis of the market rule as illustrated in **2.8.3** above. The seller can claim the consequential losses which were contemplated by the parties when the contract was made (SoGA 1979, s 54).

In addition the seller can claim for any losses or costs due to the involuntary custody of the goods, because of the buyer's failure to take delivery (SoGA 1979, s 37).

2.10.2.3 Damages for breach of warranty

In the case of a breach of warranty or where the seller elects to treat a breach of condition as breach of warranty, the seller can claim damages according to the normal rules of contract law: that is complete indemnity for the loss, which at the time of conclusion of the contract was reasonably foreseeable, unless the seller has failed to mitigate his loss.

If the buyer is late in taking delivery, the seller can also claim his expenses and losses due to this fact (SoGA 1979, s 37).

2.10.3 Linking of the two groups of remedies

If the seller uses one or more of the rights against the goods, he can still use personal remedies against the buyer. If he uses his right of lien or retention he can take the following action against the buyer:

(a) either he claims the purchase price (where the criteria are satisfied) and in addition any damages arising out of the default of the buyer; or

(b) he can use his right of resale (if the criteria are satisfied) and claim any damages from the buyer for non-acceptance and expenses for the involuntary custody for the goods.

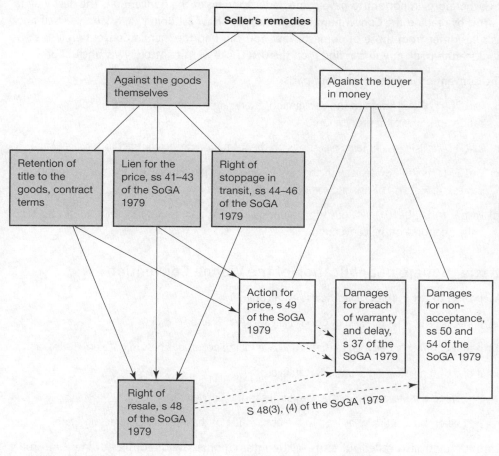

Fig 2.18 Seller's remedies

A similar right exists for stoppage in transit. However, a claim for the price will be unfruitful, as a precondition for the existence of the right of stoppage is that the buyer is insolvent.

2.11 United Nations Convention on Contracts for the International Sale of Goods 1980

2.11.1 General

The United Kingdom has not ratified the United Nations Convention on Contracts for the International Sale of Goods 1980 (CISG), which is also commonly called the Vienna Convention. However the Convention has been in force since 1 January 1988, and by September 2005 had been ratified by 65 parties (details regarding the status and contracting States can be found by accessing the 'Status of Texts' site on the UNCITRAL treaty site at http://www.uncitral.org/uncitral/en/index.html). These include the United States, most of the European Union (EU) Member States and almost all of the UK's main trading partners.

It is, therefore, important to have some understanding of the Convention. The best way to start is by reading the Convention word for word and whilst doing so, asking yourself how its rules differ from those of domestic law. You can find the Vienna Convention in a standard statute book or you can find it on the UNCITRAL website http://www.uncitral.org.

The Convention is divided into four parts.

(a) Part I (Arts 1–13) contains the Convention's general provisions, including its sphere of application and rules of interpretation.

(b) Part II (Arts 14–24) contains provisions on the formation of the contract (but not validity).

(c) Part III (Arts 25–88) deals with the sale of goods, in particular with the parties' rights and duties, the passing of risk and remedies (but not property).

(d) Part IV (Arts 89–101) sets out the final provisions, including rules regarding ratification and entry into force of the convention.

2.11.2 Sphere of application of the Vienna Convention

According to Art 1, the Convention is applicable:

(a) if there is a contract of sale of goods (see also Art 3); and

(b) if that contract is between parties who have their place of business in different States; and

(c) if one of the following situations is fulfilled:

(i) when the States are Contracting States to the Convention; or

(ii) when the conflict rules lead to the application of the law of a Contracting State.

Conflict rules, also called rules of private international law or conflict of laws, are rules that are applied to cases with an international element, in order to identify which country's law needs to be applied to the case. This is then known as the 'applicable law or proper law of the contract'. If this applicable law of the contract is the law of a Contracting State, then the Convention will apply, providing the other criteria are met. However, the parties can expressly exclude or vary the Convention's application (Art 6). As we have seen, most of the standard term contracts based on English law specifically exclude the application of the Vienna Convention.

If the parties want to use a choice of law clause to make the laws of a particular State applicable, it is essential that they are aware of all the conventions ratified by this State. Otherwise the law applicable may not turn out to be what the parties had intended. As the rights and duties of the parties differ from one legal system to another, it is crucial for the parties to know the rules of any particular legal system they select.

2.11.3 Notable features of the Vienna Convention

The obligations of the parties under the Vienna Convention are largely similar to those under domestic law; however, there are some major differences regarding the formation of the contract and the remedies. Please note that the Convention does not cover the validity of the contract or the effect of the contract on the property in the goods (Art 4). Below we shall look briefly at some of the notable differences.

2.11.3.1 Formation of contract

An offer is usually revocable. However it will not be revocable and will therefore be irrevocable in accordance with Art 16(2) where:

(a) the offer indicates this by stating it or by giving a fixed time for acceptance; or

(b) the offeree could reasonably rely on the offer being irrevocable and if he has also acted in reliance on the offer.

An acceptance becomes effective once it reaches the offeror and not before (Art 18(2)). The offeree can withdraw the acceptance if the withdrawal reaches the offeror before or at the same time as the acceptance (Art 22 together with Art 18(2)).

According to Art 19(2) the acceptance of an offer on slightly different terms, which does not materially alter the terms of the offer, still constitutes an acceptance, unless the offeror objects. Article 19 gives further guidance as to what is considered a material alteration.

2.11.3.2 Breach of contract and remedies

There are neither conditions nor warranties. However, the Convention uses a test similar to the one for innominate terms (Art 25). Only in case of a fundamental breach, which substantially deprives the innocent party of what he is entitled to expect, can the innocent party avoid the contract (Arts 49, 51(1), (2)).

If certain conditions are met, the seller may have a right to remedy the defective performance (Arts 34, 37 and 48).

Under certain circumstances the buyer has a right to demand performance of the seller's obligation, ask for substitute goods or repair (Art 46).

In case of defective delivery of the goods, the buyer may be able to reduce the price proportionally if the seller does not cure the defect (Art 50).

According to Art 39(2) there is a finite time limit for rejection of the goods for non-conformity, which is two years from physical delivery.

Article 75 states that the damages due for avoidance of the contract are measured on the basis of a substitute transaction, if the innocent party undertook this transaction in a reasonable manner within a reasonable time after the avoidance. This does not prejudice a claim for any further damages according to Art 74.

2.11.3.3 Passing of risk

The passing of risk, unlike in English law (SoGA 1979, s 20), is not connected to the passing of property, but to the control over the goods (Arts 67–69).

2.12 Revision and further reading

2.12.1 Questions

This is your opportunity to revise what you have learned and to check whether you have understood the issues covered in this chapter. I suggest that you attempt to answer these questions based on English law before you move on to the next chapter.

Question 1

What is the result of the following scenario? What are the rights of the innocent party?

(a) The cif seller does not tender the documents.

(b) The cif seller does not tender an insurance policy, but only a broker's cover note or certificate of insurance.

(c) The cif seller tenders a 'received for shipment' bill of lading.

(d) The cif seller has not taken out effective insurance; however the goods arrive safely.

(e) The fob buyer has not given a notice of readiness to the seller within the stipulated time.

(f) Goods under a cif contract have not been shipped within the shipment period.

(g) More goods have been shipped than agreed.

(h) The packaging of the goods does not comply with the particular requirements of the contract.

Question 2

S has sold tomatoes on cif terms to B. S has been paid for the tomatoes on presentation of the correct documents. The buyer had accepted the documents. On arrival of the goods B, a 'fruit & veg' merchant, realises that the goods shipped are peppers and not tomatoes as indicated on all the documents. What do you suggest to B?

(a) Can he still reject the goods?

(b) Would you consider any other action?

Question 3

S has sold tomatoes on cif terms to B. S tenders a sea waybill instead of the required bill of lading. Can the buyer reject the documents on the basis of the sale contract, even though he did not sell the goods in transit and the goods arrived safely?

Question 4

The facts are as in Question 3 above. S is still within the time limit for presentation of the documents. Can he remedy the discrepancy by retendering conforming documents to the buyer? (Please note: there are no letter of credit arrangements.)

Question 5

S sells 20 tons of Wear Dale Fluorite, a local gemstone, to B. The contract is on fob terms (Liverpool/England Incoterms 2000). The goods are shipped in accordance with the contract. During transit S learns that the buyer has become bankrupt. S knows a second buyer who would be interested in purchasing the consignment. Advise S as to his rights and options to minimise his loss. Which steps must S take?

Question 6

Goods sold under a ddp contract arrive severely damaged at their destination. The seller S threatens legal action if the buyer does not pay. Advise the buyer B as to his rights and obligations.

Question 7

S from Germany and B from England conclude a sale contract for a consignment of wooden garden furniture. S is of the opinion that this sale contract is subject to the Vienna Convention on the International Sale of Goods of 1980. Why would this be of benefit to the seller and when will this convention be applicable?

2.12.2 Further reading

(a) *Arnold Karberg & Co v Blythe, Green, Jourdain & Co* [1915] 2 KB 379, KBD concerning sale of goods — cif contracts — payment against tender of shipping documents — effect of war on contract.

(b) *Yelo v SM Machado & Co Ltd* [1952] 1 Lloyd's Rep 183, QBD concerning sale of goods — fob contract — received for shipment bill of lading — damages.

(c) *Pyrene Co Ltd v Scindia Steam Navigation Co Ltd* [1954] 2 QB 402, QBD concerning fob contracts as being a flexible instrument.

(d) *Glencore Grain Rotterdam BV v Lebanese Organisation for International Commerce (LORICO)* [1997] 2 Lloyd's Rep 386, CA concerning duties under fob contract — timing of letter of credit.

(e) *Gill & Duffus SA v Berger & Co Inc* [1984] AC 382, HL regarding cif contract — repudiation — fundamental breach — certificate final clause.

(f) *Vitol SA v Esso Australia Ltd (The Wise)* [1989] 1 Lloyd's Rep 96, QBD (Comm) and [1989] 2 Lloyd's Rep 451, CA concerning c&f contract and arrival stipulation — rejection of goods — passing of risk — short delivery — conduct amounting to waiver or estoppel.

(g) *Bunge Corporation v Tradax Export SA* [1980] 1 Lloyd's Rep 294, CA and [1981] 2 Lloyd's Rep 1, HL concerning sale of goods, fob - condition and innominate terms — notice of readiness to load — time.

(h) *Kwei Tek Chao & Others v British Traders and Shippers Ltd* [1954] 2 QB 459, QBD concerning cif contract — separate rights: right to reject documents and to reject goods.

(i) Mantijn W Hesselink, 'The European Commission's Action Plan: Towards a More Coherent European Contract Law?' (2004) 12(4) European Review of Private Law (ERPL) 397–419.

(j) Filippo Lorenzon, 'Harmonisation of European contract law: friend or foe to the shipping industry?' (2004) 10(6) Journal of International Maritime Law (JIML) 504–513

(k)   Koji Takahashi, 'Right to Terminate (Avoid) International Sales of Commodities', [2003] JBL 102–130.

(l)   Charles Debattista, 'Laytime and demurrage clauses in contracts of sale — links and connections', [2003] LMCLQ 508–524.

(m)   Charles Debattista, 'Legislative Techniques in International Trade: Madness or Method', [2002] JBL 626–637.

(n)   John N Adams, 'Damages in Sale of Goods: A Critique of the Provisions of the Sale of Goods Act and Art 2 of the Uniform Commercial Code', [2002] JBL 553–566.

(o)   Chapter II: The CISG: general issues and Chapter III: The CISG and English law compared in MG, Bridge, *International Sale of Goods: Law and Practice* (1999, Oxford: Oxford University Press).

3 Payment Methods in International Trade

3.1 General

In this chapter we shall look at the main methods of payment likely to be used in an international trade transaction. We will concentrate on an overview, showing the interaction of these payment methods with the international trade transaction, rather than study all the permutations of the payment systems and intricacies of banking law.

The choice of payment system will depend on many considerations. A bargaining factor between the parties may be whether the buyer will be given a credit period and if banks have to be involved in the payment transaction, who is to pay for their services. The extra costs incurred by such arrangements need to be considered before agreeing on the contract price.

The minimum details the parties should agree on are:

(a) mode;

(b) time;

(c) place; and

(d) currency of payment.

While considering the different payment methods, the parties have to take into account the various risks they are subjected to.

(a) Commercial risks, which depend on the business relationship between the trading partners, the solvency and reliability of the other party, the likelihood of any contractual disputes arising, the physical distance between the parties, the arrangements regarding control over the goods and any knowledge of local customs and regulations.

(b) Economic risks, which include any other issues concerning the countries both parties are trading from, for example the political situation there, and the stability and reliability of the banks involved.

(c) Financial risks, which involve dealing with foreign exchange, the interest rates and the strain on the working capital.

The seller is likely to want payment as soon as possible and before he parts with the goods, whereas the buyer may not want to pay until he has control over the goods; he may also favour a credit period. Thus mercantile custom has developed methods which will allow the parties to reconcile some of their conflicting interests. They mostly provide for the involvement of banks and the usage of documents to create constructive possession of the goods. We shall concentrate on the predominant ones.

3.1.1   Payment mechanisms effected via banks

The two major payment forms used in international trade are documentary credits and documentary collection. For fob or cif sale contracts they are by far the most suitable methods of payment.

(a) A documentary credit arrangement, also called letter of credit, enables payment by which the seller receives an independent undertaking from a bank, to pay a certain amount of money on fulfilment of certain conditions. This payment term is the most appropriate in the international sale context. The buyer initiates the letter of credit; the subsequent exchange of the documents and the price will usually be effected in the seller's country. The conditions for payment under the letter of credit are to tender, within a stipulated time, to a particular bank at a stipulated place, specified documents representing the goods. These documents are the same documents that are relevant for the fulfilment of the sale contract. They will depend on the nature of the sale contract and will comprise, under a cif contract for example, the transport document, the insurance policy, the commercial invoice and any other specified documents.

(b) Another payment form, drawing on the services of the banks, is a collection arrangement. It is initiated by the seller and is to be effected at the buyer's place of business. The seller instructs a bank to collect the purchase price from the buyer, usually against tender of the documents. It only offers limited security to the seller, who has to send the goods to the buyer without any guarantee for his payment.

(We are going to discuss these methods in more detail at **3.3** and **3.4**, but first want to concentrate on an overview of the possible payment mechanisms.) Letters of credit or collection arrangements can be used on their own, or in combination with bills of exchange.

3.1.2   Bills of exchange – an outline

A bill of exchange, also called a draft, is a written order by the drawer to the drawee to pay a certain amount of money, either at demand or on sight of the draft (sight bill) or at a specific time thereafter (term bill). Payment has to be made to a specified person, the payee. A bill of exchange in its simplest form is a written order by the seller (drawer) to the buyer (drawee) to pay the specific purchase price to the seller or another person (payee). The payment is due either on presentation of the bill or at a specific time thereafter, in which case the buyer has received a credit period. The bill is then called a term bill. On presentation, the buyer needs to sign the bill (accept the bill), which thereafter is delivered to the payee. The payee, having received the accepted draft, has two choices. He can either hold the bill until its maturity in order to present it to the buyer for payment on the due date, or he can negotiate the bill to another person. Negotiating the bill means that the payee sells the bill to a third party before payment under the bill is due. He thus obtains money for the draft in advance of the bill's maturity. However, the value given for it is reduced by any charges and interest rates the third party may claim. Thus this process is also called discounting the bill. (For a more detailed explanation of bills of exchange see **3.2** below, including illustrations, and see also the appendix at the end of this book containing an example of a blank bill of exchange.)

A bill of exchange provides a much better security to the seller if it has been avalised (signed) by a bank, thus adding a secure paymaster to the obligation of the buyer, guaranteeing the payment. A bill of exchange can be used by itself, to give credit to the buyer and enabling the seller to receive value immediately by negotiating the bill. It can also be used in conjunction with the delivery of the transport documents, then called a 'documentary bill'. A documentary bill can either be sent directly from seller to buyer (see **3.1.3** below) or via the banks as intermediaries in collection arrangements or letters of credit.

Another way of payment by bill of exchange is if the buyer uses a banker's draft to effect payment. In such a case, the buyer obtains from his bank an order drawn on its correspondent bank in the seller's country, naming the seller as payee. This has valuable advantages for the seller. Once the draft has been issued, the seller is guaranteed payment from a secure paymaster, a bank in his home country. The seller can also sell the bill at a discount, thus obtaining money straight away. The buyer, however, may not be enthusiastic to use this method, because the draft cannot be revoked once issued. Thus, a buyer agreeing on this payment method may in turn want to obtain security for the satisfactory performance of the seller's duties (see **3.5**).

3.1.3 Direct payment

The parties can use payment forms minimising the involvement of banks, also called direct payment. Here are some examples.

(a) If the exporter is not familiar with the financial status of the buyer or if other circumstances demand it, the seller can ask for 'payment in advance'. If the seller is in a particularly strong position, he may even be able to contract on 'cash with order' terms, thus obtaining the payment before manufacturing begins or before the goods are sent to the buyer. The seller is thus reducing his risk in the export transaction to a minimum.

(b) Another possibility is to arrange for an exchange of the goods or documents against the purchase price: 'cash on delivery' or 'cash against documents'. These terms are particularly suitable in 'ex works' contracts. There are other specific variants of 'cash against documents', for example 'documents against acceptance of a bill of exchange' (explained in item (c) below), or documentary collection, using a bank as intermediary in the exchange of documents against payment, to increase security (as explained above at **3.1.1(b)**).

(c) The method using a documentary bill of exchange, that is a draft to which the transport documents are attached, involves the seller sending the bill of exchange with documents directly to the buyer. The idea is that the buyer is only allowed to use the transport documents once he has honoured the bill, either by accepting it (term bill) or by paying (sight bill). This is backed up by s 19(3) of the SoGA 1979 providing that the buyer only obtains property in the goods if he honours the bill of exchange. However this protection for a seller, who accordingly retains his right of disposal of the goods, is very limited. A third party purchasing the goods from the defaulting buyer in good faith can still obtain a good title according to s 9 of the Factors Act 1889 or s 25 of the SoGA 1979 (see *Cahn & Mayer v Pockett's Bristol Channel Steam Packet Co Ltd*, CA). Thus it might be worth using banks as intermediaries in a collection arrangement (see **3.1.1** above and **3.3** below) to ensure that transport documents are only tendered once the bill of exchange has been honoured.

(d) To trade 'on open account' is suitable when the exporter is acquainted with the financial status of the buyer and there is no risk of insolvency. In such a case the exporter sends the documents to the buyer, who in turn remits the price either when the documents arrive (sight payment) or at a specified time. Payment can be effected using a variety of means, for example via telegraphic transfer (T/T), mail transfer (M/T) or by SWIFT transfer (SWIFT standing for an independent network operated by the Society for Worldwide Interbank Financial Telecommunication). These remittances are mostly carried out through the buyer's bank communicating with a bank in the seller's country, instructing it to pay the seller. Trading on open account is particularly suitable where the exporter sells the goods to his own subsidiary or branch or if the trading partners are involved in two-way trading (for example involving one of the trading partners delivering the raw materials and also acting as buyer for the finished product manufactured by the other partner).

3.1.4 Risk ladder

The above payment forms have been structured on the basis of whether the banks are crucially involved in securing the payment transaction. Figure 3.1 illustrates the level of risk incurred by the seller and the buyer respectively when choosing a particular payment form. The chart has at the top those payment systems which afford best security to the seller, whereas those at the bottom afford better security to the buyer.

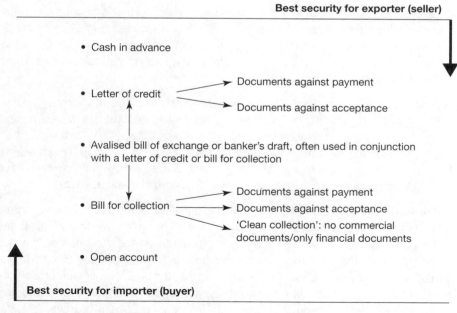

Best security for exporter (seller)

- Cash in advance

- Letter of credit
  - ➤ Documents against payment
  - ➤ Documents against acceptance

- Avalised bill of exchange or banker's draft, often used in conjunction with a letter of credit or bill for collection

- Bill for collection
  - ➤ Documents against payment
  - ➤ Documents against acceptance
  - ➤ 'Clean collection': no commercial documents/only financial documents

- Open account

Best security for importer (buyer)

Fig 3.1 Payment facilities risk ladder

Cash in advance gives the seller the best security, only having to part with the goods once paid, and in turn is the most dangerous for the buyer. The buyer at the time of payment does not know whether the goods conform to the contract. On the other hand, payment on open account does not give much security to the seller. The buyer, however, by the time he has to pay, has either received the transport documents or even the goods themselves.

Using a letter of credit, the seller's duty to ship the goods is postponed until after receipt of the letter of credit, whereas in a collection agreement he has to send the goods on their way in advance of the buyer's duty to pay.

An avalised bill of exchange can be used in conjunction with a letter of credit or a collection arrangement or on its own. The aval (signature of a guarantor) adds a secure paymaster to the obligation, thus giving a better standing to any credit arrangement.

3.1.5 Performance guarantees

It is not just the seller who might worry about payment. Where the buyer pays the contract price in advance of receipt and inspection of the goods, he too has an interest in securing himself against the seller's failure to perform the contract as agreed. The buyer might want to be able to access the sum of money which he would have been entitled to withhold on delivery of damaged goods. The buyer's concerns can be met by setting up in his favour a guarantee from a creditworthy third party, to be used in the event that the seller should default. The seller has to initiate this arrangement, which would most likely be one of the following: a performance bond; an advance payment bond; a performance guarantee; or a standby letter of credit (for details see **3.5** below).

We shall now investigate these payment forms and guarantee arrangements a little closer.

3.2 Bills of exchange in detail

3.2.1 General

The primary source of law relating to bills of exchange is the Bills of Exchange Act (BoEA) 1882. The Act, a truly remarkable piece of legislation drafted by Sir Mackenzie Chalmers, is still valid, mostly unchanged. It is recommended that you acquaint yourself with the law at this point by reading the Act, preferably as a whole. At the very least look at the section headings, and refer to those sections as soon as reference is made to them.

In s 2 the BoEA 1882 starts by giving an interpretation of the terms used. Then, in s 3(1) a bill of exchange is defined as:

> *A bill of exchange is an unconditional order in writing, addressed by one person to another, signed by the person giving it, requiring the person to whom it is addressed to pay on demand or at a fixed or determinable future time a sum certain in money to or to the order of a specified person, or to bearer.*

Let us look at the bill of exchange by first clarifying the terminology used to describe the players in a bill of exchange transaction. Thereafter we will look at examples of how the bill of exchange can be used between the parties to an international sale contract before we look at the individual criteria of the bill of exchange.

The parties to a bill of exchange are identified by the following names.

(a) The *drawer* draws the bill, that is, he gives the order to pay. He must also sign the bill.

(b) The person to whom the bill is addressed/on whom the bill is drawn is called the *drawee*.

(c) The drawee is called the *acceptor* once he has indicated his willingness to pay. If the bill is to be paid at a future date (term bill), the drawee accepts the bill by writing his acceptance on the face of it and signing it, thus becoming an acceptor.

(d) The person identified in the bill to whom the bill is payable or to whose order the bill is made out (order bill) is called the *payee*. If the bill is drawn payable to the bearer (bearer bill), the person in possession of it is called the *bearer*.

(e) A bill of exchange can be transferred from one person to another. This process is called negotiation. An order bill can be transferred by indorsement and delivery by the payee or a subsequent transferee; he is then called *indorser*. The person to whom the bill is indorsed, the recipient, is called the *indorsee*. A bearer bill on the other hand is negotiated by mere delivery.

(f) The payee or indorsee who is in possession of the bill is called the *holder*; likewise the bearer, in case of a bearer bill.

(g) Where a third party guarantees payment of the bill, either to back up or in addition to the acceptor or an indorser, this third party is called *avaliser* or guarantor. Only term bills can be avalised as the aval takes place after acceptance. Usually, bills are avalised by banks. An aval of a bank with good standing has great commercial value. However the bank is likely to charge highly for this service.

In the introduction to payment systems at **3.1.2** above, we saw that the seller may draw a bill of exchange on the buyer for payment of the purchase price. If the bill is payable on demand or sight, it needs to be paid on first presentation. No credit has been given. If the bill is a term bill, it is sent to the buyer for acceptance. The buyer has to write his acceptance on the bill and sign it. The bill is then sent back to the seller for his safekeeping until its maturity date. When the bill is paid at or after its maturity, by or on behalf of the buyer (the drawee or acceptor), the bill is discharged (see BoEA 1882, s 59(1)). This basic scenario is illustrated in Fig 3.2 for a sight bill and in Fig 3.3 for a term bill of exchange.

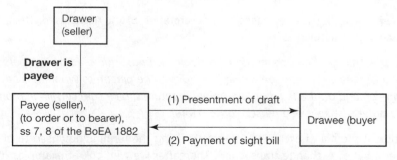

Fig 3.2 Illustration of a basic sight bill of exchange between seller and buyer, the seller being the payee

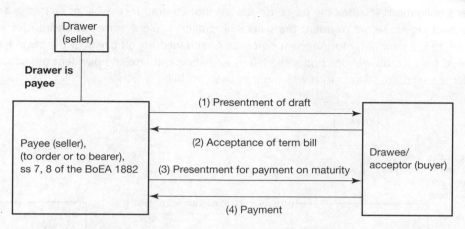

Fig 3.3 *Illustration of a basic term bill of exchange between seller and buyer, the seller being the payee*

An example of a term bill of exchange drawn by the seller on the buyer is given in Fig 3.4.

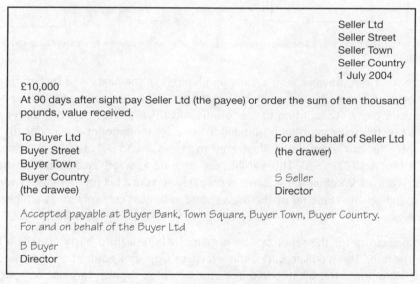

Fig 3.4 *Term bill of exchange payable 90 days after sight, drawn by the seller on the buyer*

The bill has been sent to the buyer, who has accepted the bill of exchange (see BoEA 1882, s 17). Thus, the seller (drawer) and buyer (drawee) have both signed the bill and are liable under it (see BoEA 1882, s 23). In our case the drawer is also the payee. The drawer thus only becomes liable once the bill is negotiated to another person (see **3.2.3** below).

Where the seller already owes money to his bank or any other third party he might draw the bill of exchange directly payable to the bank or the other third party, who is therefore named as payee (see Fig 3.5). The bill is then transferred to the payee who will claim acceptance and/or payment from the buyer. Once the buyer has paid the payee, the

...ons towards the payee for the amount covered by the bill of exchange are ...rged. Before payment the seller still remains liable despite having transferred ...to the third party for payment purposes. Simultaneously on payment the buyer has ...illed his own obligations under the bill of exchange and also the payment obligation under the separate sale contract which gave rise to the bill.

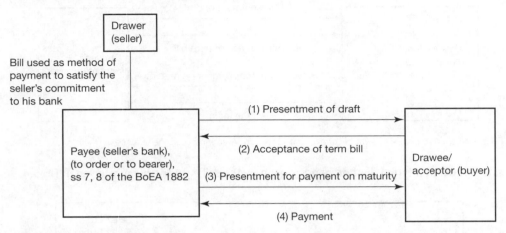

Fig 3.5 Illustration of a basic term bill of exchange drawn by the seller on the buyer naming seller's bank as payee

Where the seller has drawn a term bill naming himself as the payee and he later requires money before the maturity of the bill, he has the option of discounting the bill to a bank or other third party. Discounting (or negotiation) is usually effected with full recourse. That is to say, the seller negotiating the bill is liable for the amount due under the bill if the acceptor (in our example as illustrated in Figs 3.3 and 3.4, the buyer) does not honour it (BoEA 1882, s 55). This liability can only be avoided by discounting the bill 'without recourse'. Whether a transferee is prepared to take a bill on these terms will very much depend on the standing of the drawee and will most certainly be at a higher discount charge.

Additional security for the seller can be obtained where a third party, usually a bank, avalises the bill. The avaliser backs the acceptor's/buyer's commitment to pay and becomes liable under the bill in addition to the acceptor. An aval can also be sought to back the indorser's liability under the bill or to cover the liability of all immediate parties, the acceptor and anyone liable on recourse.

Figure 3.6 shows a term bill of exchange drawn by the seller on the buyer. The top half shows the interaction of the parties to a bill of exchange without indorsement, the bottom half with indorsement. The dotted lines show the situation where the bill has been avalised.

Another possibility is that the buyer draws a bill of exchange on his bank naming the seller as payee. The seller then has a secure paymaster, but can also discount the bill to another in order to obtain early payment. It would then look as shown in Fig 3.7:

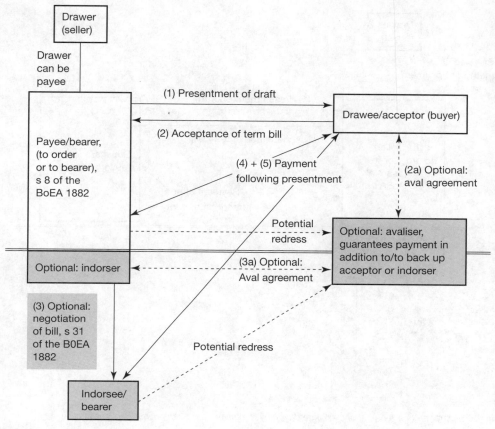

Fig 3.6 Bill of exchange:

(a) top half, above horizontal lines only: without indorsement;

(b) including bottom half: with indorsement;

(c) including dotted lines: bill of exchange that is avalised.

3.2.2 Essential criteria

If the criteria in s 3(1) of the BoEA 1882 are not fulfilled, the instrument is not a bill of exchange (BoEA 1882, s 3(2)) and will not give the same protection to the holder. The criteria that must be satisfied under s 3 of the BoEA 1882 are as follows.

3.2.2.1 The bill must signify an order by the drawer to the drawee and not just a request

It must not allow any discretion to the drawee as to whether to pay. The order must be unconditional. Section 3(2) of the BoEA 1882 states that an order is conditional if it can only be paid out of a particular fund. However, the order is unconditional if the direction to pay is unqualified but the order only indicates that the drawee is to reimburse himself from a particular account. This means the order is not dependent on whether enough funds are available on this particular account. An example of the latter is a cheque drawn on a particular account: the cheque gives the bank an order to pay the amount stated, but at the same time allows the bank to reimburse itself by debiting the account on which the cheque is drawn.

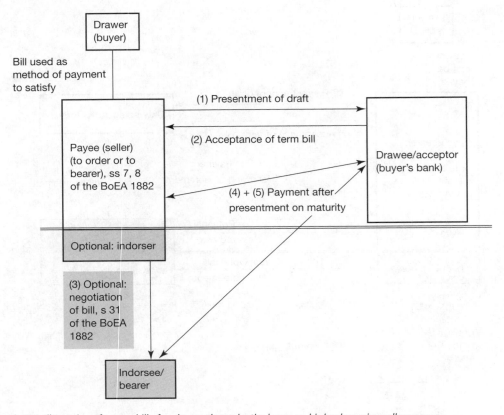

Fig 3.7 Illustration of a term bill of exchange drawn by the buyer on his bank naming seller as payee

The bill of exchange is separate from the underlying contract of sale. Thus any defences available under the sale contract do not interfere with the obligation to honour the bill of exchange. If the parties intend to interconnect the two, the order so created is not a bill of exchange.

3.2.2.2 The bill must be in writing but this does not have to be on paper

It can also be drawn on more unusual material. For example, some bills in favour of the Inland Revenue have been drawn on a cow and a piece of underwear. It remains to be seen how this criterion is met in order to create an 'electronic bill of exchange' which can be placed within the ambit, and thus the protection, of the Act.

3.2.2.3 The bill must be addressed by one person to another

The parties to the bill must be clear. The drawee and payee must be named or at least be otherwise ascertainable (BoEA 1882, ss 6 and 7). According to s 5 of the BoEA 1882 the drawer and payee can be the same person, as can the drawee and the payee. An example of the former is a seller drawing a bill payable to himself on the buyer. However, where the drawer and drawee are the same person, the holder has the choice of whether he wishes to treat the instrument as a bill of exchange or as a promissory note (BoEA 1882, s 5(2)).

3.2.2.4 The bill must be signed by the drawer

The reason is that the drawer becomes liable under the bill for the amount stated. According to s 23 of the BoEA 1882, the drawer, as well as the indorser and acceptor, only become liable under the bill once they have signed it. However the signature does not have to be made in person but can, for example, be given by an agent. It suffices that the signature is given by or under the authority of the person who is to be represented (BoEA 1882, s 91(1)). The agent signing on behalf of a principal does not become personally liable (BoEA 1882, s 26).

Section 25 of the BoEA 1882 specifies rules regarding signature by procuration. (When signing by procuration, the agent who signs the bill for the principal adds the clause that he signs 'per procuration' or 'pp' or 'per pro'. This has the effect under s 25 of the BoEA 1882 that the principal is only bound if the agent in so signing acted within the actual limits of his authority.)

Most importantly, s 24 of the BoEA 1882 stipulates that a forged or otherwise unauthorised signature is wholly inoperative. However this is subject to certain estoppels. The drawer may be precluded from setting up the forgery or want of authority as a defence against a claimant in accordance with s 24 of the BoEA 1882, if, for example, he becomes aware of the forgery but does not do anything about it. The acceptor (BoEA 1882, s 54(2)(a)) and the indorser (BoEA 1882, s 55(2)(b)) are excluded from setting up the forgery for reasons such as the existence of the drawer and the genuineness of his signature.

3.2.2.5 The order must provide for payment either on demand (BoEA 1882, s 10), or at a fixed or determinable future time (BoEA 1882, s 11)

Where the bill is payable on or at a fixed time after the occurrence of a specific event (BoEA 1882, s 11(2)), the event must be certain to happen; it must not be a contingency. Thus, 'payment x days after sight' is possible, but 'payment x days after acceptance' is not acceptable, as the latter event is uncertain (see *Korea Exchange Bank v Debenhams (Central Buying) Ltd*, CA).

3.2.2.6 The order must be to pay 'a sum certain in money'.

According to s 9(1) of the BoEA 1882 this can include interest, payment by instalments, payment according to an indicated rate of exchange, or a rate ascertainable by the bill.

3.2.2.7 The bill must be payable to or to the order of a specified person or to the bearer

Unless the bill is a bearer bill the payee must be named or otherwise identifiable (BoEA 1882, s 7). If, however, the payee is a fictitious or non-existing person, the bill can be treated as a bearer bill (BoEA 1882, s 7(3)).

3.2.2.8 Summing up

If any of the information in **3.2.2.1** to **3.2.2.7** above is not provided by the drawer, the instrument may be converted into a bill of exchange by an authorised person filling in the gaps with the necessary information (BoEA 1882, s 20). The question of whether an instrument is in fact a bill of exchange is of great importance, because a bill of exchange is a negotiable instrument. As such it affords very good security to a holder for value in good faith and is an invaluable tool for trade.

3.2.3 The bill as a negotiable instrument

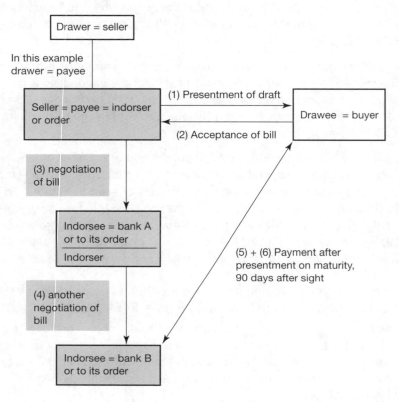

Fig 3.8 Example of an order bill of exchange payable at 90 days after sight drawn by the seller on the buyer and negotiated twice to banks

A bill can be negotiated unless its transfer is expressly prohibited by the bill (BoEA 1882, s 8(1)) (see Fig 3.8). A bearer bill is negotiated by delivery; an order bill by indorsement which has to be completed by delivery (BoEA 1882, s 8(2) and s 31(2), (3)). The indorsement must be written on the bill itself, it must be for the entire bill and unconditional. (Details regarding indorsement are set out in ss 31–35 of the BoEA 1882, and details on negotiability in ss 36, 37.)

In our example in Fig 3.4 the indorser, the payee Seller Ltd, would write on the back of the document: 'pay Bank A or order' together with signing the bill in order to effect a special indorsement. Otherwise the indorser would only sign the bill at the back without adding the name of the indorsee, thus effecting a blank indorsement, which would make the bill a bearer bill from thereon.

The important effect of negotiation is the passing of a good title in the bill to the trans-feree, thus making it a very valuable commercial tool. Where the transferee takes the bill as a holder in due course, he gains an indefeasible title regardless of any previous defects (see BoEA 1882, s 29 and s 38). According to s 30 of the BoEA 1882, there is a presumption that a holder has received the bill for value and as holder in due course. However this presumption can be rebutted and successful rebuttal leads to the holder being susceptible to any defects of and defences under the bill.

Section 29(1) of the BoEA 1882 defines a holder in due course as a person who has taken a bill:

(a) which is complete and regular on its face;

(b) before it was overdue;

(c) in case of earlier dishonour of the bill, without having notice that it has previously been dishonoured;

(d) in good faith;

(e) for value; and

(f) without notice, at the time of negotiation, of any defect in the title of the person negotiating it to him.

Section 90 of the BoEA 1882 defines an act done in 'good faith' as being done honestly, irrespective of whether it was done negligently, and s 2 defines a 'holder' as a payee or indorsee who is in possession of a bill, or a bearer thereof. Section 27 of the BoEA 1882 stipulates that a holder for value has given a valuable consideration, sufficient to support a simple contract or an antecedent debt or liability. In our example in Fig 3.8 bank A and then bank B having negotiated the bill, will have become holders in due course. They will have negotiated it before it was overdue and they will have paid for the bill, and thus received the bill for value.

Any holder who derives his title to the bill through a holder in due course, provided that he was not party to any illegality affecting the bill, has the same rights as this previous holder in due course (see BoEA 1882, s 29(3)). Thus, certain defects in a bill can be 'cured' by transfer to a holder in due course. Accordingly, one of the original/immediate parties to the bill (for example the drawer/seller), to whom the bill is returned because of dishonour, can sue the acceptor (for example the buyer) as a holder in due course by derivation (see *Jade International Stahl und Eisen GmbH & Co KG v Robert Nicholas*, CA). Thus any contractual rights and liabilities and equities which might be permitted in any proceedings on the bill between the immediate parties to the bill of exchange cannot be taken into account. The holder in due course by derivation has a right to immediate payment.

A party becomes liable under the bill of exchange once he has signed it (BoEA 1882, s 23), unless he has signed 'without recourse'. An acceptor becomes liable as from acceptance and according to the tenor of his acceptance (BoEA 1882, s 54(1)). The rules regarding the presentment for acceptance and excuses for non-presentment are detailed in s 41 of the BoEA 1882. Acceptance precludes the drawee (now called acceptor) from raising the defences stipulated in s 54(2) of the BoEA 1882 against any holder in due course. Similarly, the commitment of the drawer and indorser is set out in s 55(1) and (2) of the BoEA 1882. An avaliser, who signs the bill in order to back the bill and to guarantee its payment, becomes liable 'as an indorser' of the bill (BoEA 1882, s 56). According to s 57 of the BoEA 1882, such liability is for the amount of the bill, interest thereon and any cost for noting or protesting a dishonoured bill.

Even though all signatories are liable in principle under the bill, the primary liability rests upon the drawee. The drawer and indorsers are only liable on recourse. Thus, only where the drawee (in our example as illustrated at Fig 3.8, the buyer) defaults with payment of the bill on maturity, can the holder or indorsee of the bill turn to the other parties who have signed the bill and approach them for payment (in our example at Fig 3.8 bank B can turn to bank A, or the seller who is the drawer). In such a case the party presented with the bill must pay it; the bill is then returned to this party, who can take redress from any other party who has signed the bill before him, or from the drawee who defaulted.

In order to receive payment under the bill, it needs to be duly presented for payment according to the requirements of s 45 or of s 46 of the BoEA 1882. (The latter applies where there are excuses for any delay or non-presentment.) If the bill is not presented accordingly, the drawer and indorsers are discharged from their liability under the bill.

Sections 47–52 of the BoEA 1882 determine whether a bill has been dishonoured by the drawer or acceptor, and the consequences and procedure thereafter. If the bill is dishonoured, notice of this dishonour must be given to the drawer and any indorser, otherwise they are discharged (BoEA 1882, ss 48–50). If a foreign bill is dishonoured the bill must be protested by a notary according to s 51(2) and ss 93, 94 of the BoEA 1882 in order to preserve all rights under the bill. Unless it is specifically provided for, protest is not necessary for an inland bill under English law (BoEA 1882, s 51(1)), however many other legal systems require this procedure. Thus it is important to determine in advance which legal system is going to govern the bill of exchange. Section 72 of the BoEA 1882 contains rules as to which law should be applied.

Protest, however, is a necessary step for acceptance or payment for honour: had the drawer or any indorser given the name of a person to whom the holder may resort in case of need, the holder has the choice whether or not to resort to this 'referee in case of need' (BoEA 1882, s 15). If he chooses to do so, protest for non-payment must have been made (BoEA 1882, s 67(1)). Sections 65–68 of the BoEA 1882 deal with acceptance and payment of the bill for honour after protest: provided certain circumstances are met, any party not yet liable under the bill can intervene and accept or pay the bill for the honour of any party liable under the bill.

3.2.4 The bill as an important tool in international trade

As we have seen, a bill of exchange is a very useful tool in trade transactions. The following characteristics of a bill of exchange contribute to its value.

(a) Every obligation under the bill must be expressed in writing and must be signed (BoEA 1882, ss 3, 23). Therefore the instrument itself shows all the relevant details, which helps to establish a good level of certainty and ease of proof.

(b) The obligations set out in the bill can be easily transferred by negotiation (BoEA 1882, ss 8, 31), so that the holder can obtain money in advance of maturity of the bill.

(c) The performance of the obligations can only be claimed by a person in possession of the document, called the holder (see BoEA 1882, s 2 in conjunction with, for example, ss 38, 45(1), 59).

(d) A person acquiring the bill by negotiation obtains good security and may even obtain a better right than his predecessor (BoEA 1882, s 38(2)). Thus an indorsee or other holder in due course acquires the rights under the bill free from any defences based on the underlying sale contract.

(e) The bill of exchange can be combined with other methods of payment to ensure that the bill is honoured before the transport documents are tendered to the buyer.

(f) The holder of a bill is entitled to bring an action for summary judgment, to which defences based on the underlying contract are generally irrelevant and not admissible. Thus the defendant cannot set off for any liquidated damages or counterclaim, unless the action is between the immediate parties to the bill of exchange in this capacity. Otherwise the action can only fail where the defences of fraud, invalidity or failure of consideration can be established. Action for summary judgment based on the bill of exchange is recognised in most countries. In England the procedure is set out in Part 24 of the Civil Procedure Rules 1998. The procedure for a summary judgment allows the court to decide a claim without trial, and is thus much faster and cheaper.

3.2.5 Bills of exchange and conflict of laws

International bills of exchange can pose difficult questions of conflict of laws. An example of this is to be found in *G & H Montage GmbH v Irvani*, CA, where the court had to determine which rules of law to apply to an aval and thus which requirements the aval had to meet (see BoEA 1882, s 72). Under German law the avaliser was treated as a guarantor and not as an indorser, whereas under English law the latter would be the case. No notice of dishonour had been given to the avaliser, which was necessary under English law to preserve the rights against this party (BoEA 1882, ss 56 and 48(1)). The question of which law was to prevail and thus whether the avaliser was in fact to be understood as a guarantor or an indorser was decisive to the outcome of the case.

In order to harmonise the law on bills of exchange and promissory notes, UNCITRAL adopted a Convention on International Bills of Exchange and International Promissory Notes in 1988, the text of which can be found on http://www.uncitral.org. The convention is not yet in force. Of the 10 ratifications necessary before it can come into force, it has only received five as of the end of September 2005. So for the time being, the split remains between the civil law jurisdictions (which largely have adopted the three Geneva Conventions on the Unification of the Law relating to Bills of Exchange of 7 June 1930 and the further three Geneva Conventions on the Unification of the Law relating to Cheques of 19 March 1931) and the Anglo-American system (applicable in the United Kingdom, most Commonwealth countries, the United States and other common law jurisdictions).

3.3 Collection arrangements

3.3.1 General

If the parties have not arranged for payment to take place in the seller's country, the seller is likely to have to collect the purchase price at the buyer's place of business. This can be done in a variety of ways. The seller can directly send the buyer a bill of exchange or a documentary bill, in the hope and trust that the buyer will fulfil his part of the bargain by accepting or paying the bill accordingly. Often, however, the seller employs a third party, to make sure the buyer's obligations are met before the latter gains possession of the documents of title to the goods.

This third party can be the seller's own subsidiary in the buyer's country, an agent or his forwarders. Commonly the exporter will instruct his bank to collect the purchase price; in most cases this means arranging for the acceptance or payment of a bill of exchange. These collection arrangements are commonly governed by the Uniform Rules for Collections (1995 revision) (URC 522) sponsored by the International Chamber of Commerce (ICC) in Paris. The URC 522 can be purchased, with or without commentaries, from the ICC, whose contact details can be found at http://www.iccwbo.org. Information about the countries, territories and banks adhering to these rules can also be obtained from the ICC. The URC 522 have not got the force of law in England and thus apply only if the parties incorporate them into their contract.

3.3.2 Functioning of collection agreements

A collection arrangement, as illustrated in Fig 3.9 works in the following way.

(a) The seller/exporter, having shipped the goods to the buyer, instructs his bank to organise the collection of the price. This bank is called the *remitting bank* and is acting as the agent of the seller. It will fulfil its duties either through its own branch office abroad or by employing a subagent which will be a bank in the buyer's country. This bank is called the *collecting bank*. If the collecting bank presents the documents to the buyer, it is called the *presenting bank*.

Under the law of agency only the remitting bank has a contractual relationship with the seller. It is liable for the transaction as a whole, whether carried out by itself or through a subagent (a collecting bank). However, a relationship between the seller and the collecting bank may be created if the seller (principal) contemplates that a subagent will perform part of the contract and authorises the remitting bank as his agent to create privity of contract between himself and the collecting bank (the subagent) (see *Calico Printers' Association Ltd v Barclays Bank Ltd*, KBD). In such a case the collecting bank becomes directly liable to the seller.

This cause of action seems to be envisaged by the URC 522 in Art 3 (listing not only the principal and the remitting bank but also the collecting and presenting bank as parties to the collection), together with Art 11(a) and (b). According to the latter article the remitting bank contracts with a collecting bank for the account and risk of the principal and assumes no liability for any breach of contract of the collecting bank. This seems to suggest that the parties, by incorporating the UCP 522 into their contract, have also intended to create privity of contract between the principal and the collecting bank (in support of this argument see Rix J in *Bastone & Firminger Ltd v Nasima Enterprises (Nigeria) Ltd*, QBD (Comm)).

The collection instructions to the bank, which should contain precise and detailed orders covering all eventualities, are usually given on a 'documentary bill lodgement form' (an example can be found in the appendix). First of all, the seller will have to choose the kind of collection he wants:

(i) collection of payment and/or acceptance; or

(ii) delivery of documents against payment and/or against acceptance (documentary collection); or

(iii) delivery of documents on other terms and conditions (see URC 522, Art 2).

Below and in Fig 3.9, we shall concentrate on a documentary collection as being the most complex and most useful version for the exporter.

When using this method, the seller should also state the procedure to be followed if the bill of exchange is dishonoured; whether the documents should be given to a representative in case of need; whether, and how, the goods are to be stored; and which insurance is to be taken out in case the documents cannot be released etc. He will give the financial documents (for example the bill of exchange) and the commercial documents (for example the invoice, document of title to the goods and any other documents, such as the insurance policy, certificates, etc) to the remitting bank together with the instructions.

(b) The remitting bank will then hand the documents together with the instructions to the collecting bank.

(c) The collecting bank will present the documents to the importer/buyer (called the drawee in this context, see URC 522, Art 3) and release them against payment of a sight bill or acceptance of a term bill, in accordance with the instructions of the principal/seller. If the bill is a term bill, the collecting bank may be required to hold it until its maturity and then to re-present it to the buyer for payment.

If the collecting bank releases the documents contrary to the instructions of the principal, it is liable in damages for breach of contract and for conversion of the documents. The liability of the collecting bank will be to the seller only where there is a contract between the seller and the collecting bank, otherwise it will be to the remitting bank, which in turn is liable to the seller. However where the URC 522 apply, Art 3 together with Art 11(a) and (b) seem to suggest that the collecting bank is directly liable to the principal because of privity. In any event, the liability of the remitting bank for acts of the collecting bank is excluded by Art 11(b) of the URC 522.

The collecting bank may be in a difficult situation, if the documents are to be delivered to one of the bank's customers who is not yet able to pay. If it releases the documents prematurely in order to give him the chance to raise funds, it is liable for any failure of its customer. If it refuses, it may lose its customer. Unless a solution is found to which the seller agrees, the bank will remain liable if the documents are handed over to the buyer before payment is made.

(d) Once payment is received by the collecting bank, it is transferred to the remitting bank, which in turn will credit the seller's account or otherwise pass on the payment.

When using bills of exchange in the collection process, a seller who requires the funds earlier than the maturity of the bill, can also discount the bill to the remitting bank. However, this usually will be 'with recourse', meaning the seller remains liable under the bill of exchange if the buyer does not perform his obligations under the bill.

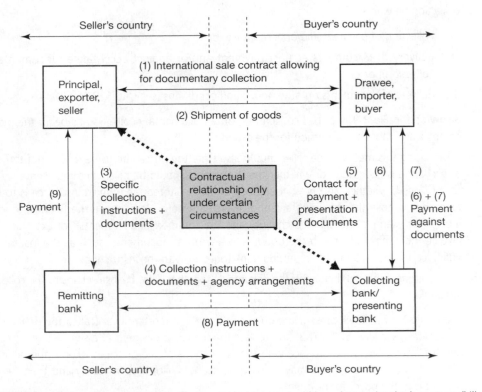

Fig 3.9 *Functioning of a documentary collection against payment within an international sale contract (bill of exchange not being discounted)*

By their use of an intermediary, collection arrangements provide a certain level of security to the seller. However the goods are dispatched to the buyer's country before the buyer has to make any payment for the goods. Thus the seller runs the risk of having to find another purchaser of his goods in the foreign country if the buyer does not fulfil his contractual obligations. In addition, the seller might still lose the goods despite having reserved his right of disposal, if the buyer gains possession of the documents and sells the goods to a *bona fide* purchaser (see s 9 of the Factors Act 1889 and s 25 of the SoGA 1979). These risks and others can be avoided by using a documentary credit instead.

3.4 Documentary credits

3.4.1 General

Using a documentary credit, also called letter of credit (l/c), for payment purposes has several advantages for the seller. The seller does not have to ship the goods until the buyer has opened the letter of credit and the seller has received advice of the opening from the bank (see *Bunge Corporation v Vegetable Vitamin Foods (Pte) Ltd,* QBD (Comm) and *Pavia & Co SpA v Thurmann-Nielsen*, CA). The letter of credit, being an independent undertaking of a bank, adds a secure paymaster to the buyer's obligation to pay the purchase price. At the same time, the letter of credit is fully independent of the underlying sale contract. This has the advantage that the seller knows he will get paid under the letter of credit if he fulfils its conditions for payment. Any disputes based on the sale contract cannot interfere with the payment, unless it is proven that the seller (who is the beneficiary of the credit) is acting fraudulently. Thus, once the seller has the letter of credit in hand, he can avail himself of a payment tool which, as long as he can meet the criteria, provides good security.

To take advantage of this the seller/beneficiary must bear in mind that the letter of credit sets out the conditions for payment. The bank will stick to these conditions regardless of the terms of the sale contract. Therefore the seller should check the terms of the letter of credit as soon as he has received it to make sure that:

(a) the letter of credit is consistent with the terms of the sale contract and does not vary or negate any stipulations of the sale contract to the detriment of the seller;

(b) he can comply with the time constraints for presentation of the documents;

(c) the documents listed for presentation are as agreed in the sale contract; and

(d) he can fulfil the particular requirements of the terms of the letter of credit, including the dates and times, as stipulated therein.

Any failure to meet the criteria in the letter of credit will result in the bank rejecting the documents. The seller will not get paid. SITPRO (Simplifying International Trade) Ltd is the trade facilitation body in the UK dedicated to simplifying the international trading process. It provides briefings to inform traders of the requirements, also giving tips for best practice and checklists for dealing with letters of credit. According to SITPRO Ltd's briefing 'Letters of Credit – An introduction' (updated January 2004), surveys show that well in excess of 50% of first presentations fail, due to documentary discrepancies. These documents, which focus on the needs of an international trader, can be accessed via the SITPRO homepage at http://www.sitpro.org.uk, or directly at http://www.sitpro.org.uk/trade/financial.html and http://www.sitpro.org.uk/trade/lettcred.html.

If the seller detects any discrepancy between the sale contract and the letter of credit he must inform the buyer at once, and either insist on fulfilment of the terms as set out in the sale contract or renegotiate them. Otherwise he is bound by the alterations as set out in the letter of credit. Similarly, the seller needs to renegotiate a change immediately with the buyer if he realises that he is no longer in a position to fulfil some of the stipulations in the credit. Otherwise he risks not getting paid.

If the requirements of a letter of credit cannot be fulfilled, the seller is at the buyer's mercy. The buyer has the opportunity to use the market situation in his favour. Where the market is rising the buyer can instruct the bank to accept the documents regardless of the discrepancies. In a falling market, however, he can give instructions to reject the documents. The latter option enables the buyer either to buy the goods cheaper elsewhere, or to renegotiate with the seller for a lower purchase price. The seller, whose goods have already been dispatched and might even have arrived at the destination, is in a vulnerable position and might have to agree to a bad bargain.

3.4.2 Functioning of a letter of credit

So how does a letter of credit work? Please consult Fig 3.10 for a graphic explanation.

3.4.2.1 First the parties to the sale contract agree on payment by letter of credit

The parties have to choose which particular credit terms they want to use. The seller may accept a letter of credit from the buyer's bank in the buyer's country. This means, however, that the seller must claim from the bank in the buyer's country. Some of the difficulties caused by the distance and a different country can be overcome by involving another bank in the seller's country. In such a case, the bank opening the letter of credit in the buyer's country, called the issuing bank, will employ a bank in the seller's country to contact the seller and act as recipient of the documents.

If this bank in the seller's country acts only as an agent of the issuing bank without entering into a contractual relationship with the seller, it is called the advising bank or nominated bank. It only advises the seller of the opening of the letter of credit by the issuing bank and as the nominated bank facilitates the exchange of documents against payment.

If it adds its own undertaking to the letter of credit, it has contractually bound itself towards the seller/beneficiary to pay the sum of money as stipulated in the letter of credit. It is confirming the issuing bank's undertaking and thus is called the confirming bank. This latter arrangement (the confirmed letter of credit) is of greater advantage to the seller, as he now has the added benefit of a secure paymaster in his own country, possibly even at his place of business. If something goes wrong he can sue this confirming bank rather than having to sue a foreign bank in a foreign country and legal system. This additional service however can be costly and it will be important to agree in the sale contract who is to pay for the letter of credit arrangements and any confirmation of the credit.

3.4.2.2 The buyer must initiate the letter of credit

The buyer must contact his bank and apply for the opening of a letter of credit in favour of the seller and in accordance with the terms of the sale contract. The credit will usually incorporate the Uniform Customs and Practices for Documentary Credits (UCP), as developed by the International Chamber of Commerce. Many banks across the world apply these banking rules. The current version is the 1993 revision (publication number 500), which came into effect on 1 January 1994 and is cited as UCP 500. The UCP have to be incorporated into the contract (as clarified by UCP 500, Art 1). As contractual terms they have precedence over common law rules.

Since April 2002 the new electronic supplement to the Uniform Customs and Practices of Documentary Credits has also come into effect, the eUCP which will, if incorporated into the contract, provide the rules for electronic or partially electronic presentation of documents.

The UCP 500 and eUCP can be purchased from the International Chamber of Commerce directly (http://www.iccwbo.org). You can also find the UCP 500 and eUCP in the appendix of the cases and materials book by Paul Todd (*Cases & Materials on International Trade Law* (2003)). The UCP 500 can also be found in the statute book by Francis Rose (*Blackstone's Statutes on Commercial & Consumer Law* (2005)) and on the website of the Golden Gate University on International Transportation at http://internet.ggu.edu/~emilian/ PUBL500.htm. You are strongly advised to read the UCP 500 alongside this part of the textbook.

3.4.2.3 Involvement of another bank

Depending on what type of credit has been chosen, a bank, usually situated in the seller's area, will become involved alongside the issuing bank. The former bank can do so by either adding its own undertaking or merely by facilitating the procedures. The following types of credit exist.

(a) Revocable or irrevocable credits (UCP 500, Arts 6, 8 and 9)

An irrevocable credit is a *definite* undertaking by the issuing bank to pay according to the stipulated conditions. An irrevocable credit can neither be cancelled nor amended without the prior agreement of all the parties involved, in particular the beneficiary (UCP 500, Art 9d). However a revocable credit on the other hand can be altered unilaterally by the issuing bank (UCP 500, Art 8a) and the buyer. The intention behind a letter of credit is to provide additional security to the seller, and a revocable credit does not do this. Therefore the default position is that a credit will be irrevocable unless stated otherwise (UCP 500, Art 6c).

(b) Unconfirmed or confirmed letter of credit (UCP 500, Arts 7–9)

As pointed out above, the bank in the seller's country can either get contractually involved with the seller and add its own undertaking to the letter of credit, thereby confirming it (UCP 500, Art 9b – confirming bank) or it can simply advise the opening of the letter of credit without entering into a direct relationship with the seller/beneficiary (UCP 500, Art 7 – advising bank). Confirmation can only be added to an irrevocable credit (UCP 500, Art 9b). Only this type is secure enough so that another bank would back it as it cannot freely be altered.

(c) Sight credit, deferred payment credit, acceptance credit or negotiation credit (UCP 500, Art 10)

These types signify the way payment is to be effected. A straight credit provides either for payment on presentation of the documents (sight credit), or for payment at some future date, for example 90 days after the date of the bill of lading (deferred payment credit), not involving a negotiable instrument. A bill of exchange is essential to an acceptance or negotiation credit. In an acceptance credit the seller draws a bill of exchange either on the nominated bank, the issuing bank or the buyer. In a negotiation credit, the nominated bank is authorised to negotiate a bill of exchange drawn by the seller on the buyer or issuing bank (see UCP 500, Arts 9a, b and 10).

It becomes evident from the above that the best option for the seller is the irrevocable and confirmed sight credit in order to secure payment and effect it as soon as possible.

3.4.2.4 Opening of the letter of credit

Once the letter of credit has been opened, the seller needs to be advised of its opening by the advising or confirming bank. Only then will the buyer's obligations towards the seller to open the letter of credit be fulfilled (see *Bunge Corporation v Vegetable Vitamin Foods*

(Pte) Ltd, QBD (Comm)). As the opening of the letter of credit is a condition precedent to the seller's duty to ship the goods (see *Garcia v Page & Co Ltd,* KBD and *Glencore Grain Rotterdam BV v Lebanese Organisation for International Commerce,* CA), this is a vital step. If the buyer has not opened the letter of credit in time, the seller can treat the contract as repudiated and claim damages. However he can waive the breach of condition and load the goods after late opening of the letter of credit. As the seller is not obliged to ship the goods without having the letter of credit in hand, any contractual provision in the sale contract that the seller will pay any demurrage for the loading period has to be read in this context. Laytime as between the parties to the sale contract does not commence until after the condition precedent for the loading operation, ie the opening of the letter of credit, is fulfilled (*Kronos Worldwide Ltd v Sempra Oil Trading SARL,* CA)

The letter of credit must be opened in time to enable the shipment of the goods. This has been held to be at the beginning of the shipment period (*Pavia & Co SpA v Thurmann-Nielsen,* CA) or at a reasonable time before the shipment date (*Plasticmoda SpA v Davidsons (Manchester) Ltd,* CA), unless the parties have fixed a specific time for the opening of the credit. The basis for this general rule is that the seller is entitled to assurance that he will get paid before he even ships the goods.

3.4.2.5 Checking the details of the letter of credit

Once the seller has received advice of the opening of the letter of credit, the seller needs to check the details of the letter of credit. If the letter of credit is compliant with the sale contract he must ship the goods. The seller must ensure he holds all the shipping documents (for example a shipped bill of lading, certificate of inspection, insurance policy etc) in accordance with the stipulations in the credit.

Where the buyer has not opened the credit as stipulated by the sale contract, the seller can claim damages for breach of condition. The buyer's failure is tantamount to a repudiatory breach, thus allowing the seller to treat the contract as having been discharged. However, should the seller choose to act upon a non-conforming letter of credit, he should reserve his rights to claim damages, otherwise he may be treated as having waived the buyer's breach altogether (see *Soproma SpA v Marine & Animal By-Products Corporation,* QBD (Comm) and *Enrico Furst & Co v WE Fischer Ltd,* QBD (Comm)).

3.4.2.6 Seller presents the documents

Now, after shipment of the goods and having obtained the shipping documents from the carrier, the seller can present the documents against payment or acceptance. He can present the documents to either the issuing bank, or confirming bank if the letter of credit is a confirmed one, or any nominated bank for this purpose. Presentation of the documents must take place at the stipulated location, within the stipulated time for presentation and before expiry of the credit (UCP 500, Arts 42 – 45; Arts 46 and 47 provide definitions of the terms used in this context). If no expiry date for presentation of the documents is provided, the latest date will be 21 days after the date of shipment (UCP 500, Art 43).

3.4.2.7 Bank checks the documents

The issuing bank, or confirming bank if the letter of credit is a confirmed one, or nominated bank acting on their behalf, will then check the documents against the terms of the credit. According to Arts 13 and 14 of the UCP 500, the bank has to ascertain whether the documents appear on their face to be in compliance with the terms and conditions of the credit. Examination of the documents has to be completed within a reasonable time (see *Banker's Trust Co v State Bank of India*, CA), not exceeding seven banking days after receipt of the documents. The outcome needs to be communicated to the party from whom the documents were received. The bank must give reasons if it rejects the documents. All discrepancies leading to the refusal must be itemised in this notice, which is binding on the bank. Thus, the bank cannot reject the documents a second time for reasons which were already in existence at the time of the first presentation and which had not been brought forward then.

On rejection, the bank needs to return or hold the documents at the disposal of the presenter. This enables the seller/beneficiary to attempt to remedy the discrepancies and to re-present the documents at a later date, as long as he is within the expiry date of the credit and for presentation of the documents. Thus, Art 14 of the UCP 500 implies a right to cure a defective tender. Should the bank fail to comply with these rejection provisions it is precluded from claiming that the documents are not compliant (UCP 500, Art 14e; applied in *Bayerische Vereinsbank Aktiengesellschaft v National Bank of Pakistan*, QBD (Comm)).

3.4.2.8 Non-compliance by a bank

If a bank does not comply with the letter of credit instructions, or pays against discrepant documents, it does so at its own risk. This means it risks not getting reimbursed. Sometimes the banks try to find a compromise, by paying 'under reserve' against non-conforming documents. This has been held to mean that the beneficiary is bound to repay the money on demand to the confirming bank if the issuing bank does not accept the documents (*Banque de l'Indochine et de Suez SA v JH Rayner (Mincing Lane) Ltd*, CA). Another possibility is that the bank may pay against indemnity. This means that the beneficiary will have to indemnify the bank in case of any loss or damage arising from the defects in the documents. However, whether this is adequate security will depend on the standing of the beneficiary.

3.4.2.9 Payment

Once the documents are accepted, payment has to be effected in the stipulated way. The bank having paid the beneficiary will then seek reimbursement from the issuing bank and the issuing bank will claim reimbursement from its customer and hand down the documents, each party being entitled to examine the documents and reject them if they do not conform to the instructions.

3.4.2.10 Choice of law in case of dispute

Difficulties may arise over the choice of law applicable to a dispute. This raises interesting points of private international law which will be discussed later in this book (**Chapter 6** at **6.4**). At this point, however, it is important that you appreciate the separate contractual relationships between the parties involved in such a transaction. They all need to be examined individually to determine the law governing the parties' rights and duties. These are:

(a) The sale contract between seller (beneficiary of the credit) and buyer (applicant for the credit) providing for payment by letter of credit.

Resulting therefrom are the letter of credit arrangements between:

(b) the applicant for the credit and the issuing bank;

(c) the issuing bank and the advising, confirming or nominated bank;

(d) the confirming bank, if any, and the beneficiary;

(e) the issuing bank and the beneficiary.

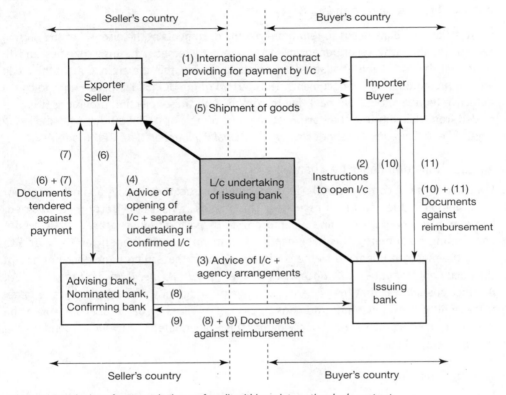

Fig 3.10 *Functioning of payment by letter of credit within an international sale contract*

3.4.3 Fundamental principles

Letters of credit, both at common law and under the UCP, are based on two fundamental principles:

(a) the autonomy of the credit; and

(b) the doctrine of strict compliance.

3.4.3.1 Autonomy of the credit

The principle of autonomy of the credit as stipulated in Arts 3a, 4 and 15 of the UCP 500, means that the letter of credit is separate and independent from the underlying sale contract. Any disputes relating to the sale contract do not affect the letter of credit. All that matters is that the conditions in the letter of credit are met. Thus, an initial sale of goods transaction with physical duties to dispatch the goods and to perform other acts is transformed into a paper trail, where only the documents matter. Due to this nature and the fact that all the relevant evidence is in paper form, it is often possible to obtain a summary judgment against a bank which does not honour its obligation under an irrevocable credit or an irrevocable and confirmed credit.

There is only one exception to the principle of strict autonomy: fraud or illegality. If the documents are fraudulent *and* the beneficiary (the seller) is involved in the fraud, the bank can refuse to pay (see *United City Merchants (Investments) Ltd v Royal Bank of Canada (The American Accord)*, HL). However, this exception is not lightly applied. Fraud must actually be proven and not just be a possibility (see *Society of Lloyd's v Canadian Imperial Bank of Commerce*, QBD (Comm) and *Bolivinter Oil SA v Chase Manhattan Bank NA*, CA). The bank can also withhold payment if the letter of credit was part of a scheme developed to mislead and thus part of an offence. In such a case the letter of credit could not be enforced for public policy reasons where it was used to secure a contract which had been entered into for purposes which breached the law, even if it was the law of a foreign but friendly State. This was argued in a case where money was lent to a company, partly secured by letter of credit, in order to enable the company to commit an accountancy offence (*Mahonia Limited v JP Morgan Chase Bank (No 1) and (No 2)*, both QBD (Comm)).

Unless this is the case, the buyer's attempts to obtain an interlocutory injunction from the courts to prevent the bank from paying until the fraud question has been tried will be unsuccessful. The same will apply with attempts to restrain the seller from calling on the letter of credit or from dealing with the amount of the letter of credit by way of freezing injunction (formerly a Mareva injunction) (see *Hamzeh Malas & Sons v British Imex Industries Ltd*, CA). There must be a very good reason to disrupt the payment mechanism of a letter of credit and thus call into question the assurance of payment it entails (see also *Intraco Ltd v Notis Shipping Corporation (The Bhoja Trader)*, CA in a case involving a demand guarantee).

On the other hand, a bank cannot be held liable if it has paid upon the tender of forged documents, as long as it has complied with the instructions in the credit and its duty to inspect the documents (*Gian Singh & Co Ltd v Banque de l'Indochine*, PC (Singapore)). Article 15 of the UCP 500 reflects this approach and states that the bank shall not be responsible 'for the form, sufficiency, accuracy, genuineness, falsification or legal effect of any document...'.

3.4.3.2 Doctrine of strict compliance

The principle of strict compliance provides that the bank can reject any document which is not in strict conformity with the terms of the credit (UCP 500, Art 14). The banks, who deal in finance and not with goods (UCP 500, Art 4), cannot be aware of all trade customs and usages. Thus their remit is to deal with documents only, without getting embroiled in the facts and practices of a particular trade. Even the slightest discrepancy enables a bank to reject. In *Equitable Trust Co of New York v Dawson Partners Ltd*, HL, Lord Sumner expressed this doctrine in the following way: 'There is no room for documents which are almost the same, or which will do just as well.'

Soproma SpA v Marine & Animal By-Products Corporation, QBD (Comm) is a good example of the application of the doctrine of strict compliance. In this case the tendered documents did not fully comply with the letter of credit. In particular, the bill of lading had several defects:

(a) it did not state that it was to order and thus negotiable;

(b) it contained a statement as to 'freight collect' instead of the required opposite 'freight prepaid';

(c) the analysis certificate showed a protein content of 3% less than the required minimum; and

(d) the commercial invoice and the bill of lading showed a slightly different name for the product sold, namely 'Fish Full Meal' instead of 'Fishmeal'.

In this case all the differences, apart from the description of the goods, were held to be material and to justify the rejection of the documents. As for the description of the goods the then equivalent of Art 37c of the UCP 500 provided that it was enough that the commercial invoice corresponded with the letter of credit. The other documents only had to describe the product in a way that was not inconsistent with the credit requirements. However where the UCP did not apply, it has been held that the description of the goods in the different documents has to tally, otherwise rejection by the bank is justified under the doctrine of strict compliance (*J H Rayner & Co Ltd v Hambros Bank Ltd*, CA).

Articles 20–38 of the UCP 500 clarify how the particular documentary requirements can be satisfied and detail the criteria to be met by the various transport documents. Article 39 of the UCP 500 allows for slight variations in amount, quantity and unit price. Whilst some of these articles relax the doctrine of strict compliance as long as their many stipulations are met, others demand additional requirements. In general, all documents must link together by clearly and unequivocally relating to the same goods. Under the common law position, however, where the UCP do not apply, it has been held that there is no room for a *de minimis* approach as in Art 39 of the UCP 500. In such a case the bank is entitled to reject the documents even if the discrepancy in the quantity is minimal (*Moralice (London) Ltd v E D & F Man*, QBD).

Tender of the documents has to be made exactly as called for in the letter of credit and to the person/bank indicated therein. These stipulations cannot be bypassed or short-circuited by tendering directly to the buyer, otherwise the tender is ineffective (*Soproma SpA v Marine & Animal By-Products Corporation*, QBD (Comm)). The letter of credit operates as conditional payment of the purchase price between the seller and the buyer. The seller is bound to use this payment method. If he fails to obtain payment due to his own fault, for example his failure to produce the correct documents, the seller cannot claim payment from the buyer directly. On the contrary, the buyer is discharged (*Shamsher Jute Mills Ltd v Sethia (London) Ltd*, QBD (Comm)). Only under exceptional circumstances can the seller demand payment from the buyer directly against tender of the documents, for example when the bank, which has been chosen as intermediary, becomes insolvent (*E D & F Man Ltd v Nigerian Sweets & Confectionery Co Ltd*, QBD (Comm)).

The doctrine of strict compliance operates with regard to the terms of the letter of credit only (remember the principle of autonomy of the credit). Any details in the sale contract differing from the credit are irrelevant for this purpose. A seller who wishes to use a letter of credit must comply with its terms. However, does this mean that the buyer can unilaterally change the details of the letter of credit? The opening by the buyer of a letter of credit not in conformity with the sale contract is understood as an offer of the buyer to alter the sale contract. The seller can object to the alterations and hold the buyer to the contract (*Glencore Grain Rotterdam BV v Lebanese Organisation for International Commerce*, CA).

However, if the seller does not challenge the alterations he may be bound by them. This has been held in cases where the seller, without objecting to or querying the alterations, shipped the goods (*Panoutsos v Raymond Hadley Corporation of New York*, CA), requested an extension of time (*Enrico Furst & Co v WE Fischer Ltd*, QBD (Comm)), tendered the documents under previous instalments (*WJ Alan & Co v El Nasr Export & Import Co*, CA) or objected to only some defects in the letter of credit but not to others (*Ficom SA v Sociedad Cadex Ltda*, QBD (Comm)). By using a letter of credit without objection, even though its terms do not comply with the sale contract, the seller is deemed to have agreed to change the sale contract in accordance with the suggestions the buyer has made in the letter of credit. Thus the sale contract has been altered, whether the seller intended this or not, and the seller is compelled to fulfil the new requirements. It is, therefore, very important that the seller scrutinises the letter of credit, regardless of whether he is under time pressure or not. Sometimes immense time pressure builds up, when the buyer is late with the opening of the credit, but this must not deter the seller from examining whether or not the chosen payment term will ultimately lead to payment.

3.4.4 Other types of credit

Depending on their business needs the parties may choose to use a special type of letter of credit.

3.4.4.1 Revolving credit

A *revolving credit* can be used between parties who are in regular trading contact. The buyer can give standing instructions to its bank to open a revolving credit, which cannot at any time exceed a maximum limit for drawings by the seller. The exporter can draw on the credit for each of the envisaged transactions, without the buyer repeatedly having to open another credit.

3.4.4.2 Packing credit

A *packing credit* or *anticipatory credit* enables the exporter to obtain payment before the goods are shipped. He will get paid against the production of specific documents prior to shipment, for example a warehouse receipt or a forwarder's certificate, affirming that the goods have been received for shipment. This credit particularly assists smaller exporters not familiar with shipping practice.

3.4.4.3 Red clause credit

Similarly a *red clause credit* is a letter of credit which entitles the seller to draw on it by way of advance against certain documents, such as a warehouse receipt. After shipment he presents the transport documents to the bank and will receive the balance of purchase price minus the advance.

3.4.4.4 Back-to-back credit

Back-to-back credits, also called countervailing credits, are mainly used in the external trade (when a merchant buys goods in one overseas country and sells them in another) and in string contracts. In the latter scenario, the same goods are sold and resold by several middlemen before they are purchased by the final buyer. The ultimate buyer opens a confirmed credit in favour of his immediate seller. This seller then uses this credit as security to open a letter of credit for his own supplier. If there are more middlemen, this can be repeated with each of them using the credit received as security to open another credit for his own supplier. The credits are usually on exactly the same terms and conditions as the initial letter of credit by the ultimate buyer, known as overriding credit. Only the details relating to the prices and invoices will vary in accordance with each sale contract in the chain. Back-to-back credits only allow the bank to take recourse against the preceding middleman who might not have any substantial assets. Thus, banks are not too enthusiastic about offering this service.

3.4.4.5 Transferable credit

Another method to finance supply transactions is to use a *transferable credit*. This form is specifically covered by Art 48 of the UCP 500. A credit is only transferable if it is expressly designated to be transferable by the issuing bank (UCP 500, Art 48b). The beneficiary of a transferable credit may request the bank authorised to pay, accept or negotiate (the transferring bank) to make the credit available in whole or in part to one or more other parties (the secondary beneficiary/ies) (UCP 500, Art 48a). Once the bank has consented to the transfer, the secondary beneficiary can obtain payment by presenting the required documents in his own name.

It is not sufficient that the credit is designated to be transferable, but the bank must expressly consent to the transfer as well as the manner and extent of it (UCP 500, Art 48c; *Bank Negara Indonesia 1946 v Lariza (Singapore) Pte Ltd)*, PC). It seems that a bank approached to give its consent is under no obligation to effect the transfer, however in practice it is unlikely to refuse without good reason, as long as adequate transfer charges are paid. The credit transfer will be on the same terms as the original credit. However, the credit transfer will usually involve some changes within the other details of the transaction; for example, the price may be reduced, the invoice substituted and any presentation times may be altered within the limits of the original credit.

Similarly, as with back-to-back credits, the prudent seller will want to make sure that he does not disclose his supplier otherwise he risks getting bypassed in the future. Thus the seller must ensure that the documentary requirements allow for the appropriate changes to be made in a transfer. Unless otherwise stated in the credit, a credit made transferable can, according to Art 48g of the UCP 500, be transferred only once.

A transferable credit governed by the UCP 500 is automatically divisible and can be transferred in parts to more than one secondary beneficiary as long as partial shipments are not excluded by the credit. In case of a transferable credit subject to English law, not incorporating the UCP, divisibility does not seem to be automatic. Thus, care needs to be taken on the opening of a credit to make sure that all intended future transactions are permissible.

3.4.4.6 Assignment of the proceeds of the credit

Another weaker form of providing security to another based on a letter of credit is by way of *assignment of the proceeds of the credit*. As it focuses on the proceeds only, without touching on the right to perform under the credit, it is not dependent on the credit's transferability (UCP 500, Art 49). The rules regarding the assignment of the proceeds will depend upon the law applicable to the transaction. In English law these are the rules governing the legal assignment of things in action under s 136 of the Law of Property Act 1925. It requires the assignment to be absolute and not in part, and made in writing by the assignor. Written notice must be given to the debtor. The disadvantage here is that the assignee has no or little opportunity to ensure that payment under the letter of credit takes place. If no proceeds are realised, the value of the assignment is nominal.

3.5 Standby credits and guarantees

3.5.1 Standby credits

A standby letter of credit, like an ordinary letter of credit, is an independent undertaking by a bank to pay the beneficiary on production of certain documents. The ordinary letter of credit is intended to secure the payment of the purchase price on tender of the transport documents. The standby credit, on the other hand, aims at protecting the beneficiary in case of default by the other party to the (underlying) contract. An example might be that the seller is asked to provide a standby credit in favour of the buyer (beneficiary) in case of shipment of unsatisfactory goods. The buyer may want to be sure that any damages will be paid, particularly if he has parted with the purchase price before he has had a chance to examine the goods.

The document that needs to be tendered to activate the credit is as prescribed by the credit agreement. For example it may be a statement by the beneficiary that the goods are defective or that the applicant has not fulfilled his duties under the underlying contract, or simply a demand by the beneficiary. Thus the beneficiary is in a stronger position to recover damages; in fact he may be able to claim the balance of the credit straightaway. Any disputes about the soundness of the allegations of the beneficiary and therefore the fulfilment of the obligations under the underlying contract, might have to be discussed or litigated at a later date. Thus the functioning of a standby credit is similar to a bank guarantee or a performance bond.

Standby letters of credit can incorporate the UCP 500 if the parties so choose. However, since 1 January 1999 the parties may instead choose the separate code for standby credits, the International Standby Practices (ISP 98). These latter rules have been developed by the International Chamber of Commerce (ICC) in collaboration with the Institute for International Banking Law and Practice and are designed to be compatible with the United Nations Convention on Independent Guarantees and Standby Letters of Credit (New York, 1995). Compared with the UCP 500, the ISP 98 prescribe slightly less onerous requirments for standby letters of credit.

3.5.2 Guarantees and performance bonds

A guarantee under common law is a secondary obligation by a third party to pay the creditor in case the principal debtor defaults with his obligations. This concept is illustrated in Fig 3.11 for the example of a seller providing a guarantee for the satisfactory performance of his obligations under the sale contract.

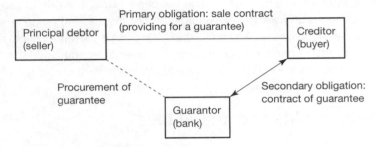

Fig 3.11 *Guarantee under common law procured by the seller*

The liability of the guarantor will depend on the terms of the contract of guarantee but, as the guarantee is accessory in nature, it will only reach as far as the liability of the principal debtor (principle of co-extensiveness). Any action that discharges the debtor will also discharge the guarantor. To be enforceable, the guarantee must be in writing or evidenced in writing and signed by the guarantor. A bank acting as guarantor will usually ask for a counter-indemnity from its customer, the debtor, enabling it to recover in full all sums paid together with interest on them.

Different types of guarantee must be distinguished, for example conditional and 'autonomous guarantees'. A conditional guarantee is dependent on the destiny of the primary obligation. It is normally activated by the non-performance of the underlying obligation, in our example the unsatisfactory performance of the seller's duties. This means that the guarantor can become involved in disputes between the parties to the underlying contract. Thus, banks may be reluctant to issue conditional guarantees and prefer other forms of guarantee instead.

In international trade, most 'guarantees' will not be guarantees in the strict common law sense, but an independent, autonomous undertaking by the guarantor to pay if the conditions of the guarantee are fulfilled. They may be in the form of a demand guarantee, performance bond, advance (or repayment) guarantee, performance guarantee or standby letter of credit. A demand guarantee is unconditional and payable upon first demand by the beneficiary against presentation of specified documents. Performance bonds, performance guarantees and, as we have seen, standby letters of credit work similarly.

Thus, these forms of independent guarantee provide an autonomous tool for the reimbursement of the beneficiary up to a specified amount upon the occurrence of certain stipulated events. This independent guarantee is usually activated by the beneficiary making certain written allegations regarding the unsatisfactory performance of the principal debtor's duties arising from the underlying contract. Except in case of fraud (see *Bolivinter Oil SA v Chase Manhattan Bank NA*, CA and *United Trading v Allied Arab Bank*,

CA), any disputes as to the correctness of these allegations cannot interfere with the payment under the independent guarantee (see *Edward Owen Engineering Ltd v Barclays Bank International*, CA). These can only be resolved at the level of the underlying contract.

Therefore, the independent guarantee provides an easy accessible pool for the beneficiary to retrieve damages, without having to pursue an action against a party based in a different country. However, at some stage the parties will have to account to each other, so that the beneficiary will be compensated for the loss actually suffered, not more and not less (*Cargill International SA v Bangladesh Sugar and Food Industries Corporation*, QBD (Comm) and CA), unless this duty is expressly excluded. Even though there is a danger of abuse by the beneficiary, not having to prove the breach of the underlying contract, the autonomous guarantee provides for the necessary and intended legal and commercial certainty for the third party guarantor.

The ICC's Uniform Rules for Demand Guarantees (URDG, with their ICC brochure number 458), promulgated by the ICC in April 1992, have attempted to codify international market practice and to balance the relationship between the paying party and the beneficiary more evenly. They can be incorporated into the contract to govern the relationship between the parties. The 1978 Uniform Rules for Contract Guarantees (URCG, ICC publication 325) have not been withdrawn by the ICC and are thus still available for incorporation into performance bonds. The URCG, which best protected the seller against unfair calls, but made the bond conditional and the conditions quite onerous on the beneficiary, have not achieved widespread acceptance. The 1992 URDG instead now recognise the importance of the autonomy principle of the independent guarantee.

Not as precise in keeping the guarantee and the underlying contract separate is the UN Convention on Independent Guarantees and Standby Letters of Credit, adopted in 1995 by the United Nations Conference on International Trade Law (UNCITRAL) in New York. This Convention has been in force since 1 January 2000, but in September 2005 still only had eight parties; the UK is not a party.

3.6 Forfaiting and factoring

Alongside the above forms of payment and financing international trade transactions, other forms of financing or debt collection have been developed which are designed to help the seller/supplier of the goods to ease his cash flow during the buyer's credit period. Depending on the form chosen, the financing institution might also take on the full risk of effecting payment and thus protect the exporter against buyer risks, exchange rate fluctuations and risks associated with a particular country. The transaction is then undertaken 'without recourse' and the financing institution will usually charge a higher price or commission.

These forms of financing are generally separate from the underlying sale contract. Where the financing institution cannot obtain payment from the buyer/importer, the success of a claim for indemnification will depend on whether the debt collection was arranged with recourse or not. However, an agreement on a non-recourse basis is unlikely to protect a seller who defaults under the sale contract without legal excuse. Thus, the seller's failure to fulfil the obligations under the sale contract may be held against him where the financing house cannot obtain payment from the buyer on these grounds.

3.6.1 Forfaiting

In forfaiting, the bank or other financing institution undertakes to collect payment under a negotiable instrument (a bill of exchange or promissory note (see BoEA 1882, ss 83–89)) from the buyer without recourse to the seller. The negotiable instrument must be backed by an aval or a separate guarantee of a bank with good standing. The forfaiter who takes the discounted bill of exchange or promissory note 'without recourse' therefore takes the risk of effecting payment from the avaliser or guarantor. For long or middle term contracts it is common for the bills or promissory notes to be drawn in a series over the duration of a contract allowing for payment by instalments. In such a case the exporter has the advantage of being able to obtain payment as agreed with the forfaiter straight away and is no longer concerned with the collection.

As illustrated in Fig 3.12 the seller, for example, draws a term bill of exchange on the buyer, but already 'without recourse' to himself. The buyer then accepts the bill and procures the backing of his bank. The seller can now indorse the bill again 'without recourse' to his bank and obtain payment for the discounted bill right away.

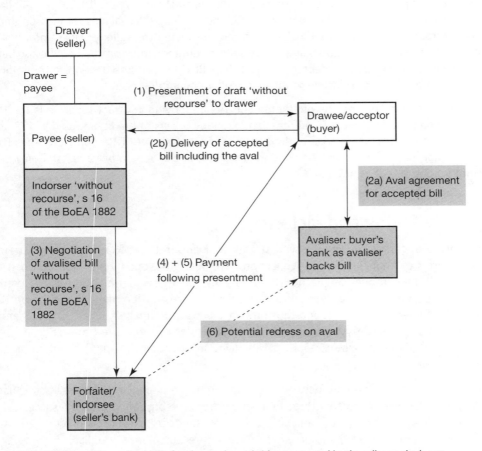

Fig 3.12 Forfaiting of an avalised bill of exchange drawn 'without recourse' by the seller on the buyer

3.6.2 Factoring

Factoring is the purchase of either all or selected book debts (receivables) by the factor. Thus the factor takes on the financial burden of the export transaction. He provides finance to the exporter and collects the price. Where the finance is provided on a non-recourse basis the factor also bears the status, transaction and exchange risks. In recourse finance, however, the exporter only receives an advance payment but must reimburse the factor in the event that the buyer fails to pay. Particularly where all the book debts are taken on by the factor, the exporter has the advantage of being able to concentrate on the essence of his business whereas the factor takes on the collection of payment and credit control.

The factor can handle the collection himself or via correspondents (direct export factoring) or he can use another factor in the buyer's country. Using such a two factor system (also called indirect factoring), the factor used by the exporter (export factor) enters into an arrangement with the import factor who takes on the credit risks of the exporter's customers situated in his country and collects payment. The advantage here is that both factors deal with customers in their own countries and thus can best assess their respective creditworthiness. The contractual responsibilities only work along the chain, where rights of recourse might also be exercised (see Fig 3.13). There is no contractual relationship between the seller/exporter and the import factor. The detailed rights and responsibilities depend on the arrangement between the parties.

Due to the importance of international factoring, conventions have been developed to provide for unified rules in this area.

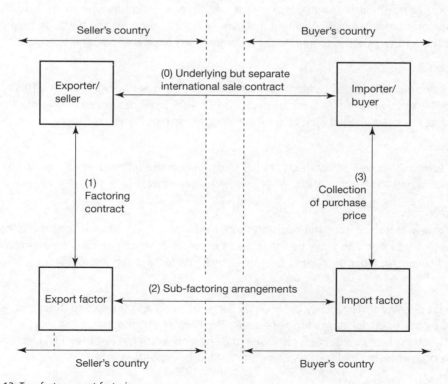

Fig 3.13 Two factor export factoring

The International Institute for the Unification of Private Law (UNIDROIT, whose website can be found at http://www.unidroit.org) adopted the Convention on International Factoring in Ottawa in 1988. The convention came into force in May 1995, but in September 2005 had been ratified by only six States. It has been criticised for its limited scope and failure to address several important issues. It can be found in I Carr and R Kidner, *Statutes & Conventions on International Trade* (4th edn, London: Cavendish, 2003), or on the web at: http://www.unidroit.org/english/conventions/1988factoring/main.htm.

UNCITRAL developed a draft convention on the Assignment of Receivables in International Trade which was adopted in New York in 2001. Five countries must ratify the convention in order for it to come into force. In September 2005 this had not yet been achieved. It can be found at http://www.uncitral.org/uncitral/en/uncitral_texts/payments.html.

3.7 Revision and further reading

3.7.1 Questions

This is your opportunity to revise what you have learned and to check whether you have understood the issues covered in this chapter. I suggest that you attempt to solve the problem questions below before you move on to the next chapter.

Question 1

Seller S and buyer B both situated in different countries are discussing different payment options. They have had no previous dealings with each other and are uncertain about each other's trustworthiness. The buyer also requires a credit period. Advise them as to their options for arranging secure payment including a credit period for the buyer. In doing so advise them as to who has to initiate the recommended payment form and bear its costs.

Question 2

S has sold tomatoes on cif terms to B. Stipulated shipment period was 1.11.05–10.11.05. Payment is to be effected via letter of credit. On 1.11.05 S still has not received notice that the credit has been opened. Can he treat the contract as repudiated?

Question 3

As question 2 above for the facts, but B had opened the letter of credit on 1.10.05. However, S had not been notified. What are the consequences?

Question 4

S has received notice from the advising bank that a revocable letter of credit has been opened in his favour. Can S rely on the terms of the sales contract providing for an irrevocable and confirmed letter of credit to be opened by B? Would you suggest any action?

Question 5

S did not discover a discrepancy between the letter of credit and the sale contract and presents the documents for payment to the bank. The bank rejects the documents on the basis that the letter of credit requires a certificate of inspection which has not been included in the list of documents required by the sale contract. What is S's position:

(a) with regard to the bank?

(b) with regard to the buyer B?

Question 6

As in question 2 above for the facts. S ships the goods on 11.11.05 and tenders the documents including the bill of lading stating the actual shipment date to the bank. The bank consults with the buyer whether to accept the documents. The market has fallen in the meantime. What is your advice to the buyer? Distinguish between the rights of rejection:

(a) under the letter of credit;

(b) under the sale contract, where no letter of credit exists.

Question 7

As in question 2 above for the facts. S tenders a sea waybill instead of the required bill of lading.

(a) Can the bank reject the documents?

(b) Where no letter of credit exists, can the buyer on the basis of the sale contract reject the documents even though he did not sell the goods in transit and the goods arrived safely?

Question 8

As in question 7 above for the facts. S is still within the time limit for presentation of the documents. Can he remedy the discrepancy by retendering conforming documents:

(a) to the bank under the letter of credit?

(b) to the buyer directly, even though a letter of credit is in place?

(c) to the buyer where no letter of credit arrangement exists?

Question 9

S sells a consignment of oranges to B. Payment is to be effected by documentary collection. The remitting bank uses the services of the presenting bank. The presenting bank hands the documents to the buyer for inspection. The buyer uses the documents and takes delivery from the carrier. The buyer does not pay. Advise S as to his rights and possible claims.

Question 10

S and B have chosen payment by letter of credit. However, B wants security in case the goods arrive damaged. Advise the parties as to their options.

Question 11

S draws a term bill of exchange on B. B accepts the bill, which is avalised by B-bank. S negotiates the bill to S-bank. On maturity S-bank presents the bill to B for payment. B refuses to pay. Advise S-bank as to its rights and options to secure payment under the bill.

3.7.2 Further reading

(a) *Glencore Grain Rotterdam BV v Lebanese Organisation for International Commerce (LORICO)* [1997] 2 Lloyd's Rep 386 concerning letters of credit and opening of credit.

(b) *Glencore International and Another v Bank of China* [1996] 1 Lloyd's Rep 135 concerning letters of credit — requirements/inspection of documents.

(c) *Bankers Trust v State Bank of India* [1991] 2 Lloyd's Rep 443 concerning letters of credit and rejection of documents.

(d) *G & H Montage GmbH (formerly Grunzweig und Hartmann Montage GmbH) v Irvani* [1990] 2 All ER 225, [1990] 1 Lloyd's Rep 14, CA concerning bills of exchange — conflict of laws — guarantees — signatures.

(e) *Bolivinter Oil SA v Chase Manhattan Bank NA* [1984] 1 Lloyd's Rep 251, CA concerning autonomy of letters of credit, performance bonds and guarantees — *ex parte* restraining injunctions.

(f) *Soproma SPA v Marine & Animal By-Products Corporation* [1966] 1 Lloyd's Rep 367 concerning letters of credit and the principle of strict compliance.

(g) *Korea Exchange Bank v Debenhams* [1979] 1 Lloyd's Rep 548 regarding bills of exchange and certainty of date of payment.

(h) *Jade International Steel Stahl und Eisen GmbH & Co KG v Robert Nicholas* [1978] QB 917 concerning bills of exchange — right of holder — holder in due course.

(i) *Alan, WJ & Co v El Nasr Export & Import Co* [1972] 2 QB 189 concerning letters of credit being conditional payment — variation of contract terms.

(j) *United City Merchants (Investments) Ltd v Royal Bank of Canada* [1983] 1 AC 168 concerning letter of credit and fraud.

(k) Duncan Sheehan, 'Rights of Recourse in Documentary (And Other) Credit Transactions', [2005] JBL 326–345.

(l) EP Ellinger, 'The UCP-500: considering a new revision', [2004] LMCLQ 31–45.

(m) Mark Williams, 'Documentary Credits and Fraud: English and Chinese Law Compared', [2004] JBL 155–170.

(n) Alexia Ganotaki, 'Documentary credits: another original story', [2003] LMCLQ 151–157 concerning letters of credit — defective documents.

(o) Benjamin Parker, 'Fraudulent Bills of Lading and Bankers' Commercial Credits: Deceit, Contributory Negligence and Directors' Personal Liability', [2003] LMCLQ 1–6.

(p) Xiang Gao, 'Presenters Immune from the Fraud Rule in the Law of Letters of Credit', [2002] LMCLQ 10–38.

(q) Howard N Bennett, 'Unclear or Ambiguous Instructions in the World of Documentary Credits', [2001] LMCLQ 24–26.

(r) Lars Gorton, 'Draft UNCITRAL Convention on Independent Guarantees', [1997] JBL 240–253.

(s) Charles Debattista, 'Performance Bonds and Letters of Credit: A Cracked Mirror Image', [1997] JBL 289–305.

(t) EP Ellinger, 'The Uniform Rules for Collection', [1996] JBL 382–387.

(u) C G J Morse, 'Letters of Credit and the Rome Convention', [1994] LMCLQ 560–571.

(v) Chapters on bills of exchange and financing international trade in LS Sealy, RJA Hooley, *Commercial Law, Text, Cases and Materials,* (3rd edn, London: Butterworths, 2003).

(w) Chapters on bills of exchange and financing international trade in R Bradgate, *Commercial Law,* (3rd edn, London: Butterworths, 2000 reprinted in 2002).

4 Contracts of Affreightment

4.1 Introduction

In accordance with the terms of the international sale contract one of the parties to this sale contract will have to arrange for the carriage of the goods to the agreed destination. For example, under a contract based on 'ex works' or on 'f terms' the importing buyer must arrange for the carriage of the goods, whereas under 'c terms' or 'd terms' this duty falls on the exporting seller. This might be a single carriage by sea, air, road or rail (unimodal) or via a variety of means (multimodal or combined transport). Depending on the mode of transport, different legal rules apply. Due to the international character of the carriage, international conventions have been drawn up to unify the relevant laws as much as possible. Each international convention needs to be ratified by the country that wishes to give it effect. Thus, the first question is: which laws govern each particular transportation of goods? Subsequent questions are: are there any conventions and, if yes, do they apply to the specific scenario? Even if a country has not ratified the relevant convention, it may still be applicable if the parties chose to incorporate it into their carriage contract.

At present, English law has given effect to the following carriage conventions.

(a) In relation to sea carriage, the Hague Rules as amended by the Brussels Protocol 1968 (the Hague-Visby Rules) are incorporated into English law by the Carriage of Goods by Sea Act 1971.

(b) The Warsaw Convention on Carriage by Air of 12 October 1929, as amended in The Hague on 28 September 1955, was incorporated into English law for air carriage of passengers and cargo by the Carriage by Air Act 1961 and the Carriage by Air (Supplementary Provisions) Act 1962. The new Montreal Convention for the Unification of Certain Rules for International Carriage by Air of 28 May 1999, which came into force on 4 November 2003, has been ratified by the United Kingdom: it is given effect by the Carriage by Air Act 1961 as amended and came into force on 28 June 2004. Between Convention States the Montreal Convention 1999 prevails over the Warsaw Convention (Montreal of the Convention 1999, Art 55).

(c) Road carriage is governed by the Convention on International Carriage of Goods by Road of 19 May 1956 (CMR) which was incorporated into English law by the Carriage of Goods by Road Act 1965.

(d) In relation to rail carriage, the Convention concerning International Carriage of Goods by Rail of 9 May 1980 (COTIF 1980) has been given effect by virtue of the International Transport Conventions Act 1983. As part of this Convention in Annexe B the Uniform Rules concerning the Contract of International Carriage of Goods by Rail (CIM) are in force. An updated version of this Convention, COTIF 1999, is at the time of writing not yet in force.

The main focus in this chapter will be on the carriage of goods by sea as more than 90% of the world's trade (measured in weight) is carried by sea. Once the principles that can be deduced from the law on sea carriage have been learned and understood, this knowledge can be used to study the rules on carriage by air or land, thereby identifying the common as well as the differing issues.

4.2 Carriage of goods by sea

4.2.1 General

In order to facilitate your understanding, relevant standard documents, such as bills of lading, non-negotiable sea waybills, multimodal transport bills, charterparty contracts and shipping instructions, have been appended to this book. Please study each form as soon as it is introduced in this chapter.

4.2.1.1 Arranging the contract and execution of the carriage

The contract of carriage, to ship the goods from one port to another, is agreed between the shipper (our exporter or importer, as the case may be) and the carrier or charterer (the latter is a person who hires the whole vessel for a period of time or a voyage). However, both parties might use the services of an intermediary to arrange the contract. The shipper may instruct a forwarder to secure shipping space and the carrier may use a loading broker to arrange cargo for his ship.

A contract of carriage so procured between a cif seller/exporter and the carrier may, for simplified example, be executed in the following simplified way: the shipowner/carrier directly or via his loading broker communicates the name of the ship, details of and closing date for loading to the forwarding agent or the shipper. A sailing card, which is a printed notice of these details, is often used for this purpose. When the shipper sends the goods to the docks he includes shipping instructions for the carrier (see Appendix to this book) and a shipping note for the superintendent of the docks (setting out the details of the goods and stating the vessel on which they are to be shipped; see Appendix to this book). Where and how the goods have to be delivered to the vessel depends on the contract or on the custom of the particular port. Unless the aforementioned clarify the matter, under common law, the place of delivery is alongside the ship or within reach of her tackle by the shipper at his expense.

The goods are then inspected by tally clerks. They record the date of loading, note down the particulars and condition of the goods, the quantity (for example by counting the number of packages or taking the weight or other measurements), and any identification marks and state whether or not the goods or their packaging show any defects or markings. On this basis the mate's receipt is issued, including all the remarks as to order and condition which the tally clerks have identified. The ship's officer in charge signs the mate's receipt after loading is complete. The function of the mate's receipt is twofold: it is an acknowledgement by the shipowner/carrier of having received the goods in the stated condition (therefore the goods are now in his possession and at his risk); and it is, even though not a document of title, prima facie evidence of the ownership of the goods. The holder of the mate's receipt or the person named therein can demand the issue of the bill of lading. The shipowner/carrier is within his rights and duties under the contract of carriage in doing so, unless he has knowledge to the contrary.

The signed mate's receipt is taken to the shipowner's/carrier's clerks to be compared with the draft bill of lading. The latter is usually pre-prepared by the shipper or his agent in a set of two or three original bills, having obtained the required forms of bills of lading used by the shipping company from a stationer. Any qualifications on the mate's receipt are added onto the bill of lading which is then signed on behalf of the shipowner/carrier and handed to the shipper. It is worth mentioning that the particulars of all bills of lading are entered on the ship's manifest, which contains all the ship's cargo and has to be produced to naval, port, consular and customs authorities. Thus it is a good document to remember when certain evidence is needed, for example if it is suspected that the bill of lading has been forged.

However in modern liner practice (where consignments of goods are carried by a shipping line which operates a regular service between the specified ports) the mate's receipt is often replaced. The goods delivered for shipment are accompanied by either a standard shipping note or a dangerous goods note. After shipment this note is signed to acknowledge receipt and passed back to the shipper. It is also common now for the carrier to prepare the bill of lading based on the details that were provided by the shipper when he booked the shipping space.

Whilst the ship is on its journey, the bill of lading together with the other transport documents is transferred from the shipper/seller/exporter (who is called the consignor) to the buyer/importer (who is called the consignee) in accordance with the sale contract. At this point it will be of particular importance whether the bill of lading has been issued 'clean', that is, stating the goods to be in good order and condition, or 'claused', including qualifying remarks relating to their condition. Under a cif contract the buyer is only bound to accept clean documents. This means that the seller is at the buyer's mercy if the bill is claused. If the tender of documents is conducted via a bank under a letter of credit the documents will be rejected, unless the buyer instructs the bank otherwise. If the seller cannot perform his obligation to tender clean documents, the buyer can use his strong position to renegotiate the contract price or buy the goods elsewhere and claim damages from the seller.

The fact that clean transport documents are of such significance has led to dishonest business practices. But even if the carrier issues a clean transport document against a letter of indemnity from the shipper (promising to indemnify the carrier against any claims resulting from this action), this is illegal and risky. The carrier is liable towards any third party, holding the bill of lading and is bound by the statements on the bill. If the goods arrive damaged, but are said to have been shipped in good order and condition, the deterioration must have been taking place whilst in the custody of the carrier. Proof to the contrary is not admissible under English law (CoGSA 1992, s 4).

Once the ship has arrived at its destination, the goods are handed over to the consignee on production of the bill of lading. Without particular agreement, or differing port custom, the carrier has to deliver the goods over the ship's rail to the consignee in order to discharge his duties. All costs incurred after that are to be borne by the consignee. Often delivery takes place to a dock company or appropriate warehouse and not directly into the physical custody of the consignee. It is the duty of the consignee to ascertain the arrival of the ship and its readiness to unload. The shipowner's/carrier's responsibility for the goods ceases once the goods have been delivered to the consignee according to the contract of carriage or custom or as stipulated by law. If he delivers goods for which a bill of lading has been issued without production of the bill, he does so at his own risk. Once one bill of the set has been accepted and delivery made, the others are void.

4.2.1.2 Different types of carriage and contracts

Liner and tramp services

Depending on the amount and type of cargo, the transport arrangements will differ. Particularly with smaller consignments, the shipper can use a 'liner vessel' if a ship opera- tor maintains a regular and scheduled transport line including the port of loading and discharge envisaged by the shipper. Where a liner vessel is not suitable, the goods must be booked onto a 'tramp ship' which does not operate under a regular schedule, but calls at any port where cargo can be obtained.

Liner services will often use containers into which the goods are loaded. Containers in standard size are available as general-purpose containers, but also as non-standard con- tainers, for example providing refrigeration or ventilation or tank containers for liquid cargo. The exporter can book his cargo as full container load (fcl) or less than full con- tainer load (lcl). The containers can be sealed after they have been fully loaded. They thus provide better protection from damage and theft. Containers also lend themselves for combined transport by more than one mode of transport where a carrier may offer a door-to-door service rather than just a port-to-port carriage.

Charterparty (chp)

If a full shipload is to be transported and particularly where cargo is carried in bulk the whole vessel is chartered. Commodities such as agricultural products (eg grain, rice, sugar, cocoa, coffee, tea) and raw materials (eg metals, ores, oils) are typically carried in bulk. The contract of carriage, hiring the entire vessel, is called a charterparty. All the terms of the contract are set out in the charterparty.

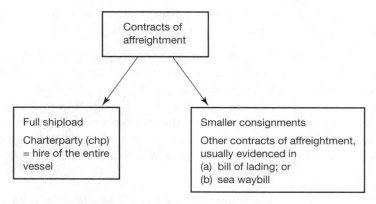

Fig 4.1 Type of contract of carriage depends on volume of cargo

Bill of lading contract (bol)

If a lesser quantity of goods or individually packaged goods are shipped along with other cargo this is mostly done under a bill of lading or similar carriage document, which evidences the contract of carriage. For ease of reference, in the following these contracts are called 'bill of lading contracts'. However, it needs to be noted that the 'bill of lading contract' is concluded prior to the issue of the bill of lading. As between the shipper and the carrier, this initial contract of carriage will prevail. The bill of lading only evidences the terms of this contract that has already been partly performed by loading the goods. Thus, a special term agreed in the contract, whether oral or in writing, may override the general clause printed on the bill of lading. This had been decided with respect to an oral agreement for direct shipment between the parties, even though the bill of lading provided for liberty regarding the route, as well as direct or indirect shipment (*Ardennes (Cargo Owners) v Ardennes (Owners) (The Ardennes)*, KBD).

However, as between the carrier and a third party which has become the lawful holder of the bill of lading, the bill of lading will constitute the contract of carriage (see Fig 4.2). The reason being that the third party holder may well be unaware of the terms arranged between the original shipper and the carrier, if they are not included in the bill of lading. As he steps into the shipper's rights and liabilities of the contract of carriage, he will not be bound by any terms other than those expressed in the bill of lading.

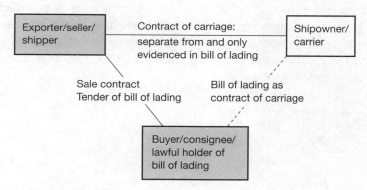

Fig 4.2 Bill of lading carriage contract based on cif sale scenario

This principle (that the third party holder of the bill is only bound by terms apparent from the bill of lading) is particularly obvious where a bill of lading is issued under a charterparty. An example of such a scenario might be the following. A shipper hires the entire vessel to ship his cargo. However, he wants to perform his duties under many international sale contracts by means of this carriage. Thus, several bills of lading are issued, each covering the goods for one particular buyer. This shipper/charterer is bound by the charterparty as against the carrier and the bill of lading as contract of carriage is irrelevant between these parties. The bill only acts as receipt for the goods. However, as between the carrier and any third party buyer becoming holder of the bill of lading, the bill of lading will in fact represent the contract of carriage (see in this respect *The Nea Tyhi*, QBD (Admlty)).

Charterparty bill of lading

If such a bill of lading, however, refers to the charterparty and incorporates some of its clauses, it is called a 'charterparty bill of lading' (see Fig 4.3). Only in this case will the clauses of the charterparty be relevant to a third party holder/indorsee of the bill and only in so far as they have been validly incorporated. Any incorporation must be made in clear and unambiguous words, which are apt to describe the charterparty clause that is intended to be included. For example in *Kish v Taylor*, HL the consignees had to pay freight as specified in the bill of lading which also incorporated the terms of the charterparty with the following clause: 'all other conditions as per charterparty dated the 18th day of December, 1907, all the terms, provisions and exceptions contained in which charter are herewith incorporated and form part hereof.' It was held that the charterparty term providing the carrier with a lien on the cargo for charterparty dead freight was validly incorporated in the bill of lading contract. Charterparty terms providing for liens for charterparty freight or demurrage have also been held to be incorporated.

However, clauses that are classed as only ancillary to the main purpose of the contract of carriage, for example arbitration or choice of jurisdiction clauses, will only be validly included where specific reference is made to them (see *Siboti K/S v BP France SA*, QBD (Comm) and *Federal Bulk Carriers v C Itoh & Co (The Federal Bulker)*, CA). Clauses such as 'all terms, conditions and exceptions as per charterparty' are not sufficient, unless the term is classed as part of the main purpose of the contract of carriage.

As a last requirement of incorporation, the relevant terms must not conflict with the Hague-Visby Rules or any express terms of the bill of lading. In a case of inconsistency of the terms sought to be incorporated and the remaining clauses of the bill of lading, the latter will prevail. Please have a look at the standard form contract for a charterparty bill of lading in the appendices to this book.

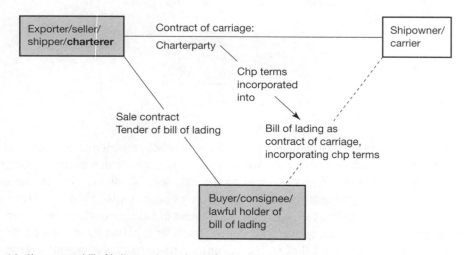

Fig 4.3 Charterparty bill of lading carriage where cif seller is the charterer

4.2.1.3 Which legal rules apply?

Depending on the type of carriage contract, different rules of law apply (as illustrated at Fig 4.4). Under a charterparty, the rights and duties are mainly governed by common law, unless the parties have agreed to incorporate the rules of an international convention. The common law provides for strict liability of the carrier for the goods in his charge. However, the parties are free to negotiate their rights and duties in detail and the carrier is free to limit his liability. Thus the contract terms are of major significance with the rules of common law filling the gaps.

Under a bill of lading contract the shipper consigning a significantly smaller amount is in a less strong bargaining position than a charterer wishing to hire an entire ship. In order to stop the carrier abuse this power imbalance, these contracts are generally governed by international conventions incorporated into the different legal systems (which, in the UK, is done by Act of Parliament). The rights and duties of the parties to the carriage contract are defined by these legal rules and any variation is subject to strict limitations safeguarding certain minimum rights of the shipper. In turn the carrier's liability is reduced, compared with the strict common law position.

The following international conventions relating to bills of lading have been developed for this purpose.

(a) The International Convention for the Unification of Certain Rules Relating to Bills of Lading of 25 August 1924 (done in Brussels), known as the Hague Rules (HR). It was incorporated into English law by the Carriage of Goods by Sea Act (CoGSA) 1924.

(b) The Hague Rules were revised by the Brussels Protocol of 23 February 1968 (the Protocol to amend the International Convention for the Unification of Certain Rules of Law Relating to Bills of Lading signed at Brussels on 25 August 1924). The result is known as the Hague-Visby Rules (HVR), which are also commonly referred to as the Hague Rules as amended by the Brussels Protocol 1968. The Hague-Visby Rules were incorporated into English law by the Carriage of Goods by Sea Act (CoGSA) 1971, entering into force on 23 June 1977. Thereafter the UK repealed the CoGSA 1924. In order not to be bound by the Hague Rules internationally the UK also denounced its ratification of the Hague Rules and repeated the denunciation each time a protocol amending the Hague Rules was ratified. By this action it seems clear that the UK no longer wants to be bound by the Hague Rules, but only by the Hague-Visby Rules.

(c) In 1978 revision, this time fundamental, again took place. The United Nations Convention on the Carriage of Goods by Sea 1978, known as the Hamburg Rules, was adopted by a United Nations Conference on 30 March 1978 in Hamburg. The Hamburg Rules came into force on 1 November 1992, but still, as of September 2005, only have 30 parties, most of which are not major seafaring countries. The lack of support for the Hamburg Rules by the big shipping nations is most likely due to their emphasis in favour of the shipper, whereas the Hague and Hague-Visby Rules afford substantial limitation of liability to the carrier. The United Kingdom has not ratified the Hamburg Rules; the Hague-Visby Rules still apply by virtue of the CoGSA 1971.

(d) In 2002 UNCITRAL began deliberations on a Draft Instrument on the Carriage of Goods [Wholly or Partly] [by Sea] which in its current state is a combination of the approaches taken in the Hague and Hamburg Rules. The progress of the draft instrument can be reviewed at http://www.uncitral.org/uncitral/en/index.html by accessing the link to 'Commissions & Working Groups', following 'Working Group III'.

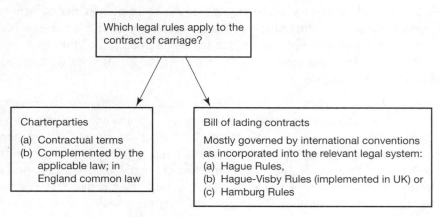

Fig 4.4 *Relevant legal rules for a contract of carriage*

Like the United Kingdom, many of the countries that adopted the Hague Rules have not ratified all or even any of the revised rules. Thus, the laws of some States (for example the United States of America) only provide for the application of the Hague Rules, the laws of other States (for example the United Kingdom) incorporate the Hague-Visby Rules, and the laws of yet other States provide for the application of the Hamburg Rules (for example Austria or Egypt). In addition there are countries which have not adopted any of the afore-mentioned rules, but have developed and apply their own (for example Australia has used the conventions as a basis for its Carriage of Goods By Sea Act 1991, but does not qualify as 'contracting State' to any of the above). The intended harmonisation of the law relating to sea carriage had been quite well achieved by the first set of rules, the Hague Rules. However that harmonisation has been fractured by the attempts to improve the provisions. To prevent further fragmentation work has begun on the new UNCITRAL Draft Instrument on the Carriage of Goods.

Thus, for the time being, a variety of regimes applies across the world, depending on which law governs the parties' contract of carriage. The first steps therefore must be to determine the law applicable to the carriage contract in order to define the rights and duties of the parties and to determine the contracting States to any convention which might be applicable.

Both the Hague and Hague-Visby Rules have been signed at Brussels and are deposited with the Belgian Government. Their status and the identity of the contracting States can be researched by accessing http://www.diplomatie.be/en/treaties/default.asp. The contracting States to the Hamburg Rules, having been adopted by UNCITRAL, can be determined by accessing the website at http://www.uncitral.org/uncitral/en/index.html, following the link to 'UNCITRAL Texts & Status'. According to s 2 of the CoGSA 1971, implementing the Hague-Visby Rules (HVR), 'Her Majesty by Order in Council certifies' the contracting States to the HVR and this order shall be conclusive evidence of the matters so certified. You can find this order inter alia in *Halsbury's Laws of England* (Shipping and Navigations Volume 43(2), Chapter 14).

4.2.1.4 When are the Hague-Visby Rules applicable?

It is assumed in the following that English law is the applicable law. As we have seen, the HVR have been given effect in the UK by virtue of the CoGSA 1971. When are these Rules applicable? Here we need to look at both, ie the CoGSA 1971 and the HVR which are appended as a Schedule to the Act. As the CoGSA 1971 gives the force of law to this convention, it has the potential to modify its application for the UK. Thus, the implementing legislation of an international convention must always be consulted. In a discussion of the convention and its implementing national legislation you can easily identify which piece of legislation is referred to by looking at the citation: the provisions of an English Act of Parliament are expressed in sections and the provisions of the HVR, as for all other conventions and treaties, in articles. However please note that the provisions of the CoGSA only apply in the United Kingdom; they are not part of the HVR as such.

The HVR apply if the following criteria are fulfilled.

Documentary application

The HVR apply to contracts of carriage covered by a bill of lading or similar document of title (CoGSA 1971, s 1(4) and HVR, Art I(a)). This also includes non-negotiable bills of lading, which have been confirmed to be a document of title and to be within the meaning of Art I(b) of the HVR (see *JI MacWilliam Co Inc v Mediterranean Shipping Co SA (The Rafaela S)*, CA, affirmed by HL). It does not matter if a damaging event occurred on loading and thus that no bill was issued. For the Rules to be applicable, it suffices that the parties contemplated the issue of a bill of lading (*Parsons Corporation v CV Scheepvaartonderneming Happy Ranger (The Happy Ranger)*, CA). This view is consistent with the understanding that the bill of lading contract has already been concluded before the issue of the bill (*Ardennes (Cargo Owners) v Ardennes (Owners)*, KBD). The contract is normally concluded orally, based on the sailing announcements of the carrier and the negotiations between the parties. Once a bill of lading contract is concluded, even if orally, it is a contract 'of carriage covered by a bill of lading' (see HVR, Art I(b)) whether or not the bill of lading has already been issued.

According to the provisions of the HVR, the Rules do not apply to non-negotiable transport documents, such as sea waybills, data freight receipts, or similar transport documents which only acknowledge the receipt of the goods; however in the UK, by virtue of s 1(6)(b) of the CoGSA 1971, the parties can choose to give the Rules 'the force of law' if they mark the receipt as a non-negotiable document and expressly opt for the application of the Rules 'as if the receipt were a bill of lading'.

Where the parties chose to incorporate the Rules voluntarily into their contract it is crucial to establish to what extent they wanted the Rules to govern the relationship, whether as a 'matter of law' or as a 'matter of contract'. Where the parties have given the Rules 'the force of law' all the provisions of the Rules apply and the parties cannot reduce the liability of the carrier below the accepted limit. If the HVR have the force of law, Art III(8) of the HVR is applied in an uncompromising manner. Any clauses limiting the liability of the carrier below the threshold of the Rules will be null and void in such a case.

The wide scope of Art III(8) of the HVR is well illustrated in *Owners of Cargo on Board the Morviken v Owners of the Hollandia (The Hollandia), (The Morviken)*, HL. Cargo was shipped by the claimants on a Dutch vessel from Scotland to the Dutch West Indies with carrier D. The bill of lading provided for jurisdiction of the Dutch courts and the application of the law of the Netherlands, which incorporated the Hague Rules. The claimant arrested *The Hollandia*, one of D's vessels, when it put into an English port. Based on the bill of lading clauses D applied for a stay of action in England invoking the jurisdiction of the courts in the Netherlands. However the House of Lords upheld the decision of the Court of Appeal holding that the jurisdiction clause was ineffective. If the courts of the Netherlands were to hear the case they would apply the Hague Rules as part of the applicable law. The liability regime of the Hague Rules however was below the threshold of the Hague-Visby Rules applicable in the UK. The consequence would be that the carrier could escape some of the liability if the jurisdiction clause were given effect. The Hague-Visby Rules scheduled to the CoGSA 1971, however, had to be treated as if they were part of directly enacted statute law in the UK. All the requirements for statutory application of the HVR were fulfilled. Thus, in the given circumstances, the jurisdiction clause was invalid in accordance with Art III(8) of the HVR, which provides that any 'clause, covenant or agreement in a contract of carriage relieving the carrier or the ship from liability for loss or damage to, or in connection with the goods...or lessening such liability otherwise than as provided in these Rules shall be null and void and of no effect'.

Where the parties on the other hand have chosen to incorporate the HVR, which otherwise would not be applicable and they have only given contractual application to the HVR, the consequences of incorporation seem not to be as drastic. Where the intention of the parties was purely to restate the position under the Rules as a basis, but still to allow for alterations of the regime by varying some of the provisions, any such variation of liability would be valid. This was assumed by Steyn J in a case where the sea waybill expressly incorporated the Rules, but also provided for limitations of liability below the threshold of the Rules. He held that the parties had not intended to give the Rules the 'force of law' as set out in s 1(6) of the CoGSA 1971, because they had not incorporated the Rules by using the words 'as if it were a bill of lading'. Section 1(6) of the CoGSA 1971 only conferred a statutory force on a voluntary tie if these exact words were used (see *Browner International Transport Ltd v Monarch SS Co Ltd (The European Enterprise)*, QBD (Comm)).

However, Steyn J's decision is contrary to the earlier decision by Lloyd J in *McCarren & Co Ltd v Humber International Transport Ltd and Truckline Ferries (Poole) Ltd (The Vechscroon)*, QBD (Comm)), where it was held that the Rules applied with 'the force of law', despite these words not being used. Lloyd J argued that there was no reason why Parliament should have intended to draw a distinction between incorporating the Rules into a non-negotiable receipt and incorporating the Rules 'as if it were a bill of lading'. These conflicting decisions show that it is of utmost importance for the parties to state clearly which effect is intended by the incorporation.

In *Dairy Containers Ltd v Tasman Orient Line CV (The Tasmanian Discoverer)*, PC (New Zealand) a similar question arose: however it was outside the scope of the UK CoGSA 1971. The bill of lading contract was neither governed by any international convention nor by the national law of the load or discharge ports, Korea and New Zealand respectively. The contract incorporated the Hague Rules, but with the additional clause that the limitation of liability under the Hague Rules was deemed to be £100 Sterling per package or unit. The cargo was damaged and the cargo claimants argued that the limitation of liability would fall foul of Art 3(8) and Art 9 of the Hague Rules. Article 9 of the Hague Rules provides that the monetary units under the Hague Rules are to be gold value, which made a big difference. However the Court of Appeal, as affirmed by the Privy Council, held that the issue was a matter of the construction of the contract. In *Dairy Containers* the wording was clear as to the incorporation of the Rules to this limited extent. Thus the claimant's argument failed and the liability of the carrier was limited to £100 Sterling per package.

From Art I(b) of the HVR it is clear that the Rules do not apply to charterparties. However they will apply to bills of lading issued under a charterparty as soon as, but only once they have been transferred to a third party holder. Article V of the HVR affirms that the provisions of the Rules do not apply to charterparties. However, where a ship under a charterparty issues bills of lading they must comply with the terms as set out in the Rules (HVR, Art V). This ensures compliance of any bill of lading with the Rules. Despite the initial scope of the Rules, the parties of a charterparty are free to opt for the application of the Rules. This often is done via a so-called 'clause paramount'. This clause means that regardless of any wide exceptions used in the carriage contract, the Rules are paramount and thus override any contradicting contractual clauses (see *Adamastos Shipping Co Ltd v Anglo Saxon Petroleum Co Ltd*, HL).

Neither do the Rules apply to live animals and deck cargo (HVR, Art I(c)). In order to be classified as deck cargo for this purpose two criteria must be fulfilled: the contract of carriage must state that the goods are carried on deck; and the goods must in fact be so carried. Often the contract of carriage will only give the carrier the option to carry the goods on deck. This is done by way of a so-called 'liberty clause'. This clause does not state that the goods are or will be carried on deck, but only entitles the carrier to choose whether to do so. Such liberty clauses have been held to be insufficient to exclude the application of the Rules (see *Svenska Tractor Aktiebolaget v Maritime Agencies (Southampton)*, QBD). On the other hand, a choice of the parties to apply the Rules to deck cargo is given effect by s 1(6), (7) of the CoGSA 1971 as if Art I(c) of the HVR did not exclude them.

Territorial application

By virtue of Art X of the HVR the Rules apply for the carriage of goods between the ports of two different States where:

(a) the bill of lading has been issued in a contracting State; or

(b) the goods have been loaded in a contracting State; or

(c) the parties have chosen the Rules' application either directly or indirectly.

The parties can indirectly opt for the application of the Rules by contractually providing for a governing law which gives effect to them. However, it may not be enough to choose 'English law' in order for the HVR to apply. English law in this respect comprises common law and the HVR (by virtue of the CoGSA 1971). If the parties want to apply the HVR outside their initial territorial application, they should express this directly by specifically choosing the application of the HVR and not just generally the use of English law (see *Hellenic Steel Co v Svolmar Shipping Co Ltd (The Komninos S)*, CA). In the *Komninos S* the bill of lading had provided for jurisdiction of the 'British courts', from which the Court of Appeal inferred that they had intended English law to apply. However, as the HVR had not been incorporated and their statutory application requirements were not fulfilled in this case it was held that the HVR did not apply.

According to s 1(3) of the CoGSA 1971 the application of the HVR also includes UK coastal waters. The fulfilment of the requirement set out in Art X of the HVR that carriage must be between ports of two different States is not necessary in so far as shipment takes place in UK coastal waters.

The application requirements of the Hague-Visby Rules are illustrated at Fig 4.5.

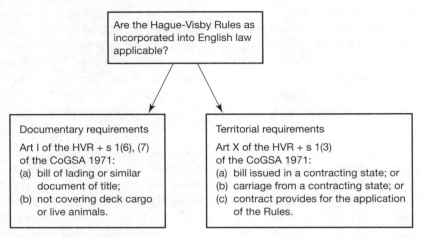

Fig 4.5 Application test for the HVR

Where the contract of carriage is not governed by the HVR, neither by legal implication nor by contractual agreement, the common law rules apply. Common law also applies to any issues beyond the ambit of the Rules, for example with regard to freight or the shipowner's lien.

So what exactly is covered by the Hague-Visby Rules? The HVR were developed to ensure that the shipper had at least a minimum protection against a carrier who was likely to attempt to exclude any liability for the cargo. The HVR burden the carrier with a certain level of liability from which he cannot escape (HVR, Art III(8)), but, in turn, afford him and his servants exceptions (HVR, Art IV and Art IV bis) and limitations of his liability (HVR, Art IV(5) for a limitation in value calculated per package and HVR, Art III(6) for a one year limit to bringing claims against the carrier). The HVR also provide for the shipper's liability if he ships dangerous cargo without prior permission of the carrier.

The details in relation to the rights and liabilities of the carrier and the shipper under these rules will be discussed at **4.2.3** and **4.2.4**. First we want to concentrate on more general issues.

The CoGSA 1971 giving the Hague-Visby Rules the force of law in the UK must not be confused with the CoGSA 1992. The latter could be classed as a misnomer because it is not an updated version of the 1971 Act, nor is it in conflict with the CoGSA 1971. It covers a different area altogether, updating and repealing the Bill of Lading Act 1855. By virtue of the CoGSA 1992, a third party to which delivery under the transport document has to be made, who is not privy to the carriage contract between the shipper and the carrier, acquires rights of suit and liabilities as if it were a party to the contract.

4.2.2 Types and nature of carriage documents

In this section we are going to examine the nature and functions of different carriage documents and in particular those of the bill of lading.

4.2.2.1 Mate's receipt

As we have seen at 4.2.1.1 above, the mate's receipt is signed when the goods are loaded on board ship. It is an acknowledgement by the carrier of having received the goods into his custody in the condition stated therein. Based on the markings in the mate's receipt the bill of lading is issued. Until that time the goods are held by the carrier subject to the exceptions and conditions of his usual bill of lading unless the parties have agreed on other conditions in the carriage contract. Even though the mate's receipt is not usually a document of title, it is prima facie evidence of the ownership of the goods. The carrier is in his rights to issue bills of lading to the holder of (or the person named in) the mate's receipt, unless the carrier has knowledge of the fact that another person is the owner of the goods (see *Nippon Yusen Kaisha v Ramjiban Serowgee*, PC).

4.2.2.2 Bill of lading

Functions of the bill of lading
We touched upon the three major functions of the bill of lading at **2.5.4.1** (see also Fig 4.6).

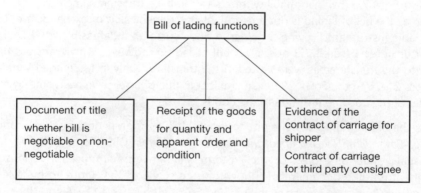

Fig 4.6 Functions of the bill of lading

Document of title
A document of title is a document recognised by law, which represents the goods for which it is issued. Transfer of such a document vests in the transferee the right to possession of the goods and possibly also the property in them. Mercantile custom has developed such a function for the bill of lading, which has long been recognised by law (see the House of Lords decision of 1793 in *Lickbarrow v Mason*). Particularly in international trade where the goods are usually in transit for a long time, the parties' interests are likely to be as follows: the seller will want to get paid as soon as possible; the buyer may have an interest in selling the goods on before they arrive; or the buyer may want to use the goods as security for obtaining credit. Thus, the goods are represented by the bill of lading to enable the parties to meet their business needs.

Transfer of the bill of lading transfers possession of the goods. Transfer of property is only effected if and when the parties to the sale contract intend this to happen. Property might be intended to pass together with the transfer of the bill, however it can also be dependent on other events, such as payment of the purchase price. Transfer of the bill of lading to an agent at the port of destination usually aims at enabling him to take delivery from the carrier, so that he can consequently fulfil the seller's obligations towards the buyer. Transfer of the bill to a bank is usually done in order to create a pledge on the goods rather than to transfer property.

Only a person holding the bill of lading can claim delivery of the goods. A carrier who delivers the goods without insisting on production of the bill of lading does so at his own risk. In practice he may want to do so only against a letter of indemnity by the consignee, but this is still very risky, as the carrier is responsible for the damage caused by his breach of contract (see *Sze Hai Tong Bank v Rambler Cycle Co Ltd*, PC (Singapore); *Kuwait Petroleum Corporation v I & D Oil Carriers (The Houda)*, CA and *SA Sucre Export v Northern River Shipping (The Sormovskiy 3068)*, QBD (Admlty)). The consignee or his bank, having given the indemnity, may dispute their obligation or may be insolvent. The carrier is then left to compensate the loss caused to his contract partner without necessarily being backed by a solvent consignee or whilst having to incur further cost in order to obtain a judgment in his favour against the consignee or his bank.

As we have seen at **2.5.4.1** above, there are negotiable and non-negotiable bills of lading (see also Fig 4.7). This 'negotiability' refers to the bill's transferability. It is a bit of a misnomer, as the bill of lading is not a negotiable instrument. Bills of exchange *are*, however, negotiable instruments, giving a holder in due course an indefeasible title regardless of any prior defects (see **3.2.3** above). A bill of lading, however, only transfers the same rights to the transferee as were vested in the transferor. Only in the limited situations set out in ss 21–25 of the SoGA 1979 can a defect in title of a seller be overcome by means of transfer of the document of title to the goods.

Where the bill of lading is a straight consigned bill it is non-negotiable (*International Air and Sea Cargo GmbH v Owners of the Chitral (The Chitral)*, QBD (Comm)). However, such a bill, usually under an express or implied term, still has to be produced in order to obtain delivery. It is still a document of title within the scope of the Hague-Visby Rules (see *JI MacWilliam Co Inc v Mediterranean Shipping Co SA (The Rafaela S)*, CA and HL).

To show its negotiability an order bill needs to include such words as 'or order or assigns' (*Henderson & Co v The Comptoir d'Escompte de Paris*, PC (Hong Kong)) beside the name of the consignee or, depending on the form, the word 'order' in the consignee box, adding the name of the consignee as notify party. 'Bearer bills' which are made out to the bearer are seldom used; they are transferred by mere delivery and thus provide little security to the purchaser.

Please compare the standard forms for negotiable and non-negotiable transport documents in this respect, which are appended to this book. Under a normal cif or c & f contract, whether under common law or under Incoterms 2000, the buyer is entitled to a negotiable bill of lading unless the parties have agreed otherwise (see *Soproma SpA v Marine & Animal By-Products Corporation*, QBD (Comm) and *Henderson & Co v The Comptoir d'Escompte de Paris*, PC (Hong Kong) for the common law position).

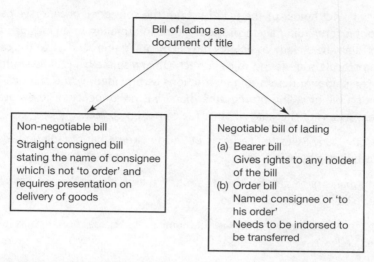

Fig 4.7 Illustration of negotiability of bills of lading

Receipt for the goods

As you can verify by looking at the transport documents included in the appendices, the bills of lading and other carriage documents all bear a section for the quantity and description of the goods, allowing for the insertion of details such as their weight, marks or number of packages. The bills also describe the goods to be in apparent good order and condition, unless comments to the contrary are inserted into the bill. In the latter event, the bill is then called 'claused' as opposed to a 'clean' bill without qualifying remarks as to the goods' quality and condition.

The statements regarding the description of the goods, the date of shipment and particularly the goods' order and condition are essential with respect to three separate contracts: the sale contract, the letter of credit (if applicable) and obviously the carriage contract. Under the sale contract the buyer can reject the bill of lading if it does not correspond with the goods sold or if it is claused (see **2.5.4.1** above as well as **2.9.1**). The sale contract invariably calls for a clean bill of lading. The buyer has no means of checking the goods before they arrive, by which time he has usually paid for the goods. Thus, he needs to be able to rely on the transport document to describe the goods accurately in quantity, quality and shipment date.

The letter of credit also requires a clean transport document (Art 32(b) of the UCP 500) unless the parties have varied this requirement. If the seller cannot present a clean bill of lading showing the date of shipment as stipulated in the credit, the bank will reject the documents and the seller will not get paid. The only way to avoid deadlock is for the seller to contact the buyer to see whether he still wants the goods even in the condition as described by the carriage document. If this is so, the buyer will advise the bank to pay regardless of the discrepancies, but will most likely first renegotiate the price with the seller. Otherwise the seller has to find a different buyer for his goods and will be liable for any damages caused to the buyer due to non-delivery.

With respect to the carriage contract there is a need to distinguish between two different relationships: that between the carrier and the shipper and that between the carrier and the third party lawful holder of the bill of lading (the consignee or indorsee of the bill). The shipper or his forwarding agent provides all the information to be included in the bill of lading. Unusually he already completes the bill of lading and sends it to the carrier who signs it if the particulars are found to be correct. Otherwise the bill is at least prepared on the basis of the shipping details and instructions as provided by the shipper. The third party holder of a bill of lading on the other hand has no influence on the statements in the bill, nor any means of checking whether the content is correct.

Under the Hague-Visby Rules the carrier is bound to issue a bill of lading on demand of the shipper including statements as to:

(a) the leading marks necessary for identification of the goods, marked in a manner which remains legible until arrival of the goods;

(b) the quantity of the goods, either by weight, number of packages or pieces, as furnished by the shipper; and

(c) the apparent order and condition of the goods.

However the carrier is not bound to show any marks, number, quantity or weight which he suspects not to be accurately representing the goods or which he has no reasonable means of checking (HVR, Art III(3)). The statement with respect to order and condition only covers their apparent state or apparent defects. The carrier does not guarantee that the goods are perfect or that they are in anyway fulfilling the condition required by the sale contract.

In favour of the shipper, who has usually provided the information on the bill of lading to the carrier, the bill is only prima facie evidence of the receipt of the goods as described. Proof of the contrary is admissible (see HVR, Art III(4)). On the other hand, in favour of the consignee or indorsee of the bill of lading the bill is conclusive evidence (see HVR, Art III(4)). The shipper, however, is deemed to have guaranteed the accuracy of the information provided in respect of quantity and marks (but not condition). If the carrier relies on this information and incurs liability towards a third party (usually the third party consignee) the shipper has to compensate for the loss of the carrier (HVR, Art III(5)).

At common law the carrier need not make any representations about quantity in the bill of lading. Often the quantity is stated, but with the addition that the quantity is 'unknown to the carrier' or it is 'as provided by the shipper'. In such a case the carrier is in fact not making any representation at all (*New Chinese Antimony Co Ltd v Ocean Steamship Co Ltd*, CA; also on this point but under the Hague Rules see *Noble Resources Ltd v Cavalier Shipping Corporation (The Atlas)*, QBD (Comm)). However, if the carrier states the quantity without any qualifications the bill is prima facie evidence in favour of the shipper (*Smith v Bedouin*, HL) and conclusive evidence in favour of the third party lawful holder of the bill of lading (CoGSA 1992, s 4, which brings bills of lading governed by common law in line with the position of a bill under the HVR). Representations as to leading marks on the bill of lading at common law were not taken to be conclusive evidence at least as long as these marks were not material to the description of the goods (see *Parsons v New Zealand Shipping Co*, CA and *Compania Importadora de Arroces Collette y Kamp SA v P & O Steam Navigation Co*, KBD).

Due to the importance of a clean bill of lading to the sale contract and the letter of credit, the carrier is at times approached by the shipper to issue a clean bill contrary to the facts, often against a letter of indemnity. Such an indemnity, however, is illegal and completely worthless for the carrier if both parties, the exporter and the carrier, know that the bill should have never been issued clean, because they conspire fraudulently to induce the consignee to accept the bill and pay the purchase price which he otherwise would not (see *Brown, Jenkinson & Co Ltd v Percy Dalton (London) Ltd*, CA).

In order to be able to issue bills of lading without becoming liable for misrepresentations, but also without inconveniencing his client (the shipper), carriers use certain innocent qualifying remarks such as 'quantity unknown', 'quality unknown', 'condition unknown'. However the carrier cannot negate specific statements made on the bill with the qualifying clause that they are unknown, in cases where he was required to make such representations, for example where the shipper demanded the statements as set out in Art III(3) of the HVR. In such a case the qualifying clause is ineffective.

However, if the carrier clearly marks the quantity 'unknown' he does not make a statement which can be held against him (see *Noble Resources Ltd v Cavalier Shipping Corporation (The Atlas)*, QBD (Comm); *Agrosin Pty Ltd v Highway Shipping Co Ltd (The Mata K)*, QBD (Comm), but see also *Rederi AB Gustav Erikson v Dr Fawzi Ahmed Abou Ismail (The Herroe and The Askoe)*, QBD (Comm) and *New Chinese Antimony Co Ltd v Ocean Steamship Co Ltd*, CA).

Qualifying clauses as to 'condition unknown' cannot be used to nullify the statement on the bill that the goods have been received in apparent good order and condition, where the goods on loading showed apparent defects (see *The Skarp*, PD & A). Detailed analysis of the relevant case law is necessary for each individual case to determine whether a specific qualifying clause is effective.

Evidence of the contract of carriage
As discussed at **4.2.1.2** above, the bill of lading evidences the carriage contract which was concluded between the shipper and the carrier long before the bill of lading was issued (*Ardennes (Cargo Owners) v Ardennes (Owners) (The Ardennes)*, KBD). However, as between the carrier and a bona fide transferee, the bill of lading constitutes the contract of carriage. Any arrangements between the shipper and the carrier which have not been entered into the bill of lading cannot be relied upon.

By virtue of s 4 of the CoGSA 1992 the bill of lading is conclusive evidence in favour of a person having become the lawful holder of the bill with respect to the shipment of the goods, but also of the binding effect of the bill. In *Alimport v Soubert Shipping Co Ltd*, QBD (Comm) the ship owner alleged that the bill was not effective and thus gave no title to sue to the holder because the agent had backdated the bill of lading, for which he had not authority. His arguments were not upheld: the bill was effective and gave conclusive evidence of the contract.

Types of bills of lading
Most types of bills of lading have already been discussed:

(a) negotiable or non-negotiable bills of lading in the first part of this section (ie at **4.2.2.2** above);

(b) charterparty bills of lading at **4.2.1.2** above;

(c) shipped and received for shipment bills of lading at **2.5.4.1** above and;

(d) clean or claused bills of lading earlier in this section (ie at **4.2.2.2** above).

Therefore, in the following, we are only going to touch upon those types not yet introduced:

Through bills of lading

These are used when the goods are transported by more than one means of transport and the sea carriage is only one part of it, or where the sea transport is divided into separate legs. Rather than having to take out several carriage contracts the shipper can take out one 'through bill' for the whole journey. The shipper only deals with the carrier who signs the through bill, charging an inclusive freight and undertaking to arrange for the transhipment with the on-carriers. The delivery of the goods at their destination will be by the last on-carrier against one part of the original through bill of lading. The principal contract of sea carriage is superimposed upon the other contracts for the on-carriage. Based on this one through bill of lading, the CoGSA 1971 incorporating the Hague-Visby Rules applies where the bill was issued in a contracting State or the goods shipped from a port of a contracting State, even after transhipment of the goods in a foreign port. Whether the shipper can sue the on-carrier directly under the contract will depend on whether the main carrier had contracted solely with the shipper only using the on-carriers as servants or sub-contractors, or whether he acted as agent for the on-carriers in contracting with the shipper.

However under a 'false through bill' the contracting carrier only takes responsibility for the part of the voyage performed by him. In addition he acts as freight forwarder to select with reasonable care the second carrier for the on-journey. In such an event the shipper can sue the second carrier only in bailment, because there is no privity of contract between them.

Container bills of lading

Container bills of lading are issued by container shipping lines for multimodal transport of goods in containers. The goods are usually dispatched from a container freight station inland to their place of destination. The container bill thus is mostly a 'received for shipment' bill and not a 'shipped on board' bill, as the carrier acknowledges the receipt of the goods inland. It is a genuine bill of lading to which the Hague or Hague-Visby Rules apply in so far as the sea carriage is concerned. With respect to the other parts of the carriage, the respective compulsory rules of national law or international conventions will also apply.

Switch bills of lading

Switch bills of lading are bills which are issued in return for the surrender of the original set of bills under which the cargo was shipped. The switch bills include certain alterations of the terms of the bill, the details of the cargo and /or shipment or the name and address of the shipper. There are plenty of commercial reasons why certain alterations may be useful, such as not to disclose the source of the cargo (see for example *Noble Resources Ltd v Cavalier Shipping Corp, (The Atlas)*, QBD (Comm)), but such a practice also lends itself to fraudulent practices. Great care needs to be taken to ensure that the original bills are surrendered and that the switch bills are issued with the authority of the carrier and that the terms of the bills are identical. Otherwise plenty of legal problems can be the result.

Electronic bills of lading

An in-depth discussion of electronic bills of lading and e-commerce is beyond the scope of this introductory book. However, some information is included in order to inspire you to undertake your own further research. In the age of electronic commerce the logical question is whether the traditional paper bill of lading can be replaced by an electronic bill.

In order to achieve the same aim as the paper bill of lading an electronic bill must fulfil the three functions of the traditional bill of lading. An electronic bill should be suitable as receipt for the cargo and evidence of the contract of carriage. However, problems arise with the function of a document of title, requiring possession of the bill, the transfer of it and the security the bill is supposed to provide for the unpaid seller, the buyer and the banks. Another issue is whether the CoGSA 1971 and the CoGSA 1992 would apply to an electronic bill as both Acts require a bill of lading or similar 'document' which seems to assume a paper form. The Law Commission's Report 'Rights of Suit in Respect of Carriage of Goods by Sea' (HC 250, 1991), recommending the enactment of the CoGSA 1992, Part VI of the Report briefly touches on documents forming part of an electronic record. The report briefly highlights the technical and legal problems that still need to be overcome to eliminate the physical transfer and suggests that instead of dealing with the issues within the CoGSA 1992, it could be left for the Secretary of State to make provision by regulations once the paperless transactions became common. These recommendations have been implemented by s 1(5) and (6) of the CoGSA 1992, but so far no regulations have appeared. Similar questions as to applicability arise for any of the international carriage conventions; only the draft UNCITRAL instrument includes specific provisions for electronic commerce.

On the practical side, one of the main challenges is that the bill of lading as document of title is transferred by (indorsement and) delivery, which requires physical possession. Various attempts have been made to facilitate electronic commerce and also to introduce a secure electronic replacement for the paper bill of lading. The UNCITRAL Model Law on Electronic Commerce 1996 (as amended in 1998) and the UNCITRAL Model Law on Electronic Signatures adopted in 2001 aim to provide solutions for many issues affecting the legal effects of electronic documents and signatures. The texts of these model laws can be accessed on UNCITRAL's website via the 'UNCITRAL Texts & Status' link at http://www.uncitral.org/uncitral/en/index.html or found in an international trade law statute book.

The Comité Maritime International (CMI) predicted the importance of electronic bills of lading and in 1990 adopted the CMI Uniform Rules for Electronic Bills of Lading. Under this system the shipper as the original holder irrevocably informs the carrier of the new holder using a 'private key', which is a unique combination of numbers and/or letters to secure the transaction. The Uniform Rules can be found in a statute book or at the CMI website at http://www.comitemaritime.org/cmidocs/rules_idx.html.

A step in the development of trade by using electronic bills of lading was taken with the Bolero project, Bolero standing for 'Bill of Lading Electronic Registry Organisation'. It was initiated by the International Chamber of Commerce and was initially sponsored by SWIFT, the 'Society for Worldwide Interbank Financial Transmission' and TT Club, the 'Through Transport Mutual Insurance Association Ltd'. Bolero is designed not just for single transactions but also to be able to cope with an entire chain sale transaction on-line. Apart from replacing the paper bill with an electronic bill it provides a registry where the 'indorsement' is monitored and recorded. Information about Bolero Association Ltd and Bolero International Ltd can be found at http://www.boleroassociation.org/ and http://www.bolero.net/respectively. The Bolero Rulebook, which is the agreement between the users of the service and Bolero Association Ltd as well as Bolero International Ltd can be accessed at http://www.boleroasso-ciation.org/downloads/rulebook1.pdf or it can be found in Paul Todd *Cases & Materials Book on International Trade Law* (2003). The 'Bolero legal guides' at http://www.bolero.net/deci-sion/legal/ may also be of interest. The system was launched in September 1999 and its first live transaction was carried out via Bolero.net in February 2000.

A legal framework is provided inter alia in the UK by the Electronic Communications Act 2000 that deals with electronic signatures, encryption technology and reliance on third parties as registers. The UK Act is consistent with the UNCITRAL Model Law on Electronic Commerce. The EU Directive 2000/31/EC on Certain Aspects of Information Society Services, in particular Electronic Commerce, in the Internal Market (EU Directive on Electronic Commerce) of 8 June 2000 ([2000] OJ L178/1) covers various legal aspects of information society services and is worth consulting.

To further the development of e-commerce the International Chamber of Commerce is also developing strategies and tools to provide secure online contracting. The eUCP are only just one example of the development work undertaken by the ICC, in this case to enable the presentation of electronic records as tender of documents under a letter of credit. Further information can be found on the ICC's website at http://www.iccwbo.org/.

4.2.2.3 Sea waybill

A sea waybill is a non-negotiable transport document. It is a receipt of the goods by the carrier and it evidences the carriage contract, but it is not a document of title. Its produc-tion by the consignee is not necessary; delivery is obtained on satisfactory identification. The advantage of a sea waybill is that delivery of the goods is not delayed by a slow trans-mission of the transport documents to the consignee, as may happen in case of a bill of lading.

A sea waybill is sufficient as a transport document if the buyer does not intend to sell the goods while in transit. The sea waybill is mostly issued in a 'received for shipment' form, but can be notated once the goods are loaded on board. It is not a good tender instead of a bill of lading but, if the parties so provide, a sea waybill can even be acceptable under a letter of credit arrangement (see UCP 500, Art 24). The Hague-Visby Rules do not apply to a sea waybill, but the Rules can be expressly incorporated into the contract. Additionally, there are the CMI Uniform Rules for Sea Waybills adopted by the CMI in 1990, which may be voluntarily incorporated into the contract of carriage. These Rules can be found via the CMI's documents site at http://www.comitemaritime.org/cmidocs/rules_idx.html.

The sea waybill is not the only non-negotiable transport document; there are others, such as the non-negotiable bill of lading or a mere receipt by the carrier.

Even though a straight consigned bill of lading is a non-negotiable transport document, the non-negotiable bill of lading is still a bill of lading within the meaning of the CoGSA

1971 and the Hague-Visby Rules (dealing with the shipper–carrier relationship and the carrier's liabilities for the cargo). Thus, the HVR apply to the straight consigned bill of lading, but not to the sea waybill.

The CoGSA 1992, which governs the rights and liabilities between the carrier and the third party entitled to delivery of the goods under the relevant transport document, applies to both these categories and also any ship's delivery order. However it treats the non-negotiable bill of lading in the same category as a sea waybill. In order to qualify as a bill of lading under this Act, the bill must be negotiable (see CoGSA 1992, s 1(2)(a) and s 1(3) which ought to be read: 'References to this Act to a sea waybill are references to any documents which is not a [transferable] bill of lading [in the sense of s 1(2) above] but…').

4.2.2.4 Delivery order

A whole consignment on board a vessel, particularly in case of bulk cargo, may have been sold in parts to separate buyers. Delivery orders can be used to divide a whole consignment into different parts to fulfil the obligations in respect of these individual buyers, even if the consignment was initially covered by only one bill of lading. Generally, a delivery order is an order addressed by the owner of the goods to the custodian of the goods, such as the carrier or the agent of the shipper, to deliver the goods to the holder of the order or to hold the goods for him. In the latter case the seller's obligation under the sale contract to deliver the goods is only fulfilled once the custodian has 'attorned' to the buyer, meaning he confirms holding the goods for him (see SoGA 1979, s 29(4)). There are two different forms of delivery orders, which need to be distinguished (see *Peter Cremer GmbH v General Carriers SA (The Dona Mari)*, QBD (Comm)):

(a) Ship's delivery order

   The ship's delivery order is an order directed to the carrier to deliver the goods to the holder. It is issued by or on behalf of the carrier or by the shipper.

(b) Merchant's delivery order

   A merchant's delivery order is issued by the shipper/seller undertaking to deliver to his buyer. Where the goods are consigned to the freight forwarder or agent of the shipper at the place of destination it is directed to this agent, ordering delivery of the goods to the holder of the document (see *Comptoir d'Achat et de Vente du Boerenbond Belge SA v Luis de Ridder Limitada (The Julia)*, HL).

The difference between these documents is important, because only the holder of a ship's delivery order has a right of suit against the carrier (see CoGSA 1992, ss 1(4) and 2(3)), but in turn also incurs liabilities (see CoGSA 1992, s 3(1), (2)). This is not the case for a merchant's delivery order (see *The Dona Mari*).

4.2.3 Duties and liabilities of the carrier under the contract of carriage

The liabilities of the carrier will depend on whether the regime for the carriage contract is common law or the Hague-Visby Rules. However, both systems cover common duties which we will examine below. The main difference is that common law implies three undertakings of the carrier into the carriage contract: the seaworthiness of the ship; not to deviate from the route; and to proceed without undue delay. However, the parties to the contract are free to alter the position, and this has led to the use of elaborate standard contracts by carriers excluding most of their liability. Only a contract partner with great bargaining power had the chance to change the terms of the contract to accommodate his needs.

First under the Hague Rules and now under the Hague-Visby Rules in force in the UK, the bill of lading contracts are subject to a statutory scheme of liability of the carrier. The carrier's liability is limited, unlike for example the absolute duty to provide a seaworthy vessel under common law. In turn, however, these liabilities cannot be reduced and the shipper can hold the carrier responsible to at least a certain minimum level. On the other hand, the parties are free to increase the carrier's liabilities contractually, should they wish to do so.

Unfortunately the regime drawn up by the Hague Rules and the Hague-Visby Rules was developed by looking at the common exclusions used so far in practice and thus its system of liabilities and immunities of the carrier is rather diverse, lacking a common basis. The Hamburg Rules were developed, amongst other reasons, to remedy this lack of a single basis for liability. However the UK has not become party to them. Thus, in the following we shall concentrate on common law and the Hague-Visby Rules.

4.2.3.1 Seaworthiness

The duty to provide a seaworthy ship means the vessel must in all respects be fit to load, store, carry and discharge the cargo, fit to encounter the ordinary perils of the sea during the voyage. The test is the standard of an ordinarily careful and prudent owner sending his ship to sea, having regard to the nature and probable circumstances of the specific voyage. If the ship has a defect which a prudent owner would remedy before sending the vessel to sea, the ship is not seaworthy (see *McFadden & Co v Blue Star Line*, KBD). The obligation of seaworthiness does not just encompass the physical state of the vessel as in the case of a defective engine (see *Hong Kong Fir Shipping Co v Kawasaki Kisen Kaisha*, CA and *Union of India v NV Reederij Amsterdam (The Amstelslot)*, HL) or a defective compass (see *Paterson Steamships Ltd v Robin Hood Mills (The Thordoc)*, PC (Canada)), or in the case of instability of the vessel due to cargo stowage (see *Kish v Taylor*, HL and *The Friso*, QBD (Admlty)), but also requires full competence and adequacy of the crew (see *Papera Traders Co Ltd v Hyundai Merchant Marine Co Ltd (The Eurasian Dream) (No 1)*, QBD (Comm); *Manifest Shipping Co Ltd v Uni-Polaris Insurance Co Ltd (The Star Sea)*, QBD (Comm); *Owners of Cargo Lately Laden on Board the Makedonia v Owners of the Makedonia (The Makedonia)*, PD&A; *Hong Kong Fir Shipping Co v Kawasaki Kisen Kaisha*, CA and *Standard Oil Co of New York v Clan Line Steamers Ltd*, HL) and correct mapping for the voyage (*Owners of Cargo Lately Laden on Board the Torepo v Owners of the Torepo (The Torepo)*, QBD (Admlty) and *Cheikh Boutros Selim El-Khoury v Ceylon Shipping Lines (The Madeleine)*, QBD (Comm)).

Seaworthiness also includes cargoworthiness, requiring that the vessel is able to carry the particular cargo safely to the port of destination, for example it needs adequate facilities for the carriage and storage of the cargo. This is not the case where the holds need to be fumigated before being in a fit state to receive the cargo (see *Tattersall v National Steamship Co*, QBD and *Compania de Naveira Nedelka SA v Tradex Internacional SA (The*

Tres Flores), CA) or where the contract provides for the shipment of frozen meat, but the ship's refrigerating system is defective (*Cargo per Maori King v Hughes*, CA).

The consequences of unseaworthiness differ. In *Hong Kong Fir Shipping Co v Kawasaki Kisen Kaisha*, CA, where the issue arose under a charterparty, seaworthiness was classed as an innominate term. Only if the breach of the term is so serious as to frustrate the commercial purpose of the contract and cannot be rectified within a reasonable time can the charterer treat the contract as repudiated (see also *Stanton v Richardson*, Ex Ch). Otherwise he is left only being able to claim damages.

The mere acceptance of the chartered vessel does not amount to a waiver of the right to claim damages or to treat the contract as repudiated, where unseaworthiness has not been discovered until after the ship has set sail (*Marbienes Compania Naviera SA v Ferrostaal AG (The Democritos)*, QBD (Comm) [1975] 1 Lloyd's Rep 386, 397 and *Hong Kong Fir Shipping Co v Kawasaki Kisen Kaisha*, CA). Where the breach is serious enough, the contract can be repudiated even after the commencement of the performance or voyage. The result of such repudiation is that the carrier can no longer rely on any of the contract clauses. Also, the contractual freight is no longer due; however, some reasonable payment will have to be made where the goods arrive safely despite the unseaworthiness. This is of particular interest in cases of charterparty contracts where the parties can allocate the risks and liabilities freely, but of less interest under a bill of lading contract where the relevant Rules govern the liability of the carrier by force of law. However, the shipper under a bill of lading can still claim against the carrier for any damages caused by the unseaworthiness of the vessel.

At common law the carrier is under an absolute obligation to provide a seaworthy ship. This duty attaches at the time when the ship sails, the beginning of the voyage, not before and not after (see *McFadden & Co v Blue Star Line*, KBD). However, this absolute duty under common law can be excluded by express provision in the contract. In order for such an exclusion clause to be effective and upheld by the courts it must be expressed clearly and unambiguously (see *Nelson Line (Liverpool) Ltd v James Nelson & Sons Ltd*, HL).

Under the Hague-Visby Rules (Art III(1)) the carrier only has to exercise due diligence to make the ship seaworthy (see also CoGSA 1971, s 3). The details as to seaworthiness required by Art III(1) of the HVR are in effect the same as under common law, just that under the latter it is an absolute duty. However, the difference in outcome is not too dissimilar as the duty to exercise due diligence to make the ship seaworthy is not restricted merely to personal diligence of the carrier. He is also liable if his servants or agents fail to observe due diligence and even if independent contractors repairing the ship act negligently (see *Riverstone Meat Co Pty Ltd v Lancashire Shipping Co Ltd (The Muncaster Castle)*, HL). The duty as to seaworthiness under the Hague-Visby Rules cannot be excluded or reduced (HVR, Art III(8)).

Article IV of the HVR stipulates a list of events in which the carrier's liability is excluded, but these clauses can only be successfully invoked if the carrier has observed his due diligence obligation at the beginning of the voyage to make the ship seaworthy (HVR, Art IV(1)). Thus, the carrier cannot rely on an excepted peril of the sea, if the immediate cause of the loss is unseaworthiness rather than the peril (see *Standard Oil of New York v Clan Line*

Steamers, HL; *Maxine Footware Ltd v Canadian Government Merchant Marine*, PC Canada and *Robin Hood Flour Mills Ltd v NM Paterson & Sons Ltd (The Farrandoc)*, Ex Ct (Canada)).

The seaworthiness obligation of Art III(1) of the HVR is an overriding duty even with respect to the shipper's duty of Art IV(6) of the HVR not to ship dangerous cargo without the carrier's prior consent (see *Mediterranean Freight Services Ltd v BP Oil International Ltd (The Fiona)*, CA). Thus, where the unseaworthiness caused the dangerous cargo to react resulting in damage, the carrier cannot claim indemnity in accordance with Art IV(6) of the HVR, because the damage would not have occurred had the carrier not breached his duty to provide a seaworthy ship.

4.2.3.2 Care for the cargo and excepted perils

At common law the carrier is liable for the loss or damage to the goods in his custody, irrespective of his fault (see *McFadden & Co v Blue Star Line*, KBD). However in the event of damage or loss caused by act of God, act of the Queen's enemies or inherent vice he is not liable. The parties can alter this position and long exclusion clauses are often inserted into contracts which are not subject to the Rules.

Under the Hague-Visby Rules (Art III(2)) 'the carrier shall properly and carefully load, handle, stow, carry, keep, care for, and discharge the goods carried': this duty is subject to the exclusions enumerated in Art IV of the HVR. The duty is to take reasonable care, to adopt a system which is sound in relation to the circumstances of which the carrier has or ought to have knowledge and in relation to what is general practice in the carriage of goods by sea (see *Albacora SRL v Westcott & Laurance Line Ltd (The Maltasian)*, HL). The duty to care for the cargo is a continuous obligation from the time of loading until discharge.

Examples where the courts have assumed liability based on Art III(2) of the HVR are cases where damage was caused by bad stowage (see *Ministry of Food v Lamport & Holt Line Ltd*, QBD), or during loading operations by the negligence of the carrier's servants (see *Pyrene Co Ltd v Scindia Navigation Co Ltd*, QBD). Liability was also accepted for the loss of a tractor, carried on deck without an agreement to do so, which was not securely fastened and was washed overboard (*Svenska Tractor Aktiebolaget v Maritime Agencies (Southampton) Ltd*, QBD).

Please take a moment to read the HVR, particularly Arts III and IV. The exceptions provided for in Art IV of the HVR are plenty and will not be duplicated in this text. They include the exceptions which are also accepted under common law. Only particular issues of some exceptions will be raised in the following.

Article IV(2)(a) of the HVR alleviates the carrier from liability for act, neglect or fault of the master or his servants in the navigation or management of the ship. (Please note that the servants or agents of the carrier, but not independent contractors, are entitled to the same defences as the carrier (HVR, Art IV bis (2)) if a claim is made against them directly.) Article IV(2)(a) of the HVR includes two separate exclusions: fault of neglect in navigation; and negligent management of the vessel.

In *Kawasaki Kisen Kaisha Ltd v Whistler International Ltd (The Hill Harmony)*, HL) the navigation exclusion was invoked to cover the master's decision to sail a different route from that ordered by the charterer. The Hague-Visby Rules had been incorporated into the charterparty. However, this argument was rejected as it was held that the choice between two safe routes was an issue of employment of the vessel and not of navigation, and so the exception was not applicable.

The exclusion for negligent management of the ship does not extend to the care for the cargo. This is a separate duty. However an overlap of the duties to manage the ship and to care for the cargo can cause problems. For example in *Gosse Millerd Ltd v Canadian Government Merchant Marine Ltd*, HL cargo stored in a hold had been damaged due to the fact that not all hatch covers had been replaced by repairers. This was classed as lack of care for the cargo resulting in liability of the carrier as the hatch covers were designed to protect the cargo. A situation where the primary objective of the negligent conduct, however, was the safety of the vessel which in turn damaged the cargo, falls within the scope of the management exception (see the Canadian case of *Kalamazoo Paper Co v CPR Co*, Supreme Court of Canada).

To avail himself successfully of the exclusion clause 'perils, dangers and accidents of the sea' (HVR, Art IV(2)(c)) the carrier must show that the damage was caused by something beyond the normal action of the sea and waves, by 'something which could not be foreseen as one of the necessary incidents of the adventure' (as per Lord Herschell in *The Xantho*, HL a case at common law). In *Canada Rice Mills Ltd v Union Marine and General Insurance Co Ltd*, the Privy Council agreed that the accidental entry of seawater caused by a severe storm was classed as having resulted from a peril of the sea just as was any action taken to prevent such incursion of seawater. In this case ventilators and hatches had been repeatedly closed during severe weather to prevent the incursion of seawater and the closure had caused heat damage to the cargo. The cargo was held to have been damaged by a peril of the sea.

Frequently the immunity of 'inherent defect' of the cargo (HVR, Art IV(2)(m)) is also alleged). The nature of perishable goods to deteriorate falls within this exception. However the carrier is expected to exercise the degree of care the goods require. He must keep the cargo dry, but is not responsible for damage to the cargo caused by the inherent moisture content of it (*Jahn (t/a CF Otto Weber) v Turnbull Scott Shipping Co Ltd (The Flowergate)*, QBD (Comm)). Where so required, the carrier must refrigerate the goods. However, he only needs to apply a system which is sound in the light of the knowledge which he had or ought to have had of the nature of the goods. Within that limit he is generally permitted to keep to the shipper's instructions. Any deterioration caused despite these precautions falls within the exclusion of inherent vice (see *Albacora SRL v Westcott & Laurance Line Ltd (The Maltasian)*, HL).

4.2.3.3 Burden of proof

In practice one of the decisive issues is the burden of proof. It can be very difficult to prove exactly how the damage to the cargo was caused, whether it was due to the unseaworthiness of the vessel or due to an excepted peril. The opinions in relation to who bears the burden of proof are conflicting:

(a) whether it is the cargo owner who has to prove the unseaworthiness because this would support his claim; or

(b) whether it is for the carrier to show that the ship was seaworthy at the outset of the journey; or

(c) in case of the Hague-Visby Rules, whether he observed due diligence in this respect.

There seems to be a majority view that the burden rests with the cargo owner to establish the vessel's unseaworthiness and that this in fact caused the damage or loss. This puts the cargo owner in a very difficult position, naturally not having all the facts and details about the vessel's condition and maintenance at hand. This has often led to a readiness of the courts to treat the presence of seawater in a hold as prima facie evidence of the unseaworthiness of the ship. Based on this practice, the burden of proof can look as in the *The Hellenic Dolphin*, QBD (Admiralty) (see also HVR, Art IV(1)).

(a) The cargo owner can raise a prima facie case by proving loss or damage to his cargo.

(b) The carrier must prove an excepted peril, if he wants to rely on it. Liability for such a peril can be excluded either due to stipulations in the contract, common law or the Rules (depending which regime is applicable). Please note however that if the carrier wants to avail himself of the exception of 'any other cause without fault or privity of the carrier' under Art IV(2)(q) of the HVR he additionally needs to prove that he did not act negligently.

(c) For all other exceptions, the cargo owner may be able to prove the carrier's negligence in order to disengage the exception unless, as in Art IV(2)(a), (b) of the HVR the exception specifically allows for negligence.

(d) Where the carrier has successfully proved an excepted peril the cargo owner must prove that the damage was caused due to the unseaworthiness of the vessel at the beginning of the voyage, rather than the excepted peril.

(e) Once this is established the carrier can still escape his liability under the HVR if he can prove that he observed due diligence to make the ship seaworthy. Please note that this is the very stage where common law and the Rules differ: under common law the duty to provide a seaworthy vessel is absolute.

4.2.3.4 Duty to issue a bill of lading

Under a charterparty the shipowner is normally required by express contractual terms to issue a bill of lading, even where the shipper is the charterer. The latter may wish to trade with the goods whilst in transit and thus needs the bill of lading to be potentially able to transfer property and/or possession to a buyer. It is normal practice that bills of lading are issued to the charterer.

Where the Hague Rules or the HVR apply, the shipper can demand the issue of a bill of lading from the carrier under Art III(3) and (7) of the HVR; Rule 3 entitles the shipper to demand a 'received for shipment' bill and Rule 7 a 'shipped' bill.

The bill of lading is usually issued either by the master of the ship or by any other agent of the shipowner. The issue and content of the bill of lading is of particular importance due to the consequences connected with it (please reread HVR, Art III(4) and (5) and CoGSA 1992, s 4).

(a) Once a bill of lading is issued the content is prima facie evidence of receipt of the goods, their quantity, leading marks and their apparent order and condition.

(b) Once the bill has been transferred to a third party, evidence to the contrary is not permissible (HVR, Art III(4)). This is in line with the provision of s 4 of the CoGSA 1992, which states that the bill of lading in the hands of a lawful holder is conclusive evidence of the fact that the goods have either been shipped or received for shipment by the carrier.

(c) However, the shipper who furnishes the carrier with the particulars of the goods on the bill of lading is liable towards the carrier if the latter incurs any liability due to inaccuracy of the statements furnished (HVR, Art III(5)).

4.2.3.5 Deviation and delay

At common law there is an implied undertaking not to deviate unreasonably from the agreed route. If no route is agreed the carrier has to stick to the usual route, or otherwise to the direct route. Also, the voyage must be carried out without undue delay. A breach of the latter duty, however, will mostly also be a breach of the duty not to deviate. Any exclusion of this undertaking must be in express, clear and unambiguous terms. However, departure from the proper route is permissible if there are good grounds for doing so, that is in order to save human life or to avoid danger to the ship or cargo, and also under a charterparty where the deviation is necessary because of some default on the part of the charterer.

Only where the deviation is voluntary and unjustified will it constitute a breach of this duty (see *Rio Tinto Co v Seed Shipping Co*, KBD). This is not the case where the ship is blown off course in a storm.

By virtue of Art IV(4) of the HVR 'any deviation in saving or attempting to save life or property at sea or any reasonable deviation' is allowed and does not constitute a breach of the Rules nor of the contract of carriage. Thus the Rules take a more relaxed approach than the common law. Besides saving life they also permit deviation merely for the purpose of saving property at sea and where otherwise 'reasonable'. When is a deviation reasonable within the meaning of Art IV(4) of the HVR? Whether a deviation is reasonable is a question of fact that has been interpreted narrowly. Lord Atkin in *Stag Line Ltd v Foscolo, Mango & Co Ltd*, HL [1932] AC 328, 343–4 summarised as follows:

> the true test seems to be what departure from the contract voyage might a prudent person controlling the voyage at the time make and maintain, having in mind all the relevant circumstances existing at the time, including the terms of the contract and the interests of all parties concerned, but without obligation to consider the interests of any one as conclusive.

Only in a very few reported English cases has a shipowner been able to rely successfully on this exception.

What are the consequences of a voluntary and unjustified deviation? Under the traditional view it constituted a fundamental breach of the contract of carriage which entitled the shipper to a choice of whether to:

(a) treat the contract as repudiated with the consequence that the future contractual obligations ceased (including the obligation to pay freight) and the carrier lost the benefit of all his contractual immunities and exceptions under the Rules; or

(b) waive the breach (affirm the contract) and only claim damages for loss due to instances which are not covered by any of the exceptions.

The reason for such a strict approach was that in the past the cover for marine cargo insurance was lost on deviation. Nowadays, however, clause 8.3 of the Institute Cargo Clauses A, B and C provides that cargo insurance shall remain in force during any deviation. (The Institute Cargo Clauses are commonly used in cargo insurance to determine and allocate the agreed extent of cover.) Thus the modern view with respect to deviation might be more appropriate.

Under the modern view the doctrine of fundamental breach is rejected and with it the automatic consequence that the party in breach could no longer rely on the exclusion clauses in the contract. Rather it is suggested solving the issues arising out of a breach by use of the normal principles of contract law (see *Suisse Atlantique Société D'Armement SA v NV Rotterdamsche Kolen Centrale*, HL and *Photo Production Ltd v Securicor Transport Ltd*, HL) or by considering deviation as a category sui generis (as per Lord Wilberforce in *Photo Production Ltd v Securicor Transport Ltd* [1980] 1 Lloyd's Rep 545, 550). The effect is that the consequences of the breach will depend on the terms of the contract. The question whether the party in breach can still rely on exclusion clauses is a matter of the construction of the contract.

It was held that the numerous cases applying or discussing the doctrine of fundamental breach were now superseded by the enactment of the Unfair Contract Terms Act 1977, which mainly protects the consumer. The parliamentary choice not to regulate over the whole field of contract had to be accepted. That meant that in the commercial field, where parties were not of unequal bargaining power and where risks could be protected by insurance, there was no reason for judicial intervention and the parties should be left to apportion the risks as they saw fit (see *Photo Production Ltd v Securicor Transport Ltd*, HL).

The approach in *Suisse Atlantique* and in *Photo Production v Securicor* was adopted in *Kenya Railways v Antares Co Pte Ltd (The Antares) (No 1)*, CA, where it was claimed that the carrier who had breached the contract of carriage by unauthorised deck carriage would no longer be able to rely on the HVR time bar due to fundamental breach. Lloyd L J, however, stated that the doctrine of fundamental breach no longer existed, in the following words: 'The death knell sounded in *Suisse Atlantique*... The corpse was buried in *Photo Production Ltd v Securior*...'. Consequently the carrier could rely on the time bar of Art III(6) of the HVR. In this decision Lloyd L J expressed his view that the deviation cases should now be assimilated into the ordinary law of contract.

4.2.3.6 Variation of liability

Under the Hague-Visby Rules the carrier's liability can be increased by inserting such an agreement into the bill of lading (HVR, Art V), but it cannot be reduced. A clause to this effect is null and void by virtue of Art III(8) of the HVR. To illustrate the application of Art III(8) of the HVR, ie that the carrier cannot contract out of his duties imposed by the HVR, see *Owners of Cargo on Board the Morviken v Owners of the Hollandia (The Hollandia)*, HL *(also known as The Morviken)*. The contract of carriage included a choice of forum clause in favour of the Netherlands' courts and a clause choosing Dutch law as the applicable law. The Netherlands, however, had not implemented the HVR, but only the Hague Rules. In so far as the application of the Hague Rules would lead to a reduced protection of the shipper, the House of Lords held that the choice of forum clause was ineffective, because it would lead to the case being heard in the Netherlands where the lesser liability regime of the Hague Rules would be applied. It would thus have the effect of relieving the carrier from some of his mandatory liability under the HVR and so was null and void according to Art III(8) of the HVR. The choice of forum clause, however, did not ex facie offend Art III(8) of the HVR because the reducing effect of the clause depended on the occurrence of a subsequent condition which might or might not arise. If other aspects in relation to the contract of carriage were in dispute, unrelated to the carrier's liability, the choice of jurisdiction would be effective.

The choice of forum was only invalid because the Hague-Visby Rules had mandatory effect. In a case where the bill of lading was issued and the goods loaded in a non-contracting State, the Rules would not be applicable and thus no conflict would arise. In this context see also *The Komninos S*, CA where an implied choice of English law did not automatically include the HVR in a case where they had no mandatory effect.

A choice of law clause would be ineffective to the same extent as a choice of forum clause if on its application the carrier's liability would be limited to a level below that of the Hague-Visby Rules. However, in *RA Lister & Co v EG Thomson (Shipping) Ltd and PT Djakarta Lloyd (The Benarty)*, CA the Court of Appeal upheld a choice of law and jurisdiction clause which allowed the carrier to invoke a statutory limitation in respect of tonnage which was less than the package limitation of the HVR. The carrier successfully invoked Art VIII of the HVR and could rely on the statute in force under the chosen applicable law to limit his liability. Thus, if the effect of a clause was a lower protection than under the HVR, the validity of the clause depended on its aim. Was it an intended avoidance of the higher limits of the HVR, or the application of a different system altogether, which had its own provisions of limitation of liability? In *The Benarty* it had been a different system, aligning limitation with tonnage rather than the number of packages. Therefore the clause was upheld.

A similar evaluation of the facts and of Art III(8) of the Hague Rules and the Hague-Visby Rules was taken in *Pyrene v Scindia*, QBD, affirmed by *GH Renton & Co v Palmyra Trading Corporation of Panama (The Caspiana)*, HL and now reaffirmed by the House of Lords in *Jindal Iron and Steel Co Ltd v Islamic Solidarity Shipping Company Jordan Inc (The Jordan II)*. Article III(8) of the Rules renders void any clauses designed to lessen the carrier's liability while performing the services. However where the parties agreed on the content of these services and allocated obligations usually performed by the carrier to the shipper and consignee, these clauses were valid. In *The Jordan II*, a charterparty bill of lading incorporated a fiost clause (free in out stowed and trimmed) from the charterparty under which the duty to load, stow and discharge the goods was transferred away from the shipowner. Loading the stowing was to be undertaken by the shipper and discharge by the receiver of the cargo. Even though, under Art III(2) of the Rules, the carrier had amongst others the duty to handle, load and stow the cargo carefully, these obligations could be transferred by agreement, without being invalidated by Art III(8).

4.2.3.7 Limitation of liability and limitation of action

The Hague-Visby Rules provide that any defences or limitations under the Rules apply to all actions, whether in contract or tort (HVR, Art IV bis (1)).

Monetary value

Under common law there is no set limit, but an express limitation of the sum payable in the event of liability is valid. The Hague-Visby Rules on the other hand provide for a maximum limit of the carrier's liability calculated on the basis of special drawing rights as defined by the International Monetary Fund per package or kilogram of gross weight (HVR, Art IV(5)(a), (c), (d)). This limitation does not apply, however, where the shipper declares the nature and value of the goods and this is inserted into the bill of lading. In such a case, the amount as included in the bill serves as prima facie evidence of the goods' nature and value (HVR, Art IV(5)(a), (f), (h)). The parties are free to fix other maximum amounts by virtue of Art IV(5)(g) of the HVR, as long as they are not less than the amounts calculated under Art IV(5)(a) of the HVR.

Where goods are consolidated into a transport device such as a container, Art IV(5)(c) of the HVR provides that the container is the package for the purposes of the limitation, unless the bill of lading enumerates the number of packages or units contained therein. Only in that event will the enumerated parcels be taken as individual packages (see *River Gurara (owners of cargo lately on board) v Nigerian National Shipping Line Ltd (The River Gurara)*, CA).

The carrier cannot avail himself of the package limitation if the damage was caused by his act or omission done with the intent to cause damage or which was reckless and envisaged possible damage (HVR, Art IV(5)(e)).

Time bar

The general period under the Limitation Act 1980 within which an action in contract must be brought is six years from the damaging event. Under the Hague-Visby Rules, however, Art III(6) contains a time bar of one year from delivery of the goods, subject to a variation under Art III(6 bis) of the HVR. This time bar is not just one of limitation but extinguishes the claim altogether. In order to avoid a claim falling foul of this hurdle, an action must be instituted in court or before arbitrators in pursuance of an arbitration agreement (for arbitration see *TB&S Batchelor & Co Ltd v Owners of the SS Merak (The Merak)*, CA).

Even where goods have not been loaded, an action is still subjected to the time limit; it starts to run from the date when the goods should have been delivered, had the loading obligation been fulfilled (*Cargill International SA v CPN Tankers (Bermuda) Ltd (The Ot Sonja)*, CA).

Thus, the time of 'delivery' is crucial in order to determine whether an action is time-barred or not. The meaning of the term 'delivery' under a bill of lading relates to the transfer of possession to the consignee. It is not interchangeable with 'discharge'. However it is not always easy to determine when 'delivery' under Art III(6) of the HVR took place.

Trafigura Beheer BV v Golden Stavraetos Maritime Inc (The Sonia), CA dealt with the fact that the cargo was not delivered at the initial destination but, as agreed between the parties at this destination, carried to another place. The Court of Appeal held that in order to determine when 'delivery' under the contract took place, one had to ask whether the delivery was made on the basis of the initial contract, albeit with amendments or whether it took place under a totally separate and distinct transaction. Where it was delivered under a separate transaction, the time limit started to run from the time when the cargo ought to have been delivered under that contract. However where the on-journey was still part of the same contract, only with some alterations, 'delivery' only took place at the final destination. Thus, the one-year time limit of Art III(6) of the HVR only started ticking at that later date.

Convention on Limitation of Liability for Maritime Claims

In addition to the above provisions, by virtue of s 185 of the Merchant Shipping Act (MSA) 1995 incorporating the Convention on Limitation of Liability for Maritime Claims 1976, shipowners, carriers and salvors are entitled to limit their liability in certain circumstances specified by the Convention. In addition, s 186 of the MSA 1995 excludes liability of the owner or charterer of a United Kingdom ship in the following circumstances:

(a) where property on board ship was lost or damaged due to a fire on board; or

(b) where valuables, such as gold, silver or jewels, got lost or damaged due to theft, robbery or other dishonest behaviour, unless their nature and value was declared in writing at the time of shipment.

Even where the Hague-Visby Rules apply, and thus Art III(8), these statutory provisions still take effect (see HVR, Art VIII).

Limitations and defences in favour of third parties

Article IV bis (2) – (4) of the HVR admits the same defences and limits to liability of the carrier to his servants and agents, but not to independent contractors (see *Midland Silicones Ltd v Scruttons Ltd sub nom Scruttons v Midland Silicones Ltd*, HL, however, for a case involving the Hague Rules without a provision equivalent to Art IV bis of the HVR).

In order to protect independent contractors as well as servants and agents the carrier must insert a Himalaya clause (so called after the case *Adler v Dickson (The Himalaya)*, CA) into the contract of carriage. In order to avoid any problems due to lack of privity of contract, the carrier needs to conclude such a provision as agent of the third party. Such a clause needs to meet three conditions:

(a) the contract of carriage must make clear that the exceptions, defences and limits to liability are intended to cover the carrier as well as the third party;

(b) the carrier is contracting for these provisions in his capacity as carrier and also as agent for the third party; and

(c) the carrier should have authority from the third party to act on its behalf or the third party should at least agree to this in hindsight.

Cases where such a clause has been upheld in favour of the third party include: *New Zealand Shipping Co Ltd v AM Satterthwaite & Co Ltd (The Eurymedon)*, PC and *Port Jackson Stevedoring Pty v Salmond and Spraggon (Australia) Pty*, PC (Australia).

The law of bailment was also used to bypass the doctrine of privity of contract. In *KH Enterprise (Cargo Owners) v Pioneer Container (Owners) (The Pioneer Container)*, PC (Hong Kong) the contract of carriage provided for the subcontracting of carriage 'on any terms'. The Privy Council held that the subcontractor, as sub-bailee, could rely on the terms of the (main) contract of carriage, including the exclusive jurisdiction clause. (See also *The Mahkutai*, PC (Hong Kong), where Lord Goff discusses the development of Himalaya clauses and the acceptance of them by the English courts in order to accommodate commercial need.)

These problems due to the doctrine of privity have been alleviated to a great extent by the Contracts (Rights of Third Parties) Act 1999, which came into force on 11 May 2000. Where a third party is expressly identified in the contract by name, class or description (1999 Act, s 1(3)), it may in its own right enforce a contractual clause which (a) either expressly provides that it may, or (b) where the term purports to confer a benefit on this party (1999 Act, s 1(1)(a) and (b)). In the latter event, the contract on its true construction must not show that the contract parties had not intended the term to be enforceable by that other person (1999 Act, s 1(2)). However, with regard to the carriage of goods by sea, and also the carriage by road, rail or air where the contract of carriage is subject to the appropriate international transport convention, s 6(5) of the Contracts (Rights of Third Parties) Act 1999 restricts its application: a third party shall not be able to avail itself of any positive rights, but only of exclusions or limitations of liability. This stipulation ensures that the compulsory provisions of the international transport conventions cannot be circumvented and that no other conflict arises.

4.2.4 Duties and liabilities of the shipper under the contract of carriage

4.2.4.1 Freight

Freight is the remuneration paid by the shipper to the shipowner/carrier under the contract of carriage for shipping the goods to the agreed destination. As a general rule of common law freight is payable to the carrier once the goods are delivered at the port of destination. If the goods are lost at sea, nothing is payable. If all the goods arrive, but they are damaged, the full freight is payable and cannot be deducted from a claim of damages against the carrier (see *Dakin v Oxley*).

However, the parties can agree to payment on other terms and this is mostly done in modern practice. The CoGSA 1971 does not qualify this liberty and different types of freight arrangements are now known. Please look through the documents at the back of this book, charterparties and bills of lading, to gain an understanding of the terms used in practice. Many bill of lading contracts provide for freight to be non-refundable and payable regardless of the arrival of the ship and delivery of the goods. Under charterparties (see **4.2.7** below), freight or hire may be payable in monthly instalments.

Freight is mostly calculated by weight or measurement. In case of slight variations of the weight due to the nature of the goods, for example changes in moisture, it is calculated on what is in fact shipped.

Freight is payable by the shipper, who has concluded the contract of carriage with the shipowner. However, the consignee of the cargo can also become liable. As we have seen in Chapter 2, the lawful holder of the transport documents has transferred to him and vested in him all rights of suit as if he were a party to the contract of carriage (CoGSA 1992, s 2(1)). This position, on the other hand, also attracts certain liabilities. These liabilities, however, are only imposed on the lawful holder/consignee where he activates his position by either demanding delivery from the carrier or by making a claim under the contract of carriage (CoGSA 1992, s 3(1)). Once the lawful holder of the bill of lading approaches the carrier with one of these demands, the carrier in turn can claim freight from the holder of the bill. The responsibility to pay the freight also still remains with the shipper (CoGSA 1992, s 3(3)).

The parties can alter the default position by agreeing on another solution, taking into account the several other types of freight.

(a) Lump sum freight is sometimes arranged under charterparties and seldom under bill of lading contracts. It is freight due for the use of an entire ship, or part thereof, regardless of whether the space has been filled or not. As long as the carrier delivers some or all of the cargo he has earned the lump sum freight.

(b) Prepaid freight becomes due in advance, usually on shipment or signing of the bill of lading. If it is true advance freight, which is non-refundable and does not just serve as a loan to the shipowner, it remains with the carrier even if the goods are lost. If the ship never sails, however, it has not earned the freight; the latter must be refunded. Prepaid and advance freight are commonly used in bill of lading contracts, but the exact stipulations vary. Advance freight is part of the insurable value of the goods and can be insured by the shipper because it is non-refundable.

(c) Pro rata freight is only payable in exceptional circumstances. As a general rule, no freight is payable where the goods do not arrive at the agreed destination. The carrier cannot unilaterally decide to deliver the cargo short of the agreed port of discharge and then charge freight in proportion to the completed voyage. However, where the parties have agreed on a new contract, for example if the goods by choice of the cargo owner are delivered to an intermediate port rather than the port of destination, or if the carrier has only loaded part of the cargo he can claim pro rata freight.

(d) Back freight is payable if the goods are not unloaded as envisaged, but carried further: for example if the shipper/seller uses his right of stoppage in transit and the goods need either to be taken back or delivered to a different destination. The shipper is then liable for any additional freight as back freight. Where the cargo owner fails to take delivery the carrier must deal with the cargo in the owner's interest and at the latter's expense. The carrier might choose to either land or warehouse the goods, carry them on to another port or return them to the port of loading. Any expenses thus incurred by the carrier can be claimed as back freight.

(e) Dead freight is payable as damages if the shipper does not honour the carriage contract and never delivers the goods. If the carrier cannot fill the freight space with other cargo, or if he can only find cargo for which less freight is paid, he can claim the difference as damages from the initial shipper.

4.2.4.2 Dangerous goods

The shipper is not allowed to ship dangerous goods without prior consent of the carrier. The reason for the shipper's duty to notify the carrier in advance is that the shipowner can refuse the cargo or take necessary precautions. Often the contract of affreightment will contain an express clause as to this obligation. However, the shipper does not need to notify the carrier where the carrier or members of his crew know or reasonably ought to know of the dangerous character of the goods.

At common law this is an implied undertaking by the shipper. Should he nevertheless ship dangerous cargo, the shipper is strictly liable for any damage caused. Once the carrier consents to carry the cargo, the shipper has discharged his obligations and cannot be held responsible at common law for any resulting damage.

Under Art IV(6) of the Hague-Visby Rules, it is provided that any dangerous cargo shipped without the carrier being aware of its nature and character and consenting to such a shipment, can at any time be discharged or destroyed without compensation to the shipper. The shipper must pay for any damage or expenses incurred from such a shipment. And even where the goods are shipped with knowledge and consent of the carrier, if the goods become a danger to the ship, the carrier can land them, destroy them, or render them innocuous without incurring any liability towards the shipper other than general average (see at **4.2.4.3** and **5.3.4** below for an explanation of general average).

What constitutes dangerous cargo? Courts have held that the dangerous nature of the cargo does not depend on the cargo being listed as a dangerous substance, but is to be found in the surrounding circumstances as a whole. The contract and the facts have to be read together. Then one has to ask whether the shipowner on the true construction of the contract has contracted to bear the risk inherent in the particular shipment.

Cargo which either causes physical damage to the ship or to other cargo or which presents a threat is classed as dangerous. For example inflammable or explosive substances fall within this category, as does cargo which needs government permission not obtained in advance, thus delaying discharge operations (see *Mitchell, Cotts & Co v Steel Bros & Co*, KBD) or cargo that is infested with a pest and so the ship is ordered to leave the port of destination with its cargo (*Effort Shipping Co Ltd v Linden Management SA (The Giannis NK)*, HL). In the last case it did not matter that the shipper did not know about the beetle infestation; it was ruled that the duty not to ship dangerous cargo in Art IV(6) of the HVR imposes strict liability and overrides the principle that the shipper is not liable to the carrier without act, fault or neglect on his behalf as enshrined in Art IV(3) of the HVR. However the duty of the carrier to make the ship seaworthy (HVR, Art III (1)) was held to override Art IV(6) of the HVR where the damage resulted from the unseaworthiness (see *Mediterranean Freight Services Ltd v BP Oil International Ltd (The Fiona)*, CA).

4.2.4.3 General average and other expenses

Sometimes the carrier has to incur expenses in order to save the cargo or to save the whole adventure, including the ship, the cargo and the freight. Where the carrier incurred reasonable expenses to save the goods, for example he bought feed for animals shipped on board, the shipper or the consignee claiming the cargo becomes liable to compensate the carrier for doing so.

Loss or damage incurred by one party to the marine adventure is called particular average. Depending on the circumstances this party might have a cause of action against another for the loss. At other times, in peculiar circumstances, loss is incurred or expenses are made to save the whole adventure and thus the common interest of the shipowner, the freight earner and the cargo owner in the success of the voyage. This is called general average. All parties must contribute to the cost incurred or compensate one of the parties for any damage caused to its interest. But this is only the case if the sacrifice was reasonably incurred to avert danger threatening all three interests (ship, freight and cargo), and the sacrifice must have benefited all parties involved. Payments due by the holders of the interests in the voyage to the party or parties which incurred the damage are called general average contributions. The shipper or the consignee of the cargo claiming delivery of the cargo will be liable for such contributions, and insurance cover for these contributions is available together with the insurance for the goods (for a more detailed explanation please see Chapter 5 at **5.3.4**).

4.2.4.4 Shipowner's lien with regard to shipper's duties

Under common law the shipowner has a possessory lien on all the goods carried on the same voyage to the same consignee under the same contract of carriage. He can withhold delivery until the following payments in relation to these goods have been made:

(a) any freight that is payable on delivery,

(b) general average contributions, and

(c) any expenses incurred by the shipowner for protecting and preserving the goods.

As soon as he duly delivers the goods, the shipowner loses his common law lien. In practice the lien is extended, by express agreement between the parties, beyond the limits of the common law provision, for example for charges other than those already mentioned and also often authorising the shipowner to realise his lien by selling the goods. Please have a look at the clauses used in practice by studying the carriage documents at the back of this book.

4.2.5 Transfer of rights and liabilities under the transport documents — Carriage of Goods by Sea Act 1992

As we have seen (at **2.5.6** and **2.6.3** above) the CoGSA 1992 is not in conflict with the CoGSA 1971 implementing the Hague-Visby Rules, but replaces the Bill of Lading Act 1855. The 1992 Act is of great practical importance as under common law the contract of carriage is normally concluded between the shipper and the carrier (unless the shipper specifically acted as agent for the consignee). Between the consignee or indorsee and the carrier there is no privity of contract. However, once the risk of loss of or damage to the goods under the sale contract has passed to the buyer/consignee or indorsee, he has a strong interest in the safe arrival of the goods and thus in the proper performance of the carriage contract. This interest is irrespective of the passing of property. In order to be able to sue in tort, the consignee or indorsee must have had a possessory or proprietary right in the goods at the time of damage. The consignee or indorsee must also be able to prove negligence on behalf of the carrier. Thus a claim in tort is not easy to establish. The gap is now filled by the Carriage of Goods by Sea Act 1992.

In the past, under the Bill of Lading Act 1855 the statutory transfer of rights of suit under the carriage contract was limited to a third party having received property of the goods by reason of the consignment or indorsement of a bill of lading only. Thus the transfer of rights of suit to the consignee was only effected in limited cases. The 'new' law, in force since 16 September 1992, by virtue of the CoGSA 1992 confers rights and liabilities with respect to bills of lading irrespective of a transfer of property. The 1992 Act is, unlike the Bill of Lading Act 1855, not limited to bills of lading but also covers sea waybills and delivery orders. The 1992 Act also deals with non-negotiable bills of lading but, being incapable of transfer, they do not fall within the bill of lading category of the Act (see CoGSA 1992, s 1(2)), but are treated as a sea waybill (see CoGSA 1992, s 1(3) and s 5(1)).

It is worth reading the six sections of the Act in full. As an introduction, however, just a few sections are highlighted in the following paragraphs.

4.2.5.1 Rights of suit against the carrier

The third party lawful holder of a bill of lading (as defined in CoGSA 1992, s 5(2)) or the person to whom delivery is to be made under a sea waybill or a delivery order has all rights of suit against the carrier as if he were party to the carriage contract (CoGSA 1992, s 2(1)). However no rights of suit are transferred where the holder has obtained the bill at a time when it no longer gives right to possession of the goods unless one of the two following circumstances are met:

(a) the transfer of the bill was effected in pursuance of a contractual obligation concluded prior to the moment when the bill ceased to be a transferable document of title (ie prior to delivery of the goods to the holder); and

(b) where possession of the bill is a result of the rejection of the goods (CoGSA 1992, s 2 (2)).

Once the rights of suit have transferred to the lawful holder of the bill of lading, any rights of suit vested in the original party or any intermediate holders of the bill are extinguished (CoGSA 1992, s 2(5)). Please note: the rights of suit of the original shipper under a sea waybill or delivery order are not prejudiced. Since property and the right of suit under the CoGSA 1992 are unrelated, the damage might be sustained by a person who is not the holder of the transport document. In such an event the holder of the transport document can claim on behalf of another for the damage sustained by that other person (see CoGSA 1992, s 2 (4)). However he is under no obligation to do so.

Where a ship's delivery order for unascertained goods forming part of a bulk cargo is concerned, any rights vested in a person by virtue of the order are 'confined to rights in respect of the goods to which the order relates' and leave the rest of the bulk cargo 'untouched' (see CoGSA 1992, s 2(3) with its correlation for liabilities in s 3(2)).

4.2.5.2 Liabilities under shipping documents

The third party holder in whom the rights under s 2(1) of the CoGSA 1992 are vested can also become liable under the transport document 'as if he had been a party to that contract', for example for freight and expenses incurred by the shipowner/carrier with respect to the cargo. In order to become liable, however, transfer of the transport document to the lawful holder is not enough. The holder must approach the carrier:

(a) either to take or demand delivery of the goods;

(b) or to make a claim under the contract of carriage;

(c) or having demanded delivery before those rights were vested in him, ie where the consignee demands delivery from the carrier before receipt of the bill of lading from the seller/shipper (see CoGSA 1992, s 3(1)).

These rules follow the principle of mutuality that where the holder of the bill wishes to enforce the contract against the carrier, he must also accept the corresponding contractual liabilities. The third party holder is therefore in charge: only once he claims against the carrier will he be subject to liability. He can avoid any liability by selling the goods before delivery is sought and without making any other claim. Where the holder only keeps the bill as security, no liability is incurred unless and until he seeks to realise his security.

So which precise action is needed to activate this liability? Lord Hobhouse in *Borealis AB v Stargas Ltd (The Berge Sisar)*, HL, clarified that 'demanding delivery' in s 3(1)(a) and (c) of the CoGSA 1992 referred to a formal demand by the holder, asserting his contractual rights as transferred by s 2(1) against the carrier to have the goods delivered to him. Allowing the vessel to berth at its import jetty and taking samples of the cargo did not amount to such a demand, but was common co-operation between the players. 'Taking delivery' is seen as the voluntary transfer of possession of the goods from the carrier to the holder for which ordinarily the bill of lading is surrendered. Again co-operation in discharge operations alone would not qualify. Unloading of the vessel was in the common interest of the ship and the cargo and typically required co-operation.

'Making a claim' in the sense of s 3(1)(b) of the CoGSA 1992 referred to a formal claim of the holder against the carrier asserting the carrier's legal liability under the contract of carriage. According to his Lordship the liability under s 3(1)(c) of the CoGSA 1992 clearly depends on whether the person taking or demanding delivery would become the lawful holder of the bill with respective rights of suit by operation of s 2(1) of the CoGSA 1992. For example the consignee took delivery of the goods from the carrier (probably against a letter of indemnity) before the bill of lading was transferred to him; however subsequently he became the lawful holder of the bill.

The principle of mutuality was held to be crucial in the application of the act, which meant that once a lawful holder had transferred his rights of suit under s 2(1) of the CoGSA 1992 by subsequent indorsement, his liability was also discharged (*The Berge Sisar*). For an illustration of the principle of mutuality, see Fig 4.8.

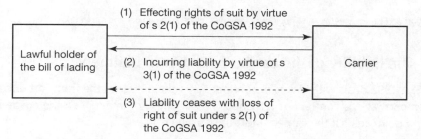

Fig 4.8 Principle of mutuality under CoGSA 1992

On the other hand, the original party to the contract of carriage is not released from its duties by means of transfer despite the fact of losing his rights of suit (CoGSA 1992, s 3(3)). However this intention is clearly stipulated in the Act.

Making the necessary alterations, the same principles apply to sea waybills and delivery orders. Liability under a ship's delivery order of a larger bulk cargo is restricted to the goods to which the order relates (CoGSA 1992, see s 3(2)).

4.2.5.3 Bill of lading as conclusive evidence

By virtue of s 4 of the CoGSA 1992 a bill of lading is conclusive evidence between the carrier and a person having become the lawful holder of the bill with respect to the goods as represented under the bill of having been shipped or received for shipment.

4.2.5.4 Summary chart

To summarise and illustrate the working of the Carriage of Goods by Sea Act 1992 as between the seller, the buyer and the carrier, please study Fig 4.9.

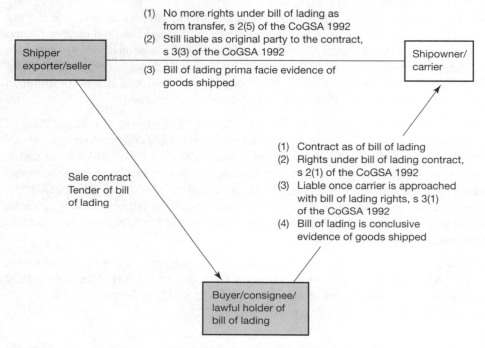

Fig 4.9 Rights and liabilities between shipper and carrier and bill of lading holder and carrier under the CoGSA 1992

4.2.6 The liability of the carrier in tort or in bailment

The CoGSA 1992 deals with claims in contract, 'as if the holder of the transport document had been party to the contract of carriage'. The Act does not impinge on the possibility of bringing a claim against the carrier in tort or in bailment.

4.2.6.1 Carrier's liability in tort

Irrespective of the rights and duties under the contract of carriage, the carrier also owes a duty of care in tort. Where the Hague-Visby Rules apply, the carrier can avail himself of the same defences and limits of liability, whether the claim is based on contract or tort (HVR, Art IV bis (1)). However, according to the decision of the House of Lords in *Leigh and Sillivan Ltd v Aliakmon Shipping Co Ltd (The Aliakmon)*, a claim in the tort of negligence requires the claimant either to have had property in or a possessory title to the goods or at least possession of the goods at the time when the damage occurred. It is not necessary that the claimant has suffered loss. Where a buyer obtains the proprietary or possessory rights only after the damaging event took place he has no right of action in tort.

Towards a person having an immediate right to possession, the carrier is also liable in tort for conversion or wrongful interference if he wrongly delivers the goods to a person not entitled to them (see *Chabbra Corporation Pte Ltd v Jag Shakti (Owners) (The Jag Shakti)*, PC and *The Winkfield*, CA).

4.2.6.2 Carrier's liability in bailment

Where the claimant has no title to sue under the contract or by way of operation of the CoGSA 1992, he nevertheless may be able to sue the carrier successfully in bailment. Under the common law concept of bailment the bailee voluntarily assumes possession of the goods of another (the bailor). The bailee has to take reasonable care of the goods and must not convert the goods. The bailee is liable for the goods while in his charge, unless he proves absence of fault. The person entitled to immediate possession of the goods can sue the bailee for breach of his duties. This right of action is not limited to the immediate bailor, but can extend to the head bailor (in case of sub-bailment) or a third party owner (see *KH Enterprise (Cargo Owners) v Pioneer Container (Owners) (The Pioneer Container)*, PC (Hong Kong)). However the claimant must show attornment, that is, that the bailee holds the goods for him, which often is a problem in cases of succession of title.

The terms on which the bailee accepts custody of the goods are mostly found in a contract, for example the contract of carriage under which the carrier accepts the goods into his care. In such a case the bailment is classed as bailment on terms and the terms of the carriage contract are relevant to define the bailee's duties and also the limitations of his liability. The bailee may in turn pass possession to another person, who is called the sub-bailee. The carrier for example may sub-bail the goods to a warehouse or to another carrier in case of transhipment. The terms of their sub-bailment will also be applicable towards the head bailor where the head bailor has consented to sub-bailment either in general on any terms or specifically on the relevant terms.

To claim in bailment might be particularly useful in the following events:

(a) where the bill of lading was made out by the charterer and in his name, but the cargo owner wants to sue the shipowner;

(b) where the bill of lading provides for transhipment, the damaging event occurs after the goods have been transhipped and the cargo owner wants to sue the second carrier; and

(c) where the shipper has lost his right to claim against the carrier by virtue of s 2(5) CoGSA 1992 because he transferred the bill of lading, provided possession has not completely passed to the new holder (see *East West Corporation v DKBS 1912*, CA).

4.2.7 Charterparties

As we have touched on before (see **4.2.1.2** above), the contract for the hire of the entire vessel is called a charterparty. The contract is governed by common law unless the parties expressly incorporate one of the carriage conventions, for example the Hague-Visby Rules, into their contract. As we have seen, charterparty contracts and bill of lading contracts are based on different legal rules due to the different bargaining power of the players in each of the contracts. Figure 4.10 briefly contrasts some of the practical and legal differences between charterparties and bill of lading contracts.

Charterparty (chp)	Bill of lading (bol) contract
(a) Full shipload	(a) Smaller consignments
(b) Usually conducted as 'tramp service'	(b) Can also be conducted by 'liner service'
(c) Contract and freight according to market demand	(c) Freight tariffs on liner service; otherwise freight is negotiable
(d) Contract terms are freely negotiable — common law applies	(d) Mandatory international rules generally apply, eg Hague-Visby Rules (incorporated into English law by the CoGSA 1971)
(e) Contract of carriage is charterparty. Bills of lading can be issued under chp, however chp still governs the relationship between charterer and shipowner	(e) Contract of carriage is evidenced in bill of lading. Chp bills of lading only take effect when transferred to third party
(f) Right of suit between the contract parties based on chp	(f) Right of suit: between parties to the contract of carriage based on contract; but also the lawful holder of bol (s 2 (1) of the CoGSA 1992) based on bol ('as if')

Fig 4.10 Comparison between charterparties and bills of lading issues

The charterparty is binding between the charterer and the shipowner, but it is not relevant to the third party consignee. As between the latter and the carrier the transport document (bill of lading) will prevail. This is illustrated in Figs 4.11 – 4.13, using simple examples of a cif seller and a fob buyer as charterer of the vessel, differentiating between the various types of charterparties. Only where the terms of the charterparty have been clearly incorporated into the bill of lading will the charterparty be of any relevance to the holder of the bill of lading.

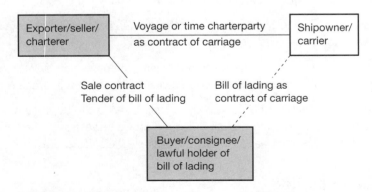

Fig 4.11 Contracts of carriage: charterparty and bill of lading where cif seller charters the vessel

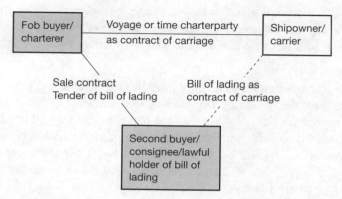

Fig 4.12 *Contracts of carriage: charterparty and bill of lading where the buyer has chartered the vessel and resold the goods in transit*

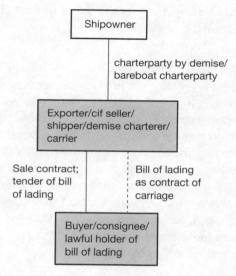

Fig 4.13 *Contracts of carriage: bareboat charterparty and bill of lading where the seller has chartered the vessel by demise and sold his goods on a cif basis*

The implied duties at common law, as discussed above, on the shipowner/carrier to provide a seaworthy vessel, not to deviate and to dispatch without undue delay and also the obligation of the shipper not to ship dangerous cargo are all relevant to the charterparty. Further duties between the parties depend on the type of charterparty. There are three main categories of charterparties: voyage, time and bareboat charterparties. In most cases, well-established form contracts are used to determine the parties' respective rights and duties. Please see the appended charterparty form contracts at the back of this book for each of the categories and compare and contrast their terms. For a detailed study of charterparties please consult a textbook on carriage of goods by sea (see **8.2.3** below).

4.2.7.1 Voyage and time charterparty

Under a voyage and time charterparty the charterer hires the vessel for a specific voyage or for a determined period of time. The shipowner remains responsible for the running of the vessel and, unless otherwise agreed, is the legal carrier of the goods. Thus a third party holder of the bill of lading can and will have to sue the shipowner as the carrier, if the contract is not performed to his satisfaction. In the case of a bareboat charterparty this is different.

Voyage charterparty

Under a voyage charterparty the charterer hires the vessel for a single voyage or consecutive journeys, from the named port of loading to the port of destination. The charterer contracts to provide full cargo for the ship and to pay freight for it. If less than the agreed quantity is loaded he is liable for dead freight. The parties usually provide for a 'laytime and demurrage' clause (see **2.7.4** above) which allows a specified amount of time for loading and discharge. If the stipulated time is exceeded the charterer has to pay damages for detention or, where specified, liquidated damages called demurrage. The carrier will usually have a lien on the cargo for the payment of any outstanding demurrage or freight. (Where a charterparty bill of lading has successfully incorporated these terms under the charterparty into the bill of lading contract, these terms will impact on the position of the bill of lading holder. Thus it is important for the holder of a bill of lading to watch out for any incorporations clauses and be aware of their reach.)

Time charterparty

Under a time charterparty the charterer hires the vessel for a specific period of time and pays hire in regular intervals (usually monthly) for the services of the ship, regardless of the amount in fact carried. Payment of the hire by the stipulated time is of utmost importance; otherwise the shipowner may be able to withdraw the vessel. The charterer employs and directs the vessel in accordance with the charterparty, but is generally only entitled to send it to safe ports, carrying lawful cargo. As the use of the vessel is his for the specified period of hire the charterer bears the risk of speedy performance of the vessel and any delays during the voyages or the cargo handling. In order for the charterer to plan and calculate, he will want to obtain some performance warranties from the shipowner about the ship's consumption, its speed, and its performance to load and discharge etc. Breach of these terms can give rise to claims of damages or even to repudiation of the contract, depending on the facts and severity of the breach.

4.2.7.2 Bareboat charterparty

The bareboat charterparty, also called charterparty by demise, operates as a lease of the vessel rather than a contract of carriage. The charterer takes possession of the vessel and runs it as if he were the owner. He takes complete control over the ship and full responsibility for its navigation and management. He is the legal carrier and responsible to answer any claims. JF Wilson, *Carriage of Goods by Sea* (5th edn, Harlow: Pearson Education, 2004), 7 describes the difference between a demise charterparty and a voyage or time charterparty as follows: the former is comparable with a contract of hire of a self-drive car as opposed to using the services of a taxi in the cases of a voyage or time charterparty.

4.2.7.3 Who is the legal carrier?

In practice one of the big problems for the cargo claimant is to identify the legal carrier in order to be able to instigate proceedings against the correct party, even more so where multiple charterparties exist. Where the Hague Rules or the Hague-Visby Rules apply, the cargo claimant only has one year to bring suit against the carrier, so if he accidentally sues another his claim against the true carrier may be time barred. Also, under many jurisdictions he risks having to pay the legal costs of the party that was wrongly sued.

As a general rule, the shipowner remains the actual and legal carrier under a time and voyage charterparty, whereas under a bareboat charterparty the demise charterer mans and runs the ship and thus performs as the actual and legal carrier.

However the charterer may arrange the bill of lading contract as principal party and issue the bill in his name, thus binding himself as carrier. Or he might have given the master permission to sign in his name and on his behalf. The charterer can also be caught where he signs the bill of lading without clarifying that he does so 'on behalf of the master and owners' of the vessel. To ensure that he, the charterer, does not incur liability as the legal carrier he can insert clauses in the bill of lading identifying the shipowner as the carrier.

Often conflicting statements with respect to the carrier's identity make it essential to check all the terms of the contract and the relevant case law as to their validity. If the face of the bill of lading indicates the carrier without doubt, but the reverse of the bill contains a carrier clause to the contrary, the name on the face of the bill should prevail (for a more detailed discussion of the topic see *Homburg Houtimport BV v Agrosin Private Ltd (The Starsin)*, HL). Regardless of who is the carrier under the bill of lading, the shipowner or demise charterer still owes the cargo claimant a duty of care under the law of bailment and thus may be liable. Usually the bailment is classed as a bailment on terms, which are the terms of the bill of lading (see *KH Enterprise (Cargo Owners) v Pioneer Container (Owners) (The Pioneer Container)*, PC (Hong Kong) and *The Mahkutai*, PC (Hong Kong)).

4.2.8 Hamburg Rules

Another legal regime for carriage contracts other than charterparties is the United Nations Convention on the Carriage of Goods by Sea 1978, known as the 'Hamburg Rules'. The convention has been in force since 1 November 1992 and differs in quite a few aspects from the Hague and Hague-Visby regime. Its emphasis is shifted towards the interests of the cargo owner rather than the protection of the carrier as in the Hague and Hague-Visby Rules. This might be the reason why most of the major seafaring countries have not ratified this convention, including the United Kingdom. Please read the Hamburg Rules alongside the following brief discussion and compare its stipulations with those of the Hague-Visby Rules.

The scope of the Hamburg Rules (Art 2) extends to any contract of carriage by sea between two different States, regardless of the transport document used. So sea waybills, booking notes and other non-negotiable transport documents are also included, not just bills of lading as under the Hague-Visby regime. However, the Hamburg Rules do not apply to charterparties. The territorial application is similar to that of the Hague-Visby Rules, but it also covers inward voyages. Thus, the Hamburg Rules might be applicable where the port of discharge is in a contracting State (Art 2(1)(b)). 'Goods' within the ambit of the Hamburg Rules (Art 1(5) and Art 9) include live animals as well as deck cargo.

The Hamburg Rules in Art 4 provide for the responsibility of the carrier during the entire period in which he is in charge of the goods. The liability regime is based on a single concept, the fault of the carrier, which is presumed if the goods are lost or damaged whilst in his charge. However the carrier can rebut this presumption and prove that all measures were taken that could reasonably be expected so as to avoid the occurrence that caused the loss and its consequences (see Hamburg Rules, Art 5). Thus, the burden of proof is on the carrier, which has important practical implications. However there is one exception and that is damage or loss by fire. Here the claimant has to prove that either the fire or the damage resulting from the fire arose due to fault or neglect on the carrier's behalf (see Hamburg Rules, Art 5 (4)).

Similar to Art III(8) of the HVR, Art 23 of the Hamburg Rules asserts that all stipulations are null and void which derogate directly or indirectly from the Rules' provisions to the detriment of the shipper, but the carrier can increase his liability. The limitation period is two years (Hamburg Rules, Art 20) instead of only one under the Hague-Visby Rules and the 'package' limitation is higher than under the Hague-Visby Rules (see Hamburg Rules, Arts 6 and 26).

The Hamburg Rules are also better designed to cope with modern practices of through transport by distinguishing between the carrier (any person by whom or in whose name the sea carriage contract was concluded) and the actual carrier (any other person who is entrusted with the performance of the carriage or part of it (see Hamburg Rules, Art 1(1), (2)). The carrier remains liable for all stages, even if performed by the actual carrier (Hamburg Rules, Art 10). However, if the actual carrier is named in the contract of carriage, the carriers' liability can be excluded in so far as the claimant can sue the named carrier in a 'competent court' (Hamburg Rules, Art 11).

4.2.9 UNCITRAL draft instrument on the carriage of goods [wholly or partly] [by sea]

So far there are three international conventions on sea transport which have received varied support, besides which some countries have implemented their own rules of law on sea carriage. The intended harmonisation thus was not achieved. To fill the gap UNCITRAL is negotiating a draft instrument on the carriage of goods. The draft so far aims to apply to carriage of goods which involves at least a sea leg across the borders, but can also include the to-carriage and on-carriage. The instrument is aimed to apply to contracts of carriage regardless of the type of transport document used, but again does not apply to charterparties. It applies to deck cargo and caters for electronic transport documents.

The liability regime is a mixture of the Hamburg and Hague-Visby approach. The carrier's liability, as in the Hamburg Rules, is based on fault with a reversed burden of proof, but also includes a list of events in which the carrier is presumed not to be at fault. The latter events mirror most of the Hague-Visby exceptions; however here the presumptions can be rebutted. The draft also includes package and time limitations.

Provisions are drafted to cover the shipper's duties, freight, general average, delivery to the consignee, rights of control, transfer or rights under the transport documents, rights of suit and time for suit. The instrument also includes rules on jurisdiction, arbitration and the relationship with other conventions.

The UNCITRAL website at http://www.uncitral.org/uncitral/en/index.html shows the detailed reports and the progress under 'Commissions & Working Groups', 'Working Group III', which are recommended for further study.

4.3 Aspects of carriage of goods by air and land

In the following we are going to discuss very briefly some aspects of these forms of transport, to give you an indication where to start any further research. The features are largely similar to those pertinent to the carriage of goods by sea and you should be able to transfer and adapt your knowledge and understanding developed under the previous heading (**4.2**).

4.3.1 Carriage of goods by air

The law relating to carriage of goods by air, like the rules on sea carriage, is governed by three different convention regimes. If neither of them applies we have to turn to the rules with respect to non-convention carriage, which in England are the common law rules on the common carrier. In principle, the common carrier is absolutely responsible for any loss or damage to the cargo unless defences such as act of God, act of the Queen's enemies, inherent vice in the goods, general average sacrifice or the owner's own fault or negligence can be pleaded and proved.

The pertinent conventions are the following.

(a) The first highly successful regime with 151 parties, the Warsaw Convention on Carriage by Air of 12 October 1929, was given effect in the United Kingdom by the Carriage by Air Act 1932. This Act was later replaced by the Carriage by Air Act (CAA) 1961 to give effect to the amended Warsaw Convention, which was ratified by 135 parties. However the initial 1929 Convention is still applicable as part of English law with respect to those few countries remaining signatories only to the old convention. The unamended Warsaw Convention is still contained in Schedule 2 to the Carriage by Air Acts (Application of Provision) Order 1967.

(b) The Warsaw Convention as amended in The Hague on 28 September 1955 was incorporated into English law by the Carriage by Air Act 1961 and is set out in its Schedule 1. The amended Warsaw Convention was supplemented by the Guadalajara Convention 1961 (the Convention Supplementary to the Warsaw Convention for the Unification of Certain Rules relating to International Carriage by Air performed by a person other than the Contracting Carrier) to ameliorate the position of cases where the contracting carrier and the actual carrier are different persons. The Guadalajara Convention is implemented by the Carriage by Air (Supplementary Provisions) Act 1962. Further amendment of the Warsaw Conventions took place by virtue of the Montreal Additional Protocols 1975 Nos 1 – 4. They all concern the limits of the carrier's liability. Protocols Nos 1 and 2 replaced the original gold franc with the Special Drawing Rights as defined by the International Monetary Fund, No 1 for the unamended Convention and No 2 for the Warsaw Convention as amended by the Hague Protocol. No 3 relates to another Protocol known as the Guatemala Protocol, both concerning the carrier's liability for passengers, and No 4 raises the limits of liability with respect to cargo and postal items. The Montreal Additional Protocols Nos 1, 2 and 4 are in force in the United Kingdom; No 3 has yet to enter into force after the deposit of the thirtieth instrument of ratification. The Warsaw Convention as amended by the Hague Protocol and the Montreal Additional Protocols Nos 2 and 4 is appended to the Carriage by Air Act 1961 in Schedule 1A.

(c) The new Montreal Convention for the Unification of Certain Rules for International Carriage by Air of 28 May 1999, which came into force on 4 November 2003, has been ratified by the United Kingdom: it is given effect to by the Carriage by Air Act 1961 as amended and has the force of law as of 28 June 2004. The Montreal Convention has also been ratified by the European Union in its own right with the entry into force date of 28 June 2004. As of September 2005 it had 66 parties. It consolidates, updates and unifies the provisions of the Warsaw Convention with all its amendments and also, for the first time, addresses the allocation of liability between the contractual carrier and another carrier actually performing the carriage. Between States party to the other Carriage by Air Conventions, the Montreal Convention 1999 prevails over the Warsaw Conventions and its amendments (Montreal Convention 1999, Art 55). This is also set out in s 1(4) of the Carriage by Air Act 1961, which provides that for any carriage by air the applicable provisions of the most recent Convention have the force of law.

In England, therefore, the law on air carriage is now mainly governed by the Carriage by Air Act 1961 and the Carriage by Air (Supplementary Provisions) Act 1962, both incorporating the above-mentioned conventions. The conventions determine the legal liabilities and relationships between the air carrier and either the passenger or the cargo consignor and/or consignee. The provisions are in principle quite similar to the ones of the sea carriage conventions which have already been discussed in detail. Please take some time to consult the full text of the amended Warsaw Convention (WC) and the Montreal Convention (MC) and compare their contents for further study. They are appended to the Carriage by Air Act 1961 and can be found in I Carr and R Kidner, *Statutes and Conventions on International Trade Law* (2003). Many of their provisions are similar or identical but there are also a few distinct differences. We are not going into detail, but will set out a few basic principles.

The conventions apply to so-called international carriage, defined in Arts 1(2) (ie of both conventions). This is carriage between two different contracting States, whether or not there is a stop or transhipment in another state, or carriage with the place of departure and landing in the same contracting State, where there is an agreed stop in another State. The carrier must issue an air waybill or a cargo receipt (Arts 4 – 11), but if he does not do so, or if he misses out some of the particulars, no sanctions are attached. (Under the unamended Warsaw Convention of 1929, Art 9 the carrier who had not issued an air consignment note or included all the particulars as required by Art 8 could not avail himself of any limitation of liability.) The air waybill or the cargo receipt is prima facie evidence of the conclusion of the carriage contract, the acceptance of the cargo and the conditions of carriage stated therein. It is also a receipt relating to weight or number of packages and other information if the specific conditions are met (Arts 11).

Liability is automatically on the carrier for destruction, loss or damage to the cargo or for delay, if it took place whilst the goods were in the charge of the carrier unless he proves certain exceptions (Arts 18, 19). He can avail himself of limitations in respect of the financial limit (Arts 22) and also of a two-year limitation period (WC, Art 29 and MC, Art 35). On top of this the claimant is required to submit a written complaint forthwith after discovery of the damage, within 7 days from the date of receipt for a baggage claim, 14 days for a cargo claim and 21 days in case of delay (WC, Art 26 and MC, Art 31). Both conventions provide rules for successive carriage and combined carriage, but only the Montreal Convention deals with carriage by a person other than the contractual carrier (MC, Arts 39 – 46). The conventions set out rules with respect to jurisdiction (WC, Art 28 and MC, Art 33) and the Montreal Convention even makes express provision for written arbitration agreements (MC, Art 34). The parties cannot limit the liability of the carrier to below that of the provisions of the convention; such an agreement is null and void (WC, Art 23 and MC, Art 47) and mandatory provisions cannot be avoided (WC, Art 32 and MC, Art 49).

The air waybill is not a document of title, but this is not an issue as the nature of the goods transported and the speed of the carriage do not lend themselves to sale and resale during transit. However, the sale contract needs to be contemplated accordingly and even if the parties agree 'cif air München' or 'fob Paris airport' these terms need to be understood and adapted accordingly. Apart from these considerations the sale contract can take all kinds of variations similar to those used for sea transport.

4.3.2 Carriage of goods by road and rail

Even though Britain is an island, international conventions on the carriage of goods by road and rail are nevertheless increasing in importance due to the Channel Tunnel and 'Ro-Ro vessels'. Ro-Ro ships are designed for lorries, with their containers, to 'roll on and off' the vessel before and after the sea transit. Please read the stated conventions and acts alongside this very brief introduction. They can be found in a comprehensive international trade or commercial law statute book or on the internet, for example at http://www.jus.uio.no/lm/.

4.3.2.1 Carriage of goods by road

Carriage of goods by road is governed by the Convention on International Carriage of Goods by Road of 19 May 1956 (CMR). The CMR was incorporated into English law by the Carriage of Goods by Road Act 1965 and is contained in the Act's Schedule. The abbreviation CMR stems from its French name: 'Convention relative au contrat de transport des Merchandises par Route'.

The CMR applies to road carriage contracts against remuneration where the place of taking over the goods and the place of delivery are located in two different States, at least one of which is a contracting State (CMR, Art 1). The convention is, however, not applicable between the United Kingdom and the Republic of Ireland (see the protocol of signature). By virtue of Art 2 of the CMR the convention is also applicable where the vehicle carrying the goods is carried for part of the journey by rail, sea or inland waterways or air. However, to the extent that it is proved that any loss, damage or delay was caused by the other means of transport without any act or omission of the road carrier, the liability of the carrier by road is to be determined according to the convention governing the other means of transport. The road carrier's situation must not be worse than it would have been had the contract been concluded for only that particular part of the journey, based on that specific other liability scheme (CMR, Art 2). The carrier is liable for his own acts and omissions and also for those of any servants, agents or any other person whose services he uses in the performance of the carriage (CMR, Art 3).

The carrier has to make out a consignment note which confirms the contract of carriage. The consignment note must be made out in three copies and is to contain specified particulars (CMR, Arts 4 – 9). It is prima facie evidence of the carriage contract and its conditions as well as of the receipt of the goods (CMR, Art 9(1)). The sender providing information about the goods, weight, number of packages, marks, etc is liable for any inaccuracy in his statements (CMR, Arts 7 and 11(2)). The carrier must check the information provided as well as the apparent order and condition of the goods, including their packaging. If the consignment note is not claused with specific reservations by the carrier, it is presumed that the goods were in apparent good order and condition and that the marks and numbers correspond with the note (CMR, Arts 8 and 9(2)).

The carrier is liable for loss or damage to the goods or any delay whilst the goods are in his charge; however, several exceptions are set out in Art 17 of the CMR to alleviate this general liability of the carrier. These exceptions mostly have to be proved by the carrier (CMR, Art 18). The amount of compensation to be paid by the carrier as well as the upper limit of his liability is calculated in accordance with Art 23 of the CMR. In order to preserve his claim the consignee taking delivery has to check the goods and make reservations. In case of apparent loss or damage reservations have to be made on delivery, where the damage was not apparent they have to be made in writing within 7 days, and in case of delay within 21 days (CMR, Art 30). Article 31 of the CMR sets out rules for jurisdiction and procedural matters. The general limitation period for any action is one year, unless the longer three-year period applies in case of wilful misconduct (CMR, Art 32).

The liability with respect to successive carriers is dealt with in Arts 34 – 40 of the CMR. Where a carriage which is governed by a single contract is performed by successive road carriers, every carrier is party to the whole contract and is liable for the whole operation by reason of his acceptance of the goods and the consignment note (CMR, Art 34). Any derogation from the convention provisions is null and void (CMR, Art 41).

The consignment note is not a document of title. Road transport therefore does not lend itself to buying and selling of the goods in transit. However, road carriage has the advantage of enabling door-to-door service, based on one carriage contract. Thus, it is particularly useful for sale contracts concluded on ex works or delivery terms, whether the goods are delivered at the place of destination or at the frontier. For example the mode 'free on truck' (fot) is essentially an ex works contract, but additionally requiring the seller to load the goods on the carrying vehicle.

4.3.2.2 Carriage of goods by rail

International transport of goods by rail is governed by the International Convention concerning the Carriage of Goods by Rail (CIM: the abbreviation is derived from its French name 'Convention Internationale concernant le transport des Merchandises par chemin de fer'). The CIM was initially concluded in 1961 and remains in force although it is now an integral part of the Convention concerning the International Carriage of Goods by Rail (COTIF 1980) (COTIF 1980, Art 3). All the Member States to COTIF 1980 constitute the Intergovernmental Organisation for International Carriage by Rail called OTIF, which has as its principal aim to 'establish a uniform system of law applicable to the carriage of passengers, luggage and goods in international through traffic by rail between Member States, and to facilitate the application and development of this system' (COTIF 1980, Art 2). COTIF 1980 has since been amended by the Protocol of 20 December 1990. Further amendments will take place with the coming into force of the 1999 Protocol of Vilnius, which is a revised and updated version of COTIF 1980 and the CIM. The amended convention (COTIF 1999) will come into force once two-thirds of the existing Member States of OTIF have ratified the 1999 Protocol (see the 1999 Protocol, Art 4 and COTIF 1980, Art 20 § 2). As of September 2005 this had still not come into force.

COTIF 1980 (as amended by the 1990 Protocol) and thus the Uniform Rules concerning the Contract of International Carriage of Goods by Rail in Appendix B to COTIF 1980, have been given effect in the United Kingdom by virtue of the International Transport Conventions Act 1983.

The CIM 1980 is applicable to contracts of carriage by rail under a through consignment note which is made out for a route over the territories of at least two Member States using transport lines designated as international (see CIM 1980, Art 1). In general, the carrier is liable for all loss or damage arising while the goods are in his charge as well as for any delays. However he can avail himself of various exceptions (CIM 1980, Art 36 and burden of proof in Art 27) as well as an overall financial limit (see CIM 1980, Arts 40, 42 and 45). The limitation period is one year unless the two-year period is triggered by specified events as set out in Art 58 of the CIM 1980.

The transport document is a consignment note which is not a document of title. The terms of a sale contract providing for this transport method can vary depending on the choices of the parties and on the overall journey of the goods. For example 'free on rail' (for) is a contract providing essentially for ex works terms but additionally making the seller responsible for delivering the goods into the care of the railway carrier.

4.3.3 Multimodal transport

The legal problems are compounded by using multimodal transport or combined transport methods. In combined transport a freight forwarder, container operator or multi-modal transport operator concludes a single contract of carriage to ship the goods to their destination by using at least two or more different forms of transport. The transport operator takes on the full and sole responsibility towards the cargo owner for the goods for the whole transit. The contractual rights of the cargo owner depend solely on the single multimodal transport contract, despite the fact that the transport operator has subcontracted different stages to individual unimodal carriers.

Combined transport needs to be distinguished from 'through transport' where one unimodal carrier is responsible for his leg of the journey, but contracts the other stages only as agent for the cargo owner. Thus this carrier acts as principal while he carries the goods, but negotiates independent contracts on behalf of the cargo owner for the other stages. Thus each carrier is only responsible for his leg of the transport and the rights and responsibilities depend on the individual unimodal terms and conventions. In this case it becomes crucial for the exporter or importer to be able to determine during which leg of the transit the damage occurred. Only then can he successfully sue the responsible party.

Multimodal transport is particularly interesting due to containerisation of goods. Container trade has its own particular features, issues and sale contract terms, such as 'delivered at container depot' or 'free arrival station' (which should not be confused with free alongside ship, which has the same initials). Where the exporter intends to fill a whole container, 'full container load' (fcl), he may get a door-to-door container which is filled at his premises and unloaded at the business premises of the buyer. In case of a 'less than full container load' (lcl) the exporter will usually have to send the goods to the container freight station, where they are loaded.

Problems can arise with respect to the different legal rules governing the different legs of the transit, which are based on different liability schemes. For example under the Hague Rules and the Hague-Visby Rules the carrier is only liable if he acted negligently, whereas under the Warsaw Convention and the CIM or CMR liability is strict. In practice it may be difficult to discern and prove where during transit the damage occurred. In order to cope with these issues the UN Convention on International Multimodal Transport of Goods was adopted in Geneva on 24 May 1980. It expresses the principle of uniform liability of the transport operator in Art 16. The Convention enters into force twelve months after 30 States have ratified it. As of May 2005 the Convention had been raitified by only one-third of the required parties.

However the ICC (International Chamber of Commerce) and UNCTAD (United Nations Conference on Trade and Development) have developed the UNCTAD/ICC Rules for Multimodal Transport Documents (ICC No 481), which came into force on 1 January 1992. They are largely based on the UN Draft Convention and supersede the ICC Uniform Rules for a Combined Transport Document (ICC No 298). The UNCTAD/ICC Rules only apply if the parties incorporate them into their contract. Some of the form contracts used in practice provide for their application, for example the BIMCO Negotiable Multimodal Transport Bill of Lading (MULTIDOC 95) which you can find in the appendix to this book. Organisations such as FIATA, the International Federation of Freight Forwarders Associations (http://www.fiata.com/), also offer a variety of documents.

Bearing the above in mind please consult the BIMCO MULTIDOC 95 in the appendix to this book and read the UNCTAD/ICC Rules in your own time. You can purchase the latter from the International Chamber of Commerce or find them via the website of UNCTAD at www.unctad.org or directly at http://r0.unctad.org/ttl/docs-legal/nm-rules/UNCTAD-ICC%20Rules.pdf. They are also printed in the appendix to *Day & Griffin, The Law of International Trade*, (3rd edn, London: Butterworths, 2003).

4.4 Revision and further reading

4.4.1 Questions

This is your opportunity to revise what you have learned and to check whether you have understood the issues covered in this chapter. I suggest that you attempt to advise the parties in the scenarios below before you move on to the next chapter.

Question 1

S ships goods from England to France. Which legal rules apply to the carriage contract to define the rights and duties of the carrier?

Question 2

Does it matter whether a bill of lading has been issued for the goods in Question 1?

Question 3

Do the Hague-Visby Rules apply to shipment of goods from a port in Scotland to a port in England?

Question 4

The goods, shipped from England under bills of lading, are damaged in transit due to entry of seawater into the holds. The carrier claims they would not have been damaged had they been packaged properly.

(a) Is the carrier liable for the damage?

(b) The shipper claims that the vessel was not seaworthy. Does this make a difference? Who has the burden of proof?

(c) Other goods are also damaged due to a fire on board the vessel. Will the shipper's claim be successful in that regard?

(d) Another bill of lading states that a container containing 1,000 boxes are shipped. The goods are destroyed during the journey due to a fault of the carrier. The goods were very valuable. Are there any restrictions as to when and how much the cargo owner can claim?

(e) Has the carrier earned freight for each of the consignments shipped under the above bills of landing? Can he delay delivery of the goods until freight has been paid?

Question 5

On which bases can the cargo owner sue the carrier, if he has not shipped the goods himself?

Question 6

S wants to ship goods from various countries with carrier C. Both are keen to incorporate the Hague-Visby Rules into the contract of carriage. Knowing that the UK is a signatory to the Rules they therefore stipulate that English law shall govern the contract. Does this clause achieve their aim?

Question 7

Goods are shipped under a bill of lading from England to Egypt. They arrive damaged despite a clean bill of lading. Neither the cargo owner nor the carrier can prove the cause for the damage. Will the Hamburg Rules apply? Will the carrier be liable?

Question 8

Carrier C has arrived at the port of destination and has another shipment to load. Keen to get the goods of the previous journey unloaded, he wants to know whether he can deliver to Buyer B the goods of a consignment for which a non-negotiable bill of lading had been issued. B has not yet received the bill of lading due to delays in the document transfer but can validly prove his identity as the buyer identified in the bill. He even offers a letter of indemnity to the carrier. C asks you for advice and wants an explanation as to the validity and standing of such a letter of indemnity.

Question 9

S from England ships containerised goods with carrier C to Germany. C is to arrange through-transport to Austria. The goods are damaged in transit due to the carelessness of the train operator on the second leg of the journey. Who is responsible for the damage and according to which Rules?

Question 10

T has newly opened his business as multimodal transport operator. He seeks your advice as to which conventions are pertinent in the areas of carriage of goods by sea, air, road and rail and on multimodal transport. He also wants to know whether the UK has implemented the relevant conventions. He also wants you to explain and summarise the common features of the carriage of goods by sea, air, road and rail conventions.

4.4.2 Further reading

(a) *JI MacWilliam Co Inc v Mediterranean Shipping Co SA; (The Rafaela S)* [2003] EWCA Civ 556, CA affirmed by [2005] 2 WLR 554, HL concerning bill of lading — carriage of goods by sea — straight bill of lading — Hague Rules — Carriage of Goods by Sea Act 1971

(b) *Daewoo Heavy Industries Ltd v Klipriver Shipping Ltd (The Kapitan Petko Voivoda)* [2003] EWCA Civ 451, CA concerning bills of lading — breach of contract — charterparty — deck cargo — limit of liability — Hague Rules

(c) *Homburg Houtimport BV v Agrosin Private Ltd (The Starsin)* [2003] 2 WLR 711, HL concerning charterparty — bill of lading — negligent stowage of cargo — identity and liability of carrier — Himalaya clause — bailment

(d) *Hong Kong Fir Shipping Co Ltd v Kawasaki Kisen Kaisha Ltd* [1962] 2 QB 26, CA concerning charterparty — contract — frustration — seaworthiness

(e) Richard Williams, 'The developing law relating to deck cargo', [2005] 11.2 JIML 100–109

(f) Michael F Sturley, 'Solving the Scope-of-Application Puzzle: Contracts, Trades, and Documents in the UNCITRAL Transport Law Project', [2005] 11.1 JIML 22–41

(g) KF Haak and Maih Hoeks, 'Arrangements of intermodal transport in the field of conflicting conventions', [2004] 10.5 JIML 422–433

(h) Simon Baughen, 'Charterer's bills and shipowners' liabilities: a black hole for cargo claimants?' [2004] 10.3 JIML 248–253

(i) James Marissen, 'Is using a "straight" bill of lading still straightforward? The decision in *The Rafaela S*', [2004] 10.3 JIML 274–290

(j)   William Tetley, 'Interpretation and Construction of the Hague, Hague/Visby and Hamburg Rules', [2004] 10.1 JIML 30–70

(k)   Benjamin Parker, 'Liability for incorrectly clausing bills of lading', [2003] LMCLQ 201

(l)   Paul Todd, 'Representations in Bills of Lading', [2003] JBL 160–180

(m)   Caslav Pejovic, 'Delivery of goods without a bill of lading: revival of an old problem in the Far East', [2003] 9.5 JIML 448–460

(n)   Simon Baughen, 'Defining the Ambit of Article III r.8 of the Hague Rules: Obligations and Exceptions Clauses', [2003] 9.2 JIML 115–122

(o)   Stephen Girvin, 'Contracting Carriers, Himalaya Clauses and Tort in the House of Lords; *The Starsin*', [2003] LMCLQ 311

(p)   William Tetley, 'The Himalaya Clause — revisited', [2003] 9.1 JIML 40–64

(q)   Malcolm Clarke, 'Transport Documents: their transferability as documents of title; electronic documents', [2002] LMCLQ 356

(r)   Hugh Beale and Lowri Griffiths, 'Electronic commerce: formal requirements in commercial transactions' [2002] LMCLQ 467

(s)   Sze Ping-Fat, 'The Common Carrier's Strict Liability: a Concept or a Fallacy', [2002] JBL 235–249

(t)   Chinyere Ezeoke, 'Allocating onus of proof in sea cargo claims: the contest of conflicting principles' [2001] LMCLQ 261

(u)   Caslav Pejovic, 'Documents of title in carriage of goods by sea: present status and possible future directions', [2001] JBL 461–488

(v)   Malcolm Clarke, 'The transport of goods in Europe: patterns and problems of uniform law' [1999] LMCLQ 36–70

(w)   Charles Debattista, 'Carriage Conventions and their Interpretation in English Courts', [1997] JBL 130–142

(x)   Regina Asariotis, 'Implications of a "British" Jurisdiction Clause', [1992] JBL 321–325.

5 Marine Cargo Insurance

5.1 Introduction

Marine insurance is the oldest form of insurance; it was known in England in the fourteenth century. The first English statute was passed in 1601. Many of the principles developed for marine insurance are valid in insurance law in general. Marine insurance is insurance which provides cover against losses incurred by marine perils, typically to the ship, cargo or freight for which different covers are available. Marine insurance includes a variety of types to insure a variety of risks, for example: cargo insurance, hull and machinery insurance for the ship, mortgagee indemnity insurance, loss of hire insurance, port risk insurance, liability insurance for passengers, crew and merchandise etc. As we are looking at this subject from the international merchant's point of view we will concentrate on cargo insurance. Many of the general principles, however, are similarly valid for the other types of insurance.

Cargo insurance covers the physical damage or loss of the goods in transit. It is thus an important means of minimising some of the risks inherent in the international trade transaction. An exporter has an interest in the goods until he is paid, but also as long as the goods can still be rejected. Similarly, the importer should be aware of the passing of risk of damage and loss of the goods in the international sale contract. Any deterioration of the goods, once the risk has passed to him, is at his cost. One might argue that this would not be a problem as he may qualify for compensation by the carrier, however the liability of the carrier is often limited, either by international conventions or contract clauses (see **Chapter 4**). Even when the carrier is finally held to be liable, the carrier's financial standing might be uncertain, thus additional security in form of insurance is advisable. Depending on the terms chosen for the sale contract between the exporter and importer, insurance may have to be provided. For example, the exporter must insure the goods in order to comply with the obligations under a sale contract on cif or cip terms.

Marine cargo insurance can be effected not only for the sea voyage, but also for the other legs of the journey, thus making sure that the goods are covered at all times. Other types of cargo insurance are largely formed on the basis of the *marine* insurance cover. In general, they are mostly a matter of the individual contract rather than a widely spread and adopted system. Thus, in the following, we will concentrate on the marine cargo insurance to understand the basic principles, which also underlie other types of cargo insurance.

Marine insurance law has been standardised to a great level. In the UK it is governed by the Marine Insurance Act (MIA) 1906, which codified the case law that had developed over centuries of litigation on marine insurance issues. The Act was drafted by Sir Mackenzie Chalmers, who also drafted the Bills of Exchange Act 1882 and the Sale of Goods Act 1893. Appended to the 1906 Act, in its Schedule, is the former standard form policy, known as the 'Lloyd's SG Policy' (ship and goods policy) which nowadays has been replaced by the 'Lloyd's Marine Policy' and the 'Institute Cargo Clauses'.

Marine cargo insurance can be taken out either with Lloyd's underwriters or with marine insurance companies. Steeped in tradition, insurance with Lloyd's can only be effected via a Lloyd's broker, who has access to the Lloyd's facilities, whereas an insurance company can be contacted directly. To form a liaison between the Lloyd's underwriters and insurance companies, to create standard form clauses for all insurers, and to discuss and report on marine insurance developments to its members, the Institute of London Underwriters was established. Amongst other services, it has developed the new Lloyd's Marine Policy and Companies Marine Policy as well as the Institute Cargo Clauses, setting out the policy and standard terms for insurance contracts, introduced on 1 January 1982. The Institute Cargo Clauses are contractual by nature and have to be incorporated if the parties wish to apply them. They have proven to be very popular and are used almost universally. The Companies Marine Policy and the Institute Cargo Clauses can be found in Indira Carr and Richard Kidner *Statutes and Conventions on International Trade* (4th edn, London: Cavendish, 2003), together with the Lloyd's Marine Policy in the appendices of Susan Hodges, *Cases & Materials on Marine Insurance Law* (London: Cavendish, 1999).

The cargo insurance taken out by a merchant will be dependent on the details agreed in the policy and the terms of the cover, usually a particular set of Institute Cargo Clauses. The above mentioned Marine Policies are both subject to the exclusive jurisdiction of the English courts and the Institute Cargo Clauses provide for English law and practice to be applied (Institute Cargo Clauses, clause 19). Thus, governing law will be English law, ie the Marine Insurance Act 1906 and common law. However, other insurance policies and clauses exist which may provide for the law and jurisdiction of a different country to be applied in such an event. In the following, we are concerned with the English perspective.

Figure 5.1 illustrates the legal basis for a marine insurance contract under English Law. The contract details are set out by the policy and any terms describing the extent of cover, such as a particular set of Institute Cargo Clauses. The legal framework for the whole is provided by the Marine Insurance Act 1906 and common law.

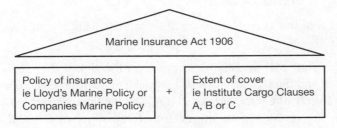

Fig 5.1 The marine insurance contract and the legal requirements

It is thus highly recommended that you now read at least the headings of the Marine Insurance Act 1906 and of the Institute Cargo Clauses, to develop a basic idea. However, you should definitely read each section of the Act or clause of the Cargo Clauses as soon as it is mentioned in the following text. This will enable you to find your way through the primary sources without necessarily having to resort to a textbook in the future.

5.2 Making the insurance contract

5.2.1 Assured – insurer – broker relationship

The contract of insurance is made between the insurer and the assured, who is called the proposer whilst he is seeking insurance and before the contract is effected. The proposer in our example is the international merchant, either the exporter or the importer, depending on the requirements set out in the sale contract. The insurance policy or certificate forms part of the transport documents. If no particular cover is agreed, the merchant must insure the goods against risks customarily covered in the particular trade, concerning the relevant type of goods and their envisaged voyage. However, where the sale contract is based on Incoterms 2000, he need only provide minimum cover. Very different levels of cover exist. A merchant relying on another to take out suitable insurance should therefore give detailed instructions to ensure his needs are met.

Usually the merchant (the proposer) will use a broker to effect the insurance. The broker, even though paid by the insurer, acts as agent for the assured. The proposer informs the broker of all relevant details regarding the adventure he wants to insure. The broker makes a memorandum of the cover sought, called the 'slip'. This slip is then presented to underwriters who, if they are prepared to take the risk, initial the slip together with the proportion they intend to cover. The broker takes the slip to different underwriters until the whole risk is covered. Presentation of the slip to an underwriter constitutes the offer, the initialling by the underwriter, which is called 'writing a line', is the acceptance of the insurance offer. The contract is now complete between the parties, on the terms set out in the slip. The broker will now prepare the policy and take it to the insurer's office, in the case of a Lloyd's policy to the Lloyd's Policy Signing Office, to get it checked, signed and sealed on behalf of the underwriters. Sections 22–31 of the MIA 1906 cover the legal requirements regarding the policy and set out that the policy must contain:

(a) the name of the assured or the person effecting insurance on his behalf (s 23(1));

(b) the signature by or on behalf of the insurer (s 24(1)); and

(c) sufficient details of the subject matter, in order for it to be designated with reasonable certainty (s 26(1)).

The policy should state identical terms to those on the slip. If there is a discrepancy between the policy and the slip, the latter will prevail (per Scrutton LJ in *Symington & Co v Union Insurance Society of Canton Ltd (No 2)*, CA). The binding contract between the parties is made on the terms and to the extent of the slip (see *General Reinsurance Corporation v Forsakringsaktiebolaget Fennia Patria*, CA). However, a marine insurance contract is only admissible evidence once embodied in a policy adhering to the legal requirements of the Act (MIA 1906, s 22). Only once a policy has been issued can the slip be used as admissible evidence to prove the terms of the contract (MIA 1906, s 89).

The broker normally sends a 'cover note' to the assured, letting him know that cover has been arranged, stating the agreed terms. This is prudent business practice but not a legal obligation on the broker (*United Mills Agencies Ltd v RE Harvey, Bray & Co*, KBD). Depending on the nature of the particular insurance contract, the cover note takes a specific form. A 'closed cover note' is sent if all details are finalised as to cargo and shipment, the insurance being definite. An 'open cover note' is used if further instructions are necessary regarding the cargo, voyage or value shipped under the insurance. The latter usually occurs where the assured took out a 'floating policy' or an 'open cover', both designed to insure not just a single voyage, but several shipments, which might not all be substantiated yet.

A broker's cover note is merely an advice between the broker and the assured that cover has been obtained. It cannot take the place of the insurance document required by the sale contract. Where the assured exporter sends this cover note to the importer, the importer can reject it and insist on a policy. The importer is not required to accept a certificate of insurance issued by a broker or the assured. The certificate entitles the holder to demand the issue of the policy and to claim under the insurance. However unless the parties have agreed otherwise or trade usage suggests differently, such a certificate will not suffice (as discussed at **2.5.4.2** above). Nor will a letter of insurance given by the assured exporter to the importer, confirming that insurance has been effected, be sufficient.

Payment of the premium and issue of the policy are concurrent conditions (MIA 1906, s 52). Invariably, policies contain a recital of payment, acknowledging payment of the premium. Such acknowledgement is conclusive evidence between the insurer and the assured; however this is not the case as between the insurer and the broker (MIA 1906, s 54). The broker himself is directly responsible to the insurer for the premium (MIA 1906, s 53(1)). The broker in turn has a lien on the policy against the assured for the premium and his charges (MIA 1906, s 53(2)). The broker is thus an important intermediary in the conclusion of the insurance contract and the payment of the premium, having defined duties and responsibilities towards both parties. However, where the insurer has to make payment to the assured, the insurer is directly responsible to the assured, who is his contracting party (MIA 1906, s 53(1)), and not to the broker.

5.2.2 Insurable interest

The contract of marine insurance is a contract of indemnity (MIA 1906, s 1). The assured is to be put in the position he would be in without the loss or damage. Under no circumstances is he to receive more than he lost. Thus, a valid insurance contract can only be concluded if the assured has an insurable interest. Otherwise the contract is void (MIA 1906, s 4). It must not be the case that the assured has an interest in the failure of the adventure. The Marine Insurance (Gambling Policies) Act 1909 even makes gambling on marine adventures a criminal offence. However, some genuine commercial interests are not always recognised as an insurable interest by law. Thus, insurers may agree to insure goods without proof of insurable interest under a so-called 'honour policy' or 'ppi' (policy proof of interest). These policies do not carry any legal obligation under the MIA 1906

(MIA 1906, s 4(2)) or any other statute, thus are not enforceable and are entirely dependent on the honour of the insurer.

Insurable interest had been defined in the House of Lords decision of *Lucena v Craufurd*, 100 years before being substantially incorporated into s 5 of the MIA 1906. The concept of insurable interest is fairly wide and is fulfilled if the person insuring property will suffer some form of loss as a result of its damage, loss or destruction. The interest must be in the insured goods themselves and does not cover the interest of a shareholder in the company owning the goods (see *Macaura v Northern Assurance*, HL). Looking at the issue from a merchant's perspective, a person has an insurable interest in each of the following events.

(a) He has property in the goods. According to s 14(3) of the MIA 1906 the owner of goods has an insurable interest.

(b) He is in possession or has a right to immediate possession of the goods. For example, a bailee or carrier entrusted with the goods for which he is liable to the cargo owner for any damage or loss. However, he must hold the excess of his interest for the owner of the goods (*Hepburn v A Tomlinson (Hauliers) Ltd*, HL). The buyer having possession of the goods also has an insurable interest.

(c) He bears the risk of loss or damage to the goods. A cif or fob buyer has an insurable interest as from shipment of the goods (MIA 1906, s 7(2)), even if the goods are unascertained (MIA 1906, s 8; see also *John Gillanders Inglis v William Ravenhill Stock*, HL and *Leigh and Sillivan Ltd v Aliakmon Shipping Co Ltd (The Aliakmon)*, HL). The buyer has an interest in the profits which he would have made on a resale had the goods arrived undamaged.

(d) He has a contingent interest or defeasible interest in the goods (MIA 1906, s 7). The unpaid seller for example has a contingent interest, because he might exercise his right of stoppage in transit. Even a fob seller or c & f seller has a contingent interest in the goods during transit. The seller also has a defeasible interest until such time as the buyer has lost his right to reject the goods.

(e) He made payment or a contribution towards the adventure. A buyer having prepaid some of the or the entire purchase price has an interest with regard to the paid amount. The master or any member of the crew has an insurable interest in respect of his wages (MIA 1906, s 11) and a person advancing the freight with regard to this amount, unless it is repayable in case of loss (MIA 1906, s 12). According to s 13 of the MIA 1906 the assured has an insurable interest with respect to the insurance charges.

In summary, a seller has an insurable interest particularly as owner, risk bearer or as unpaid seller for any security rights. A buyer has an insurable interest once he takes possession or becomes the owner of the goods, when risk passes or if he made advance payment. The insurable interest does not have to be with the assured at the time the contract is made, but at least at the time of the loss (MIA 1906, s 6(1)). The latter requirement is abrogated if the goods are insured on a 'lost or not lost' basis.

5.2.3 Assignment of policy

The insurance is not automatically passed on together with the assignment of the insured subject matter (MIA 1906, s 15). It has to be assigned specifically according to ss 50 and

51 of the MIA 1906. Usually this is done by indorsement and delivery of the policy (see MIA 1906, s 50(3)). The insurer does not have to consent to the assignment; unless the insurance policy contains express terms to the contrary it is assignable (MIA 1906, s 50(1)). The assignee can only assign the rights he had vested in him at the time of the assignment; he must have an insurable interest in the policy at the time (MIA 1906, s 51). However, the policy can be assigned after the loss took place (MIA 1906, ss 50 (1) and 51). Once assigned, the assignee can sue in his own name and to the full value of the insurance, irrespective of how much he paid for the goods. The insurer, in turn, is entitled to make all defences that would have been available against the original assured (MIA 1906, s 50(2)). Thus the assignee's claim will fail where the assignor had lost his insurable interest before assignment took place, for example where the assured buyer rejects the goods finally before he assigns the policy to the seller (MIA 1906, s 51). Where the assured had breached one of his duties whilst negotiating the insurance contract, the insurer can successfully avoid the policy even as against the assignee (MIA 1906, ss 17–20, 50(2)).

Thus, in an international sale contract it is particularly important that the parties agree not just on the transfer of the goods, but also on the assignment of the insurance policy covering the goods in transit. This is normally implied in a cif contract, as tender of the insurance policy is part of the obligations under these terms, but might have to be stated expressly if the sale contract is concluded on other terms. If the buyer of the goods has become the assignee of the policy and he rejects the goods on arrival, he needs to have agreed to reassign the policy to the seller before he loses his insurable interest by a final rejection of the goods (MIA 1906, s 51). Otherwise the seller can no longer claim under the insurance he initially took out.

5.2.4 General insurance principles

English contract law, subject to some exceptions, has no general duty of utmost good faith (*Walford v Miles*, HL). However insurance law provides such an exception. Marine insurance contracts, like other insurance contracts, are based on utmost good faith (uberrimae fidei) (MIA 1906, s 17) which includes:

(a) the duty to disclose all material facts (MIA 1906, ss 18, 19); and

(b) the duty not to make any misrepresentations (MIA 1906, s 20).

The duties to disclose all material facts as well as not to make any misrepresentations apply pre-contractually and are designed to give the insurer all the information which is material for his choice of whether to accept the risk and for which premium. The duty to observe utmost good faith (MIA 1906, s 17), however, is wider and applies to both parties of the insurance contract, mainly before the contract is made, but also to a lesser extent after conclusion of the contract.

In certain circumstances the duty of utmost good faith, ie to disclose all material facts and not to make any misrepresentation, applies or recurs post-contractually when a contract of insurance can be renewed, but also where the insurance contract provides for the inclusion of a particular risk or variation on information provided by the assured. One such example is under a 'held covered clause' which requires the assured to inform the insurer of a certain fact, for example the change of destination of the ship. The insurer will then insure the additional journey against a premium and on conditions to be arranged (for an example see clause 10 of the Institute Cargo Clauses). The aim of these duties is then to act in utmost good faith with respect to the additional cover sought.

The remedy for breach of the duty of utmost good faith is avoidance of the contract. However in order for the insurer to avoid the contract, the breach of the assured must concern a fact which is material to the insurer. It must have induced the insurer into the making of the contract even if it was not a decisive element (see *Pan Atlantic Insurance Co Ltd v Pine Top Insurance Co Ltd*, HL).

The duty to observe utmost good faith is without prejudice to other common law or statutory remedies which may be relevant, for example under the Misrepresentation Act 1967 or the common law duty not to make fraudulent claims.

After this general introduction let us look at the individual issues in more detail. We shall start with the general duty to observe utmost good faith before looking at the subcategories of disclosure and of making correct representations. Thereafter we shall look at the consequences of a breach of these duties.

Figure 5.2 gives a brief overview of the fundamental insurance principles and when they are applicable.

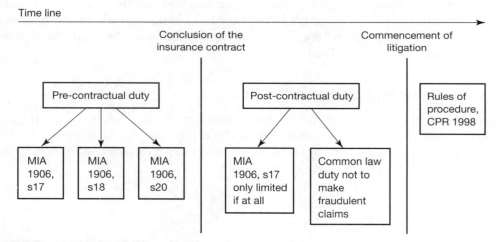

Fig 5.2 The fundamental insurance principles

5.2.4.1 Utmost good faith

The relationship between the parties to the marine insurance contract is based on utmost good faith (MIA 1906, s 17; see also *Greenhill v Federal Insurance Co*, CA). Where this duty is not observed by either party, the other party may avoid the contract (MIA 1906, s 17), providing that the misrepresented or undisclosed matter is material. The obligation to observe utmost good faith is mainly a pre-contractual duty which must be observed before the conclusion of the contract, but also applies post-contractually in limited circumstances and to a lesser degree. For example, concealment of material facts known to the proposer before the contract is effected will lead to the insurer avoiding the policy.

However the assured does not have to disclose every piece of information obtained after the contract was made (see *Niger Co Ltd v Guardian Assurance Co Ltd*, CA, affirmed by HL), nor does he need to disclose every piece of information he receives after having made an honest claim (see *Manifest Shipping Co Ltd v Uni-Polaris Insurance Co Ltd (The Star Sea)*, HL). The scope of the post-contractual duty seems to be limited to circumstances of repudiatory breach or fraudulent intent (see *The Star Sea* and *K/S Merc-Scandia XXXXII v Certain Lloyd's Underwriters (The Mercandian Continent)*, CA). However, once litigation commences the procedural rules as provided under the Civil Procedure Rules 1998 govern the extent of disclosure, and s 17 of the MIA 1906 is no longer relevant (*The Star Sea*).

5.2.4.2 Post-contractual duty to observe utmost good faith versus common law duty not to make fraudulent claims

Where a fraudulent claim was made against the insurance contract, insurers have pleaded a breach of the post-contractual duty of utmost good faith. If this was accepted it would enable the insurer to avoid the contract ab initio, which is a very severe sanction. However it seems that courts are reluctant to accept this argument and are more inclined to apply the common law rule on fraudulent claims (see *Agapitos v Agnew (The Aegeon) (No 1)*). Where a fraudulent claim is made or where an honest claim is maintained by using a fraudulent device or a claim knowingly exaggerated by the insured, the insured forfeits the claim and the insurer is discharged (*Agapitos v Agnew* and *Eagle Star Insurance Co Ltd v Games Video Co (GVC) SA (The Game Boy)*, QBD (Comm)). The forfeiture covers all of the claim, any genuine parts as well as the one known to be untrue or exaggerated. Thus the existence of a genuine loss suffered by the assured is irrelevant; the insurer is discharged due to the fraudulent action. However the common law rule is not given retrospective effect on prior and separate claims which have already been settled under the same policy before any fraud occurred (see *Axa General Insurance Ltd v Clara Gottlieb and Joseph Meyer Gottlieb*, CA)

The common law rule, like the duty of utmost good faith, does not extend to the making of a fraudulent claim during litigation (*Agapitos v Agnew*). As soon as litigation commences the procedural rules prevail.

There are some important differences between the fraud rule of common law and the duty to observe utmost good faith as in s 17 of the MIA 1906. The sanction of s 17 of the MIA requires materiality of the fraudulent misrepresentation or undisclosed matter (see also *K/S Merc-Scandia XXXXII v Certain Lloyd's Underwriters (The Mercandian Continent)*, CA), whereas under the fraud rule there is no such requirement (*Agapitos v Agnew*). The consequences also differ: the fraudulent behaviour in making a claim only discharges the insurer, but does not give the right to avoid the contract ab initio (see *Agapitos v Agnew*).

5.2.4.3 Disclosure

The proposer must disclose to the insurer every material fact he knows or should know of. In case this is not observed the insurer may avoid the contract in accordance with s 18(1) of the MIA 1906. Every circumstance is material that is likely to influence the insurer's decision on whether to insure the risk or at what price (MIA 1906, s 18(2)). Certain information, however, does not need to be disclosed, particularly where the fact reduces the risk of the insurer, or where the insurer is presumed to know the circumstance (MIA 1906, s 18(3)).

What is material and whether the knowledge would have influenced a prudent insurer to act differently, must be tested at the time of placing the risk and not in hindsight. Where the proposer is the subject of allegations or investigations, he must disclose these facts. Where this undisclosed information would have been material and relevant for the insurer in deciding whether and on what terms to insure the risk, the insurer was held to be able to avoid the contract (*Brotherton v Aseguradora Colseguros SA (No 2)*, CA). However where the insurer aimed at avoiding the policy at a time when it was clear that the undisclosed allegations were untrue, the insurer was prevented from doing so by his duty of utmost good faith (see *Drake Insurance Plc v Provident Insurance Plc*, CA)

To what extent must an exporter of goods describe the nature of the cargo? The subject-matter must be designated with reasonable certainty (MIA 1906, s 26) and must clearly relate to the goods in question, otherwise they are not insured (*Mackenzie v Whitworth*, CA). The description of goods as 'clocks' was held not to be sufficient to disclose the fact that the goods shipped included Rolex watches and other high value brand watches (*WISE Underwriting Agency Ltd v Grupo Nacional Provincial SA*, QBD (Comm)). If the goods shipped are ordinary and lawful cargo, no specific details besides the general description are necessary. However, if in doubt, it is best to state further particulars to be on the safe side. On the other hand, the proposer must disclose if goods are of an unusual and particularly dangerous kind.

Where circumstances regarding the cargo are disclosed, which would put an ordinary careful insurer on inquiry, the insurer is treated as having waived further information according to s 18(3)(c) of the MIA 1906 where he fails to inquire (see *WISE v Grupo* and, on the issue of waiver, refer to *Container Transport International Inc v Oceanus Mutual Underwriting Association (Bermuda) Ltd (No 1)*, CA). Cover for deck cargo must be arranged specifically unless there is a usage in the particular trade to carry those goods on deck (see MIA 1906, Sched 1, r 17 and *British and Foreign Marine Insurance Co v Gaunt*, HL).

This duty of disclosure cannot be avoided by employing an agent (MIA 1906, s 19). In such a case, it is the disclosure by the agent towards the insurer that counts, not the one between assured and agent. The agent has to disclose every material circumstance known to him or which he is deemed to know. As agent he is deemed to know all facts which in the ordinary course of his business he ought to know or which ought to have been communicated to him. However, an insurer cannot avoid a contract just because a material circumstance known to the assured was not disclosed, if the assured's knowledge came too late to communicate it to the agent (MIA 1906, s 19(b)).

5.2.4.4 Representations

According to s 20 of the MIA 1906, every material representation made by the proposer or his agent during negotiations must be true. Otherwise, the insurer may avoid the contract. A representation is material if it would influence the judgment of a prudent insurer in fixing the premium or in deciding whether to insure the risk (MIA 1906, s 20(2)). Representations can be made as to a matter of fact or a belief or expectation. In the latter case, the representation must be made in good faith (MIA 1906, s 20(5)) whereas matters of fact must be substantially correct (MIA 1906, s 20(4)). The duty to make true representations concerns the time before the conclusion of the contract. Any representation can be withdrawn or corrected before the contract is finally made (MIA 1906, s 20 (6)).

Under 'held covered clauses', however, innocent discrepancies in the description of the goods are not sanctioned by the consequences of misrepresentation or the lack of disclosure. A held covered clause is sometimes inserted into the insurance contract to allow such innocent discrepancies. The latter must be caused by an innocent misdescription or mistake by the assured. Once the assured discovers the discrepancy he must give prompt notice to the insurer who, depending on the circumstances, is entitled to charge an additional premium. Without the clause, any material misdescription in the goods — regardless of its reason — allows the insurer to avoid the contract. Held covered clauses are also used to allow for changes in destination, an example of which is clause 10 of the Institute Cargo Clauses A, B, and C. However the assured must give prompt notice of the change to the insurer. The conditions and premium are then fixed accordingly.

5.2.4.5 Consequences of breach

The breach of utmost good faith, the failure to disclose or the misrepresentation must concern a fact that is material in order to allow the insurer to avoid the contract. The insurer must show that the non-disclosure or misrepresentation induced him into entering into the contract on the agreed terms. However, it need not have been a decisive influence (see *Pan Atlantic Insurance Co Ltd v Pine Top Insurance Co Ltd*, HL and *Marc Rich & Co AG v Portman*, QBD (Comm) affirmed by CA). What is material and whether the knowledge would have influenced a prudent insurer to act differently must be tested at the time of placing the risk and not in hindsight (*Brotherton v Aseguradora Colseguros SA (No 2)*, CA).

Once there is a breach of one of the above obligations, the other party can elect whether to affirm or to avoid the contract. It is irrelevant whether the party in breach acted fraudulently, negligently or innocently. The aggrieved party can avoid the contract until it has affirmed it or is deemed to have affirmed it. In order to affirm, the party needs to fulfil the following criteria:

(a) it needs to have full actual knowledge of the facts;

(b) it needs to know that the non-disclosure or misrepresentation creates the right to avoid;

(c) it needs to have had reasonable time in which to decide on the cause of action; and

(d) it must have communicated unequivocally to the other party either by words or conduct that it made an informed choice to affirm the contract.

If after a reasonable time after acquiring full knowledge the insurer has not taken any action, he is deemed to have affirmed the contract (see *Liberian Insurance Agency v Mosse*, QBD). Where an insurance contract has been cancelled at a time when the insurer knew that it had a right to avoid the contract on the basis of non-disclosure, this cancellation can amount to an affirmation of the contract (*WISE Underwriting Agency Ltd v Grupo Nacional Provincial SA*, CA).

Where the aggrieved party chooses to avoid the contract, it is void ab initio. Unless the breach was fraudulent or illegal on behalf of the assured or his agent, the premium has to be returned to the assured (MIA 1906, s 84).

5.3 Kinds of insurance cover

5.3.1 Types of policies

5.3.1.1 Valued and unvalued policies

According to s 27(1) of the MIA 1906, a policy can be either valued or unvalued. A valued policy specifies the agreed value of the subject matter (MIA 1906, s 27(2)), whereas an unvalued policy only states the upper limit and leaves the insurable value to be subsequently ascertained (MIA 1906, s 28). In the latter case the insurable value will be the prime cost of the subject matter insured plus expenses of and incidental to shipping plus any insurance charges upon the whole (MIA 1906, s 16(3)). It should be noted that the buyer's anticipated profits are not included.

On the other hand, under a valued policy these anticipated profits are usually included in the value declared. A certain percentage (for example about 10–15%) is added to the invoice value of the goods including any shipping and insurance charges. The amount fixed in the policy will be conclusive evidence between the assured and the insurer as to the insurable value, unless the assured acted fraudulently (MIA 1906, s 27(3)). The valued policy is the norm in export practice. Where it transpires that the insured value under an ordinary policy is too low, for example if the market is rising, the assured can take out a so-called 'increased value' policy to cater for this difference.

Whether a marine policy is a valued or an unvalued policy depends on the actual words used. Where the words 'sum insured' were used without any indication as to valuation, they denoted an unvalued insurance. This was the guidance given in ss 27 and 28 of the MIA 1906 (see *Thor Navigation Inc v Ingosstrakh Insurance Co Ltd*, QBD (Comm)).

5.3.1.2 Voyage, time and mixed policies

Section 25 of the MIA 1906 states that a policy is:

(a) a *voyage policy*, if it insures the subject matter from one place to another, thus for a particular journey;

(b) a *time policy*, if it covers the subject matter for a definite period of time; and

(c) a *mixed policy*, if both aspects are included, ie the journey and the duration.

A time policy often contains a 'continuation clause' to cater for a prolonged journey, as long as the assured notifies the insurer.

5.3.1.3 Floating policy, open cover and blanket policy

Floating policy

According to s 29 of the MIA 1906 a floating policy describes the general terms and leaves the name of the ship or ships and other particulars to a subsequent declaration. These particulars are usually unknown to the assured at the time when the floating policy is effected. The floating policy is a single policy, usually for a limited period, covering all shipments falling within its scope. As long as the assured declares all consignments promptly, all the shipments made under a floating policy are insured. It has an overall value, from which each declared consignment value is deducted until the policy is exhausted. The floating policy is thus an aggregation of voyage policies.

To stop the assured from only declaring shipments which have incurred losses, certain conditions have to be fulfilled:

(a) the assured must declare all consignments falling within the insurance cover provided;

(b) all these declarations must be made in order of dispatch or shipment and as soon as possible after shipment. However, an omission or erroneous declaration can be corrected provided it is made in good faith (MIA 1906, s 29(3));

(c) where the value has not been declared until after notice of loss or arrival, the policy is treated as unvalued for the particular declaration (MIA 1906, s 29(4)).

Open cover
Where more flexibility is sought, the parties can arrange an open cover. This is not a policy, but a document by which the insurer undertakes to issue policies, including floating policies, from time to time within the terms of the cover. Declarations of each shipment must be made and the cover is written off accordingly. Thus, the open cover is very similar to the floating policy. However, a floating policy is usually for 12 months whereas an open cover can be either for a limited period of time or permanent. Also, under a floating policy the assured actually holds a policy, whereas under an open cover the assured does not receive one, but is entitled to demand a policy if required.

Blanket policy
In case the assured prefers not having to declare each single consignment, he can take out a blanket policy. Here, for a lump sum and over a period of time, all shipments falling within the terms are insured. Thus, no consignment is uninsured due to forgetfulness or other reasons.

All the forms discussed at **5.3.1.3** have in common that the assured seller will not be able to tender a specific insurance policy for the goods sold to his buyer, as all policies/covers relate to multiple shipments. The seller, therefore, needs to make sure that the buyer agrees in the sale contract on the tender of an insurance certificate or different insurance document which the seller is able to obtain.

5.3.2 Warranties

Warranties in marine insurance law are important terms which govern the contractual relationship between the parties. There are promissory warranties, covered in ss 33–41 of the MIA 1906, denoting a condition to be fulfilled by the assured, and exceptive warranties (nowadays called exclusions). Under the latter category, the insurer is excepted from liability if the indicated circumstances are fulfilled; for an example of this see the exclusions in Clauses 4–7 of the Institute Cargo Clauses A, B and C (they are discussed at **5.3.3** below within the extent of cover).

According to s 33(1) of the MIA 1906 a promissory warranty is 'a warranty by which the assured undertakes that some particular thing shall or shall not be done, or that some condition shall be fulfilled, or whereby he affirms or negatives the existence of a particular state of facts.' These warranties can be express or implied (MIA 1906, s 33(2)). A warranty in marine insurance law is not comparable with a warranty in ordinary contract law; rather it is comparable to a condition. If a promissory warranty in marine insurance law is not fulfilled or if it is breached, the insurer is discharged from liability from the date of the breach of warranty. However, any liability incurred before the breach is not prejudiced (MIA 1906, s 33(3)). For this sanction to apply it is not necessary that the breach was material to the risk (MIA 1906, s 33(3)); a causal link between breach and loss is irrelevant. According to the House of Lords, the fulfilment of the promissory warranty is a condition precedent to the liability of the insurer (*Bank of Nova Scotia v Hellenic Mutual War Risks Association (Bermuda) Ltd (The Good Luck)*, HL). It is easy to see why warranties have such a strong standing: they contribute to determining the risk which the underwriter had agreed to cover. Once the cover is agreed, it would not be helpful to open debate between the parties in every case on whether the breach of a warranty had increased the risk or caused the damage or not.

According to s 34(3) of the MIA 1906 the insurer has the option to waive the breach. Where it chooses to do so, the insurer remains bound by the contract.

The parties to a marine insurance contract can expressly incorporate any legally valid warranty into their policy or expressly alter the warranties implied by the MIA (MIA 1906, s 35), which are:

(a) warranty of seaworthiness (MIA 1906, s 39);

(b) warranty of cargoworthiness (MIA 1906, s 40(2)); and

(c) warranty of legality (MIA 1906, s 41).

In order to ascertain which warranty is implied by the MIA 1906, we need to discern what kind of policy has been agreed. Under a voyage policy there is an implied warranty that the ship is seaworthy (MIA 1906, s 39(1)) and cargoworthy (MIA 1906, s 40(2)) at the beginning of the voyage. Under a time policy, on the other hand, there are no such implied warranties. However, where, with privity of the assured, the ship is sent to sea in an unseaworthy state, the insurer is not liable for any loss or damage caused by the unseaworthiness (MIA 1906, s 39(5)).

Where a specific warranty is included into the insurance contract, a warranty has to be construed practically, so that it bears commercial sense. It has to be interpreted by looking at the meaning of the words and considering the rationale behind them (*Brownsville Holdings Ltd v Adamjee Insurance Co Ltd (The Milasan)*, QBD (Comm) and *Eagle Star Insurance Co Ltd v Games Video Co (GVC) SA (The Game Boy)*, QBD (Comm)).

5.3.3 Extent of cover

Once the type of policy has been discerned, the extent of the cover provided needs to be decided upon, also taking into account any exclusions. As we have seen, the Institute Cargo Clauses developed by the Institute of London Underwriters have received great support and are widely used, together with the Lloyd's Marine Policy (used by Lloyd's Underwriters) or the Companies Marine Policy (used by insurance companies which are members of the Institute of London Underwriters) developed by the Institute. Both the policy and the cargo clauses were introduced on 1 January 1982.

Unlike the old Lloyd's SG Policy appended to the MIA 1906, the Lloyd's Marine Policy (and also the Companies Marine Policy) does not contain the terms of the insurance. It only forms a schedule into which certain information needs to be inserted, usually the policy number, the name of the assured, details as to the vessel, voyage, cargo, agreed value (if any), duration of cover, amount insured and premium. Clauses and endorsements, special conditions and warranties are agreed as inserted or attached. The extent of the cover provided is thus determined by which sets of clauses are chosen.

There are the Institute Cargo Clauses A, B, and C, covering the cargo against certain groups of risks typical for the journey, as well as the Institute Strike Clauses and the Institute War Clauses. These last two need to be taken out specifically if the risks based on strike or war are to be insured. The Institute Cargo Clauses A, B and C provide insurance cover to different extents. Clauses A are an 'all risks' cover, whereas Clauses B and C only insure against the specified risks stated, with Clauses C providing only minimum cover. Please take the time to read the Clauses. You can find them together with the Companies Marine Policy in I Carr and R Kidner, *Statutes and Conventions on International Trade Law,* 2003).

The typical scope of cover is as follows.

(a) One of the Institute Cargo Clauses A, B or C is selected.

(b) These all include a 'warehouse to warehouse' or 'transit' provision, clause 8. Thus the goods are covered during the whole of the journey and not just whilst at sea. By virtue of clause 8.1 the cover commences once 'the goods leave the warehouse or place of storage at the place named herein for the commencement of the transit' and thus does not include pre-transit storage. However, where an individually agreed clause has been inserted, extending the cover to the time of delivery and storage before the commencement of the transit, this clause will take precedence over the incorporated Institute Cargo Clauses with the effect that the insurer has to indemnify the assured for loss or damage incurred during this stage (see *Eurodale Manufacturing Ltd v Ecclesiastical Insurance Office Plc*, CA).

How long does the cover last? We need to distinguish two separate categories on the basis of the overall transport intended for the goods (see *Bayview Motors Ltd v Mitsui Marine & Fire Insurance Co Ltd*, CA). Where the goods are only transported to the final destination named in the policy without further transport being contemplated after arrival, clause 8.1.1 specifies that transit ends when the goods are delivered to the consignee or final warehouse. Where goods are temporarily stored in a transit shed after arrival at the interim destination for which the policy has been obtained, in readiness to re-embark on another onward journey, cover does not end there, but extends for a limited period of 60 days from discharge of the ship until the goods commence the onward transport (see Institute Cargo Clauses, clause 8.1.3 and 8.2).

Transit also ends where the goods are delivered to a warehouse or place of storage, where the assured elects to store the goods other than in the ordinary course of transit or for allocation and distribution (Institute Cargo Clauses, clause 8.1.2). Any of the above events will stop transit, whichever occurs first.

(c) All Institute Cargo Clauses cover possible deviation of the ship, any transhipment or any variation of the adventure resulting from a liberty of the carrier under the contract of carriage (see Institute Cargo Clauses, clause 8.3).

(d) All Institute Cargo Clauses have the same exclusions, which are listed in clauses 4, 5, 6 and 7. In addition, unless the policy provides otherwise, the sections of the MIA 1906 are applicable. So the insurer can avail himself of s 55(2) of the MIA 1906, which excludes liability for any loss attributable to wilful misconduct of the assured, delay, and ordinary wear and tear, ordinary leakage and breakage, inherent vice or loss proximately caused by rats and vermin. However, where the agreed Institute Cargo Clauses vary the provisions of the MIA 1906, the contractually agreed clauses will prevail.

(e) Clause 16, the 'duty of the assured clause', imposes a duty on the assured to undertake all reasonable acts to minimise the loss as does s 78(3), (4) of the MIA 1906. However, under clause 16 the assured will be reimbursed, which is not foreseen in the MIA 1906.

(f) If necessary, additional cover is available in the form of the Institute War Clauses (Cargo) and Institute Strikes Clauses (Cargo) for example. Otherwise, cover for these risks is specifically excluded by clauses 6 and 7 of the Institute Cargo Clauses.

We will briefly discuss some of the exclusion clauses because they are important. Clause 4 is the general exclusion clause. Clause 4.1 mirrors s 55(2)(a) of the MIA 1906 and excludes any loss which is 'attributable to the wilful misconduct of the assured'. Clause 4.2 excludes 'ordinary leakage' and 'ordinary wear and tear'. This refers to ordinary transit losses due to the nature of the goods or the way they are handled during transit. 'Insufficiency or unsuitability of packing', including stowage in a container or liftvan prior to the start date of the insurance, is excluded by clause 4.3 and 'damage caused by inherent vice or nature of the subject matter insured' by clause 4.4.

Whether the packaging is sufficient is a question of fact, measured against the standards and practices in industry. The packaging has to enable the cargo to withstand the normal conditions of the voyage (see *FW Berk & Co Ltd v Style*, QBD). Goods, insufficiently packaged, can also fall within the inherent vice category (see also *Berk v Style*). Damage caused by inherent vice only means that it was caused by the natural tendencies of the goods, without the intervention of any chance external element (see *Soya GmbH Mainz KG v White*, HL). Thus, no special abnormal weakness is necessary; the goods' normal and ordinary tendency to self-degenerate is enough.

Institute Cargo Clauses A do not exclude 'deliberate damage or deliberate destruction of the subject matter' by a person's wrongdoing; however Clauses B and C do, by means of their clause 4.7. All clauses exclude damage attributable to the unseaworthiness of the vessel in their clause 5, but only where the assured was privy to the unseaworthiness. Thus, in the case of a voyage policy, clause 5 contractually changes the effect which s 39 of the MIA 1906 would otherwise have. Privity means that the assured has either positive knowledge of the unseaworthiness or 'blind-eye-knowledge', which means that the assured is ignoring the true state of the ship (see *Manifest Shipping Co Ltd v Uni-Polaris Insurance Co Ltd (The Star Sea)*, CA and QBD).

5.3.4 General average

The law of general average is set out in s 66 of the MIA 1906. The idea of general average is based on the interests involved in a marine adventure. These are usually:

(a) the interest in the ship by the shipowner;

(b) the interest in the freight by the carrier; and

(c) the interest in the cargo by the cargo owner or person bearing the risk of loss or damage to the goods.

Sometimes, an extraordinary sacrifice has to be made affecting one or more of these interests, or an extraordinary expenditure has to be incurred, in order to rescue the property of all parties involved in the common adventure. For example, if the ship has encountered an extreme storm, got damaged and therefore risks running aground, it might be better to damage the cargo on board voluntarily in an attempt to repair the ship and thus save the remainder of all three interests. By entering a port of refuge and warehousing the goods while the vessel is repaired, costs incurred reasonably are likely to be general average expenditure.

General average is defined in s 66(1), (2) of the MIA 1906 as:

(a) an extraordinary sacrifice or expenditure

(b) directly caused by or as a direct consequence of

(c) a voluntary act

(d) reasonably made or incurred

(e) in time of peril

(f) for the purpose of preserving the property endangered by the peril.

Because these sacrifices and expenditures are made in the interest and for the benefit of all parties to the common adventure, the cost or damage is shared between the owners of all interests. This is called adjusting the general average. This adjustment is done either in accordance with the law at the port of destination or the last port if the journey has been broken up beforehand. Where the parties have included rules into their contract stating how to adjust the general average, then these rules will prevail.

The International Law Association has developed standard rules to create some form of uniformity. These rules are known as the York-Antwerp Rules. The current Rules are the 1994 Rules; however, the 1974 Rules may also still be relevant, particularly in adjusting older contracts. The York-Antwerp Rules do not enjoy the force of law and so they need to be incorporated into the contract of carriage if the parties wish to apply them. Professional general average adjusters can be appointed to give their impartial and independent service in the matter.

It is important to distinguish the different contractual relationships that are affected by the law of general average:

(a) the contract of carriage of the goods (see MIA 1906, s 66(3)); and

(b) the insurance contract (see MIA 1906, s 66 (4), (5)).

The interests between the parties to the marine adventure/the carriage contract have to be adjusted. However, the assured will be covered by his insurance for his contribution to the general average sacrifice or expenditure caused by an insured peril (MIA 1906, s 66(5)). In addition, he will recover the damage to the subject matter according to his insurance contract, irrespective of any general average contributions owed by the other parties to the adventure (MIA 1906, s 66(4)). Once the assured has been indemnified, the insurer is subrogated to these general average contributions and can claim them itself (MIA 1906, s 79(1); see **5.4.6** below). However, the liability of the insurer only goes as far as the general average loss or expenditure was caused in connection with the avoidance of an insured peril (MIA 1906, s 66(6)); any other peril will not suffice.

5.4 The insurance claim

5.4.1 Liability and causation

According to s 55(1) of the MIA 1906 the insurer is not liable for every possible damage or loss. The loss must be proximately caused by a peril which was insured. Thus, the particular risk must be covered by the specific policy that was taken out. As the cover is mostly determined by the incorporation of a set of Institute Cargo Clauses, the perils causing the damage must be covered in the chosen clauses. Only under the 'all risks cover' of the Institute Cargo Clauses A is the assured relieved from proving this point. Also, the peril must not be specifically excluded, either by specific arrangement under the policy, under clauses 4–7 of the Institute Cargo Clauses, or by s 55(2) of the MIA 1906.

The proximate cause test is used unless the parties have agreed a different standard. In Institute Cargo Clauses B and C, under clause 1.1, the risk is determined in a different way. Instead of using the test of causation, the damage must only be 'reasonably attributable' to the risks specified under clause 1.1. However, for risks under clause 1.2 and under Institute Cargo Clauses A for all risks, the proximate cause test will have to be applied. This can be a difficult task, if the damage had been caused by a number of events, some of which were insured and others not.

The House of Lords defined the meaning of 'proximate cause' in *Leyland Shipping Co Ltd v Norwich Union Fire Insurance Society Ltd*, HL. In this case a ship was insured against perils of the sea, but damage or loss due to hostilities was excluded. The ship was torpedoed. She was taken to the nearby harbour and moored alongside the quay. However a gale came up causing the vessel to range and bump against the quay. It was feared that the vessel would sink and block the quay. She was thus ordered to leave and either to be beached or to be anchored in the outer harbour. On anchorage there was much motion by wind and waves. The front of the vessel was down and hit the ground on a very low tide. However, the rest of the vessel was afloat causing great strain to which the vessel finally gave way and became a total loss. The question was whether the loss was caused by the hostilities as argued by the insurers, or by the perils of the sea as contended by the assured. The House of Lords confirmed the decision of the Court of Appeal that the loss had been proximately cased by the torpedo. It was held that the train of causation from the act of hostility to the loss was unbroken. The ship had never been out of immediate danger since the torpedo had struck. There had been no new intervening cause of loss. The test of proximity was not solved by looking at the order of time, but by what was proximate in effectiveness. Causation was not a chain but a net. 'At each point influences, forces, events, precedent and simultaneous, meet, and the radiation from each point extends infinitely. At the point where these various influences meet it is for the judgment as upon a matter of fact to declare which of the causes thus joined at the point of effect was the proximate and which was the remote cause' (as per Lord Shaw at [1918] AC 350, 369).

Thus, what is proximately caused has to be determined by using common sense standards, looking at which cause was effective to what extent (for further examples see *Reischer v Borwick*, CA and *JJ Lloyd Instruments Ltd v Star Insurance Co Ltd (The Miss Jay Jay)*, CA). It is not necessary that the insured peril was the immediate cause. However, if one of two dominant causes is explicitly excluded, the insurer does not have to pay.

5.4.2 Burden of proof

The assured must prove that the loss or damage suffered falls within a risk which is covered by the effected insurance policy. In case of a broad risk, such as the 'perils of the sea', the cause needs to be narrowed down with some degree of particularity (see *Rhesa Shipping Co SA v Edmunds (The Popi M)*, HL). The assured must also prove that the subject matter had been undamaged at the outset. Thereafter, the burden of proof shifts to the insurer to show that the risk is not in fact covered or has actually been excluded. Below is a short checklist to illustrate the relevant questions to be answered and proven by the different parties.

5.4.2.1 Check list/burden of proof

Claimant/assured/assignee has to show and prove:

(a) position of the claimant:
   (i)   assured or assignee;
   (ii)   insurable interest;

(b) insurance cover:
   (i)   what kind of policy: voyage, time, etc?
   (ii)   duration of cover;
   (iii) was the actual risk insured?

(c) Proximately caused by insured peril (MIA 1906, s 55) or reasonably attributable to risk insured under clause 1.1 of the Institute Cargo Clauses B and C

Defendant/insurer has to show and prove:

(a) breach of utmost good faith which is material;

(b) lack of compliance with promissory warranty;

(c) relevant exclusion clauses.

5.4.3 Total and partial loss

Different actions are necessary and the measure of indemnity has to be determined differently depending on whether the loss is total or partial (see MIA 1906, ss 56–63). For example, a partial loss has occurred if either some of the loaded cargo is washed overboard and lost whereas the remainder of the cargo arrives safely, or if all of the cargo arrives but slightly damaged.

Where the cargo arrives, but is no longer identifiable as a commercial product due to severe deterioration, this is a total loss. A total loss can be either an actual or constructive total loss (MIA 1906, ss 56(2), 57, 58 and 60). Actual total loss means that all the cargo is either destroyed, irretrievably lost or it has lost its commercial identity (MIA 1906, s 57(1)). Thus, the assured has no choice but to claim for the whole loss.

In case of a constructive total loss, the assured has two options (MIA 1906, s 61). He might choose to repair the subject matter and claim for partial loss, or he may abandon the subject matter and claim for a total loss. Section 60(2) of the MIA 1906 gives specific examples for a constructive total loss:

(a) where the assured is deprived of the possession of his ship or goods and it is unlikely that he can recover the insured subject matter or its retrieval is uneconomic;

(b) where the ship is so badly damaged by an insured peril that the costs of repairing would exceed her value when repaired; or

(c) where the goods are so badly damaged that their repair and forwarding to the destination would exceed their value on arrival.

If the assured does not notify the insurer of his decision to abandon the subject matter with reasonable diligence, he can only claim for a partial loss (MIA 1906, s 62), unless the notice was unnecessary in accordance with s 62(7) of the MIA 1906 (see *Kastor Navigation Co Ltd v Axa Global Risks (UK) Ltd (The Kastor Too)*, CA). Once notice of abandonment has been given and the insurer has accepted it, the insurer has the right to take over the subject matter and property passes to the insurer.

5.4.4 Measure of indemnity

In order to determine the measure of indemnity (MIA 1906, ss 67–78) one has to differentiate between a valued and unvalued policy and a total and partial loss. Section 68 of the MIA 1906 provides that in a case of total loss the measure of indemnity is the sum fixed in a valued policy and the insurable value of the subject matter in the case of an unvalued policy. In a case of partial loss, the amount of indemnity is apportioned according to the rules set out in s 71 of the MIA 1906. The partial loss for goods that arrive damaged is determined as follows: the proportion of the difference between the wholesale price of the goods had they arrived undamaged, and the wholesale price of the damaged goods is identified. Then the sum fixed under a valued policy, or the insurable value under an unvalued policy, is reduced by this proportion. The result is the amount the assured can claim.

5.4.5 Double insurance and underinsurance

In a case where the subject matter is insured under more than one policy and the sums insured would exceed the indemnity allowed by the MIA 1906, the assured is over-insured by double insurance (MIA 1906, s 32(1)). This has the effect that the assured is not entitled to receive more than the indemnity allowed under the Act. Should he receive more, he is deemed to hold such excess in trust for the insurers. The assured can choose from which insurer he wishes to claim how much of the indemnity until the limit is reached (MIA 1906, s 32(2)). The insurers between themselves have to contribute rateably to the amount (MIA 1906, s 80).

If the assured has not insured the whole value of the subject matter, he is only entitled to indemnity with regard to the proportion of the value that was insured. With regard to the rest, he is deemed to be his own insurer (MIA 1906, s 81).

5.4.6 Subrogation

For the same loss or damage, the assured will often not just have a claim against the insurer, but also a claim against another person, for example the carrier of the goods in transit or the owner of the other ship that collided with the insured ship etc. The assured, however, must not take advantage of the damaging event and claim twice. The party which is finally bearing the loss has the right to compensation from the person having caused the loss. If the insurer pays the assured, it is the former who can claim against the third party. In case the assured has already been compensated by the third party, the insurer can claim any money received from the assured. Thus, once and in so far as the insurer has indemnified the assured, the former becomes subrogated to all rights and remedies of the assured in respect of the insured subject matter (MIA 1906, s 79).

The insurer can claim in his own name, but only within the limits of the rights that the assured had vested in himself, and to the extent that the insurer has indemnified the assured. The latter hurdle can be overcome by the assured assigning all his right against the third party to the insurer, so that the insurer can recover the full amount of any claim.

In a case of total loss, the insurer also becomes entitled to take over the interest of the assured in the remainder, for example the damaged goods or the ship wreck. This means the insurer becomes the owner of the damaged subject matter and therefore can retain any benefits, from salvage for example. In case of a partial loss, the ownership stays with the assured and thus the right to any proceeds from the damaged property.

5.5 Revision and further reading

5.5.1 Questions

This is your opportunity to revise what you have learned and to check whether you have understood the issues covered in this chapter. I suggest that you attempt to answer the following questions before you move on to the next chapter.

Question 1

Buyer B insures the goods purchased on fob terms for the transit against all risks. After inspection on arrival he rejects the goods for breach of condition.

(a) Has he had an insurable interest and if so for how long? Has he lost his insurable interest or can he still assign his policy to the seller?

(b) The seller also insured the goods for transit. When and for how long has he got an insurable interest? Did it matter that risk had passed on shipment to the buyer?

Question 2

Seller S ships the contracted goods on a vessel which is unseaworthy. He insures the goods under the Lloyd's Marine Policy and Institute Cargo Clauses C.

(a) Is this insurance cover sufficient so that the seller can fulfil his obligations under a cif sale contract with buyer B? Does it matter whether the cif contract is based on Incoterms 2000 or not?

(b) With respect to the assured–insurer relationship, does it matter whether S knew of the unseaworthiness of the vessel before he concluded the insurance contract?

(c) S assigns the policy to buyer B. B wants to claim under the insurance policy for damage to the cargo due to entry of seawater in the course of a very severe storm. What defences against the claim may the insurer wish to plead?

Question 3

The goods shipped and insured as above are explosives.

(a) Does it matter whether this fact is communicated to the insurer?

(b) A fire breaks out on board ship. The explosive goods are thrown overboard. Does the insurer have to pay for this? Does general average have a role to play?

Question 4

Insurance policy as in Question 2. The goods are damaged by the overturning of the lorry that is to bring the goods to the port.

(a) Is this damage covered although it occurred before shipment?

(b) The goods are no longer usable for the initial purpose, but can be retreated to become a different product. Can the assured claim for any damage? If so, on what basis?

(c) Half of the goods are totally damaged and useless. What is the measure of indemnity the assured can claim?

Question 5

The seller obtains insurance cover under the Companies Marine Policy of the Institute of London Underwriters, on Institute Cargo Clauses B and ships the goods from England to China. He did not disclose that he was accused of fraud in respect of another cargo claim; however he knows that he is innocent. Only part of the goods arrives as some have been lost overboard on loading and discharge from the vessel.

(a) Buyer B from China, having been assigned the policy, wants to sue the insurer in his home country. Which country's courts would have jurisdiction to hear the case and which law is applicable?

(b) After the fraud claim has been settled and the seller has been found innocent, can the insurer avoid the policy on the basis of lack of disclosure?

(c) If the insurer cannot avoid the policy, will B be indemnified? Was the particular risk insured?

(d) If the insurer were to pay, can it sue the carrier for the loss? If so, on which basis?

5.5.2 Further reading

(a) *Manifest Shipping Co Ltd v Uni-Polaris Insurance Co Ltd (The Star Sea)* [1995] 1 Lloyd's Rep 651, QBD Commercial Court, concerning utmost good faith — seaworthiness; see also [1997] 1 Lloyd's Rep 360, CA; [2001] 2 WLR 170, HL

(b) *Kyzuna Investments Ltd v Ocean Marine Mutual Insurance Association (Europe)* [2000] 1 Lloyd's Rep 505 concerning marine insurance — valued or unvalued policy

(c) *Colonia Versicherung AG v Amoco Oil Co* [1997] 1 Lloyd's Rep 261, CA, concerning assignment of policy and subrogation

(d) *Cepheus Shipping Corporation v Guardian Royal Exchange Assurance plc* (The Capricorn) [1995] 1 Lloyd's Rep 622 concerning marine insurance — subject matter of policy — insurable interest

(e) *Pan Atlantic Insurance Co Ltd v Pine Top Insurance Co Ltd* [1994] 2 Lloyd's Rep 427 concerning marine insurance — duty of disclosure and consequences of breach — misrepresentation

(f) *TM Noten BV v Paul Charles Harding* [1990] 2 Lloyd's Rep 283, CA concerning marine insurance — exception for loss and damage — inherent vice exclusion

(g) *Canada Rice Mills Ltd v Union Marine & General Insurance Co Ltd* [1941] AC 55 concerning marine insurance — insured peril — proximate cause

(h) André Naidoo and David Oughton, 'The Confused Post-Formation Duty of Good Faith in Insurance Law: From Refinement to Fragmentation to Elimination?', [2005] JBL 346–371

(i) Tania McDonald, 'The insurable interest of international buyers on cif terms', [2004] 10.5 JIML 413–421

(j) Andrew Longmore, 'Good faith and breach of warranty: are we moving forwards or backwards?' [2004] LMCLQ 158–171

(k) Tania McDonald, 'The marine insurance contract and assignment under the English Marine Insurance Act 1906', [2003] 9.2 JIML 123–136

(l) Peter MacDonald Eggers, 'Remedies for the failure to observe the utmost good faith', [2003] LMCLQ 249–278

(m) Malcolm Clarke, 'Wisdom after the event: the duty to mitigate insured loss' [2003] LMCLQ 525–543

(n) Baris Soyer, 'Defences available to a marine insurer', [2002] LMCLQ 199–213

(o) HY Yeo, 'Post-Contractual Good Faith — Change in Judicial Attitude?' [2003] 66.3 MLR 425–440

(p) Anthony George, 'The new Institute Cargo Clauses' [1986] LMCLQ 438–456

(q) Donald R O'May, 'The new Marine Policy and Institute Clauses' [1985] LMCLQ 191–200

6
International Dispute Resolution

6.1 General

As we have seen in the previous chapters above (and see **1.4** above in particular), international trade by its very nature involves contracts and transactions with an international element. The parties to a contract within the international trade ambit may be situated in different legal systems or the contract may otherwise point to another country. For example, the international element can be the fact that the contracted goods between two salesmen situated in one country are delivered to a place in another country, that the goods are being carried between the ports of different countries, that the banks involved in a letter of credit agreement are situated in different countries or that the foreign assured took out insurance with Lloyd's in London. Each contract within the international trade transaction has to be examined individually.

If the parties to a contract get into a dispute about their respective rights and duties, for example if one party alleges a breach of contract by the other, or if one party repudiates the contract but the other party wants to continue with it, the first issue must be to determine the applicable law. Once the relevant legal system is identified, this law needs to be applied to solve the dispute. The facts of the case need to be established as they then form the basis for ascertaining the respective rights and duties of the parties.

However, in order to identify the applicable law, we need to be aware that the law of different countries may take different approaches. Each country has its own rules of private international law, also called conflict of law rules, to determine which law is applicable. Some countries have harmonised this approach by becoming party to pertinent conventions. Thus, which law will be identified as the applicable law depends on the country that is deciding on the matter and on the rules which this country applies in the process. For example, if an English court has to decide which laws to apply to an international scenario it will use English conflict rules, whereas a court in Spain will use Spanish conflict rules. If these countries were party to the same convention on the applicable law (in the example above, the Rome Convention on the Law Applicable to Contractual Obligations (1980)), one would hope that the outcomes found by both courts were the same; if this is not the case very different outcomes are possible. Even where the countries have ratified the same convention, there are other possible areas of discrepancy. The courts of the different con-tracting States may interpret the crucial Articles of the convention in a different way, thus possibly leading to different outcomes. In addition, before applying the relevant interna-tional convention the court needs to determine which convention might be applicable. In order to do so the court needs to categorise the issue in dispute. It does so by using its rules of private international law and the categorisation approach taken by any pertinent conventions, eg to determine whether the issue in dispute is a matter of contract or tort. The outcome will usually depend on the rules of law applicable in the forum state. Only where the matter is classed as a contractual issue will the court apply the relevant conven-tion to identify the applicable law to the contract, which in the UK is the Rome Convention on the Law Applicable to Contractual Obligations (1980).

Therefore it makes sense to ask first in which forum the case will be heard. The applicable law will be determined by using the private international law rules of this forum. Thus, we must first determine which country's court has jurisdiction to try the case, unless the courts have no jurisdiction at all. Where the parties have a valid arbitration agreement, this will prevail and the correct arbitration tribunal must be consulted.

The order in which to ask the relevant questions is set out at Fig 6.1 below.

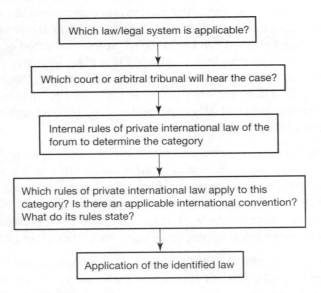

Fig 6.1 Identification of the applicable law

Whilst considering which countries' courts have jurisdiction, a claimant must also address the issue of enforcement of a judgment. The judgment is only as valuable to the claimant as the enforcement prospects in the country where the defendant's assets are situated. Where the courts of several countries are likely to assume jurisdiction, the claimant should choose the courts of the country which will apply a law favourable to him (this process of selection is called forum shopping), but which will also enable recognition and enforce-ment in the State where the defendant has his assets. Another consideration might be the length of time it takes in different countries to obtain a judgment and/or the time for enforcement. It could also be important to know whether interlocutory remedies are available to secure the claimant's interests. Where time is of the essence, for example where the defendant is likely to become bankrupt, it might be advantageous to file the claim with the courts of the country where the assets are situated. This can ensure speedy enforcement and might allow for a freezing injunction or other provisional remedies.

Therefore any case with international scope will involve three main questions before individual rights and duties can be assessed and enforced.

(a) Which country's courts will have jurisdiction to try the case or is there a valid arbitration agreement?

(b) Which law will be applied to solve the dispute?

(c) Is the judgment or arbitral award enforceable in the relevant country?

The fewest problems arise where the parties have agreed on choice of law and jurisdiction clauses. The courts generally uphold such clauses if they are validly incorporated into the contract. It cannot be stressed enough how important these clauses are. Only when the parties know which legal system governs their relationship will they be able to determine their respective rights and duties. Thus together choice of law and jurisdiction clauses serve two important purposes: first by providing the parties with certainty as to their respective rights and duties, therefore avoiding conflict; and secondly, where a dispute cannot be avoided, by providing the legal framework in which to decide the matter. Proceedings to determine the jurisdiction and applicable law can often be more costly and time extensive than the dispute as to the substance, ie with respect to the parties' rights and duties under the pertinent law. Clarity in this respect thus saves resources.

We shall start by looking at the topic of jurisdiction.

6.2 Jurisdiction and enforcement of judgments

6.2.1 General

The court must have jurisdiction in law to hear and decide a case. Different jurisdictional rules apply whether the action is based on a claim against a person (jurisdiction *in personam*) or on a right that should be respected by people generally, such as ownership of property (jurisdiction *in rem*). In the latter case the action is directed against an item of property, a thing (*res*), for example a ship, or cargo, or any immovable property. From the point of view of an export transaction, both areas of jurisdiction are important; the jurisdiction *in personam* is relevant for all matters of contract, but an action *in rem* may at times be useful to secure the position of the claimant (for example the arrest of cargo or the ship), to protect his property rights or to obtain security.

The court uses its conflict of law rules to determine the question of 'international jurisdiction'. Where the State in which the court is situated is party to a jurisdiction convention or a bilateral jurisdiction agreement, the rules of this instrument will prevail where and in so far as they are applicable. If no international agreements are pertinent, the conflict rules inherent to the particular legal system are applied, which in England are the common law rules, subject to statutory alterations. Usually different international agreements and national rules govern the different subject areas. For example civil and commercial matters will have different jurisdiction rules from matrimonial matters or matters of parental responsibility.

The order in which to ask the relevant questions to determine jurisdiction is set out at Fig 6.2 below.

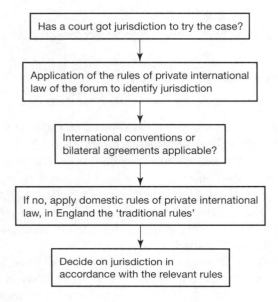

Fig 6.2 *Identifying jurisdiction*

We will now examine the position in England in relation to international trade, which is the subject area of 'civil and commercial matters'. The United Kingdom has ratified two important conventions on the jurisdiction and enforcement of judgments in civil and commercial matters: the Brussels Convention 1968 (BC) and the Lugano Convention 1988 (LC). Both have been given the force of law in the United Kingdom by virtue of the Civil Jurisdiction and Judgments Act 1982. In addition, as a Member State of the European Union (EU), the United Kingdom is bound by Council Regulation 44/2001/EC since it came into force in 2002. Apart from these 'European instruments' the 'traditional rules' of private international law govern the subject: these are provided by common law and legislation (see mainly Parts 6 and 74 of the Civil Procedure Rules (CPR) 1998).

Before applying the rules of a convention or international agreement, the exact scope of its application must be examined. Only if the scenario falls within its scope can the instrument be used to determine the jurisdiction. However where and in so far as either of the above-mentioned European instruments applies, it takes priority over the traditional rules (see Fig 6.3). Only if none of them are applicable or if their provisions direct the use of the traditional rules (for example Art 4 of Regulation 44/2001/EC) can the latter be consulted. We shall therefore consider the European rules first.

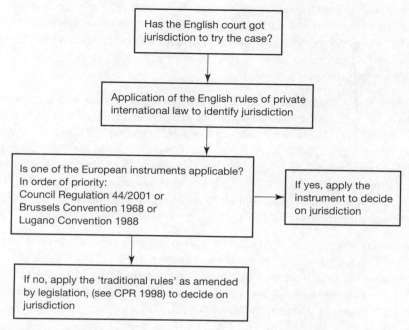

Fig 6.3 Identifying jurisdiction in England

6.2.2 The European rules in overview

As we have seen, there are three European instruments which are potentially applicable. Where pertinent, Council Regulation 44/2001/EC has priority over the Brussels Convention 1968. The Lugano Convention 1988 is a parallel convention to the Brussels Convention 1968. The rules are mostly identical, but they cover the relationship between different States.

(a) Council Regulation 44/2001/EC has been in force since 1 March 2002. It replaces the Brussels Convention of 27 September 1968 on the Jurisdiction and Enforcement of Judgments in Civil and Commercial Matters between all the Member States of the European Union except Denmark. Denmark opted out from taking part in this scheme. As a Council Regulation, it is directly effective in the Member States and thus enforceable in the United Kingdom without the need for any implementing legislation. However, in order to provide the necessary framework for Reg 44/2001 in the UK, the Civil Jurisdiction and Judgments Order 2001 (SI 2001/3929) was drafted.

Since the enlargement of the European Union on 1 May 2004 the Member States are Austria, Belgium, Cyprus, the Czech Republic, Denmark, Estonia, Finland, France, Germany, Greece, Hungary, Ireland, Italy, Latvia, Lithuania, Luxembourg, Malta, the Netherlands, Poland, Portugal, Slovakia, Slovenia, Spain, Sweden and the United Kingdom. In the nomenclature of Reg 44/2001, Member States include all of the above-mentioned, with the exception of Denmark as it has opted out (Reg 44/2001, Art 1(3)).

Regulation 44/2001 can be found in a relevant statute book or it can be accessed on 'Europa', the official information server of the EU at http://www.europa.eu.int. Information on the subject can be found on the site for judicial co-operation in civil matters within the

European Union at http://www.europa.eu.int/scadplus/leg/en/s22003.htm. The text of the consolidated version of the original text of Reg 44/2001 including any amendments (mainly due to the enlargement process) can be found by searching the Eur-Lex website for consolidated legislation or can be accessed directly at http://europa.eu.int/eur-lex/en/consleg /pdf/2001/en_2001R0044_do_001.pdf .

(b) The Brussels Convention of 27 September 1968 on the Jurisdiction and Enforcement of Judgments in Civil and Commercial Matters is applicable in legal proceedings instituted before 1 March 2002 between the then EU Member States (pre-2004 accession, which are Austria, Belgium, Denmark, Finland, France, Germany, Greece, Ireland, Italy, Luxembourg, the Netherlands, Portugal, Spain, Sweden, United Kingdom) and after this date for matters between Denmark and those 14 EU Member States. The Brussels Convention 1968 (BC) has been given legislative effect in the United Kingdom and enacted as Schedule I to the Civil Jurisdiction and Judgments Act (CJJA) 1982 (see CJJA1982, s 2).

(c) The Lugano Convention of 16 April 1988 on the Jurisdiction and Enforcement of Judgments in Civil and Commercial Matters now applies between those 14 EU Member States, Poland and the remaining EFTA (European Free Trade Association) States which have not acceded to the European Union, namely Iceland, Norway and Switzerland, but not Liechtenstein. The implementation in the United Kingdom of the Lugano Convention has been effected as Schedule 3C to the CJJA 1982 (see CJJA 1982, s 3A).

The Brussels Convention and the Lugano Convention are very similar to each other. Many of their provisions are substantially the same. As a result the EFTA Member States to the Lugano Convention have agreed to observe the rulings of the European Court of Justice in the interpretation of the Brussels Convention in relation to these provisions. Also Reg 44 is based on the provisions of the Brussels Convention, but makes some considerable changes to some of them. Please read the Brussels and Lugano Conventions alongside the following brief explanation of Reg 44/2001, to become aware of the many features they share in common, but also of their differences. The full text of the conventions can be found in a comprehensive conflict of laws statute book or on the web, for example at the site of the Court of Justice for the Brussels and Lugano Conventions http://www.curia.eu.int/common/ recdoc/convention /en/. Their status can be reviewed by accessing the sites of the depositories: for the Brussels Convention, the Council of the European Union (http://ue.eu.int/ cms3_fo/index.htm) at http://ue.eu.int/cms3_fo/showPage.asp?id=252&lang =en&mode=g; and for the Lugano Convention, the Swiss Federal Council at http://www.eda.admin.ch/eda/ e/home/foreign/ intagr.html. However, the Foreign and Commonwealth Office also provides some status information (in English) at http://www.fco.gov.uk/Files/kfile/statusbrussels,0.pdf.

We will now turn to a short discussion of Reg 44/2001, making some references to the Brussels Convention.

6.2.3 Jurisdiction under Council Regulation 44/2001/EC

6.2.3.1 General
Questions of interpretation of this fundamental statute on jurisdiction for the EU Member States are referred to the European Court of Justice (ECJ) under the Preliminary Rulings

Procedure of Art 234 (ex Art 177) EC (ie of the Treaty establishing the European Community as amended). The ECJ also has jurisdiction to interpret the Brussels Convention 1968 (see CJJA 1982, Sch 2, giving effect to the 1971 Protocol to the Brussels Convention), but not the Lugano Convention. This means that the Member States to Reg 44/2001 and the Brussels Convention must follow the precedents set by the ECJ, which in turn leads to a more harmonious approach in interpretation. In this context please note that the terminology in Reg 44/2001 is interpreted according to its European meaning and not according to a national interpretation of the same word. Except for provisions of Reg 44/2001 which have been materially altered, the interpretation by the ECJ of the Brussels Convention remains authoritative.

Regulation 44/2001 only confers jurisdiction on the courts of the Member States, one of which is the United Kingdom (not England). Thus, if according to Reg 44/2001 jurisdiction is assigned to a court within the United Kingdom, the case still needs to be allocated internally between the courts of England and Wales, Scotland and Northern Ireland. This is done in accordance with Sch 4 to the CJJA 1982, as amended by Sch 2 to the Civil Jurisdiction and Judgments Order 2001.

The following basic principles are pertinent to both Reg 44/2001 and the Brussels Convention.

(a) Rules restricting the right of the defendant to defend the claim in the courts of his country of domicile are interpreted restrictively.

(b) A restrictive interpretation is given to rules of non-recognition of judgments of other Member States.

(c) It is assumed that the courts of each Member State are equally competent.

6.2.3.2 Scope: civil and commercial matters

For a good understanding of the topic it is essential that you read the full text of Reg 44 and the Convention Articles as soon as they are referred to below.

The scope of Reg 44/2001 as set out in Art 1 of Reg 44/2001 covers civil and commercial matters, for example contractual issues between trading partners. This is irrespective of the nature of the court or tribunal involved. The scope of Reg 44/2001 does not extend to revenue, customs or administrative matters. Certain areas are also specifically excluded in Art 1(2) (a–d) of Reg 44/2001. The exclusion of most interest to us is arbitration in Art 1(2)(d). Thus, it does not interfere with existing international conventions on arbitration.

Once a claim falls within the ambit of Reg 44/2001 and an English court has jurisdiction in accordance with Reg 44/2001, it does not matter whether the defendant is domiciled in England (UK) or in another Member State. The claimant can serve process without needing the permission necessary under the traditional English rules.

Difficulties with the scope of Reg 44/2001 arise where the courts are asked to rule on the validity of an arbitration agreement. The question whether a dispute falls within the scope of Reg 44/2001 or not, must be decided solely by reference to the subject matter of the dispute. If it is arbitration it is outside the scope of Reg 44/2001 (Reg 44/2001, Art 1(2)(d)). For example where the courts are asked to appoint an arbitrator, with or without having to deal with the preliminary issue of the validity of the arbitration agreement, the dispute is outside the scope of Reg 44/2001 and the Brussels Convention 1968 (see *Case C-190/89 Marc Rich & Co AG v Societa Italiana Impianti PA (The Atlantic Emperor)*, ECJ). If the subject matter of the dispute is the performance of the contract, for example the correct delivery of the goods, and the defendant disputes jurisdiction of the courts alleging an arbitration agreement, it is submitted that the courts can still assume jurisdiction based on Reg 44/2001 or the Brussels Convention 1968 to try the case and then decide on the preliminary issue of jurisdiction/the validity of the arbitration agreement.

Further difficulties arise where a judgment has been pronounced in one country on the basis that the arbitration agreement is invalid if the judgment is being enforced in another country according to whose laws the arbitration agreement is valid. In this case, according to the laws of the enforcement State, the judgment itself is in breach of the arbitration agreement. However, under the Convention, enforcement of a Member State's judgment can only be refused in specified events. One of those is if the decision is contrary to public policy (Reg 44/2001, Art 34). However by virtue of Art 35(3) of Reg 44/2001 this does not include considerations relating to jurisdiction. It is thus submitted that such a judgment has to be enforced regardless. The provisions in Reg 44/2001 are based on the principles of mutual respect, trust and co-operation between the Member States; review of the other court's jurisdiction would jeopardise these.

However, can an English court grant an anti-suit injunction against a defendant who has brought an action in another country in breach of an arbitration agreement? Such an injunction is addressed to the defendant, who is the claimant in the foreign court, preventing him from carrying on those foreign proceedings (see *Aggeliki Charis Compania Maritima SA v Pagnan SpA (The Angelic Grace)*, CA). As the subject matter of the English proceedings is the arbitration agreement, it was argued that these proceedings fall outside the scope of Reg 44/2001 or the Brussels Convention 1968, which meant that an anti-suit injunction could be issued (*Navigation Maritime Bulgare v Rustal Trading Ltd & others (The Ivan Zagubanski)*, QBD (Comm); *Through Transport Mutual Insurance Association (Eurasia) Ltd v New India Assurance Co Ltd (The Hari Bhum)*, CA and *West Tankers Inc v RAS Riunione Adriatica di Sicurta (The Front Comor)*, QBD (Comm)).

This issue was discussed in *Toepfer International GmbH v Société Cargill France*, CA. The Court of Appeal decided to refer the case to the ECJ for a preliminary ruling on the issue. However, it was never decided by the ECJ because the case was settled beforehand. The Court of Appeal asked first whether the arbitration exception of Art 1(4) of the BC 1968 (Reg 44/2001, Art 1(2)(d) Reg) extended to anti-suit proceedings and secondly whether these anti-suit proceedings were based on the same cause of action for which Art 21 of the BC 1968 (Reg 44/2001, Art 27) required a court seised second to stay the proceedings. Despite the fact that there is no preliminary ruling on exactly the same issue, it is submitted that interference with the jurisdiction of another Member State is not acceptable (see Reg 44/2001, Art 27), regardless of the line of argument. *Case C-159/02 Gregory Paul Turner v (1) Felix Fareed Ismail Grovit (2) Harada Ltd (3) Changepoint SA*, ECJ and *Case C-116/02 Erich Gasser GmbH v MISAT SrL*, ECJ both point strongly in this direction. In *Turner v Grovit* the issue of an anti-suit injunction in support of an exclusive jurisdiction agreement was held to be incompatible with the European regime. In *Erich Gasser v MISAT* it was held that a court seised second, even though it claimed a jurisdiction clause in its favour, had to stay proceedings until the court seised first had ruled upon its jurisdiction (BC 1968, Art 21 and Reg 44/2001, Art 27).

6.2.3.3 Temporal scope

According to Art 66 of Reg 44/2001 it only applies to legal proceedings instituted after it came into force on 1 March 2002 (Reg 44/2001, Arts 66 and 76). For proceedings started before this time the Brussels Convention 1968 will continue to apply between the pre-2004 Accession EU Member States.

6.2.3.4 Territorial scope

As we have seen, as between the Member States of the European Union Reg 44/2001 does not apply in respect of Denmark where the Brussels Convention 1968 is still applicable (see **6.2.2** above). This is also true for enforcement proceedings. Regulation 44/2001 only applies to enforcement proceedings relating to judgments of a court of one of the Member States (as defined in Reg 44/2001). This therefore again excludes Denmark (Reg 44/2001, Art 1(3)). The Brussels Convention 1968 will still be pertinent to deal with enforcement actions from Denmark, and the Lugano Convention 1988 with those from the Lugano States (see **6.2.2**, **item (c)** above).

6.2.3.5 Relation to other instruments

Articles 67–72 of Reg 44/2001 provide the rules to determine how Reg 44/2001 interacts with other international instruments. Where there is Community legislation in force which provides for jurisdiction and enforcement in specific matters or national legislation implementing it, this legislation will not be overridden by Reg 44/2001 (Reg 44/2001, Art 67). Articles 68 and 70 of Reg 44/2001 (BC 1968, Arts 54–56) set out the extent to which specific conventions and treaties are superseded by Reg 44/2001.

Article 71 of Reg 44/2001 (BC 1968, Art 57) provides that other conventions to which the Member States are party and which govern the jurisdiction, recognition and enforcement of judgments in relation to particular matters shall not be affected. Article 71 of Reg 44/2001 (BC 1968, Art 57) thus introduces an exception to the general rules that Reg 44/2001 (or the Brussels Convention 1968) takes precedence over other conventions signed by the Contracting States on jurisdiction and enforcement of judgments. The purpose of that exception is to ensure compliance with the rules of jurisdiction laid down by these specialised conventions, which take into account the special features of the matters to which they relate.

In this respect, for matters involving international trade and shipping, the Arrest Convention 1952 (International Convention for Unification of Certain Rules relating to the Arrest of Seagoing Ships 1952) is worth mentioning. Article 7 of the Arrest Convention 1952 gives the courts in which country the arrest was made jurisdiction to determine the case on its merits. Thus, the jurisdiction rules of Reg 44/2001 (or the Brussels Convention 1968) are supplanted by the rules of the Arrest Convention or any other 'Art 71 of Reg 44/2001 convention'.

In Case C-148/03 *Nurnberger Allgemeine Versicherungs AG v Portbridge Transport International BV* the ECJ held that jurisdiction derived from a specialised convention, whose rules of jurisdiction are upheld by virtue of Art 57 of the BC 1968 (or Reg 44/2001, Art 71), was classed as jurisdiction derived from a provision of the Brussels Convention 1968 in the sense of Art 20 of the BC 1968 (Reg 44/2001, Art 26). (According to Art 20 of the BC 1968, where a defendant, who is domiciled in another Contracting State than the State where he is sued, does not enter an appearance, the court shall of its own motion declare that it has no jurisdiction unless its jurisdiction is derived from the provisions of this Convention.) This meant that the court seised could accept jurisdiction on the basis of the rules of the specialised convention (in the present case CMR, Art 31(1)), even though the defendant did not enter an appearance in the court and contested jurisdiction. From this it follows that the jurisdictional rules of these specialised conventions are at least supported, if not deemed incorporated, by the Brussels regime (ie, BC 1968 and Reg 44/2001).

This is in line with the argument of the ECJ in *Case C-406/92 The Tatry*. Here the ECJ decided that although its jurisdictional rules were precluded by such a specialised international convention, the Brussels Convention 1968 still applied in relation to matters on which the specialised convention was silent. Thus, where the specialised international convention (in *The Tatry* it was the Arrest Convention 1952) did not provide any rules with respect to pending proceedings and related actions, the rules of the Brussels Convention 1968 (or now Reg 44/2001) were applicable in so far. If proceedings had already been started in another court for the same cause of action, the court seised first had priority. This means that whilst the initial court decides on its jurisdiction the court seised second has to stay its proceedings and it must decline jurisdiction in favour of the initial court, if and where the latter finally assumes jurisdiction (see BC 1968, Art 21 and Reg 44/2001, Art 27).

According to the ECJ in *The Tatry* it did not matter if one action was *in personam* and the other *in rem*. For the purposes of Arts 21 and 22 of the BC 1968 (Reg 44/2001, Arts 27 and 28) there was no difference so long as they concerned the same (Reg 44/2001, Art 21; BC 1968, Art 27) or a related cause of action (Reg 44/2001, Art 22; BC 1968, Art 28). Thus, the Brussels Convention 1968 or Reg 44/2001 will apply to fill gaps where a particular convention is silent.

In the English case *The Bergen (No 1)*, it was held by the Admiralty Court that in the case of conflict between Art 7 of the Arrest Convention 1952 (jurisdiction in the country of arrest) and Art 17 of the BC 1968 (jurisdiction agreement; see also Reg 44/2001, Art 23) Art 57 of the BC 1968 (see Reg 44/2001, Art 71) required the court to give priority to the Arrest Convention 1952. However where there is an exclusive foreign jurisdiction clause, the English court (having jurisdiction based on the Arrest Convention 1952) has discretion to stay its proceedings. It will usually do so unless strong reasons to the contrary can be shown (*Aratra Potato Co Ltd and Another v Egyptian Navigation Co (The El Amira)*, CA). But this approach taken by the English courts is now called into question by the decision of the ECJ in Case C-181/02 *Owusu v Jackson*, which has outlawed the application of the doctorine of forum non-conveniens in matters covered by the Brussels regime (see **6.2.6.2** below). If the specialist convention is supported by the rules of Reg 44/2001 (or the BC 1968), does this also mean that the court's traditional rules of forum non-conveniens are overridden? It is submitted that it is likely that the ECJ would take this point of view.

6.2.3.6 Jurisdiction rules

The jurisdiction regime is set out in Arts 2–30 of Reg 44/2001 (BC 1968, Arts 2–23). The basic rule for jurisdiction under Reg 44/2001 or BC 1968 is that a person domiciled in a Member State must be sued in the courts of that Member State (Reg 44/2001, Art 2 and BC 1968, Art 2), irrespective of nationality. Articles 59 and 60 of Reg 44/2001 (BC 1968, Arts 52, 53) provide guidance on what amounts to domicile. For individuals, Art 59(1) of Reg 44/2001 points to the internal law of the court to determine the domicile of the defendant. In England that is set out in Sch 1, para 9 to the Civil Jurisdiction and Judgments Order (CJJO) 2001 for Reg 44/2001, and in ss 41 and 42 of the CJJA 1982 for the purposes of the Brussels and Lugano Conventions and the allocation of jurisdiction within the United Kingdom. In general an individual is domiciled in the United Kingdom if he is resident in the UK and if the nature and circumstances of his residence indicate that he has a substantial connection to the UK. He is domiciled in a particular part of the UK if he is resident there and has a substantial connection to the part (CJJO 2001, Sch 1, para 9(2), (3)). The domicile of a company or other legal person is where this legal person has its statutory seat, its central administration or its principal place of business (Reg 44/2001, Art 60).

However there are many exceptions to the rule of Art 2 of Reg 44/2001 and there are other jurisdiction rules that have priority over the domicile jurisdiction of Art 2 of Reg 44/2001. Where a court of one country is best equipped to try the case (for example because the dispute involves immovable property situated in this country), it has exclusive jurisdiction. Article 22 of Reg 44/2001 sets out when this applies. A person can enter an appearance before a court without contesting jurisdiction and thus is classed as having agreed to this forum (Reg 44/2001, Art 24). In specific scenarios where there is typically a power imbalance between the parties, the weaker party has more choices about where to sue the other (Reg 44/2001, Arts 8–21). Next in line are jurisdiction agreements. If the agreement does not contravene any of the aforementioned rules it will be accepted according to Art 23 of Reg 44/2001, overruling the domicile jurisdiction of Art 2 of Reg 44/2001. A jurisdiction agreement has to fulfil the criteria set out in Art 23 of Reg 44/2001, in particular in relation to the form, which in international trade has to accord with the trade usage, otherwise in writing or in a form established between the parties.

In addition to the rule in Art 2 of Reg 44/2001, the defendant can also be sued in other courts where Arts 5–7 of Reg 44/2001 apply. Of particular interest for us are the rules in Art 5(1) of Reg 44/2001. They give alternative jurisdiction to a court at the place of performance of the obligation. In a contract for the sale of goods this is the place where the goods were delivered or ought to have been delivered. Where the contract does not provide for a specific place of performance, this has to be identified by the court. The court will determine the *lex contractus* (the law applicable to the contract) and will then apply the *lex contractus* to locate the place of performance (see *Case C-440/97 GIE Groupe Concorde v Master of the Vessel 'Suhediwarno Panjan'*, ECJ). If there is more than one place and country of performance, the court determines the issue by reference to where the principal obligation had to be performed. As the Rome Convention on the Law Applicable to Contractual Obligations 1980 provides the choice of law rules for contractual issues for all EU Member States the outcome is not as unpredictable as it may seem at first.

The case of *Union Transport Group plc v Continental Lines SA*, is an example of a decision on the principal place of performance (Reg 44/2001, Art 5(1)) in a charterparty dispute for failure to nominate and provide a vessel to carry the cargo. In this case the House of Lords held that the obligation to nominate a vessel under a charterparty was such a principal obligation, and that non-performance of it gave jurisdiction to the courts at the place where the nomination should have taken place, irrespective of the envisaged port of loading. According to the House of Lords, nomination of a vessel had the effect that the nominated vessel became 'written' into the contract, which then would have determined the ship that would have had to perform the charterparty. Therefore it was the principal obligation in this context.

Article 5(3) of Reg 44/2001 provides for jurisdiction in matters of tort at the place where the harmful event occurred; Art 5(5) of Reg 44/2001 provides for jurisdiction for a claim arising out of the operations of a branch, agency or other establishment, at the place where the establishment is situated. Article 5(7) of Reg 44/2001 provides for jurisdiction for salvage claims in respect of cargo or freight at the place where the cargo or freight is arrested. As the Arrest Convention 1952 only applies to the arrest of a ship and not of other property, Art 5(7) of Reg 44/2001 is very important.

In cases where there are co-defendants, counterclaims or multiple defendants the rules of Art 6 of Reg 44/2001 provide for jurisdiction to combine these matters. In particular, Art 7 of Reg 44/2001 provides that the courts of a Member State, which have jurisdiction to hear actions relating to the liability of a ship, also have jurisdiction over claims for limitation of such a liability.

Article 4(1) of Reg 44/2001 allows for the internal jurisdictional rules of a Member State to be applied where the defendant has no domicile in one of the Member States, provided Art 22 of Reg 44/2001 (on exclusive jurisdiction) and Art 23 of Reg 44/2001 (on jurisdiction agreements) do not lead to another court's jurisdiction. Any claimant domiciled in a Member State has the same rights to those jurisdiction rules as a national of that State (Reg 44/2001, Art 4(2) and Annexe I, which in England are in particular the rules of CPR 1998, Part 6). The provision of Art 4 of Reg 44/2001 does not take the jurisdiction outside the scope of Reg 44/2001, but provides subject to the limitations set out in Reg 44/2001 (Arts 22, 23 and 27), for the application of the rules of the internal law of the forum. This is of significance for the enforcement of a judgment derived from an Art 4 of Reg 44/2001 court. The judgment must be recognised and enforced according to the rules of chapter III of Reg 44/2001.

6.2.3.7 Loss of jurisdiction

The jurisdiction identified according to the above rules can be lost if a court of another Member State was already seised of a claim involving the same cause of action (Reg 44/2001, Arts 29 and 27) Please note that the notion of exclusive jurisdiction in Art 29 of Reg 44/2001 only refers to the jurisdiction derived from Art 22 of Reg 44/2001 and not from a jurisdiction agreement under Art 23 of Reg 44/2001 (see *Case C-351/89 Overseas Union Insurance Ltd v New Hampshire Insurance Co*, ECJ). As discussed at **6.2.3.5** above, *Case C-406/92 The Tatry*, ECJ gives a good example of the working of Art 27 of Reg 44/2001 (BC 1968, Art 21) where the proceedings at the court first seised were given priority.

The practice of many Member States had been to accept an exclusive jurisdiction clause in their favour and to try a case despite the fact that another Member State's court had already been seised of the case. The European Court of Justice in *Case C-116/02 Erich Gasser GmbH v MISAT SrL* made clear that this practice contravenes the rules of the Brussels Convention 1968 and thus also of Reg 44/2001.

Where related actions are pending in the courts of different Member States, Art 28 of Reg 44/2001 provides for a voluntary stay of action in the court seised second or, where the cases are pending at first instance, for a voluntary consolidation of the actions. According to Art 28(3) of Reg 44/2001, actions are related 'where they are so closely connected that it is expedient to hear and determine them together' in order to avoid irreconcilable judgments which might result from entertaining separate proceedings. Where the proceedings of the court seised first are still pending at first instance and the proceedings can be consolidated in this court, the court seised second can, on application of one of the parties, decline jurisdiction. In any other case it can stay proceedings to await the outcome of the action pending before the court first seised, before continuing its proceedings. This puts the court seised second in the position to take the judgment of the court seised first into account.

6.2.3.8 Protective measures

Protective measures can either be sought in conjunction with the main action or, to a limited extent, in another court in accordance with the rules of Art 31 of Reg 44/2001. Art 31 of Reg 44/2001 allows these actions for provisional measures in accordance with the rules of the internal law of the State whose court is seised of such an application. But, any provisional measure granted under Art 31 of Reg 44/2001 (or BC 1968, Art 24) must:

(a) be truly provisional, which means it must be wholly reversible; and

(b) can only relate to assets within the territorial jurisdiction of the court seised.

For example a freezing injunction or 'Mareva injunction' (see *Mareva Compania Naviera SA v International Bulk Carriers*, CA, the case that gave the name to these injunctions), designed to prevent the defendant from transferring or concealing assets in order to defeat justice, can be granted by an English court as long as it is limited to the assets situated in England even if the main proceedings are pending in a different Member State. Even in a case where the parties had excluded litigation in favour of arbitration, a court was still held to have jurisdiction to grant a provisional or protective measure on the basis of (the then) Art 24 of the BC 1968 (now Reg 44/2001, Art 31) (Case C-391/95 *Van Uden Maritime BV v Deco Line*, ECJ).

Anti-suit injunctions against proceedings pending in another Member State are, however, not permitted, as we have already seen above at **6.2.3.2** (see Case C-159/02 *Gregory Paul Turner v (1) Felix Fareed Ismail Grovit (2) Harada Ltd (3) Changepoint SA*, ECJ).

6.2.3.9 Checklist

Generally, the following checklist can be used in the order set out below to identify which jurisdiction rules will be predominant:

(a) *Jurisdiction*

    (i)   Exclusive jurisdiction, Art 22 of Reg 44/2001.

    (ii)   Jurisdiction by appearance, Art 24 of Reg 44/2001.

    (iii)   Jurisdiction in matters relating to insurance, Arts 8–14 of Reg 44/2001; *or*

    (iv)   jurisdiction over consumer contracts, Arts 15–17 of Reg 44/2001; *or*

    (v)   jurisdiction over individual contracts of employment, Arts 18–21 of Reg 44/2001.

    (vi)   Jurisdiction agreements, Art 23 of Reg 44/2001.

    (vii)   General provisions — rule on domicile, Art 2 of Reg 44/2001.

    (viii) Special jurisdiction — rules regarding contracts, multiple defendants and related proceedings, Arts 5 – 7 of Reg 44/2001.

    (ix)   Jurisdiction in cases of lack of domicile within a Member State, Art 4 of Reg 44/2001.

(b) *Loss of Jurisdiction, Arts 27 – 30 of Reg 44/2001*

    (i)   Excusive Jurisdiction, Art 29 of Reg 44/2001

    (ii)   Lis pendens, Art 27 of Reg 44/2001

    (iii)   Related actions, Art 28 of Reg 44/2001

(c) *Protective measures, Art 31 of Reg 44/2001.*

6.2.4 Recognition and enforcement of judgments under Council Regulation 44/2001/EC

Once we have identified which country's courts have jurisdiction to try the case we also need to make sure that a judgment of such a court will be enforceable in the country where the defendant has his assets. Where a defendant does not pay the sum due voluntarily, the judgment will need to be enforced if the claimant wants to assert his position. Otherwise the fees and time spent on the legal proceedings are lost for no gain. Recognition, on the other hand, is sought (see **6.2.4.1** below) where a defendant obtained a judgment in his favour. He then has an interest in using this judgment in order to prevent the claimant from restarting proceedings elsewhere.

6.2.4.1 Recognition

Recognition of a judgment means that the claim is treated as having been determined once and for all. For judgments *in personam* the effect is limited to the parties, as opposed to judgments *in rem*, where the effect is attached to the property in question. Whether the claim has been decided in favour or against the claimant does not matter. Any party will be estopped from contradicting the outcome in subsequent proceedings; the matter is then *res judicata*, meaning that the action cannot be reopened or challenged by the original parties or their successors in interest.

A judgment is recognised in accordance with Arts 33–37 of Reg 44/2001, without the need to comply with any special procedure. The judgment must be as follows.

(a) An original adjudication in the sense of a 'judgment' as in Art 32 of Reg 44/2001 of a court of a Member State. This generally includes interlocutory and provisional measures and also extends to judgments based on Art 4 of Reg 44/2001 (where the internal rules of the Member State are used to allocate jurisdiction). However it does not extend to the registration of an arbitral award 'as a judgment'. The latter is done in some States in order to enforce an arbitral award. Article 32 of Reg 44/2001 also excludes court settlements and authentic instruments which are covered in Arts 57 and 58 of Reg 44/2001 instead. However a judgment by consent still falls within the ambit of Art 32 of Reg 44/2001 (see *Landhurst Leasing Plc v Marcq*, CA).

(b) From a court of a Member State, to be enforced in a Member State.

(c) An adjudication given after 1 March 2002 if enforcement is sought on the basis of the Regulation (Reg 44/2001, Art 66(2)), otherwise enforcement must be sought under the Brussels Convention 1968.

(d) An adjudication of a civil and commercial matter in accordance with Art 1(1) and (2) of Reg 44/2001.

(e) Not impeachable for specific jurisdictional errors, for example breach of the jurisdictional rules set out for insurance and consumer contracts and also for exclusive jurisdiction under Art 22 of Reg 44/2001. Only those errors set out in Art 35(1) of Reg 44/2001 will qualify. Subject to para (1) jurisdiction may not be reviewed, not even as a matter of public policy (Reg 44/2001, Art 35(3)).

(f) Not impeachable for specific substantive reasons. Only the reasons set out in Art 34 of Reg 44/2001 will qualify. They are: if recognition is manifestly contrary to public policy; in certain circumstances where the judgment was given in default of appearance; where the judgment is irreconcilable with a judgment of the Member State between the same parties; or where the judgment is irreconcilable with an earlier judgment of another State between the same parties involving the same cause of action. However the latter only refers to irreconcilability to judgments only; court settlements are not taken into account in this context (see *Case C-414/92 Solo Kleinmotoren GmbH v Boch*, ECJ).

(g) Not excluded from recognition by another Treaty (Reg 44/2001, Art 72 in conjunction with BC 1968, Art 59).

6.2.4.2 Enforcement

A judgment which is enforceable in the Member State in which it was given will be enforced in another Member State. This, however, requires that on the application of the interested party the judgment has first been declared enforceable in the other Member State or, for the United Kingdom, that the judgment has been registered for enforcement in the part of the United Kingdom where enforcement is sought (Reg 44/2001, Art 38). Registration for enforcement in England is based on s 4 of the CJJA 1982 for the Brussels and Lugano Conventions and the CJJO 2001 provides in Sch I the framework for Reg 44/2001. The procedure is covered in Part 74(I) of the CPR 1998.

A judgment will automatically be declared enforceable once the formalities have been fulfilled (Reg 44/2001, Art 41). The declaration of enforceability is served on the party against whom enforcement is sought and the applicant is notified (Reg 44/2001, Art 42). Either party can now appeal against the decision on the declaration of enforceability (Reg 44/2001, Art 43). The applicant might want to appeal in case his application has not been successful or has only been partially successful. Appeal is the first chance the respondent has to object to the enforcement. If he chooses to appeal he has to file it within one month of service of the declaration of enforceability (Reg 44/2001, Art 43(5)). A further appeal is limited in the United Kingdom to a single further appeal on a point of law (Reg 44/2001, Art 44 referring to Annexe IV).

The only grounds for appeal are the reasons set out in Arts 34 and 35 of Reg 44/2001, which are also the reasons for refusing recognition (Reg 44/2001, Art 45). Under no circumstances may the judgment be reviewed as to its substance (Reg 44/2001, Art 45(2)). However, where the judgment that is to be enforced in another Member State is irreconcilable with a judgment given by a court in the enforcement country in a dispute between the same parties (Reg 44/2001, Art 34(3) and BC 1968, Art 27(3)), recognition and enforcement must be denied (see *Case C-80/00 Italian Leather SpA v WECO Polstermöbel GmbH & Co*, ECJ), there is no discretion.

Where enforcement has been sought whilst the judgment itself can still be appealed in the country of origin, Art 46 of Reg 44/2001 provides rules on how to proceed with the enforcement. The enforcement proceedings may be stayed until the judgment is final.

6.2.5 The European Enforcement Order

Regulation 805/2004/EC of the European Parliament and of the Council of 30 April 2004 ([2004] OJ L143/15) creating a European Enforcement Order for Uncontested Claims (hereafter the EEO Reg) applies from 21 October 2005, with the exception of some of the general and final provisions which apply from 21 January 2005 (EEO Reg, Art 33). The Regulation creates a European enforcement order for uncontested claims and has the same scope as Reg 44/2001 (EEO Reg, Art 2). It aims to permit the free circulation of judgments, court settlements and authentic instruments based on uncontested claims throughout the Member States, without any intermediate proceedings needing to be brought in the Member State of enforcement prior to recognition and enforcement (EEO Reg, Art 1). To enable this to occur, the EEO Reg lays down minimum standards for the enforcement order.

The EEO Reg does not affect the possibility of enforcing a claim under Reg 44/2001 (EEO Reg, Art 27). The EEO Reg can be accessed via the Europa home page: http://www.europa.eu.int or by searching the Eur-Lex website: http://europa.eu.int/eur-lex/en/index.html under 'legislation'; some information can also be found at http://www.europa.eu.int/scadplus/leg/en/s22003.htm.

6.2.6 Jurisdiction under the traditional rules

6.2.6.1 Sphere of application

The traditional rules of English law are applicable where Reg 44/2001 provides for the application of the internal law of a State where the court is situated (see Reg 44/2001, Arts 4 and 31) and where an English court is seised. Where the traditional rules are applied in the context of Reg 44/2001, interpretation of these rules may require a more 'autonomous international' approach (see *Raiffeisen Zentralbank Österreich AG v Five Star Trading LLC*, CA ([2001] 1 Lloyd's Rep 597, para 33).

The traditional rules are also applicable when the matter is outside the European rules, for example because it is not a civil or commercial matter according to Art 1 of Reg 44/2001 or Art 1 of the BC 1968 or because it falls within the excluded matters. A judgment based on these traditional rules without being anchored in any way in Reg 44/2001 or the Brussels or Lugano Conventions is also outside their scope for recognition purposes.

6.2.6.2 Jurisdiction in general

Jurisdiction under the traditional rules is established by service of process: the claim form must be served on the defendant. If the defendant is present in England he can be served with process as of right, thus establishing jurisdiction of the English courts over him. The defendant does not need to be domiciled in England; it is sufficient if he is served while present in England, even if he is only on a visit. The service of documents is governed by Part 6 of the Civil Procedure Rules 1998 (SI 1998/3132). Part 6 of the CPR governs the procedure from 1 May 2000; prior to the CPR the matter was governed by Ord 11 of the Rules of the Supreme Court (RSC). Authorities based on Ord 11 RSC are still pertinent. Part 6 of the CPR can be found in an international trade or conflict of laws statute book or can be accessed via the HMSO site: http://www.hmso.gov.uk. You should read the sections of the CPR and any other statute or legal text as and when this text refers to them.

If the defendant is not present in England the claimant needs the permission of the court to serve the claim form outside England. Once permission is granted and service completed, jurisdiction is established. In order to receive the permission three criteria have to be met by the claimant's request:

(a) Each of the claims pleaded has to fall within one or more categories of 6.20 CPR. These paragraphs require in general a close connection to England, either by means of a concluded contract, an action taken, an act committed, damages sustained in England or in another similar way. If a claim is made in respect of a contract it is sufficient that the contract is governed by English law or that the contract contains a jurisdiction clause in favour of English courts (CPR, 6.20(5)). There are no formal requirements for a jurisdiction agreement, in contrast to the provisions in Art 23 of Reg 44/2001.

(b) England must be 'the proper place in which to bring the claim' (CPR, r 6.21(2A)). This means that it must be shown that England is clearly or distinctly the most appropriate forum.

(c) Each of the claims must have a reasonable prospect of success (CPR, r 6.21(1)(b)). Therefore the claimant must show a good arguable case on the merits of his claim, which means that the court does not need to be persuaded of the success on a balance of probability, but there must at least be a reasonable chance, even if below 50% (see *Seaconsar Far East Ltd v Bank Markazi Jomhouri Islami Iran*, HL). English courts do not have the same powers as courts in many civil jurisdictions to hear evidence before deciding on jurisdiction. Therefore under common law a lower threshold to anchor jurisdiction is required. However, this may be an area of concern for civil law countries, particularly where a judgment derived from this jurisdiction qualifies for automatic recognition based on Arts 4, 38 and 41 of Reg 44/2001.

If a defendant wants to *contest jurisdiction* he must make an application under Part 11 of the CPR otherwise any steps he undertakes in the action may be interpreted as submission to the jurisdiction. The defendant must first acknowledge the service in accordance with

Part 11 of the CPR and then, within the period for filing a defence, must contest jurisdiction supported by evidence (CPR, r 11(4)).

The defendant can also apply for a stay of action on the basis that another court should adjudicate the case (CPR, Part 11). There are two main reasons for seeking to stay proceedings in England: first that the *forum conveniens* is elsewhere (see *Spiliada Maritime Corporation v Cansulex Ltd (The Spiliada)*, HL); and secondly that bringing the action in an English court is in breach of contract because, for example, there is a valid arbitration agreement or a jurisdiction agreement giving jurisdiction to another country's courts. An action *in rem* can be stayed just as well as an action *in personam* (see *Aratra Potato Co Ltd and Another v Egyptian Navigation Co (The El Amira)*, CA, where the stay of an action *in rem* against a ship was considered).

At common law there are no stringent rules of priority between different courts as in the Brussels regime (see Reg 44/2001, Arts 27 and 28 or BC 1968, Arts 21 and 23). A balance and order between the jurisdiction of different States is instead achieved by applying the doctrine of *forum non conveniens* and by issuing anti-suit injunctions. In the former, the court limits its own jurisdiction in favour of a more appropriate court, whereas in the latter the court indirectly places limits on the foreign court's jurisdiction by ordering the claimant to halt the foreign proceedings. Under the doctrine of *forum non conveniens* jurisdiction is discretionary. The English court will stay the action where the defendant can show that there is another competent court in which the case can be most suitably tried, where the foreign court is clearly and distinctly more appropriate.

These rules are applicable at common law, but cannot be used to interfere with the European scheme of jurisdiction. The ECJ has held that both approaches are inappropriate under the Brussels regime. Anti-suit injunctions would violate the principles of mutual trust and competence between the Member States (see *Case C-159/02 Turner v Grovit*, ECJ) and considerations of *forum non conveniens* would interfere with the predictability and legal certainty of the jurisdictional rules to which the Brussels regime aspires (see *Case C-181/02 Owusu v Jackson*, ECJ; see also **6.2.6.3** below).

6.2.6.3 Forum shopping

Forum shopping means that the claimant selects a court most favourable to him, for example because the *lex fori* (which is the procedural law used by the court; it is always the law of the country in which the court is situated) contains rules which work in support of the claimant or because of the choice of law rules which this court applies lead to a substantive law of benefit to the claimant. In order to limit forum shopping, which sometimes leads to a race to see who can file a claim first, the traditional English rules have developed a three pronged approach.

(a) The defendant can seek a stay of proceedings on the basis that the English court is a *forum non conveniens*. The English court therefore limits its own jurisdiction. Please note that this is only possible within the ambit of the traditional rules. The European rules do not have any provision for this; a court thus cannot decline jurisdiction if no other claim is already pending. In *Owusu v Jackson* the ECJ has clarified that once a court has jurisdiction in accordance with the Brussels regime, it cannot decline its jurisdiction in favour of a more convenient forum. Such an approach would undermine the predictability of the rules laid down by the Brussels Convention 1968 and consequently undermine the principle of legal certainty which was the basis of the Convention.

(b) A party to a dispute may bring an action for declaration of non-liability, without waiting for the other party — the natural claimant — to start proceedings. This action itself looks suspiciously like forum shopping, but is particularly effective under the scheme of Reg 44/2001, as the court seised first will prevail (Reg 44/2001, Art 27, BC 1968, Art 21 and *Case C-406/92 The Tatry*, ECJ).

(c) The defendant can seek an anti-suit injunction from an English court against an action by the claimant pending in a foreign court, whereby the English court indirectly places limitations on the jurisdiction of the foreign court by restraining the claimant under the foreign proceedings from continuing his action.

As we have already seen at **6.2.3.2** above anti-suit injunctions have their own dynamic and problems within the European context (see *Case C-159/02 Turner v Grovit*, ECJ and *Toepfer International GmbH v Société Cargill France*, CA), falling foul of the rules for related action and the spirit of mutual trust and competence between the Member States. However, outside the jurisdictional rules of Reg 44/2001 or the Brussels or Lugano Conventions they are applicable. The following requirements need to be satisfied in order to obtain such an injunction (see *Aggeliki Charis Compania Maritima SA v Pagnan SpA (The Angelic Grace)*, CA).

(a) The court must have personal jurisdiction over the defendant. Therefore he must be served with process, either as of right within England or outside with permission of the court according to Part 6 of the CPR, (CPR, rr 6.20 and 6.21). (However, where jurisdiction would be derived from Reg 44/2001, the rules of Art 27 of Reg 44/2001 on cases pending before courts of other Member States will restrict the jurisdiction.)

(b) England is or would be the natural home for litigating the substantive dispute.

(c) The respondent must be shown as acting vexatiously or oppressively in having brought the action before the foreign court. This includes an action brought against an 'English jurisdiction' clause or an arbitration clause.

Even if only applied in cases falling outside the European rules, it needs to be borne in mind that there is a risk that judgments will clash following an anti-suit injunction. First, it seems very likely that the English injunction will not find recognition in the country where proceedings are taking place. Secondly, a judgment obtained in the foreign court despite an English anti-suit injunction will not be recognised nor will it be enforced in England.

6.2.6.4 Jurisdiction for interim relief

An English court can, for example, grant a freezing injunction to restrain a party from removing its assets from the jurisdiction or from dealing with the assets in a manner that is aimed at diminishing them. This injunction was formerly known as a Mareva injunction after *Mareva Compania Naviera SA v International Bulk Carriers*, CA and is now granted by virtue of s 37 of the Supreme Court Act 1981 in accordance with the procedure set out in Part 25 of the CPR.

Interim relief, including provisional and protective measures can be sought in three cases:

(a) in support of an action in English courts;

(b) in support of a civil or commercial claim pending before a court of a Reg 44/2001 State (Reg 44/2001, Art 31) or a Brussels or Lugano State (BC 1968 and LC 1988, Art 24).

(c) in support of other actions in foreign courts (CJJA 1982, s 25).

The same rules as to service of process (CPR, Part 6) are to be observed, even where the jurisdiction is based on Art 31 of Reg 44/2001, because Art 31 of Reg 44/2001 only provides for jurisdiction in accordance with the internal law of the State whose court is seised with the protective measure. Therefore 'service out' needs the permission of the English court.

6.2.7 Recognition and enforcement under the traditional rules

6.2.7.1 General

The common law rules deal with judgments of the Member States in so far as they fall outside the scope of Reg 44/2001, and with the recognition and enforcement of judgments from the courts of all other countries.

Where a party just wants the recognition of the judgment, it only needs to plead *res judicata* (this means that the scenario has already been determined by the courts and thus no more action can be taken based on the same cause).

If the party wants to enforce a judgment it must follow a set procedure. It can either register the judgment for enforcement if it is a 'priority judgment' or it must commence an enforcement action at common law, founded on the foreign judgment. The judgment is then scrutinised to see if it fulfils the relevant criteria.

6.2.7.2 Recognition of judgments

In order to be recognised the foreign judgment must fulfil various conditions. The case is scrutinised regarding the existence of a valid connection between the foreign court and the parties (whether the court had jurisdiction in accordance with the English rules), the nature of the judgment and limited objections against the judgment. Thus in order to be recognised the judgment must be:

(a) final and conclusive;

(b) from a court that has international jurisdiction according to the rules of English private international law (international jurisdiction in this sense requires the defendant/respondent either to have submitted to the jurisdiction of the court (see CJJA 1982, s 33(1)), or to have been present or resident within the jurisdiction of the court at the time when proceedings were instituted);

(c) on the merits of the case between the same parties involving the same cause of action; and

(d) indefeasible by defences against recognition.

There are certain defences at common law that can be raised successfully against the recognition of a foreign judgment. They are as follows:

(a) the violation of a valid arbitration agreement or a valid agreement on the jurisdiction of a court;

(b) the absence of local jurisdiction of the foreign court;

(c) fraud;

(d) want of natural or substantive justice;

(e) public policy being offended;

(f) res judicata in England.

In general a judgment cannot be reviewed on its merits; allegations that the foreign court erred in its reasoning are not acceptable. However, a limited review is held under the defences of violation of an arbitration or choice of court agreement, and allegations of fraud.

The effects of recognition at common law are first that it paves the way to enforcement; secondly that the cause of action between the parties will be regarded as *res judicata* against the defendant; and thirdly that a partially successful claimant is precluded under s 34 of the CJJA 1982 from suing for a second time on the same cause of action.

6.2.7.3 Enforcement of the judgment in overview

To summarise, before we look at the enforcement criteria at common law, there are broadly three different schemes in England to give effect to foreign judgments.

(a) Judgments from other parts of the United Kingdom (in accordance with CJJA 1982, Schs 6 and 7), other Member States of the European Union under Reg 44/2001 (in accordance with the CJJO 2001, Sch I) or under the Brussels or Lugano Convention (in accordance with CJJA 1982, s 4) are given effect to most readily. Here legislation has been implemented to provide rules that are easy to satisfy and which offer a swift procedure for enforcement (see CPR, Part 74).

(b) Judgments from States party to bilateral agreements with the United Kingdom are dealt with under the relevant statutory provision (see the Administration of Justice Act 1920 and the Foreign Judgments (Reciprocal Enforcement) Act 1933) that reflects the recognition and enforcement under common law, but benefits from a simplified enforcement procedure (see CPR, Part 74).

(c) Judgments from other countries are given effect according to the rules and the procedure at common law alone.

6.2.7.4 Enforcement by action at common law

In order for a judgment for payment of a debt to be enforced, the claimant must bring an action at common law which is founded on the foreign judgment. The claimant has to commence original proceedings by service of a claim form and can then apply under r 24.2 of the CPR for a summary judgment on the basis that the defendant has no grounds to defend himself successfully. If this is accepted, the judgment will be registered for enforcement. However, if the defendant can show that he has a prospect of successfully defending the claim, the case will proceed to trial in the usual way, dismissing the application for summary judgment.

In order to qualify for enforcement the judgment must satisfy three criteria:

(a) the judgment must be for a debt or a fixed sum of money;

(b) the judgment must be final and conclusive;

(c) the judgment must not be for tax or a penalty.

6.2.7.5 Enforcement by statutory registration

The Administration of Justice Act 1920 and the Foreign Judgments (Reciprocal Enforcement) Act 1933 provide for reciprocal enforcement of judgments in respect of particular countries. The 1920 Act applies to many colonial and Commonwealth territories, most of which are smaller, but also some larger jurisdictions such as Malaysia, Singapore and New Zealand. The 1933 Act applies to judgments from Australia and Canada, and also from Guernsey, Jersey, India, the Isle of Man, Israel, Pakistan, Suriname and Tonga. The full list of States can be found in *Halsbury's Laws of England* (Conflict of Laws, Volume 8(3), Chapter 4). The substantive requirements for enforcement are very close to those at common law, but the procedure is greatly simplified. The above statutes allow the claimant to register the judgment for enforcement, rather than having to start original proceedings, giving the judgment the same force and effect for the purpose of enforcement as if it were an English one.

6.3 Arbitration as a form of alternative dispute resolution

6.3.1 General

Arbitration is a form of alternative dispute resolution that is, in comparison with mediation and conciliation, rather more akin to a judicial settlement. In mediation and conciliation the parties appoint an independent 'go-between' to help them solve the dispute amicably and to come to a mutual acceptable agreement. Arbitration, on the other hand, gives powers to decide the outcome of the case to the arbitrators in a similar way to a court. Proceedings are mostly defined by pre-existing rules, which can make them more formal and thus more like a court. Arbitration, however can have a number of advantages over trial in court.

(a) The arbitrators are usually selected from technical experts in the trade or subject concerned and so can provide expert knowledge themselves whereas a court needs to hear expert witnesses.

(b) The dispute may be resolved quicker and in a less antagonistic manner, thereby probably preventing the destruction of the basis for future business relationships between the parties.

(c) The proceedings are kept more informal; location, time and venue can be arranged to suit the parties.

(d) Confidentiality and privacy of the proceedings can be a huge advantage; there are no public hearings and the award is not publicised, unlike court decisions. Thus negative publicity can be avoided and business details do not need to be disclosed to the public.

(e) Arbitration proceedings can be more cost effective than trial in court, although the cost of experts in the trade should not be underestimated. However the cost of institutional arbitration (conducted by a specialist arbitral institution) can be quite high. It is therefore advisable to consider the relevant costs for the envisaged form of arbitration before agreeing on a particular arbitration clause.

(f) Unlike the courts, the arbitrators are not bound by a system of precedents. However this can be a disadvantage as outcomes can be unpredictable and lack consistency.

(g) The parties are free to choose the substantive rules according to which the dispute must be solved. They can opt for the rules of law of a particular country or they can provide for the use of 'internationally accepted principles of law governing contractual relations', the *lex mercatoria* or law merchant, or they can simply allow the arbitrators to apply whatever law they deem to be appropriate (for an example see *Deutsche Schachtbau- und Tiefbohrgesellschaft mbH v R' As al-Khaima National Oil Co*, CA reversed on other grounds, where the arbitrators applied the *lex mercatoria*).

Arbitration ends with an award (much like a judgment) to the advantage of one of the parties unless the parties have been able to agree an amicable solution. In general the award given by an arbitration tribunal is final and can be enforced by the courts.

In deciding whether to arrange for arbitration or litigation in case of dispute, the parties must evaluate the respective benefits of these methods, one aspect of which will be fast and effective enforcement. The New York Convention on the Recognition and Enforcement of Foreign Arbitral Awards 1958 has received widespread support with, as of September 2005, 137 parties (see the list of signatories to be found on the UNCITRAL website http://www.uncitral.org/uncitral/en/index.html under the category of 'status of texts'), whereas there is not yet an equivalent for the enforcement of judgments. This gap, however, may be filled to some extent by the new Convention on Choice of Court agreements drafted by the Hague Conference on Private International Law and concluded on 30 June 2005 (see http://www.hcch.net and follow the links 'work in progress' and 'judgments' or access directly at http://www.hcch.net/index_en.php?act=progress. listing&cat=4).

The parties can choose between ad hoc arbitration and institutional arbitration. Ad hoc arbitration leaves it up to the parties to prescribe the procedure and first of all the mode of appointment of the arbitrator. The parties can set out specific rules or they can choose the application of one of the standard sets of arbitration rules, for example the UNCITRAL Arbitration Rules or the ICC Arbitration Rules. They can also leave the appointment of the arbitrator to a third person, who is respected by both sides. The arbitrator will control the proceedings himself within the limits of any incorporated rules or provisions made by the parties and the law. Where the parties have not chosen any particular rules, the proceedings will be conducted in accordance with the rules of law at the place of arbitration. In the case of arbitration proceedings in England this would generally be the Arbitration Act 1996.

If the parties choose institutional arbitration, they agree on proceedings conducted by a specialist arbitral institution which uses its own rules of arbitration. Examples of such institutions are the International Chamber of Commerce, the London Court of International Arbitration, the American Arbitration Association and regional arbitration institutions, such as those of Zurich, Stockholm and Vienna. Some trade organisations, for example the Grain and Feed Trade Association (GAFTA) and the Federation of Oils, Seeds and Fats Association Ltd (FOSFA), also provide arbitration services based on their own rules for their members. The advantages of the services of a trade organisation are that the parties will use a tried and tested form of contract of their trade organisation, which provides for arbitration and choice of law clauses as well as for the procedure by which the arbitration is conducted, thus reducing the points of dispute to a minimum.

6.3.2 International arbitration

Arbitration is international either by virtue of the nature of the dispute or the identity of the parties. Some arbitral rules may differentiate between domestic and international arbitration. (In England, the Arbitration Act (AA) 1996 distinguished between domestic and international arbitration in ss 85–87. However these sections never came into force and can thus be disregarded.)

For international arbitration two decisions need to be taken first, before deciding the dispute.

(a) Which law, known as the *lex arbitri*, is applicable to the arbitration proceedings?

(b) Which is the applicable substantive law, for example the proper law of the contract?

Both laws can differ, just as in the case of court proceedings. Court proceedings will always be conducted in accordance with the procedural law of the forum, but the substantive law applicable to the dispute is determined separately. It is similar with arbitration. The *lex arbitri* is either governed by the set of rules, the parties have adopted or by the rules of law governing arbitration proceedings at the place of the arbitration. This, under most rules is where the seat of the arbitration is located. Under s 3 of the AA 1996 the seat of arbitration is determined by the juridical seat, and the fact that evidence is taken in a different country does not change the seat of arbitration. In *Naviera Amazonica Peruana SA v Compania Internacional de Sugeros del Peru* the Court of Appeal pointed out that the arbitrator can conduct the hearings at any convenient place, not affecting the seat of the arbitration. Where the seat of arbitration is situated in England the provisions of the AA 1996 apply (AA 1996, s 2(1)). However, some provisions of the Act may still apply, for example the provisions in respect of stay of proceedings and enforcement of the award, regardless of whether the seat of arbitration is in England or not (AA 1996, s 2(2)–(5)).

The *lex arbitri* governs the conduct of the arbitration. The law of the specific country determines what exactly is determined by it. As a general rule, however, the likelihood is that matters regarding jurisdiction of the arbitrators, the proceedings, form and finality of the award are covered.

An attempt to harmonise the *lex arbitri* has been made by the UNCITRAL Model Law, which, to a large extent, has been taken into account in the enactment of the AA 1996. Harmonisation of procedural rules has further been achieved by the wide acceptance of the New York Convention on the Recognition and Enforcement of Foreign Arbitral Awards 1958 to which the UK is a signatory, because the *lex arbitri* is also of great importance in respect of enforcement.

The proper law of the contract, the law applicable to the substance of the case, needs to be determined thereafter. Often the parties have chosen the law which they wish to apply (for example English law, another country's law or *lex mercatoria*), or the rules they have chosen to govern the arbitration may provide details on how to identify the applicable law. Where the arbitration procedure is to be conducted in accordance with the AA 1996, s 46 of the AA 1996 provides rules to identify the proper law: the tribunal must either decide the dispute in accordance with the law chosen by the parties, or, where the parties so agree, in accordance with any such considerations as agreed by them or determined by the tribunal. The latter seems to make room for the applications of trade customs and the law merchant. If the parties have made no choice of law or rules, the tribunal must determine the applicable law by using the conflict of law rules which it considers applicable (AA 1996, s 46(3)). The tribunal will need to characterise the scenario and determine whether the dispute concerns, for example, a question of contract or tort. Then it will need to apply the conflict rules relevant to this category. For example, the Contracts (Applicable Law) Act 1990 makes provision as to the law applicable to contractual obligations in the case of conflict of laws and the Private International Law (Miscellaneous Provisions) Act 1995 for the law applicable to torts and delicts.

We shall now have a look at arbitration under English law and consider briefly the procedure, as well as recognition and enforcement of arbitral awards.

6.3.3 Arbitration in England

English arbitration is governed by the AA 1996. The Act provides rules in respect of the conduct of arbitration and its procedure, the appointment and jurisdiction of the arbitration tribunal, any possible intervention of the courts and the recognition and enforcement of arbitral awards. Please take a look at the Arbitration Act 1996 to get an overview of the sections contained in it and read the provisions of the Act as and when referred to in this chapter. Please remember that ss 85–87 of the AA 1996, distinguishing between domestic and international arbitration, never came into force (due to problems of discrimination associated with such a distinction, at least under European Community law).

The following is a very brief summary of English arbitration to give you some insight into the basic principles on which this subject is based.

The English law on arbitration has been reformed by the AA 1996 which took on board many of the proposals in the Model Law on International Commercial Arbitration 1985 adopted by the United Nations Commission on International Trade Law (the UNCITRAL Model Law), and which repealed the Arbitration Acts of 1975 and 1979, Part I and s 42(2) of the Arbitration Act of 1950 and the Consumer Arbitration Agreements Act 1988.

Arbitration is governed by the principles of non-intervention of the courts (AA 1996, s 1(c)) and the freedom of the parties to decide how they want their dispute resolved (AA 1996, s 1 (b)).

An arbitration agreement (see AA 1996, ss 6–8) governed by the AA 1996 determines which disputes are submitted to the jurisdiction of the arbitration tribunal. The arbitration agreement must be in writing (AA 1996, s 5) although there is a very low threshold to fulfil this requirement. The agreement need not be signed by the parties, need not be contained in the same document and even oral acceptance of a written offer has been held to be within this ambit. An oral agreement is not invalid, but just not governed by the AA 1996 (AA 1996, s 81), with the effect that common law will be applicable.

In the event that a party takes recourse to a court despite the matter being bound by a valid arbitration agreement, s 9 of the AA 1996 sets out that a court will stay the proceedings before it in order to give priority to the agreement. Thus, one of the parties cannot unilaterally avoid the arbitration clause by filing a claim in court. The court will uphold the arbitration agreement and stay proceedings if requested by the defendant unless it is satisfied that the arbitration agreement is null and void or inoperative. It is at this point that several jurisdictions come to different conclusions: depending on the requirements for a valid arbitration agreement, particularly in form, an agreement may be valid under the laws of country X, but invalid under the laws of country Z. Thus, it becomes crucial in which country's courts a claim is filed and which law is applied to determine the validity of the arbitration agreement. This also explains why a party may wish to resort to an anti-suit injunction. Where this party is sued in a country whose law does not recognise the arbitration agreement, this injunction may be the only way to 'enforce' the arbitration agreement by stopping the proceedings in that country. However, as we have seen at **6.2.3.2** above, the use of anti-suit injunctions between courts of EU Member States is not acceptable. Discrepancies in the laws must be accepted; they can only be avoided by harmonising the law (see the efforts in respect of a 'European Contract Law' at http://www.europa.eu.int/scadplus/leg/en/lvb/l33158.htm).

Sections 15–17 of the AA 1996 give details about appointment and numbers of the arbitrators; an even number of arbitrators will normally require a chairperson or an umpire. The court has the power to remove an arbitrator where necessary (AA 1996, s 24), for example where the arbitrator is not suitably qualified as required by the arbitration agreement.

The tribunal itself can rule on its own jurisdiction (AA 1996, s 30), but the court under s 32 of the AA 1996 can review this decision. The tribunal's powers in relation to procedural and evidential matters are set out in s 34 of the AA 1996 and its general duties in s 33 of the AA 1996. Section 34(2)(g) of the AA 1996, for example, gives the tribunal the opportunity to employ an inquisitorial procedure, which means it does not need to wait for the initiative of the parties.

The arbitrators can appoint experts or legal advisors (AA 1996, s 37), make inter alia orders for security of costs and order a witness or a party to be examined on oath (AA 1996, s 38), and make provisional awards (AA 1996, s 39). The parties are free to agree on the powers which the tribunal can exercise as regards remedies. In the absence of any agreement the tribunal has similar powers to a court in ordering payment, or in ordering a party to do or not to do a thing (AA 1996, s 48) and to award interest (AA 1996, s 49).

The award given has to be accompanied by reasons (AA 1996, s 52(4)), in default of which the court can be employed within 28 days to order the tribunal to give reasons (AA 1996, s 70(4)). However the parties can agree to dispense with reasons; this is then interpreted as excluding the court's jurisdiction under s 69 of the AA 1996 (AA 1996, s 69(1)). The parties must be notified of the award by service without delay (AA 1996, s 55). However the tribunal can withhold the award because of non-payment of fees (AA 1996, s 56).

Unless otherwise agreed, costs usually follow the event (AA 1996, ss 61, 62). The English arbitration award can be enforced in England as a judgment by leave of the court (AA 1996, s 66). Unless otherwise agreed by the parties, the award is deemed to be made at the seat of arbitration (AA 1996, s 53), which is particularly important for further proceedings and recognition and enforcement matters.

As we have seen (AA 1996, s 1(c)) the court only plays a limited role in the arbitration procedure. It has the power to extend the time for the beginning of arbitral proceedings (AA 1996, s 12). It can appoint an arbitrator (AA 1996, s 18) and remove an arbitrator on specific grounds (AA 1996, s 24). The court can assist in various matters set out in ss 42 and 44 of the AA 1996, for example to order a party to comply with a peremptory order of the tribunal or to assist the tribunal by making certain orders. The court can also be called on by a party to determine a preliminary point of law or jurisdiction (AA 1996, ss 45 and 32).

The arbitral award is deemed to be final, except for the challenges specified in the Act (AA 1996, s 58). Subject to the supplementary provisions of s 70 of the AA 1996, a review of the award is possible under ss 67–69 AA 1996 only:

(a) for lack of substantive jurisdiction (as set out in AA 1996, ss 30 and 82);

(b) for serious irregularity (for example the tribunal exceeding its powers, not complying with its general duties, failing to deal with all the issues or the award being against public policy); and

(c) on points of law.

One of the supplementary requirements of an appeal, as set out in s 70 of the AA 1996, is that the applicant has exhausted any arbitral appeals or reviews provided for by the Act (AA 1996, s 70(2)). Also, the application or appeal must be brought within 28 days of the date of the award (AA 1996, s 70(3)).

In *Pioneer Shipping Ltd v BTP Tioxide Ltd (The Nema)*, [1982] AC 724, 739–740 the House of Lords gave guidance, setting out that the court's discretion in allowing judicial review on a point of law must be exercised sparingly. It distinguished between one-off contracts and contracts involving a question of general importance, the former of which should only be reviewable if the arbitrator was obviously wrong. The emphasis of finality of an award, highlighted in this judgment, has been confirmed by the AA 1996 in s 69. The House of Lords' distinction concerning the importance of the disputed issue is set out in s 69(3)(c) of the AA 1996.

Once the court is allowed to intervene, it can either confirm the award or vary it, remit the award to the tribunal or set it aside (AA 1996, s 69(7)).

6.3.4 Enforcement of arbitral awards in overview

6.3.4.1 General

Once an award has been made, the unsuccessful party may wish to prevent enforcement. This can be done by actively or passively challenging the award. An active challenge to overturn the initial award is made in the courts of the seat of arbitration, unless that seat and the procedural law applied to the arbitration are different. A passive challenge means that the defeated party alleges in the enforcement proceedings that requirements for recognition and enforcement are not met.

Each jurisdiction has its own requirements that must be fulfilled before a foreign judgment or arbitral award is enforced. Certain of these conditions are common to most jurisdictions, and international agreements to harmonise the law have produced good effects. Generally, a party wishing to enforce an arbitral award should consider the following questions.

(a) Is the award final and binding?

(b) In which country are the assets of the defeated party situated?

(c) Will recognition and enforcement of the specific award be permitted there?

(d) If the assets are situated in more than one country, will all of those jurisdictions permit the recognition and enforcement of the award? Which jurisdiction will be most suitable?

(e) Are international agreements or reciprocal treaties binding both States involved (ie the State where the award was made and the enforcement State)?

(f) Are there any time limits for starting the enforcement procedure?

With respect to the recognition and enforcement of arbitral awards, the United Kingdom is party to the following conventions:

(a) the Geneva Convention for the Execution of Foreign Arbitral Awards 1927, which was given the force of law in England by virtue of Part II of the Arbitration Act 1950 (which is still in force); and

(b) the New York Convention on the Recognition and Enforcement of Foreign Arbitral Awards 1958, which was given effect by ss 9, 100–103 of the AA 1996.

The New York Convention has been (as of September 2005) ratified by 137 States. Where a State is party to both the Geneva and the New York Conventions, the New York Convention will prevail (New York Convention 1958, Art VII(2), the full text of which can be found at http://www.uncitral.org/uncitral/en/index.html under the category of 'UNCITRAL Texts & Statutes'). The New York Convention 1958 is applicable to the enforcement of foreign awards. It seeks to create a uniform system whereby an arbitral award is made enforceable, but it does not provide a procedure for enforcement. The latter is to be determined by the individual countries. The New York Convention stipulates the rule of non-intervention to arbitral proceedings by courts. It sets out specific requirements for the recognition and enforcement and allows for specific grounds on which the enforcement may be refused.

6.3.4.2 Overview of enforcement of foreign awards in England

There are broadly four ways of enforcing a foreign arbitral award in England:

(a) in the case of New York Convention awards, by applying for enforcement of the award under ss 100–103 of the AA 1996;

(b) in the case of Geneva Convention awards which are not also New York Convention awards, by applying for enforcement in accordance with Part II of the AA 1950 (in particular s 37), which continues to apply by virtue of s 99 of the AA 1996;

(c) by bringing an action at common law on the award (under the summary procedure of CPR, Part 24) or by applying for a summary enforcement under s 66 of the AA 1996 (see also AA 1950, s 36(1)). In s 104 of the AA 1996 it is explicitly clarified that these enforcement procedures are also open to New York Convention awards;

(d) by enforcing the respective foreign award under ss 9(3)(a), (5) and 12(1) of the Administration of Justice Act 1920, or under s 10A of the Foreign Judgments (Reciprocal Enforcement) Act 1933, or for awards in other parts of the UK in accordance with s 18(2)(e) of the CJJA 1982.

6.3.4.3 Provisions of the CJJA 1982

Sections 32 and 33 of the CJJA 1982, applicable to the enforcement of a judgment of a foreign court, back up the legislative decisions taken in the AA 1996 to recognise arbitration agreements between parties and to support the finality of an award so obtained. Section 32 of the CJJA 1982 provides for non-recognition of a judgment that did not give effect to a valid arbitration agreement and s 33 of the CJJA 1982 highlights steps which do not amount to a submission to the foreign court's jurisdiction, inter alia appearing in court in order to contest jurisdiction. However, this only goes as far as other specified instruments, including the European rules, do not require the recognition and enforcement.

6.3.5 Enforcement of New York Convention awards

Section 100 of the AA 1996 defines which awards fall within the scope of this Part of the AA 1996. An award is a New York Convention award in the sense of Part III of the AA 1996 if, at the date when recognition and enforcement is sought, the State in which the award is made is a signatory to the Convention. It could be argued, therefore, that accession to the New York Convention has a retroactive effect, because it is irrelevant whether or not the State was already a Convention State at the time when the *award* was made.

Section 101 of the AA 1996 states that foreign awards are to be recognised as binding between the parties and may be relied on by way of defence. They may be enforced by leave of the court in the same manner as if they were judgments of that court.

The enforcement provisions in ss 101–104 of the AA 1996 and those in s 36 of the AA 1950 are very similar. Under the AA 1996 a New York Convention award may be enforced in the following ways.

(a) By applying for leave of the court to enforce the award in the same manner as if it were a judgment of that court (s 101(2)). The procedure in the English courts will follow the Practice Direction, Arbitrations PD 49G, which supplements Part 49 of the CPR and replaces, with modifications, the former Ord 73 of the RSC.

(b) By applying for the terms of this award to be entered as a judgment (s 101(3)), following the procedure in PD 49G. This may be beneficial if the party wishes to register the judgment in a foreign court in order to enforce it there.

(c) By entering into a separate action on the award to enforce it finally (1996, s 104). This will be an action for damages in the amount of the award on breach of the arbitration contract and is of particular use if the successful party cannot supply the evidence required in s 102 of the AA 1996. Every arbitration agreement, irrespective of the arbitration being foreign or domestic, has an implied term that any award given in accordance with the agreement will be carried out. Such proceedings are not arbitration proceedings, so the usual provisions apply to them (PD 49G, para 30.1).

(d) By using the enforcement procedure under s 66 of the AA 1996 (Part I) according to s 104 of the AA 1996, again using the procedure set out in PD 49G. This should be considered carefully as it may be more difficult to meet the slightly differing criteria under Part I than it is to meet those of Part III of the AA 1996.

Section 102 of the AA 1996 sets out the requirements of evidencing the award as stated in Art IV of the New York Convention 1958. Section 103 of the AA 1996 provides for grounds on which recognition and enforcement may be refused. The refusal in these cases is discretionary, but nevertheless refusal can only be made in the cases provided for. They are:

(a) incapacity of a party to the arbitration agreement;

(b) invalidity of the arbitration agreement;

(c) absence of notice given to the other party of the appointment of the arbitrator or of the proceedings or where the respondent was otherwise unable to present his or her case;

(d) excess of jurisdiction conferred by the arbitration agreement;

(e) the composition of the tribunal or the procedure applied was contrary to the agreement or the relevant *lex arbitri*;

(f) the award is not yet binding or has been set aside or suspended;

(g) lack of arbitrability of the matter in dispute;

(h) recognition of enforcement is contrary to public policy (see *Westacre Investments Inc v Jugoimport SDPR Holding Co Ltd*, CA and *Soleimany v Soleimany*, CA).

6.3.6 Enforcement under the Administration of Justice Act 1920, the Foreign Judgments (Reciprocal Enforcement) Act 1933 and the Civil Jurisdiction and Judgments Act 1982

According to s 12(1) of the 1920 Act and s 10A of the 1933 Act these Acts apply to 'an award in proceedings on an arbitration if the award has, in pursuance of the law in force in the place where it was made, become enforceable in the same manner as a judgment given by a court in that place'. The procedure is essentially similar to that for judgments and the defences are the same (see 1920 Act, s 9(3) and (5), and 1933 Act, s 10A).

For enforcement of UK arbitral awards in other parts of the UK, s 18(2)(e) of the CJJA 1982 provides that 'an arbitration award which has become enforceable in the part of the United Kingdom in which it was given in the same manner as a judgment given by a court of law in that part' falls within the meaning of judgment under this section. This enforcement method is parallel to the possibility of enforcing the award at common law or by recourse to s 66 of the AA 1996 (see AA 1996, s 2(2)(b)).

6.4 Applicable law

6.4.1 General

The forum seised with the dispute will first determine the applicable law before it can apply this law to the facts. Even though it makes sense for a court to use its own law, for example an English court to use English law, this is not the default position for cases with an international element. Each case needs to be examined and the law applicable to it determined individually. Thus, it helps if the parties can agree on both the jurisdiction and the applicable law. If the parties choose the law of a country and also assign jurisdiction to a forum within that country, the resources are used in the most efficient and cost effective way. The judges can only be expected to be experts in their own legal system. If foreign law needs to be applied in the English courts, the content of the foreign law needs to be pleaded and proven by the parties.

How is the applicable law determined? Initially every jurisdiction developed its rules of private international law to answer this question; at common law it was the doctrine of the 'proper law of the contract'. However, in order to prevent forum shopping, harmonisation efforts have been made and over the years the 15 Member States of the European Union pre-2004 accession (namely Austria, Belgium, Denmark, Finland, France, Germany, Greece, Ireland, Italy, Luxembourg, the Netherlands, Portugal, Spain, Sweden and the United Kingdom) adopted and acceeded to the Rome Convention on the Law Applicable to Contractual Obligations 1980. As a consequence, the common law doctrine has been superseded and is only applicable outside the scope of the Rome Convention.

On 14 April 2005 all 25 Member States of the European Union signed the Convention on the Accession of the Czech Republic, the Republic of Estonia, the Republic of Cyprus, the Republic of Latvia, the Republic of Lithuania, the Republic of Hungary, the Republic of Malta, the Republic of Poland, the Republic of Slovenia and the Slovak Republic to the Convention on the Law Applicable to Contractual Obligations opened for signature in Rome on 19 June 1980, and to the First and Second Protocols on its interpretation by the Court of Justice of the European Communities (see [2005] OJ C169/1). All Member States declared to take the necessary steps to ratify this Convention within a reasonable time and, if possible, before December 2005.

The Convention will come into force between the States which have ratified it, on the first day of the third month following the deposit of the second instrument of ratification with the Secretary-General of the Council of the European Union (Accession Convention, Arts 4 and 5(1)). Thereafter it will enter into force for every Signatory State which ratifies the Convention on the first day of the third month following the deposit of its instrument of ratification (Accession Convention, Art 5(2)). As of September 2005 the Convention has not yet come into force.

Until all Member States have ratified the Convention it is necessary to check whether the Convention has yet become binding for the relevant state. You can do so by searching the agreements database of the Council of the European Union via the home page of the Council at http://ue.eu.int/cms3_fo/index.htm or directly at http//ue.eu.int/cms3_applications /Applications/accords/search.asp?lang=EN&cmsID=297. You can also access the website of the Council of the European Union via the Europa website at http://europa .eu.int, under the heading 'institutions'.

The Rome Convention goes hand in hand with Reg 44/2001 on jurisdiction and the recognition and enforcement of judgments in civil and commercial matters, as most of the contractual obligations covered by the Rome Convention will fall within the ambit of Reg

44/2001. Both instruments work together to reduce the scope for forum shopping. In the area of applicable law, the Rome Convention is only a first step and further harmonisation efforts within the European Union are being made. There are efforts to modernise the Rome Convention and to convert it into a Community instrument, but there are also efforts to develop a Community instrument on the law applicable to non-contractual obligations (see http://www.europa.eu.int or direct at http://www.europa.eu.int/scadplus/ leg/en/ s22003.htm).

On signing the 2005 Accession Convention to the Rome Convention the Member States also made a declaration, requesting the Commission to submit, as soon as possible, but the latest by end of 2005, a proposal for a Regulation on the law applicable to contractual obligations.

6.4.2 Rome Convention

The Rome Convention on the Law Applicable to Contractual Obligations (RC) 1980, with the exception of Arts 7(1) and 10(1)(e), has been incorporated into English law by the Contracts (Applicable Law) Act 1990 (see 1990 Act, s 2). The 1990 Act, including the RC 1980 in Sch 1, can be found in an international trade or conflict of laws statute book. The RC 1980 and the Contracts (Applicable Law) Act 1990 came into force on 1 April 1991 (see Contracts (Applicable Law) Act 1990 (Commencement No 1) Order 1991 (SI 1991/707)). The RC 1980 applies to contracts made after that date involving a choice between the laws of different countries (RC 1980, Arts 1(1) and 17).

One of the basic principles of the RC 1980 is the autonomy of the parties of a contract to choose their respective rights and obligations, part of which is to determine the applicable law. However there are some obstacles which need to be taken into account by the parties in order to make sure that their choice will be upheld.

6.4.2.1 Interpretation

Section 3 of the 1990 Act provides that the Conventions appended to the Act are to be interpreted in accordance with the principles laid down by, and any relevant decisions of, the ECJ. Judicial notice is to be taken of any decisions or opinions expressed by the ECJ. References to the ECJ for a preliminary ruling in accordance with the Brussels Protocol are permissive but not mandatory. Both the Brussels Protocol and the Second Protocol that has been drafted for this purpose, finally came into force on 1 August 2004. (The Brussels Protocol, which is to be found in Sch 3 to the 1990 Act, and the Second Protocol ([1998] OJ L48/17) are both appended to the consolidated version of the RC 1980 at [1998] OJ C27/34.)

The report of Professor Mario Giuliano and Professor Paul Lagarde of 31 October 1980, published in the Official Journal of the European Communities at [1980] OJ C282/1, may be considered in ascertaining the meaning or effect of any provision of the Convention (by virtue of Contracts (Applicable Law) Act 1990, s 3(3)(a)). The report can be accessed via the Eur-Lex web-site: http://europa.eu.int/eur-lex.

Article 18 of the RC 1980 provides for autonomous interpretation of the convention in order to achieve uniformity across the Member States: 'regard shall be had to their international character'. As with all Community legislation, it is to be interpreted purposively.

Please note that the same terms may be interpreted in a different way depending on whether they are used in the convention or in the national law of a State. For example, the same term used in the CPR will be interpreted in the light of the rules of English law, whereas the term used in a Community instrument will have international character which is reflected in a purposive interpretation.

So far, there are no preliminary rulings of the ECJ that would ensure a common interpretation of the Rome Convention. The Protocols enabling the ECJ to give rulings have only recently come into force. Thus, in the past the different Contracting States, despite the requirement of an autonomous and purpositive interpretation, have developed their own understanding as to the meaning of the articles of the RC 1980. This means that it is possible that the courts of one country might identify a different applicable law than the courts of another State. It is therefore necessary in each case to identify the exact meaning given to the relevant stipulation of the RC 1980 in the particular State, until and unless the matter is clarified by the ECJ.

6.4.2.2 Scope

The RC 1980 applies regardless of territorial connections or whether or not the contract or dispute has any connection with a Contracting State. It applies on the basis that a court in a Contracting State has jurisdiction. Thus, within the jurisdiction of the English courts, common law rules are only applicable where the subject matter falls outside the scope of the RC 1980.

The law identified by the RC 1980 will be applied, regardless of whether it is the law of a Contracting State or not (RC 1980, Art 2). The law that is specified by the RC 1980 is the substantive law of a country and not its conflict of law rules (RC 1980, Art 15).

The RC 1980 deals with: 'contractual obligations in any situation involving a choice between the laws of different countries' (RC 1980, Art 1(1)). This is interpreted in a European sense, and so for example, also includes gifts and promises to give, even though they are not supported by consideration (see Giuliano–Lagarde Report [1980] OJ C282/1). The RC 1980 applies in England to contracts made after 1 April 1991 (RC 1980, Art 17).

However, various matters have been excluded from the RC 1980's scope (RC 1980, Art 1(2)–(4)), mostly because they have already been dealt with under other instruments or agreements. The most interesting exclusions from our point of view are the following.

(a) By virtue of Art 1(2)(c) of the RC 1980 obligations arising out of the negotiable character of a bill of exchange, promissory note or other negotiable instrument are excluded. (In England these matters are governed by the Bills of Exchange Act 1882, s 72.) This exception only covers the aspect of negotiability of these instruments and not for example any contract clauses providing for payment by way of a bill of exchange.

(b) The RC 1980 does not apply to arbitration agreements or agreements on the choice of court. These subjects lie within the sphere of procedure and one could argue they are therefore better placed within the ambit of the *lex fori*. Another reason for their exclusion is that they are, to some extent, regulated by other international instruments, such as the New York Convention of 1958 for arbitration and the Brussels regime for jurisdiction.

(c) Matters of evidence and procedure are also excluded (see RC 1980, Art 1(2)(h)). However, in so far as the applicable law makes presumptions of law or regulates the burden of proof, these rules will prevail (RC 1980, Art 14(1)). In addition, proof of a contract or an act intended to produce legal effect, can be effected by using a mode of proof recognised either by the law of the forum or any other law referred to in Art 9 of the RC 1980 under which the act or contract is formally valid (RC 1980, Art 14 (2)).

(d) By virtue of Art 1(3) and (4) of the RC contracts of insurance are excluded in so far as they cover risks situated in the territories of EU Member States and are not concerned with re-insurance. Whether or not a risk falls within these territories is determined by the internal law of the forum. For this purpose s 2(1A) of the Contracts (Applicable Law) Act 1990 clari-fies which internal rules these are in England. The reason behind this exclusion is that the European Community has made efforts to harmonise the law of insurance and has pro-duced Directives to this effect, which have been implemented by the Member States (see for the UK the Financial Services and Markets Act 2000 (Law Applicable to Contracts of Insurance) Regulations 2001 (SI 2001/2653 as amended by SI 2001/3542)). However, the risk of most marine insurance contracts will fall outside the ambit of the exclusion and will thus be within the scope of the Convention.

Article 20 of the RC 1980 provides that the Convention shall not affect the application of pre-existing and future provisions of Community legislation and national law implement-ing EC legislation. Also, by virtue of Art 21 of the RC 1980, the 'Convention shall not prejudice the application of international conventions to which a Contracting State is, or becomes, a party'. The Rome Convention 1980 only helps to assert the applicable law. Once the applicable law is found this law will be applied and with it any conventions such as the Hague-Visby Rules for the carriage of goods by sea or the CISG for international sale contracts which are part of the applicable substantive law.

As we have seen, the RC 1980 applies to cases with a choice of law between different coun-tries. By virtue of Art 19(1) of the RC 1980, a territorial unit of a State, which has its own rules of law in respect of contractual obligations, is deemed to be a country in this context. Thus, even though both are part of the United Kingdom, England and Scotland would be understood as different 'countries'. In respect of the difference in law between the different parts of the United Kingdom, s 2(3) of the Contracts (Applicable Law) Act 1990 provides, despite Art 19 (2) of the RC 1980, that the RC 1980 is also to be used to determine the applicable law in a conflict between English and Scottish law.

6.4.2.3 Express choice of governing law – Art 3 of the RC 1980

Article 3 of the RC 1980 highlights the principle of party autonomy. The parties are free to choose the law to govern their contract. They can even choose different laws to govern different parts of it, they can choose a foreign law not otherwise connected to the con-tract and they can alter their choice. In order for Art 3 of the RC 1980 to be pertinent two criteria have to be fulfilled:

(a) the parties must have made a choice; and

(b) that choice must be express or demonstrated with reasonable certainty (RC 1980, Art 3(1)).

To ensure that a choice of law clause will be upheld, it is of utmost importance that the stipulations as to choice of law are expressed as simply and clearly as possible. The RC

1980 is meant to operate as a full, complete, and sufficient code for the determination of the governing law, independently from any national law. This principle should be borne in mind whilst analysing whether a choice of law exists and whether this choice is express or demonstrable. Contract terms that are not identifiable by means of the RC 1980 should therefore be avoided, as it is not in the parties' interest to litigate first over the governing law before they can even address the dispute itself.

The Giuliano-Lagarde Report ([1980] OJ C282/1 at 17) gives some examples where the parties could have made an implied choice in favour of a particular law:

(a) A contract made using a standard form which is governed by a particular system of law, such as a Lloyd's Marine Policy, might indicate the choice of this legal system.

(b) Where the parties to a contract had previous dealings with each other under contracts including express choice of law clauses, the situation as a whole might indicate that the same law is also to apply to the new contract.

(c) A choice of forum clause might lead to the conclusion that the law of the forum has been chosen; however, this is subject to the other terms of the contract and all other circumstances.

(d) Where the parties refer to specific articles or sections of a particular law, this might indicate that the parties intend this legal system to apply.

(e) Where the parties to an arbitration agreement chose a place for the arbitration, and other circumstances indicate that the arbitrators are to apply the law of that place, this would indicate the choice of law of the parties.

In *Egon Oldendorff v Libera Corp (No 2)*, QBD (Comm), for example, the place of arbitration and the fact that the parties had used a well-known English charterparty based on English law was held to demonstrate the parties' intention to apply English law to the contract.

The law chosen has to be the law of a specific country. This will be the domestic law of the country (RC 1980, Art 15), rather than its rules of private international law. The parties however cannot avoid the application of mandatory rules of their own legal system by choosing the application of a foreign law. The mandatory rules of the legal system that was derogated from remain applicable by virtue of Art 3(3) of the RC 1980.

6.4.2.4 Absence of express choice, Art 4 of the RC 1980

In the absence of a valid choice of law clause, Art 4 of the RC 1980 provides for the application of the law of the country to which the contract is most closely connected. A severable part of the contract that has closer connection with another country may, by way of exception, be governed by the law of this other country. Article 4 of the RC 1980 in paras (2)–(4) provides presumptions as to where the closest connection lies.

The following presumptions may be of particular interest.

(a) Article 4(2) RC 1980 presumes that the contract has its closest connection to the country in which the characteristic performer is situated. In the case of a business transaction it will be the country in which the party effecting the characteristic performance has its principal place of business, or where the place of business is situated through which, in accordance with the contract, the performance is effected. For example, in the case of a contract of the sale of goods the characteristic performance is the one of the seller. Thus, by virtue of Art 4(2) of the RC 1980, the law of the country where the seller has his place of business is the applicable law. See also *Bank of Baroda v Vysya Bank*, QBD (Comm) for an example of this presumption in relation to a dispute between the issuing and confirming bank of a letter of credit. It was held that the characteristic performance is the one of the guarantor: the honouring of the letter of credit towards the seller.

(b) For a contract of carriage of goods, a closer connection is necessary in order to invoke a presumption: at the time when the contract is concluded the place of business of the carrier must coincide with either the place of loading or discharge, or with the principal place of business of the consignor (RC 1980, Art 4(4)). Only where these requirements are met will there be a presumption of the applicable law to the carriage contract. Otherwise the closest connection must be established in accordance with Art 4(1) 1980 RC.

Please note, however, that the presumptions given in Art 4(2)–(4) of the RC 1980 may be made *inapplicable* according to Art 4(5) of the RC 1980 if the circumstances as a whole point to a closer connection with another country. An example of this may be where the performance of the obligation takes place in another country to which other factors also point.

However, should the presumptions of Art 4(2)–(4) of the RC 1980 be easily rebutted in favour of Art 4(5)? The aim and effect of using presumptions is to create certainly and predictability. The parties must be able to identify the applicable law clearly and easily. On the other hand, Art 4(5) of the RC 1980 allows for flexibility to cater best for the circumstances of each individual case. How stringent should the requirements be therefore in order to displace the presumption? In different courts and countries different views have been advanced, following either the so-called 'strong presumption' or 'weak presumption' theory. Even within England different decisions have been based on different approaches. Overall, however, there seems to be a trend in English courts to treat the *place of performance* as a more significant element in determining the centre of gravity than the *place of business* of the characteristic performer. Thus they seem to favour a more flexible approach, more readily displacing the presumptions of Art 4(2)–(4) of the RC 1980 (see *Bank of Baroda v Vysya Bank*, QBD (Comm); *Marconi Communications International Ltd v PT Pan Indonesia Bank Ltd*, CA; *Kenburn Waste Management Ltd v Bergmann*, CA upholding ChD; and *Definitely Maybe (Touring) Ltd v Marek Lierberberg Konzertagentur GmbH (No 2)*, QBD (Comm)).

Now that the Protocols to the Rome Convention (see **6.4.2.1**) have come into force, these differences could be abolished by a ruling of the ECJ. This, however, presupposes that one of the Contracting States refers a question as to the interpretation of Art 4 (5) of the RC 1980 to the ECJ in accordance with the relevant procedure (see First and Second Protocol).

6.4.2.5 Modifications

The general rules of choice of law and close connection are modified for certain consumer contracts (RC 1980, Art 5; but note that Art 5 is not applicable to contracts of carriage) and individual employment contracts (RC 1980, Art 6). These rules act on two levels.

(a) On default of a choice of law by the parties these rules determine a law with which the weaker contracting party (the consumer or employee) seems to have the closest connection.

(b) If the parties have chosen the applicable law, the mandatory rules of the law that would govern the contract following the rule above cannot be avoided.

Mandatory rules are rules of such importance that they must not be contracted out of, and they must even be applied irrespective of the governing law. Apart from the provisions in Arts 5 and 6 of the RC 1980 references to mandatory rules can be found in four cases.

(a) Article 3(3) of the RC 1980 so that the mandatory rules of the ordinarily applicable law cannot be avoided by choosing a different law to govern the contract.

(b) Article 7(1) of the RC 1980 to cater for the mandatory rules of a country with which the case has a close connection; please remember that Art 7(1) has not been enacted in England by the Contracts (Applicable Law) Act 1990, s 2(2).

(c) Article 7(2) of the RC 1980 to allow for the application of rules of the forum which are mandatory irrespective of the law otherwise applicable.

(d) Article 16 of the RC 1980 by which the application of a rule of the law specified by the RC 1980 can be avoided if it is manifestly incompatible with the public policy of the forum.

The Hague-Visby Rules as enacted by the Carriage of Goods by Sea Act 1971 are an example of such mandatory rules referred to in Art 7(2) of the RC 1980. The Hague-Visby Rules apply irrespective of the law applicable to the carriage contract in so far as the limits of liability provided by the Rules cannot be reduced. Any clause purporting such an effect is null and void (HVR, Art III(8)). Similarly it was held in *Owners of Cargo on Board the Morviken v Owners of the Hollandia (The Hollandia), (The Morviken)*, HL that Art III(8) of the HVR prevented the giving of effect to a forum selection clause which would have had the effect of a lesser liability regime being applied by that chosen court. Thus, both the choice of forum and the choice of law clause were restricted in their application due to the mandatory application of the liability regime of the Hague-Visby rules as set out in Art III(8) of the HVR.

6.4.2.6 Domain of the governing law

Article 10 of the RC 1980 provides the scope of the governing law. It covers issues of interpretation and performance of the contract, consequences of the breach within the limits of the powers conferred on the court by its procedural law (RC 1980, Art 1(2)(h)), the extinction of its obligations, prescription and limitation of actions. (The Foreign Limitation Periods Act 1984 had already brought English private law in line with the principle that the issues on limitation are attached to the governing law.) Please note that, by virtue of s 2(2) of the Contracts (Applicable Law) Act 1990, Art 10(1)(e) of the RC 1980 has been excluded from application in the UK. Article 10(1)(e) of the RC 1980, if applied in the UK, would lead to the consequences of nullity of contract being governed by the law applicable to the contract rather than, as under UK law, according to the choice of law rules for restitutionary obligations.

The formal validity of the contract is covered by Art 9 of the RC 1980 which refers to the law governing the contract or the law at the place where the contract was made. Compliance with the requirements of one of these laws will suffice. The material validity is covered by Art 8 of the RC 1980, the rules of which point mainly to the law that would govern the contract if it were valid.

6.4.3 Common law rules on contractual obligations

English courts developed the doctrine of the 'proper law of the contract', where the choice of law process is broken into three stages.

(a) Express choice: the parties are free to make an express choice of law. This choice is upheld as long as it is bona fide, legal and not contrary to public policy.

(b) Implied choice: in the absence of an express choice the proper law may be inferred from the circumstances, such as the use of a particular standard form (see *Amin Rasheed Shipping Corporation v Kuwait Insurance Co*, HL), the use of an arbitration agreement (see *Compagnie Tunisienne de Navigation SA v Compagnie d'Armement Maritime SA*, HL) or of a jurisdiction clause (see *Hellenic Steel Co v Svolamar Shipping Co Ltd (The Komninos S)*, CA).

(c) Closest and most real connection: in the absence of any express or implied choice the contract is to be governed by the 'objective proper law', which is determined by looking for the law with which the transaction has its closest and most real connection (for example by looking at the place of performance of the contract, the domicile of the parties and any other relevant circumstances).

Since 1 April 1991 the proper law doctrine is only applicable where the issue falls outside the scope of the Rome Convention 1980, that is to say when the subject matter is not a 'contractual obligation' in the sense of Art 1 of the RC 1980, bearing in mind the exclusions in Art 1(2) RC 1980. The proper law doctrine and the RC 1980 approach are very similar, yet different in some aspects. Under the proper law doctrine a court, in the absence of a choice of law, would evaluate all the facts of the case in order to find the closest and most real connection, whereas under the RC 1980 the approach is to apply one of the presumptions of Art 4(2)–(4) of the RC 1980. At times it seems that the interpretation of the RC 1980 by English courts is still slightly influenced by the initial proper law approach, for example with respect to the court's readiness to dis-apply the presumption in favour of a more close connection (RC 1980, Art 4 (5)).

6.4.4 Checklist for the applicable law to contractual obligations

A brief checklist follows of all the aspects that need to be borne in mind while identifying the applicable law.

6.4.4.1 Which rules of private international law are applicable?

(a) Rome Convention 1980:

   (i)   applicable throughout the 15 pre-2004 accession EU Member States and to other member states upon ratification of the 2005 Accession Convention;

   (ii)   in England for contracts after 1 April 1991;

   (iii) also applicable for conflict of laws within the United Kingdom (between the laws of England, Scotland and Northern Ireland);

(iv)   for contractual obligations within the scope of the RC 1980;

(v)   as long as no other more specific convention applies, Art 21 of the RC 1980.

(b) Common law:

(i)   for contracts made before 1 April 1991; and

(ii)   for contracts in areas not covered by the RC 1980.

6.4.4.2 Choice of law rules of the Rome Convention 1980

(a) Express choice of governing law, Art 3.

(b) Absence of express choice, Art 4.

(c) Modification: certain consumer contracts, Art 5.

(d) Modification: individual employment contracts, Art 6.

(e) Modification: mandatory rules. Apart from the provisions in Arts 5 and 6 references to those mandatory rules can be found in four cases:

(i)   Art 3(3);

(ii)   Art 7(1) (please remember that Art 7(1) has no force of law in England: see the Contracts (Applicable Law) Act 1990, s 2 (2));

(iii)   Art 7(2); and

(iv)   Art 16 (reference to public policy).

6.4.5 Applicable law to non-contractual obligations

6.4.5.1 General

Where the issue in question is characterised as a non-contractual obligation, the Rome Convention 1980 and the common law doctrine of the proper law of the contract are not applicable. As we have seen at **6.4.1** above there are efforts to create a Community instrument (the so-called Rome II Regulation) in order to fill the gap, but the process has not yet been completed (search at http://www.europa.eu.int or see http://www.europa.eu.int /scadplus/leg/en/s22003.htm). In the absence of Community legislation, each country has to apply its own rules of private international law to determine the applicable law. Most claims covering non-contractual obligations will be in the area of tort and restitution. For claims in tort, most countries apply, as a basic rule, the law of the place where the tort occurred, also called the *lex loci delicti*. However, problems arise for example where the tortious act was committed in a different country from where the damage occurred and one might be better advised to find the 'proper law of the tort', by asking to which country the tort is most closely connected.

6.4.5.2 Torts and delicts

In England the law applicable to non-contractual obligations, before 1 May 1996, was found by using the rules of common law. However since 1 May 1996, according to ss 13 and 14 of the Private International Law (Miscellaneous Provisions) Act (PILMPA) 1995 and art 2 of the Private International Law (Miscellaneous Provisions) Act 1995 (Commencement) Order 1996 (the 1996 Commencement Order) the applicable law for torts is determined as follows:

(a) by using the rules of common law for torts that occurred before 1 May 1996 (see PILMPA 1995, s 14(1) and the 1996 Commencement Order, para 2;

(b) by using the rules of common law for claims alleging defamation, malicious falsehood, and similar complaints (PILMPA 1995, Art 13);

(c) by applying the 1995 Act for all other tort claims.

Let us look briefly at the common law perspective on the applicable law for torts and proceed thereafter to the provisions of the PILMPA 1995.

The starting point in determining the law applicable to torts under the common law rules is the location of the tort. This location is easy to determine if the damage occurred at the same place where the tortious act was committed. However where the damage occurred at different locations, one has to identify the place where in substance the cause of action arose (see *Metall und Rohstoff AG v Donaldson Lufkin & Jenrette Inc*, CA). Regardless of the international character of the case and the parties involved, if the cause of action arose in England, English domestic law applies. If however the cause of action arose in a foreign country, but is heard in an English court, the double actionability rule will apply. This means that the claimant will have to show that the claim will be successful under both:

(a) English domestic law as the *lex fori* in which the facts of the case need to give rise to liability as a tort; and

(b) the domestic *lex loci delicti*, where the tort occurred, as a civil liability.

In the course of time two exceptions were made to the double actionability rule, now known as the rule of double actionability with double flexibility:

(a) first if an issue or the whole dispute was more closely connected to another law the *lex loci delicti* was replaced by this other law;

(b) secondly another more closely connected law could replace the English law as *lex fori*.

Part III of the PILMPA 1995 provides for the abolition of the double actionability rule (with or without double flexibility) in cases other than defamation (PILMPA 1995, ss 10 and 13). The Act provides a general rule in s 11 that the applicable law is the law of the place where the tort or delict occurred. In cases where the elements of those events take place in different countries one has to look at where the damage was sustained in cases of personal injury or damage to property and the law of that country will then apply. Otherwise one has to identify where the most significant element of those events occurred. However in the event that another law is substantially more appropriate to determine the issues arising in the case or any of those issues, s 12 provides for a displacement of the general rule.

In *Harding v Wealands*, considering the applicable law to a road accident, the Court of Appeal gave some guidance on the interaction between ss 11 and 12 of the PILMPA 1995. It held that where the law of the place where the tort occurred was also the national law of one of the parties involved, it was difficult to envisage circumstances that would render it substantially more appropriate under s 12 of the PILMPA 1995 that any issue could be tried by reference to some other law.

6.4.5.3 Restitution

For restitutionary matters English conflict of law rules provide for application of the proper law of the obligation (see *Macmillan Inc v Bishopsgate Investment Trust plc (No 3)*, CA). This proper law of the obligation is determined as the:

(a) law applicable to the contract if there was a contract between the parties from which the obligation arose;

(b) *lex situs* of the obligation arising out of a transaction involving immovable property; and

(c) law of the country where the enrichment occurs in any other circumstances.

6.5 Dispute resolution checklist

Please find below a brief checklist, which can be used to recall the necessary conflict of laws issues. The steps below are to help identify the form and rules of dispute resolution and enforcement, as well as the applicable law.

6.5.1 Form of dispute resolution

6.5.1.1 Arbitration

(a) Proceedings and jurisdiction: institutional arbitration or, in England, the English Arbitration Act 1996.

(b) Recognition and enforcement of arbitral awards:

   (i)   Geneva Convention, which obtained the force of law in England from Part II of the Arbitration Act 1950;

   (ii)   New York Convention 1958, which obtained the force of law in England from Part III, ss 100–104 of the Arbitration Act 1996.

6.5.1.2 Litigation in the courts

(a) Jurisdiction:

   (i)   Regulation 44/2001/EC (Reg 44/2001);

   (ii)   the Brussels Convention of 27 September 1968;

   (iii) the Lugano Convention of 16 April 1988;

   (iv) national rules of private international law, in England the common law rules as amended by statutory provisions (CPR, Part 6).

(b) Recognition and enforcement of judgments:

   (i)   Regulation 44/2001/EC Chapter III;

   (ii)   Brussels Convention of 27 September 1968; Title III;

   (iii) Lugano Convention of 16 April 1988, Title III;

   (iv) National rules of private international law, in England the common law rules, subject to the application of the Administration of Justice Act 1920 and the Foreign Judgments (Reciprocal Enforcement) Act 1933.

6.5.2 Applicable law

(a) Contractual obligations:

    (i)   Rome Convention 1980, Contracts (Applicable Law) Act 1990

    (ii)   National rules of private international law, in England the common law rules on contractual obligations.

(b) Non-contractual obligations:

    (i)   National rules of private international law, in England the Private International Law (Miscellaneous Provisions) Act 1995, Part III and the common law rules on non-contractual obligations.

6.6 Revision and further reading

6.6.1 Questions

This is your opportunity to revise what you have learned and to check whether you have understood the issues covered in this chapter. I suggest that you attempt to answer the questions below before you move on to the next chapter. In doing so explain your findings and refer to the relevant legal provisions.

Question 1

S, a UK company based in Scotland, agreed to sell iron products to B Co, Bombay, India. The contract, negotiated and signed in London, stipulated that the goods were sold on ddp terms. No agreement has been made as to the law governing the contract and as to which country's courts would have jurisdiction over any disputes arising under the contract of sale. The goods arrive damaged due to improper loading and packaging. B now sues S for breach of contract and files its claim for damages with a Scottish court at the place of S's business.

(a) Explain whether this Scottish court has jurisdiction to try the case.

(b) Which law would the Scottish court apply to the sale contract? Give reasons for your decision.

Question 2

A, domiciled in Spain, sells a crane to B, who is domiciled in the Netherlands. The crane is to be delivered to a building site in Portugal. B wants to sue A for damages due to defects in the crane.

(a) Explain which courts will accept jurisdiction.

(b) Which law will the relevant court apply to the contract and why?

Question 3

A, an exporter from South Africa, and B, an importer with his place of business in Bulgaria, have concluded a contract on the sale of goods. They have agreed on the jurisdiction of the English courts. The performance of the contract causes dispute.

(a) A wants to sue B in the English courts. Explain whether the English courts will accept jurisdiction.

(b) Which law will the English court apply to the contract?

(c) Which jurisdiction rules would apply if B was domiciled in Belgium?

Question 4

Company A, with a seat in Romania, has concluded a sale contract with B, domiciled in England. The contract should have been performed in England, however A did not deliver the goods to B. B wants to sue for breach of contract.

(a) Explain whether the English courts will accept jurisdiction.

(b) Which law would an English court apply to the contract and why?

Question 5

Seller A, domiciled in England, sells goods to buyer B from Japan. The contract provides for the application of English law. A wants to sue B for the purchase price in the English courts.

(a) Explain whether the English courts will accept jurisdiction.

(b) Which law would an English court apply to the contract and why?

Question 6

A sued B in Sweden for damages resulting from alleged breach of contract. The Swedish court rejects the claim in its final judgment. A now starts proceedings in England regarding the same claim and cause of action. What can B do?

Question 7

Judgment in favour of A was given in a court of a Member State of the EU and is now to be enforced in another Member State. The enforcing Member State however is of the opinion that the adjudicating court had erred when accepting jurisdiction. It had ignored a jurisdiction agreement between the parties which would have led to the courts of another Member State. Will the enforcing court recognise the judgment?

Question 8

A sued B in England for damages resulting from alleged breach of contract. Before the court gives a judgment the parties settle the case in an agreement before the English court, providing that B has to pay £10,000 to A.

(a) How can this agreement be enforced?

(b) Later A regrets his choice and sues B in Italy for the whole amount of damages again. The Italian court ignores the previous settlement and finds in favour of A. A now wants to enforce the Italian judgment in the English courts. B opposes this idea. Will the judgment be enforced? What is the procedure for this?

Question 9

S and B have entered into negotiations for a sale contract. They wonder whether they should add an arbitration agreement into their contract.

(a) Advise them as to the advantages and disadvantages of such an agreement.

(b) Are there any formal requirements for the arbitration agreement?

Question 10

S and B agree on arbitration to be the means of solving any disputes arising out of their contract. However B sues S before the English courts. What can S do to uphold the arbitration agreement?

Question 11

English arbitration proceedings end with an award in B's favour. S is adamant that this award is wrong. He wants the English courts to review the whole case. Will he be successful in obtaining a 'review' by the courts?

Question 12

B has succeeded in arbitration against S in a New York Convention state. B now wants to enforce this arbitral award in England.

(a) Explain whether and how this is possible.

(b) S wants to oppose the enforcement of the arbitral award. What are the possible challenges he can submit?

Question 13

S does not agree with the arbitral award made in a New York Convention State in B's favour. He wants to sue B on the same grounds as disputed in the foreign arbitration proceedings, but this time in the English courts. Will he be successful?

6.6.2 Further reading

(a) Case C-159/02 *Gregory Paul Turner v (1) Felix Fareed Ismail Grovit (2) Harada Ltd (3) Changepoint SA (2004)*, [2004] All ER (EC) 485 including the Advocate General's opinion concerning anti-suit injunctions within the European jurisdiction regime

(b) Case C-116/02 *Erich Gasser GmbH v MISAT SrL* [2004] 1 Lloyd's Rep 222 concerning Brussels Convention 1968 — jurisdiction clauses — lis pendens

(c) Case C-80/00 *Italian Leather SpA v WECO Polstermöbel GmbH & Co* [2002] ECR I–4995 concerning Brussels Convention 1968 — enforcement of provisional measure – irreconcilability within the meaning of Art 27(3) of the Brussels Convention 1968

(d) *Hiscox v Outhwaite* [1992] 2 Lloyd's Rep 435 concerning enforcement of arbitral awards and the interpretation of the term 'convention award'

(e) *Union Transport Group plc v Continental Lines SA* [1992] 1 Lloyd's Rep 229, HL concerning jurisdiction in the EC — place of performance of obligation — charterparty

(f) *Spiliada Maritime Corporation v Cansulex Ltd* [1987] AC 460 concerning *forum non conveniens*

(g) *Amin Rasheed Shipping Corporation v Kuwait Insurance Co* [1984] 1 AC 50 concerning when to serve out of jurisdiction – how to ascertain the proper law of the contract

(h) *The Hollandia* (also known as *The Morviken*) [1983] 1 Lloyd's Rep 1 concerning the limits of a choice of law clause — Art III(8) of the Hague-Visby Rules

(i) *Mareva Compania Naviera SA v International Bulk Carriers* [1975] 2 Lloyd's Rep 509 concerning the Mareva injunction

(j) Convention on choice of court agreements of 30 June 2005 concluded by the Hague Conference on Private International Law, details to be found on www.hcch.net

(k) Edwin Peel, 'Forum non conveniens and European ideals', [2005] LMCLQ 363–377

(l) Adrian Briggs, 'Forum non conveniens and ideal Europeans', [2005] LMCLQ 378–382

(m) Haris P Meidnais, 'Public policy and ordre public in the private international law of the EU: traditional positions and modern trends', [2005] 30.1 ELRev 95–110

(n) William E O'Brian, 'Choice of law under the Rome Convention: the dancer or the dance', [2004] LMCLQ 375–386

(o) Jonathan Hill, 'Choice of law in contract under the Rome Convention: the approach taken by the UK courts', [2004] ICLQ 325–350

(p) Gordon Blanke, 'The turning tides of Turner', [2004] 25.10 Bus LR 261–270

(q) Chee Ho Tham, 'Damages for breach of English jurisdiction clauses: more than meets the eye', [2004] LMCLQ 46–71

(r) Yvonne Baatz, 'Who decides on Jurisdiction Clauses? *Erich Gasser v MISAT*', [2004] LMCLQ 25–29

(s) Ana M Lopez-Rodriguez, 'The Rome Convention of 1980 and its revision at the crossroads of the European contract law project', [2004] 12.2 ERPL 167–191

(t) Louis Flannery, 'Anti-suit Injunctions in Support of Arbitration', [2003] EBLR 143–159

(u) Adrian Briggs, 'Choice of Law?' [2003] LMCLQ 12–38

(v) Adrian Briggs, 'On drafting agreements on choice of law', [2003] LMCLQ 389–395

(w) Xandra E Kramer, Case Comment: Case C-80/00, *Italian Leather SpA v WECO Polstermöbel GmbH & Co*, Judgment of the Court (Fifth Chamber of 6 June 2002, [2002] ECR I-4995; [2003] 40 CMLRev 953–964

(x) Rolf Herber, 'Jurisdiction and arbitration — should the new Convention contain rules on these subjects?' [2002] LMCLQ 405–417

(y) Christopher Tillman, 'The Relationship between Party Autonomy and the Mandatory Rules in the Rome Convention', [2002] JBL 45–77

(z) J Fawcett, 'Non-exclusive jurisdiction agreements in private international law', [2001] LMCLQ 234–260

(aa) David Jackson, 'Fitting English maritime jurisdiction into Europe — or vice versa?' [2001] LMCLQ 219–233; however please bear in mind the developments since this article was written with respect to anti-suit injunctions (the ECJ decision on *Turner v Grovit*) and the coming into force of Reg 44/2001.

(bb) CGJ Morse, 'Letters of credit and the Rome Convention' [1994] LMCLQ 560–571

(cc) Regina Asariotis, 'Implications of a "British" Jurisdiction Clause', [1992] JBL 321–325.

For future developments please research the following topics via the Europa home page http://www.europa.eu.int or directly at http://www.europa.eu.int/eur-lex/lexlen/index.htm:

(a) conversion of the Rome Convention 1980 on the law applicable to contractual obligations into a Community instrument and its modernisation, particularly the Green Paper (COM (2002) 654 final) and opinions thereon;

(b) proposal for a Regulation on the law applicable to non-contractual obligations ('Rome II Regulation'), COM (2003) 427 final and opinions thereon;

(c) Regulation 805/2004/EC creating a European enforcement order for uncontested claims;

(d) Commission proposal for a Regulation establishing a European small claims procedure of 15 March 2005, COM (2005) 87 final.

7
The Bigger Picture

7.1 Introduction

The international trade transaction needs to be understood as a whole, consisting of a multitude of contracts which, at least from the seller's and buyer's perspective, are interrelated. A stipulation in one of the contracts or a decision taken within one contractual relationship can have the power to affect one or all of the others. For example:

(a) any actions under a letter of credit are likely to influence the sale contract, in particular the seller's payment;

(b) the questions of whether the seller or the buyer can sue the carrier and whether the claimant has an insurable interest or not will depend on the progress of the sales transaction (relevant aspects are, eg: who bears the risk; who has property; who is in possession of the transport document; has the seller been paid);

(c) also, the decision of either the seller or the buyer to claim against the insurer of the goods will affect the right to claim damages from the carrier, due to subrogation.

A good way of improving your understanding of the relevant questions and connections is to read as many court decisions as possible.

In this chapter we want to concentrate on some case studies to look at examples of these interconnected relationships, but we also want to create a deeper understanding by linking the separate chapters of this book together. The case studies are used as an educational tool. They do not claim to be realistic. In practice at least, parties who regularly trade internationally will have their standard terms of contract, which usually include choice of law clauses and often jurisdiction clauses. However, even then problems might arise if both parties have conflicting standard terms. It may be questionable whether these standard terms have been sufficiently incorporated into the contract. Different legal systems will have different standards. Thus, in practice many more precautions are usually taken than in the following case studies. However, some of the questions which are relevant in the case studies might still surface in practice in one way or another.

The cases start with setting out the scenario and follow with a brief discussion of the critical issues. The aim is to facilitate an awareness of the problems or issues rather than to provide the reader with all possible details of a solution. You may want to attempt to draw up your own answer plan first before reading and looking at the outline answer. Whether your advice is required as such or as part of an assessment at university, you should concentrate on following the criteria listed below whilst formulating your advice.

7.1.1 Identification of essential issues/relevance of the content of your advice

Your reader or tutor is not interested in all the aspects of international trade law you have ever heard of. He consults you to obtain a solution to the specific problem. Thus you need to discriminate between relevant and irrelevant information.

7.1.2 Accuracy of the content and correct application of relevant legal principles:

The content of your advice must be correct. If there is conflicting authority or if the outcome is unclear, you must inform your reader of these aspects and advise of the best procedure. If you have not received all the facts you need to form a conclusive opinion, you should ask the person seeking your advice to provide you with the necessary information or you or he should investigate further. If this is not possible, or if further investigations do not lead to a clarification in the matter, you need to cover all eventualities in your advice.

7.1.3 Structured approach and presentation

It is essential that you structure your advice, so that all parties involved can find and identify the required details easily.

7.1.4 Clarity of expression

You should pitch your advice, so that every party concerned can understand and follow your explanations.

7.1.5 Appropriate use of authority and level of research

Regardless of whether you are researching for a factual situation or for an assessment at University, you need to make sure that you have used the latest authority and are up to date. Your statements should be backed up with the appropriate statutes and case-law.

7.2 Case study 1 Steel Girders

7.2.1 Scenario

Sell Co, a company based in Mozambique, has sold 2,000 steel girders of best quality to Buyer Ltd, seated in Portsmouth. The contract, written in English, was negotiated and agreed upon during the visit of Sell Co's representative to England. It is based on Buyer Ltd's standard terms. The goods are to be shipped from Beira in Mozambique to Portsmouth, England. The parties have termed the contract an extended fob contract and have agreed the following:

I. Sell Co is to ship the goods from Beira to Portsmouth before 15 August 2005, make all shipping arrangements, pay the carrier and the insurance premium, and tender the bill of lading together with the other documents to Buyer Ltd via its bank in England.

II. Sell Co is to take out marine insurance (Institute Cargo Clauses A) for the steel girders and tender the insurance policy to Buyer Ltd.

III. Buyer Ltd is to pay a lump sum to Sell Co on tender of the documents for the arrangements made by Sell Co. However, the price of the steel girders has to be specified individually for accountancy reasons.

IV. Payment is to be effected by letter of credit (l/c) in pounds sterling.

V. Property is to pass on the tender of the documents.

VI. In case of any disputes arising, the matter shall be dealt with by arbitration in London.

Buyer Ltd has now opened a letter of credit (incorporating the UCP 500) and Sell Co has received advice of the opening of the credit in its favour. The letter of credit requires a bill of lading with a shipment period of 1 July–10 August 2005 and has an expiry date of 21 days after shipment. Sell Co has only checked the letter of credit to confirm that the amount accords with the contract.

The goods are shipped on 10 August 2005 on the ship '*Hope*' which has been chartered by Charley Ltd from the shipowner, Ocean Enterprise Corporation under a charterparty by demise. Both shipping companies have their place of business in Beira. Sell Co has pre-prepared a bill of lading for the ship's master to sign, which is wrongly dated 11 August 2005. The bill states the goods as compliant with the commercial invoice and to be in good order and condition. The immaculate condition is verified by a certificate of inspection, issued on loading.

When Sell Co presents the documents to the issuing bank they are rejected on the basis that the date on the bill of lading is not within the period stated in the letter of credit and that the insurance certificate is not acceptable.

Sell Co contacts the ship's master and asks him to sign a bill of lading dated 10 August 2005. Sell Co then re-tenders the second bill of lading, the insurance policy and all the other documents stipulated in the contract to the bank. The bank contacts Buyer Ltd for instructions as to whether they should pay Sell Co according to the credit, as they suspect fraud or forgery because of the altered date of shipment.

In the meantime, the price for steel girders has fallen dramatically and the goods have arrived in Portsmouth. A representative of Buyer Ltd sees the steel girders in the hold of the ship stored beside logs of wood which are obviously damp. The steel girders are rusty and Buyer Ltd is therefore keen to avoid its contractual obligations.

Buyer Ltd now seeks your advice and asks you to explain the following:

1. Which law will be applicable to the contract and any arbitration proceedings between Sell Co and itself?

2. Is the sale contract an extended fob contract, or is it a cif contract after all?

3. Was the bank's first rejection of the documents valid? What is the nature and effect of the arrangement between Sell Co and Buyer Ltd providing for a letter of credit?

4. Can the ship's master lawfully alter the bill of lading? Can Sell Co make a corrective tender, thus using the second bill of lading?

5. Can the bank reject the documents a second time because of alleged fraud?

6. In the event that the bank has to pay and accept the documents, can Buyer Ltd reject the goods?

7. Can Buyer Ltd sue the carrier under the bill of lading contract if it should choose to accept the goods? Who in fact is the carrier, Ocean Enterprise Corporation or Charley Ltd?

8. Who will have to bear the cost of the damage to the steel girders and what is the position of the marine insurers in this respect?

Advise Buyer Ltd. (In answering questions 2 to 8 you are to assume that English law is the law applicable to the sale contract.)

7.2.2 Points of discussion

7.2.2.1 Introduction

In the following we will identify the critical issues relevant to the scenario between Sell Co and Buyer Ltd and will advise Buyer Ltd concerning its questions 1 to 8.

7.2.2.2 Analysis

Question 1 Applicable law to the arbitration proceedings and the sale contract

(a) To determine the law governing the arbitration proceedings and in the absence of a choice of the procedural law, the English conflict of law rules point to the law at the seat of arbitration. The seat has been chosen by the parties to be London. Therefore English law is to be applicable for the conduct of the arbitration proceedings, (see AA 1996, ss 3 and 2(1)). As the arbitration agreement is in writing, the AA 1996 applies (AA 1996, s 4).

The validity of such an arbitration agreement has to be determined according to the English conflict rules. These are the common law rules, because the scope of Art 1(2)(d) of the Rome Convention 1980, included in Sch 1 to the Contracts (Applicable Law) Act 1990, does not extend to arbitration. According to these rules, the validity of the arbitration clause is determined by the law governing the contract of which the arbitration agreement is a term. This is in our case English law, as identified under item (b) below.

Please note that Reg 44/2001 (see Reg 44/2001 Art 1(2)(d)) and the Brussels and Lugano Conventions (for each see Art 1(4)) do *not* apply to arbitration.

Section 46(3) of the AA 1996 provides that the tribunal, in the absence of a choice of substantive law, is to decide the dispute according to 'the law determined by the conflict rules which it considers applicable'. In our case, with the seat of arbitration in London, this leads to the application of the English conflict rules.

(b) The law applicable to the sale contract, according to the English conflict of law rules, is determined by the Contracts (Applicable Law) Act 1990. The 1990 Act gives effect to the Rome Convention (RC) 1980, which is appended to the Act in Sch I. The scope of the RC is set out in its Art 1. As seen in item (a) above, it specifically excludes arbitration agreements (RC 1980, Art 1(2)(d)). The law of a contract can be determined either by express or determinable choice (RC 1980, Art 3) or, in the absence of such a choice, by establishing with which country the case is most closely connected (RC 1980, Art 4).

Have the parties chosen an applicable law? They have not made an explicit choice, but is there an implied choice which was demonstrated with reasonable certainty? In *Egon Oldendorff v Libera Corp (No 2)* it was highlighted that the choice of seat of arbitration would be one of several aspects to be taken into consideration. In *Egon Oldendorff v Libera Corp (No. 2)* the choice of English law was made on the basis that more than one factor pointed to England: the place of arbitration and the fact that the parties had used a well-known English charterparty. The English charterparty defining the rights and obligations of the parties to the carriage contract was based on English law. This combination showed that the parties had intended to apply English law to their contract. Thus, choice of seat of arbitration is only an indication which could lead, together with other agreed terms or circumstances, to the conclusion that a choice of substantive law was implied by the particular combination (see also Giuliano–Lagarde Report [1980] OJ C282/1 at 17). In our scenario a choice of English law could be implied by taking the following factors into account: the choice of seat of arbitration in England coinciding with the contract having been based on the English buyer's standard terms, the contract having been concluded in England and in English language and England being the place of tender of the documents.

However if one concludes differently, one needs to ascertain the applicable law as follows:

In the absence of choice, Art 4 of the RC 1980 sets out the rules to identify to which country the case has the closest connection and Art 4(2)–(4) states various presumptions to that end. The application of Art 4(2) of the RC 1980 would lead to the law of the place where Sell Co has its principal place of business (Mozambique, leading to Mozambique law), as Sell Co is effecting the characteristic performance (delivery of the merchandise). However according to Art 4(5) of the RC 1980, these presumptions are not to be used if the case is more closely connected to another country.

This leads us to the following questions: (1) Is the case in fact more closely connected to another country, in this instance England? (2) When can the presumption of Art 4(2) of the RC 1980 be disregarded in favour of Art 4(5) of the RC 1980?

In our case, a closer connection to England could be argued by taking into account the following elements of the contract: it was concluded in England; it was drafted in English; it was based on the standard terms of the English party to the contract; the payment was to be made in pounds sterling; the seat of arbitration was chosen to be in England; the place of tender of the documents was England; and in addition, the goods were to be shipped to England. Therefore, the main emphasis of the case seems to point to England.

Will this lead to the application of English law to the sale contract? This will be the case if one assumes this connection to be enough in order to rebut the presumption of Art 4(2) of the RC 1980. However, what is the aim and effect of using presumptions? One has to balance the wish for flexibility to cater best for the circumstances of each individual case on the one hand against certainty and predictability of the applicable law on the other hand. How stringent should the requirements be in order to displace the presumption? Different views have been advanced by different courts. Overall, however, it seems likely that an English court would adopt the more flexible approach in favour of Art 4(5) of the RC 1980, leading to English law being applied to this sale contract (see *Bank of Baroda v Vysya Bank*, QBD (Comm); *Kenburn Waste Management Ltd v Bergmann*, CA upholding ChD; and *Definitely Maybe (Touring) Ltd v Marek Lierberberg Konzertagentur GmbH (No 2)*, QBD (Comm)).

Question 2 Sale contract

Here we need to focus on the distinction between fob variants and cif contracts. The extended fob and the cif contracts should be compared (see **Chapter 2** above). Labelling is not enough; it depends on the exact arrangements between the parties as to which trade term is the relevant one, bearing in mind any further duties that are owed under the contract (see *Pyrene Co Ltd v Scindia Navigation Co Ltd*, QBD; *NV Handel My J Smits Import-Export v English Exporters (London) Ltd*, QBD (Comm) and *The Parchim*, PC (UK)).

Here, the parties seem to have intended a cif contract: they have opted for the property to be transferred on tender of the documents. Payment is to be made in one lump sum. This is to cover the goods and all services undertaken by the seller, in particular the shipping and insurance arrangements. Payment of a lump sum indicates that the parties did not intend the price to vary, subject to market fluctuations in the shipping and insurance business. This means that the seller is bearing the risk of any changes in the market, which he should have included in the price. The specification of the price for the steel girders individually was only for accountancy reasons, rather than setting out each individual price for the different services undertaken by the seller.

Question 3 Bank

(a) The law applicable to the letter of credit is English law, as the characteristic performance (RC 1980, Art 4(2)) under the letter of credit is the undertaking by the issuing bank in England; England is also the place where the documents had to be tendered.

b) The letter of credit incorporated the UCP 500. Therefore the rights and duties of the parties to the letter of credit have to be identified in accordance with these rules.

The law relating to letters of credit is based on two fundamental principles: the autonomy of the credit (UCP 500, Arts 3a and 4) and the doctrine of strict compliance (UCP 500, Arts 13 and 14; also see *Equitable Trust Co of New York v Dawson Partners Ltd*, HL and *Soproma SpA v Marine & Animal By-Products Corporation*, QBD (Comm)). Are these principles complied with?

There are two aspects to be looked at: the insurance certificate and the shipment date. In both cases we need to distinguish between the sale contract and the autonomous letter of credit.

(i) Certificate of insurance: under a cif contract, the buyer is entitled to an insurance policy and nothing less will suffice according to a rather old authority (*Diamond Alkali Export Corp v Bourgeois*, KBD). However, if the buyer wants to insist on tender of a policy he needs to instruct his bank accordingly. Unless otherwise stipulated in the letter of credit, banks will accept insurance certificates, as long as they fulfil the criteria of Art 34d of the UCP 500.

(ii)   Shipment date: the required shipment date as stipulated in the letter of credit is not complied with, but this date in the letter of credit is not in accordance with the date in the sale contract, on which the parties had initially agreed. The buyer cannot unilaterally alter the shipment period by providing for a different date in the letter of credit. However, such a change in the letter of credit is understood as an offer to alter the date. A seller who does not challenge the changed date is deemed to have agreed to the alteration, if he acts upon receipt of the discrepant credit and for example ships the goods (*Panoutsos v Hadley*, CA). Thus, Sell Co is deemed to have consented to the alteration and so has to comply with the requirements to that end. Sell Co is too late to challenge the buyer about this alteration. It has to produce a bill of lading that conforms with the set dates. The bank, only being concerned with the letter of credit, can reject the documents on the basis of non-compliance. The reason for the discrepancy is irrelevant. Thus, the bank was right in rejecting the documents.

(c)   The letter of credit is the form of payment arranged for in the sale contract. The obligation of Buyer Ltd to pay for the goods and the services of Sell Co is effected by letter of credit, and nothing else. Only if the bank is insolvent or liquidated and the seller can no longer get payment by means of the letter of credit, can he claim payment directly from the buyer. The buyer's obligation to pay is 'frozen' due to the letter of credit; it will only 'come back to life' where the seller *without fault of his own* has exhausted all remedies against the bank unsuccessfully. Where the seller fails to comply with his obligations under the letter of credit he runs the risk of not getting paid at all. He cannot simply wait for expiry of the credit and then claim payment from the buyer directly.

However, as the documents are only exchanged against payment, the buyer will receive neither the transport documents nor the goods. Whether the buyer will instruct the bank nonetheless to accept the discrepant documents will most certainly depend on the current market situation and on the strength of a business relationship between the parties. In our case, the buyer does not seem to be willing to accept discrepant documents as he is keen to avoid the contract.

Question 4 Second bill of lading

(a)   The alteration of the bill of lading in relation to the contract of carriage does not pose a problem, as it is only the correction of a genuine mistake which was amended by the carrier (see *Mendala III Transport v Total Transport Corp (The Wilomi Tanana)*, QBD (Comm)).

(b)   So far as the corrective tender is concerned, Sell Co wants to re-tender documents to the bank under the letter of credit, not to the buyer under the sale contract. In the former case, the possibility to re-tender to the bank is implied in the stipulation of Art 14 of the UCP 500, particularly Art 14(c), (d) and (e). Sell Co can re-tender as long as it complies within the time limit/expiry of the letter of credit. The tender of non-conforming documents to the bank has not breached the letter of credit. The effect of wrongful tender to the bank only means that the seller will not get paid.

Whether the seller is free to make a corrective tender of documents to the buyer *under the sale contract* (without letter of credit arrangement) is controversial, even though the case of *Borrowman Phillips & Co v Free & Hollis*, CA suggests this is possible (see **2.5.5** above). Such a scenario, however, needs to be strictly differentiated from a case where payment and thus tender of documents is effected via a letter of credit. Therefore, Sell Co is within its rights to make a corrective tender using the second bill of lading, as long as it does so within the time limits of the letter of credit.

Question 5 Rejection of second tender:

According to the principle of autonomy of the letter of credit (UCP 500, Arts 3, 4 and 15) the bank must pay the seller once complying documents have been presented. This duty exists irrespective of any problems with the underlying sale contract. However, there is one exception: fraud or forgery. The payer can refuse to pay if he can prove that the beneficiary was involved in fraud or forgery (*Society of Lloyd's v Canadian Imperial Bank of Commerce*, QBD (Comm)). This fraud exception is applied in a very narrow sense, as pointed out by the House of Lords (*United City Merchants (Investments) Ltd v Royal Bank of Canada (The American Accord)*), so as not to compromise the function of letters of credit as an important commercial tool.

The bank is liable to the beneficiary of the letter of credit for any damage arising due to non-payment if alleged fraud or forgery cannot be proved. Thus, the bank should be very careful in accepting any instructions of the buyer not to pay. Under Art 15 of the UCP 500, the bank assumes no liability or responsibility for the form and accuracy of the documents or for the description, packing, etc of the goods represented by the documents. Therefore, if in doubt whether the fraud exception can be proven, the bank is safer to pay under the letter of credit than to withhold payment and risk being sued by the seller for breach of its undertaking.

Thus allegations of fraud are insufficient and further investigations should be made, should the bank wish to withhold payment. As it happens in our case no forgery has taken place. The altered bill of lading only states the true date of shipment. The bank will have to pay under the letter of credit and Buyer Ltd should instruct it to do so.

Question 6 Possible rejection of the goods

The potential rights of Buyer Ltd to reject the documents and to reject the goods are separate remedies. Sell Co owes has a dual obligation under the cif contract: shipment of the contracted goods and tender of documents (see *Kwei Tek Chao & Others v British Traders and Shippers Ltd*, QBD and *Bergerco USA v Vegoil Ltd*, QBD (Comm)). The documents are correct and cannot be rejected. The only possibility could be to reject the goods. The seller has to ship goods of satisfactory quality which, according to s 14(2), (6) of the SoGA 1979, is an implied condition of the contract. It does not matter in what condition the goods arrive, but whether the seller at the relevant time of shipment has fulfilled his duties under the sale contract. The question is therefore the origin of the rust. The certificate of inspection together with the clean bill of lading suggests that, on shipment, the goods were in a condition and quality conforming to the sale contract. Once the goods were shipped, the risk of deterioration and damage passed to Buyer Ltd. Thus, it cannot reject the goods on grounds of unsatisfactory quality due to rust.

Question 7 Liability of carrier

(a) The carrier could be liable under the contract of carriage. First of all, however, we need to determine the applicable law. Previously we had only determined the law applicable to the sale contract between Sell Co and Buyer Ltd. Now we are concerned with the relationship between the carrier and the consignor and/or consignee under the contract of carriage. We have to assume that the parties have not chosen any particular law, as no further information is provided. (In practice you would investigate, get the bill of lading and search it for any applicable law clauses.) The applicable law is determined by using the rules of private international law. Each country provides its own rules of private international law, but might have acceded to international conventions in order to harmonise the approach. All 15 of the pre-2004 accession Member States of the European Union have ratified or acceded to the Rome Convention 1980. Thus, if the question of the applicable law was asked in proceedings before a court or arbitral tribunal in England, the Rome Convention 1980, enacted into English law by the Contracts (Applicable Law) Act 1990, would provide the rules. In the absence of a choice of law, Art 4(4) of the RC 1980 will provide the test to find the country with which the contract of carriage has the closest connection and this country will provide the applicable law. This is the country where the carrier has his place of business and where also loading took place, namely Mozambique.

(b) Even without having further details of Mozambiquan law — in practice one would consult an expert in the particular country's legal system — we can continue our study on the basis that Mozambique is a contracting State to the Hague Rules (HR). According to Art 10 of the HR the contract of carriage is governed by the Hague Rules, because the bill of lading was issued in Beira in Mozambique and thus in a contracting State. According to Art 3(2) of the HR the carrier has a duty to stow the goods properly and carefully. This had not been done by loading and stowing damp wood and steel products besides each other in the same hold. The carrier is therefore liable for the damage caused. According to Art 3(8) of the HR this liability (ie under HR, Art 3) cannot be excluded. However, the carrier may avail himself of the limitation of his liability under the Hague Rules: Art 4(5) of the HR provides for a financial limitation of liability and Art 3(6) of the HR for a time limit in which claims can be brought against the carrier.

(c) However, it was not the buyer who initially concluded the carriage contract with the carrier. Under English law, s 2(1) of the CoGSA 1992, this does not stop the buyer from claiming against the carrier on the basis of the contract. Once the buyer is a lawful holder of the bill of lading he can sue the carrier for any damages for which the latter is liable, as if the buyer had been party to the contract of carriage. This presupposes that the bank accepts the documents and forwards them to Buyer Ltd. On tender and acceptance of the documents the property in the goods has transferred to the buyer and the latter could, under English law, also sue as owner of the goods in tort (*Leigh and Sillivan Ltd v Aliakmon Shipping Co Ltd (The Aliakmon)*, HL). However the damage occurred due to the negligent storage which took place before the possessory and proprietary rights vested in the buyer and so a tortious claim would fail. To determine whether the above would be similar under the applicable Mozambiquan law we would need to contact our expert again.

(d) In a charterparty by demise the charterer runs the vessel as if he were the owner for the duration of the charterparty. The master of the ship is employed by the charterer and signs the bills of lading in his name. Therefore the charterer, Charley Ltd, is the carrier.

Question 8 Final bearer of cost

a) The insurer will only pay if the insurance policy covered the particular risk that has manifested. Thus it is crucial what specific cover Sell Co had effected. The seller under a cif contract under common law has to take out appropriate insurance according to the custom of the particular trade. Here, however, the parties have agreed that Sell Co would take out policy. Comparing the cover provided by the different Institute Cargo Clauses, oven beneficial. Only the all risks cover of the Institute Cargo Clauses A insures the risk, namely the failure on behalf of the carrier to observe his duty of care in stor-rgo, which resulted in the deterioration.

(b) Clause 19 of the Institute Cargo Clauses determines English law as the applicable law to the insurance contract. Marine insurance law in England is governed by the MIA 1906.

(c) In order to claim under the contract of insurance the claimant must have an insurable interest in the subject matter insured at the time of the damage (see s 5 of the MIA 1906 and *Lucena v Craufurd*, HL). The party in whom the property in the goods is vested has an insurable interest, but so also does the party who bears the risk. A buyer also has an interest in the profit which he would have made had the goods arrived, and the unpaid seller has an interest in the goods because he may want to exercise his right of stoppage in transit. In a cif contract risk passes on shipment and property passes on tender of documents, but this is only conditional property, which re-vests in the seller if upon examination the buyer finds the goods not to be in accordance with the contract. In the meantime the seller retains a reversionary interest in the goods. (For conditional property see *Kwei Tek Chao & Others v British Traders and Shippers Ltd*, QBD and *Taylor & Sons Ltd v Bank of Athens*, KBD.)

So unless Buyer Ltd has accepted documents and goods and has paid Sell Co, Sell Co still has an insurable interest. Buyer Ltd has an interest as long as it has not finally rejected the documents or the goods. It is most likely that Buyer Ltd itself will have to claim from the insurance for the damage, as it cannot lawfully reject the goods. If Buyer Ltd cannot reject the goods, it will have to bear the cost of the damage unless it can obtain payment from either the insurer or the carrier. As the insurance covers the risk it seems easier to claim from the insurer rather than claim against the carrier, which can avail itself of the package limitation. Buyer Ltd however can only claim against the insurer if Sell Co had assigned the insurance policy to it (MIA 1906, ss 15 and 50), which usually takes place on tender of the documents.

(d) Once the insurer has paid for the loss, it can claim against any party who has caused the damage or loss and is liable for it (subrogation according to s 79 of the MIA 1906). This is the carrier in our scenario. Thus, the loss is finally borne by the carrier, Charley Ltd to the extent of its liability and solvency, and beyond this by the insurer. It might not be effective to sue Charley Ltd, who as demise charterer may be lacking in assets.

7.2.2.3 Conclusion

The English arbitration tribunal will apply English law to the procedure — here the Arbitration Act 1996 — and also English law to the sale contract between Sell Co and Buyer Ltd. However, the contract of carriage between Sell Co and Charley Ltd — who, as a demise charterer is the legal carrier — is governed by the Hague Rules. Charley Ltd is responsible and liable for the damage to the steel girders. Buyer Ltd cannot reject the goods as they have been delivered on board ship in a condition satisfying the sale contract, nor can Buyer Ltd reject the documents, even though the first rejection was justified, because on second tender all documents were in compliance with the letter of credit. Buyer Ltd is advised to claim against the insurer in order to recover the damage caused by the carelessness of Charley Ltd. The insurer in turn is subrogated to Buyer Ltd's claim against the carrier.

7.3 Case study 2 Didgeridoos

7.3.1 Scenario

Bubble World Products Ltd (BWP Ltd), an English company, has concluded a contract with Sounds of Australia Music Company (SAM Co) for the purchase of 5 containers, each containing 2,000 didgeridoos. BWP Ltd sells these typical Australian musical instruments in its shops in a small quantity, about 100 a month. However, for the 'Australian Week', a one-off international event to be held in Southampton from 1 to 10 August 2005, BWP Ltd predicts a record demand due to its advertising campaign promoting didgeridoos as the 'must' in fashion.

The sale contract, cif Southampton Incoterms 2000, provides for shipment of the goods from Fremantle, Australia in the month of April 2005. SAM Co is to produce a certificate of quality by Check Co, an independent agency, which is to be final as to the quality and condition of the goods. The contract is to be governed by English law. Payment is to be effected by confirmed letter of credit. The contract states that BWP Ltd wants the goods at its disposal no later than 1 July 2005.

SAM Co insures the goods with 'Safety Net' under Institute Cargo Clauses C for the journey and has booked the containers on the ship '*Wavelength*', to be loaded around 10 April 2005.

However the ship '*Wavelength*' sails on 15 April 2005 without the goods, as SAM Co has not received the confirmed letter of credit and is not prepared to ship the goods without it. BWP Ltd urges SAM Co to ship the goods, promising to open the letter of credit within the shipment period. On 30 April SAM Co finally receives confirmation of the letter of credit which provides for shipment in April/May 2005. SAM Co takes all possible steps to ship the goods immediately and manages to secure shipping space with the English carrier Sink Co, loading to take place on 1 May 2005. The containerised goods are to be carried 'according to the custom of the trade'. A clean bill of lading is issued stating this, however without mentioning the goods' storage on deck. The contract of carriage is to be governed by English law and the Hague-Visby Rules are to apply.

SAM Co has packaged the goods with great care for carriage below deck. It obtained a certificate of quality, stating that the goods are in immaculate order and condition and comply with the requirements of the sale contract. The containerised goods are loaded on deck and get damaged during the journey due to heavy storms, whereby seawater enters the containers dampening the contents. The packaging has not provided for such conditions, therefore it does not prevent the water from damaging the didgeridoos, particularly their hand-painted finish.

The goods arrive on 20 July 2005 damaged. BWP Ltd's bank (House Bank) has already paid the contract price to the confirming bank. After examination of the goods BWP Ltd wishes to avoid the contract or at the very least receive adequate compensation. However it is aware of the time problem in that the event is due to commence on 1 August. SAM Co is of the opinion that it has fully complied with the contract terms and requires to be compensated for the expenses incurred due to the ship '*Wavelength*' setting sail without the didgeridoos. House Bank, Sink Co and Safety Net, having been threatened with 'legal action' by BWP Ltd, do not want to pay anything.

Advise all of the above the parties as to their rights and obligations.

7.3.2 Points of discussion

7.3.2.1 Introduction

In the following we are going to advise BWP Ltd and SAM Co, House Bank, Safety Net, and Sink Co in turn.

7.3.2.2 Analysis

Question 1 BWP Ltd and SAM Co:

Discussion of the contract terms

(a) English law is applicable to the sale contract. This was agreed on in the sale contract. According to Art 3 of Sch I to the Contracts (Applicable Law) Act 1990, incorporating the Rome Convention 1980 into English law, the parties are free to choose the applicable law.

In English law the Incoterms have not got the force of law, but they can be incorporated into the contract, thus derogating from the common law rules and the Sale of Goods Act 1979 where applicable.

(b) Have the parties concluded a cif contract or, in fact, an arrival contract? Due to the explicit wording 'cif Southampton' and the vagueness regarding the date of arrival, the cif terms will override the arrival stipulation.

The courts construe stipulations as to the arrival of goods within a cif contract restrictively. The insertion of such a date is only taken to mean that this is the expected date or time period of arrival, not a guaranteed one (see *Vitol SA v Esso Australia Ltd (The Wise)*, QBD (Comm) (the case was remitted to the Commercial Court on other grounds) and *Erg Petroli SpA v Vitol SA (The Ballenita and The BP Energy)*, QBD (Comm)). Thus, SAM Co has fulfilled its contractual obligations by loading the cargo on board a vessel which, in the ordinary course of events, would enable the cargo to arrive within the stipulated period.

(c) Under a cif Incoterms 2000 contract, goods need only be insured with minimum cover — Institute Cargo Clauses C therefore will be sufficient, even if in practice the 'all risks cover', Institute Cargo Clauses A, is preferred.

(d) The carriage contract has to be on the usual terms by the usual route. Terms of contract state that goods are going to be carried according to custom of trade which is therefore in line with the cif obligations of the seller.

Rights of rejection for BWP Ltd

(a) The potential rights of BWP Ltd to reject the documents and to reject the goods are separate remedies. Thus it does not matter that the bank as well as BWP Ltd have accepted the documents (BWP Ltd used the documents to obtain the goods from the carrier). SAM Co is responsible under the cif contract for both shipment of the contracted goods and tender of the documents (see *Kwei Tek Chao & Others v British Traders and Shippers Ltd*, QBD and *Bergerco USA v Vegoil Ltd*, QBD (Comm)).

(b) The goods were only shipped after the shipment period provided in the sale contract had expired. Does this enable BWP Ltd to reject the goods?

First, this right would have been waived due to acceptance of the documents showing the date of shipment. Goods cannot be rejected on grounds which were noticeable and not raised on acceptance of the documents (see *Panchaud Frères SA v Etablissements General Grain Co*, CA); however the right to reject on other grounds is not lost (*Vargas Pena Apezteguia y Cia SAIC v Peter Cremer GmbH & Co*, QBD (Comm)).

Secondly, BWP Ltd itself had offered to alter the sale contract by having opened a letter of credit providing for a longer shipment period. By using this letter of credit the seller is deemed to have agreed to the alterations, which in our case was favourable to SAM Co. Looking at previous case law, it seems that the slightest dealings with the letter of credit without objection to the altered passage is read as consent by the seller (see *Panoutsos v Hadley*, CA; *Enrico Furst v Fischer*, QBD (Comm) and *Alan v El Nasr*, CA). The sale contract has been changed to reflect the dates as shown in the letter of credit. The buyer cannot reject on these grounds.

(c) Is there a possibility to reject on the basis of the late arrival, after 1 July? We have already discussed that the arrival date goes against the spirit and core of a cif contract and that in our case on evaluation of the contract terms, the strong stipulation as a cif contract over-rides the arrival stipulation. Therefore the arrival date is only a date by which the goods are expected to arrive, without attaching any condition to it. However, SAM Co needs to ship the goods on a suitable vessel so that the goods will arrive in the ordinary course of events by the stipulated date. One could assume that SAM Co has fulfilled its obligation, as long as it takes out a usual carriage contract by the usual route. It has allowed two months for the journey with loading on 1 May and suggested arrival before or on 1 July.

Anyway, even if this assumption cannot be made or if the arrival date has been interpreted as a condition of the original contract, BWP Ltd might not be able to rely on the lateness of the goods' arrival. By opening the letter of credit one month late, BWP Ltd, by its own con-duct, is either deemed to have waived the arrival condition or is at least estopped from insisting on strict performance of the contract. Another line of argument can be that BWP Ltd, by means of the late opening of the letter of credit on changed shipment terms, has offered to alter the terms of the contract not only as to the shipment period, but also as to the arrival date. Thus, it is very unlikely that BWP Ltd would succeed in rejecting the goods on these grounds.

(d) Can BWP Ltd reject the goods on the basis that they did not comply with the sale contract? The seller is responsible for suitable packaging of the goods in order to ensure their safe arrival at the port of destination (see SoGA 1979, s 14(1), (2) and s 32(2) regarding the fit-ness for purpose and the satisfactory quality, which is a condition). In our case the goods were only packaged for under deck transport, however the carriage contract concluded by SAM Co provided for transport customary to the trade. In the container trade deck transport is typical – at least on a container ship. Therefore SAM Co has not complied with its contrac-tual obligations to ensure the goods' arrival in satisfactory quality, because it contracted for the shipment with an option for deck carriage.

The bill of lading was issued clean, meaning that the goods were in good order and condi-tion on loading. The certificate of quality stated the goods to be in conformity with the requirements of the contract. The contract includes a certificate final clause as to the quality and condition of the goods. This means that the certificate is binding between the seller and the buyer and usually no proof of facts to the contrary is admissible. But does this cover the problem that the goods were insufficiently packaged to withstand the journey, taking account of the liberty clause in the contract of carriage for deck storage? This will depend on the ambit of the quality certificate and its interpretation.

BWP Ltd may be able to reject the goods on the basis of breach of condition, if one is of the opinion that the packaging in relation to the concluded carriage contract was not included in the certificate final clause (SoGA 1979, s 14(2), (6) and s 32(2)). Section 15A of the SoGA 1979, which excludes the repudiation of a contract in cases of only minor damage, is deemed not to be applicable to international sale contracts (SoGA 1979, s 15A(2)).

(e) The goods do not seem to be seriously damaged. It is mainly the hand-painted finish which has suffered. Thus, in order to minimise its loss in the event that it does not win the argument regarding the certificate final clause, BWP Ltd may be better advised to accept the goods and claim damages from the seller in accordance with s 11(2) of the SoGA 1979. It can then sell the goods during the 'Australian Week', with or without attempted repairs.

SAM Co's right to compensation
SAM Co may have a claim for compensation due to the fact that the letter of credit was not issued on time. It might have had to pay extra costs for warehousing the goods at the port and for dead freight (or even demurrage, depending on the particular carriage contract) for the breach of the carriage contract for the planned shipment aboard the 'Wavelength'. Failure in opening a letter of credit amounts to breach of a condition and the seller can treat the contract as repudiated or demand damages.

BWP Ltd eventually opened the letter of credit, but was it on time? A letter of credit has to be opened in good time to allow the seller to ship the goods after receipt of the letter of credit (*Glencore Grain Rotterdam BV v Lebanese Organisation for International Commerce*, CA). It therefore has to be with the seller at least by the beginning of the shipment period (see *Pavia & Co SpA v Thurmann-Nielsen*, CA).

By shipping the goods after receipt of the letter of credit SAM Co has waived its right to treat the contract as repudiated (*Soproma SpA v Marine & Animal By-Products Corporation*, QBD (Comm)). However, can SAM Co claim damages (by analogy with SoGA 1979, s 11(2)) for dead freight and other expenses incurred due to the lateness of the letter of credit? Generally the answer is yes, but there might be a problem if SAM Co was deemed to have waived its right to these damages. SAM Co and BWP Ltd were in negotiations regarding the lateness of the letter of credit, knowing that the goods had been booked onto 'Wavelength'. SAM Co held firm as to its need to have a letter of credit in place before shipping the goods. There is no further indication that SAM Co has waived its right to claim damages for its expenses for 'Wavelength'. However, could shipment after receipt of the late letter of credit and without reservation of the right to compensation be enough to constitute a waiver? It seems unlikely, but in practice it is certainly best to reserve the right to compensation explicitly, indicating that expenses have been incurred.

Question 2 House Bank

The relationship between the English company BWP Ltd and its English bank will be governed by English law, as there is no express choice of law clause to the contrary. Are the

UCP 500 applicable to their relationship? The UCP have not got the status of law in England and thus are only applicable if they have been incorporated into letter of credit contract. However it is common banking practice to incorporate the UCP 500 and the fundamental principles regarding letters of credit are the same under common law and the UCP 500.

Therefore, whether the UCP are incorporated or not, regard needs to be given to the two fundamental principles: the autonomy of credit (see *Hamzeh Malas & Sons v British Imex Industries Ltd*, CA and UCP 500, Arts 3, 4 and 15) and the doctrine of strict compliance (see *Equitable Trust Co of New York v Dawson Partners Ltd*, HL and *Soproma SpA v Marine & Animal By-Products Cooperation*, QBD (Comm) and UCP 500, Art 14).

According to the principle of autonomy of the letter of credit (if UCP 500 are incorporated see Arts 3, 4 and 15 thereof) the bank has to pay the seller on presentation of complying documents, regardless of any problems with the underlying sale contract. The issue as to whether the shipment date in the sale contract could be altered via the letter of credit is an independent issue as the letter of credit is totally autonomous from the underlying sale contract.

As the documents tendered conformed with the requirements of the letter of credit (this can be assumed as no indication to the contrary is provided), particularly the date of shipment, the bank only fulfilled its obligations under the letter of credit by paying SAM Co. Any issues or problems concerning the sale contract and the goods themselves are irrelevant. Thus, BWP Ltd has no grounds to claim against the bank.

Question 3 Safety Net

The insurance policy that SAM Co effected provided for cover according to the Institute Cargo Clauses C. Entry of sea, lake or river water is *not* included in this cover (see Institute Cargo Clauses C and compare with clause 1.2.3 of Institute Cargo Clauses B). Also, damage due to insufficient packing is excluded (Clause 4.3). Therefore, there is no valid claim against Safety Net and there is no need to explore the insurance issue any further.

Question 4 Sink Co

(a) The main question to start with is the applicable law to the carriage contract. This is not to be confused with the choice of law the parties to the sale contract (SAM Co and BWP Ltd) have undertaken. Here we deal with a different issue, namely the carriage contract, initially between SAM Co and Sink Co. The parties to the carriage have chosen the application of English law. This choice of law is acceptable under the English conflict of law rules, here Art 3 of the RC 1980.

English law of carriage of goods by sea consists of common law and of the Carriage of Goods by Sea Act 1971, incorporating the Hague-Visby Rules (HVR). The latter are only applicable, if either the bill of lading is issued in a contracting State (HVR, Art X(a)) or the goods are shipped from a port in a contracting State (HVR, Art X(b)) or if the parties have chosen the law of a State giving effect to the Rules or have directly incorporated the Rules (HVR, Art X (c)).

Art X(a) and (b) of the HVR do not lead to the application of the HVR, as the goods were shipped from a port in Australia, where the bill of lading was also issued. Australia has not become a contracting State to the HVR, even though it has adopted the HVR in general and implemented them whilst adding its own amendments. However, Art X(c) of the HVR is fulfilled, as the parties to the carriage contract have explicitly provided for the HVR to apply.

The mere choice of English law might not have been sufficiently clear to mean the application of the HVR, as common law also provides rules for the carriage of goods (see *Hellenic Steel Co v Svolamar Shipping Co Ltd (The Komninos S)*, CA). In *The Komninos S* the parties had provided for jurisdiction of the 'British courts', from which the court inferred that they had intended English law to apply, however the HVR had not been incorporated and thus did not apply where carriage was from a non-contracting state.

(b) Because the parties have chosen the HVR to apply, according to ss 1(6) and (7) of the CoGSA 1971, it does not matter whether or not the contract is a bill of lading contract (HVR, Art I(b)) or the goods are classed as deck cargo (HVR, Art I(c)). Even without the explicit choice, these hurdles would be overcome. First, in our case we have a bill of lading contract. Secondly, the Rules do not apply to deck cargo, but only if two conditions are fulfilled, namely that the goods must be carried on deck and the contract of carriage must state this fact. 'Carriage according to customs of the trade' does not seem to be clear enough to fulfil the second condition. It only gives the carrier the option to choose the storage place (liberty clause), without discharging it from the obligations of the Rules (*Svenska Tractor Aktiebolaget v Maritime Agencies (Southampton)*, QBD).

(c) Is the carrier liable under the Rules for the damage caused due to the deck storage? According to the carriage contract, as evidenced in the bill of lading, the carrier was entitled to carry the goods according to the custom of the trade. In container trade it is customary to carry containers on deck. Thus, the contract provided a liberty clause for the carrier to choose the storage place. Against this background, we need to evaluate the carrier's duty to stow and care for the cargo (HVR, Art III(2)) in the light of the exclusion of his liability for damages due to inadequate packing (HVR, Art IV(2)(n)).

(i) Due to the contractual liberty clause with regard to the deck carriage the carrier is not precluded from using the defence of insufficient packing as against SAM Co, the party with whom it concluded the contract. Thus, any claim of the shipper SAM Co, against the carrier for any damage derived from deck storage is excluded.

(ii) Will this be the same for BWP Ltd, the lawful holder of the bill of lading? (As House Bank had paid SAM Co, we can assume BWP Ltd has received the bill of lading tendered by SAM Co.) The carrier might have forfeited its defence that the packaging was insufficient. The bill of lading had not been 'claused' to the effect that it stated that the goods were in fact carried on deck. Therefore, a third party purchasing the goods could not see straight away that the goods were carried as deck cargo and could not assess the risk accordingly (see *Encyclopaedia Britannica Inc v The Hong Kong Producer and Universal Marine Corporation*, US CA, and see also *J Evans & Sons (Portsmouth) Ltd v Andrea Merzario Ltd*, CA, where a forwarder was held responsible for the loss of deck cargo, which he had orally promised to store below deck). Thus, the carrier is liable for the damage, because it would not have occurred had the goods been shipped below deck (see also *Silver v Ocean Steamship Co Ltd*, CA).

(iii) The next pertinent question is whether the carrier can use the package limitation in Art IV(5) of the HVR against BWP Ltd, despite the carrier's lack of care for the cargo as identified above? According to the decision in *Daewoo Heavy Industries Ltd v Klipriver Shipping Ltd (The Kapitan Petko Voivoda)*, CA (overruling *Wibau Maschinenfabrik Hartman SA v Mackinnon Mackenzie (The Chanda)*, QBD (Comm)) and also *Parsons*

Corporation v CV Scheepvaartonderneming Happy Ranger (The Happy Ranger), CA it can, because Art IV(5)(a) of the HVR states that the limitation is to apply 'in any event'. Whether the 'package' is the container, or the different parcels within, will depend on the details set out in the bill of lading (HVR, Art IV(5)(c)). It is thus very important to enumerate on the bill of lading the parcels which are contained in such a transport device. Otherwise any compensation will be nominal because, in the absence of such enumeration, each container is understood as one parcel only.

7.3.2.3 Conclusion

BWP Ltd can successfully claim damages against Sink Co but only to the amount limited by Art IV(5) of the HVR. BWP Ltd has no claims against Safety Net or House Bank. Any rights of BWP Ltd against SAM Co will depend on the content and interpretation of the certificate's final clause. Thus BWP Ltd may be left with some of the damage and without adequate remedy in this respect. It may be well advised to try to sell the goods during the event in order to minimise its loss. SAM Co, on the other hand, can claim for damages against BWP Ltd due to the lateness of the letter of credit.

8

A Guide to Further Reading

After you have developed an understanding of international trade law you may wish to deepen and widen your knowledge. You might also need to research specific areas in depth. In order to help you with your research a selection of books related to international trade law is listed below. These books can be your first point of call when continuing your study and research. Efforts have been made to state the current edition of any books as of autumn 2005. Please always check to make sure that you are consulting the most recent and up-to-date version of each book.

8.1 Textbooks and Cases and Materials Books in International Trade Law

These textbooks in international trade law or related areas are listed alphabetically by surname of the author. A short summary is provided to give you an initial indication of the content.

S Baughen, *Shipping Law* (3rd edn, London: Cavendish, 2004), concerning the areas of dry shipping (issues around the carriage of goods), wet shipping (collisions, salvage and marine pollution), jurisdiction and procedural aspects.

J Birds, NJ Hird, *Birds' Modern Insurance Law* (6th edn, London: Sweet & Maxwell, 2004), concerning the relevant principles of insurance law with specific coverage of life insurance, liability insurance, motor vehicle insurance and employers liability insurance. However, it does not give a detailed account of marine insurance.

I Carr, *International Trade Law* (3rd edn, London: Cavendish, 2005), a comprehensive textbook going into a lot of detail.

JCT Chuah, *Law of International Trade* (3rd edn, London: Sweet & Maxwell, 2005), provides a lot of detailed analysis of the relevant case law.

CMV Clarkson, J Hill, *Jaffey on the Conflict of Laws* (2nd edn, London: Butterworths, 2002), for a deeper study of conflict of laws, also known as private international law.

L D'Arcy, C Murray, B Cleave, *Schmitthoff's Export Trade: The Law and Practice of International Trade* 10th edn, London: Sweet & Maxwell, 2000), for a detailed study of international trade law providing insight into the practical side of this trade.

M Dockray, *Cases & Materials on the Carriage of Goods by Sea* (3rd edn, London: Cavendish, 2004), for an in-depth study of the aspects of carriage of goods by sea.

B Griffin, *Day & Griffin: The Law of International Trade* (3rd edn, London: Butterworths Lexis Nexis, 2003), a short textbook in international trade law, introducing the reader to key cases in this area.

R Hayward, *Conflict of Laws* (4th edn, London: Cavendish, due 2006), for a more comprehensive study of conflict of laws, also known as private international law.

S Hodges, *Cases and Materials on Marine Insurance Law* (1st edn, London: Cavendish, 1999, reprinted 2002), for an in-depth study of marine insurance law using cases and materials.

D McClean, K Beevers, *Morris, The Conflict of Laws* (6th edn, London: Sweet & Maxwell, 2005).

A Redfern, M Hunter, *Law and Practice of International Commercial Arbitration*, (4th edn, London: Sweet & Maxwell, student edition, 2004), for a focus on international commercial arbitration.

P Sellman, *The Law of International Trade*, Textbook, (5th edn, London: Old Bailey Press, 2005), in conjunction with P Sellman, *The Law of International Trade, Revision Workbook* (4th edn, London: Old Bailey Press, 2004), and P Sellman, *The Law of International Trade, 150 Leading Cases* (2nd edn, London: Old Bailey Press, 2004), provides a good and instructive study pack.

P Todd, *Cases and Materials on International Trade Law* (1st edn, London: Sweet & Maxwell, 2003), covering cases and materials in the areas of contract of sale, finance and carriage.

JF Wilson, *Carriage of Goods by Sea*, (5th edn, Harlow, Pearson Education, 2004), a textbook for an in-depth study of the aspects of carriage of goods by sea.

8.2 Practitioner guides

These practitioner guides are arranged first by topic and then alphabetically by surname of the author. These are comprehensive books with detailed information and are very useful reference books.

8.2.1 General

R Goode, *Transactional Commercial Law; International Instruments and Commentary* (Oxford: Oxford University Press, 2004).

8.2.2 Sale of goods

M G Bridge, *International Sale of Goods: Law and Practice* (Oxford: Oxford University Press, 1999).

C Debattista, *Sale of Goods carried by Sea* (2nd edn, London: Butterworths, 1998).

A G Guest, *Benjamin's Sale of Goods* (6th edn, London: Sweet & Maxwell, 2003).

J Ramberg, *ICC Guide to Incoterms 2000* (Paris: International Chamber of Commerce Publishing, 1999).

D M Sassoon, *CIF and FOB Contracts* (4th edn, London: Sweet & Maxwell, 1995).

P Schlechtriem, I Schwenzer, *Commentary on the UN Convention on the International Sale of Goods (CISG)* (2nd edn, Oxford: Oxford University Press, 2005).

8.2.3 Carriage of goods

M Clarke, *Carriage of Goods by Road: CMR* (4th edn, London: LLP, 2003).

M Clarke, *Contracts of Carriage by Air* (London: LLP Professional Publishing, 2002).

M Clarke, D Yates, *Carriage of Goods by Land and Air* (London: LLP, 2004).

J Cooke, T Young, A Taylor, J D Kimball, D Martowski, *Voyage Charters* (2nd edn, London: LLP Professional Publishing, 2001).

N Gaskell, R Asoriotis, Y Baats, *Bills of Lading: Law and Contracts*, (London: LLP Professional Publishing, 2000).

D A Glass, *Freight Forwarding and Multimodal Transport Contracts* (London: LLP Professional Publishing, 2004).

J Schofield, *Laytime and Demurrage* (5th edn, London: LLP Professional Publishing, 2004).

G H Treitel, F M B Reynolds, *Carver on Bills of Lading*, (London: Sweet & Maxwell, 2001).

M Wilford, T Coghlin, J D Kimball, *Time Charters*, (5th edn, London: LLP Professional Publishing, 2003).

8.2.4 Payment methods

W Hedley, R Hedley, *Bills of Exchange and Banker's Documentary Credits* (4th edn, London: LLP Professional Publishing, 2001).

R Jack, A Malek, D Quest, *Documentary Credits* (3rd edn, London: Butterworths, 2000).

G Penn, A Haynes, *Law and Practice of International Banking* (2nd edn, London: Sweet & Maxwell, 2004).

8.2.5 Marine insurance

F D Rose, *Marine Insurance: Law and Practice* (London: LLP Professional Publishing, 2004).

B Soyer, *Warranties in Marine Insurance* (2nd edn, London: Cavendish Publishing, 2005).

8.2.6 Arbitration

C Ambrose, K Maxwell, *London Maritime Arbitration* (2nd edn, London: LLP Professional Publishing, 2002).

P Binder, *International Commercial Arbitration and Conciliation in UNCITRAL Model Law*, (London: Sweet & Maxwell, 2004).

G Petrochilos, *Procedural Law in International Arbitration* (Oxford: Oxford University Press, 2004).

A Redfern, M Hunter, *Law and Practice of International Commercial Arbitration* (4th edn, London: Sweet & Maxwell, 2004).

A Tweedale, K Tweedale, *Arbitration of Commercial Disputes; International and English Law and Practice* (Oxford: Oxford University Press, 2005).

8.2.7 International dispute resolution

A Briggs, P Rees, *Civil Jurisdiction and Judgments* (4th edn London: LLP Professional Publishing, 2005).

J Collins, C G J Morse, J D McClean, A, Briggs, *Dicey and Morris on the Conflict of Laws* (13th edn, London: Sweet & Maxwell, 2000) and T C Hartley, J D McClean, C J D, Morse, *Dicey and Morris on the Conflict of Laws*, 1st supplement to the 13th edn (London: Sweet & Maxwell, 2001).

J Fawcett, J, Harris, J, Bridge, M, *International Sale of Goods in the Conflict of Laws* (Oxford: Oxford University Press, 2005).

S Geeroms, *Foreign Law in Civil Litigation*, (Oxford: Oxford University Press, 2004).

J Hill, *International Commercial Disputes in English Courts*, (3rd edn, Oxford: Hart Publishing, 2005).

D Jackson, *Enforcement of Maritime Claims* (4th edn, London: LLP Professional Publishing, 2005).

D Joseph, *Jurisdiction and Arbitration Agreements and their Enforcement* (London: Sweet & Maxwell, 2005).

A Layton, H Mercer, *European Civil Practice* (2nd edn, London: Sweet & Maxwell, 2004).

J A Pontier, E Burg, *EU Principles on Jurisdiction and Recognition and Enforcement of Judgments in Civil and Commercial Matters* (Cambridge: Cambridge University Press, 2004).

8.3 Statute books

The importance and usefulness of statute books to enhance your understanding has already been pointed out at **1.2** above. Please find a selection listed alphabetically by the surname of the author.

I Carr, R Kidner, *Statutes and Conventions on International Trade Law* (4th edn, London: Cavendish Publishing, 2003), including Institute Cargo Clauses.

J Chuah, R Earle, *Statutes and Conventions of Private International Law* (2nd edn, London: Cavendish Publishing, 2004), particularly for legislation in the area of private international law and international dispute resolution.

Cracknell's Statutes: Conflict of Laws (3rd edn, London: Old Bailey Press, 2005), particularly for legislation in the area of private international law/international dispute resolution.

Cracknell's Statutes: Law of International Trade (5th edn, London: Old Bailey Press, 2005).

ICC Supplement to UCP 500 for electronic presentation (eUCP) (Paris: International Chamber of Commerce Publishing, 2002).

ICC Uniform Customs and Practice for Documentary Credits, UCP 500 (Paris: International Chamber of Commerce Publishing, 1993).

ICC Uniform Rules for Collections, UCR 522 (Paris: International Chamber of Commerce Publishing, 1995).

F Rose, *Statutes on Commercial & Consumer Law, 2005–2006* (14th edn, Oxford: Oxford University Press, 2005), including the ICC Uniform Customs and Practice for Documentary Credits.

UNCTAD/ICC Rules for multimodal transport documents (Paris: International Chamber of Commerce Publishing, 1992).

8.4 Journals and newsletters

The journals listed alphabetically below might help with your in-depth research and also if you want to keep your knowledge up to date. They mainly contain interesting and topical articles, relevant court decisions and digests. Some of the journals are accessible online.

Arbitration Law Monthly, Informa Legal Publishing UK.

Business Law International, Sweet & Maxwell.

International and Comparative Law Quarterly, Oxford University Press on behalf of the British Institute of International and Comparative Law.

International Arbitration Law Review, Sweet & Maxwell.

International Trade Law and Regulation, Sweet & Maxwell.

Journal of Business Law, Sweet & Maxwell.

Journal of International Banking Law, Sweet & Maxwell.

Journal of International Maritime Law, Lawtext Publishing.

Lloyd's Law Reports, Informa Legal Publishing UK.

Lloyd's List Law Reports, Informa Legal Publishing UK.

Lloyd's Maritime and Commercial Law Quarterly, Informa Legal Publishing UK (formerly LLP Professional Publishing).

Lloyd's Maritime Law Newsletter, Informa Legal Publishing UK.

P & I International, Informa Legal Publishing UK.

Shipping and Trade Law, Informa Legal Publishing UK.

8.5   Online sources

The web makes a multitude of sources available but you are well advised to check the reliability of your source. Listed below are a number of sites of reputable bodies and organisations which contain relevant information in the area of international trade law.

The website of the United Nations Commission on International Trade Law (UNCITRAL) can be accessed via http://www.uncitral.org with access to the full text version of its adopted texts. At http://www.uncitral.org/uncitral/en/index.html you can find information as to the contracting States to the UNCITRAL Conventions and States adopting the Model Laws on International Trade Law.

The website of the International Institute for the Unification of Private Law (UNIDROIT) can be found at http://www.unidroit.org. Amongst other information you can find there the full text and status of UNIDROIT conventions and the text of its model laws, principles and guides.

The International Civil Aviation Organisation (ICAO) (http://www.icao.int/) has its treaty collection at http://www.icao.int/icao/en/leb/, where you can find information on the treaties, their status and their depositary. The ICAO itself is depositary for many of the multinational treaties on international air law. For those you can find a list of the contracting States with the respective date of entry into force on ICAO's site.

The Intergovernmental Organisation for International Carriage by Rail (OTIF) (http://www.otif.org) was set up as a consequence of the Convention of 9 May 1980 (COTIF). It holds all the information on the COTIF convention and protocols, their full texts, contracting States, entry into force and developments at http://www.otif.org/html/e/ pres_convention.php and provides useful addresses and links.

The Comité Maritime International (CMI) is a non-governmental organisation which contributes to the unification of maritime law. Amongst other work it has produced Uniform Rules on Sea Waybills and Electronic Bills of Lading, which the parties can incorporate into their contract, and the CMI Draft Instrument on Carriage of Goods. The documents and much more information can be accessed via the CMI home page at http://www.comitemaritime.org/home.htm. It also provides information about the status of maritime conventions and a database of decisions on maritime conventions.

The website of Lex Mercatoria can be accessed at http://www.jus.uio.no/lm/. It provides plenty of information on international commercial law. Of particular interest is that via this site you can access the full text of most international conventions in this area of law.

The British Academy Portal website gives search options in law in general, including good links to sites concerning international trade and private international law at http://www.britac.ac.uk/

portal/bysection.asp?section=S1. You can also access this site via the home page on http://www.britac.ac.uk/portal/.

The website of SITPRO Simplifying International Trade Ltd can be found at http://www.sitpro.org.uk, offering checklists and briefings relevant to international trade issues. SITPRO Ltd is the trade facilitation body in the UK dedicated to simplifying the international trading process.

The international shipping organisation BIMCO offers many trade facilitation activities. It has drafted and developed many maritime contracts and other related forms. Sample documents can be viewed via its website at http://www.bimco.dk/.

The International Maritime Organisation (IMO) facilitates co-operation on technical matters relevant to the shipping industry and particularly on safety at sea; see http://www.imo.org.

Http://www.iccwbo.org/ is the website for the International Chamber of Commerce. There you can find its publications, particularly the Incoterms, Uniform Customs and Practice for Documentary Credits (UCP), Uniform Rules for Collections (URG) and the UNCTAD/ICC Rules for Multimodal Transport Documents.

The United Nations Economic Commission for Europe focuses on implementing international standards and trade facilitation measures. It offers various publications, including sets of general conditions and standard forms in specialised areas. Please see http://www.unece.org.

The United Nations Conference on Trade and Development (UNCTAD) seeks to integrate developing countries in a development-friendly way into the world economy. UNCTAD's work also aims at harmonising international trade, development and regional economic policies. More information can be found on its website at http://www.unctad.org.

Http://www.asil.org/resource/treaty1.htm is a website of the American Society of International Law called 'ASIL Guide to Electronic Resources for International Law' providing information and links in areas including private international law, international commercial arbitration, international sale of goods and international organisations.

Http://vlib.org/ is a website of Indiana University and provides a lot of information and links in various areas including dispute resolution and maritime law.

For recent case law relating to the Brussels and Lugano Conventions on jurisdiction and the enforcement of judgments in civil and commercial matters see http://curia.eu.int/common/recdoc/convention/en/index.htm.

Http://www.hcch.net is the website of the Hague Conference on Private International Law. Of particular interest is the information (including the full text and the full status report) about the conventions negotiated by this Conference which can be found at http://www.hcch.net/e/conventions/index.html, as well as the information on its work in progress at http://www.hcch.net/e/workprog/, including the draft of a worldwide jurisdiction and recognition convention (http://www.hcch.net/e/workprog/jdgm.html).

The World Trade Organisation's website is http://www.wto.org.

Europa, the official information server of the EU can be found on http://www.europa.eu.int. The site for judicial co-operation in civil matters within the European Union can be directly accessed at http://www.europa.eu.int/scadplus/leg/en/s22003.htm and the text of legislation in force in its initial form as well as in its consolidated version can be accessed via http://europa.eu.int/eur-lex/en/lif/reg/en_register_1920.html.

For House of Lords judgments delivered since 14 November 1996, see http://www.publications.parliament.uk/pa/ld199697/ldjudgmt/ldjudgmt.htm or access them via the main parliament site: http://www.parliament.uk.

You can find UK legislation including Acts of Parliament, statutory instruments and explanatory notes on the internet via the HMSO site (Her Majesty's Stationary Office) at http://www.opsi.gov.uk.

Government publications can be found via http://www.open.gov.uk.

The web address for the UK's Foreign & Commonwealth Office is http://www.fco.gov.uk. At http://www.fco.gov.uk/treaty you can find information about the treaties for which the UK is the depositary. You can also find links to the sites of other countries which are depositaries of treaties and to the respective information. It also contains a link to the Treaty Enquiry Service.

In addition there are many websites of international organisations, companies, law firms and lecturers, which provide legal information, newsletters or updates on cases.

Appendices

Appendix A) Overview of the Incoterms 2000

The Incoterms 2000 can be purchased from the International Chamber of Commerce directly (http://www.iccwbo.org). You can also find the fob and cif terms of the Incoterms 2000 in the appendix of the cases & materials book by Paul Todd (Cases & Materials on International Trade Law, Sweet and Maxwell).

E terms:

- Exw 'ex works' (…named place)
  Here the seller minimises his risk by making the goods available only at his premises.

F terms:

- Fca 'free carrier' (…named place)
  The seller must deliver the goods to the carrier at the named place. The buyer must arrange for the main carriage or, if agreed, the seller must do this on the buyer's behalf.

- Fas 'free alongside ship' (…named port of shipment)
  The seller must deliver the goods alongside a ship, nominated by the buyer. This term is to be used for sea carriage only.

- Fob 'free onboard ship' (… named port of shipment)
  The seller must load the goods over the ship's rail, and carriage is arranged for by the buyer. This term is to be used for sea carriage only.

Under f-Terms the seller arranges and pays for any pre-carriage in the country of export and completes all customs and export formalities. The main carriage is to be arranged by the buyer. Risk and property pass once seller has delivered the goods at the agreed place.

C terms:

- Cfr 'cost and freight' (…named port of destination)
  The seller must arrange for carriage and load the goods over the ship's rail. He does **not** have to arrange for insurance. This term is to be used for sea carriage only.

- Cif 'cost, insurance and freight' (…named port of destination)
  The seller must arrange for carriage & insurance and load the goods over the ship's rail. This term is to be used for sea carriage only.

- Cpt 'carriage paid to' (…named place of destination)
  The seller must arrange for carriage and deliver goods into custody of carrier. He does **not** have to arrange for insurance.

- Cip 'carriage and insurance paid to' (…named place of destination)
  The seller must arrange for carriage & insurance and deliver the goods into custody of the carrier.

Under c-Terms the seller arranges and pays for the main carriage but risk passes when the goods are loaded (under cfr and cif), or given into custody of the first carrier (under cpt and cip); property passes once the bill of lading/transport documents are tendered. Export formalities must be cleared by the seller; import formalities are the buyer's duty.

D terms:

- Daf 'delivered at frontier' (… named place)
  The buyer must take delivery at the frontier. This term is to be used for carriage by road or rail only.

- Des 'delivered ex ship' (…named port of destination)
  The buyer must take delivery from the ship at the agreed destination. This term is to be used for sea carriage only.

- Deq 'delivered ex quay' (…named port of destination)
  The buyer must take delivery of the goods from the quay at the agreed destination. This term is to be used for sea carriage only.

- Ddu 'delivered duty unpaid' (…named place of destination)
  The buyer must take delivery of the goods from the named place of destination.

- Ddp 'delivered duty paid' (…named place of destination)
  The buyer must take delivery of the goods from the named place of destination. All import formalities and charges are the seller's responsibility.

Under d-Terms, the seller must make the goods available upon arrival at the agreed destination, therefore his cost and risk is maximised, under ddp even covering the import clearance. Apart from ddp, the duty to complete all import formalities is with the buyer.

Parties to an international sale contract should stipulate clearly, if they wish to apply the Incoterms 2000 and not the common law interpretation of a trade term. The following is an example of such an express incorporation clause: cif (port of destination, i.e. Hamburg) Incoterms 2000.

Effective 1st January 2003

Gafta No.100

Copyright
THE GRAIN AND FEED TRADE ASSOCIATION

CONTRACT FOR SHIPMENT OF FEEDINGSTUFFS
IN BULK
TALE QUALE - CIF TERMS

*delete/specify as appropriate   Date ....

1 **SELLERS** ....
2
3 **INTERVENING AS BROKERS** ....
4
5 **BUYERS** ....
6 have this day entered into a contract on the following terms and conditions. Wherever the word "cakes" is used, this is agreed to mean
7 goods of the contractual description.
8
9 **1.   GOODS-**
10   Broken cakes and/or meal in a proportion, having regard to the characteristics of the goods and methods of handling, to be taken and
11   paid for as cakes. Goods in bulk but Buyers agree to accept up to 15% in stowage bags, such bags to be taken and paid for as cakes
12   and any cutting to be paid for by Buyers. Sellers have the option of shipping the whole or part of the quantity in excess of 15% in
13   bags, in which case the excess over 15% shall be delivered in bulk and Sellers shall be responsible for cutting the excess bags which
14   remain their property.
15
16 **2.   QUANTITY-** .... 2% more or less.
17   Sellers shall have the option of shipping a further 3% more or less than the contract quantity. The excess above 2% or the deficiency
18   below 2% shall be settled on the quantity thereof at shipment at market value on the last day of discharge of the vessel at the port of
19   destination; the value to be fixed by arbitration, unless mutually agreed. Should Sellers exercise the option to ship up to 5% more, the
20   excess over 2% shall be paid for provisionally at contract price. The difference between the contract price and the market price
21   calculated in accordance with the provisions of this clause shall be adjusted in a final invoice. In the event of more than one shipment
22   being made, each shipment shall be considered a separate contract, but the margin of the mean quantity sold shall not be affected
23   thereby.
24
25 **3.   PRICE AND DESTINATION** - At ....
26   * per tonne of 1000 kilograms   }
27   } gross weight, cost, insurance and freight to ....
28   * per ton of 1016 kilograms or 2240 lbs. }
29
30 **4.   BROKERAGE**...per tonne, to be paid by Sellers on the mean contract quantity, goods lost or not lost,
31   contract fulfilled or not fulfilled unless such non-fulfilment is due to the cancellation of the contract under the terms of the
32   Prohibition or Force Majeure Clause. Brokerage shall be due on the day shipping documents are exchanged or, if the goods are
33   not appropriated then brokerage shall be due on the 30th consecutive day after the last day for appropriation.
34
35 **5.   QUALITY-**
36   *   **Warranted to contain** .... at time and place of discharge.
37
38   Not less than ....% of oil and protein combined, and not more than 2.50% of sand and/or silica. Should the whole, or
39   any portion, not turn out equal to warranty, the goods must be taken at an allowance to be agreed or settled by arbitration as
40   provided for below, except that for any deficiency of oil and protein there shall be allowances to Buyers at the following rates,
41   viz.: 1% of the contract price for each of the first 3 units of deficiency under the warranted percentage; 2% of the contract price
42   for the 4th and 5th units and 3% of the contract price for each unit in excess of 5 and proportionately for any fraction thereof.
43   When the combined content of oil and protein is warranted within a margin (as for example 40%/42%) no allowance shall be made
44   if the analysis ascertained as herein provided be not below the minimum, but if the analysis results are below the minimum
45   warranted the allowance for deficiency shall be computed from the mean of the warranted content. For any excess of sand and/or
46   silica there shall be an allowance of 1% of the contract price for each unit of excess and proportionately for any fraction thereof.
47   Should the goods contain over 5% of sand and/or silica the Buyers shall be entitled to reject the goods, in which case the contract
48   shall be null and void for such quantity rejected.
49
50   The goods are warranted free from castor seed and/or castor seed husk, but should the analysis show castor seed husk not
51   exceeding 0.005%, the Buyers shall not be entitled to reject the goods, but shall accept them with the following allowances: 0.75%
52   of contract price if not exceeding 0.001%, 1% of contract price if not exceeding 0.002%, and 1.50% of contract price if not
53   exceeding 0.005%. Should the first analysis show the goods free from castor seed and/or castor seed husk such analysis shall be
54   final but in the event of the first analysis showing castor seed husk to be present a second sample may be analysed at the request of
55   either party and the mean of the two analyses shall be taken as final. Should the parcel contain castor seed husk in excess of
56   0.005% Buyers shall be entitled to reject the parcel, in which case the contract shall be null and void for such quantity rejected.

100/1

57 Nevertheless, should Buyers elect to retain the parcel they shall be entitled to a further allowance for any excess over 0.005% of
58 castor seed husk, to be settled by agreement or arbitration. For the purpose of sampling and analysis each mark shall stand as a
59 separate shipment. The right of rejection provided by this clause shall be limited to the parcel or parcels found to be defective.
60

61   * **Official** .... certificate of inspection, at time of loading into the ocean carrying vessel, shall be final as to
62   quality.
63

64   * **Sample**, at time and place of shipment about as per sealed sample marked...........................in possession of ....
65   the word "about" when referring to quality shall mean the equivalent of 0.50% on contract price. Analysis as per arrival sample.
66 Difference in quality shall not entitle Buyers to reject except under the award of arbitrator(s) or board of appeal, as the case may be,
67 referred to in the Arbitration Rules specified in the Arbitration Clause.
68 **Condition** – Shipment shall be made in good condition.
69

70 **6.**   **PERIOD OF SHIPMENT**- as per bill(s) of lading dated or to be dated ....
71 The bill(s) of lading to be dated when the goods are actually on board. Date of the bill(s) of lading shall be accepted as proof of date of
72 shipment in the absence of evidence to the contrary. In any month containing an odd number of days, the middle day shall be accepted
73 as being in both halves of the month.
74

75 **7.**   **SALES BY NAMED VESSELS**- For all sales by named vessels, the following shall apply: -
76 (a) Position of vessel is mutually agreed between Buyers and Sellers;
77 (b) The word "now" to be inserted before the word "classed" in the Shipment and Classification Clause;
78 (c) Appropriation Clause cancelled if sold "shipped".
79

80 **8.**   **SHIPMENT AND CLASSIFICATION** - Shipment from ....
81 direct or indirect, with or without transhipment by first class mechanically self-propelled vessel(s) suitable for the carriage of the
82 contract goods, classed in accordance with the Institute Classification Clause of the International Underwriting Association in force at
83 the time of shipment.
84

85 **9.**   **EXTENSION OF SHIPMENT**- The contract period for shipment, if such be 31 days or less, shall be extended by an additional
86 period of not more than 8 days, provided that Sellers serve notice claiming extension not later than the next business day following the
87 last day of the originally stipulated period. The notice need not state the number of additional days claimed.
88 Sellers shall make an allowance to Buyers, to be deducted in the invoice from the contract price, based on the number of days by
89 which the originally stipulated period is exceeded, in accordance with the following scale: -
90   1 to 4 additional days, 0.50%;
91   5 or 6 additional days, 1%;
92   7 or 8 additional days 1.50% of the gross contract price.
93 If, however, after having served notice to Buyers as above, Sellers fail to make shipment within such 8 days, then the contract shall be
94 deemed to have called for shipment during the originally stipulated period plus 8 days, at contract price less 1.50%, and any settlement
95 for default shall be calculated on that basis. If any allowance becomes due under this clause, the contract price shall be deemed to be
96 the original contract price less the allowance and any other contractual differences shall be settled on the basis of such reduced price.
97

98 **10. APPROPRIATION**-
99 (a) Notice of appropriation shall state the vessel's name, the approximate weight shipped, and the date or the presumed date of the
100 bill of lading.
101 (b) The notice of appropriation shall within (i) 10 consecutive days if shipped from the U.S. Gulf and/or U.S. and/or Canadian
102 Atlantic/Lake Ports, (ii) 14 consecutive days if shipped from any other port, from the date of the bill(s) of lading be served by or
103 on behalf of the Shipper direct on his Buyers or on the Selling Agent or Brokers named in the contract. The Non-Business Days
104 Clause shall not apply.
105 (c) Notice of appropriation shall, within the period stated in sub-clause (b) be served by or on behalf of subsequent Sellers on
106 their Buyers or on the Selling Agent or Brokers named in the contract, but if notice of appropriation is received by subsequent
107 Sellers on the last day or after the period stated in sub-clause (b) from the date of the bill of lading, their notice of appropriation
108 shall be deemed to be in time if served: -
109

110   (1)   On the same calendar day, if received not later than 1600 hours on any business day, or
111

112   (2)   Not later than 1600 hours on the next business day, if received after 1600 hours or on a non-business day.
113

114 (d) A notice of appropriation served on a Selling Agent or Brokers named in the contract shall be considered an appropriation
115 served on Buyers. A Selling Agent or Brokers receiving a notice of appropriation shall serve like notice of appropriation in
116 accordance with the provisions of this clause. Where the Shipper or subsequent Sellers serves the notice of appropriation on the
117 Selling Agent, such Selling Agent may serve notice of appropriation either direct to the Buyers or to the Brokers.
118 (e) The bill of lading date stated in the notice of appropriation shall be for information only and shall not be binding, but in fixing
119 the period laid down by this clause for serving notices of appropriation the actual date of the bill of lading shall prevail.
120 (f) Every notice of appropriation shall be open to correction of any errors occurring in transmission, provided that the sender is
121 not responsible for such errors, and for any previous error in transmission which has been repeated in good faith.
122 (g) Should the vessel arrive before receipt of the appropriation and any extra expenses be incurred thereby, such expenses shall
123 be borne by Sellers.
124 (h) When a valid notice of appropriation has been received by Buyers, it shall not be withdrawn except with their consent.

125   (i) In the event of less than 95 tonnes being tendered by any one vessel Buyers shall be entitled to refund of any proved extra expenses
126   for sampling, analysis and lighterage incurred thereby at port of discharge.
127

128   **11.**   **PAYMENT**-
129   (a) **Payment** .... % of invoice amount by cash in ....
130   * In exchange for and on presentation of shipping documents;
131   * In exchange for shipping documents on or before arrival of the vessel at destination, at Buyers' option;
132   Sellers, however, have the option of calling upon Buyers to take up and pay for documents on or after ....
133   consecutive days from the date of the bill(s) of lading.
134

135   (b) **Shipping documents** – shall consist of - 1. Invoice. 2. Full set(s) of on board Bill(s) of Lading and/or Ship's Delivery
136   Order(s) and/or other Delivery Order(s) in negotiable and transferable form. Such other Delivery Order(s) if required by Buyers,
137   to be countersigned by the Shipowners, their Agents or a recognised bank. 3. Policy (ies) and/or Insurance Certificate(s) and/or
138   Letter(s) of Insurance in the currency of the contract. The Letter(s) of Insurance to be certified by a recognised bank if required
139   by Buyers. 4. Other documents as called for under the contract. Buyers agree to accept documents containing the Chamber of
140   Shipping War Deviation Clause and/or other recognised official War Risk Clause.
141   (c) In the event of shipping documents not being available when called for by Buyers, or on arrival of the vessel at destination,
142   Sellers may provide other documents or an indemnity entitling Buyers to obtain delivery of the goods and payment shall be made
143   by Buyers in exchange for same, but such payment shall not prejudice Buyers' rights under the contract when shipping documents
144   are eventually available.
145   (d) Should Sellers fail to present shipping documents or other documents or an indemnity entitling Buyers to take delivery, Buyers
146   may take delivery under an indemnity provided by themselves and shall pay for the other documents when presented. Any
147   recoverable extra expenses, including the costs of such indemnity or extra charges incurred by reason of the failure of Sellers to
148   provide such documents, shall be borne by Sellers, but such payment shall not prejudice Buyers' rights under the contract when
149   shipping documents are eventually available.
150   (e) Should shipping documents be presented with an incomplete set of bill(s) of lading or should other shipping documents be
151   missing, payment shall be made provided that delivery of such missing documents is guaranteed, such guarantee to be
152   countersigned, if required by Buyers, by a recognised bank.
153   (f) Costs of collection shall be for account of Sellers, but if Buyers demand presentation only through a bank of their choice, in
154   that event any additional collection costs shall be borne by Buyers.
155   (g) No obvious clerical error in the documents shall entitle Buyers to reject them or delay payment, but Sellers shall be responsible
156   for all loss or expense caused to Buyers by reason of such error and Sellers shall on request furnish an approved guarantee in
157   respect thereto.
158   (h) Amounts payable under this contract shall be settled without delay. If not so settled, either party may notify the other that a
159   dispute has arisen and serve a notice stating his intention to refer the dispute to arbitration in accordance with the Arbitration
160   Rules.
161   (i) **Interest** – If there has been unreasonable delay in any payment, interest appropriate to the currency involved shall be charged.
162   If such charge is not mutually agreed, a dispute shall be deemed to exist which shall be settled by arbitration. Otherwise interest
163   shall be payable only where specifically provided in the terms of the contract or by an award of arbitration. The terms of this
164   clause do not override the parties' contractual obligation under sub-clause (a).
165

166   **12.**   **DUTIES, TAXES, LEVIES, ETC**.- All export duties, taxes, levies, etc., present or future, in country of origin, shall be for Sellers'
167   account. All import duties, taxes, levies, etc., present or future, in country of destination, shall be for Buyers' account.
168

169   **13.**   **DISCHARGE**- Discharge shall be as fast as the vessel can deliver in accordance with the custom of the port, but in the event of
170   shipment being made under liner bill(s) of lading, discharge shall be as fast as the vessel can deliver in accordance with the terms of
171   the bill(s) of lading. The cost of discharge from hold to ship's rail shall be for Sellers' account, from ship's rail overboard for Buyers'
172   account. If documents are tendered which do not provide for discharging as above or contain contrary stipulations, Sellers shall be
173   responsible to Buyers for all extra expenses incurred thereby. Discharge by grab(s) shall be permitted unless specifically excluded at
174   time of contract. If shipment is effected by lash barge, then the last day of discharge shall be the day of discharging the last lash barge
175   at the port of destination.
176

177   **14.**   **WEIGHING**-the terms and conditions of GAFTA Weighing Rules No. 123 are deemed to be incorporated into this contract.
178   Unless otherwise agreed, final settlement shall be made on the basis of gross delivered weights at time and place of discharge at
179   Buyers' expense. If the place of destination is outside the port limits, Buyers agree to pay the extra expenses incurred by Sellers
180   or their agents for weighing. No payment shall be made for increase in weight occasioned by water and/or oil during the voyage.
181   If final at time and place of loading, as per GAFTA registered superintendents' certificate at Sellers' choice and expense, (in
182   which case the Deficiency Clause will not apply).
183

184   **15.**   **DEFICIENCY**- Any deficiency in the bill of lading weight shall be paid for by Sellers and any excess over bill of lading weight
185   shall be paid for by Buyers at contract price, (unless the Pro-rata clause applies).
186

187   **16.**   **SAMPLING, ANALYSIS AND CERTIFICATES OF ANALYSIS**- the terms and conditions of GAFTA Sampling Rules No.124,
188   are deemed to be incorporated into this contract. Samples shall be taken at the time of discharge on or before removal from the
189   ship or quay, unless the parties agree that quality final at loading applies, in which event samples shall be taken at time and place
190   of loading. The parties shall appoint superintendents, for the purposes of supervision and sampling of the goods, from the GAFTA
191   Register of Superintendents. Unless otherwise agreed, analysts shall be appointed from the GAFTA Register of Analysts.
192

193   **17.**   **INSURANCE**- Sellers shall provide insurance on terms not less favourable than those set out hereunder, and as set out in detail in
194   GAFTA Insurance Terms No.72 viz.:-
195   (a) Risks Covered:-

196	Cargo Clauses (WA), with average payable, with 3% franchise or better terms	- Section 2 of Form 72
197	War Clauses (Cargo)	- Section 4 of Form 72
198	Strikes, Riots and Civil Commotions Clauses (Cargo)	- Section 5 of Form 72

199 (b) Insurers - The insurance to be effected with first class underwriters and/or companies who are domiciled or carrying on business in
200 the United Kingdom or who, for the purpose of any legal proceedings, accept a British domicile and provide an address for service of
201 process in London, but for whose solvency Sellers shall not be responsible.
202 (c) Insurable Value - Insured amount to be for not less than 2% over the invoice amount, including freight when freight is payable on
203 shipment or due in any event, ship and/or cargo lost or not lost, and including the amount of any War Risk premium payable by
204 Buyers.
205 (d) Freight Contingency - When freight is payable on arrival or on right and true delivery of the goods and the insurance does not
206 include the freight, Sellers shall effect insurance upon similar terms, such insurance to attach only as such freight becomes payable, for
207 the amount of the freight plus 2%, until the termination of the risk as provided in the above mentioned clauses, and shall undertake
208 that their policies are so worded that in the case of particular or general average claim the Buyers shall be put in the same position as if
209 the c.i.f. value plus 2% were insured from the time of shipment.
210 (e) Certificates/Policies - Sellers shall serve all policies and/or certificates and/or letters of insurance provided for in this contract,
211 (duly stamped if applicable) for original and increased value (if any) for the value stipulated in (c) above. In the event of a certificate of
212 insurance being supplied, it is agreed that such certificate shall be exchanged by Sellers for a policy if and when required, and such
213 certificate shall state on its face that it is so exchangeable. If required by Buyers, letter(s) of insurance shall be guaranteed by a
214 recognised bank, or by any other guarantor who is acceptable to Buyers.
215 (f) Total Loss - In the event of total or constructive total loss, or where the amount of the insurance becomes payable in full, the
216 insured amount in excess of 2% over the invoice amount shall be for Sellers' account and the party in possession of the policy (ies)
217 shall collect the amount of insurance and shall thereupon settle with the other party on that basis.
218 (g) Currency of Claims - Claims to be paid in the currency of the contract.
219 (h) War and Strike Risks/Premiums - Any premium in excess of 0.50% to be for account of Buyers. The rate of such insurance not to
220 exceed the rate ruling in London at time of shipment or date of vessel's sailing whichever may be adopted by underwriters. Such
221 excess premium shall be claimed from Buyers, wherever possible, with the Provisional Invoice, but in no case later than the date of
222 vessel's arrival, or not later than 7 consecutive days after the rate has been agreed with underwriters, whichever may be the later,
223 otherwise such claim shall be void unless, in the opinion of Arbitrators, the delay is justifiable. Sellers' obligation to provide War Risk
224 Insurance shall be limited to the terms and conditions in force and generally obtainable in London at time of shipment.
225 (i) Where Sellers are responsible for allowances or other payments to Buyers under Rye Terms or other contractual terms, (and which
226 risks are also covered by the insurance provided by Sellers), the Buyers, on receipt of settlement, shall immediately return to Sellers
227 the insurance documents originally received from them and shall, if required, subrogate to Sellers all right of claim against the Insurers
228 in respect of such matters.
229

230 **18. PROHIBITION**- In case of prohibition of export, blockade or hostilities or in case of any executive or legislative act done by or on
231 behalf of the government of the country of origin or of the territory where the port or ports of shipment named herein is/are situate,
232 restricting export, whether partially or otherwise, any such restriction shall be deemed by both parties to apply to this contract and to
233 the extent of such total or partial restriction to prevent fulfilment whether by shipment or by any other means whatsoever and to that
234 extent this contract or any unfulfilled portion thereof shall be cancelled. Sellers shall advise Buyers without delay with the reasons
235 therefor and, if required, Sellers must produce proof to justify the cancellation.
236

237 **19. FORCE MAJEURE, STRIKES, ETC**- Sellers shall not be responsible for delay in shipment of the goods or any part thereof
238 occasioned by any Act of God, strike, lockout, riot or civil commotion, combination of workmen, breakdown of machinery, fire, or
239 any cause comprehended in the term "force majeure". If delay in shipment is likely to occur for any of the above reasons, the Shipper
240 shall serve a notice on Buyers within 7 consecutive days of the occurrence, or not less than 21 consecutive days before the
241 commencement of the contract period, whichever is the later. The notice shall state the reason(s) for the anticipated delay.
242

243 If after serving such notice an extension to the shipping period is required, then the Shipper shall serve a further notice not later than 2
244 business days after the last day of the contract period of shipment stating the port or ports of loading from which the goods were
245 intended to be shipped, and shipments effected after the contract period shall be limited to the port or ports so nominated.
246

247 If shipment be delayed for more than 30 consecutive days, Buyers shall have the option of cancelling the delayed portion of the
248 contract, such option to be exercised by Buyers serving notice to be received by Sellers not later than the first business day after the
249 additional 30 consecutive days. If Buyers do not exercise this option, such delayed portion shall be automatically extended for a further
250 period of 30 consecutive days. If shipment under this clause is prevented during the further 30 consecutive days extension, the
251 contract shall be considered void. Buyers shall have no claim against Sellers for delay or non-shipment under this clause, provided that
252 Sellers shall have supplied to Buyers, if required, satisfactory evidence justifying the delay or non-fulfilment.
253

254 **20. NOTICES**- All notices required to be served on the parties pursuant to this contract shall be communicated rapidly in legible form.
255 Methods of rapid communication for the purposes of this clause are defined and mutually recognised as: - either telex, or letter if
256 delivered by hand on the date of writing, or telefax, or E-mail, or other electronic means, always subject to the proviso that if
257 receipt of any notice is contested, the burden of proof of transmission shall be on the sender who shall, in the case of a dispute,
258 establish, to the satisfaction of the arbitrator(s) or board of appeal appointed pursuant to the Arbitration Clause, that the notice was
259 actually transmitted to the addressee. In case of resales/repurchases all notices shall be served without delay by sellers on their
260 respective buyers or vice versa, and any notice received after 1600 hours on a business day shall be deemed to have been received
261 on the business day following. A notice to the Brokers or Agent shall be deemed a notice under this contract.
262

263 **21. NON-BUSINESS DAYS**- Saturdays, Sundays and the officially recognised and/or legal holidays of the respective countries and any
264 days, which GAFTA may declare as non-business days for specific purposes, shall be non-business days. Should the time limit for
265 doing any act or serving any notice expire on a non-business day, the time so limited shall be extended until the first business day
266 thereafter. The period of shipment shall not be affected by this clause.
267

268 **22. PRO RATA**-

269 (a) Should any of the above mentioned quantity form part of a larger quantity of the same or a different period of shipment of bags of
270 the same mark, or of a similar quality, whether in bags or bulk or whether destined to more than one port, no separation or distinction
271 shall be necessary.
272 (b) All loose collected, damaged goods and sweepings shall be shared by and apportioned pro-rata in kind between the various
273 Receivers thereof at the port of discharge named in the contract, buying under contracts containing this clause. In the event of this not
274 being practicable or any of them receiving more or less than his pro-rata share or apportionment, he shall settle with the other(s) on a
275 pro-rata basis in cash at the market price and each Receiver shall bear his proportion of the depreciation in market value. The pro-rata
276 statement shall be established by the Sellers or their Representatives in conjunction with the Receivers or their Representatives.
277 (c) The above pro-rata apportionment between Receivers shall have no bearing on the establishment of final invoices with Sellers and
278 for the purpose of these invoices, the total quantity of loose collected, damaged goods and sweepings shall be regarded as delivered to
279 those Receivers who did not receive their full invoiced quantity.
280 (d) In the case of excess or deficiency, the difference between the invoiced and the total delivered quantity shall be settled at the market
281 price by final invoices to be rendered by Receivers, who have received more or less than that paid for, to their immediate Sellers
282 without taking into consideration the above pro-rata apportionment between Receivers.
283 (e) If an excess quantity is delivered to one or more Receiver and a deficient quantity is delivered to one or more Receiver, the excess
284 and deficiency shall be settled between them at the market price. Invoices shall be established with immediate Sellers for any balance
285 resulting from this settlement.
286 (f) All Shippers, Sellers and Buyers of any part of such larger quantity as aforesaid under contracts containing this clause shall be
287 deemed to have entered into mutual agreements with one another to the above effect, and to agree to submit to arbitration all questions
288 and claims between them or any of them in regard to the execution of this clause as aforesaid in accordance with the Arbitration
289 Clause of this contract. Sellers and Buyers shall serve all reasonable assistance in execution of this clause. All Sellers shall be
290 responsible for the settlement by the respective Buyers in accordance with this clause within a reasonable time.
291 (g) The market price wherever mentioned in this clause shall be the market price on the last day of discharge of the vessel in the port
292 of destination, such price to be fixed by arbitration unless mutually agreed.
293 (h) In the event of this clause being brought into operation, any allowances payable in respect of condition, or quality, or under any of
294 the other guarantees contained in this contract, shall be based upon the actual weight received by the Buyers and not on the pro-rata
295 weight.
296 (i) In the event of any conflict in terms of apportionment applicable to the port of discharge the method published by GAFTA shall,
297 where applicable, take precedence over sub-clauses (b) to (h) above.
298 (j) In the event that sub-clause (a) applies or that the goods subsequently become co-mingled, and that the goods were shipped by more
299 than one Shipper and destined for one or more ports of discharge then, after the adjustment between Receivers under the terms of this
300 clause, the Shippers shall settle pro-rata between themselves in proportion to their bill of lading quantities. Such settlements shall be
301 made in cash and, in the event of two or more discharging ports being involved, then the settlement price shall be the average of the
302 market prices on the last day of discharge in the respective ports.
303
304 **23. DEFAULT** - In default of fulfilment of contract by either party, the following provisions shall apply: -
305 (a) The party other than the defaulter shall, at their discretion have the right, after serving notice on the defaulter to sell or purchase, as
306 the case may be, against the defaulter, and such sale or purchase shall establish the default price.
307 (b) If either party be dissatisfied with such default price or if the right at (a) above is not exercised and damages cannot be mutually
308 agreed, then the assessment of damages shall be settled by arbitration.
309 (c) The damages payable shall be based on, but not limited to, the difference between the contract price and either the default price
310 established under (a) above or upon the actual or estimated value of the goods, on the date of default, established under (b) above.
311 (d) In no case shall damages include loss of profit on any sub-contracts made by the party defaulted against or others unless the
312 arbitrator(s) or board of appeal, having regard to special circumstances, shall in his/their sole and absolute discretion think fit.
313 (e) Damages, if any, shall be computed on the quantity appropriated if any but, if no such quantity has been appropriated then on the
314 mean contract quantity, and any option available to either party shall be deemed to have been exercised accordingly in favour of the
315 mean contract quantity.
316 (f) Default may be declared by Sellers at any time after expiry of the contract period, and the default date shall then be the first
317 business day after the date of Sellers' advice to their Buyers. If default has not already been declared then (notwithstanding the
318 provisions stated in the Appropriation Clause) if notice of appropriation has not been served by the 10th consecutive day after the last
319 day for appropriation laid down in the contract, the Seller shall be deemed to be in default and the default date shall then be the first
320 business day thereafter.
321
322 **24. CIRCLE** - Where Sellers re-purchase from their Buyers or from any subsequent buyer the same goods or part thereof, a circle shall be
323 considered to exist as regards the particular goods so re-purchased, and the provisions of the Default Clause shall not apply. (For the
324 purpose of this clause the same goods shall mean goods of the same description, from the same country of origin, of the same quality,
325 and, where applicable, of the same analysis warranty, for shipment to the same port(s) of destination during the same period of
326 shipment). Different currencies shall not invalidate the circle.
327 Subject to the terms of the Prohibition Clause in the contract, if the goods are not appropriated, or, having been appropriated
328 documents are not presented, invoices based on the mean contract quantity shall be settled by all Buyers and their Sellers in the circle
329 by payment by all Buyers to their Sellers of the excess of the Sellers' invoice amount over the lowest invoice amount in the circle.
330 Payment shall be due not later than 15 consecutive days after the last day for appropriation, or, should the circle not be ascertained
331 before the expiry of this time, then payment shall be due not later than 15 consecutive days after the circle is ascertained.
332 Where the circle includes contracts expressed in different currencies the lowest invoice amount shall be replaced by the market price
333 on the first day for contractual shipment and invoices shall be settled between each Buyer and his Seller in the circle by payment of the
334 differences between the market price and the relative contract price in currency of the contract.
335 All Sellers and Buyers shall give every assistance to ascertain the circle and when a circle shall have been ascertained in accordance
336 with this clause same shall be binding on all parties to the circle. As between Buyers and Sellers in the circle, the non-presentation of
337 documents by Sellers to their Buyers shall not be considered a breach of contract. Should any party in the circle prior to the due date
338 of payment commit any act comprehended in the Insolvency Clause of his contract, settlement by all parties in the circle shall be
339 calculated at the closing out price as provided for in the Insolvency Clause, which shall be taken as a basis for settlement, instead of
340 the lowest invoice amount in the circle. In this event respective Buyers shall make payment to their Sellers or respective Sellers shall
341 make payment to their Buyers of the difference between the closing out price and the contract price.

100/5

25. INSOLVENCY- If before the fulfilment of this contract, either party shall suspend payments, notify any of the creditors that he is unable to meet debts or that he has suspended or that he is about to suspend payments of his debts, convene, call or hold a meeting of creditors, propose a voluntary arrangement, have an administration order made, have a winding up order made, have a receiver or manager appointed, convene, call or hold a meeting to go into liquidation (other than for re-construction or amalgamation) become subject to an Interim Order under Section 252 of the Insolvency Act 1986, or have a Bankruptcy Petition presented against him (any of which acts being hereinafter called an "Act of Insolvency") then the party committing such Act of Insolvency shall forthwith serve a notice of the occurrence of such Act of Insolvency on the other party to the contract and upon proof (by either the other party to the contract or the Receiver, Administrator, Liquidator or other person representing the party committing the Act of Insolvency) that such notice was served within 2 business days of the occurrence of the Act of Insolvency, the contract shall be closed out at the market price ruling on the business day following the serving of the notice.

If such notice has not been served, then the other party, on learning of the occurrence of the Act of Insolvency, shall have the option of declaring the contract closed out at either the market price on the first business day after the date when such party first learnt of the occurrence of the Act of Insolvency or at the market price ruling on the first business day after the date when the Act of Insolvency occurred.

In all cases the other party to the contract shall have the option of ascertaining the settlement price on the closing out of the contract by re-purchase or re-sale, and the difference between the contract price and the re-purchase or re-sale price shall be the amount payable or receivable under this contract.

26. DOMICILE- This contract shall be deemed to have been made in England and to be performed in England, notwithstanding any contrary provision, and this contract shall be construed and take effect in accordance with the laws of England. Except for the purpose of enforcing any award made in pursuance of the Arbitration clause of this contract, the Courts of England shall have exclusive jurisdiction to determine any application for ancillary relief, the exercise of the powers of the Court in relation to the arbitration proceedings and any dispute other than a dispute which shall fall within the jurisdiction of arbitrators or board of appeal of the Association pursuant to the Arbitration Clause of this contract. For the purpose of any legal proceedings each party shall be deemed to be ordinarily resident or carrying on business at the offices of The Grain and Feed Trade Association, England, (GAFTA) and any party residing or carrying on business in Scotland shall be held to have prorogated jurisdiction against himself to the English Courts or if in Northern Ireland to have submitted to the jurisdiction and to be bound by the decision of the English Courts. The service of proceedings upon any such party by leaving the same at the offices of The Grain and Feed Trade Association, together with the posting of a copy of such proceedings to his address outside England, shall be deemed good service, any rule of law or equity to the contrary notwithstanding.

27. ARBITRATION-
(a) Any dispute arising out of or under this contract shall be settled by arbitration in accordance with the GAFTA Arbitration Rules, No. 125, in the edition current at the date of this contract, such Rules forming part of this contract and of which both parties hereto shall be deemed to be cognisant.
(b) Neither party hereto, nor any persons claiming under either of them shall bring any action or other legal proceedings against the other of them in respect of any such dispute until such dispute shall first have been heard and determined by the arbitrator(s) or a board of appeal, as the case may be, in accordance with the Arbitration Rules and it is expressly agreed and declared that the obtaining of an award from the arbitrator(s) or a board of appeal, as the case may be, shall be a condition precedent to the right of either party hereto or of any persons claiming under either of them to bring any action or other legal proceedings against the other of them in respect of any such dispute.

28. INTERNATIONAL CONVENTIONS-
The following shall not apply to this contract: -
(a) The Uniform Law on Sales and the Uniform Law on Formation to which effect is given by the Uniform Laws on International Sales Act 1967;
(b) The United Nations Convention on Contracts for the International Sale of Goods of 1980; and
(c) The United Nations Convention on Prescription (Limitation) in the International Sale of Goods of 1974 and the amending Protocol of 1980.
(d) Incoterms
(e) Unless the contract contains any statement expressly to the contrary, a person who is not a party to this contract has no right under the Contract (Rights of Third Parties) Act 1999 to enforce any term of it.

Sellers .... Buyers ....

Printed in England and issued by

GAFTA
(THE GRAIN AND FEED TRADE ASSOCIATION)
GAFTA HOUSE, 6 CHAPEL PLACE, RIVINGTON ST, LONDON EC2A 3SH

100/6

253

Effective from 1ˢᵗ November 2003

Gafta No.119
Copyright
THE GRAIN AND FEED TRADE ASSOCIATION

GENERAL CONTRACT FOR FEEDINGSTUFFS IN BAGS OR BULK
FOB TERMS

* delete/specify as applicable　　　　　　　　　　　　　Date ....

1　**SELLERS** ....
2
3　**INTERVENING AS BROKERS** ....
4
5　**BUYERS**...
6　have this day entered into a contract on the following terms and conditions.
7
8　**1.　GOODS**-
9　　If in bags, in new and/or second-hand bags of suitable strength to withstand ordinary wear and tear to port of destination. Bags of each
10　　mark shall be of uniform weight and shall be properly marked. If in bulk, Buyers may call for up to 10% in stowage bags, such bags
11　　to be taken and paid for as goods and any cutting to be paid for by Buyers. Buyers have the option of calling for an additional quantity
12　　to be shipped in bags, in which case they will be responsible for providing the extra bags and any additional costs incurred, but shall
13　　not be required to pay for the extra bags as goods.
14
15　**2.　QUANTITY**- .... 5% more or less at Buyers' option.
16　　In the event of the quantity contracted being a full and complete cargo and/or cargoes the margin of contract quantity shall be 10%
17　　more or less, any excess or deficiency over 5% shall be settled at the FOB price on date of last bill of lading; value shall be fixed by
18　　arbitration unless mutually agreed. In the event of more than one delivery being made each delivery shall be considered a separate
19　　contract, but the margin on the mean quantity sold shall not be affected thereby. Each mark/parcel shall stand as a separate delivery.
20
21　**3.　PRICE**- at ....
22　　* per tonne of 1000 kilograms　　　　　}
23　　　　　　　　　　　　　　　　　　　　}gross weight, delivered Free on Board Buyers' vessel at ....
24　　* per ton of 1016 kilograms or 2240 lbs.　}
25
26　**4.　BROKERAGE**...................................per tonne, to be paid by Sellers on the mean contract quantity, goods lost or not lost,
27　　contract fulfilled or not fulfilled unless such non-fulfilment is due to the cancellation of the contract under the terms of the
28　　Prohibition or Force Majeure Clause. Brokerage shall be due on the day shipping documents are exchanged, or if the goods are
29　　not delivered then the brokerage shall be due on the 30ᵗʰ consecutive day after the last day for delivery.
30
31　**5.　QUALITY**- ....
32
33　　***Official** ....certificate of inspection, at time of loading into the ocean carrying vessel, shall be final as to quality.
34
35　　***Sample**, at time and place of shipment about as per sealed sample marked ....in possession of ....
36
37　　Warranted to contain not less than...
38　　% of oil and protein combined and not more than 2.50% of sand and/or silica. Should the whole, or any portion, not turn out equal
39　　to warranty, the goods must be taken at an allowance to be agreed or settled by arbitration as provided for below, except that for
40　　any deficiency of oil and protein there shall be allowances to Buyers at the following rates, viz.: 1% of the contract price for each
41　　of the first 3 units of deficiency under the warranted percentage; 2% of the contract price for the 4th and 5th units and 3% of the
42　　contract price for each unit in excess of 5 and proportionately for any fraction thereof. When the combined content of oil and
43　　protein is warranted within a margin (as for example 40%/42%) no allowance shall be made if the analysis ascertained as herein
44　　provided be not below the minimum, but if the analysis results below the minimum warranted the allowance for deficiency shall
45　　be computed from the mean of the warranted content. For any excess of sand and/or silica there shall be an allowance of 1% of
46　　the contract price for each unit of excess and proportionately for any fraction thereof. Should the goods contain over 5% of sand
47　　and/or silica the Buyers shall be entitled to reject the goods, in which case the contract shall be null and void, for such quantity
48　　rejected. For the purpose of sampling and analysis each mark/parcel shall stand as a separate shipment. The right of rejection
49　　provided by this Clause shall be limited to the mark/parcel or marks/parcels found to be defective.
50
51　　**Condition**. Delivery shall be made in good condition.
52　**6.　PERIOD OF DELIVERY**
53　　**Delivery during** .... at Buyers' call.

119/1

54
55   **Nomination of Vessel**- Buyers shall serve not less than ....consecutive days notice of the name and
56   probable readiness date of the vessel and the estimated tonnage required. Buyers have the right to substitute the nominated vessel,
57   but in any event the original delivery period and any extension shall not be affected thereby. Provided the vessel is presented at the
58   loading port in readiness to load within the delivery period, Sellers shall if necessary complete loading after the delivery period
59   and carrying charges shall not apply. In case of re-sales a provisional notice shall be passed on without delay, where possible, by
60   telephone and confirmed on the same day in accordance with the Notices Clause.
61
62   **7.**   **SHIPMENT AND CLASSIFICATION**- Shipment by first class mechanically self-propelled vessel(s) suitable for the carriage of
63   the contract goods, classed in accordance with the Institute Classification Clause of the International Underwriting Association in
64   force at the time of shipment, excluding tankers and vessels which are either classified in Lloyd's Register or described in Lloyd's
65   Shipping Index as "Ore/Oil" vessels.
66
67   **8.**   **LOADING -** Vessel(s) to load in accordance with the custom of the port of loading unless otherwise stipulated. Bill of lading shall
68   be considered proof of delivery in the absence of evidence to the contrary.
69
70   **9.**   **EXTENSION OF DELIVERY**- The contract period of delivery shall be extended by an additional period of not more than 30
71   consecutive days, provided that Buyers serve notice claiming extension not later than the next business day following the last day of
72   the delivery period. In this event Sellers shall carry the goods for Buyers' account and all charges for storage, interest, insurance and
73   other such normal carrying expenses shall be for Buyers' account, unless the vessel presents in readiness to load within the contractual
74   delivery period.
75   Any differences in export duties, taxes, levies etc, between those applying during the original delivery period and those applying
76   during the period of extension, shall be for the account of Buyers. If required by Buyers, Sellers shall produce evidence of the
77   amounts paid. In such cases the Duties, Taxes, Levies Clause shall not apply.
78   Should Buyers fail to present a vessel in readiness to load under the extension period, Sellers shall have the option of declaring Buyers
79   to be in default, or shall be entitled to demand payment at the contract price plus such charges as stated above, less current FOB
80   charges, against warehouse warrants and the tender of such warehouse warrants shall be considered complete delivery of the contract
81   on the part of Sellers.
82
83   **10.**   **ICE** - ....
84
85   **11.**   **PAYMENT**-
86   (a) By cash in .... against the
87
88   following shipping documents ....
89   (b) No clerical error in the documents shall entitle the Buyers to reject them or delay payment, but Sellers shall be responsible for all
90   loss or expense caused to Buyers by reason of such error, and Sellers shall on request of Buyers furnish an approved guarantee in
91   respect thereto.
92   (c) Amounts payable under this contract shall be settled without delay. If not so settled, either party may notify the other that a dispute
93   has arisen and serve a notice stating his intention to refer the dispute to arbitration in accordance with the Arbitration Rules.
94   (d) **Interest** – If there has been unreasonable delay in any payment, interest appropriate to the currency involved shall be charged. If such
95   charge is not mutually agreed, a dispute shall be deemed to exist which shall be settled by arbitration. Otherwise interest shall be payable
96   only where specifically provided in the terms of the contract or by an award of arbitration. The terms of this clause do not override the
97   parties' contractual obligation under sub-clause (a).
98
99   **12.**   **EXPORT LICENCE** - if required, to be obtained by Sellers.
100
101   **13.**   **DUTIES, TAXES, LEVIES, ETC**.- All export duties, taxes, levies, etc., present or future, in country of origin, or of the territory
102   where the port or ports of shipment named herein is/are situate, shall be for Sellers' account.
103
104   **14.**   **INSURANCE**- Marine and war risk insurance including strikes, riots, civil commotions and mine risks to be effected by Buyers with
105   first class underwriters and/or approved companies. Buyers shall supply Sellers with confirmation thereof at least 5 consecutive days
106   prior to expected readiness of vessel(s). If Buyers fail to provide such confirmation, Sellers shall have the right to place such
107   insurance at Buyers' risk and expense.
108
109   **15.**   **WEIGHING**- the terms and conditions of GAFTA Weighing Rules No.123 are deemed to be incorporated into this contract.
110   Final at time and place of loading, as per GAFTA registered superintendent certificate at Sellers' choice and expense. Buyers
111   have the right to attend at loading.
112
113   **16.**   **SAMPLING, ANALYSIS AND CERTIFICATE OF ANALYSIS**- the terms and conditions of GAFTA Sampling Rules No. 124,
114   are deemed to be incorporated into this contract. Samples shall be taken at time and place of loading. The parties shall appoint
115   superintendents, for the purposes of supervision and sampling of the goods, from the GAFTA Register of Superintendents. Unless
116   otherwise agreed, analysts shall be appointed from the GAFTA Register of Analysts
117
118   **17.**   **PROHIBITION**- In case of prohibition of export, blockade or hostilities or in case of any executive or legislative act done by or on
119   behalf of the government of the country of origin or of the territory where the port or ports of shipment named herein is/are situate,
120   restricting export, whether partially or otherwise, any such restriction shall be deemed by both parties to apply to this contract and to

121 the extent of such total or partial restriction to prevent fulfilment whether by shipment or by any other means whatsoever and to that
122 extent this contract or any unfulfilled portion thereof shall be cancelled. Sellers shall advise Buyers without delay with the reasons
123 therefor and, if required, Sellers must produce proof to justify the cancellation.
124

18. LOADING STRIKES-
125
126 (a) Should delivery of the goods or any part thereof be prevented at any time during the last 28 days of guaranteed time of delivery or
127 at any time during guaranteed contract period if such be less than 28 days, by reason of riots, strikes or lock-outs at port(s) of loading
128 or elsewhere preventing the forwarding of the goods to such port(s), then Sellers shall be entitled at the resumption of work after
129 termination of such riots, strikes or lock-outs to as much time, not exceeding 28 days, for delivery from such port(s) as was left for
130 delivery under the contract prior to the outbreak of the riots, strikes or lock-outs, and in the event of the time left for delivery under
131 the contract being 14 days or less, a minimum extension of 14 days shall be allowed.
132 (b) In the event of further riots, strikes or lock-outs occurring during the time by which the guaranteed time of delivery has been
133 extended by reason of the operation of the provisions of paragraph (a), the additional extension shall be limited to the actual duration of
134 such further riots, strikes or lock-outs. In case of non-delivery under the above circumstances the date of default shall be similarly
135 deferred.
136 (c) If delay in delivery is likely to occur for any of the above reasons, Sellers shall serve notice on their Buyers within 7 consecutive
137 days of the occurrence, or not less than 21 consecutive days before the commencement of the contract period, whichever is later, if
138 they intend to claim an extension for delivery, such notice shall limit the port(s) for delivery after expiry of contract period to those for
139 which an extension is claimed.
140 (d) If required by Buyers, Sellers must provide documentary evidence to establish any claim for extension under this clause.
141

19. FORCE MAJEURE - ....
142
143

20. CIRCLE- Where Sellers re-purchase from their Buyers or from any subsequent Buyer the same goods or part thereof, a circle shall be
144
145 considered to exist as regards the particular goods so re-purchased, and the provisions of the Default Clause shall not apply. (For the
146 purpose of this clause the same goods shall mean goods of the same description, from the same country of origin, of the same quality,
147 and, where applicable, of the same analysis warranty, for delivery from the same port(s) of loading during the same period of
148 delivery). Different currencies shall not invalidate the circle.
149 Subject to the terms of the Prohibition Clause in the contract, if the circle is established before the goods are delivered, or if the goods
150 are not delivered invoices based on the mean contract quantity, or if the goods have been delivered invoices based on the delivered
151 quantity, shall be settled by all Buyers and their Sellers in the circle by payment by all Buyers to their Sellers of the excess of the
152 Sellers' invoice amount over the lowest invoice amount in the circle. Payment shall be due not later than 15 consecutive days after the
153 last day for delivery, or, should the circle not be ascertained before the expiry of this time, then payment shall be due not later than 15
154 consecutive days after the circle is ascertained.
155 Where the circle includes contract expressed in different currencies the lowest invoice amount shall be replaced by the market price on
156 the first day for contractual delivery and invoices shall be settled between each Buyer and his Seller in the circle by payment of the
157 differences between the market price and the relative contract price in the currency of the contract.
158 All Sellers and Buyers shall give every assistance to ascertain the circle and when a circle shall have been ascertained in accordance
159 with this clause same shall be binding on all parties to the circle. As between Buyers and Sellers in the circle, the non-presentation of
160 documents by Sellers to their Buyers shall not be considered a breach of contract. Should any party in the circle prior to the due date
161 of payment commit any act comprehended in the Insolvency Clause of this contract, settlement by all parties in the circle shall be
162 calculated at the closing out price as provided for in the Insolvency Clause, which shall be taken as a basis for settlement, instead of
163 the lowest invoice amount in the circle. In this event respective Buyers shall make payment to their Sellers or respective Sellers shall
164 make payment to their Buyers of the difference between the closing out price and the contract price.
165

21. NOTICES- All notices required to be served on the parties pursuant to this contract shall be communicated rapidly in legible form.
166
167 Methods of rapid communication for the purposes of this clause are defined and mutually recognised as: - either telex, or letter if
168 delivered by hand on the date of writing, or telefax, or E-mail, or other electronic means, always subject to the proviso that if
169 receipt of any notice is contested, the burden of proof of transmission shall be on the sender who shall, in the case of a dispute,
170 establish, to the satisfaction of the arbitrator(s) or board of appeal appointed pursuant to the Arbitration Clause, that the notice was
171 actually transmitted to the addressee. For the purpose of serving notices in a string, any notice received after 1600 hours on a
172 business day shall be deemed to have been received on the business day following. In case of resales/repurchases all notices shall
173 be served without delay by sellers on their respective buyers or vice versa. A notice to the Brokers or Agent shall be deemed a
174 notice under this contract.
175

22. NON-BUSINESS DAYS- Saturdays, Sundays and the officially recognised and/or legal holidays of the respective countries and any
176
177 days, which GAFTA may declare as non-business days for specific purposes, shall be non-business days. Should the time limit for
178 doing any act or serving any notice expire on a non-business day, the time so limited shall be extended until the first business day
179 thereafter. The period of delivery shall not be affected by this clause.
180

23. DEFAULT- In default of fulfilment of contract by either party, the following provisions shall apply: -
181
182 (a) The party other than the defaulter shall, at their discretion have the right, after serving notice on the defaulter, to sell or purchase,
183 as the case may be, against the defaulter, and such sale or purchase shall establish the default price.
184 (b) If either party be dissatisfied with such default price or if the right at (a) above is not exercised and damages cannot be mutually
185 agreed, then the assessment of damages shall be settled by arbitration.
186 (c) The damages payable shall be based on, but not limited to, the difference between the contract price and either the default price
187 established under (a) above or upon the actual or estimated value of the goods, on the date of default, established under (b) above.

188 (d) In all cases the damages shall, in addition, include any proven additional expenses which would directly and naturally result in the
189 ordinary course of events from the defaulter's breach of contract, but shall in no case include loss of profit on any sub-contracts made
190 by the party defaulted against or others unless the arbitrator(s) or board of appeal, having regard to special circumstances, shall in
191 his/their sole and absolute discretion think fit.
192 (e) Damages, if any, shall be computed on the quantity called for if any but, if no such quantity has been declared then on the mean
193 contract quantity, and any option available to either party shall be deemed to have been exercised accordingly in favour of the mean
194 contract quantity.
195

196 **24. INSOLVENCY**- If before the fulfilment of this contract, either party shall suspend payments, notify any of the creditors that he is
197 unable to meet debts or that he has suspended or that he is about to suspend payments of his debts, convene, call or hold a meeting of
198 creditors, propose a voluntary arrangement, have an administration order made, have a winding up order made, have a receiver or
199 manager appointed, convene, call or hold a meeting to go into liquidation (other than for re-construction or amalgamation) become
200 subject to an Interim Order under Section 252 of the Insolvency Act 1986, or have a Bankruptcy Petition presented against him (any of
201 which acts being hereinafter called an "Act of Insolvency") then the party committing such Act of Insolvency shall forthwith serve a
202 notice of the occurrence of such Act of Insolvency on the other party to the contract and upon proof (by either the other party to the
203 contract or the Receiver, Administrator, Liquidator or other person representing the party committing the Act of Insolvency) that such
204 notice was thus served within 2 business days of the occurrence of the Act of Insolvency, the contract shall be closed out at the market
205 price ruling on the business day following the serving of the notice. If such notice has not been served, then the other party, on learning
206 of the occurrence of the Act of Insolvency, shall have the option of declaring the contract closed out at either the market price on the
207 first business day after the date when such party first learnt of the occurrence of the Act of Insolvency or at the market price ruling on
208 the first business day after the date when the Act of Insolvency occurred. In all cases the other party to the contract shall have the option
209 of ascertaining the settlement price on the closing out of the contract by re-purchase or re-sale, and the difference between the contract
210 price and the re-purchase or re-sale price shall be the amount payable or receivable under this contract.
211

212 **25. DOMICILE**-This contract shall be deemed to have been made in England and to be performed in England, notwithstanding any
213 contrary provision, and this contract shall be construed and take effect in accordance with the laws of England. Except for the
214 purpose of enforcing any award made in pursuance of the Arbitration Clause of this contract, the Courts of England shall have
215 exclusive jurisdiction to determine any application for ancillary relief, the exercise of the powers of the Court in relation to the
216 arbitration proceedings and any dispute other than a dispute which shall fall within the jurisdiction of arbitrators or board of appeal
217 of the Association pursuant to the Arbitration Clause of this contract. For the purpose of any legal proceedings each party shall be
218 deemed to be ordinarily resident or carrying on business at the offices of The Grain and Feed Trade Association, (GAFTA),
219 England, and any party residing or carrying on business in Scotland shall be held to have prorogated jurisdiction against himself to
220 the English Courts or if in Northern Ireland to have submitted to the jurisdiction and to be bound by the decision of the English
221 Courts. The service of proceedings upon any such party by leaving the same at the offices of The Grain and Feed Trade
222 Association, together with the posting of a copy of such proceedings to his address outside England, shall be deemed good
223 service, any rule of law or equity to the contrary notwithstanding.
224

225 **26. ARBITRATION**-
226 (a) Any dispute arising out of or under this contract shall be settled by arbitration in accordance with the GAFTA Arbitration Rules,
227 No. 125, in the edition current at the date of this contract, such Rules forming part of this contract and of which both parties hereto
228 shall be deemed to be cognisant.
229 (b) Neither party hereto, nor any persons claiming under either of them shall bring any action or other legal proceedings against the
230 other of them in respect of any such dispute until such dispute shall first have been heard and determined by the arbitrator(s) or a board
231 of appeal, as the case may be, in accordance with the Arbitration Rules and it is expressly agreed and declared that the obtaining of an
232 award from the arbitrator(s) or a board of appeal, as the case may be, shall be a condition precedent to the right of either party hereto
233 or of any persons claiming under either of them to bring any action or other legal proceedings against the other of them in respect of
234 any such dispute.
235

236 **27. INTERNATIONAL CONVENTIONS**-
237 The following shall not apply to this contract: -
238 (a) The Uniform Law on Sales and the Uniform Law on Formation to which effect is given by the Uniform Laws on International
239 Sales Act 1967;
240 (b) The United Nations Convention on Contracts for the International Sale of Goods of 1980; and
241 (c) The United Nations Convention on Prescription (Limitation) in the International Sale of Goods of 1974 and the amending Protocol
242 of 1980.
243 (d) Incoterms
244 (e) Unless the contract contains any statement expressly to the contrary, a person who is not a party to this contract has no right
245 under the Contract (Rights of Third Parties) Act 1999 to enforce any term of it.

Sellers.. Buyers ....

119/4

INVOICE RECHNUNG FACTURE FACTURA فاتورة

Seller (name, address, VAT reg no.)		Invoice number		
		Invoice date (tax point)	Seller's reference	U N I C
		Buyer's reference	Other reference	
(c) SITPRO 1992	Consignee VAT no.	Buyer (if not consignee) VAT no.		
		Country of origin of goods	Country of destination	
		Terms of delivery and payment		
Vessel/flight no. and date	Port/airport of loading			
Port/airport of discharge	Place of delivery			
Shipping marks; container number	No. and kind of packages; description of goods	Commodity code	Total gross wt (Kg)	Total cube (m3)
			Total net wt (Kg)	

Item/packages	Gross/net/cube Description	Quantity	Unit price	Amount
			Invoice total	

Name of signatory

Place and date of issue

Signature

It is hereby certified that this invoice shows the actual price of the goods described, that no other invoice has been or will be issued, and that all particulars are true and correct.

SITPRO Licensee No. 000.

V5

INCORPORATING BILL OF EXCHANGE		**ADDITIONAL COPY** FOREIGN BILL AND/OR DOCUMENTS FOR COLLECTION

Drawer/exporter	Drawer's/exporter's reference(s) (to be quoted by bank in all correspondence)
Consignee	Drawee (if not consignee)
To (bank)	For bank use only

FORWARD DOCUMENTS ENUMERATED BELOW BY AIR MAIL. FOLLOW SPECIAL INSTRUCTIONS AND THOSE MARKED X

Bill of exchange	Commercial invoice	Certified/consular invoice	Certificate of origin	Insurance policy/ certificate	Bill of lading	Parcel post receipt	Air waybill
Combined transport document	Other documents and whereabouts of any missing original bill of lading						

RELEASE DOCUMENTS ON	ACCEPTANCE	PAYMENT	If unaccepted		protest	do not protest
If documents are not taken up on arrival of goods	warehouse goods	do not warehouse	and advise reason by		telex/cable	airmail
	insure against fire	do not insure	If unpaid		protest	do not protest
Collect ALL charges			and advise reason by		telex/cable	airmail
Collect correspondent's charges ONLY			Advise acceptance and due date by		telex/cable	airmail
Return accepted bill by airmail			Remit proceeds by		telex/cable	airmail
In case of need refer to					for guidance	accept their instructions

SPECIAL INSTRUCTIONS: 1. Represent on arrival of goods if not honoured on first presentation.

Cut

(C) SITPRO 1987

THIS FORM SHOULD ONLY BE USED IN CONJUNCTION WITH THE BRITISH BANKERS' ASSOCIATION APPROVED FORM "FOREIGN BILL AND/OR DOCUMENTS FOR COLLECTION"

Date of bill of exchange

BILL of EXCHANGE for _____

At

pay against this sole of exchange to our order the sum of:

DRAWEE

FOR VALUE RECEIVED

Signature

SITPRO Licensee No. 000.

259

BILLS OF EXCHANGE - FIRST/ SECOND/ THIRD OF EXCHANGE

Date of bill of exchange

At

BILL of EXCHANGE for

pay against this **first** of exchange to our order the sum of:

DRAWEE

SITPRO
(C)
1993

FOR VALUE RECEIVED

Signature

SITPRO Licensee No. 000.

Date of bill of exchange

At

BILL of EXCHANGE for

...ains ...nd of exchange to our order the sum of:

DRAWEE

SITPRO
(C)
1993

FOR VALUE RECEIVED

Signature

SITPRO Licensee No. 000.

Date of bill of exchange

At

BILL of EXCHANGE for

pay against this **third** of exchange to our order the sum of:

DRAWEE

SITPRO
(C)
1993

FOR VALUE RECEIVED

Signature

SITPRO Licensee No. 000.

(c) BBA/SITPRO 1976/1981/1987

AUTHORISED BY THE BRITISH BANKERS' ASSOCIATION

FOREIGN BILL AND/OR DOCUMENTS FOR COLLECTION

Drawer/exporter	Drawer's/exporter's reference(s) (to be quoted by bank in all correspondence)
Consignee	Drawee (if not consignee)
To (bank)	For bank use only

FORWARD DOCUMENTS ENUMERATED BELOW BY AIR MAIL. FOLLOW SPECIAL INSTRUCTIONS AND THOSE MARKED X

Bill of exchange	Commercial invoice	Certified/consular invoice	Certificate of origin	Insurance policy/ certificate	Bill of lading	Parcel post receipt	Air waybill
Combined transport document	Other documents and whereabouts of any missing original bill of lading						

RELEASE DOCUMENTS ON	ACCEPTANCE	PAYMENT	If unaccepted		protest	do not protest
If documents are not taken up on arrival of goods	warehouse goods	do not warehouse	and give reason		telex/cable	airmail
	insure against fire	do not insure	If unpaid		protest	do not protest
Collect ALL charges			and give reason by		telex/cable	airmail
Collect correspondent's charges ONLY			Advise acceptance and due date by		telex/cable	airmail
Return accepted bill by airmail			Remit proceeds by		telex/cable	airmail
In case of need refer to					for guidance	accept their instructions

SPECIAL INSTRUCTIONS: Represent on arrival of goods if not honoured on first presentation.

Date of bill of exchange	Bill of exchange value/amount of collection
Tenor of bill of exchange	
Bill of exchange claused	
	Please collect the above-mentioned bill and/or documents subject to the Uniform Rules for Collections (1978 Revision), International Chamber of Commerce, Publication No. 322. I/We agree that you shall not be liable for any loss, damage, or delay however caused which is not directly due to the negligence of your own officers or servants.
	Date and signature

SITPRO Licensee No. 000.

SAMPLE

A.B.C. Bank plc
Application Form For A Documentary Credit

1 PLEASE ISSUE AN IRREVOCABLE DOCUMENTARY CREDIT

☐ BY AIRMAIL

☐ BY AIRMAIL PRE-ADVISE BY TELE-TRANSMISSION

☐ BY TELE-TRANSMISSION FULL PARTICULARS

2 **APPLICANT** (full name and address)

3 **BENEFICIARY**
IN FAVOUR OF (full name and address)

4 **CURRENCY AND AMOUNT** (in figures and words)

5 **EXPIRY DATE**

(Country)

6 AVAILABLE BY DRAFT(S) AT ☐ SIGHT ☐ DAYS SIGHT ☐ DAYS FROM DATE OF _____

FOR _____ % OF INVOICE DRAWN ON YOU/YOUR CORRESPONDENTS OR BY DEFERRED PAYMENT AT _____

7 DOCUMENTS REQUIRED WHICH MUST BE PRESENTED NOT LATER THAN _____ DAYS AFTER THE DATE
OF THE ISSUANCE OF THE TRANSPORT DOCUMENT

8 TRANSPORT DOCUMENT

9 COMMERCIAL INVOICE

10 INSURANCE

11 OTHER DOCUMENTS

12 INSURANCE TO BE EFFECTED BY _____ (BUYER/SELLERS)

13 COVERING (GOODS DESCRIPTION)

14 TERMS OF SHIPMENT (CIF, FOB, ETC.)

15 SHIPMENT/DESPATCH/TAKING IN CHARGE AT/FROM _____ TO _____
NOT LATER THAN _____

16 PART SHIPMENTS ALLOWED/NOT ALLOWED TRANSHIPMENT ALLOWED/NOT ALLOWED

17 SPECIAL CONDITIONS/OTHER INSTRUCTIONS

EXCEPT AS OTHERWISE EXPRESSLY STATED THIS DOCUMENTARY CREDIT IS SUBJECT TO UNIFORM CUSTOMS AND PRACTICE FOR DOCUMENTARY CREDITS
PROVISIONS OF THE INTERNATIONAL CHAMBER OF COMMERCE PUBLICATION NO. 500.

(c) BBA/SITPRO 1992

LETTER OF CREDIT PRESENTATION FORM

AUTHORISED BY THE BRITISH BANKERS' ASSOCIATION

Drawer/exporter	Drawer's/exporter's reference(s)	
	Issuing bank L/C no.	Your reference no.
	Issuing bank	
To (bank)	Value of the drawing	

DOCUMENTS ENCLOSED (state no. of copies)

Bill of exchange	Commercial invoice	Certified Consular Invoice	Certificate of origin	
Insurance policy/certificate	Transport documents	L/C for endorsement	OTHER DOCUMENTS	
			Document	Copies

Dear Sirs,

We have much pleasure in enclosing the above document[s] to th[e]
Letter of Credit referred to above.
We trust you will find the documents to be in order and [...] forw[ard] to
receiving your settlement as shown below.
Should you discover any discrepancies please [...]us as [...]n
below BEFORE taking any action.

SAMPLE

FOR TERM DRAFTS
We request you to *discount/negotiate [...] inter[...]
Please *retain/return accepte[d] [d]raft(s) to [...]
*Delete as appropriate

PAYMENT INSTRU[CTI]ONS

☐ For GBP [ster]ling item[s ...] rem[it] proceeds to
our ac[cou]nt no. :
held

[...] :

Sort code no.

☐ For currency items - (please specify)
:
:
:
Forward contact reference (if any)
:

☐ For GBP sterling items please remit proceeds to
us by cheque

☐ OTHER - (please specify)
:
:
:
:

DISCREPANCIES/SPECIAL INSTRUCTIONS

Contact details (eg. fax. telex nos.)	Company/telephone no.
	Name of signatory
	Place and date
	Signature

SITPRO Licensee No. 000.

39

263

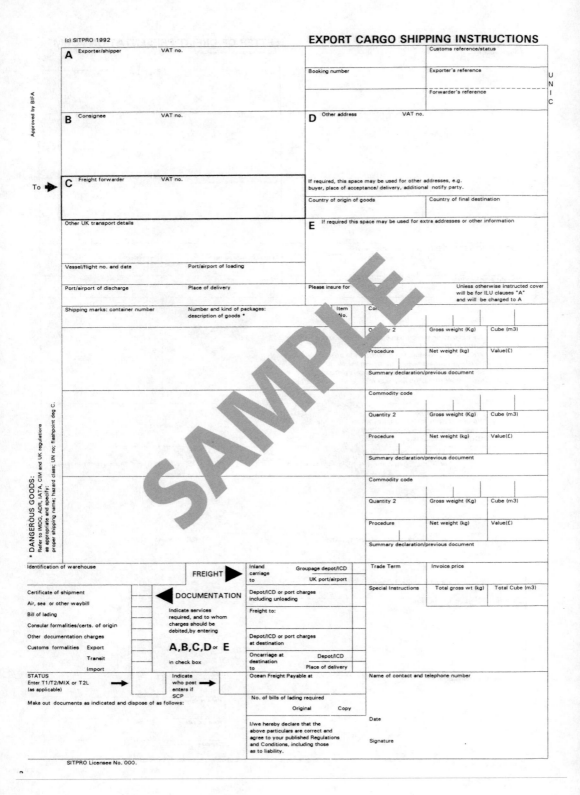

© SITPRO 1999

STANDARD SHIPPING NOTE - FOR NON - DANGEROUS GOODS ONLY

IMPORTANT USE THE DANGEROUS GOODS NOTE IF THE GOODS ARE CLASSIFIED AS DANGEROUS ACCORDING TO APPLICABLE REGULATIONS SEE BOX 10A

Exporter	1	Customs reference/status	2
		Booking number	3	Exporters reference	4
			Forwarder's reference	5
Consignee	6		
Freight forwarder	7	International carrier	8
		For use of receiving authority only	
Other UK transport details (e.g. ICD, terminal, vehicle bkg. ref. receiving dates)	9		

The Company preparing this note declares that, to the best of their belief, the goods have been accurately described, their quantities, weights and measurements are correct and at the time of despatch were in good order and condition; that the goods are not classified as being dangerous by reference to relevant national and international regulations applicable to the intended modes of transport. **10A**

| Vessel/flight no. and date | Port/airport of loading | 10 |
| Port/airport of discharge | Destination | 11 |

TO THE RECEIVING AUTHORITY — please receive the shipment the goods described below subject to your published regulations and conditions (including those as to liability)

Shipping marks	Number and kind of packages; descripion of goods; non-hazardous special stowage requirements	12	Gross weight (kg) of goods	13A	Cube (m²) of goods	14

For use of Shipping company only

Total gross weight of goods

Total cube of goods

| Container identification number/ vehicle registration number | 16 | Seal number(s) | 16A | Container/vehicle size and type | 16B | Tare (kg) | 16C | Total gross weight (including tare) (kg) | 16D |

HAULIER DETAILS	**DOCK/TERMINAL RECEIPT**		17
	RECEIVING AUTHORITY REMARKS	Name and telephone number of company preparing this note
Hauliers name	Received the above number of packages/containers/trailers in apparent good order and condition unless stated hereon.	
Vehicle reg. no		Name/status of declarant
		Place and date
Drivers signature	Receiving authority signature and date	Signature of declarant

265

© SITPRO 1999

DANGEROUS GOODS NOTE

Exporter	1	Customs reference/status	2
		Booking number	3	Exporter's reference	4
			Forwarder's reference	5

| Consignee | 6 | DSHA Notification (in accordance with DSHA Regulations (as amended)) given by: | 6A |

| | Shipper | Cargo agent | Transport operator | Shipping line |

| Freight forwarder | 7 | International carrier | 8 |

For use of receiving authority only

| Other UK transport details (e.g. ICD, terminal, vehicle bkg. ref., receiving dates) | 9 |

I hereby declare that the contents of this consignment are fully and accurately described below by the proper shipping name, and are classified, packaged, marked and labelled/placarded and are in all respects in proper condition for transport according to the applicable international and national governmental regulations and in accordance with the provisions shown overleaf. The shipper must complete and sign box 17. — 10A

| Vessel | Port of loading | 10 |

TO THE RECEIVING AUTHORITY
Please receive for shipment the goods described below subject to your published regulations and conditions (including those as to liability).

| Port of discharge | Destination | 11 |

| Shipping marks | Number and kind of packages; description of goods; | 12 | Net weight (kg) of goods | 13 | Gross weight (kg) of goods | 13A | Cube (m³) of goods | 14 |

SPECIFY: Proper Shipping Name*, Hazard Class, UN No. Additional information (if applicable) see over. For RID/ADR/CDG Road requirements see notes overleaf

SAMPLE

* Proper Shipping Name - Trade names alone are unacceptable

CONTAINER/VEHICLE PACKING CERTIFICATE

I hereby declare that the goods described above have been packed/loaded into the container/vehicle identified below in accordance with the provisions shown overleaf.

THIS DECLARATION MUST BE COMPLETED AND SIGNED FOR ALL CONTAINER/VEHICLE LOADS BY THE PERSON RESPONSIBLE FOR PACKING/LOADING

Name of company	15	Total gross weight of goods	Total cube of goods
Name/Status of declarant			
Place and date			
Signature of declarant			

| Container identification number/ vehicle registration number | 16 | Seal number(s) | 16A | Container/vehicle size and type | 16B | Tare (kg) | 16C | Total gross weight (including tare) (kg) | 16D |

DOCK/TERMINAL RECEIPT

HAULIER DETAILS

RECEIVING AUTHORITY REMARKS

Received the above number of packages/containers/trailers in apparent good order and condition unless stated hereon.

| Name and telephone number of shipper preparing this note | 17 |

Haulier's name

Name/status of declarant

Vehicle reg. no.

Place and date

Driver's signature

Receiving authority signature and date

Signature of declarant

630 Non-completion of any boxes is a subject for resolution by the contracting parties

ADDITIONAL INFORMATION (Box 12) – Number and kind of packages; description of goods

The following information must also appear with the proper shipping name, hazard class/division and UN Number:
(a) packaging group – where assigned;
(b) the words "MARINE POLLUTANT" for substances so designated in the IMDG Code;
(c) the minimum closed cup (cc) flashpoint in °C – if 61°C or less;
(d) subsidiary hazards not communicated in the proper shipping name; and
(e) the words "SALVAGE PACKAGING" for dangerous goods transported in salvage packaging together with the description of the goods.

Additional information is required for:
(f) substances and articles in Class 1 and 2;
(g) certain substances in Classes 4.1 and 5.2;
(h) infectious substances (Class 6.2);
(i) radioactive materials (Class 7);
(j) empty packaging/tanks containing residues;
(k) waste dangerous goods;
(l) dangerous goods consigned as limited quantities; and
(m) dangerous goods requiring a weathering certificate.

RID/ADR/CDG Road Information

For hazardous goods moved under RID/ADR or CDG Road Regulations the following information must be given:

(a) a description (including the substance identification number for RID/ADR);
(b) the class;
(c) the item number together with any letter for RID/ADR OR the UN number for CDG Road;
(d) the initials RID/ADR; and
(e) any extra information required to determine the transport category and the control te____ture ___ emergency temperature where appropriate (for CDG Road).

Refer to the IMDG Code, RID Regulations, ADR Agreement, CDG Road Regula___ and the SI___ ___ Completion Guide for further details.

CONTAINER/VEHICLE PACKING CERTIFCATE (box 15)
The signature given overleaf in box 15 must be that of the person c____ the ___ ___hicle operation.

It is certified that:
1. the container/vehicle was clean, dry and apparently fit to rec___ g___
2. if the consignment includes goods of class 1, other than d___ 1.4, ___tainer is structurally serviceable in conformity with section 12 of the introduction to Class 1 of the IMDG Code;
3. no incomplete goods have been packed into the container/____ ___ss s___lly authorised by the Competent Authority;
4. all packages have been externally inspected for d___ge and ___ly ___ packages packed;
5. drums have been stowed in an upright position ___ ___erw___ auth___ed by the Competent Authority;
6. all packages have been properly packed and se___ ___ in ___ ___ ___ner/vehicle;
7. when materials are transported in bulk packaging ___ ___rgo ___ ___ evenly distributed in the container/vehicle;
8. the packages and the container/vehicle ___ ___ been pr___ly mar___, labelled and placarded. Any irrelevant marks, labels and placards have been removed;
9. when solid carbon dioxide (CO_2 – dry i___s u___ ___ooli___ purposes, the vehicle or freight container is externally marked or labelled in a conspicuous place e.g. at the door end, ___ the DANGEROUS CO₂ GAS (D___ ___E) INS___ VENTILATE THOROUGH___ ___EFORE EN___ ___ING
10. when this Dangerous Go___ Note ___ed a ___ontainer/vehicle packing certificate only, not a combined document, a Dangerous Goods Declaration signed by the ___ ___ ___ ___ ___ has been issued/received to cover each dangerous goods consignment packed in the container.

Note: The container packing certificate is n___ ___quired for tanks.

THE SHIPPER'S DECLARATION (Box ___) covers the following regulations

The International Maritime Dangerous Goods code (IMDG Code), as revised or re-issued from time to time by the International Maritime Organisation.

Annex 1 (RID) to the Uniform Rules concerning the Contract for international Carriage of Goods by Rail (CIM), as revised or re-issued from time to time.

European Agreement concerning the international carriage of dangerous goods by road (ADR) as revised or re-issued from time to time.

The Carriage of Dangerous Goods by Road Regulations 1996 – S.I. 2095/1996 (the CDG Road Regulations), or any amending or replacement regulations.

If signing the document for the ADR Agreement or CDG Road Regulations the shipper is confirming that in accordance with the applicable Regulations:
i) the dangerous goods as presented may be carried;
ii) the dangerous goods and any packaging, intermediate bulk container or tank in which they are contained are in a fit condition for carriage and are properly labelled; and
iii) where several packages are packed together in an overpack or in a single container, that this mixed packaging is not prohibited.

© SITPRO 1987

HOUSE AIR WAYBILL (Air Consignment Note)

Consignor/shipper (name, address. a/c no.) CRN HAWB no.

HAWB issued by Master Air Waybill no.

Consignee (name, address, a/c no.)

Agent (name, city)

Place of departure and requested routeing

It is agreed that the goods described herein are accepted subject to issuer's conditions of contract. If the carriage involves an ultimate destination or stop in a country other than the country of departure, the Warsaw Convention may be applicable and the Convention governs and in most cases limits the liability of carriers in respect of loss of, damage or delay to cargo. Agreed stopping places are those places (other than the places of departure or destination) detailed under "Routeing" herein and/or those places shown in the timetables of any carriers performing carriage under and scheduled stopping places for the route.

by from

to Place of delivery Amount of insurance

Handling information: marks or numbers on packages: number of packages: method of packing: nature and quantity of goods Gross weight (kg) Dimensions or volume (m³)/declared value for Customs

SAMPLE

Format approved by
The Institute of Freight Forwarders Ltd.
HM Customs & Excise
and SITPRO, London, 1987

Prepaid	Weight charge	Collect	Other charges	Rate class		Chargeable weight	Rate		Charge	Total
				Commodity item no.						

Total prepaid Total collect Shipper certifies that the particulars on the face hereof are correct Executed on (place and date)

Currency conversion rates cc charges in dest. currency Signature of shipper or his agent Signature of issuer

Form No. 805/80 Published and Sold by FORMECON SERVICES Ltd. Gateway, Crewe CW1 1YN Tel. 0270 500800 SITPRO Approved Licensee No.21

268

SHIPPER'S LETTER OF INSTRUCTIONS FOR ISSUING AIR WAYBILL(AIR CONSIGNMENT NOTE)

This form is based on IATA Recommended Practice No. 1650

Shipper

Shipper's Reference:

Consignee

Name of Airline

Freight forwarder or Airline (Name and Address)

You are hereby requested and authorised upon receipt of the consignment described herein to prepare and sign the Air Waybill and other necessary documents on our behalf and despatch the consignment in accordance with your/airline's Conditions of Contract.

I certify that the contents of this consignment are properly identified by name. Insofar as any part of the consignment contains restricted articles, such part is in proper condition for carriage by air according to the International Air Transport Association's Restricted Articles Regulations.

Airport of Departure and Requested Routing

Airport of destination

Insurance - Amount Requested

Marks and Numbers	No. and Kind of Packages; Description of Goods	Gross Wt.(kg)	Measurement(m3)

AIR FREIGHT CHARGES

(mark one to apply)

☐ PREPAID
☐ COLLECT (if service available)

OTHER CHARGES at origin (Mark one to apply)

☐ PREPAID
☐ COLLECT (if service available)

INSURANCE AMOUNT REQUESTED (SEE ABOVE)

DECLARED VALUE

For Carriage

For Customs

SHIPPER'S C.O.D.

HANDLING INFORMATION AND REMARKS

DATE

SIGNATURE

105

ORIGINAL

THIS CERTIFICATE REQUIRES ENDORSEMENT IN THE EVENT OF ASSIGNMENT

CLAIMS SETTLEMENT INSTRUCTIONS

1. Lloyd's Settling Agent nearest destination is authorised to adjust and settle on behalf of the Underwriters, and to purchase on behalf of the Corporation of Lloyd's, in accordance with Lloyd's Standing Regulations for the Settlement of Claims Abroad, any claim which may arise on this Certificate.

2. If Lloyd's Agents are not to deal with claims, it should be clearly marked by an 'X' in the adjacent box and claim papers sent to :- A. Short & Co. Ltd., 1 London Road, London EC9 1OC.

Certificate of Insurance No. C 0000/

This is to Certify that there has been deposited with the Council of Lloyd's a Contract effected by *A. Short & Co. Ltd.,* of Lloyd's, acting on behalf of *Bodgit and Scarpa Ltd.,* with Underwriters at Lloyd's, for insurances attaching thereto during the period commencing the *First* day of *March,* 1997, and ending the *Twenty-eighth* day of *February, 1998,* both days inclusive, and that the said Underwriters have undertaken to issue to *A. Short & Co. Ltd.,* Policy/Policies of Insurance at Lloyd's to cover, up to *US$5,000,000 (or equivalent in other currencies),* in all by any one *steamer and/or conveyances, or sending by air and/or post,* General Merchandise and/or Goods and/or Equipment of any nature whatsoever including but not limited to Rice, Sugar, Motor Spare Parts, Bicycles, Generator Sets, Raw Jute, Jute Goods, from any port or ports, place or places in *the World,* to any port or ports, place or places in *the World, including all transhipments as and when occurring,* and that *Bodgit and Scarpa Ltd.,* are entitled to declare against the said Contract insurances attaching thereto.

Conveyance	From		
			for the Council of Lloyd's.
			Dated at Lloyd's, London, 20th May, 1998.
Via/To	To	INSURED VALUE/Currency	
Marks and Numbers		Interest	

© Lloyd's, 1998.

We hereby declare for Insurance under the said Contract interest as specified above so valued subject to the special conditions stated below and on the back hereof.

Institute Cargo Clauses (A) or Institute Cargo Clauses (Air) (excluding sendings by Post) as applicable. Excluding rust, oxidisation, discoloration, twisting and bending.
Institute War Clauses (Cargo) or Institute War Clauses (Air Cargo) (excluding sendings by Post) or Institute War Clauses (sendings by Post) as applicable.
Institute Strikes Clauses (Cargo) or Institute Strikes Clauses (Air Cargo) as applicable.
Institute Classification Clause.
Institute Radioactive Contamination Exclusion Clause.
Institute Replacement Clause.

Underwriters agree losses, if any, shall be payable to the order of BODGIT AND SCARPA LTD., on surrender of this Certificate.
In the event of loss or damage which may result in a claim under this Insurance, immediate notice must be given to the Lloyd's Agent at the port or place where the loss or damage is discovered in order that he may examine the goods and issue a survey report. The survey agent will normally be the Agent authorised to adjust and settle claims in accordance with the terms and conditions set forth herein, but where such Agent does not hold the requisite authority, he will be able to supply the name and address of the appropriate Settling Agent.

(Survey fee is customarily paid by claimant and included in valid claim against Underwriters.)

SEE IMPORTANT INSTRUCTIONS ON REVERSE

This Certificate not valid unless the Declaration be signed by
BODGIT AND SCARPA LTD.

Dated

Signed

LLOYD'S

Brokers : A. Short & Co. Ltd.,
1 London Road, London EC9 1OC.

Authorised Signatory
9405CM

SPECIMEN

IMPORTANT INSTRUCTIONS IN EVENT OF CLAIM

DOCUMENTATION OF CLAIMS

To enable claims to be dealt with promptly, the Assured or their Agents are advised to submit all available supporting documents without delay, including when applicable:-

1. Original policy or certificate of insurance.

2. Original or copy shipping invoices, together with shipping specification and/or weight notes.

3. Original Bill of Lading and/or other contract of carriage.

4. Survey report or other documentary evidence to show the extent of the loss or damage.

5. Landing account and weight notes at final destination.

6. Correspondence exchanged with the Carriers and other parties regarding their liability for the loss or damage.

IMPORTANT
LIABILITY OF CARRIERS, BAILEES OR OTHER THIRD PARTIES

It is the duty of the Assured and their Agents, in all cases, to take such measures as may be reasonable for the purpose of averting or minimising a loss and to ensure that all rights against Carriers, Bailees or other third parties are properly preserved and exercised. In particular, the Assured or their Agents are required:-

1. To claim immediately on the Carriers, Port Authorities or other Bailees for any missing packages.

2. In no circumstances, except under written protest, to give clean receipts where goods are in doubtful condition.

3. When delivery is made by Container, to ensure that the Container and its seals are examined immediately by their responsible official. If the Container is delivered damaged or with seals broken or missing or with seals other than as stated in the shipping documents, to clause the delivery receipt accordingly and retain all defective or irregular seals for subsequent identification.

4. To apply immediately for survey by Carriers' or other Bailees' Representatives if any loss or damage be apparent and claim on the Carriers or other Bailees for any actual loss or damage found at such survey.

5. To give notice in writing to the Carriers or other Bailees within 3 days of delivery if the loss or damage was not apparent at the time of taking delivery.

Note.- The Consignees or their Agents are recommended to make themselves familiar with the Regulations of the Port Authorities at the port of discharge.

NOTE.- The Institute Clauses incorporated herein are deemed to be those current at the time of commencement of the risk.

It is necessary for the Assured when they become aware of an event which is "held covered" under this Insurance to give prompt notice to Underwriters and the right to such cover is dependent upon compliance with this obligation.

Lloyd's Agents referred to herein are not insurers and are not liable for claims arising on this Certificate. The service of legal proceedings upon Lloyd's Agents is not effective service for the purpose of starting legal proceedings against Underwriters.

This insurance shall be subject to the exclusive jurisdiction of the English Courts.

Printed in England by G. Harmsworth & Co. Ltd., Farringdon Point, 29-35 Farringdon Road, London EC1M 3JB. 9405CM

1. Shipbroker	**RECOMMENDED** **THE BALTIC AND INTERNATIONAL MARITIME COUNCIL** **UNIFORM GENERAL CHARTER (AS REVISED 1922, 1976 and 1994)** (To be used for trades for which no specially approved form is in force) **CODE NAME: "GENCON"** Part I	
	2. Place and date	
3. Owners/Place of business (Cl. 1)	4. Charterers/Place of business (Cl. 1)	
5. Vessel's name (Cl. 1)	6. GT/NT (Cl. 1)	
7. DWT all told on summer load line in metric tons (abt.) (Cl. 1)	8. Present position (Cl. 1)	
9. Expected ready to load (abt.) (Cl. 1)		
10. Loading port or place (Cl. 1)	11. Discharging port or place (Cl. 1)	
12. Cargo (also state quantity and margin in Owners' option, if agreed; if full and complete cargo not agreed state "part cargo") (Cl. 1)		
13. Freight rate (also state whether freight prepaid or payable on delivery) (Cl. 4)	14. Freight payment (state currency and method of payment; also beneficiary and bank account) (Cl. 4)	
15. State if vessel's cargo handling gear shall not be used (Cl. 5)	16. Laytime (if separate laytime for load. and disch. is agreed, fill in a) and b). If total laytime for load. and disch., fill in c) only) (Cl. 6)	
17. Shippers/Place of business (Cl. 6)	a) Laytime for loading	
18. Agents (loading) (Cl. 6)	b) Laytime for discharging	
19. Agents (discharging) (Cl. 6)	c) Total laytime for loading and discharging	
20. Demurrage rate and manner payable (loading and discharging) (Cl. 7)	21. Cancelling date (Cl. 9)	
	22. General Average to be adjusted at (Cl. 12)	
23. Freight Tax (state if for the Owners' account) (Cl. 13 (c))	24. Brokerage commission and to whom payable (Cl. 15)	
25. Law and Arbitration (state 19 (a), 19 (b) or 19 (c) of Cl. 19; if 19 (c) agreed also state Place of Arbitration) (if not filled in 19 (a) shall apply) (Cl. 19)		
(a) State maximum amount for small claims/shortened arbitration (Cl. 19)	26. Additional clauses covering special provisions, if agreed	

It is mutually agreed that this Contract shall be performed subject to the conditions contained in this Charter Party which shall include Part I as well as Part II. In the event of a conflict of conditions, the provisions of Part I shall prevail over those of Part II to the extent of such conflict.

Signature (Owners)	Signature (Charterers)

Printed by The BIMCO Charter Party Editor

PART II
"Gencon" Charter (As Revised 1922, 1976 and 1994)

1. It is agreed between the party mentioned in Box 3 as the Owners of the Vessel named in Box 5, of the GT/NT indicated in Box 6 and carrying about the number of metric tons of deadweight capacity all told on summer loadline stated in Box 7, now in position as stated in Box 8 and expected ready to load under this Charter Party about the date indicated in Box 9, and the party mentioned as the Charterers in Box 4 that:
The said Vessel shall, as soon as her prior commitments have been completed, proceed to the loading port(s) or place(s) stated in Box 10 or so near thereto as she may safely get and lie always afloat, and there load a full and complete cargo (if shipment of deck cargo agreed same to be at the Charterers' risk and responsibility) as stated in Box 12, which the Charterers bind themselves to ship, and being so loaded the Vessel shall proceed to the discharging port(s) or place(s) stated in Box 11 as ordered on signing Bills of Lading, or so near thereto as she may safely get and lie always afloat, and there deliver the cargo.

2. **Owners' Responsibility Clause**
The Owners are to be responsible for loss of or damage to the goods or for delay in the delivery of the goods only in case the loss, damage or delay has been caused by personal want of due diligence on the part of the Owners or their Manager to make the Vessel in all respects seaworthy and to secure that she is properly manned, equipped and supplied, or by the personal act or default of the Owners or their Manager.
And the Owners are not responsible for loss, damage or delay arising from any other cause whatsoever, even from the neglect or default of the Master or crew or some other person employed by the Owners on board or ashore for whose acts they would, but for this Clause, be responsible, or from unseaworthiness of the Vessel on loading or commencement of the voyage or at any time whatsoever.

3. **Deviation Clause**
The Vessel has liberty to call at any port or ports in any order, for any purpose, to sail without pilots, to tow and/or assist Vessels in all situations, and also to deviate for the purpose of saving life and/or property.

4. **Payment of Freight**
(a) The freight at the rate stated in Box 13 shall be paid in cash calculated on the intaken quantity of cargo.
(b) *Prepaid.* If according to Box 13 freight is to be paid on shipment, it shall be deemed earned and non-returnable, Vessel and/or cargo lost or not lost.
Neither the Owners nor their agents shall be required to sign or endorse bills of lading showing freight prepaid unless the freight due to the Owners has actually been paid.
(c) *On delivery.* If according to Box 13 freight, or part thereof, is payable at destination it shall not be deemed earned until the cargo is thus delivered. Notwithstanding the provisions under (a), if freight or part thereof is payable on delivery of the cargo the Charterers shall have the option of paying the freight on delivered weight/quantity provided such option is declared before breaking bulk and the weight/quantity can be ascertained by official weighing machine, joint draft survey or tally.
Cash for Vessel's ordinary disbursements at the port of loading to be advanced by the Charterers, if required, at highest current rate of exchange, subject to two (2) per cent to cover insurance and other expenses.

5. **Loading/Discharging**
(a) Costs/Risks
The cargo shall be brought into the holds, loaded, stowed and/or trimmed, tallied, lashed and/or secured and taken from the holds and discharged by the Charterers, free of any risk, liability and expense whatsoever to the Owners. The Charterers shall provide and lay all dunnage material as required for the proper stowage and protection of the cargo on board, the Owners allowing the use of all dunnage available on board. The Charterers shall be responsible for and pay the cost of removing their dunnage after discharge of the cargo under this Charter Party and time to count until dunnage has been removed.
(b) Cargo Handling Gear
Unless the Vessel is gearless or unless it has been agreed between the parties that the Vessel's gear shall not be used and stated as such in Box 15, the Owners shall throughout the duration of loading/discharging give free use of the Vessel's cargo handling gear and of sufficient motive power to operate all such cargo handling gear. All such equipment to be in good working order. Unless caused by negligence of the stevedores, time lost by breakdown of the Vessel's cargo handling gear or motive power - pro rata the total number of cranes/winches required at that time for the loading/discharging of cargo under this Charter Party - shall not count as laytime or time on demurrage.
On request the Owners shall provide free of charge cranemen/winchmen from the crew to operate the Vessel's cargo handling gear, unless local regulations prohibit this, in which latter event shore labourers shall be for the account of the Charterers. Cranemen/winchmen shall be under the Charterers' risk and responsibility and as stevedores to be deemed as their servants but shall always work under the supervision of the Master.
(c) Stevedore Damage
The Charterers shall be responsible for damage (beyond ordinary wear and tear) to any part of the Vessel caused by Stevedores. Such damage shall be notified as soon as reasonably possible by the Master to the Charterers or their agents and to their Stevedores, failing which the Charterers shall not be held responsible. The Master shall endeavour to obtain the Stevedores' written acknowledgement of liability.
The Charterers are obliged to repair any stevedore damage prior to completion of the voyage, but must repair stevedore damage affecting the Vessel's seaworthiness or class before the Vessel sails from the port where such damage was caused or found. All additional expenses incurred shall be for the account of the Charterers and any time lost shall be for the account of and shall be paid to the Owners by the Charterers at the demurrage rate.

6. **Laytime**
* *(a) Separate laytime for loading and discharging*
The cargo shall be loaded within the number of running days/hours as indicated in Box 16, weather permitting, Sundays and holidays excepted, unless used, in which event time used shall count.
The cargo shall be discharged within the number of running days/hours as indicated in Box 16, weather permitting, Sundays and holidays excepted, unless used, in which event time used shall count.
* *(b) Total laytime for loading and discharging*
The cargo shall be loaded and discharged within the number of total running days/hours as indicated in Box 16, weather permitting, Sundays and holidays excepted, unless used, in which event time used shall count.
(c) Commencement of laytime (loading and discharging)
Laytime for loading and discharging shall commence at 13.00 hours, if notice of readiness is given up to and including 12.00 hours, and at 06.00 hours next working day if notice given during office hours after 12.00 hours. Notice of readiness at loading port to be given to the Shippers named in Box 17 or if not named, to the Charterers or their agents named in Box 18. Notice of readiness at the discharging port to be given to the Receivers or, if not known, to the Charterers or their agents named in Box 19.
If the loading/discharging berth is not available on the Vessel's arrival at or off the port of loading/discharging, the Vessel shall be entitled to give notice of readiness within ordinary office hours on arrival there, whether in free pratique or not, whether customs cleared or not. Laytime or time on demurrage shall then count as if she were in berth and in all respects ready for loading/ discharging provided that the Master warrants that she is in fact ready in all respects. Time used in moving from the place of waiting to the loading/ discharging berth shall not count as laytime.
If, after inspection, the Vessel is found not to be ready in all respects to load/ discharge time lost after the discovery thereof until the Vessel is again ready to load/discharge shall not count as laytime.
Time used before commencement of laytime shall count.
* *Indicate alternative (a) or (b) as agreed, in Box 16.*

7. **Demurrage**
Demurrage at the loading and discharging port is payable by the Charterers at the rate stated in Box 20 in the manner stated in Box 20 per day or pro rata for any part of a day. Demurrage shall fall due day by day and shall be payable upon receipt of the Owners' invoice.
In the event the demurrage is not paid in accordance with the above, the Owners shall give the Charterers 96 running hours written notice to rectify the failure. If the demurrage is not paid at the expiration of this time limit and if the vessel is in or at the loading port, the Owners are entitled at any time to terminate the Charter Party and claim damages for any losses caused thereby.

8. **Lien Clause**
The Owners shall have a lien on the cargo and on all sub-freights payable in respect of the cargo, for freight, deadfreight, demurrage, claims for damages and for all other amounts due under this Charter Party including costs of recovering same.

9. **Cancelling Clause**
(a) Should the Vessel not be ready to load (whether in berth or not) on the cancelling date indicated in Box 21, the Charterers shall have the option of cancelling this Charter Party.
(b) Should the Owners anticipate that, despite the exercise of due diligence, the Vessel will not be ready to load by the cancelling date, they shall notify the Charterers thereof without delay stating the expected date of the Vessel's readiness to load and asking whether the Charterers will exercise their option of cancelling the Charter Party, or agree to a new cancelling date.
Such option must be declared by the Charterers within 48 running hours after the receipt of the Owners' notice. If the Charterers do not exercise their option of cancelling, then this Charter Party shall be deemed to be amended such that

PART II
"Gencon" Charter (As Revised 1922, 1976 and 1994)

the seventh day after the new readiness date stated in the Owners' notification 149
to the Charterers shall be the new cancelling date. 150
The provisions of sub-clause (b) of this Clause shall operate only once, and in 151
case of the Vessel's further delay, the Charterers shall have the option of 152
cancelling the Charter Party as per sub-clause (a) of this Clause. 153

10. Bills of Lading 154
Bills of Lading shall be presented and signed by the Master as per the 155
"Congenbill" Bill of Lading form, Edition 1994, without prejudice to this Charter 156
Party, or by the Owners' agents provided written authority has been given by 157
Owners to the agents, a copy of which is to be furnished to the Charterers. The 158
Charterers shall indemnify the Owners against all consequences or liabilities 159
that may arise from the signing of bills of lading as presented to the extent that 160
the terms or contents of such bills of lading impose or result in the imposition of 161
more onerous liabilities upon the Owners than those assumed by the Owners 162
under this Charter Party. 163

11. Both-to-Blame Collision Clause 164
If the Vessel comes into collision with another vessel as a result of the 165
negligence of the other vessel and any act, neglect or default of the Master, 166
Mariner, Pilot or the servants of the Owners in the navigation or in the 167
management of the Vessel, the owners of the cargo carried hereunder will 168
indemnify the Owners against all loss or liability to the other or non-carrying 169
vessel or her owners in so far as such loss or liability represents loss of, or 170
damage to, or any claim whatsoever of the owners of said cargo, paid or 171
payable by the other or non-carrying vessel or her owners to the owners of said 172
cargo and set-off, recouped or recovered by the other or non-carrying vessel 173
or her owners as part of their claim against the carrying Vessel or the Owners. 174
The foregoing provisions shall also apply where the owners, operators or those 175
in charge of any vessel or vessels or objects other than, or in addition to, the 176
colliding vessels or objects are at fault in respect of a collision or contact. 177

12. General Average and New Jason Clause 178
General Average shall be adjusted in London unless otherwise agreed in Box 179
22 according to York-Antwerp Rules 1994 and any subsequent modification 180
thereof. Proprietors of cargo to pay the cargo's share in the general expenses 181
even if same have been necessitated through neglect or default of the Owners' 182
servants (see Clause 2). 183
If General Average is to be adjusted in accordance with the law and practice of 184
the United States of America, the following Clause shall apply: "In the event of 185
accident, danger, damage or disaster before or after the commencement of the 186
voyage, resulting from any cause whatsoever, whether due to negligence or 187
not, for which, or for the consequence of which, the Owners are not 188
responsible, by statute, contract or otherwise, the cargo shippers, consignees 189
or the owners of the cargo shall contribute with the Owners in General Average 190
to the payment of any sacrifices, losses or expenses of a General Average 191
nature that may be made or incurred and shall pay salvage and special charges 192
incurred in respect of the cargo. If a salving vessel is owned or operated by the 193
Owners, salvage shall be paid for as fully as if the said salving vessel or vessels 194
belonged to strangers. Such deposit as the Owners, or their agents, may deem 195
sufficient to cover the estimated contribution of the goods and any salvage and 196
special charges thereon shall, if required, be made by the cargo, shippers, 197
consignees or owners of the goods to the Owners before delivery.". 198

13. Taxes and Dues Clause 199
(a) *On Vessel* -The Owners shall pay all dues, charges and taxes customarily 200
levied on the Vessel, howsoever the amount thereof may be assessed. 201
(b) *On cargo* -The Charterers shall pay all dues, charges, duties and taxes 202
customarily levied on the cargo, howsoever the amount thereof may be 203
assessed. 204
(c) *On freight* -Unless otherwise agreed in Box 23, taxes levied on the freight 205
shall be for the Charterers' account. 206

14. Agency 207
In every case the Owners shall appoint their own Agent both at the port of 208
loading and the port of discharge. 209

15. Brokerage 210
A brokerage commission at the rate stated in Box 24 on the freight, dead-freight 211
and demurrage earned is due to the party mentioned in Box 24. 212
In case of non-execution 1/3 of the brokerage on the estimated amount of 213
freight to be paid by the party responsible for such non-execution to the 214
Brokers as indemnity for the latter's expenses and work. In case of more 215
voyages the amount of indemnity to be agreed. 216

16. General Strike Clause 217
(a) If there is a strike or lock-out affecting or preventing the actual loading of the 218
cargo, or any part of it, when the Vessel is ready to proceed from her last port or 219

at any time during the voyage to the port or ports of loading or after her arrival 220
there, the Master or the Owners may ask the Charterers to declare, that they 221
agree to reckon the laydays as if there were no strike or lock-out. Unless the 222
Charterers have given such declaration in writing (by telegram, if necessary) 223
within 24 hours, the Owners shall have the option of cancelling this Charter 224
Party. If part cargo has already been loaded, the Owners must proceed with 225
same, (freight payable on loaded quantity only) having liberty to complete with 226
other cargo on the way for their own account. 227
(b) If there is a strike or lock-out affecting or preventing the actual discharging 228
of the cargo on or after the Vessel's arrival at or off port of discharge and same 229
has not been settled within 48 hours, the Charterers shall have the option of 230
keeping the Vessel waiting until such strike or lock-out is at an end against 231
paying half demurrage after expiration of the time provided for discharging 232
until the strike or lock-out terminates and thereafter full demurrage shall be 233
payable until the completion of discharging, or of ordering the Vessel to a safe 234
port where she can safely discharge without risk of being detained by strike or 235
lock-out. Such orders to be given within 48 hours after the Master or the 236
Owners have given notice to the Charterers of the strike or lock-out affecting 237
the discharge. On delivery of the cargo at such port, all conditions of this 238
Charter Party and of the Bill of Lading shall apply and the Vessel shall receive 239
the same freight as if she had discharged at the original port of destination, 240
except that if the distance to the substituted port exceeds 100 nautical miles, 241
the freight on the cargo delivered at the substituted port to be increased in 242
proportion. 243
(c) Except for the obligations described above, neither the Charterers nor the 244
Owners shall be responsible for the consequences of any strikes or lock-outs 245
preventing or affecting the actual loading or discharging of the cargo. 246

17. War Risks ("Voywar 1993") 247
(1) For the purpose of this Clause, the words: 248
(a) The "Owners" shall include the shipowners, bareboat charterers, 249
disponent owners, managers or other operators who are charged with the 250
management of the Vessel, and the Master; and 251
(b) "War Risks" shall include any war (whether actual or threatened), act of 252
war, civil war, hostilities, revolution, rebellion, civil commotion, warlike 253
operations, the laying of mines (whether actual or reported), acts of piracy, 254
acts of terrorists, acts of hostility or malicious damage, blockades 255
(whether imposed against all Vessels or imposed selectively against 256
Vessels of certain flags or ownership, or against certain cargoes or crews 257
or otherwise howsoever), by any person, body, terrorist or political group, 258
or the Government of any state whatsoever, which, in the reasonable 259
judgement of the Master and/or the Owners, may be dangerous or are 260
likely to be or to become dangerous to the Vessel, her cargo, crew or other 261
persons on board the Vessel. 262
(2) If at any time before the Vessel commences loading, it appears that, in the 263
reasonable judgement of the Master and/or the Owners, performance of 264
the Contract of Carriage, or any part of it, may expose, or is likely to expose, 265
the Vessel, her cargo, crew or other persons on board the Vessel to War 266
Risks, the Owners may give notice to the Charterers cancelling this 267
Contract of Carriage, or may refuse to perform such part of it as may 268
expose, or may be likely to expose, the Vessel, her cargo, crew or other 269
persons on board the Vessel to War Risks; provided always that if this 270
Contract of Carriage provides that loading or discharging is to take place 271
within a range of ports, and at the port or ports nominated by the Charterers 272
the Vessel, her cargo, crew, or other persons onboard the Vessel may be 273
exposed, or may be likely to be exposed, to War Risks, the Owners shall 274
first require the Charterers to nominate any other safe port which lies 275
within the range for loading or discharging, and may only cancel this 276
Contract of Carriage if the Charterers shall not have nominated such safe 277
port or ports within 48 hours of receipt of notice of such requirement. 278
(3) The Owners shall not be required to continue to load cargo for any voyage, 279
or to sign Bills of Lading for any port or place, or to proceed or continue on 280
any voyage, or on any part thereof, or to proceed through any canal or 281
waterway, or to proceed to or remain at any port or place whatsoever, 282
where it appears, either after the loading of the cargo commences, or at 283
any stage of the voyage thereafter before the discharge of the cargo is 284
completed, that, in the reasonable judgement of the Master and/or the 285
Owners, the Vessel, her cargo (or any part thereof), crew or other persons 286
on board the Vessel (or any one or more of them) may be, or are likely to be, 287
exposed to War Risks. If it should so appear, the Owners may by notice 288
request the Charterers to nominate a safe port for the discharge of the 289
cargo or any part thereof, and if within 48 hours of the receipt of such 290
notice, the Charterers shall not have nominated such a port, the Owners 291
may discharge the cargo at any safe port of their choice (including the port 292
of loading) in complete fulfilment of the Contract of Carriage. The Owners 293
shall be entitled to recover from the Charterers the extra expenses of such 294
discharge and, if the discharge takes place at any port other than the 295
loading port, to receive the full freight as though the cargo had been 296

PART II
"Gencon" Charter (As Revised 1922, 1976 and 1994)

carried to the discharging port and if the extra distance exceeds 100 miles, 297
to additional freight which shall be the same percentage of the freight 298
contracted for as the percentage which the extra distance represents to 299
the distance of the normal and customary route, the Owners having a lien 300
on the cargo for such expenses and freight. 301

(4) If at any stage of the voyage after the loading of the cargo commences, it 302
appears that, in the reasonable judgement of the Master and/or the 303
Owners, the Vessel, her cargo, crew or other persons on board the Vessel 304
may be, or are likely to be, exposed to War Risks on any part of the route 305
(including any canal or waterway) which is normally and customarily used 306
in a voyage of the nature contracted for, and there is another longer route 307
to the discharging port, the Owners shall give notice to the Charterers that 308
this route will be taken. In this event the Owners shall be entitled, if the total 309
extra distance exceeds 100 miles, to additional freight which shall be the 310
same percentage of the freight contracted for as the percentage which the 311
extra distance represents to the distance of the normal and customary 312
route. 313

(5) The Vessel shall have liberty:- 314
(a) to comply with all orders, directions, recommendations or advice as to 315
departure, arrival, routes, sailing in convoy, ports of call, stoppages, 316
destinations, discharge of cargo, delivery or in any way whatsoever which 317
are given by the Government of the Nation under whose flag the Vessel 318
sails, or other Government to whose laws the Owners are subject, or any 319
other Government which so requires, or any body or group acting with the 320
power to compel compliance with their orders or directions; 321
(b) to comply with the orders, directions or recommendations of any war 322
risks underwriters who have the authority to give the same under the terms 323
of the war risks insurance; 324
(c) to comply with the terms of any resolution of the Security Council of the 325
United Nations, any directives of the European Community, the effective 326
orders of any other Supranational body which has the right to issue and 327
give the same, and with national laws aimed at enforcing the same to which 328
the Owners are subject, and to obey the orders and directions of those who 329
are charged with their enforcement; 330
(d) to discharge at any other port any cargo or part thereof which may 331
render the Vessel liable to confiscation as a contraband carrier; 332
(e) to call at any other port to change the crew or any part thereof or other 333
persons on board the Vessel when there is reason to believe that they may 334
be subject to internment, imprisonment or other sanctions; 335
(f) where cargo has not been loaded or has been discharged by the 336
Owners under any provisions of this Clause, to load other cargo for the 337
Owners' own benefit and carry it to any other port or ports whatsoever, 338
whether backwards or forwards or in a contrary direction to the ordinary or 339
customary route. 340

(6) If in compliance with any of the provisions of sub-clauses (2) to (5) of this 341
Clause anything is done or not done, such shall not be deemed to be a 342
deviation, but shall be considered as due fulfilment of the Contract of 343
Carriage. 344

18. General Ice Clause 345
Port of loading 346
(a) In the event of the loading port being inaccessible by reason of ice when the 347
Vessel is ready to proceed from her last port or at any time during the voyage or 348
on the Vessel's arrival or in case frost sets in after the Vessel's arrival, the 349
Master for fear of being frozen in is at liberty to leave without cargo, and this 350
Charter Party shall be null and void. 351
(b) If during loading the Master, for fear of the Vessel being frozen in, deems it 352
advisable to leave, he has liberty to do so with what cargo he has on board and 353
to proceed to any other port or ports with option of completing cargo for the 354
Owners' benefit for any port or ports including port of discharge. Any part 355
cargo thus loaded under this Charter Party to be forwarded to destination at the 356
Vessel's expense but against payment of freight, provided that no extra 357
expenses be thereby caused to the Charterers, freight being paid on quantity 358
delivered (in proportion if lumpsum), all other conditions as per this Charter 359
Party. 360
(c) In case of more than one loading port, and if one or more of the ports are 361
closed by ice, the Master or the Owners to be at liberty either to load the part 362
cargo at the open port and fill up elsewhere for their own account as under 363
section (b) or to declare the Charter Party null and void unless the Charterers 364
agree to load full cargo at the open port. 365

Port of discharge 366
(a) Should ice prevent the Vessel from reaching port of discharge the 367
Charterers shall have the option of keeping the Vessel waiting until the re- 368
opening of navigation and paying demurrage or of ordering the Vessel to a safe 369
and immediately accessible port where she can safely discharge without risk of 370
detention by ice. Such orders to be given within 48 hours after the Master or the 371
Owners have given notice to the Charterers of the impossibility of reaching port 372

of destination. 373
(b) If during discharging the Master for fear of the Vessel being frozen in deems 374
it advisable to leave, he has liberty to do so with what cargo he has on board and 375
to proceed to the nearest accessible port where she can safely discharge. 376
(c) On delivery of the cargo at such port, all conditions of the Bill of Lading shall 377
apply and the Vessel shall receive the same freight as if she had discharged at 378
the original port of destination, except that if the distance of the substituted port 379
exceeds 100 nautical miles, the freight on the cargo delivered at the substituted 380
port to be increased in proportion. 381

19. Law and Arbitration 382
* (a) This Charter Party shall be governed by and construed in accordance with 383
English law and any dispute arising out of this Charter Party shall be referred to 384
arbitration in London in accordance with the Arbitration Acts 1950 and 1979 or 385
any statutory modification or re-enactment thereof for the time being in force. 386
Unless the parties agree upon a sole arbitrator, one arbitrator shall be 387
appointed by each party and the arbitrators so appointed shall appoint a third 388
arbitrator, the decision of the three-man tribunal thus constituted or any two of 389
them, shall be final. On the receipt by one party of the nomination in writing of 390
the other party's arbitrator, that party shall appoint their arbitrator within 391
fourteen days, failing which the decision of the single arbitrator appointed shall 392
be final. 393
For disputes where the total amount claimed by either party does not exceed 394
the amount stated in Box 25** the arbitration shall be conducted in accordance 395
with the Small Claims Procedure of the London Maritime Arbitrators' 396
Association. 397
* (b) This Charter Party shall be governed by and construed in accordance with 398
Title 9 of the United States Code and the Maritime Law of the United States and 399
should any dispute arise out of this Charter Party, the matter in dispute shall be 400
referred to three persons at New York, one to be appointed by each of the 401
parties hereto, and the third by the two so chosen; their decision or that of any 402
two of them shall be final, and for purpose of enforcing any award, this 403
agreement may be made a rule of the Court. The proceedings shall be 404
conducted in accordance with the rules of the Society of Maritime Arbitrators, 405
Inc.. 406
For disputes where the total amount claimed by either party does not exceed 407
the amount stated in Box 25** the arbitration shall be conducted in accordance 408
with the Shortened Arbitration Procedure of the Society of Maritime Arbitrators, 409
Inc.. 410
* (c) Any dispute arising out of this Charter Party shall be referred to arbitration at 411
the place indicated in Box 25, subject to the procedures applicable there. The 412
laws of the place indicated in Box 25 shall govern this Charter Party. 413
(d) If Box 25 in Part 1 is not filled in, sub-clause (a) of this Clause shall apply. 414
* *(a), (b) and (c) are alternatives; indicate alternative agreed in Box 25.* 415
** *Where no figure is supplied in Box 25 in Part 1, this provision only shall be void but* 416
the other provisions of this Clause shall have full force and remain in effect. 417

Ship Brokers	THE BALTIC AND INTERNATIONAL MARITIME COUNCIL (BIMCO) GENERAL TIME CHARTER PARTY

PART I

	1. Place and Date of Charter
2. Owners/Disponent Owners/Place of business (State full name, address, telex and fax. No.)	3. Charterers/Place of business (State full name, address, telex and fax. No.)
4. Vessel's Name	5. Vessel's Description Flag:
6. Period of Charter (Cl. 1(a))	Year Built:
6(a). Margin on Final Period (Cl. 1(a))	Class: M/tons Deadweight (Summer):
7. Optional Period and Notice (Cl. 1(a))	GT/NT:
8. Delivery Port/Place or Range (Cl. 1(b))	Grain/Bale Capacity: Speed capability in knots (about):
9. Earliest Delivery Date/Time (Cl. 1(c))	10. Cancellation Date/Time (Cl. 1(c)(d))	Consumption in m/tons at above speed (about):
11. Notices of Delivery (Cl. 1(e))	12. Intended First Cargo (Cl. 1(f))	(Speed and Consumption on Summer dwt in good weather, max. windspeed 4Bft)

13. Trading Limits and Excluded Countries (Cl. 2(a)

14. Excepted Countries (Cl. 2(b))

(continued overleaf)

Copyright, published by
The Baltic and International Maritime Council (BIMCO), Copenhagen
Issued: September 1999

Printed by The BIMCO Charter Party Editor

(Continued) **"GENTIME" General Time Charter Party** PART I

15. Excluded Cargoes (Cl. 3(b))		

16. Hazardous Cargo Limit (Cl. 3(c))	17. Redelivery Port/Place or Range (Cl. 4(a))	18. Notices of Redelivery (Cl. 4(c))

19. Fuel Quantity on Delivery (Cl. 6(a))	20. Fuel Quantity on Redelivery (Cl. 6(a))	21. Fuel Price on Delivery (Cl. 6(c))	22. Fuel Price on Redelivery (Cl. 6(c))

23. Fuel Specifications (Cl. 6(d))			

24. Hire (Cl. 8(a))	25. Owner´s Bank Account (Cl. 8(b))

26. Grace Period (Cl. 8(c))	27. Max. Period for Requisition (Cl. 9(c))	28. General Average Adjustment (Cl. 14(b))

29. Supercargo (Cl. 15(f))	30. Victualling (Cl. 15(g))	31. Representation (Cl. 15(h))	32. Hold Cleaning by Crew (Cl. 15(m))

33. Lumpsum for Hold Cleaning on Redelivery (Cl. 15(m))	34. Vessel´s Insured Value (Cl. 20(a))

35. Law and Arbitration (state Cl. 22(a), 22(b) or 22(c) of Cl. 22 as agreed; if 22(c) agreed, place of arbitration must be stated (Cl. 22))	36. Commission and to whom payable (Cl. 23)

37. Additional Clauses

It is agreed that this Contract shall be performed subject to the conditions contained in this Charter Party consisting of PART I including any additional clauses agreed and stated in Box 37 and PART II as well as Appendix A attached thereto. In the event of any conflict of conditions, the provisions of PART I and Appendix A shall prevail over those of PART II to the extent of such conflict but no further.

Signature (Owners)	Signature (Charterers)

Printed by The BIMCO Charter Party Editor

"GENTIME" - General Time Charter Party
Index

PART II

"GENTIME" General Time Charter Party

It is agreed on the date shown in Box 1 between the party named in Box 2 as Owners/ Disponent Owners (hereinafter called "the Owners") of the Vessel named in Box 4, of the description stated in Box 5 and the party named in Box 3 as Charterers as follows:

1. Period and Delivery

(a) *Period* - In consideration of the hire stated in Box 24 the Owners let and the Charterers hire the Vessel for the period/trip(s) stated in Box 6.
The Charterers shall have the option to extend the Charter Party by the period(s)/ trip(s) stated in Box 7 which option shall be exercised by giving written notice to the Owners on or before the date(s) stated in Box 7.
Unless otherwise agreed, the Charterers shall have the option to increase or to reduce the final period of the Charter Party by up to the number of days stated in Box 6(a), which shall be applied only to the period finally declared.

(b) *Delivery Place* - The Owners shall deliver the Vessel to the Charterers at the port or place stated in Box 8 or a port or place within the range stated in Box 8.

(c) *Delivery Time* - Delivery shall take place no earlier than the date/time stated in Box 9 and no later than the date/time stated in Box 10. Delivery shall be effected at any time day or night, Saturdays, Sundays and holidays included.

(d) *Cancellation* - Should the Vessel not be delivered by the date/time stated in Box 10 the Charterers shall have the option to cancel the Charter Party without prejudice to any claims the Charterers may otherwise have on the Owners under the Charter Party. If the Owners anticipate that, despite their exercise of due diligence, the Vessel will not be ready for delivery by the date/time stated in Box 10, they may notify the Charterers in writing, stating the anticipated new date of readiness for delivery, proposing a new cancelling date/time and requiring the Charterers to declare whether they will cancel or will take delivery of the Vessel. Should the Charterers elect not to cancel or should they fail to reply within two (2) working days (as applying at the Charterers' place of business) of receipt of such notification, then unless otherwise agreed, the proposed new cancelling date/time will replace the date/time stated in Box 10. This provision shall operate only once and should the Vessel not be ready for delivery at the new cancelling date/time the Charterers shall have the option of cancelling this Charter Party.

(e) *Notice(s)* - The Owners shall give the Charterers not less than the number of days notice stated in Box 11 of the date/time on which the Vessel is expected to be delivered and shall keep the Charterers closely advised of possible changes in the Vessel's expected date/time of delivery. The Owners shall give the Charterers and/or their local agents notice of delivery when the Vessel is in a position to come on hire.

(f) *Vessel's Condition* - On arrival at the first port or place of loading the Vessel's holds shall be clean and in all respects ready to receive the intended cargo identified in Box 12, failing which the Vessel shall be off-hire from the time of rejection until she is deemed ready.

(g) *Charterers' Acceptance* - Acceptance of delivery of the Vessel by the Charterers shall not prejudice their rights against the Owners under this Charter Party.

2. Trading Areas

(a) *Trading Limits* - The Vessel shall be employed in lawful trades within Institute Warranty Limits (IWL) and within the trading limits as stated in Box 13 between safe ports or safe places where she can safely enter, lie always afloat, and depart.

(b) *Excepted Countries* - The Owners warrant that at the time of delivery the Vessel will not have traded to any of the countries listed in Box 14.

(c) *Ice* - The Vessel shall not be required to enter or remain in any icebound port or area, nor any port or area where lights, lightships, markers or buoys have been or are about to be withdrawn by reason of ice, nor where on account of ice there is risk that, in the ordinary course of events, the Vessel will not be able safely to enter and remain in the port or area or to depart after completion of loading or discharging. The Vessel shall not be obliged to force ice but, subject to the Owners' prior approval, may follow ice-breakers when reasonably required, with due regard to her size, construction and class. If, on account of ice, the Master considers it dangerous to remain at the port or place of loading or discharging for fear of the Vessel being frozen in and/or damaged he shall be at liberty to sail to any convenient place and there await the Charterers' new instructions.

3. Cargo - Restrictions and Exclusions

(a) *Lawful Cargoes* - The Vessel shall be employed in carrying lawful cargo. Cargo of a hazardous, injurious, or noxious nature or IMO-classified cargo shall not be carried without the Owners' prior consent in which case it shall be carried only in accordance with the provisions of sub-clause (c) of this Clause.

(b) *Excluded Cargoes* - Without prejudice to the generality of the foregoing, the following cargoes shall be excluded: livestock, arms, ammunition, explosives, nuclear and radioactive material other than radio-isotopes as described in sub-clause (d) of this clause and any other cargoes enumerated in Box 15.

(c) *Hazardous Cargoes* - If the Owners agree that the Charterers may carry hazardous, injurious, noxious or IMO-classified cargo, the amount of such cargo shall be limited to the quantity indicated in Box 16 and the Charterers shall provide the Master with evidence that the cargo has been packed, labelled and documented and shall be loaded and stowed in accordance with IMO regulations, any mandatory local requirements and regulations and/or recommendations of the competent authorities of the country of the Vessel's registry. Failure to observe the foregoing shall entitle the Master to refuse such cargo or, if already loaded, to discharge it in the Charterers' time and at their risk and expense.

(d) *Radio-active Cargoes* - Radio-isotopes, used or intended to be used for industrial, commercial, agricultural, medical or scientific purposes, may be carried subject to prior consent by the Owners and the Master, provided that they are not of such a category as to invalidate the Vessel's P & I cover.

(e) *Containers* - If cargo is carried in ISO-containers such containers shall comply with the International Convention for Safe Containers.

(f) *Deck Cargo* - Subject to the Master's prior approval, which shall not be unreasonably withheld, cargo may be carried on deck in accordance with the provisions of Clauses 17 (c) and 18.

4. Redelivery

(a) *Redelivery Place* - The Charterers shall redeliver the Vessel to the Owners at the port or place stated in Box 17 or a port or place within the range stated in Box 17, in the same order and condition as when the Vessel was delivered, fair wear and tear excepted.

(b) *Acceptance of Redelivery* - Acceptance of redelivery of the Vessel by the Owners shall not prejudice their rights against the Charterers under this Charter Party.

(c) *Notice* - The Charterers shall give the Owners not less than the number of days notice stated in Box 18 indicating the port or place of redelivery and the expected date on which the Vessel is to be ready for redelivery.

(d) *Last Voyage* - The Charterers warrant that they will not order the Vessel to commence a voyage (including any preceding ballast voyage) which cannot reasonably be expected to be completed in time to allow redelivery of the Vessel within the period agreed and declared as per Clause 1(a). If, nevertheless, such an order is given, the Owners shall have the option: (i) to refuse the order and require a substitute order allowing timely redelivery; or (ii) to perform the order without prejudice to their rights to claim damages for breach of charter in case of late redelivery. In any event, for the number of days by which the period agreed and declared as per Clause 1(a) is exceeded, the Charterers shall pay the market rate if this is higher than the rate stated in Box 24.

5. On/Off-hire Surveys

Joint on-hire and off-hire surveys shall be conducted by mutually acceptable surveyors at ports or places to be agreed. The on-hire survey shall be conducted without loss of time to the Charterers, whereas the off-hire survey shall be conducted in the Charterers' time. Survey fees and expenses shall be shared equally between the Owners and the Charterers.
Both surveys shall cover the condition of the Vessel and her equipment as well as quantities of fuels remaining on board. The Owners shall instruct the Master to co-operate with the surveyors in conducting such surveys.

6. Bunkers

(a) *Quantity at Delivery/Redelivery* - The Vessel shall be delivered with about the quantity of fuels stated in Box 19 and, unless indicated to the contrary in Box 20, the Vessel shall be redelivered with about the same quantity, provided that the quantity of fuels at redelivery is at least sufficient to allow the Vessel to safely reach the nearest port at which fuels of the required type or better are available.

(b) *Bunkering prior to Delivery and Redelivery* - Provided that it can be accomplished at scheduled ports, without hindrance to the operation of the Vessel, and by prior arrangement between the parties, the Owners shall allow the Charterers to bunker for the account of the Charterers prior to delivery and the Charterers shall allow the Owners to bunker for the account of the Owners prior to redelivery.

(c) *Purchase Price* - The Charterers shall purchase the fuels on board at delivery at the price stated in Box 21 and the Owners shall purchase the fuels on board at redelivery at the price stated in Box 22. The value of the fuel on delivery shall be paid together with the first instalment of hire.

(d) *Bunkering* - The Charterers shall supply fuel of the specifications and grades stated in Box 23. The fuels shall be of a stable and homogeneous nature and unless otherwise agreed in writing, shall comply with ISO standard 8217: 1996 or any subsequent amendments thereof as well as with the relevant provisions of Marpol. The Chief Engineer shall co-operate with the Charterers' bunkering agents and fuel suppliers and comply with their requirements during bunkering, including but not limited to checking, verifying and acknowledging sampling, readings or soundings, meters etc. before, during and/or after delivery of fuels. During delivery four representative samples of all fuels shall be taken at a point as close as possible to the Vessel's bunker manifold. The samples shall be labelled and sealed and signed by suppliers, Chief Engineer and the Charterers or their agents. Two samples shall be retained by the suppliers and one each by the Vessel and the Charterers. If any claim should arise in respect of the quality or specification or grades of the fuels supplied, the samples of the fuels retained as aforesaid shall be analysed by a qualified and independent laboratory.

(e) *Liability* - The Charterers shall be liable for any loss or damage to the Owners caused by the supply of unsuitable fuels or fuels which do not comply with the specifications and grades set out in Box 23 and the Owners shall not be held liable for any reduction in the Vessel's speed performance and/or increased bunker consumption nor for any time lost and any other consequences arising as a result of such supply.

7. Vessel's Gear and Equipment

(a) *Regulations* - The Vessel's cargo gear, if any, and any other related equipment shall comply with the law and national regulations of the countries to which the Vessel may be employed and the Owners shall ensure that the Vessel is at all times in possession of valid certificates to establish compliance with such regulations. If stevedores are not permitted to work due to failure of the Master and/or the Owners to comply with the aforementioned regulations or because the Vessel is not in possession of such valid certificates, then the Charterers may suspend hire for the time lost thereby and the Owners shall pay all expenses incurred incidental to and resulting from such failure (see Clause 11(d)).

(b) *Breakdown of Vessel's Gear* - All cargo handling gear, including derricks/cranes/ winches if any, shall be kept in good working order and the Owners shall exercise due diligence in maintaining such gear. In the event of loss of time due to a breakdown of derrick(s), crane(s) or winch(es) for any period by reason of disablement or insufficient power, the hire shall be reduced for the actual time lost thereby during loading/discharging unless the lost time is caused by negligence of the Charterers or their servants. If the Charterers continue working by using shore-crane(s) the Owners shall pay the cost of shore craneage, to an amount not exceeding the amount of hire payable to the Owners for such period.

(c) *Suez and Panama Canal* - During the currency of this Charter Party the Vessel

PART II
"GENTIME" General Time Charter Party

shall be equipped with all necessary fittings in good working order for Suez and Panama Canal transit. 172 173

(d) *Lighting* - The Owners shall ensure that the Vessel will supply, free of expense to the Charterers, sufficient lighting on deck and in holds to permit 24 hour working. 174 175

8. Hire

(a) *Rate* - The Charterers shall pay hire per day or pro rata for any part of a day from the time the Vessel is delivered to the Charterers until her redelivery to the Owners, in the currency and at the rate stated in Box 24. In the event that additional hire is payable in accordance with Clause 9(d) such hire shall be based on the rate applicable at the time of redelivery. All calculation of hire shall be made by reference to UTC (Universal Time Coordinated). 176 177 178 179 180 181 182

(b) *Payment* - Subject to sub-clause (d) payment of hire shall be made in advance in full, without discount every 15 days to the Owners' bank account designated in Box 25 or to such other account as the Owners may from time to time designate in writing, in funds available to the Owners on the due date. 183 184 185 186

(c) *Default* - In default of punctual and regular payment of hire the Owners shall have the right to withdraw the Vessel without prejudice to any other claim they may have against the Charterers under this Charter Party. 187 188 189

Where there is a failure to make punctual and regular payment of hire due to oversight, negligence, errors or omissions on the part of the Charterers or their bankers, the Owners shall give the Charterers written notice of the number of clear banking days stated in Box 26 (as recognized at the agreed place of payment) in which to rectify the failure, and when so rectified within such number of days following the Owners' notice, the payment shall stand as regular and punctual. Failure by the Charterers to pay hire within the number of days stated in Box 26 of their receiving the Owners' notice as provided herein, shall entitle the Owners to withdraw the Vessel without further notice and without prejudice to any other claim they may have against the Charterers. 190 191 192 193 194 195 196 197 198 199

Further, at any time after the period stated in Box 26, as long as hire remains unpaid, the Owners shall, without prejudice to their right to withdraw, be entitled to suspend the performance of any and all of their obligations hereunder and shall have no responsibility whatsoever for any consequences thereof in respect of which the Charterers hereby agree to indemnify the Owners. Notwithstanding the provisions of Clause 9(a)(ii), hire shall continue to accrue and any extra expenses resulting from such suspension shall be for the Charterers' account. 200 201 202 203 204 205 206

(d) *Deductions* - On production of supporting vouchers the Charterers shall be entitled to deduct from the next hire due any expenditure incurred on behalf of the Owners which is for the Owners' account under this Charter Party. If such expenditure is incurred in a currency other than that in which hire is payable, conversion into such currency for the purpose of deduction shall be effected at the rate of exchange prevailing on the date the expenditure was incurred. 207 208 209 210 211 212

(e) *Redelivery Adjustment* - Should the Vessel be on her voyage towards the port or place of redelivery at the time payment of hire becomes due, said payment shall be made for the estimated time necessary to complete the voyage, less the estimated value of the fuels remaining on board at redelivery. When the Vessel is redelivered to the Owners any difference shall be refunded to or paid by the Charterers as appropriate, but not later than thirty days after redelivery of the Vessel. 213 214 215 216 217 218

9. Off-hire

After delivery in accordance with Clause 1 hereof the Vessel shall remain on hire until redelivered in accordance with Clause 4, except for the following periods: 219 220 221

(a) *Inability to Perform Services* 222

If the Vessel is unable to comply with the instructions of the Charterers on account of: 223

(i) any damage, defect, breakdown, deficiency of, or accident to the Vessel's hull, machinery, equipment or repairs or maintenance thereto, including drydocking, excepting those occasions where Clauses 7(b) and 16(b) apply; 224 225 226

(ii) any deficiency of the Master, Officers and/or Crew, including the failure or refusal or inability of the Master, Officers and/or Crew to perform services when required; 227 228

(iii) Arrest of the Vessel at the suit of a claimant except where the arrest is caused by, or arises from any act or omission of the Charterers, their servants, agents or sub-contractors; 229 230 231

(iv) the terms of employment of the Master, Officers and/or Crew; 232

then the Vessel will be off-hire for the time thereby lost. 233

(b) *Deviation* - In the event of the Vessel deviating (which expression includes putting back, or putting into any port or place other than that to which she is bound under the instructions of the Charterers) for reasons other than to save life or property the Vessel shall be off-hire from the commencement of such deviation until the time when the Vessel is again ready to resume her service from a position not less favourable to the Charterers than that at which the deviation commenced, provided always that due allowance shall be made for any distance made good towards the Vessel's destination and any bunkers saved. However, should the Vessel alter course to avoid bad weather or the Vessel is delayed or prevented by stress of weather, the Vessel shall remain on hire and all costs thereby incurred shall be for the Charterers' account. 234 235 236 237 238 239 240 241 242 243

(c) *Requisitions* - Should the Vessel be requisitioned by any government or governmental authority during the period of this Charter Party, the Owners shall immediately notify the Charterers. The Vessel shall be off-hire during the period of such requisition and any hire or compensation paid by any government or governmental authority in respect of such requisition shall be paid to the Owners. However, if the period of requisition exceeds the number of days stated in Box 27, either party shall have the option of cancelling the balance period of the Charter Party, by giving 14 days notice of cancellation to the other. 244 245 246 247 248 249 250 251

(d) *Addition to Charter Period* - Any time during which the Vessel is off-hire under this Charter Party may be added, at the option of the Charterers, to the charter period as determined in accordance with Clause 1(a). Such option shall be declared in writing not less than one month before the expected date of redelivery, or latest one week after the event if such event occurs less than one month before the expected date of redelivery. 252 253 254 255 256 257

10. Loss of Vessel

This Charter Party shall terminate and hire shall cease at noon on the day the Vessel is lost or becomes a constructive total loss and if missing, at noon on the date when last heard of. Any hire paid in advance and not earned shall be returned to the Charterers and payment of any hire due shall be deferred until the Vessel is reported safe. 258 259 260 261 262

11. Owners' Obligations

Except as provided elsewhere in this Charter Party, the Owners shall deliver the Vessel in the Class indicated in Box 5 and in a thoroughly efficient state of hull and machinery and shall exercise due diligence to maintain the Vessel in such Class and in every way fit for the service throughout the period of the Charter Party. 263 264 265 266 267

Nothing contained in this Charter Party shall be construed as a demise of the Vessel to the Charterers and the Owners remain at all times responsible for her navigation and for the due performance of related services, including but not limited to pilotage and towage even if paid for by the Charterers. 268 269 270 271

Unless otherwise agreed, the Owners shall provide and pay for the costs of the following:- 272

(a) *Wages* - Master's, Officers' and Crew's wages. 273

(b) *Stores* - All provisions, deck and engine-room stores, including lubricants. 274

(c) *Insurance of the Vessel* (See Clause 20). 275

(d) *Crew's assistance in:-* 276

(i) preparing the Vessel's cranes, derricks, winches and/or cargo handling gear for use, 277 278

(ii) opening and closing all hatches (other than pontoon type hatches), ramps and other means of access to cargo, 279 280

(iii) docking, undocking and shifting operations in port, 281

(iv) bunkering, 282

(v) maintaining power during loading and discharging operations, 283

(vi) instructing crane drivers and winchmen in the use of the Vessel's gear, 284

The above services will be rendered by the crew if required, provided port and local regulations permit; otherwise charges for such services shall be for the Charterers' account. 285 286 287

(e) *Documentation* - Any documentation relating to the Vessel as required at the commencement of the Charter Party to permit the Vessel to trade within the limits provided in Box 13, including but not limited to international tonnage certificate, Suez and Panama tonnage certificates, certificate of registry, certificates relating to the strength, safety and/or serviceability of the Vessel's gear and certificates of financial responsibility for oil pollution as long as such oil pollution certificates can be obtained by the Owners in the market on ordinary commercial terms. 288 289 290 291 292 293 294

Such documentation shall be maintained during the currency of the Charter Party as necessary. 295 296

(f) *Deratisation* - A deratisation certificate at the commencement of the Charter Party and any renewal thereof throughout the Charter Party, except if certification is required as a result of the cargo carried or ports visited under this Charter Party in which case all expenses in connection therewith shall be for the account of the Charterers. 297 298 299 300

(g) *Smuggling* - Any fines, taxes or imposts levied in the event of smuggling by the Master, Officers and/or Crew. The Vessel shall be off-hire for any time lost as a result thereof. See also Clause 13(f). 301 302 303

12. Master

The Master shall be conversant with the English language and, although appointed by the Owners, shall at all times during the currency of this Charter Party be under the orders and directions of the Charterers as regards employment, agency or other arrangements. The Master shall prosecute all voyages with due dispatch and supervise loading and discharging operations to ensure that the seaworthiness of the Vessel is not affected. 304 305 306 307 308 309 310

The Charterers recognise the principles stated in IMO Resolution A.443 (XI) as regards maritime safety and protection of the marine environment and shall not prevent the Master from taking any decision in this respect which in his professional judgement is necessary. 311 312 313 314

13. Charterers' Obligations

The Charterers shall keep and care for the cargo at loading and discharging ports, be responsible for the stevedoring operations enumerated under sub-clause 13(d), arrange any transhipment and properly deliver the cargo at destination. 315 316 317 318

The Charterers shall furnish the Master with full and timely instructions and unless otherwise agreed, they shall provide and pay for the costs of the following throughout the currency of this Charter Party: 319 320 321

(a) *Voyage Expenses* - All port charges (including compulsory charges for shore watchmen and garbage removal), light and canal dues, pilotage, towage, consular charges, and all other charges and expenses relating to the cargo and/or to the Vessel as a result of her employment hereunder, other than charges or expenses provided for in Clause 11. 322 323 324 325 326

(b) *Bunker Fuel* (See Clause 6). - All fuels except for quantities consumed while the Vessel is off-hire. 327 328

(c) *Agency Costs* - All agency fees for normal ship's husbandry at all ports or places of call. 329 330

(d) *Stevedoring* - All stevedoring operations during the currency of this Charter Party including receipt, loading, handling, stuffing containers, stowing, lashing, securing, unsecuring, unlashing, discharging, stripping containers, tallying and delivering of all cargo. 331 332 333 334

(e) *Advances to Master* - Reasonable funds which, upon request by the Owners, are to be made available by Charterers' local agents to the Master for disbursements. The Charterers may deduct such advance funds from hire payments. 335 336 337

(f) *Contraband* - Any fines, taxes or imposts levied in the event that contraband and/or unmanifested drugs and/or cargoes are found to have been shipped as part of the cargo and/or in containers on board. The Vessel shall remain on hire during any time lost as a result thereof. However, if it is established that the Master, Officers and/or Crew are involved in smuggling then any security required shall be provided by the Owners. See also Clause 11(g). 338 339 340 341 342 343

PART II
"GENTIME" General Time Charter Party

14. Owners' Requirements   344

(a) *Maintenance* - Without prejudice to the provisions of Clause 9(a)(i), the Owners   345
shall have the right to take the Vessel out of service at any time for emergency   346
repairs, and by prior arrangement with the Charterers for routine maintenance,   347
including drydocking.   348

(b) *General Average* - General Average shall be adjusted, stated and settled at the   349
place shown in Box 28 according to the York-Antwerp Rules 1994 or any   350
subsequent modification thereto by an adjuster appointed by the Owners. Charter   351
hire shall not contribute to General Average.   352
General Average shall be adjusted in any currency at the sole option of the Owners.   353
Exchange into the currency of adjustment shall be calculated at the rate prevailing   354
on the date of payment for disbursements and on the date of completion of   355
discharge of the Vessel for allowances, contributory values etc.   356
The Charterers agree to co-operate with the Owners and their appointed adjuster   357
by supplying manifest and other information and, where required, to endeavour   358
to secure the assistance of the Charterers' local agents in the collection of security,   359
at the Owners' expense.   360

(c) *Salvage* - All salvage and assistance to other vessels shall be for the Owners'   361
and the Charterers' equal benefit after deducting the Master's and Crew's   362
proportion and all legal and other expenses including hire paid under the Charter   363
Party for time lost in the salvage, damage to the Vessel and fuel consumed. The   364
Charterers shall be bound by all measures taken by the Owners in order to secure   365
payment of salvage and to settle its amount.   366

(d) *Lien* - The Charterers warrant that they will not suffer, nor permit to be continued, 367
any lien or encumbrance incurred by them or their agents, which might have   368
priority over the title and interest of the Owners in the Vessel. In no event shall   369
the Charterers procure, nor permit to be procured, for the Vessel, any supplies,   370
necessaries or services without previously obtaining a statement signed by an   371
authorised representative of the furnisher thereof, acknowledging that such   372
supplies, necessaries or services are being furnished on the credit of the   373
Charterers and not on the credit of the Vessel or of the Owners and that the   374
furnisher claims no maritime lien on the Vessel therefor.   375
The Owners shall have a lien on all shipped cargo before or after discharge and   376
on all sub-freights and/or sub-hire including deadfreight and demurrage, for any   377
amount due under this Charter Party including but not limited to unpaid charter   378
hire, unreimbursed Charterers' expenses initially paid by the Owners, and   379
contributions in general average properly due.   380
The Charterers shall ensure that such lien is incorporated in all documents   381
containing or evidencing Contracts of Carriage issued by them or on their behalf.   382

15. Charterers' Requirements   383

(a) *Plans* - On concluding this Charter Party or as soon as practical thereafter the   384
Owners shall provide the Charterers with copies of any operational plans or   385
documents that the Charterers may reasonably request and which are necessary   386
for the safe and efficient operation of the Vessel. All documents received by the   387
Charterers shall be returned to the Owners on redelivery.   388

(b) *Flag and Funnel* - If they so require, the Charterers shall, during the currency of   389
this Charter Party, be allowed to fly their house flag and/or paint the funnel in the   390
Charterers' colours. All alterations including re-instatement shall be effected in   391
the Charterers' time and at their expense.   392

(c) *Communications Facilities* - The Owners shall permit the Charterers' use of the   393
Vessel's communication facilities at cost.   394

(d) *Logs* - The Owners shall maintain full deck and engine room logs during the   395
currency of this Charter Party and the Charterers shall have full access to all the   396
Vessel's logs, rough and official, covering this period. The Owners undertake to   397
produce all such documentation promptly upon written request of the Charterers   398
and to allow them to make copies of relevant entries.   399

(e) *Replacement of Master and Officers* - If the Charterers shall have reason to be   400
dissatisfied with the conduct of the Master or Officers, the Owners shall, on   401
receiving particulars of the complaint in writing, investigate same and, if necessary,   402
replace the offending party or parties at their expense.   403

(f) *Supercargo* - The Owners shall provide and maintain a clean and adequate room   404
for the Charterers' Supercargo if any, furnished to the same standard as officers'   405
accommodation. The Supercargo shall be victualled with the Vessel's officers. The   406
Charterers shall pay at the daily rate shown in Box 29 for his accommodation and   407
victualling. The Supercargo shall be on board at the risk and expense of the   408
Charterers and both Charterers and Supercargo shall sign the customary indemnity   409
forms.   410

(g) *Victualling* - The Owners shall, when requested and authorised in writing by the   411
Charterers or their agents, victual other officials and servants of the Charterers at   412
the rate per person per meal shown in Box 30.   413

(h) *Representation* - Expenses for representation incurred by the Master for the   414
Charterers' account and benefit shall be settled by the Charterers' payment of the   415
amount stated in Box 31, per month or pro rata. The Charterers shall indemnify the   416
Owners against all consequences and/or liabilities including customs fines which   417
may result from such representation.   418

(i) *Sub-Letting* - The Charterers shall have the right to sub-let all or part of the   419
Vessel whilst remaining responsible to the Owners for the performance of this Charter   420
Party.   421

(j) *Inspections* - The Charterers shall, upon giving reasonable notice, have the right to 422
a superficial inspection of the Vessel in their time and the Master shall within reason   423
co-operate with the Charterers to facilitate their inspection of the Vessel. The   424
Charterers shall pay for any and all expenses associated with such inspection and   425
the Charterers shall be entitled to receive a copy of the report.   426

(k) *Weather Routeing* - The Charterers may supply the Master with weather routeing   427
information during the currency of this Charter Party. In this event the Master, though   428
not obliged to follow routeing information, shall comply with the reporting procedure   429
of the Charterers' weather routeing service.   430

(l) *Laying up* - At the written request of the Charterers, the Owners shall at any time   431
provide an estimate of any economies which may be possible in the event of laying-   432
up the Vessel. The Charterers shall then have the right to order the laying-up of the   433
Vessel at any time and for any period of time at a safe berth or safe place in their   434
option, and in the event of such laying-up the Owners shall promptly take reasonable   435
steps to effect all the economies in operating costs. The laying-up port or place and   436
laid-up arrangements shall be subject to approval by the Owners' insurers. Laying-   437
up preparation and reactivation cost, and all expenses incurred shall be for the   438
Charterers' account. The Charterers shall give sufficient notice of their intention in   439
this respect to enable the Owners to make necessary arrangements for   440
decommissioning and recommissioning. The Owners must give prompt credit to   441
the Charterers for all economies achieved.   442

(m) *Cleaning* - The Charterers may request the Owners to direct the crew to sweep   443
and/or wash and/or clean the holds between voyages and/or between cargoes   444
against payment at the rate per hold stated in Box 32, provided the crew is able to   445
undertake such work and is allowed to do so by local regulations. In connection   446
with any such operation the Owners shall not be responsible if the Vessel's holds   447
are not accepted or passed.   448
In lieu of cleaning the Charterers shall have the option to re-deliver the Vessel with   449
unclean/unswept holds against the disposal of dunnage and/or waste, which shall be   450
for the disposal of dunnage and/or waste, which shall be for Charterers' account.   451

16. Sundry Matters   452

(a) *Stowaways*   453
  (i) The Charterers shall exercise due care and diligence in preventing stowaways   454
       from gaining access to the Vessel by means of secreting away in cargo or   455
       containers shipped by the Charterers.   456
  (ii) If, despite the exercise of due care and diligence by the Charterers, stowaways   457
       have gained access to the Vessel by means of secreting away in the cargo   458
       and/or containers shipped by the Charterers, this shall amount to breach of   459
       charter for the consequences of which the Charterers shall be liable and shall   460
       hold the Owners harmless and shall keep them indemnified against all claims   461
       whatsoever which may arise and be made against them. Furthermore, all time   462
       lost and all expenses whatsoever and howsoever incurred, including fines,   463
       shall be for the Charterers' account and the Vessel shall remain on hire.   464
  (iii) Should the Vessel be arrested as a result of the Charterers' breach of charter   465
       according to sub-clause (ii) above, the Charterers shall take all reasonable   466
       steps to secure that within a reasonable time, the Vessel is released and at   467
       their expense post bail or other security to obtain release of the Vessel.   468
  (iv) If, despite the exercise of due care and diligence by the Owners, stowaways   469
       have gained access to the Vessel by means other than secreting away in the   470
       cargo and/or containers shipped by the Charterers, all time lost and all expenses   471
       whatsoever and howsoever incurred, including fines, shall be for the Owners'   472
       account.   473
  (v) Should the Vessel be arrested as a result of stowaways having gained access   474
       to the Vessel by means other than secreting away in the cargo and/or containers   475
       shipped by the Charterers, the Owners shall take all reasonable steps to secure   476
       that within a reasonable time, the Vessel is released and at their expense post   477
       bail or other security to obtain release of the Vessel.   478

(b) *Stevedore Damage* - Notwithstanding anything contained herein to the contrary,   479
the Charterers shall be liable for any and all damage to the Vessel caused by   480
stevedores, provided the Master has notified the Charterers or their agents, in writing,   481
within 24 hours of the occurrence or as soon as possible thereafter but latest when   482
the damage could have been discovered by the exercise of due diligence. The   483
Master shall use his best efforts to obtain written acknowledgment by the party   484
or parties causing damage unless the damage has been made good in the   485
meantime.   486
  (i) Stevedore damage affecting the Vessel's seaworthiness and/or the safety of   487
       the crew, proper working of the Vessel and/or her equipment, shall be repaired   488
       immediately by the Charterers and the Vessel is to remain on hire until such   489
       repairs are completed and, if required, passed by the Vessel's classification   490
       society.   491
  (ii) Stevedore damage not affecting the Vessel's seaworthiness and/or the safety   492
       of the crew shall be repaired, at the Charterers' option, before or after redelivery 493
       concurrently with Owners' work. In the latter case no hire will be paid to the   494
       Owners except in so far as the time required for the repairs for which the Charterers   495
       are liable exceeds the time necessary to carry out the Owners' work.   496
  (iii) The Owners shall have the option of requiring that stevedore damage affecting   497
       the trading capabilities of the Vessel is repaired before redelivery.   498

(c) *Fumigation* - Expenses in connection with fumigations and/or quarantine ordered   499
because of cargo carried or ports visited while the Vessel is employed under this   500
Charter Party shall be for the Charterers' account. Expenses in connection with all   501
other fumigations and/or quarantine shall be for the Owners' account.   502

(d) *Anti-drug Clause* - The Charterers warrant to exercise the highest degree of care   503
and diligence in preventing unmanifested narcotic drugs and/or any other illegal   504
substances being loaded or concealed on board the Vessel.   505
Non-compliance with the provisions of this Clause shall amount to breach of warranty   506
for the consequences of which the Charterers shall be liable and shall hold the   507
Owners, the Master and the crew of the Vessel harmless and shall keep them   508
indemnified against all claims whatsoever which may arise and be made against them   509
individually or jointly. Furthermore, all time lost and all expenses incurred,   510
including fines, as a result of the Charterers' breach of the provisions of this Clause   511
shall be for the Charterers' account and the Vessel shall remain on hire.   512
Should the Vessel be arrested as a result of the Charterers' non-compliance with   513
the provisions of this Clause, the Charterers shall at their expense take all reasonable   514
steps to secure that within a reasonable time the Vessel is released and at their   515
expense post bail to secure release of the Vessel.   516
The Owners shall remain responsible for all time lost and all expenses incurred,   517
including fines, in the event that unmanifested narcotic drugs and other illegal   518

PART II
"GENTIME" General Time Charter Party

substances are found in the possession or effects of the Vessel's personnel. 519

17. Bills of Lading, Waybills and Other Contracts of Carriage 520

(a) *Signing Contracts of Carriage* 521

(i) The Master shall sign bills of lading or waybills as presented in conformity with 522 mate's receipts. If requested, the Owners may authorise the Charterers and/or 523 their agents in writing to sign bills of lading, waybills, through bills of lading, or 524 multimodal bills of lading (hereafter collectively referred to as Contracts of 525 Carriage) on the Owners' and/or Master's behalf in conformity with mate's 526 receipts without prejudice to the terms and conditions of the Charter Party. 527

(ii) In the event the Charterers and/or their agents, pursuant to the provisions of 528 sub-clause 17(a)(i) above, sign Contracts of Carriage which extend the Owners' 529 responsibility beyond the period during which the cargo is on board the Vessel 530 the Charterers shall indemnify the Owners against any claims for loss, damage 531 or expense which may result therefrom. 532

(iii) Neither the Charterers nor their agents shall permit the issue of any Contract 533 of Carriage (whether or not signed on behalf of the Owners or on behalf of the 534 Charterers or on behalf of any Sub-Charterers) incorporating, where not 535 compulsorily applicable, the Hamburg Rules or any other legislation giving 536 effect to the Hamburg Rules or any other legislation imposing liabilities in excess 537 of Hague or Hague-Visby Rules. 538

(b) *Protective Clauses* - The Charterers warrant that Contracts of Carriage issued in 539 respect of cargo under this Charter Party shall incorporate the clauses set out in 540 Appendix A. 541

(c) *Deck Cargo* - Unless the cargo is stowed in fully closed containers, placed on 542 board the Vessel in areas designed for the carriage of containers with class-approved 543 container fittings and secured to the Vessel by means of class-approved Vessel's 544 lashing gear or material, Contracts of Carriage covering cargo carried on deck 545 shall be claused: "Agreed to be shipped on deck at Charterers', Shippers' and 546 Receivers' risk, and responsibility for loss, damage or expense howsoever caused". 547

(d) *Defence of Claims* - Should the Charterers issue or cause to be issued a Contract 548 of Carriage in default of the provisions of this Clause 17, they shall be obliged upon 549 written request by the Owners to take over, pay for the defence of and pay any 550 liability established in respect of any claim brought against the Vessel and/or the 551 Owners as a result of such default. 552

(e) *Payment and Indemnity* - The Charterers shall pay for, and/or indemnify the Owners 553 against any loss, damage or expense which results from any breach of the provisions 554 of this Clause 17. 555

18. Responsibilities 556

(a) *Cargo Claims* 557

(i) *Definition* - For the purpose of this Clause 18(a), Cargo Claim means a 558 claim for loss, damage, shortage, (including slackage, ullage or pilferage), 559 overcarriage or delay to cargo including customs fines or fines in respect 560 of such loss, damage, shortage, overcarriage or delay and includes: 561
(1) any legal costs or interest claimed by the original claimant making such a 562 claim; 563
(2) all legal, Club correspondents' and experts' costs reasonably incurred in 564 the defence of or in the settlement of the claim made by the original claim- 565 ant, but shall not include any costs of whatsoever nature incurred in making 566 a claim or in seeking an indemnity under this Charter Party. 567

(ii) *Claim Settlement* - It is a condition precedent to the right of recovery by either 568 party under this Clause 18(a) that the party seeking indemnity shall have first 569 properly settled or compromised and paid the claim. 570

(iii) *Owners' Liability* - The Owners shall be liable for any Cargo Claim arising or 571 resulting from: 572
(1) failure of the Owners or their servants to exercise due diligence before or 573 at the beginning of each voyage to make the Vessel seaworthy, 574
(2) failure of the Owners or their servants properly and carefully to carry 575 keep and care for the cargo while on board; 576
(3) unreasonable deviation from the voyage described in the Contract of 577 Carriage unless such deviation is ordered or approved by the Charterers; 578
(4) errors in navigation or the management of the Vessel solely where the 579 Contract of Carriage is subject to mandatory application of legislation 580 giving effect to the Hamburg Rules. 581

(iv) *Charterers' Liability* - The Charterers shall be liable for any Cargo Claim arising 582 or resulting from: 583
(1) the stevedoring operations enumerated under Clause 13(d) unless the 584 Charterers prove that such Cargo Claim was caused by the unseaworthi- 585 ness of the Vessel, in which case the Owners shall be liable; 586
(2) any transhipment in connection with through-transport or multimodal 587 transport, save where the Charterers can prove that the circumstances 588 giving rise to the Cargo Claim occurred after commencement of the 589 loading of the cargo onto the Vessel and prior to its discharge; 590
(3) the carriage of cargo on deck unless such cargo is stowed in fully closed 591 containers, placed on board the Vessel in areas designed for the carriage 592 of containers with class-approved container fittings and secured to the 593 Vessel by means of class-approved Vessel's lashing gear or material. 594

(v) *Shared Liability* - All Cargo Claims arising from other causes than those 595 enumerated under sub-clauses (iii) and (iv), shall be shared equally between 596 the Owners and the Charterers unless there is clear and irrefutable evidence 597 that the claim arose out of pilferage or the act or neglect of one or the other 598 party or their servants or sub-contractors, in which case that party shall bear 599 the full claim. 600

(vi) *Charterers' Own Cargo* - If the cargo is the property of the Charterers, the 601 Owners shall have the same responsibilities and benefits as they would have 602 had under this Clause had the cargo been the property of a third party and 603 carried under a Bill of Lading incorporating the Hague-Visby Rules. 604

(b) *Fines, etc.* - The Charterers shall also be liable to the Owners for any losses, 605

damages, expenses, fines, penalties, or claims which the Owners may incur or 606 suffer by reason of the cargo or the documentation relating thereto failing to comply 607 with any relevant laws, regulations, directions or notices of port authorities or other 608 authorities, or by reason of any infestation, contamination or condemnation of the 609 cargo or of infestation, damage or contamination of the Vessel by the cargo. 610

(c) *Deck cargo* - The Charterers shall be liable to the Owners for any loss, damage, 611 expense or delay to the Vessel howsoever caused and resulting from the carriage 612 of cargo on deck save where the Charterers can prove that such loss, damage, 613 expense or delay was the result of negligence on the part of the Owners and/or 614 their servants. 615

(d) *Death or Personal Injury* - Claims for death or personal injury having a direct 616 connection with the operation of the Vessel shall be borne by the Owners unless 617 such claims are caused by defect of the cargo or by the act, neglect or default of the 618 Charterers, their servants, agents or sub-contractors. 619

(e) *Agency* - The Owners authorise and empower the Charterers to act as the Owners' 620 agents solely to ensure that, as against third parties, the Owners will have the 621 benefit of any immunities, exemptions or liberties regarding the cargo or its carriage. 622 Subject to the provisions of Clause 17 the Charterers shall have no authority to 623 make any contracts imposing any obligations whatsoever upon the Owners in respect 624 of the cargo or its carriage. 625

(f) *Indemnity and Limitation* - The Owners and the Charterers hereby agree to indemnify 626 each other against all loss, damage or expenses arising or resulting from any 627 obligation to pay claims, fines or penalties for which the other party is liable in 628 accordance with this Charter Party. Both the Owners and the Charterers shall retain 629 their right to limit their liability against the other party in respect of any claim brought 630 by way of indemnity, notwithstanding that the other party has been denied the right 631 to limit against any third party or has failed in whatever manner to exercise its rights 632 of limitation. 633

(g) *Time Bar* - In respect of any Cargo Claims as between the Owners and the 634 Charterers, brought under sub-clause 18(a), unless extensions of time have been 635 sought or obtained from one party by the other or notice of arbitration has been 636 given by either party, such claim(s) shall be deemed to be waived and absolutely 637 time barred upon the expiry of two years reckoned from the date when the cargo 638 was or should have been delivered. When the Hamburg Rules apply compulsorily 639 the above time bar shall be extended to three years. 640

19. Exceptions 641

As between the Charterers and the Owners, responsibility for any loss, damage, delay 642 or failure of performance under this Charter Party not dealt with in Clause 18(a), shall 643 be subject to the following mutual exceptions: 644

Act of God, act of war, civil commotions, strikes, lockouts, restraint of princes and rulers, 645 and quarantine restrictions. 646

In addition, any responsibility of the Owners not dealt with in Clause 18(a) shall be 647 subject to the following exceptions: 648

Any act, neglect or default by the Master, pilots or other servants of the Owners in the 649 navigation or management of the Vessel, fire or explosion not due to the personal fault 650 of the Owners or their Manager, collision or stranding, unforeseeable breakdown of or 651 any latent defect in the Vessel's hull, equipment or machinery. 652

The above provisions shall in no way affect the provisions as to off-hire in this Charter 653 Party. 654

20. Insurances 655

(a) *Hull and Machinery* - The Owners warrant that the Vessel is insured for Hull, 656 Machinery and basic War Risks purposes at the value stated in Box 34. 657

(b) *Protection and Indemnity (P & I)* - The Owners warrant that throughout the period 658 of the Charter Party the Vessel will be fully covered for P&I risks, including through 659 transport cover, with underwriters approved by the Charterers which approval shall 660 not be unreasonably withheld. 661

The Charterers warrant that throughout the period of the Charter Party they will be 662 covered for Charterers' liability risk by underwriters approved by the Owners which 663 approval will not be unreasonably withheld 664

21. War Risks ("Conwartime 1993") 665

(a) For the purpose of this Clause, the words: 666
(i) "Owners" shall include the shipowners, bareboat charterers, disponent owners, 667 managers or other operators who are charged with the management of the 668 Vessel, and the Master; 669
(ii) "War Risks" shall include any war (whether actual or threatened), act of war, 670 civil war, hostilities, revolution, rebellion, civil commotion, warlike operations, 671 the laying of mines (whether actual or reported), acts of piracy, acts of terrorists, 672 acts of hostility or malicious damage, blockades (whether imposed against all 673 vessels or imposed selectively against vessels of certain flags or ownership, or 674 against certain cargoes or crews or otherwise howsoever), by any person, 675 body, terrorist or political group, or the Government of any state whatsoever, 676 which, in the reasonable judgement of the Master and/or the Owners, may be 677 dangerous or are likely to be or to become dangerous to the Vessel, her cargo, 678 crew or other persons on board the Vessel. 679

(b) The Vessel, unless the written consent of the Owners be first obtained, shall not be 680 ordered to or required to continue to or through, any port, place, area or zone 681 (whether of land or sea), or any waterway or canal, where it appears that the Vessel, 682 her cargo, crew or other persons on board the Vessel, in the reasonable judgement 683 of the Master and/or the Owners, may be, or are likely to be, exposed to War Risks. 684 Should the Vessel be within any such place as aforesaid, which only becomes 685 dangerous, or is likely to be or to become dangerous, after her entry into it, she 686 shall be at liberty to leave it. 687

(c) The Vessel shall not be required to load contraband cargo, or to pass through any 688 blockade, whether such blockade be imposed on all vessels, or is imposed selectively 689 in any way whatsoever against vessels of certain flags or ownership, or against 690 certain cargoes or crews or otherwise howsoever, or to proceed to an area where 691

PART II
"GENTIME" General Time Charter Party

	she shall be subject, or is likely to be subject to a belligerent's right of search and/ or confiscation.	692 693
(d) (i)	The Owners may effect war risks insurance in respect of the Hull and Machinery of the Vessel and their other interests (including, but not limited to, loss of earnings and detention, the crew and their Protection and Indemnity Risks), and the premiums and/or calls therefor shall be for their account.	694 695 696 697
(ii)	If the Underwriters of such insurance should require payment of premiums and/or calls because, pursuant to the Charterers' orders, the Vessel is within, or is due to enter and remain within, any area or areas which are specified by such Underwriters as being subject to additional premiums because of War Risks, then such premiums and/or calls shall be reimbursed by the Charterers to the Owners at the same time as the next payment of hire is due.	698 699 700 701 702 703
(e)	If the Owners become liable under the terms of employment to pay to the crew any bonus or additional wages in respect of sailing into an area which is dangerous in the manner defined by the said terms, then such bonus or additional wages shall be reimbursed to the Owners by the Charterers at the same time as the next payment of hire is due.	704 705 706 707 708
(f)	The Vessel shall have liberty:-	709
(i)	to comply with all orders, directions, recommendations or advice as to departure, arrival, routes, sailing in convoy, ports of call, stoppages, destinations, discharge of cargo, delivery or in any other way whatsoever, which are given by the Government of the Nation under whose flag the Vessel sails, or other Government to whose laws the Owners are subject, or any other Government, or any other body or group whatsoever acting with the power to compel compliance with their orders or directions;	710 711 712 713 714 715 716
(ii)	to comply with the order, directions or recommendations of any war risks underwriters who have the authority to give the same under the terms of the war risks insurance;	717 718 719
(iii)	to comply with the terms of any resolution of the Security Council of the United Nations, any directives of the European Community, the effective orders of any other Supranational body which has the right to issue and give the same, and with national laws aimed at enforcing the same to which the Owners are subject, and to obey the orders and directions of those who are charged with their enforcement;	720 721 722 723 724 725
(iv)	to divert and discharge at any other port any cargo or part thereof which may render the Vessel liable to confiscation as a contraband carrier;	726 727
(v)	to divert and call at any other port to change the crew or any part thereof or other persons on board the Vessel when there is reason to believe that they may be subject to internment, imprisonment or other sanctions.	728 729 730
(g)	If in accordance with their rights under the foregoing provisions of this Clause, the Owners refuse to proceed to the loading or discharging ports, or any one or more of them, they shall immediately inform the Charterers. No cargo shall be discharged at any alternative port without first giving the Charterers notice of the Owners' intention to do so and requesting them to nominate a safe port for such discharge. Failing such nomination by the Charterers within 48 hours of the receipt of such notice and request, the Owners may discharge the cargo at any safe port of their own choice.	731 732 733 734 735 736 737 738
(h)	If in compliance with any of the provisions of sub-clauses (b) to (g) of this Clause anything is done or not done, such shall not be deemed a deviation, but shall be considered as due fulfilment of this Charter Party.	739 740 741

22. Law and Arbitration — 742

*) (a) This Charter Party shall be governed by and construed in accordance with English law and any dispute arising out of or in connection with this Charter Party shall be referred to arbitration in London in accordance with the Arbitration Act 1996 or any statutory modification or re-enactment thereof save to the extent necessary to give effect to the provisions of this Clause. — 743–747

The arbitration shall be conducted in accordance with the London Maritime Arbitrators Association (LMAA) Terms current at the time when the arbitration proceedings are commenced. — 748–750

The reference shall be to three arbitrators. A party wishing to refer a dispute to arbitration shall appoint its arbitrator and send notice of such appointment in writing to the other party requiring the other party to appoint its own arbitrator within 14 calendar days of that notice and stating that it will appoint its arbitrator as sole arbitrator unless the other party appoints its own arbitrator and gives notice that it has done so within the 14 days specified. If the other party does not appoint its own arbitrator and give notice that it has done so within the 14 days specified, the party referring a dispute to arbitration may, without the requirement of any further prior notice to the other party, appoint its arbitrator as sole arbitrator and shall advise the other party accordingly. The award of a sole arbitrator shall be binding on both parties as if he had been appointed by agreement. — 751–762

Nothing herein shall prevent the parties agreeing in writing to vary these provisions to provide for the appointment of a sole arbitrator. — 763–764

In cases where neither the claim nor any counterclaim exceeds the sum of USD 50,000 (or such other sum as the parties may agree) the arbitration shall be conducted in accordance with the LMAA Small Claims Procedure current at the time when the arbitration proceedings are commenced. — 765–768

*) (b) This Charter Party shall be governed by and construed in accordance with Title 9 of the United States Code and the Maritime Law of the United States and any dispute arising out of or in connection with this Charter Party shall be referred to three persons at New York, one to be appointed by each of the parties hereto, and the third by the two so chosen; their decision or that of any two of them shall be final, and for the purposes of enforcing any award, judgement may be entered on an award by any court of competent jurisdiction. The proceedings shall be conducted in accordance with the rules of the Society of Maritime Arbitrators, Inc. — 769–777

In cases where neither the claim nor any counterclaim exceeds the sum of USD 50,000 (or such other sum as the parties may agree) the arbitration shall — 778–779

be conducted in accordance with the Shortened Arbitration Procedure of the Society of Maritime Arbitrators, Inc. current at the time when the arbitration proceedings are commenced. — 780–782

*) (c) This Charter Party shall be governed by and construed in accordance with the laws of the place mutually agreed by the parties and stated in Box 35 and any dispute arising out of or in connection with this Charter Party shall be referred to arbitration at the place stated in Box 35, subject to the procedures applicable there. — 783–787

(d) If Box 35 in Part I is not appropriately filled in, sub-clause (a) of this Clause shall apply. — 788–789

*) (a), (b) and (c) are alternatives; indicate alternative agreed in Box 35 — 790

23. Commission — 791

The Owners shall pay a commission at the rate stated in Box 36 to the Broker(s) stated in Box 36 on any hire paid under this Charter Party or any continuation or extension thereof. If the full hire is not paid owing to breach of Charter Party by either of the parties the party liable therefor shall indemnify the Brokers against their loss of commission. — 792–796

Should the parties agree to cancel this Charter Party, the Owners shall indemnify the Brokers against any loss of commission but in such case the commission shall not exceed the brokerage on one year's hire. — 797–799

In signing this Charter Party the Owners acknowledge their agreement with the brokers to pay the commissions described in this Clause. — 800–801

24. Notices — 802

Any notices as between the Owners and the Charterers shall be in writing and sent to the addresses stated in Boxes 2 and 3 as the case may be or to such other addresses as either party may designate to the other in writing. — 803–805

"GENTIME" General Time Charter Party
Appendix A - Protective Clauses

A.   **WAR RISKS ("Voywar 1993")**

(1) For the purpose of this Clause, the words:

(a) "Owners" shall include the shipowners, bareboat charterers, disponent owners, managers or other operators who are charged with the management of the Vessel, and the Master; and

(b) "War Risks" shall include any war (whether actual or threatened), act of war, civil war, hostilities, revolution, rebellion, civil commotion, warlike operations, the laying of mines (whether actual or reported), acts of piracy, acts of terrorists, acts of hostility or malicious damage, blockades (whether imposed against all vessels or imposed selectively against vessels of certain flags or ownership, or against certain cargoes or crews or otherwise howsoever), by any person, body, terrorist or political group, or the Government of any state whatsoever, which, in the reasonable judgement of the Master and/or the Owners, may be dangerous or are likely to be or to become dangerous to the Vessel, her cargo, crew or other persons on board the Vessel.

(2) If at any time before the Vessel commences loading, it appears that, in the reasonable judgement of the Master and/or the Owners, performance of the Contract of Carriage, or any part of it, may expose, or is likely to expose, the Vessel, her cargo, crew or other persons on board the Vessel to War Risks, the Owners may give notice to the Charterers cancelling this Contract of Carriage, or may refuse to perform such part of it as may expose, or may be likely to expose, the Vessel, her cargo, crew or other persons on board the Vessel to War Risks; provided always that if this Contract of Carriage provides that loading or discharging is to take place within a range of ports, and at the port or ports nominated by the Charterers the Vessel, her cargo, crew, or other persons on board the Vessel may be exposed, or may be likely to be exposed, to War Risks, the Owners shall first require the Charterers to nominate any other safe port which lies within the range for loading or discharging, and may only cancel this Contract of Carriage if the Charterers shall not have nominated such safe port or ports within 48 hours of receipt of notice of such requirement.

(3) The Owners shall not be required to continue to load cargo for any voyage, or to sign Bills of Lading for any port or place, or to proceed or continue on any voyage, or on any part thereof, or to proceed through any canal or waterway, or to proceed to or remain at any port or place whatsoever, where it appears, either after the loading of the cargo commences, or at any stage of the voyage thereafter before the discharge of the cargo is completed, that, in the reasonable judgement of the Master and/or the Owners, the Vessel, her cargo (or any part thereof), crew or other persons on board the Vessel (or any one or more of them) may be, or are likely to be, exposed to War Risks. If it should so appear, the Owners may by notice request the Charterers to nominate a safe port for the discharge of the cargo or any part thereof, and if within 48 hours of the receipt of such notice, the Charterers shall not have nominated such a port, the Owners may discharge the cargo at any safe port of their choice (including the port of loading) in complete fulfilment of the Contract of Carriage. The Owners shall be entitled to recover from the Charterers the extra expenses of such discharge and, if the discharge takes place at any port other than the loading port, to receive the full freight as though the cargo had been carried to the discharging port and if the extra distance exceeds 100 miles, to additional freight which shall be the same percentage of the freight contracted for as the percentage which the extra distance represents to the distance of the normal and customary route, the Owners having a lien on the cargo for such expenses and freight.

(4) If at any stage of the voyage after the loading of the cargo commences, it appears that, in the reasonable judgement of the Master and/or the Owners, the Vessel, her cargo, crew or other persons on board the Vessel may be, or are likely to be, exposed to War Risks on any part of the route (including any canal or waterway) which is normally and customarily used in a voyage of the nature contracted for, and there is another longer route to the discharging port, the Owners shall give notice to the Charterers that this route will be taken. In this event the Owners shall be entitled, if the total extra distance exceeds 100 miles, to additional freight which shall be the same percentage of the freight contracted for as the percentage which the extra distance represents to the distance of the normal and customary route.

(5) The Vessel shall have liberty:-

(a) to comply with all orders, directions, recommendations or advice as to departure, arrival, routes, sailing in convoy, ports of call, stoppages, destinations, discharge of cargo, delivery or in any way whatsoever which are given by the Government of the Nation under whose flag the Vessel sails, or other Government to whose laws the Owners are subject, or any other Government which so requires, or any body or group acting with the power to compel compliance with their orders or directions;

(b) to comply with the orders, directions or recommendations of any war risks underwriters who have the authority to give the same under the terms of the war risks insurance;

(c) to comply with the terms of any resolution of the Security Council of the United Nations, any directives of the European Community, the effective orders of any other Supranational body which has the right to issue and give the same, and with national laws aimed at enforcing the same to which the Owners are subject, and to obey the orders and directions of those who are charged with their enforcement;

(d) to discharge at any other port any cargo or part thereof which may render the Vessel liable to confiscation as a contraband carrier;

(e) to call at any other port to change the crew or any part thereof or other persons on board the Vessel when there is reason to believe that they may be subject to internment, imprisonment or other sanctions;

(f) where cargo has not been loaded or has been discharged by the Owners under any provisions of this Clause, to load other cargo for the Owners' own benefit and carry it to any other port or ports whatsoever, whether backwards or forwards or in a contrary direction to the ordinary or customary route.

(6) If in compliance with any of the provisions of sub-clauses (2) to (5) of this Clause anything is done or not done, such shall not be deemed to be a deviation, but shall be considered as due fulfilment of the Contract of Carriage.

B.   **CLAUSE PARAMOUNT**

The International Convention for the Unification of Certain Rules of Law relating to Bills of Lading signed at Brussels on 24 August 1924 ("the Hague Rules") as amended by the Protocol signed at Brussels on 23 February 1968 ("the Hague-Visby Rules") and as enacted in the country of shipment shall apply to this Contract. When the Hague-Visby Rules are not enacted in the country of shipment, the corresponding legislation in the country of destination shall apply, irrespective of whether such legislation may only regulate outbound shipments.

When there is no enactment of the Hague-Visby Rules in either the country of shipment or in the country of destination, the Hague-Visby Rules shall apply to this Contract, save where the Hague Rules as enacted in the country of shipment or if no such enactment is in place the Hague Rules as enacted in the country of destination apply compulsorily to this Contract.

The Protocol signed at Brussels on 21 December 1979 ("the SDR Protocol 1979") shall apply where the Hague-Visby Rules apply whether mandatorily or by this Contract.

The Carrier shall in no case be responsible for loss of or damage to cargo arising prior to loading, after discharging, or while the cargo is in the charge of another carrier, or with respect to deck cargo and live animals.

C.   **GENERAL AVERAGE**

General Average shall be adjusted and settled at a port or place in the option of the Carrier according to the York-Antwerp Rules, 1994 or any subsequent amendment thereto.

D.   **HIMALAYA CLAUSE**

It is hereby expressly agreed that no servant or agent of the Carrier (including every independent contractor from time to time employed by the Carrier) shall in any circumstances whatsoever be under any liability whatsoever to the Charterers, Shippers, Consignees, owner of the goods or to any holder of a Bill of Lading issued under this Charter Party, for any loss, damage or delay of whatsoever kind arising or resulting directly or indirectly from any act, neglect or default on his part while acting in the course of or in connection with his employment.

Without prejudice to the generality of the foregoing provisions in this clause, every exemption, limitation, condition and liberty herein contained and every right, exemption from liability, defence and immunity of whatsoever nature applicable to the Carrier or to which the Carrier is entitled hereunder; shall also be available and shall extend to protect every such servant or agent of the Carrier acting as aforesaid.

For the purpose of all the foregoing provisions of this clause the Carrier is or shall be deemed to be acting as agents or trustees on behalf of and for the benefit of all persons who might be his servants or agents from time to time (including independent contractors as aforesaid) and all such persons shall to this extent be or be deemed to be parties to this contract.

E.   **NEW JASON CLAUSE**

In the event of accident, danger, damage or disaster before or after the

"GENTIME" General Time Charter Party
Appendix A - Protective Clauses

commencement of the voyage resulting from any cause whatsoever, whether due to negligence or not, for which, or for the consequences of which, the Carrier is not responsible, by statute, contract, or otherwise, the goods, shippers, consignees, or owners of the goods shall contribute with the Carrier in general average to the payment of any sacrifices, losses, or expenses of a general average nature that may be made or incurred, and shall pay salvage and special charges incurred in respect of the goods.

If a salving vessel is owned or operated by the Carrier, salvage shall be paid for as fully as if salving vessel or vessels belonged to strangers. Such deposit as the Carrier or his agents may deem sufficient to cover the estimated contribution of the goods and any salvage and special charges thereon shall, if required, be made by the goods, shippers, consignees or owners of the goods to the Carrier before delivery.

F.   BOTH-TO-BLAME COLLISION CLAUSE

If the Vessel comes into collision with another vessel as a result of the negligence of the other vessel and any act, neglect or default of the master, mariner, pilot or the servants of the Carrier in the navigation or in the management of the vessel, the owners of the goods carried hereunder will indemnify the Carrier against all loss or liability to the other or non-carrying vessel or her owners insofar as such loss or liability represents loss of, or damage to, or any claim whatsoever of the owners of said goods, paid or payable by the other or non-carrying vessel or her owners to the owners of said goods and set-off, recouped or recovered by the other or non-carrying vessel or her owners as part of their claim against the carrying Vessel or Carrier.

The foregoing provisions shall also apply where the owners, operators or those in charge of any vessels or objects other than, or in addition to, the colliding vessels or objects are at fault in respect to a collision or contact.

1. Shipbroker	**BIMCO STANDARD BAREBOAT CHARTER**
	CODE NAME: "BARECON 2001" PART I
	2. Place and date

3. Owners/Place of business (Cl. 1)	4. Bareboat Charterers/Place of business (Cl. 1)

5. Vessel's name, call sign and flag (Cl. 1 and 3)	

6. Type of Vessel	7. GT/NT

8. When/Where built	9. Total DWT (abt.) in metric tons on summer freeboard

10. Classification Society (Cl. 3)	11. Date of last special survey by the Vessel's classification society

12. Further particulars of Vessel (also indicate minimum number of months' validity of class certificates agreed acc. to Cl. 3)

13. Port or Place of delivery (Cl. 3)	14. Time for delivery (Cl. 4)	15. Cancelling date (Cl. 5)

16. Port or Place of redelivery (Cl. 15)	17. No. of months' validity of trading and class certificates upon redelivery (Cl. 15)	

18. Running days' notice if other than stated in Cl. 4	19. Frequency of dry-docking (Cl. 10(g))

20. Trading limits (Cl. 6)	

21. Charter period (Cl. 2)	22. Charter hire (Cl. 11)

23. New class and other safety requirements (state percentage of Vessel's insurance value acc. to Box 29)(Cl. 10(a)(ii))

24. Rate of interest payable acc. to Cl. 11(f) and, if applicable, acc. to PART IV	25. Currency and method of payment (Cl. 11)

Printed and sold by Fr. G. Knudtzons Bogtrykkeri A/S,
Vallensbaekvej 61, DK-2625 Vallensbaek, Fax: +45 4366 0701

continued

(continued) "BARECON 2001" STANDARD BAREBOAT CHARTER PART I

26. Place of payment; also state beneficiary and bank account (Cl. 11)	27. Bank guarantee/bond (sum and place)(Cl. 24)(optional)
28. Mortgage(s), if any (state whether 12(a) or (b) applies; if 12(b) applies state date of Financial Instrument and name of Mortgagee(s)/Place of business)(Cl. 12)	29. Insurance (hull and machinery and war risks)(state value acc. to Cl. 13(f) or, if applicable, acc. to Cl. 14(k))(also state if Cl. 14 applies)
30. Additional insurance cover, if any, for Owners' account limited to (Cl. 13(b) or, if applicable, Cl. 14(g))	31. Additional insurance cover, if any, for Charterers' account limited to (Cl. 13(b) or, if applicable, Cl. 14(g))
32. Latent defects (only to be filled in if period other than stated in Cl. 3)	33. Brokerage commission and to whom payable (Cl. 27)
34. Grace period (state number of clear banking days)(Cl. 28)	35. Dispute Resolution (state 30(a), 30(b) or 30(c); if 30(c) agreed Place of Arbitration *must* be stated (Cl. 30)
36. War cancellation (indicate countries agreed)(Cl. 26(f))	
37. Newbuilding Vessel (indicate with "yes" or "no" whether PART III applies)(optional)	38. Name and place of Builders (only to be filled in if PART III applies)
39. Vessel's Yard Building No. (only to be filled in if PART III applies)	40. Date of Building Contract (only to be filled in if PART III applies)
41. Liquidated damages and costs shall accrue to (state party acc. to Cl. 1) a) b) c)	
42. Hire/Purchase agreement (indicate with "yes" or "no" whether PART IV applies)(optional)	43. Bareboat Charter Registry (indicate "yes" or "no" whether PART V applies)(optional)
44. Flag and Country of the Bareboat Charter Registry (only to be filled in if PART V applies)	45. Country of the Underlying Registry (only to be filled in if PART V applies)
46. Number of additional clauses covering special provisions, if agreed	

PREAMBLE - It is mutually agreed that this Contract shall be performed subject to the conditions contained in this Charter which shall include PART I and PART II. In the event of a conflict of conditions, the provisions of PART I shall prevail over those of PART II to the extent of such conflict but no further. It is further mutually agreed that PART III and/or PART IV and/or PART V shall only apply and only form part of this Charter if expressly agreed and stated in the Boxes 37, 42 and 43. If PART III and/or PART IV and/or PART V apply, it is further agreed that in the event of a conflict of conditions, the provisions of PART I and PART II shall prevail over those of PART III and/or PART IV and/or PART V to the extent of such conflict but no further.

Signature (Owners)	Signature (Charterers)

PART II
"BARECON 2001" Standard Bareboat Charter

1. Definitions   1
In this Charter, the following terms shall have the   2
meanings hereby assigned to them: 3
"*The Owners*" shall mean the party identified in Box 3;   4
"*The Charterers*" shall mean the party identified in Box 4;   5
"*The Vessel*" shall mean the vessel named in Box 5 and   6
with particulars as stated in Boxes 6 to 12.   7
"*Financial Instrument*" means the mortgage, deed of   8
covenant or other such financial security instrument as   9
annexed to this Charter and stated in Box 28.   10

2. Charter Period   11
In consideration of the hire detailed in Box 22, the   12
Owners have agreed to let and the Charterers have   13
agreed to hire the Vessel for the period stated in Box 21   14
("The Charter Period").   15

3. Delivery   16
(not applicable when Part III applies, as indicated in Box 37)   17
(a) The Owners shall before and at the time of delivery   18
exercise due diligence to make the Vessel seaworthy   19
and in every respect ready in hull, machinery and   20
equipment for service under this Charter.   21
The Vessel shall be delivered by the Owners and taken   22
over by the Charterers at the port or place indicated in   23
Box 13 in such ready safe berth as the Charterers may   24
direct.   25
(b) The Vessel shall be properly documented on   26
delivery in accordance with the laws of the flag State   27
indicated in Box 5 and the requirements of the   28
classification society stated in Box 10. The Vessel upon   29
delivery shall have her survey cycles up to date and   30
trading and class certificates valid for at least the number   31
of months agreed in Box 12.   32
(c) The delivery of the Vessel by the Owners and the   33
taking over of the Vessel by the Charterers shall   34
constitute a full performance by the Owners of all the   35
Owners' obligations under this Clause 3, and thereafter   36
the Charterers shall not be entitled to make or assert   37
any claim against the Owners on account of any   38
conditions, representations or warranties expressed or   39
implied with respect to the Vessel but the Owners shall   40
be liable for the cost of but not the time for repairs or   41
renewals occasioned by latent defects in the Vessel,   42
her machinery or appurtenances, existing at the time of   43
delivery under this Charter, provided such defects have   44
manifested themselves within twelve (12) months after   45
delivery unless otherwise provided in Box 32.   46

4. Time for Delivery   47
(not applicable when Part III applies, as indicated in Box 37)   48
The Vessel shall not be delivered before the date   49
indicated in Box 14 without the Charterers' consent and   50
the Owners shall exercise due diligence to deliver the   51
Vessel not later than the date indicated in Box 15.   52
Unless otherwise agreed in Box 18, the Owners shall   53
give the Charterers not less than thirty (30) running days'   54
preliminary and not less than fourteen (14) running days'   55
definite notice of the date on which the Vessel is   56
expected to be ready for delivery.   57
The Owners shall keep the Charterers closely advised   58
of possible changes in the Vessel's position.   59

5. Cancelling   60
(not applicable when Part III applies, as indicated in Box 37)   61
(a) Should the Vessel not be delivered latest by the   62
cancelling date indicated in Box 15, the Charterers shall   63
have the option of cancelling this Charter by giving the   64

Owners notice of cancellation within thirty-six (36)   65
running hours after the cancelling date stated in Box   66
15, failing which this Charter shall remain in full force   67
and effect.   68
(b) If it appears that the Vessel will be delayed beyond   69
the cancelling date, the Owners may, as soon as they   70
are in a position to state with reasonable certainty the   71
day on which the Vessel should be ready, give notice   72
thereof to the Charterers asking whether they will   73
exercise their option of cancelling, and the option must   74
then be declared within one hundred and sixty-eight   75
(168) running hours of the receipt by the Charterers of   76
such notice or within thirty-six (36) running hours after   77
the cancelling date, whichever is the earlier. If the   78
Charterers do not then exercise their option of cancelling,   79
the seventh day after the readiness date stated in the   80
Owners' notice shall be substituted for the cancelling   81
date indicated in Box 15 for the purpose of this Clause 5.   82
(c) Cancellation under this Clause 5 shall be without   83
prejudice to any claim the Charterers may otherwise   84
have on the Owners under this Charter.   85

6. Trading Restrictions   86
The Vessel shall be employed in lawful trades for the   87
carriage of suitable lawful merchandise within the trading   88
limits indicated in Box 20.   89
The Charterers undertake not to employ the Vessel or   90
suffer the Vessel to be employed otherwise than in   91
conformity with the terms of the contracts of insurance   92
(including any warranties expressed or implied therein)   93
without first obtaining the consent of the insurers to such   94
employment and complying with such requirements as   95
to extra premium or otherwise as the insurers may   96
prescribe.   97
The Charterers also undertake not to employ the Vessel   98
or suffer her employment in any trade or business which   99
is forbidden by the law of any country to which the Vessel   100
may sail or is otherwise illicit or in carrying illicit or   101
prohibited goods or in any manner whatsoever which   102
may render her liable to condemnation, destruction,   103
seizure or confiscation.   104
Notwithstanding any other provisions contained in this   105
Charter it is agreed that nuclear fuels or radioactive   106
products or waste are specifically excluded from the   107
cargo permitted to be loaded or carried under this   108
Charter. This exclusion does not apply to radio-isotopes   109
used or intended to be used for any industrial,   110
commercial, agricultural, medical or scientific purposes   111
provided the Owners' prior approval has been obtained   112
to loading thereof.   113

7. Surveys on Delivery and Redelivery   114
(not applicable when Part III applies, as indicated in Box 37)   115
The Owners and Charterers shall each appoint   116
surveyors for the purpose of determining and agreeing   117
in writing the condition of the Vessel at the time of   118
delivery and redelivery hereunder. The Owners shall   119
bear all expenses of the On-hire Survey including loss   120
of time, if any, and the Charterers shall bear all expenses   121
of the Off-hire Survey including loss of time, if any, at   122
the daily equivalent to the rate of hire or pro rata thereof.   123

8. Inspection   124
The Owners shall have the right at any time after giving   125
reasonable notice to the Charterers to inspect or survey   126
the Vessel or instruct a duly authorised surveyor to carry   127
out such survey on their behalf:-   128
(a) to ascertain the condition of the Vessel and satisfy   129

PART II
"BARECON 2001" Standard Bareboat Charter

themselves that the Vessel is being properly repaired 130
and maintained. The costs and fees for such inspection 131
or survey shall be paid by the Owners unless the Vessel 132
is found to require repairs or maintenance in order to 133
achieve the condition so provided; 134
(b) in dry-dock if the Charterers have not dry-docked 135
her in accordance with Clause 10(g). The costs and fees 136
for such inspection or survey shall be paid by the 137
Charterers; and 138
(c) for any other commercial reason they consider 139
necessary (provided it does not unduly interfere with 140
the commercial operation of the Vessel). The costs and 141
fees for such inspection and survey shall be paid by the 142
Owners. 143
All time used in respect of inspection, survey or repairs 144
shall be for the Charterers' account and form part of the 145
Charter Period. 146
The Charterers shall also permit the Owners to inspect 147
the Vessel's log books whenever requested and shall 148
whenever required by the Owners furnish them with full 149
information regarding any casualties or other accidents 150
or damage to the Vessel. 151

9. **Inventories, Oil and Stores** 152
A complete inventory of the Vessel's entire equipment, 153
outfit including spare parts, appliances and of all 154
consumable stores on board the Vessel shall be made 155
by the Charterers in conjunction with the Owners on 156
delivery and again on redelivery of the Vessel. The 157
Charterers and the Owners, respectively, shall at the 158
time of delivery and redelivery take over and pay for all 159
bunkers, lubricating oil, unbroached provisions, paints, 160
ropes and other consumable stores (excluding spare 161
parts) in the said Vessel at then current market prices 162
at the ports of delivery and redelivery, respectively. The 163
Charterers shall ensure that all spare parts listed in the 164
inventory and used during the Charter Period are 165
replaced at their expense prior to redelivery of the 166
Vessel. 167

10. **Maintenance and Operation** 168
(a)(i) Maintenance and Repairs - During the Charter 169
Period the Vessel shall be in the full possession 170
and at the absolute disposal for all purposes of the 171
Charterers and under their complete control in 172
every respect. The Charterers shall maintain the 173
Vessel, her machinery, boilers, appurtenances and 174
spare parts in a good state of repair, in efficient 175
operating condition and in accordance with good 176
commercial maintenance practice and, except as 177
provided for in Clause 14(l), if applicable, at their 178
own expense they shall at all times keep the 179
Vessel's Class fully up to date with the Classification 180
Society indicated in Box 10 and maintain all other 181
necessary certificates in force at all times. 182
(ii) New Class and Other Safety Requirements - In the 183
event of any improvement, structural changes or 184
new equipment becoming necessary for the 185
continued operation of the Vessel by reason of new 186
class requirements or by compulsory legislation 187
costing (excluding the Charterers' loss of time) 188
more than the percentage stated in Box 23, or if 189
Box 23 is left blank, 5 per cent. of the Vessel's 190
insurance value as stated in Box 29, then the 191
extent, if any, to which the rate of hire shall be varied 192
and the ratio in which the cost of compliance shall 193
be shared between the parties concerned in order 194
to achieve a reasonable distribution thereof as 195

between the Owners and the Charterers having 196
regard, inter alia, to the length of the period 197
remaining under this Charter shall, in the absence 198
of agreement, be referred to the dispute resolution 199
method agreed in Clause 30. 200
(iii) Financial Security - The Charterers shall maintain 201
financial security or responsibility in respect of third 202
party liabilities as required by any government, 203
including federal, state or municipal or other division 204
or authority thereof, to enable the Vessel, without 205
penalty or charge, lawfully to enter, remain at, or 206
leave any port, place, territorial or contiguous 207
waters of any country, state or municipality in 208
performance of this Charter without any delay. This 209
obligation shall apply whether or not such 210
requirements have been lawfully imposed by such 211
government or division or authority thereof. 212
The Charterers shall make and maintain all arrange- 213
ments by bond or otherwise as may be necessary to 214
satisfy such requirements at the Charterers' sole 215
expense and the Charterers shall indemnify the Owners 216
against all consequences whatsoever (including loss of 217
time) for any failure or inability to do so. 218
(b) Operation of the Vessel - The Charterers shall at 219
their own expense and by their own procurement man, 220
victual, navigate, operate, supply, fuel and, whenever 221
required, repair the Vessel during the Charter Period 222
and they shall pay all charges and expenses of every 223
kind and nature whatsoever incidental to their use and 224
operation of the Vessel under this Charter, including 225
annual flag State fees and any foreign general 226
municipality and/or state taxes. The Master, officers and 227
crew of the Vessel shall be the servants of the Charterers 228
for all purposes whatsoever, even if for any reason 229
appointed by the Owners. 230
Charterers shall comply with the regulations regarding 231
officers and crew in force in the country of the Vessel's 232
flag or any other applicable law. 233
(c) The Charterers shall keep the Owners and the 234
mortgagee(s) advised of the intended employment, 235
planned dry-docking and major repairs of the Vessel, 236
as reasonably required. 237
(d) Flag and Name of Vessel - During the Charter 238
Period, the Charterers shall have the liberty to paint the 239
Vessel in their own colours, install and display their 240
funnel insignia and fly their own house flag. The 241
Charterers shall also have the liberty, with the Owners' 242
consent, which shall not be unreasonably withheld, to 243
change the flag and/or the name of the Vessel during 244
the Charter Period. Painting and re-painting, instalment 245
and re-instalment, registration and re-registration, if 246
required by the Owners, shall be at the Charterers' 247
expense and time. 248
(e) Changes to the Vessel – Subject to Clause 10(a)(ii), 249
the Charterers shall make no structural changes in the 250
Vessel or changes in the machinery, boilers, appurten- 251
ances or spare parts thereof without in each instance 252
first securing the Owners' approval thereof. If the Owners 253
so agree, the Charterers shall, if the Owners so require, 254
restore the Vessel to its former condition before the 255
termination of this Charter. 256
(f) Use of the Vessel's Outfit, Equipment and 257
Appliances - The Charterers shall have the use of all 258
outfit, equipment, and appliances on board the Vessel 259
at the time of delivery, provided the same or their 260
substantial equivalent shall be returned to the Owners 261
on redelivery in the same good order and condition as 262
when received, ordinary wear and tear excepted. The 263

PART II
"BARECON 2001" Standard Bareboat Charter

Charterers shall from time to time during the Charter 264
Period replace such items of equipment as shall be so 265
damaged or worn as to be unfit for use. The Charterers 266
are to procure that all repairs to or replacement of any 267
damaged, worn or lost parts or equipment be effected 268
in such manner (both as regards workmanship and 269
quality of materials) as not to diminish the value of the 270
Vessel. The Charterers have the right to fit additional 271
equipment at their expense and risk but the Charterers 272
shall remove such equipment at the end of the period if 273
requested by the Owners. Any equipment including radio 274
equipment on hire on the Vessel at time of delivery shall 275
be kept and maintained by the Charterers and the 276
Charterers shall assume the obligations and liabilities 277
of the Owners under any lease contracts in connection 278
therewith and shall reimburse the Owners for all 279
expenses incurred in connection therewith, also for any 280
new equipment required in order to comply with radio 281
regulations. 282
(g) Periodical Dry-Docking - The Charterers shall dry- 283
dock the Vessel and clean and paint her underwater 284
parts whenever the same may be necessary, but not 285
less than once during the period stated in Box 19 or, if 286
Box 19 has been left blank, every sixty (60) calendar 287
months after delivery or such other period as may be 288
required by the Classification Society or flag State. 289

11. Hire 290
(a) The Charterers shall pay hire due to the Owners 291
punctually in accordance with the terms of this Charter 292
in respect of which time shall be of the essence. 293
(b) The Charterers shall pay to the Owners for the hire 294
of the Vessel a lump sum in the amount indicated in 295
Box 22 which shall be payable not later than every thirty 296
(30) running days in advance, the first lump sum being 297
payable on the date and hour of the Vessel's delivery to 298
the Charterers. Hire shall be paid continuously 299
throughout the Charter Period. 300
(c) Payment of hire shall be made in cash without 301
discount in the currency and in the manner indicated in 302
Box 25 and at the place mentioned in Box 26. 303
(d) Final payment of hire, if for a period of less than 304
thirty (30) running days, shall be calculated proportionally 305
according to the number of days and hours remaining 306
before redelivery and advance payment to be effected 307
accordingly. 308
(e) Should the Vessel be lost or missing, hire shall 309
cease from the date and time when she was lost or last 310
heard of. The date upon which the Vessel is to be treated 311
as lost or missing shall be ten (10) days after the Vessel 312
was last reported or when the Vessel is posted as 313
missing by Lloyd's, whichever occurs first. Any hire paid 314
in advance to be adjusted accordingly. 315
(f) Any delay in payment of hire shall entitle the 316
Owners to interest at the rate per annum as agreed in 317
Box 24. If Box 24 has not been filled in, the three months 318
interbank offered rate in London (LIBOR or its successor) 319
for the currency stated in Box 25, as quoted by the British 320
Bankers' Association (BBA) on the date when the hire 321
fell due, increased by 2 per cent., shall apply. 322
(g) Payment of interest due under sub-clause 11(f) 323
shall be made within seven (7) running days of the date 324
of the Owners' invoice specifying the amount payable 325
or, in the absence of an invoice, at the time of the next 326
hire payment date. 327

12. Mortgage 328
(only to apply if Box 28 has been appropriately filled in) 329

*) **(a)** The Owners warrant that they have not effected 330
any mortgage(s) of the Vessel and that they shall not 331
effect any mortgage(s) without the prior consent of the 332
Charterers, which shall not be unreasonably withheld. 333
*) **(b)** The Vessel chartered under this Charter is financed 334
by a mortgage according to the Financial Instrument. 335
The Charterers undertake to comply, and provide such 336
information and documents to enable the Owners to 337
comply, with all such instructions or directions in regard 338
to the employment, insurances, operation, repairs and 339
maintenance of the Vessel as laid down in the Financial 340
Instrument or as may be directed from time to time during 341
the currency of the Charter by the mortgagee(s) in 342
conformity with the Financial Instrument. The Charterers 343
confirm that, for this purpose, they have acquainted 344
themselves with all relevant terms, conditions and 345
provisions of the Financial Instrument and agree to 346
acknowledge this in writing in any form that may be 347
required by the mortgagee(s). The Owners warrant that 348
they have not effected any mortgage(s) other than stated 349
in Box 28 and that they shall not agree to any 350
amendment of the mortgage(s) referred to in Box 28 or 351
effect any other mortgage(s) without the prior consent 352
of the Charterers, which shall not be unreasonably 353
withheld. 354
*) *(Optional, Clauses 12(a) and 12(b) are alternatives;* 355
indicate alternative agreed in Box 28). 356

13. Insurance and Repairs 357
(a) During the Charter Period the Vessel shall be kept 358
insured by the Charterers at their expense against hull 359
and machinery, war and Protection and Indemnity risks 360
(and any risks against which it is compulsory to insure 361
for the operation of the Vessel, including maintaining 362
financial security in accordance with sub-clause 363
10(a)(iii)) in such form as the Owners shall in writing 364
approve, which approval shall not be un-reasonably 365
withheld. Such insurances shall be arranged by the 366
Charterers to protect the interests of both the Owners 367
and the Charterers and the mortgagee(s) (if any), and 368
the Charterers shall be at liberty to protect under such 369
insurances the interests of any managers they may 370
appoint. Insurance policies shall cover the Owners and 371
the Charterers according to their respective interests. 372
Subject to the provisions of the Financial Instrument, if 373
any, and the approval of the Owners and the insurers, 374
the Charterers shall effect all insured repairs and shall 375
undertake settlement and reimbursement from the 376
insurers of all costs in connection with such repairs as 377
well as insured charges, expenses and liabilities to the 378
extent of coverage under the insurances herein provided 379
for. 380
The Charterers also to remain responsible for and to 381
effect repairs and settlement of costs and expenses 382
incurred thereby in respect of all other repairs not 383
covered by the insurances and/or not exceeding any 384
possible franchise(s) or deductibles provided for in the 385
insurances. 386
All time used for repairs under the provisions of sub- 387
clause 13(a) and for repairs of latent defects according 388
to Clause 3(c) above, including any deviation, shall be 389
for the Charterers' account. 390
(b) If the conditions of the above insurances permit 391
additional insurance to be placed by the parties, such 392
cover shall be limited to the amount for each party set 393
out in Box 30 and Box 31, respectively. The Owners or 394
the Charterers as the case may be shall immediately 395
furnish the other party with particulars of any additional 396

PART II
"BARECON 2001" Standard Bareboat Charter

insurance effected, including copies of any cover notes 397
or policies and the written consent of the insurers of 398
any such required insurance in any case where the 399
consent of such insurers is necessary. 400

(c) The Charterers shall upon the request of the 401
Owners, provide information and promptly execute such 402
documents as may be required to enable the Owners to 403
comply with the insurance provisions of the Financial 404
Instrument. 405

(d) Subject to the provisions of the Financial Instru- 406
ment, if any, should the Vessel become an actual, 407
constructive, compromised or agreed total loss under 408
the insurances required under sub-clause 13(a), all 409
insurance payments for such loss shall be paid to the 410
Owners who shall distribute the moneys between the 411
Owners and the Charterers according to their respective 412
interests. The Charterers undertake to notify the Owners 413
and the mortgagee(s), if any, of any occurrences in 414
consequence of which the Vessel is likely to become a 415
total loss as defined in this Clause. 416

(e) The Owners shall upon the request of the 417
Charterers, promptly execute such documents as may 418
be required to enable the Charterers to abandon the 419
Vessel to insurers and claim a constructive total loss. 420

(f) For the purpose of insurance coverage against hull 421
and machinery and war risks under the provisions of 422
sub-clause 13(a), the value of the Vessel is the sum 423
indicated in Box 29. 424

14. Insurance, Repairs and Classification 425
(Optional, only to apply if expressly agreed and stated 426
in Box 29, in which event Clause 13 shall be considered 427
deleted). 428

(a) During the Charter Period the Vessel shall be kept 429
insured by the Owners at their expense against hull and 430
machinery and war risks under the form of policy or 431
policies attached hereto. The Owners and/or insurers 432
shall not have any right of recovery or subrogation 433
against the Charterers on account of loss of or any 434
damage to the Vessel or her machinery or appurt- 435
enances covered by such insurance, or on account of 436
payments made to discharge claims against or liabilities 437
of the Vessel or the Owners covered by such insurance. 438
Insurance policies shall cover the Owners and the 439
Charterers according to their respective interests. 440

(b) During the Charter Period the Vessel shall be kept 441
insured by the Charterers at their expense against 442
Protection and Indemnity risks (and any risks against 443
which it is compulsory to insure for the operation of the 444
Vessel, including maintaining financial security in 445
accordance with sub-clause 10(a)(iii)) in such form as 446
the Owners shall in writing approve which approval shall 447
not be unreasonably withheld. 448

(c) In the event that any act or negligence of the 449
Charterers shall vitiate any of the insurance herein 450
provided, the Charterers shall pay to the Owners all 451
losses and indemnify the Owners against all claims and 452
demands which would otherwise have been covered by 453
such insurance. 454

(d) The Charterers shall, subject to the approval of the 455
Owners or Owners' Underwriters, effect all insured 456
repairs, and the Charterers shall undertake settlement 457
of all miscellaneous expenses in connection with such 458
repairs as well as all insured charges, expenses and 459
liabilities, to the extent of coverage under the insurances 460
provided for under the provisions of sub-clause 14(a). 461
The Charterers to be secured reimbursement through 462
the Owners' Underwriters for such expenditures upon 463

presentation of accounts. 464

(e) The Charterers to remain responsible for and to 465
effect repairs and settlement of costs and expenses 466
incurred thereby in respect of all other repairs not 467
covered by the insurances and/or not exceeding any 468
possible franchise(s) or deductibles provided for in the 469
insurances. 470

(f) All time used for repairs under the provisions of 471
sub-clauses 14(d) and 14(e) and for repairs of latent 472
defects according to Clause 3 above, including any 473
deviation, shall be for the Charterers' account and shall 474
form part of the Charter Period. 475
The Owners shall not be responsible for any expenses 476
as are incident to the use and operation of the Vessel 477
for such time as may be required to make such repairs. 478

(g) If the conditions of the above insurances permit 479
additional insurance to be placed by the parties such 480
cover shall be limited to the amount for each party set 481
out in Box 30 and Box 31, respectively. The Owners or 482
the Charterers as the case may be shall immediately 483
furnish the other party with particulars of any additional 484
insurance effected, including copies of any cover notes 485
or policies and the written consent of the insurers of 486
any such required insurance in any case where the 487
consent of such insurers is necessary. 488

(h) Should the Vessel become an actual, constructive, 489
compromised or agreed total loss under the insurances 490
required under sub-clause 14(a), all insurance payments 491
for such loss shall be paid to the Owners, who shall 492
distribute the moneys between themselves and the 493
Charterers according to their respective interests. 494

(i) If the Vessel becomes an actual, constructive, 495
compromised or agreed total loss under the insurances 496
arranged by the Owners in accordance with sub-clause 497
14(a), this Charter shall terminate as of the date of such 498
loss. 499

(j) The Charterers shall upon the request of the 500
Owners, promptly execute such documents as may be 501
required to enable the Owners to abandon the Vessel 502
to the insurers and claim a constructive total loss. 503

(k) For the purpose of insurance coverage against hull 504
and machinery and war risks under the provisions of 505
sub-clause 14(a), the value of the Vessel is the sum 506
indicated in Box 29. 507

(l) Notwithstanding anything contained in sub-clause 508
10(a), it is agreed that under the provisions of Clause 509
14, if applicable, the Owners shall keep the Vessel's 510
Class fully up to date with the Classification Society 511
indicated in Box 10 and maintain all other necessary 512
certificates in force at all times. 513

15. Redelivery 514
At the expiration of the Charter Period the Vessel shall 515
be redelivered by the Charterers to the Owners at a 516
safe and ice-free port or place as indicated in Box 16, in 517
such ready safe berth as the Owners may direct. The 518
Charterers shall give the Owners not less than thirty 519
(30) running days' preliminary notice of expected date, 520
range of ports of redelivery or port or place of redelivery 521
and not less than fourteen (14) running days' definite 522
notice of expected date and port or place of redelivery. 523
Any changes thereafter in the Vessel's position shall be 524
notified immediately to the Owners. 525
The Charterers warrant that they will not permit the 526
Vessel to commence a voyage (including any preceding 527
ballast voyage) which cannot reasonably be expected 528
to be completed in time to allow redelivery of the Vessel 529
within the Charter Period. Notwithstanding the above, 530

PART II
"BARECON 2001" Standard Bareboat Charter

should the Charterers fail to redeliver the Vessel within 531
the Charter Period, the Charterers shall pay the daily 532
equivalent to the rate of hire stated in Box 22 plus 10 533
per cent. or to the market rate, whichever is the higher, 534
for the number of days by which the Charter Period is 535
exceeded. All other terms, conditions and provisions of 536
this Charter shall continue to apply. 537
Subject to the provisions of Clause 10, the Vessel shall 538
be redelivered to the Owners in the same or as good 539
structure, state, condition and class as that in which she 540
was delivered, fair wear and tear not affecting class 541
excepted. 542
The Vessel upon redelivery shall have her survey cycles 543
up to date and trading and class certificates valid for at 544
least the number of months agreed in Box 17. 545

16. Non-Lien 546
The Charterers will not suffer, nor permit to be continued, 547
any lien or encumbrance incurred by them or their 548
agents, which might have priority over the title and 549
interest of the Owners in the Vessel. The Charterers 550
further agree to fasten to the Vessel in a conspicuous 551
place and to keep so fastened during the Charter Period 552
a notice reading as follows: 553
"This Vessel is the property of (name of Owners). It is 554
under charter to (name of Charterers) and by the terms 555
of the Charter Party neither the Charterers nor the 556
Master have any right, power or authority to create, incur 557
or permit to be imposed on the Vessel any lien 558
whatsoever." 559

17. Indemnity 560
(a) The Charterers shall indemnify the Owners against 561
any loss, damage or expense incurred by the Owners 562
arising out of or in relation to the operation of the Vessel 563
by the Charterers, and against any claim of whatsoever 564
nature arising out of an event occurring during the 565
Charter Period. If the Vessel be arrested or otherwise 566
detained by reason of claims or liens arising out of her 567
operation hereunder by the Charterers, the Charterers 568
shall at their own expense take all reasonable steps to 569
secure that within a reasonable time the Vessel is 570
released, including the provision of bail. 571
Without prejudice to the generality of the foregoing, the 572
Charterers agree to indemnify the Owners against all 573
consequences or liabilities arising from the Master, 574
officers or agents signing Bills of Lading or other 575
documents. 576
(b) If the Vessel be arrested or otherwise detained by 577
reason of a claim or claims against the Owners, the 578
Owners shall at their own expense take all reasonable 579
steps to secure that within a reasonable time the Vessel 580
is released, including the provision of bail. 581
In such circumstances the Owners shall indemnify the 582
Charterers against any loss, damage or expense 583
incurred by the Charterers (including hire paid under 584
this Charter) as a direct consequence of such arrest or 585
detention. 586

18. Lien 587
The Owners to have a lien upon all cargoes, sub-hires 588
and sub-freights belonging or due to the Charterers or 589
any sub-charterers and any Bill of Lading freight for all 590
claims under this Charter, and the Charterers to have a 591
lien on the Vessel for all moneys paid in advance and 592
not earned. 593

19. Salvage 594
All salvage and towage performed by the Vessel shall 595
be for the Charterers' benefit and the cost of repairing 596
damage occasioned thereby shall be borne by the 597
Charterers. 598

20. Wreck Removal 599
In the event of the Vessel becoming a wreck or 600
obstruction to navigation the Charterers shall indemnify 601
the Owners against any sums whatsoever which the 602
Owners shall become liable to pay and shall pay in 603
consequence of the Vessel becoming a wreck or 604
obstruction to navigation. 605

21. General Average 606
The Owners shall not contribute to General Average. 607

22. Assignment, Sub-Charter and Sale 608
(a) The Charterers shall not assign this Charter nor 609
sub-charter the Vessel on a bareboat basis except with 610
the prior consent in writing of the Owners, which shall 611
not be unreasonably withheld, and subject to such terms 612
and conditions as the Owners shall approve. 613
(b) The Owners shall not sell the Vessel during the 614
currency of this Charter except with the prior written 615
consent of the Charterers, which shall not be unreason- 616
ably withheld, and subject to the buyer accepting an 617
assignment of this Charter. 618

23. Contracts of Carriage 619
*) **(a)** The Charterers are to procure that all documents 620
issued during the Charter Period evidencing the terms 621
and conditions agreed in respect of carriage of goods 622
shall contain a paramount clause incorporating any 623
legislation relating to carrier's liability for cargo 624
compulsorily applicable in the trade; if no such legislation 625
exists, the documents shall incorporate the Hague-Visby 626
Rules. The documents shall also contain the New Jason 627
Clause and the Both-to-Blame Collision Clause. 628
*) **(b)** The Charterers are to procure that all passenger 629
tickets issued during the Charter Period for the carriage 630
of passengers and their luggage under this Charter shall 631
contain a paramount clause incorporating any legislation 632
relating to carrier's liability for passengers and their 633
luggage compulsorily applicable in the trade; if no such 634
legislation exists, the passenger tickets shall incorporate 635
the Athens Convention Relating to the Carriage of 636
Passengers and their Luggage by Sea, 1974, and any 637
protocol thereto. 638
*) *Delete as applicable.* 639

24. Bank Guarantee 640
(Optional, only to apply if Box 27 filled in) 641
The Charterers undertake to furnish, before delivery of 642
the Vessel, a first class bank guarantee or bond in the 643
sum and at the place as indicated in Box 27 as guarantee 644
for full performance of their obligations under this 645
Charter. 646

25. Requisition/Acquisition 647
(a) In the event of the Requisition for Hire of the Vessel 648
by any governmental or other competent authority 649
(hereinafter referred to as "Requisition for Hire") 650
irrespective of the date during the Charter Period when 651
"Requisition for Hire" may occur and irrespective of the 652
length thereof and whether or not it be for an indefinite 653

PART II
"BARECON 2001" Standard Bareboat Charter

or a limited period of time, and irrespective of whether it 654
may or will remain in force for the remainder of the 655
Charter Period, this Charter shall not be deemed thereby 656
or thereupon to be frustrated or otherwise terminated 657
and the Charterers shall continue to pay the stipulated 658
hire in the manner provided by this Charter until the time 659
when the Charter would have terminated pursuant to 660
any of the provisions hereof always provided however 661
that in the event of "Requisition for Hire" any Requisition 662
Hire or compensation received or receivable by the 663
Owners shall be payable to the Charterers during the 664
remainder of the Charter Period or the period of the 665
"Requisition for Hire" whichever be the shorter. 666
 (b) In the event of the Owners being deprived of their 667
ownership in the Vessel by any Compulsory Acquisition 668
of the Vessel or requisition for title by any governmental 669
or other competent authority (hereinafter referred to as 670
"Compulsory Acquisition"), then, irrespective of the date 671
during the Charter Period when "Compulsory Acqui- 672
sition" may occur, this Charter shall be deemed 673
terminated as of the date of such "Compulsory 674
Acquisition". In such event Charter Hire to be considered 675
as earned and to be paid up to the date and time of 676
such "Compulsory Acquisition". 677

26. War 678
 (a) For the purpose of this Clause, the words "War 679
Risks" shall include any war (whether actual or 680
threatened), act of war, civil war, hostilities, revolution, 681
rebellion, civil commotion, warlike operations, the laying 682
of mines (whether actual or reported), acts of piracy, 683
acts of terrorists, acts of hostility or malicious damage, 684
blockades (whether imposed against all vessels or 685
imposed selectively against vessels of certain flags or 686
ownership, or against certain cargoes or crews or 687
otherwise howsoever), by any person, body, terrorist or 688
political group, or the Government of any state 689
whatsoever, which may be dangerous or are likely to be 690
or to become dangerous to the Vessel, her cargo, crew 691
or other persons on board the Vessel. 692
 (b) The Vessel, unless the written consent of the 693
Owners be first obtained, shall not continue to or go 694
through any port, place, area or zone (whether of land 695
or sea), or any waterway or canal, where it reasonably 696
appears that the Vessel, her cargo, crew or other 697
persons on board the Vessel, in the reasonable 698
judgement of the Owners, may be, or are likely to be, 699
exposed to War Risks. Should the Vessel be within any 700
such place as aforesaid, which only becomes danger- 701
ous, or is likely to be or to become dangerous, after her 702
entry into it, the Owners shall have the right to require 703
the Vessel to leave such area. 704
 (c) The Vessel shall not load contraband cargo, or to 705
pass through any blockade, whether such blockade be 706
imposed on all vessels, or is imposed selectively in any 707
way whatsoever against vessels of certain flags or 708
ownership, or against certain cargoes or crews or 709
otherwise howsoever, or to proceed to an area where 710
she shall be subject, or is likely to be subject to a 711
belligerent's right of search and/or confiscation. 712
 (d) If the insurers of the war risks insurance, when 713
Clause 14 is applicable, should require payment of 714
premiums and/or calls because, pursuant to the 715
Charterers' orders, the Vessel is within, or is due to enter 716
and remain within, any area or areas which are specified 717
by such insurers as being subject to additional premiums 718
because of War Risks, then such premiums and/or calls 719
shall be reimbursed by the Charterers to the Owners at 720

the same time as the next payment of hire is due. 721
 (e) The Charterers shall have the liberty: 722
 (i) to comply with all orders, directions, recommend- 723
    ations or advice as to departure, arrival, routes, 724
    sailing in convoy, ports of call, stoppages, 725
    destinations, discharge of cargo, delivery, or in any 726
    other way whatsoever, which are given by the 727
    Government of the Nation under whose flag the 728
    Vessel sails, or any other Government, body or 729
    group whatsoever acting with the power to compel 730
    compliance with their orders or directions; 731
 (ii) to comply with the orders, directions or recom- 732
    mendations of any war risks underwriters who have 733
    the authority to give the same under the terms of 734
    the war risks insurance; 735
 (iii) to comply with the terms of any resolution of the 736
    Security Council of the United Nations, any 737
    directives of the European Community, the effective 738
    orders of any other Supranational body which has 739
    the right to issue and give the same, and with 740
    national laws aimed at enforcing the same to which 741
    the Owners are subject, and to obey the orders 742
    and directions of those who are charged with their 743
    enforcement. 744
 (f) In the event of outbreak of war (whether there be a 745
declaration of war or not) (i) between any two or more 746
of the following countries: the United States of America; 747
Russia; the United Kingdom; France; and the People's 748
Republic of China, (ii) between any two or more of the 749
countries stated in Box 36, both the Owners and the 750
Charterers shall have the right to cancel this Charter, 751
whereupon the Charterers shall redeliver the Vessel to 752
the Owners in accordance with Clause 15, if the Vessel 753
has cargo on board after discharge thereof at 754
destination, or if debarred under this Clause from 755
reaching or entering it at a near, open and safe port as 756
directed by the Owners, or if the Vessel has no cargo 757
on board, at the port at which the Vessel then is or if at 758
sea at a near, open and safe port as directed by the 759
Owners. In all cases hire shall continue to be paid in 760
accordance with Clause 11 and except as aforesaid all 761
other provisions of this Charter shall apply until 762
redelivery. 763

27. Commission 764
The Owners to pay a commission at the rate indicated 765
in Box 33 to the Brokers named in Box 33 on any hire 766
paid under the Charter. If no rate is indicated in Box 33, 767
the commission to be paid by the Owners shall cover 768
the actual expenses of the Brokers and a reasonable 769
fee for their work. 770
If the full hire is not paid owing to breach of the Charter 771
by either of the parties the party liable therefor shall 772
indemnify the Brokers against their loss of commission. 773
Should the parties agree to cancel the Charter, the 774
Owners shall indemnify the Brokers against any loss of 775
commission but in such case the commission shall not 776
exceed the brokerage on one year's hire. 777

28. Termination 778
 (a) Charterers' Default 779
The Owners shall be entitled to withdraw the Vessel from 780
the service of the Charterers and terminate the Charter 781
with immediate effect by written notice to the Charterers if: 782
 (i) the Charterers fail to pay hire in accordance with 783
    Clause 11. However, where there is a failure to 784
    make punctual payment of hire due to oversight, 785
    negligence, errors or omissions on the part of the 786

PART II
"BARECON 2001" Standard Bareboat Charter

Charterers or their bankers, the Owners shall give 787
the Charterers written notice of the number of clear 788
banking days stated in Box 34 (as recognised at 789
the agreed place of payment) in which to rectify 790
the failure, and when so rectified within such 791
number of days following the Owners' notice, the 792
payment shall stand as regular and punctual. 793
Failure by the Charterers to pay hire within the 794
number of days stated in Box 34 of their receiving 795
the Owners' notice as provided herein, shall entitle 796
the Owners to withdraw the Vessel from the service 797
of the Charterers and terminate the Charter without 798
further notice; 799

(ii) the Charterers fail to comply with the requirements of: 800
    (1) Clause 6 (Trading Restrictions) 801
    (2) Clause 13(a) (Insurance and Repairs) 802
    provided that the Owners shall have the option, by 803
    written notice to the Charterers, to give the 804
    Charterers a specified number of days grace within 805
    which to rectify the failure without prejudice to the 806
    Owners' right to withdraw and terminate under this 807
    Clause if the Charterers fail to comply with such 808
    notice; 809

(iii) the Charterers fail to rectify any failure to comply 810
with the requirements of sub-clause 10(a)(i) 811
(Maintenance and Repairs) as soon as practically 812
possible after the Owners have requested them in 813
writing so to do and in any event so that the Vessel's 814
insurance cover is not prejudiced. 815

(b) Owners' Default 816
If the Owners shall by any act or omission be in breach 817
of their obligations under this Charter to the extent that 818
the Charterers are deprived of the use of the Vessel 819
and such breach continues for a period of fourteen (14) 820
running days after written notice thereof has been given 821
by the Charterers to the Owners, the Charterers shall 822
be entitled to terminate this Charter with immediate effect 823
by written notice to the Owners. 824

(c) Loss of Vessel 825
This Charter shall be deemed to be terminated if the 826
Vessel becomes a total loss or is declared as a 827
constructive or compromised or arranged total loss. For 828
the purpose of this sub-clause, the Vessel shall not be 829
deemed to be lost unless she has either become an 830
actual total loss or agreement has been reached with 831
her underwriters in respect of her constructive, 832
compromised or arranged total loss or if such agreement 833
with her underwriters is not reached it is adjudged by a 834
competent tribunal that a constructive loss of the Vessel 835
has occurred. 836

(d) Either party shall be entitled to terminate this 837
Charter with immediate effect by written notice to the 838
other party in the event of an order being made or 839
resolution passed for the winding up, dissolution, 840
liquidation or bankruptcy of the other party (otherwise 841
than for the purpose of reconstruction or amalgamation) 842
or if a receiver is appointed, or if it suspends payment, 843
ceases to carry on business or makes any special 844
arrangement or composition with its creditors. 845

(e) The termination of this Charter shall be without 846
prejudice to all rights accrued due between the parties 847
prior to the date of termination and to any claim that 848
either party might have. 849

29. Repossession 850
In the event of the termination of this Charter in 851
accordance with the applicable provisions of Clause 28, 852
the Owners shall have the right to repossess the Vessel 853

from the Charterers at her current or next port of call, or 854
at a port or place convenient to them without hindrance 855
or interference by the Charterers, courts or local 856
authorities. Pending physical repossession of the Vessel 857
in accordance with this Clause 29, the Charterers shall 858
hold the Vessel as gratuitous bailee only to the Owners. 859
The Owners shall arrange for an authorised represent- 860
ative to board the Vessel as soon as reasonably 861
practicable following the termination of the Charter. The 862
Vessel shall be deemed to be repossessed by the 863
Owners from the Charterers upon the boarding of the 864
Vessel by the Owners' representative. All arrangements 865
and expenses relating to the settling of wages, 866
disembarkation and repatriation of the Charterers' 867
Master, officers and crew shall be the sole responsibility 868
of the Charterers. 869

30. Dispute Resolution 870
*) **(a)** This Contract shall be governed by and construed 871
in accordance with English law and any dispute arising 872
out of or in connection with this Contract shall be referred 873
to arbitration in London in accordance with the Arbitration 874
Act 1996 or any statutory modification or re-enactment 875
thereof save to the extent necessary to give effect to 876
the provisions of this Clause. 877
The arbitration shall be conducted in accordance with 878
the London Maritime Arbitrators Association (LMAA) 879
Terms current at the time when the arbitration proceed- 880
ings are commenced. 881
The reference shall be to three arbitrators. A party 882
wishing to refer a dispute to arbitration shall appoint its 883
arbitrator and send notice of such appointment in writing 884
to the other party requiring the other party to appoint its 885
own arbitrator within 14 calendar days of that notice and 886
stating that it will appoint its arbitrator as sole arbitrator 887
unless the other party appoints its own arbitrator and 888
gives notice that it has done so within the 14 days 889
specified. If the other party does not appoint its own 890
arbitrator and give notice that it has done so within the 891
14 days specified, the party referring a dispute to 892
arbitration may, without the requirement of any further 893
prior notice to the other party, appoint its arbitrator as 894
sole arbitrator and shall advise the other party 895
accordingly. The award of a sole arbitrator shall be 896
binding on both parties as if he had been appointed by 897
agreement. 898
Nothing herein shall prevent the parties agreeing in 899
writing to vary these provisions to provide for the 900
appointment of a sole arbitrator. 901
In cases where neither the claim nor any counterclaim 902
exceeds the sum of US$50,000 (or such other sum as 903
the parties may agree) the arbitration shall be conducted 904
in accordance with the LMAA Small Claims Procedure 905
current at the time when the arbitration proceedings are 906
commenced. 907
*) **(b)** This Contract shall be governed by and construed 908
in accordance with Title 9 of the United States Code 909
and the Maritime Law of the United States and any 910
dispute arising out of or in connection with this Contract 911
shall be referred to three persons at New York, one to 912
be appointed by each of the parties hereto, and the third 913
by the two so chosen; their decision or that of any two 914
of them shall be final, and for the purposes of enforcing 915
any award, judgement may be entered on an award by 916
any court of competent jurisdiction. The proceedings 917
shall be conducted in accordance with the rules of the 918
Society of Maritime Arbitrators, Inc. 919
In cases where neither the claim nor any counterclaim 920

PART II
"BARECON 2001" Standard Bareboat Charter

exceeds the sum of US$50,000 (or such other sum as the parties may agree) the arbitration shall be conducted in accordance with the Shortened Arbitration Procedure of the Society of Maritime Arbitrators, Inc. current at the time when the arbitration proceedings are commenced. 921-925

*) **(c)** This Contract shall be governed by and construed in accordance with the laws of the place mutually agreed by the parties and any dispute arising out of or in connection with this Contract shall be referred to arbitration at a mutually agreed place, subject to the procedures applicable there. 926-931

(d) Notwithstanding (a), (b) or (c) above, the parties may agree at any time to refer to mediation any difference and/or dispute arising out of or in connection with this Contract. 932-935

In the case of a dispute in respect of which arbitration has been commenced under (a), (b) or (c) above, the following shall apply:- 936-938

(i) Either party may at any time and from time to time elect to refer the dispute or part of the dispute to mediation by service on the other party of a written notice (the "Mediation Notice") calling on the other party to agree to mediation. 939-943

(ii) The other party shall thereupon within 14 calendar days of receipt of the Mediation Notice confirm that they agree to mediation, in which case the parties shall thereafter agree a mediator within a further 14 calendar days, failing which on the application of either party a mediator will be appointed promptly by the Arbitration Tribunal ("the Tribunal") or such person as the Tribunal may designate for that purpose. The mediation shall be conducted in such place and in accordance with such procedure and on such terms as the parties may agree or, in the event of disagreement, as may be set by the mediator. 944-956

(iii) If the other party does not agree to mediate, that 957 fact may be brought to the attention of the Tribunal and may be taken into account by the Tribunal when allocating the costs of the arbitration as between the parties. 958-961

(iv) The mediation shall not affect the right of either party to seek such relief or take such steps as it considers necessary to protect its interest. 962-964

(v) Either party may advise the Tribunal that they have agreed to mediation. The arbitration procedure shall continue during the conduct of the mediation but the Tribunal may take the mediation timetable into account when setting the timetable for steps in the arbitration. 965-970

(vi) Unless otherwise agreed or specified in the mediation terms, each party shall bear its own costs incurred in the mediation and the parties shall share equally the mediator's costs and expenses. 971-974

(vii) The mediation process shall be without prejudice and confidential and no information or documents disclosed during it shall be revealed to the Tribunal except to the extent that they are disclosable under the law and procedure governing the arbitration. 975-979

(Note: The parties should be aware that the mediation process may not necessarily interrupt time limits.) 980-981

(e) If Box 35 in Part I is not appropriately filled in, sub-clause 30(a) of this Clause shall apply. Sub-clause 30(d) shall apply in all cases. 982-984

*) *Sub-clauses 30(a), 30(b) and 30(c) are alternatives; indicate alternative agreed in Box 35.* 985-986

31. Notices 987

(a) Any notice to be given by either party to the other party shall be in writing and may be sent by fax, telex, registered or recorded mail or by personal service. 988-990

(b) The address of the Parties for service of such communication shall be as stated in Boxes 3 and 4 respectively. 991-993

"BARECON 2001" Standard Bareboat Charter

PART III
PROVISIONS TO APPLY FOR NEWBUILDING VESSELS ONLY
(Optional, only to apply if expressly agreed and stated in Box 37)

1. Specifications and Building Contract

(a) The Vessel shall be constructed in accordance with the Building Contract (hereafter called "the Building Contract") as annexed to this Charter, made between the Builders and the Owners and in accordance with the specifications and plans annexed thereto, such Building Contract, specifications and plans having been countersigned as approved by the Charterers. 1–8

(b) No change shall be made in the Building Contract or in the specifications or plans of the Vessel as approved by the Charterers as aforesaid, without the Charterers' consent. 9–12

(c) The Charterers shall have the right to send their representative to the Builders' Yard to inspect the Vessel during the course of her construction to satisfy themselves that construction is in accordance with such approved specifications and plans as referred to under sub-clause (a) of this Clause. 13–18

(d) The Vessel shall be built in accordance with the Building Contract and shall be of the description set out therein. Subject to the provisions of sub-clause 2(c)(ii) hereunder, the Charterers shall be bound to accept the Vessel from the Owners, completed and constructed in accordance with the Building Contract, on the date of delivery by the Builders. The Charterers undertake that having accepted the Vessel they will not thereafter raise any claims against the Owners in respect of the Vessel's performance or specification or defects, if any. Nevertheless, in respect of any repairs, replacements or defects which appear within the first 12 months from delivery by the Builders, the Owners shall endeavour to compel the Builders to repair, replace or remedy any defects or to recover from the Builders any expenditure incurred in carrying out such repairs, replacements or remedies. However, the Owners' liability to the Charterers shall be limited to the extent the Owners have a valid claim against the Builders under the guarantee clause of the Building Contract (a copy whereof has been supplied to the Charterers). The Charterers shall be bound to accept such sums as the Owners are reasonably able to recover under this Clause and shall make no further claim on the Owners for the difference between the amount(s) so recovered and the actual expenditure on repairs, replacement or remedying defects or for any loss of time incurred. 19–44

Any liquidated damages for physical defects or deficiencies shall accrue to the account of the party stated in Box 41(a) or if not filled in shall be shared equally between the parties. The costs of pursuing a claim or claims against the Builders under this Clause (including any liability to the Builders) shall be borne by the party stated in Box 41(b) or if not filled in shall be shared equally between the parties. 45–51

2. Time and Place of Delivery

(a) Subject to the Vessel having completed her acceptance trials including trials of cargo equipment in accordance with the Building Contract and specifications to the satisfaction of the Charterers, the Owners shall give and the Charterers shall take delivery of the Vessel afloat when ready for delivery and properly documented at the Builders' Yard or some other safe and readily accessible dock, wharf or place as may be agreed between the parties hereto and the Builders. Under the Building Contract the Builders have estimated that the Vessel will be ready for delivery to the Owners as therein provided but the delivery date for the purpose of this Charter shall be the date when the Vessel is in fact ready for delivery by the Builders after completion of trials whether that be before or after as indicated in the Building Contract. The Charterers shall not be entitled to refuse acceptance of delivery of the Vessel 52–68

and upon and after such acceptance, subject to Clause 1(d), the Charterers shall not be entitled to make any claim against the Owners in respect of any conditions, representations or warranties, whether express or implied, as to the seaworthiness of the Vessel or in respect of delay in delivery. 69–74

(b) If for any reason other than a default by the Owners under the Building Contract, the Builders become entitled under that Contract not to deliver the Vessel to the Owners, the Owners shall upon giving to the Charterers written notice of Builders becoming so entitled, be excused from giving delivery of the Vessel to the Charterers and upon receipt of such notice by the Charterers this Charter shall cease to have effect. 75–82

(c) If for any reason the Owners become entitled under the Building Contract to reject the Vessel the Owners shall, before exercising such right of rejection, consult the Charterers and thereupon 83–86

(i) if the Charterers do not wish to take delivery of the Vessel they shall inform the Owners within seven (7) running days by notice in writing and upon receipt by the Owners of such notice this Charter shall cease to have effect; or 87–90

(ii) if the Charterers wish to take delivery of the Vessel they may by notice in writing within seven (7) running days require the Owners to negotiate with the Builders as to the terms on which delivery should be taken and/or refrain from exercising their right to rejection and upon receipt of such notice the Owners shall commence such negotiations and/or take delivery of the Vessel from the Builders and deliver her to the Charterers; 91–98

(iii) in no circumstances shall the Charterers be entitled to reject the Vessel unless the Owners are able to reject the Vessel from the Builders; 99–101

(iv) if this Charter terminates under sub-clause (b) or (c) of this Clause, the Owners shall thereafter not be liable to the Charterers for any claim under or arising out of this Charter or its termination. 102–105

(d) Any liquidated damages for delay in delivery under the Building Contract and any costs incurred in pursuing a claim therefor shall accrue to the account of the party stated in Box 41(c) or if not filled in shall be shared equally between the parties. 106–110

3. Guarantee Works

If not otherwise agreed, the Owners authorise the Charterers to arrange for the guarantee works to be performed in accordance with the building contract terms, and hire to continue during the period of guarantee works. The Charterers have to advise the Owners about the performance to the extent the Owners may request. 111–117

4. Name of Vessel

The name of the Vessel shall be mutually agreed between the Owners and the Charterers and the Vessel shall be painted in the colours, display the funnel insignia and fly the house flag as required by the Charterers. 118–122

5. Survey on Redelivery

The Owners and the Charterers shall appoint surveyors for the purpose of determining and agreeing in writing the condition of the Vessel at the time of re-delivery. Without prejudice to Clause 15 (Part II), the Charterers shall bear all survey expenses and all other costs, if any, including the cost of docking and undocking, if required, as well as all repair costs incurred. The Charterers shall also bear all loss of time spent in connection with any docking and undocking as well as repairs, which shall be paid at the rate of hire per day or pro rata. 123–133

"BARECON 2001" Standard Bareboat Charter

PART IV
HIRE/PURCHASE AGREEMENT
(Optional, only to apply if expressly agreed and stated in Box 42)

On expiration of this Charter and provided the Charterers have fulfilled their obligations according to Part I and II as well as Part III, if applicable, it is agreed, that on payment of the final payment of hire as per Clause 11 the Charterers have purchased the Vessel with everything belonging to her and the Vessel is fully paid for. (1–7)

In the following paragraphs the Owners are referred to as the Sellers and the Charterers as the Buyers. (8–9)

The Vessel shall be delivered by the Sellers and taken over by the Buyers on expiration of the Charter. (10–11)

The Sellers guarantee that the Vessel, at the time of delivery, is free from all encumbrances and maritime liens or any debts whatsoever other than those arising from anything done or not done by the Buyers or any existing mortgage agreed not to be paid off by the time of delivery. Should any claims, which have been incurred prior to the time of delivery be made against the Vessel, the Sellers hereby undertake to indemnify the Buyers against all consequences of such claims to the extent it can be proved that the Sellers are responsible for such claims. Any taxes, notarial, consular and other charges and expenses connected with the purchase and registration under Buyers' flag, shall be for Buyers' account. Any taxes, consular and other charges and expenses connected with closing of the Sellers' register, shall be for Sellers' account. (12–27)

In exchange for payment of the last month's hire instalment the Sellers shall furnish the Buyers with a Bill of Sale duly attested and legalized, together with a certificate setting out the registered encumbrances, if any. On delivery of the Vessel the Sellers shall provide for deletion of the Vessel from the Ship's Register and deliver a certificate of deletion to the Buyers. (28–34)

The Sellers shall, at the time of delivery, hand to the Buyers all classification certificates (for hull, engines, anchors, chains, etc.), as well as all plans which may be in Sellers' possession. (35–38)

The Wireless Installation and Nautical Instruments, unless on hire, shall be included in the sale without any extra payment. (39–41)

The Vessel with everything belonging to her shall be at Sellers' risk and expense until she is delivered to the Buyers, subject to the conditions of this Contract and the Vessel with everything belonging to her shall be delivered and taken over as she is at the time of delivery, after which the Sellers shall have no responsibility for possible faults or deficiencies of any description. (42–48)

The Buyers undertake to pay for the repatriation of the Master, officers and other personnel if appointed by the Sellers to the port where the Vessel entered the Bareboat Charter as per Clause 3 (Part II) or to pay the equivalent cost for their journey to any other place. (49–53)

PART V
PROVISIONS TO APPLY FOR VESSELS REGISTERED IN A BAREBOAT CHARTER REGISTRY
(Optional, only to apply if expressly agreed and stated in Box 43)

1. Definitions

For the purpose of this PART V, the following terms shall have the meanings hereby assigned to them:
"The Bareboat Charter Registry" shall mean the registry of the State whose flag the Vessel will fly and in which the Charterers are registered as the bareboat charterers during the period of the Bareboat Charter.
"The Underlying Registry" shall mean the registry of the State in which the Owners of the Vessel are registered as Owners and to which jurisdiction and control of the Vessel will revert upon termination of the Bareboat Charter Registration. (1–12)

2. Mortgage

The Vessel chartered under this Charter is financed by a mortgage and the provisions of Clause 12(b) (Part II) shall apply. (13–16)

3. Termination of Charter by Default

If the Vessel chartered under this Charter is registered in a Bareboat Charter Registry as stated in Box 44, and if the Owners shall default in the payment of any amounts due under the mortgage(s) specified in Box 28, the Charterers shall, if so required by the mortgagee, direct the Owners to re-register the Vessel in the Underlying Registry as shown in Box 45.
In the event of the Vessel being deleted from the Bareboat Charter Registry as stated in Box 44, due to a default by the Owners in the payment of any amounts due under the mortgage(s), the Charterers shall have the right to terminate this Charter forthwith and without prejudice to any other claim they may have against the Owners under this Charter. (17–31)

BILL OF LADING

TO BE USED WITH CHARTER-PARTIES
CODE NAME: "CONGENBILL"
EDITION 1994
ADOPTED BY
THE BALTIC AND INTERNATIONAL MARITIME COUNCIL (BIMCO)

Conditions of Carriage

(1) All terms and conditions, liberties and exceptions of the Charter Party, dated as overleaf, including the Law and Arbitration Clause, are herewith incorporated.

(2) **General Paramount Clause.**
(a) The Hague Rules contained in the International Convention for the Unification of certain rules relating to Bills of Lading, dated Brussels the 25th August 1924 as enacted in the country of shipment, shall apply to this Bill of Lading. When no such enactment is in force in the country of shipment, the corresponding legislation of the country of destination shall apply, but in respect of shipments to which no such enactments are compulsorily applicable, the terms of the said Convention shall apply.

(b) Trades where Hague-Visby Rules apply.
In trades where the International Brussels Convention 1924 as amended by the Protocol signed at Brussels on February 23rd 1968 - the Hague-Visby Rules - apply compulsorily, the provisions of the respective legislation shall apply to this Bill of Lading.

(c) The Carrier shall in no case be responsible for loss of or damage to the cargo, howsoever arising prior to loading into and after discharge from the Vessel or while the cargo is in the charge of another Carrier, nor in respect of deck cargo or live animals.

(3) **General Average.**
General Average shall be adjusted, stated and settled according to York-Antwerp Rules 1994, or any subsequent modification thereof, in London unless another place is agreed in the Charter Party.
Cargo's contribution to General Average shall be paid to the Carrier even when such average is the result of a fault, neglect or error of the Master, Pilot or Crew. The Charterers, Shippers and Consignees expressly renounce the Belgian Commercial Code, Part II, Art. 148.

(4) **New Jason Clause.**
In the event of accident, danger, damage or disaster before or after the commencement of the voyage, resulting from any cause whatsoever, whether due to negligence or not, for which, or for the consequence of which, the Carrier is not responsible, by statute, contract or otherwise, the cargo, shippers, consignees or the owners of the cargo shall contribute with the Carrier in General Average to the payment of any sacrifices, losses or expenses of a General Average nature that may be made or incurred and shall pay salvage and special charges incurred in respect of the cargo. If a salving vessel is owned or operated by the Carrier, salvage shall be paid for as fully as if the said salving vessel or vessels belonged to strangers. Such deposit as the Carrier, or his agents, may deem sufficient to cover the estimated contribution of the goods and any salvage and special charges thereon shall, if required, be made by the cargo, shippers, consignees or owners of the goods to the Carrier before delivery.

(5) **Both-to-Blame Collision Clause.**
If the Vessel comes into collision with another vessel as a result of the negligence of the other vessel and any act, neglect or default of the Master, Mariner, Pilot or the servants of the Carrier in the navigation or in the management of the Vessel, the owners of the cargo carried hereunder will indemnify the Carrier against all loss or liability to the other or non-carrying vessel or her owners in so far as such loss or liability represents loss of, or damage to, or any claim whatsoever of the owners of said cargo, paid or payable by the other or non-carrying vessel or her owners to the owners of said cargo and set-off, recouped or recovered by the other or non-carrying vessel or her owners as part of their claim against the carrying Vessel or the Carrier.
The foregoing provisions shall also apply where the owners, operators or those in charge of any vessel or vessels or objects other than, or in addition to, the colliding vessels or objects are at fault in respect of a collision or contact.

For particulars of cargo, freight, destination, etc., see overleaf.

CODE NAME: "CONGENBILL". EDITION 1994

Shipper

BILL OF LADING
TO BE USED WITH CHARTER-PARTIES

B/L No.

Page 2

Reference No.

Consignee

Notify address

Draft Copy

Vessel   Port of loading

Port of discharge

Shipper's description of goods   Gross weight

Draft Copy

(of which   on deck at Shipper's risk; the Carrier not
being responsible for loss or damage howsoever arising)

Freight payable as per
CHARTER-PARTY dated

FREIGHT ADVANCE.
Received on account of freight:

Time used for loading   days   hours.

SHIPPED at the Port of Loading in apparent good order and
condition on board the Vessel for carriage to the Port
of Discharge or so near thereto as she may safely get the goods specified above.

Weight, measure, quality, quantity, condition, contents and value unknown.

IN WITNESS whereof the Master or Agent of the said Vessel has signed
the number of Bills of Lading indicated below all of this tenor and date,
any one of which being accomplished the others shall be void.

FOR CONDITIONS OF CARRIAGE SEE OVERLEAF

Freight payable at	Place and date of issue
Number of original Bs/L	Signature

Printed by the BIMCO Charter Party Editor

Page 1

Shipper (full style and address)	**BIMCO LINER BILL OF LADING**	
	CODE NAME: "CONLINEBILL 2000"	
	Amended January 1950; August 1952; January 1973; July 1974; August 1976; January 1978; November 2000.	

Consignee (full style and address) or Order	B/L No.	Reference No.
	Vessel	
Notify Party (full style and address)	Port of loading	
	Port of discharge	

PARTICULARS DECLARED BY THE SHIPPER BUT NOT ACKNOWLEDGED BY THE CARRIER

Container No./Seal No./Marks and Numbers	Number and kind of packages; description of cargo	Gross weight, kg	Measurement, m³

Draft Copy

SHIPPED on board in apparent good order and condition (unless otherwise stated herein) the total number of Containers/Packages or Units indicated in the Box opposite entitled "Total number of Containers/Packages or Units received by the Carrier" and the cargo as specified above, weight, measure, marks, numbers, quality, contents and value unknown, for carriage to the Port of discharge or so near thereunto as the vessel may safely get and lie always afloat, to be delivered in the like good order and condition at the Port of discharge unto the lawful holder of the Bill of Lading, on payment of freight as indicated to the right plus other charges incurred in accordance with the provisions contained in this Bill of Lading. In accepting this Bill of Lading the Merchant* expressly accepts and agrees to all its stipulations on both Page 1 and Page 2, whether written, printed, stamped or otherwise incorporated, as fully as if they were all signed by the Merchant. One original Bill of Lading must be surrendered duly endorsed in exchange for the cargo or delivery order, whereupon all other Bills of Lading to be void. IN WITNESS whereof the Carrier, Master or their Agent has signed the number of original Bills of Lading stated below right, all of this tenor and date.

	Total number of Containers/Packages or Units received by the Carrier	
	Shipper's declared value	Declared value charge
	Freight details and charges	

Carrier's name/principal place of business	Date shipped on board	Place and date of issue
	Number of original Bills of Lading	
	Pre-carriage by**	
Signature	Place of receipt by pre-carrier**	
.... Carrier		
or, for the Carrier		
.... as Master	Place of delivery by on-carrier**	
(Master's name/signature)		
.... as Agents		
(Agent's name/signature)		

*As defined hereinafter (Cl 1)
**Applicable only when pre-/on-carriage is arranged in accordance with Clause 8

Printed and sold by Fr. G. Knudtzons Bogtrykkeri A/S, Vallensbaekvej 61, DK-2625 Vallensbaek, Fax: +45 4366 070

BIMCO LINER BILL OF LADING

Code Name: "CONLINEBILL 2000"

1. Definition.
"Merchant" includes the shipper, the receiver, the consignor, the consignee, the holder of the Bill of Lading, the owner of the cargo and any person entitled to possession of the cargo.

2. Notification.
Any mention in this Bill of Lading of parties to be notified of the arrival of the cargo is solely for the information of the Carrier and failure to give such notification shall not involve the Carrier in any liability nor relieve the Merchant of any obligation hereunder.

3. Liability for Carriage Between Port of Loading and Port of Discharge.
(a) The International Convention for the Unification of Certain Rules of Law relating to Bills of Lading signed at Brussels on 25 August 1924 ("the Hague Rules") as amended by the Protocol signed at Brussels on 23 February 1968 ("the Hague-Visby Rules") and as enacted in the country of shipment shall apply to this Contract. When the Hague-Visby Rules are not enacted in the country of shipment, the corresponding legislation of the country of destination shall apply, irrespective of whether such legislation may only regulate outbound shipments.
When there is no enactment of the Hague-Visby Rules in either the country of shipment or in the country of destination, the Hague-Visby Rules shall apply to this Contract save where the Hague Rules as enacted in the country of shipment or, if no such enactment is in place, the Hague Rules as enacted in the country of destination apply compulsorily to this Contract.
The Protocol signed at Brussels on 21 December 1979 ("the SDR Protocol 1979") shall apply where the Hague-Visby Rules apply, whether mandatorily or by this Contract.
The Carrier shall in no case be responsible for loss of or damage to cargo arising prior to loading, after discharging, or with respect to deck cargo and live animals.
(b) If the Carrier is held liable in respect of delay, consequential loss or damage other than loss of or damage to the cargo, the liability of the Carrier shall be limited to the freight for the carriage covered by this Bill of Lading, or to the limitation amount as determined in sub-clause 3(a), whichever is the lesser.
(c) The aggregate liability of the Carrier and/or any of his servants, agents or independent contractors under this Contract shall, in no circumstances, exceed the limits of liability for the total loss of the cargo under sub-clause 3(a) or, if applicable, the Additional Clause.

4. Law and Jurisdiction.
Disputes arising out of or in connection with this Bill of Lading shall be exclusively determined by the courts and in accordance with the law of the place where the Carrier has his principal place of business, as stated on Page 1, except as provided elsewhere herein.

5. The Scope of Carriage.
The intended carriage shall not be limited to the direct route but shall be deemed to include any proceeding or returning to or stopping or slowing down at or off any ports or places for any reasonable purpose connected with the carriage including bunkering, loading, discharging, or other cargo operations and maintenance of Vessel and crew.

6. Substitution of Vessel.
The Carrier shall be at liberty to carry the cargo or part thereof to the Port of discharge by the said or other vessel or vessels either belonging to the Carrier or others, or by other means of transport, proceeding either directly or indirectly to such port.

7. Transhipment.
The Carrier shall be at liberty to tranship, lighter, land and store the cargo either on shore or afloat and reship and forward the same to the Port of discharge.

8. Liability for Pre- and On-Carriage.
When the Carrier arranges pre-carriage of the cargo from a place other than the Vessel's Port of loading or on-carriage of the cargo to a place other than the Vessel's Port of discharge, the Carrier shall contract as the Merchant's Agent only and the Carrier shall not be liable for any loss or damage arising during any part of the carriage other than between the Port of loading and the Port of discharge even though the freight for the whole carriage has been collected by him.

9. Loading and Discharging.
(a) Loading and discharging of the cargo shall be arranged by the Carrier or his Agent.
(b) The Merchant shall, at his risk and expense, handle and/or store the cargo before loading and after discharging.
(c) Loading and discharging may commence without prior notice.
(d) The Merchant or his Agent shall tender the cargo when the Vessel is ready to load and as fast as the Vessel can receive including, if required by the Carrier, outside ordinary working hours notwithstanding any custom of the port. If the Merchant or his Agent fails to tender the cargo when the Vessel is ready to load or fails to load as fast as the Vessel can receive the cargo, the Carrier shall be relieved of any obligation to load such cargo, the Vessel shall be entitled to leave the port without further notice and the Merchant shall be liable to the Carrier for deadfreight and/or any overtime charges, losses, costs and expenses incurred by the Carrier.
(e) The Merchant or his Agent shall take delivery of the cargo as fast as the Vessel can discharge including, if required by the Carrier, outside ordinary working hours notwithstanding any custom of the port. If the Merchant or his Agent fails to take delivery of the cargo the Carrier's discharging of the cargo shall be deemed fulfilment of the contract of carriage. Should the cargo not be applied for within a reasonable time, the Carrier may sell the same privately or by auction. If the Merchant or his Agent fails to take delivery of the cargo as fast as the Vessel can discharge, the Merchant shall be liable to the Carrier for any overtime charges, losses, costs and expenses incurred by the Carrier.
(f) The Merchant shall accept his reasonable proportion of unidentified loose cargo.

10. Freight, Charges, Costs, Expenses, Duties, Taxes and Fines.
(a) Freight, whether paid or not, shall be considered as fully earned upon loading and non-returnable in any event. Unless otherwise specified, freight and/or charges under this Contract are payable by the Merchant to the Carrier on demand. Interest at Libor (or its successor) plus 2 per cent. shall run from fourteen days after the date when freight and charges are payable.
(b) The Merchant shall be liable for all costs and expenses of fumigation, gathering and sorting loose cargo and weighing onboard, repairing damage to and replacing packing due to excepted causes, and any extra handling of the cargo for any of the aforementioned reasons.
(c) The Merchant shall be liable for any dues, duties, taxes and charges which under any denomination may be levied, *inter alia*, on the basis of freight, weight of cargo or tonnage of the Vessel.
(d) The Merchant shall be liable for all fines, penalties, costs, expenses and losses which the Carrier, Vessel or cargo may incur through non-observance of Customs House and/or import or export regulations.
(e) The Carrier is entitled in case of incorrect declaration of contents, weights, measurements or value of the cargo to claim double the amount of freight which would have been due if such declaration had been correctly given. For the purpose of ascertaining the actual facts, the Carrier shall have the right to obtain from the Merchant the original invoice and to have the cargo inspected and its contents, weight, measurement or value verified.

11. Lien.
The Carrier shall have a lien on all cargo for any amount due under this contract and the costs of recovering the same and shall be entitled to sell the cargo privately or by auction to satisfy any such claims.

12. General Average and Salvage.
General Average shall be adjusted, stated and settled in London according to the York-Antwerp Rules 1994, or any modification thereof, in respect of all cargo, whether carried on or under deck. In the event of accident, danger, damage or disaster before or after commencement of the voyage resulting from any cause whatsoever, whether due to negligence or not, for which or for the consequence of which the Carrier is not responsible by statute, contract or otherwise, the Merchant shall contribute with the Carrier in General Average to the payment of any sacrifice, losses or expenses of a General Average nature that may be made or incurred, and shall pay salvage and special charges incurred in respect of the cargo. If a salving vessel is owned or operated by the Carrier, salvage shall be paid for as fully as if the salving vessel or vessels belonged to strangers.

13. Both-to-Blame Collision Clause.
If the Vessel comes into collision with another vessel as a result of the negligence of the other vessel and any act, negligence or default of the Master, Mariner, Pilot or the servants of the Carrier in the navigation or in the management of the Vessel, the Merchant will indemnify the Carrier against all loss or liability to the other or non-carrying vessel or her Owner in so far as such loss or liability represents loss of or damage to or any claim whatsoever of the owner of the cargo paid or payable by the other or non-carrying vessel or her Owner to the owner of the cargo and set-off, recouped or recovered by the other or non-carrying vessel or her Owner as part of his claim against the carrying vessel or Carrier. The foregoing provisions shall also apply where the Owner, operator or those in charge of any vessel or vessels or objects other than, or in addition to, the colliding vessels or objects are at fault in respect of a collision or contact.

14. Government directions, War, Epidemics, Ice, Strikes, etc.
(a) The Master and the Carrier shall have liberty to comply with any order or directions or recommendations in connection with the carriage under this Contract given by any Government or Authority, or anybody acting or purporting to act on behalf of such Government or Authority, or having under the terms of the insurance on the Vessel the right to give such orders or directions or recommendations.
(b) Should it appear that the performance of the carriage would expose the Vessel or any cargo onboard to risk of seizure, damage or delay, in consequence of war, warlike operations, blockade, riots, civil commotions or piracy, or any person onboard to risk of loss of life or freedom, or that any such risk has increased, the Master may discharge the cargo at the Port of loading or any other safe and convenient port.
(c) Should it appear that epidemics; quarantine; ice; labour troubles, labour obstructions, strikes, lockouts (whether onboard or on shore); difficulties in loading or discharging would prevent the Vessel from leaving the Port of loading or reaching or entering the Port of discharge or there discharging in the usual manner and departing therefrom, all of which safely and without unreasonable delay, the Master may discharge the cargo at the Port of loading or any other safe and convenient port.
(d) The discharge, under the provisions of this Clause, of any cargo shall be deemed due fulfilment of the contract of carriage.
(e) If in connection with the exercise of any liberty under this Clause any extra expenses are incurred they shall be paid by the Merchant in addition to the freight, together with return freight, if any, and a reasonable compensation for any extra services rendered to the cargo.

15. Defences and Limits of Liability for the Carrier, Servants and Agents.
(a) It is hereby expressly agreed that no servant or agent of the Carrier (which for the purpose of this Clause includes every independent contractor from time to time employed by the Carrier) shall in any circumstances whatsoever be under any liability whatsoever to the Merchant under this Contract of carriage for any loss, damage or delay of whatsoever kind arising or resulting directly or indirectly from any act, neglect or default on his part while acting in the course of or in connection with his employment.
(b) Without prejudice to the generality of the foregoing provisions in this Clause, every exemption from liability, limitation, condition and liberty herein contained and every right, defence and immunity of whatsoever nature applicable to the Carrier or to which the Carrier is entitled, shall also be available and shall extend to protect every such servant and agent of the Carrier acting as aforesaid.
(c) The Merchant undertakes that no claim shall be made against any servant or agent of the Carrier and, if any claim should nevertheless be made, to indemnify the Carrier against all consequences thereof.
(d) For the purpose of all the foregoing provisions of this Clause the Carrier is or shall be deemed to be acting as agent or trustee on behalf of and for the benefit of all persons who might be his servants or agents from time to time and all such persons shall to this extent be or be deemed to be parties to this Contract of carriage.

16. Stowage.
(a) The Carrier shall have the right to stow cargo by means of containers, trailers, transportable tanks, flats, pallets, or similar articles of transport used to consolidate goods.
(b) The Carrier shall have the right to carry containers, trailers, transportable tanks and covered flats, whether stowed by the Carrier or received by him in a stowed condition from the Merchant, on or under deck without notice to the Merchant.

17. Shipper-Packed Containers, trailers, transportable tanks, flats and pallets.
(a) If a container has not been filled, packed or stowed by the Carrier, the Carrier shall not be liable for any loss of or damage to its contents and the Merchant shall cover any loss or expense incurred by the Carrier, if such loss, damage or expense has been caused by:
(i) negligent filling, packing or stowing of the container;
(ii) the contents being unsuitable for carriage in container; or
(iii) the unsuitability or defective condition of the container unless the container has been supplied by the Carrier and the unsuitability or defective condition would not have been apparent upon reasonable inspection at or prior to the time when the container was filled, packed or stowed.
(b) The provisions of sub-clause (i) of this Clause also apply with respect to trailers, transportable tanks, flats and pallets which have not been filled, packed or stowed by the Carrier.
(c) The Carrier does not accept liability for damage due to the unsuitability or defective condition of reefer equipment or trailers supplied by the Merchant.

18. Return of Containers.
(a) Containers, pallets or similar articles of transport supplied by or on behalf of the Carrier shall be returned to the Carrier in the same order and condition as handed over to the Merchant, normal wear and tear excepted, with interiors clean and within the time prescribed in the Carrier's tariff or elsewhere.
(b) The Merchant shall be liable to the Carrier for any loss, damage to, or delay, including demurrage and detention incurred by or sustained to containers, pallets or similar articles of transport during the period between handing over to the Merchant and return to the Carrier.

ADDITIONAL CLAUSE

U.S. Trade. Period of Responsibility.
(i) In case the Contract evidenced by this Bill of Lading is subject to the Carriage of Goods by Sea Act of the United States of America, 1936 (U.S. COGSA), then the provisions stated in said Act shall govern before loading and after discharge and throughout the entire time the cargo is in the Carrier's custody and in which event freight shall be payable on the cargo coming into the Carrier's custody.
(ii) If the U.S. COGSA applies, and unless the nature and value of the cargo has been declared by the shipper before the cargo has been handed over to the Carrier and inserted in this Bill of Lading, the Carrier shall in no event be or become liable for any loss or damage to the cargo in an amount exceeding USD 500 per package or customary freight unit.

Code Name: "LINEWAYBILL"

Shipper

Consignee (not to order)

NON-NEGOTIABLE
LINER SEA WAYBILL
Issued by The Baltic and International Maritime Council (BIMCO), subject to the CMI Uniform Rules for Sea Waybills.

LWB. No.

Reference No.

Notify party/address

Draft Copy

Pre-carriage by *	Place of receipt by pre-carrier *
Vessel	Port of loading
Port of discharge	Place of delivery by on-carrier *

Container No./Seal No./Marks and Numbers	Number and kind of packages, description of goods	Gross weight, kg.	Measurement, m³

NON - NEGOTIABLE

Draft Copy

Above particulars as declared by Shipper but not acknowledged by the Carrier

Total No. of Containers/Packages or Units received by the Carrier	RECEIVED for carriage in apparent good order and condition (unless otherwise stated herein) the total number of Containers/Packages or Units indicated in the Box opposite entitled "Total No. of Containers/Packages or Units received by the Carrier" and the goods as specified above, weight, measure, marks, numbers, quality, quantity, contents and value unknown for delivery at the place indicated above. The goods shipped under this Sea Waybill will be delivered to the Party named as Consignee or its authorised agent, on production of proof of identity without any documentary formalities. Should the Shipper require delivery of the goods to a party other than the Consignee stated in this Sea Waybill, then written instructions must be given to the Carrier or his agent. The Shipper shall, however, be entitled to transfer right of control of the goods to the Consignee, the exercise of such option to be noted on this Sea Waybill and to be made no later than the receipt of the goods by the Carrier. The Carrier shall exercise due care ensuring that delivery is made to the proper party. However, in case of incorrect delivery, the Carrier will accept no responsibility unless due to fault or neglect on his part.
Freight and charges	
Freight payable at	
Shipper's declared value of:	Place and date of issue
subject to payment of above extra charge. **FOR CONDITIONS OF CARRIAGE SEE NEXT PAGE.** **Note:** The Merchant's attention is drawn to the fact that in accordance with Clauses 10 to 13 and Clause 24 of this Sea Waybill, the liability of the Carrier is limited in respect of loss of or damage to the goods and delay. * Applicable only when document used as a Through Sea Waybill	Signed for .... as Carrier by .... As agent(s) only to the Carrier

Printed by the BIMCO Charter Party Editor

LINER SEA WAYBILL
Code Name: "LINEWAYBILL"

I. GENERAL PROVISIONS

1. Definitions.
"Carrier" means the party on whose behalf this Sea Waybill has been signed.
"Merchant" includes the Shipper, the Receiver, the Consignor, the Consignee and the owner of the goods.

2. Carrier's Tariff.
The terms of the Carrier's applicable Tariff on the date of shipment are incorporated herein. Copies of the relevant provisions of the applicable Tariff are available from the Carrier upon request. In the case of inconsistency between this Sea Waybill and the applicable Tariff, this Sea Waybill shall prevail.

3. Law and Jurisdiction.
Disputes arising under this Sea Waybill shall be determined by the courts and in accordance with the law at the place where the Carrier has his principal place of business.

II. PERFORMANCE OF THE CONTRACT

4. Methods and Routes of Transportation.
(a) As the Vessel is engaged in liner service the intended voyage shall not be limited to the direct route but shall be deemed to include any proceeding or returning to or stopping or slowing down at or off any ports or places for any reasonable purpose connected with the service including maintenance of the Vessel and crew, and the Vessel may sail with or without pilots, undergo repairs, adjust equipment, drydock, be towed or low vessels in all situations.
(b) Whether expressly arranged beforehand or otherwise, the Carrier shall be at liberty to carry the goods to their port of destination by the said or other vessel or vessels either belonging to the Carrier or others, or by other means of transport, proceeding either directly or indirectly to such port and to carry the goods or part of them beyond their port of destination, and to tranship, land and store the goods either on shore or afloat and reship and forward the same at the Carrier's expense but at the Merchant's risk.

5. Stowage.
(a) The Carrier shall have the right to stow goods by means of containers, trailers, transportable tanks, flats, pallets, or similar articles of transport used to consolidate goods.
(b) The Carrier shall have the right to carry containers, trailers, transportable tanks and covered flats, whether stowed by the Carrier or received by him in a stowed condition from the Merchant on or under deck without notice to the Merchant.

6. Hindrances etc. Affecting Performance.
(a) The Carrier shall use reasonable endeavours to complete the performance of this Contract.
(b) If at any time the performance of the Contract as evidenced by this Sea Waybill is or will be affected by any hindrance, risk, delay, difficulty or disadvantage of whatsoever kind, and if by virtue of sub-clause 6(a) the Carrier has no duty to complete the performance of the Contract, the Carrier (whether or not the transport is commenced) may elect to treat the performance of this Contract as terminated and place the goods at the Merchant's disposal at any place which the Carrier shall deem safe and convenient.
(c) If the Merchant has not taken delivery of the goods within the time designated by the Carrier, the Carrier shall be at liberty to put the goods in safe custody on behalf of the Merchant at the latter's risk and expense, and, if not taken delivery of, to sell the same privately or by auction after 14 days.
(d) In any event the Carrier shall be entitled to full freight for goods received for transportation and additional compensation for extra costs resulting from the circumstances referred to above.

7. Lighterage.
Any customary, local lightering in or off ports of loading or ports of discharge shall be for the account and risk of the Carrier.

8. Loading, Discharging and Delivery.
(a) Loading, discharging and delivery of the cargo shall be arranged by the Carrier's Agent unless otherwise agreed.
(b) All costs for storing and handling of the goods before loading and after discharge shall be for the Merchant's account.
(c) Loading and discharging may commence without previous notice.
(d) The Merchant or his Assigns shall tender the goods when the Vessel is ready to load and as fast as the Vessel can receive and - but only if required by the Carrier - also outside ordinary working hours notwithstanding any custom of the port.
Otherwise the Carrier shall be relieved of any obligation to load such cargo and the Vessel may leave the port without further notice and deadfreight is to be paid.
(e) The Merchant or his Assigns shall take delivery of the goods and continue to receive the goods as fast as the Vessel can deliver and - but only if required by the Carrier - also outside ordinary working hours notwithstanding any custom of the port. Otherwise the Carrier shall be at liberty to discharge the goods and any discharge shall be deemed a true fulfilment of the Contract, or alternatively to act under Clause 6.
(f) The Merchant shall bear all overtime charges in connection with tendering and taking delivery of the goods as above.
(g) The Merchant shall accept his reasonable proportion of unidentified loose cargo.

9. Optional Ports of Discharge.
The port of discharge for optional cargo must be declared to the Vessel's Agents at the first of the optional ports not later than 48 hours before the Vessel's arrival there. In the absence of such declaration the Carrier may elect to discharge at the first or any other optional port and the contract of carriage shall then be considered as having been fulfilled. Any option can be exercised for the total quantity under this Sea Waybill only.

III. CARRIER'S LIABILITY

10. Liability for Carriage Between Port of Loading and Port of Discharge.
The International Convention for the Unification of Certain Rules of Law relating to Bills of Lading signed at Brussels on 25 August 1924 ("the Hague Rules") as amended by the Protocol signed at Brussels on 23 February 1968 ("the Hague-Visby Rules") and as enacted in the country of shipment shall apply to this Contract. When the Hague-Visby Rules are not enacted in the country of shipment, the corresponding legislation of the country of destination shall apply, irrespective of whether such legislation may only regulate outbound shipments.
When there is no enactment of the Hague-Visby Rules in either the country of shipment or in the country of destination, the Hague-Visby Rules shall apply to this Contract save where the Hague Rules as enacted in the country of shipment or if no such enactment is in place, the Hague Rules as enacted in the country of destination apply compulsorily to this Contract.
The Protocol signed at Brussels on 21 December 1979 ("the SDR Protocol 1979") shall apply where the Hague-Visby Rules apply, whether mandatorily or by this Contract.
The Carrier shall in no case be responsible for loss of or damage to cargo arising prior to loading, after discharging, or while the cargo is in the charge of another carrier, or with respect to deck cargo and live animals.

11. Liability for Pre- and On-Carriage.
When engaging to receive the goods at a place other than the Vessel's Port of Loading or to deliver the goods at a place other than the Vessel's Port of Discharge, the Carrier acts as the Merchant's Agent only and shall be entitled to sub-contract the carriage on any terms. The Carrier shall not be liable for any loss or damage arising during any part of the transport other than that between the Port of Loading and Port of Discharge even though the freight for the whole transport has been collected by him.

12. Amount of Compensation.
(a) When the Carrier is liable for compensation in respect of loss of or damage to the goods, such compensation shall be calculated by reference to the value of such goods at the place and time they are delivered to the Merchant or should have been so delivered in accordance with the Contract.
(b) The value of the goods shall be fixed according to the commodity exchange price or, if there be no such price, according to the current market price or, if there be no commodity exchange price or current market price, by reference to the normal value of goods of the same kind and quality.
(c) Higher compensation than provided for in Clause 10 may be claimed only when, with the consent of the Carrier, the value for the goods declared by the Shipper which exceeds the limits laid down in Clause 10 has been stated on the face of this Sea Waybill at the place indicated. In that case the amount of the declared value shall be substituted for that limit.

13. Delay, Consequential Loss, etc.
If the Carrier is held liable in respect of delay, consequential loss or damage other than loss of or damage to the goods, the liability of the Carrier shall be limited to the freight for the transport covered by this Sea Waybill, or to the limitation amount as determined in Clause 10, whichever is the lesser.

14. Defences and Limits for the Carrier, Servants, etc.
(a) The defences and limits of liability provided in this Sea Waybill shall apply in any action against the Carrier for loss of or damage to the goods whether the action can be founded in contract or in tort.
(b) The Carrier shall not be entitled to the benefit of the limitation of liability provided for in this Sea Waybill, if it is proved that the loss or damage resulted from a personal act or omission of the Carrier done with intent to cause such loss or damage or recklessly and with knowledge that damage would probably result.
(c) The Merchant undertakes that no claim shall be made against any servant, agent or other persons whose services the Carrier has used in order to perform this Contract and if any claim should nevertheless be made, to indemnify the Carrier against all consequences thereof.
(d) However, the provisions of this Sea Waybill apply whenever claims relating to the performance of this Contract are made against any servant, agent or other persons whose services the Carrier has used in order to perform this Contract, whether such claims are founded in contract or in tort. In entering into this Contract, the Carrier, to the extent of such provisions, does so not only on his own behalf but also as agent or trustee for such persons. The aggregate liability of the Carrier and such persons shall not exceed the limits in Clause 12 and, if applicable, Clause 24.

IV. DESCRIPTION OF GOODS

15. Carrier's Responsibility.
In the absence of reservation by the Carrier, any statement in this Sea Waybill as to the quantity, order and/or condition of the goods shall as between the Carrier and the Shipper be prima facie evidence of receipt of the goods as so stated.

16. Shipper's Responsibility.
The Shipper shall be deemed to have guaranteed to the Carrier the accuracy, at the time the goods were received for carriage, of the description of the goods, marks, numbers, quantity and weight, as furnished by him, and the Shipper shall defend, indemnify and hold harmless the Carrier against all loss, damage and expenses arising or resulting from inaccuracies in or inadequacy of such particulars. The right of the Carrier to such indemnity shall in no way limit his responsibility and liability under this Sea Waybill to any person other than the Shipper. The Shipper shall remain liable even if the goods have been delivered.

17. Shipper-Packed Containers, etc.
(a) If a container has not been filled, packed or stowed by the Carrier, the Carrier shall not be liable for any loss of or damage to its contents and the Merchant shall cover any loss or expense incurred by the Carrier, if such loss, damage or expense has been caused by:
(i) negligent filling, packing or stowing of the container;
(ii) the contents being unsuitable for carriage in container; or
(iii) the unsuitability or defective condition of the container unless the container has been supplied by the Carrier and the unsuitability or defective condition would not have been apparent upon reasonable inspection at or prior to the time when the container was filled, packed or stowed.
(b) The provisions of sub-clause (i) of this Clause also apply with respect to trailers, transportable tanks, flats and pallets which have not been filled, packed or stowed by the Carrier.
(c) The Carrier does not accept liability for damage due to the unsuitability or defective condition of reefer equipment or trailers supplied by the Merchant.

18. Dangerous Goods.
(a) The Merchant shall comply with all internationally recognised requirements and all rules which apply according to national law or by reason of international Convention, relating to the carriage of goods of a dangerous nature, and shall in any event inform the Carrier in writing of the exact nature of the danger before goods of a dangerous nature are taken into charge by the Carrier and indicate to him, if need be, the precautions to be taken.
(b) Goods of a dangerous nature which the Carrier did not know were dangerous, may, at any time or place, be unloaded, destroyed, or rendered harmless, without compensation; further, the Merchant shall be liable for all expenses, loss or damage arising out of the handing over of such goods or of their carriage.
(c) If any goods shipped with the knowledge of the Carrier as to their dangerous nature shall become a danger to any person or property, the goods may in like manner be landed at any place or destroyed or rendered innocuous by the Carrier without liability on the part of the Carrier except for General Average, if any.

19. Return of Containers.
(a) For the purpose of this Clause the Consignor shall mean the person who concludes this Contract with the Carrier and the Consignee shall mean the person entitled to receive the goods from the Carrier.
(b) Containers, pallets or similar articles of transport supplied by or on behalf of the Carrier shall be returned to the Carrier in the same order and condition as handed over to the Merchant, normal wear and tear excepted, with interiors clean and within the time prescribed in the Carrier's tariff or elsewhere.
(c) (i) The Consignor shall be liable for any loss of, damage to, or delay, including demurrage, of such articles, incurred during the period between handing over to the Consignor and return to the Carrier for carriage.
(ii) The Consignor and the Consignee shall be jointly and severally liable for any loss of. damage to, or delay, including demurrage, of such articles. incurred during the period between handing over to the Consignee and return to the Carrier.

V. FREIGHT AND LIEN

20. Freight and Charges.
(a) Freight shall be deemed earned when the goods have been received for carriage and shall be paid in any event.
The Carrier's claim for any charges under this Contract shall be considered definitely payable in like manner as soon as the charges have been incurred. Interest at Libor plus 2 per cent., shall run from the date when freight and charges are due.
(b) The Merchant shall be liable for expenses of fumigation and of gathering and sorting loose cargo and of weighing on board and expenses incurred in repairing damage to and replacing of packing due to excepted causes and for all expenses caused by extra handling of the cargo for any of the aforementioned reasons.
(c) Any dues, duties, taxes and charges which under any denomination may be levied on any basis such as amount of freight, weight of cargo or tonnage of the Vessel shall be paid by the Merchant.
(d) The Merchant shall be liable for all fines and/or losses which the Carrier, the Vessel or cargo may incur through non-observance of Custom House and/or import or export regulations.
(e) The Merchant's attention is drawn to the stipulations concerning currency in which the freight and charges are to be paid, rate of exchange, devaluation and other contingencies relative to freight and charges in the relevant tariff conditions.
If no such stipulation as to devaluation exists or is applicable the following shall apply:
If the currency in which freight and charges are quoted is devalued between the date of the freight agreement and the date when the freight and charges are paid, then all freight and charges shall be automatically and immediately increased in proportion to the extent of the devaluation of the said currency.
(f) The Carrier is entitled in case of incorrect declaration of contents, weights, measurements or value of the goods to claim double the amount of freight which would have been due if such declaration had been correctly given. For the purpose of ascertaining the actual facts or verifying the freight basis, the Carrier reserves the right to obtain from the Merchant the original invoice and to have the goods inspected and the weight, measurement or value verified.

21. Lien.
The Carrier shall have a lien on the goods for any amount due under this Contract and for the costs of recovering the same, and may enforce such lien in any reasonable manner, including sale or disposal of the goods.

VI. MISCELLANEOUS PROVISIONS

22. General Average.
(a) General Average shall be adjusted at any port or place at the Carrier's option, and settled according to the York-Antwerp Rules 1994, or any modification thereof, this covering all goods, whether carried on or under deck. The New Jason Clause as approved by BIMCO shall be considered incorporated into this Sea Waybill.
(b) Such security including a cash deposit as the Carrier may deem sufficient to cover the estimated contribution of the goods and any salvage and special charges thereon shall, if required, be submitted to the Carrier prior to delivery of the goods.

23. Both-to-Blame Collision Clause.
The Both-to-Blame Collision Clause as approved by BIMCO shall be considered incorporated into this Sea Waybill.

24. U.S. Trade.
(a) In case the Contract evidenced by this Sea Waybill is subject to the Carriage of Goods by Sea Act of the United States of America, 1936 (U.S. COGSA), then the provisions stated in the said Act shall govern before loading and after discharge and throughout the entire time the goods are in the Carrier's custody.
(b) If the U.S. COGSA applies, and unless the nature and value of the goods have been declared by the Shipper before the goods have been handed over to the Carrier and inserted in this Sea Waybill, the Carrier shall in no event be or become liable for any loss of or damage to the goods in an amount exceeding USD 500 per package or customary freight unit.

Code Name: "COMBICONBILL"

B/L No.

Shipper

Reference No.

Negotiable
COMBINED TRANSPORT BILL OF LADING
Revised 1995

Consigned to order of

Notify party/address

Place of receipt

Ocean Vessel | Port of loading

Port of discharge | Place of delivery | Freight payable at | Number of original Bills of Lading

Marks and Nos. | Quantity and description of goods | Gross weight, kg, Measurement, m³

Particulars above declared by Shipper

Freight and charges

RECEIVED the goods in apparent good order and condition and, as far as ascertained by reasonable means of checking, as specified above unless otherwise stated.
The Carrier, in accordance with and to the extent of the provisions contained in this Bill of Lading, and with liberty to sub-contract, undertakes to perform and/or in his own name to procure performance of the combined transport and the delivery of the goods, including all services related thereto, from the place and time of taking the goods in charge to the place and time of delivery and accepts responsibility for such transport and such services.
One of the Bills of Lading must be surrendered duly endorsed in exchange for the goods or delivery order.
IN WITNESS whereof TWO (2) original Bills of Lading have been signed, if not otherwise stated above, one of which being accomplished the other(s) to be void.

Shipper's declared value of ......

Place and date of issue

subject to payment of above extra charge.

Signed for

.... as Carrier

Note:
The Merchant's attention is called to the fact that according to Clauses 10 to 12 and Clause 24 of this Bill of Lading, the liability of the Carrieris, in most cases, limited in respect of loss of or damage to the goods and delay.

by ....

As agent(s) only to the Carrier

Printed by the BIMCO Charter Party Editor

p.t.o.

COMBINED TRANSPORT BILL OF LADING

Adopted by The Baltic and International Maritime Council in January, 1971 (as revised 1995)

Code Name: "COMBICONBILL"

I. GENERAL PROVISIONS

1. **Applicability.**
Notwithstanding the heading "Combined Transport", the provisions set out and referred to in this Bill of Lading shall also apply, if the transport as described in this Bill of Lading is performed by one mode of transport only.

2. **Definitions.**
"Carrier" means the party on whose behalf this Bill of Lading has been signed.
"Merchant" includes the Shipper, the Receiver, the Consignor, the Consignee, the holder of this Bill of Lading and the owner of the goods.

3. **Carrier's Tariff.**
The terms of the Carrier's applicable Tariff at the date of shipment are incorporated herein. Copies of the relevant provisions of the applicable Tariff are available from the Carrier upon request. In the case of inconsistency between this Bill of Lading and the applicable Tariff, this Bill of Lading shall prevail.

4. **Time Bar.**
All liability whatsoever of the Carrier shall cease unless suit is brought within 9 months after delivery of the goods or the date when the goods should have been delivered.

5. **Law and Jurisdiction.**
Disputes arising under this Bill of Ladinq shall be determined by the courts and in accordance with the law at the place where the Carrier has his principal place of business.

II. PERFORMANCE OF THE CONTRACT

6. **Methods and Routes of Transportation.**
(1) The Carrier is entitled to perform the transport and all services related thereto in any reasonable manner and by any reasonable means, methods and routes.
(2) In accordance herewith, for instance, in the event of carriage by sea, vessels may sail with or without pilots, undergo repairs, adjust equipment, drydock and tow vessels in all situations.

7. **Optional Stowage.**
(1) Goods may be stowed by the Carrier by means of containers, trailers, transportable tanks, flats, pallets, or similar articles of transport used to consolidate goods.
(2) Containers, trailers, transportable tanks and covered flats, whether stowed by the Carrier or received by him in a stowed condition from the Merchant, may be carried on or under deck without notice to the Merchant.

8. **Hindrances etc. Affecting Performance.**
(1) The Carrier shall use reasonable endeavours to complete the transport and to deliver the goods at the place designated for delivery.
(2) If at any time the performance of the contract as evidenced by this Bill of Lading is or will be affected by any hindrance, risk, delay, difficulty or disadvantage of whatsoever kind, and if by virtue of sub-clause 8 (1) the Carrier has no duty to complete the performance of the contract, the Carrier (whether or not the transport is commenced) may elect to:
(a) treat the performance of this Contract as terminated and place the goods at the Merchant's disposal at any place which the Carrier shall deem safe and convenient;
or
(b) deliver the goods at the place designated for delivery.
(3) If the goods are not taken delivery of by the Merchant within a reasonable time after the Carrier has called upon him to take delivery, the Carrier shall be at liberty to put the goods in safe custody on behalf of the Merchant at the latter's risk and expense.
(4) In any event the Carrier shall be entitled to full freight for goods received for transportation and additional compensation for extra costs resulting from the circumstances referred to above.

III. CARRIER'S LIABILITY

9. **Basic Liability.**
(1) The Carrier shall be liable for loss of or damage to the goods occurring between the time when he receives the goods into his charge and the time of delivery.
(2) The Carrier shall be responsible for the acts and omissions of any person of whose services he makes use for the performance of the contract of carriage evidenced by this Bill of Lading.
(3) The Carrier shall, however, be relieved of liability for any loss or damage if such loss or damage arose or resulted from:
(a) The wrongful act or neglect of the Merchant.
(b) Compliance with the Instructions of the person entitled to give them.
(c) The lack of, or defective conditions of packing in the case of goods which, by their nature, are liable to wastage or to be damaged when not packed or when not properly packed.
(d) Handling, loading, stowage or unloading of the goods by or on behalf of the Merchant.
(e) Inherent vice of the goods.
(f) Insufficiency or inadequacy of marks or numbers on the goods, covering, or unit loads.
(g) Strikes or lock-outs or stoppages or restraints of labour from whatever cause whether partial or general.
(h) Any cause or event which the Carrier could not avoid and the consequence whereof he could not prevent by the exercise of reasonable diligence.
(4) Where under sub-clause 9 (3) the Carrier is not under any liability in respect of some of the factors causing the loss or damage, he shall only be liable to the extent that those factors for which he is liable under this Clause have contributed to the loss or damage.
(5) The burden of proving that the loss or damage was due to one or more of the causes or events, specified in (a), (b) and (h) of sub-clause 9 (3) shall rest upon the Carrier.
(6) When the Carrier establishes that in the circumstances of the case, the loss or damage could be attributed to one or more of the causes or events, specified in (c) to (g) of sub-clause 9 (3), it shall be presumed that it was so caused. The Merchant shall, however, be entitled to prove that the loss or damage was not, in fact, caused either wholly or partly by one or more of the causes or events.

10. **Amount of Compensation.**
(1) When the Carrier is liable for compensation in respect of loss of or damage to the goods, such compensation shall be calculated by reference to the value of such goods at the place and time they are delivered to the Merchant in accordance with the contract or should have been so delivered.
(2) The value of the goods shall be fixed according to the commodity exchange price or, if there be no such price, according to the current market price or, if there be no commodity exchange price or current market price, by reference to the normal value of goods of the same kind and quality.
(3) Compensation shall not, however, exceed two Special Drawing Rights per kilogramme of gross weight of the goods lost or damaged.
(4) Higher compensation may be claimed only when, with the consent of the Carrier, the value for the goods declared by the Shipper which exceeds the limits laid down in this Clause has been stated on the face of this Bill of Lading at the place indicated. In that case the amount of the declared value shall be substituted for that limit.

11. **Special Provisions for Liability and Compensation.**
(1) Notwithstanding anything provided for in Clauses 9 and 10 of this Bill of Lading, if it can be proved where the loss or damage occurred, the Carrier and the Merchant shall, as to the liability of the Carrier, be entitled to require such liability to be determined by the provisions contained in any international convention or national law, which provisions:
(a) cannot be departed from by private contract, to the detriment of the claimant, and
(b) would have applied if the Merchant had made a separate and direct contract with the Carrier in respect of the particular stage of transport where the loss or damage occurred and received as evidence thereof any particular document which must be issued if such international convention or national law shall apply.
(2) Insofar as there is no mandatory law applying to carriage by sea by virtue of the provisions of sub-clause 11 (1), the liability of the Carrier in respect of any carriage by sea shall be determined by the International Brussels Convention 1924 as amended by the Protocol signed at Brussels on February 23rd 1968 - The Hague/Visby Rules.
The Hague/Visby Rules shall also determine the liability of the Carrier in respect of carriage by inland waterways as if such carriage were carriage by sea. Furthermore, they shall apply to all goods, whether carried on deck or under deck.

12. **Delay, Consequential Loss, etc.**
If the Carrier is held liable in respect of delay, consequential loss or damage other than loss of or damage to the goods, the liability of the Carrier shall be limited to the freight for the transport covered by this Bill of Lading, or to the value of the goods as determined in Clause 10, whichever is the lesser.

13. **Notice of Loss of or Damage to the Goods.**
(1) Unless notice of loss of or damage to the goods, specifying the general nature of such loss or damage, is given in writing by the Merchant to the Carrier when the goods are handed over to the Merchant, such handing over is *prima facie* evidence of the Delivery by the Carrier of the goods as described in this Bill of Lading.
(2) Where the loss or damage is not apparent, the same *prima facie* effect shall apply if notice in writing is not given within three (3) consecutive days after the day when the goods were handed over to the Merchant.

14. **Defences and Limits for the Carrier, Servants, etc.**
(1) The defences and limits of liability provided for in this Bill of Lading shall apply in any action against the Carrier for loss or damage to the goods whether the action can be founded in contract or in tort.
(2) The Carrier shall not be entitled to the benefit of the limitation of liability provided for in sub-clause 10 (3), if it is proved that the loss or damage resulted from a personal act or omission of the Carrier done with intent to cause such loss or damage or recklessly and with knowledge that damage would probably result.
(3) The Merchant undertakes that no claim shall be made against any servant, agent or other persons whose services the Carrier has used In order to perform this Contract and if any claim should nevertheless be made, to indemnify the Carrier against all consequences thereof.
(4) However, the provisions of this Bill of Lading apply whenever claims relating to the performance of this Contract are made against any servant, agent or other person whose services the Carrier has used in order to perform this Contract, whether such claims are founded in contract or in tort. In entering into this Contract, the Carrier, to the extent of such provisions, does so not only on his own behalf but also as agent or trustee for such persons. The aggregate liability of the Carrier and such persons shall not exceed the limits in Clauses 10, 11 and 24, respectively.

IV. DESCRIPTION OF GOODS

15. **Carrier's Responsibility.**
The information in this Bill of Lading shall be *prima facie* evidence of the taking in charge by the Carrier of the goods as described by such information unless a contrary indication, such as "shipper's weight, load and count", "Shipper-packed container" or similar expressions, have been made in the printed text or superimposed on the Bill of Lading. Proof to the contrary shall not be admissible when the Bill of Lading has been transferred, or the equivalent electronic data interchange message has been transmitted to and acknowledged by the Consignee who in good faith has relied and acted thereon.

16. **Shipper's Responsibility.**
The Shipper shall be deemed to have guaranteed to the Carrier the accuracy, at the time the goods were taken in charge by the Carrier, of the description of the goods, marks, number, quantity and weight, as furnished by him, and the Shipper shall defend, indemnify and hold harmless the Carrier against all loss, damage and expenses arising or resulting from inaccuracies in or inadequacy of such particulars. The right of the Carrier to such indemnity shall in no way limit his responsibility and liability under this Bill of Lading to any person other than the Shipper. The Shipper shall remain liable even if the Bill of Lading has been transferred by him.

17. **Shipper-packed Containers, etc.**
(1) If a container has not been filled, packed or stowed by the Carrier, the Carrier shall not be liable for any loss of or damage to its contents and the Merchant shall cover any loss or expense incurred by the Carrier, if such loss, damage or expense has been caused by:
(a) negligent filling, packing or stowing of the container;
(b) the contents being unsuitable for carriage in container; or
(c) the unsuitability or defective condition of the container unless the container has been supplied by the Carrier and the unsuitability or defective condition would not have been apparent upon reasonable inspection at or prior to the time when the container was filled, packed or stowed.
(2) The provisions of sub-clause (1) of this Clause also apply with respect to trailers, transportable tanks, flats and pallets which have not been filled, packed or stowed by the Carrier.
(3) The Carrier does not accept liability for damage due to the unsuitability or defective condition of reefer equipment or trailers supplied by the Merchant.

18. **Dangerous Goods.**
(1) The Merchant shall comply with all internationally recognised requirements and all rules which apply according to national law or by reason of international Convention, relating to the carriage of goods of a dangerous nature, and shall in any event inform the Carrier in writing of the exact nature of the danger before goods of a dangerous nature are taken into charge by the Carrier and indicate to him, if need be, the precautions to be taken.
(2) Goods of a dangerous nature which the Carrier did not know were dangerous, may, at any time or place, be unloaded, destroyed, or rendered harmless, without compensation; further, the Merchant shall be liable for all expenses, loss or damage arising out of their handing over for carriage or of their carriage.
(3) If any goods shipped with the knowledge of the Carrier as to their dangerous nature shall become a danger to any person or property, they may in like manner be landed at any place or destroyed or rendered innocuous by the Carrier without liability on the part of the Carrier except to General Average, if any.

19. **Return of Containers.**
(1) For the purpose of this Clause the Consignor shall mean the Person who concludes this Contract with the Carrier and the Consignee shall mean the person entitled to receive the goods from the Carrier.
(2) Containers, pallets or similar articles of transport supplied by or on behalf of the Carrier shall be returned to the Carrier in the same order and condition as handed over to the Merchant, normal wear and tear excepted, with interiors clean and within the time prescribed in the Carrier's tariff or elsewhere.
(3)(a) The Consignor shall be liable for any loss of, damage to, or delay, including demurrage, of such articles, incurred during the period between handing over to the Consignor and return to the Carrier for carriage.
(b) The Consignor and the Consignee shall be jointly and severally liable for any lose of, damage to, or delay, including demurrage, of such articles, incurred during the period between handing over to the Consignee and return to the Carrier.

V. FREIGHT AND LIEN

20. **Freight.**
(1) Freight shall be deemed earned when the goods have been taken in charge by the Carrier and shall be paid in any event.
(2) The Merchant's attention is drawn to the stipulations concerning currency in which the freight and charges are to be paid, rate of exchange, devaluation and other contingencies relative to freight and charges in the relevant tariff conditions. If no such stipulation as to devaluation exists or is applicable the following shall apply:
If the currency in which freight and charges are quoted is devalued between the date of the freight agreement and the date when the freight and charges are paid, then all freight and charges shall be automatically and immediately increased in proportion to the extent of the devaluation of the said currency.
(3) For the purpose of verifying the freight basis, the Carrier reserves the right to have the contents of containers, trailers or similar articles of transport inspected in order to ascertain the weight, measurement, value, or nature of the goods.

21. **Lien.**
The Carrier shall have a lien on the goods for any amount due under this Contract and for the costs of recovering the same, and may enforce such lien in any reasonable manner, including sale or disposal of the goods.

VI. MISCELLANEOUS PROVISIONS

22. **General Average.**
(1) General Average shall be adjusted at any port or place at the Carrier's option, and to be settled according to the York-Antwerp Rules 1994, or any modification thereof, this covering all goods, whether carried on or under deck. The New Jason Clause as approved by BIMCO to be considered as incorporated herein.
(2) Such security including a cash deposit as the Carrier may deem sufficient to cover the estimated contribution of the qoods and any salvage and special charges thereon, shall, if required, be submitted to the Carrier prior to delivery of the goods.

23. **Both-to-Blame Collision Clause.**
The Both-to-Blame Collision Clause as adopted by BIMCO shall be considered incorporated herein.

24. **U.S. Trade.**
(1) In case the contract evidenced by this Bill of Lading is subject to the Carriage of Goods by Sea Act of the United States of America, 1936 (U.S. COGSA), then the provisions stated in the said Act shall govern before loading and after discharge and throughout the entire time the goods are in the Carrier's custody.
(2) If the U.S. COGSA applies, and unless the nature and value of the goods have been declared by the shipper before the goods have been handed over to the Carrier and inserted in this Bill of Lading, the Carrier shall in no event be or become liable for any loss of or damage to the goods in an amount exceeding USD 500 per package or customary freight unit.

<u>Code Name: "COMBICONWAYBILL"</u>

Shipper

Reference No.

COMBINED TRANSPORT SEA WAYBILL

Issued by The Baltic and International Maritime Council
(BIMCO), subject to the CMI Uniform Rules for Sea Waybills

Consignee (not to order)

Issued 1995

Notify party/address

Place of receipt

Ocean Vessel	Port of loading	
Port of discharge	Place of delivery	Freight payable at
Marks and Nos.	Quantity and description of goods	Gross weight, kg, Measurement, m³

Particulars above declared by Shipper

Freight and charges

RECEIVED the goods in apparent good order and condition and, as far as ascertained by reasonable means of checking, as specified above unless otherwise stated.

The Carrier, in accordance with and to the extent of the provisions contained in this Sea Waybill, and with liberty to sub-contract, undertakes to perform and/or in his own name to procure performance of the multimodal transport and the delivery of the goods, including all services related thereto, from the place and time of taking the goods in charge to the place and time of delivery and accepts responsibility for such transport and such services.

The Shipper shall be entitled to transfer right of control of the cargo to the Consignee, the exercise of such option to be noted on this Sea Waybill and to be made no later than the receipt of the cargo by the Carrier.

Shipper's declared value of ......

Place and date of issue

subject to payment of above extra charge.

Signed for

.... as Carrier

Note:

The Merchant's attention is called to the fact that according to Clauses 10 to 12 and Clause 24 of this Sea Waybill, the liability of the Carrier is, in most cases, limited in respect of loss of or damage to the goods and delay.

by ....

As agent(s) only to the Carrier

Printed by the BIMCO Charter Party Editor

p.t.o.

COMBINED TRANSPORT SEA WAYBILL
Code Name: "COMBICONWAYBILL"

I. GENERAL PROVISIONS

1. Applicability.
Notwithstanding the heading "Combined Transport", the provisions set out and referred to in this Sea Waybill shall also apply, if the transport as described in this Sea Waybill is performed by one mode of transport only.

2. Definitions.
"Carrier" means the party on whose behalf this Sea Waybill has been signed.
"Merchant" includes the Shipper, the Receiver, the Consignor, the Consignee and the owner of the goods.

3. Carrier's Tariff.
The terms of the Carrier's applicable Tariff at the date of shipment are incorporated herein. Copies of the relevant provisions of the applicable Tariff are available from the Carrier upon request. In the case of inconsistency between this Sea Waybill and the applicable Tariff, this Sea Waybill shall prevail.

4. Time Bar.
All liability whatsoever of the Carrier shall cease unless suit is brought within 9 months after delivery of the goods or the date when the goods should have been delivered.

5. Law and Jurisdiction.
Disputes arising under this Sea Waybill shall be determined by the courts and in accordance with the law at the place where the Carrier has his principal place of business.

II. PERFORMANCE OF THE CONTRACT

6. Methods and Routes of Transportation.
(1) The Carrier is entitled to perform the transport and all services related thereto in any reasonable manner and by any reasonable means, methods and routes.
(2) In accordance herewith, for instance, in the event of carriage by sea, vessels may sail with or without pilots, undergo repairs, adjust equipment, drydock and tow vessels in all situations.

7. Optional Stowage.
(1) Goods may be stowed by the Carrier by means of containers, trailers, transportable tanks, flats, pallets, or similar articles of transport used to consolidate goods.
(2) Containers, trailers, transportable tanks and covered flats, whether stowed by the Carrier or received by him in a stowed condition from the Merchant, may be carried on or under deck without notice to the Merchant.

8. Hindrances etc. Affecting Performance.
(1) The Carrier shall use reasonable endeavours to complete the transport and to deliver the goods at the place designated for delivery.
(2) If at any time the performance of the contract as evidenced by this Sea Waybill is or will be affected by any hindrance, risk, delay, difficulty or disadvantage of whatsoever kind, and if by virtue of sub-clause 8 (1) the Carrier has no duty to complete the performance of the contract, the Carrier (whether or not the transport is commenced) may elect to:
(a) treat the performance of this Contract as terminated and place the goods at the Merchant's disposal at any place which the Carrier shall deem safe and convenient; or
(b) deliver the goods at the place designated for delivery.
In any event the Carrier shall be entitled to full freight for goods received for transportation and additional compensation for extra costs resulting from the circumstances referred to above.

III. CARRIER'S LIABILITY

9. Basic Liability.
(1) The Carrier shall be liable for loss of or damage to the goods occurring between the time when he receives the goods into his charge and the time of delivery.
(2) The Carrier shall be responsible for the acts and omissions of any person of whose services he makes use for the performance of the contract of carriage evidenced by this Sea Waybill.
(3) The Carrier shall, however, be relieved of liability for any loss or damage if such loss or damage arose or resulted from:
(a) The wrongful act or neglect of the Merchant.
(b) Compliance with the instructions of the person entitled to give them.
(c) The lack of or defective conditions of packing in the case of goods which, by their nature, are liable to wastage or to be damaged when not packed or when not properly packed.
(d) Handling, loading, stowage or unloading of the goods by the Merchant.
(e) Inherent vice of the goods.
(f) Insufficiency or inadequacy of marks or numbers on the goods, covering, or unit loads.
(g) Strikes or lock-outs or stoppages or restraints of labour from whatever cause whether partial or general.
(h) Any cause or event which the Carrier could not avoid and the consequence whereof he could not prevent by the exercise of reasonable diligence.
(4) Where under sub-clause 9 (3) the Carrier is not under any liability in respect of some of the factors causing the loss or damage, he shall only be liable to the extent that those factors for which he is liable under this Clause have contributed to the loss or damage.
(5) The burden of proving that the loss or damage was due to one or more of the causes or events, specified in (a), (b) and (h) of sub-clause 9 (3) shall rest upon the Carrier.
(6) When the Carrier establishes that in the circumstances of the case, the loss or damage could be attributed to one or more of the causes or events, specified in (c) to (g) of sub-clause 9 (3) it shall be presumed that it was so caused. The Merchant shall, however, be entitled to prove that the loss or damage was not, in fact, caused either wholly or partly by one or more of these causes.

10. Amount of Compensation
(1) When the Carrier is liable for compensation in respect of loss of or damage to the goods, such compensation shall be calculated by reference to the value of such goods at the place and time they are delivered to the Merchant in accordance with the contract or should have been

delivered.
(2) The value of the goods shall be fixed according to the commodity exchange price or, if there be no such price, according to the current market price or, if there be no commodity exchange price or current market price, by reference to the normal value of goods of the same kind and quality.
(3) Compensation shall not, however, exceed two Special Drawing Rights per kilogramme of gross weight of the goods lost or damaged.
(4) Higher compensation may be claimed only when, with the consent of the Carrier, the value for the goods declared by the Shipper which exceeds the limits laid down in this Clause has been stated on the face of this Sea Waybill at the place indicated. In that case the amount of the declared value shall be substituted for that limit.

11. Special Provisions for Liability and Compensation
(1) Notwithstanding anything provided for in Clauses 9 and 10 of this Sea Waybill, if it can be proved where the loss or damage occurred, the Carrier and the Merchant shall, as to the liability of the Carrier, be entitled to require such liability to be determined by the provisions contained in any international convention or national law, which provisions:
(a) cannot be departed from by private contract, to the detriment of the claimant, and
(b) would have applied if the Merchant had made a separate and direct contract with the Carrier in respect of the particular stage of transport where the loss or damage occurred and received as evidence thereof any particular document which must be issued if such international convention or national law shall apply.
(2) Insofar as there is no mandatory law applying to carriage by sea by virtue of the provisions of sub-clause 11 (1), the liability of the Carrier in respect of any carriage by sea shall be determined by the International Brussels Convention 1924 as amended by the Protocol signed at Brussels on February 23rd 1968 - The Hague/Visby Rules.
The Hague/Visby Rules shall also determine the liability of the Carrier in respect of carriage by inland waterways as if such carriage were carriage by sea. Furthermore, they shall apply to all goods, whether carried on deck or under deck.

12. Delay, Consequential Loss, etc.
If the Carrier is held liable in respect of delay, consequential loss or damage other than loss of or damage to the goods, the liability of the Carrier shall be limited to the freight for the transport covered by this Sea Waybill, or to the value of the goods as determined in Clause 10, whichever is the lesser.

13. Notice of Loss of or Damage to the Goods
(1) Unless notice of loss of or damage to the goods, specifying the general nature of such loss or damage, is given in writing by the Merchant to the Carrier when the goods are handed over to the Merchant, such handing over is prima facie evidence of the Delivery by the Carrier of the goods as described in this Sea Waybill.
(2) Where the loss or damage is not apparent, the same prima facie effect shall apply if notice in writing is not given within three (3) consecutive days after the day when the goods were handed over to the Merchant.

14. Defences and Limits for the Carrier, Servants, etc.
(1) The defences and limits of liability provided for in this Sea Waybill shall apply in any action against the Carrier for loss or damage to the goods whether the action can be founded in contract or in tort.
(2) The Carrier shall not be entitled to the benefit of the limitation of liability provided for in sub-clause 10 (3), if it is proved that the loss or damage resulted from a personal act or omission of the Carrier done with intent to cause such loss or damage or recklessly and with knowledge that damage would probably result.
(3) The Merchant undertakes that no claim shall be made against any servant, agent or other persons whose services the Carrier has used in order to perform this Contract and if any claim should nevertheless be made, to indemnify the Carrier against all consequences thereof.
(4) However, the provisions of this Sea Waybill apply whenever claims relating to the performance of this Contract are made against any servant, agent or other person whose services the Carrier has used in order to perform this Contract, whether such claims are founded in contract or in tort. In entering into this Contract, the Carrier, to the extent of such provisions, does so not only on his own behalf but also as agent or trustee for such persons. The aggregate liability of the Carrier and such persons shall not exceed the limits in Clauses 10,11 and 24, respectively.

IV. DESCRIPTION OF GOODS

15. Carrier's Responsibility.
The information in this Sea Waybill shall be prima facie evidence of the taking in charge by the Carrier of the goods as described by such information unless a contrary indication, such as "shipper's weight, load and count", "Shipper-packed container" or similar expressions, have been made in the printed text or superimposed on the Sea Waybill. As between the Carrier and Consignee the information in the Sea Waybill shall be conclusive evidence of receipt of the goods as so stated and proof to the contrary shall not be permitted provided always that the Consignee has acted in good faith.

16. Shipper's Responsibility.
The Shipper shall be deemed to have guaranteed to the Carrier the accuracy, at the time the goods were taken in charge by the Carrier, of the description of the goods, marks, number, quantity and weight, as furnished by him, and the Shipper shall defend, indemnify and hold harmless the Carrier against all loss, damage and expenses arising or resulting from inaccuracies in such particulars. The right of the Carrier to such indemnity shall in no way limit his responsibility and liability under this Sea Waybill to any person other than the Shipper. The Shipper shall remain liable even if the goods have been delivered.

17. Shipper-packed Containers, etc.
(1) If a container has not been filled, packed or stowed by the Carrier, the Carrier shall not be liable for any loss of or damage to its contents and the Merchant shall cover any loss or expense incurred by the Carrier, if such loss,

damage or expense has been caused by:
(a) negligent filling, packing or stowing of the container;
(b) the contents being unsuitable for carriage in container; or
(c) the unsuitability or defective condition of the container unless the container has been supplied by the Carrier and the unsuitability or defective condition would not have been apparent upon reasonable inspection at or prior to the time when the container was filled, packed or stowed.
(2) The provisions of sub-clause (1) of this Clause also apply with respect to trailers, transportable tanks, flats and pallets which have not been filled, packed or stowed by the Carrier.
(3) The Carrier does not accept liability for damage due to the unsuitability or defective condition of reefer equipment or trailers supplied by the Merchant.

18. Dangerous Goods.
(1) The Merchant shall comply with all internationally recognised requirements and all rules which apply according to national law or by reason of international Convention, relating to the carriage of goods of a dangerous nature, and shall in any event inform the Carrier in writing of the exact nature of the danger before goods of a dangerous nature are taken into charge by the Carrier and indicate to him, if need be, the precautions to be taken.
(2) Goods of a dangerous nature which the Carrier did not know were dangerous, may, at any time or place, be unloaded, destroyed, or rendered harmless, without compensation; further, the Merchant shall be liable for all expenses, loss or damage arising out of their handing over for carriage or of their carriage.
(3) If any goods shipped with the knowledge of the Carrier as to their dangerous nature shall become a danger to any person or property, they may in like manner be landed at any place or destroyed or rendered innocuous by the Carrier without liability on the part of the Carrier except to General Average, if any.

19. Return of Containers
(1) For the purpose of this Clause the Consignor shall mean the person who concludes this Contract with the Carrier and the Consignee shall mean the person entitled to receive the goods from the Carrier.
(2) Containers, pallets or similar articles of transport supplied by or on behalf of the Carrier shall be returned to the Carrier in the same order and condition as handed over to the Merchant, normal wear and tear excepted, with interiors clean and within the time prescribed in the Carrier's tariff or elsewhere.
(3) (a) The Consignor shall be liable for any loss of, damage to, or delay, including demurrage, of such articles, incurred during the period between handing over to the Consignor and return to the Carrier for carriage.
(b) The Consignor and the Consignee shall be jointly and severally liable for any loss of, damage to, or delay, including demurrage, of such articles, incurred during the period between handing over to the Consignee and return to the Carrier.

V. FREIGHT AND LIEN

20. Freight.
(1) Freight shall be deemed earned when the goods have been taken in charge by the Carrier and shall be paid in any event.
(2) The Merchant's attention is drawn to the stipulations concerning currency in which the freight and charges are to be paid, rate of exchange, devaluation and other contingencies relative to freight and charges in the relevant tariff conditions. If no such stipulation as to devaluation exists or is applicable the following shall apply:
If the currency in which freight and charges are quoted is devalued between the date of the freight agreement and the date when the freight and charges are paid, then all freight and charges shall be automatically and immediately increased in proportion to the extent of the devaluation of the said currency.
(3) For the purpose of verifying the freight basis, the Carrier reserves the right to have the contents of containers, trailers or similar articles of transport inspected in order to ascertain the weight, measurement, value, or nature of the goods.

21. Lien.
The Carrier shall have a lien on the goods for any amount due under this Contract and for the costs of recovering the same, and may enforce such lien in any reasonable manner, including sale or disposal of the goods.

VI. MISCELLANEOUS PROVISIONS

22. General Average.
(1) General Average shall be adjusted at any port or place at the Carrier's option, and to be settled according to the York-Antwerp Rules 1994, or any modification thereof, this covering all goods, whether carried on or under deck. The New Jason Clause as approved by BIMCO to be considered as incorporated herein.
(2) Such security including a cash deposit as the Carrier may deem sufficient to cover the estimated contribution of the goods and any salvage and special charges thereon, shall, if required, be submitted to the Carrier prior to delivery of the goods.

23. Both-to-Blame Collision Clause.
The Both-to-Blame Collision Clause as adopted by BIMCO shall be considered incorporated herein.

24. U.S. Trade
(1) In case the contract evidenced by this Sea Waybill is subject to the Carriage of Goods by Sea Act of the United States of America, 1936 (U.S. COGSA), then the provisions stated in the said Act shall govern before loading and after discharge and throughout the entire time the goods are in the Carrier's custody.
(2) If the U.S. COGSA applies, and unless the nature and value of the goods have been declared by the shipper before the goods have been handed over to the Carrier and inserted in this Sea Waybill, the Carrier shall in no event be or become liable for any loss of or damage to the goods in an amount exceeding USD 500 per package or customary freight unit.

Code Name: "MULTIDOC 95"

MT Doc. No.

Consignor

Reference No.

Negotiable
MULTIMODAL TRANSPORT BILL OF LADING

Issued by The Baltic and International Maritime Council
(BIMCO), subject to the UNCTAD/ICC Rules for Multimodal
Transport Documents (ICC Publication No. 481).

Issued 1995

Consigned to order of

Notify party/address

Place of receipt

Ocean Vessel | Port of loading

Port of discharge | Place of delivery

Marks and Nos. | Quantity and description of goods | Gross weight, kg, Measurement, m³

Particulars above declared by Consignor

Freight and charges

RECEIVED the goods in apparent good order and condition, as far as
ascertained by reasonable means of checking, as specified above unless
otherwise stated.
The MTO, in accordance with and to the extent of the provisions contained in
this MT Bill of Lading, and with liberty to sub-contract, undertakes to perform
and/or in his own name to procure performance of the multimodal transport
and the delivery of the goods, including all services related thereto, from the
place and time of taking the goods in charge to the place and time of delivery
and accepts responsibility for such transport and such services.
One of the MT Bills of Lading must be surrendered duly endorsed in exchange
for the goods or delivery order.
IN WITNESS whereof MT Bill(s) of Lading has/have been signed in the number
indicated below, one of which being accomplished the other(s) to be void.

Consignor's declared value of ...... | Freight payable at | Place and date of issue

subject to payment of above extra charge.

Number of original MT Bills of Lading | Signed for the Multimodal Transport Operator (MTO)
.... as Carrier

Note:
The Merchant's attention is called to the fact that according
to Clauses 10 to 12 of this MT Bill of Lading, the liability of
the MTO is, in most cases, limited in respect of loss of or
damage to the goods.

by ....
As agent(s) only to the MTO

Printed by the BIMCO Charter Party Editor

p.t.o.

MULTIMODAL TRANSPORT BILL OF LADING

CODE NAME: "MULTIDOC 95"

I. GENERAL PROVISIONS

1. Applicability

The provisions of this Contract shall apply irrespective of whether there is a unimodal or a Multimodal Transport Contract involving one or several modes of transport.

2. Definitions

"Multimodal Transport Contract" means a single Contract for the carriage of Goods by at least two different modes of transport.

"Multimodal Transport Bill of Lading" (MT Bill of Lading) means this document evidencing a Multimodal Transport Contract and which can be replaced by electronic data interchange messages insofar as permitted by applicable law and is issued in a negotiable form.

"Multimodal Transport Operators" (MTO) means the person named on the face hereof who concludes a Multimodal Transport Contract and assumes responsibility for the performance thereof as a Carrier.

"Carrier" means the person who actually performs or undertakes to perform the carriage, or part thereof, whether he is identical with the Multimodal Transport Operator or not.

"Merchant" includes the Shipper, the Receiver, the Consignor, the Consignee, the holder of this MT Bill of Lading and the owner of the Goods.

"Consignor" means the person who concludes the Multimodal Transport Contract with the Multimodal Transport Operator.

"Consignee" means the person entitled to receive the Goods from the Multimodal Transport Operator.

"Taken in charge" means that the Goods have been handed over to and accepted for carriage by the MTO.

"Delivery" means

(i) the handing over of the Goods to the Consignee; or

(ii) the placing of the Goods at the disposal of the Consignee in accordance with the Multimodal Transport Contract or with the law or usage of the particular trade applicable at the place of delivery; or

(iii) the handing over of the Goods to an authority or other third party to whom, pursuant to the law or regulations applicable at the place of delivery, the Goods must be handed over.

"Special Drawing Rights" (SDR) means the unit of account as defined by the International Monetary Fund.

"Goods" means any property including live animals as well as containers, pallets or similar articles of transport or packaging not supplied by the MTO, irrespective of whether such property is to be or is carried on or under deck.

3. MTO's Tariff

The terms of the MTO's applicable tariff at the date of shipment are incorporated herein. Copies of the relevant provisions of the applicable tariff are available from the MTO upon request. In the case of inconsistency between this MT Bill of Lading and the applicable tariff, this MT Bill of Lading shall prevail.

4. Time Bar

The MTO shall, unless otherwise expressly agreed, be discharged of all liability under this MT Bill of Lading unless suit is brought within nine months after:

(i) the Delivery of the Goods; or

(ii) the date when the Goods should have been delivered; or

(iii) the date when, in accordance with sub-clause 10 (e) failure to deliver the Goods would give the Consignee the right to treat the Goods as lost.

5. Law and Jurisdiction

Disputes arising under this MT Bill of Lading shall be determined by the courts and in accordance with the law at the place where the MTO has his principal place of business.

II. PERFORMANCE OF THE CONTRACT

6. Methods and Routes of Transportation

(a) The MTO is entitled to perform the transport in any reasonable manner and by any reasonable means, methods and routes.

(b) In accordance herewith, for instance, in the event of carriage by sea, vessels may sail with or without pilots, undergo repairs, adjust equipment, drydock and tow vessels in all situations.

7. Optional Stowage

(a) Goods may be stowed by the MTO by means of containers, trailers, transportable tanks, flats, pallets, or similar articles of transport used to consolidate Goods.

(b) Containers, trailers, transportable tanks and covered flats, whether stowed by the MTO or received by him in a stowed condition, may be carried on or under deck without notice to the Merchant.

8. Delivery of the Goods to the Consignee

The MTO undertakes to perform or to procure the performance of all acts necessary to ensure Delivery of the Goods:

(i) when the MT Bill of Lading has been issued in a negotiable form "to bearer", to the person surrendering one original of the document; or

(ii) when the MT Bill of Lading has been issued in a negotiable form "to order", to the person surrendering one original of the document duly endorsed; or

(iii) when the MT Bill of Lading has been issued in a negotiable form to a named person, to that person upon proof of his identity and surrender of one original document; if such document has been transferred "to order" or in blank, the provisions of (ii) above apply.

9. Hindrances, etc. Affecting Performance

(a) The MTO shall use reasonable endeavours to complete the transport and to deliver the Goods at the place designated for Delivery.

(b) If at any time the performance of the Contract as evidenced by this MT Bill of Lading is or will be affected by any hindrance, risk, delay, difficulty or disadvantage of whatsoever kind and if by virtue of sub-clause 9 (a) the MTO has no duty to complete the performance of the Contract, the MTO (whether or not the transport is commenced) may elect to

(i) treat the performance of this Contract as terminated and place the Goods at the Merchant's disposal at any place which the MTO shall deem safe and convenient; or

(ii) deliver the Goods at the place designated for Delivery.

(c) If the Goods are not taken Delivery of by the Merchant within a reasonable time after the MTO has called upon him to take Delivery, the MTO shall be at liberty to put the Goods in safe custody on behalf of the Merchant at the latter's risk and expense.

(d) In any event the MTO shall be entitled to full freight for Goods received for transportation and additional compensation for extra costs resulting from the circumstances referred to above.

III. LIABILITY OF THE MTO

10. Basis of Liability

(a) The responsibility of the MTO for the Goods under this Contract covers the period from the time the MTO has taken the Goods into his charge to the time of their Delivery.

(b) Subject to the defences set forth in Clauses 11 and 12, the MTO shall be liable for loss of or damage to the Goods as well as for delay in Delivery, if the occurrence which caused the loss, damage or delay in Delivery took place while the Goods were in his charge as defined in sub-clause 10 (a), unless the MTO proves that no fault or neglect of his own, his servants or agents or any other person referred to in sub-clause 10 (c) has caused or contributed to the loss damage or delay in Delivery.

However, the MTO shall only be liable for loss following from delay in Delivery if the Consignor has made a written declaration of interest in timely Delivery which has been accepted in writing by the MTO.

(c) The MTO shall be responsible for the acts and omissions of his servants or agents, when any such servant or agent is acting within the scope of his employment, or of any other person of whose services he makes use for the performance of the Contract, as if such acts and omissions were his own.

(d) Delay in Delivery occurs when the Goods have not been delivered within the time expressly agreed upon or, in the absence of such agreement, within the time which it would be reasonable to require of a diligent MTO, having regard to the circumstances of the case.

(e) If the Goods have not been delivered within ninety (90) consecutive days following the date of Delivery determined according to Clause 10 (d) above, the claimant may, in the absence of evidence to the contrary, treat the Goods as lost.

11. Defences for Carriage by Sea or Inland Waterways

Notwithstanding the provisions of Clause 10 (b), the MTO shall not be responsible for loss, damage or delay in Delivery with respect to Goods carried by sea or inland waterways when such loss, damage or delay during such carriage results from:

(i) act, neglect or default of the master, mariner, pilot or the servants of the Carrier in the navigation or in the management of the vessel;

(ii) fire, unless caused by the actual fault or privity of the Carrier;

(iii) the causes listed in the Hague-Visby Rules article 4.2 (c) to (p);

however, always provided that whenever loss or damage has resulted from unseaworthiness of the vessel, the MTO can prove that due diligence has been exercised to make the vessel seaworthy at the commencement of the voyage.

12. Limitation of Liability

(a) Unless the nature and value of the Goods have been declared by the Consignor before the Goods have been taken in charge by the MTO and inserted in the MT Bill of Lading, the MTO shall in no event be or become liable for any loss of or damage to the Goods in an amount exceeding:

(i) when the Carriage of Goods by Sea Act of the United States of America, 1936 (US COGSA) applies USD 500 per package or customary freight unit; or

(ii) when any other law applies, the equivalent of 666.67 SDR per package or unit or two SDR per kilogramme of gross weight of the Goods lost or damaged, whichever is the higher.

(b) Where a container, pallet or similar article of transport is loaded with more than one package or unit, the packages or other shipping units enumerated in the MT Bill of Lading as packed in such article of transport are deemed packages or shipping units. Except as aforesaid, such article of transport shall be considered the package or unit.

(c) Notwithstanding the above-mentioned provisions, if the Multimodal Transport does not, according to the Contract, include carriage of Goods by sea or by inland waterways, the liability of the MTO shall be limited to an amount not exceeding 8.33 SDR per kilogramme of gross weight of the Goods lost or damaged.

(d) In any case, when the loss of or damage to the Goods occurred during one particular stage of the Multimodal Transport, in respect of which an applicable international convention or mandatory national law would have provided another limit of liability if a separate contract of carriage had been made for that particular stage of transport, then the limit of the MTO's liability for such loss or damage shall be determined by reference to the provisions of such convention or mandatory national law.

(e) If the MTO is liable in respect of loss following from delay in Delivery, or consequential loss or damage other than loss of or damage to the Goods, the liability of the MTO shall be limited to an amount not exceeding the equivalent of the freight under the Multimodal Transport Contract for the Multimodal Transport.

(f) The aggregate liability of the MTO shall not exceed the limits of liability for total loss of the Goods.

(g) The MTO is not entitled to the benefit of the limitation of liability if it is proved that the loss, damage or delay in Delivery resulted from a personal act or omission of the MTO done with the intent to cause such loss, damage or delay, or recklessly and with knowledge that such loss, damage or delay would probably result.

13. Assessment of Compensation

(a) Assessment of compensation for loss of or damage to the Goods shall be made by reference to the value of such Goods at the place and time they are delivered to the Consignee or at the place and time when, in accordance with the Multimodal Transport Contract, they should have been so delivered.

(b) The value of the Goods shall be determined according to the current commodity exchange price or, if there is no such price, according to the current market price or, if there is no commodity exchange price or current market price, by reference to the normal value of Goods of the same kind and quality.

14. Notice of loss of or Damage to the Goods

(a) Unless notice of loss of or damage to the Goods, specifying the general nature of such loss or damage, is given in writing by the Consignee to the MTO when the Goods are handed over to the Consignee, such handing over is prima facie evidence of the Delivery by the MTO of the Goods as described in the MT Bill of Lading.

(b) Where the loss or damage is not apparent, the same prima facie effect shall apply if notice in writing is not given within six consecutive days after the day when the Goods were handed over to the Consignee.

15. Defences and Limits for the MTO, Servants, etc.

(a) The provisions of this Contract apply to all claims against the MTO relating to the performance of the Multimodal Transport Contract, whether the claim be founded in contract or in tort.

(b) The Merchant undertakes that no claim shall be made against any servant, agent or other persons whose services the MTO has used in order to perform the Multimodal Transport Contract and if any claim should nevertheless be made, to indemnify the MTO against all consequences thereof.

(c) However, the provisions of this Contract apply whenever claims relating to the performance of the Multimodal Transport Contract are made against any servant, agent or other person whose services the MTO has used in order to perform the Multimodal Transport Contract, whether such claims are founded in contract or in tort. In entering into this Contract, the MTO, to the extent of such provisions, does so not only on his own behalf but also as agent or trustee for such persons. The aggregate liability of the MTO and such persons shall not exceed the limits in Clause 12.

IV. DESCRIPTION OF GOODS

16. MTO's Responsibility

The information in the MT Bill of Lading shall be prima facie evidence of the taking in charge by the MTO of the Goods as described by such information unless a contrary indication, such as "shipper's weight, load and counts", "shipper-packed container" or similar expressions, have been made in the printed text or superimposed on the document. Proof to the contrary shall not be admissible when the MT Bill of Lading has been transferred, or the equivalent electronic data interchange message has been transmitted to and acknowledged by the Consignee who in good faith has relied and acted thereon.

17. Consignor's Responsibility

(a) The Consignor shall be deemed to have guaranteed to the MTO the accuracy, at the time the Goods were taken in charge by the MTO, of all particulars relating to the general nature of the Goods, their marks, number, weight, volume and quantity and, if applicable, to the dangerous character of the Goods as furnished by him or on his behalf for insertion in the MT Bill of Lading.

(b) The Consignor shall indemnify the MTO for any loss or expense caused by inaccuracies in or inadequacies of the particulars referred to above.

(c) The right of the MTO to such indemnity shall in no way limit his liability under the Multimodal Transport Contract to any person other than the Consignor.

(d) The Consignor shall remain liable even if the MT Bill of Lading has been transferred by him.

18. Return of Containers

(a) Containers, pallets or similar articles of transport supplied by or on behalf of the MTO shall be returned to the MTO in the same order and condition as when handed over to the Merchant, normal wear and tear excepted, with interiors clean and within the time prescribed in the MTO's tariff or elsewhere.

(b) (i) The Consignor shall be liable for any loss of, damage to, or delay, including demurrage, of such articles, incurred during the period between handing over to the Consignor and return to the MTO for carriage.

(ii) The Consignor and the Consignee shall be jointly and severally liable for any loss of, damage to, or delay, including demurrage, of such articles, incurred during the period between handing over to the Consignee and return to the MTO.

19. Dangerous Goods

(a) The Consignor shall comply with all internationally recognised requirements and all rules which apply according to national law or by reason of international convention, relating to the carriage of Goods of a dangerous nature, and shall in any event inform the MTO in writing of the exact nature of the danger before Goods of a dangerous nature are taken in charge by the MTO and indicate to him, if need be, the precautions to be taken.

(b) If the Consignor fails to provide such information and the MTO is unaware of the dangerous nature of the Goods and the necessary precautions to be taken and if, at any time, they are deemed to be a hazard to life or property, they may at any place be unloaded, destroyed or rendered harmless, as circumstances may require, without compensation and the Consignor shall be iable for all loss, damage, delay or expenses arising out of their being taken in charge, or their carriage, or of any service incidental thereto.

The burden of proving that the MTO knew the exact nature of the danger constituted by the carriage of the said Goods shall rest upon the person entitled to the Goods.

(c) If any Goods shipped with the knowledge of the MTO as to their dangerous nature shall become a danger to the vessel or cargo, they may in like manner be landed at any place or destroyed or rendered innocuous by the MTO without liability on the part of the MTO except to General Average, if any.

20. Consignor-packed Containers, etc.

(a) If a container has not been filled, packed or stowed by the MTO, the MTO shall not be liable for any loss of or damage to its contents and the Consignor shall indemnify any loss or expense incurred by the MTO if such loss, damage or expense has been caused by:

(i) negligent filling, packing or stowing of the container;

(ii) the contents being unsuitable for carriage in container; or

(iii) the unsuitability or defective condition of the container unless the container has been supplied by the MTO and the unsuitability or defective condition would not have been apparent upon reasonable inspection at or prior to the time when the container was filled, packed or stowed.

(b) The provisions of sub-clause (a) of this Clause also apply with respect to trailers, transportable tanks, flats and pallets which have not been filled, packed or stowed by the MTO.

(c) The MTO does not accept liability for damage due to the unsuitability or defective condition of reefer equipment or trailers supplied by the Merchant.

V. FREIGHT AND LIEN

21. Freight

(a) Freight shall be deemed earned when the Goods have been taken into charge by the MTO and shall be paid in any event.

(b) The Merchant's attention is drawn to the stipulations concerning currency in which the freight and charges are to be paid, rate of exchange, devaluation and other contingencies relative to freight and charges in the relevant tariff conditions. If no such stipulation as to devaluation exists or is applicable the following provision shall apply:

If the currency in which freight and charges are quoted is devalued or revalued between the date of the freight agreement and the date when the freight and charges are paid, then all freight and charges shall be automatically and immediately changed in proportion to the extent of the devaluation or revaluation of the said currency. When the MTO has consented to payment in other currency than the above mentioned currency, then all freight and charges shall - subject to the preceding paragraph - be paid at the highest selling rate of exchange for banker's sight draft current on the day when such freight and charges are paid. If the banks are closed on the day when the freight is paid the rate to be used will be the one in force on the last day the banks were cpen.

(c) For the purpose of verifying the freght basis the MTO reserves the right to have the contents of containers, trailers or similar articles of transport inspected in order to ascertain the weight, measurement, value, or nature of the Goods. If on such inspection it is found that the declaration is not correct, it is agreed that a sum equal either to five times the difference between the correct freight and the freight charges or to double the correct freight less the freight charges, whichever sum is the smaller, shall be payable as liquidated damages to the MTO notwithstanding any other sum having been stated on this MT Bill of Lading as the freight payable.

(d) All dues, taxes and charges levied on the Goods and other expenses in connection therewith shall be paid by the Merchant.

22. Lien

The MTO shall have a lien on the Goods for any amount due under this Contract and for the costs of recovering the same, and may enforce such lien in any reasonable manner, including sale or disposal of the Goods.

VI. MISCELLANEOUS PROVISIONS

23. General Average

(a) General Average shall be adjusted at any port or place at the MTO's option, and to be settled according to the York-Antwerp Rules 1994, or any modification thereof, this covering all Goods, whether carried on or under deck. The New Jason Clause as approved by BIMCO to be considered as incorporated herein.

(b) Such security including a cash deposit as the MTO may deem sufficient to cover the estimated contribution of the Goods and any salvage and special charges thereon, shall, if required, be submitted to the MTO prior to Delivery of the Goods.

24. Both-to-Blame Collision Clause

The Both-to-Blame Collision Clause as adopted by BIMCO shall be considered incorporated herein.

25. U.S. Trade

In case the Contract evidenced by this MT Bill of Lading is subject to U.S COGSA, then the Provisions stated in said Act shall govern before loading and after discharge and throughout the entire time the Goods are in the Carrier's custody.

Draft Copy

Draft Copy

Code Name: "MULTIWAYBILL"

Consignor

MT Doc. No.

Reference No.

Consignee (not to order)

MULTIMODAL TRANSPORT WAYBILL

Issued by The Baltic and International Maritime Council
(BIMCO), subject to the UNCTAD/ICC Rules for Multimodal
Transport Documents (ICC Publication No. 481) and to
the CMI Uniform Rules for Sea Waybills.

Issued 1995

Notify party/address

Place of receipt

Ocean Vessel	Port of loading

Port of discharge	Place of delivery

Marks and Nos.	Quantity and description of goods	Gross weight, kg, Measurement, m³

Particulars above declared by Consignor

Freight and charges

RECEIVED the goods in apparent good order and condition and, as far as
ascertained by reasonable means of checking, as specified above unless
otherwise stated.

The MTO, in accordance with and to the extent of the provisions contained in
this MT Waybill, and with liberty to sub-contract, undertakes to perform and/
or in his own name to procure performance of the multimodal transport and
the delivery of the goods, including all services related thereto, from the place
and time of taking the goods in charge to the place and time of delivery and
accepts responsibility for such transport and such services.

The Consignor shall be entitled to transfer right of control of the cargo to the
Consignee, the exercise of such option to be noted on this MT Waybill and to
be made no later than the receipt of the cargo by the Carrier.

Consignor's declared value of ......

subject to payment of above extra charge.

Note:
The Merchant's attention is called to the fact that according
to Clauses 10 to 12 of this MT Waybill, the liability of the
MTO is, in most cases, limited in respect of loss of or
damage to the goods.

Freight payable at

Place and date of issue

Signed for the Multimodal Transport Operator (MTO)
.... as Carrier

by ....
As agent(s) only to the MTO

Printed by the BIMCO Charter Party Editor

p.t.o.

Draft Copy

NON - NEGOTIABLE

Draft Copy

MULTIMODAL TRANSPORT WAYBILL

CODE NAME: "MULTIWAYBILL 95"

I. GENERAL PROVISIONS

1. Applicability
The provisions of this Contract shall apply irrespective of whether there is a unimodal or a Multimodal Transport Contract involving one or several modes of transport.

2. Definitions
"Multimodal Transport Contract" means a single Contract for the carriage of Goods by at least two different modes of transport.
"Multimodal Transport Waybill" (MT Waybill) means this document evidencing a Multimodal Transport Contract and which can be replaced by electronic data interchange messages insofar as permitted by applicable law and is issued in a non-negotiable form clearly indicating a named Consignee.
"Multimodal Transport Operator" (MTO) means the person named on the face hereof who concludes a Multimodal Transport Contract and assumes responsibility for the performance thereof as a Carrier.
"Carrier" means the person who actually performs or undertakes to perform the carriage, or part thereof, whether he is identical with the Multimodal Transport Operator or not.
"Merchant" includes the Shipper, the Receiver, the Consignor, the Consignee and the owner of the Goods.
"Consignor" means the person who concludes the Multimodal Transport Contract with the Multimodal Transport Operator.
"Consignee" means the person entitled to receive the Goods from the Multimodal Transport Operator.
"Taken in charge" means that the Goods have been handed over to and accepted for carriage by the MTO.
"Delivery" means
(i) the handing over of the Goods to the Consignee; or
(ii) the placing of the Goods at the disposal of the Consignee in accordance with the Multimodal Transport Contract or with the law or usage of the particular trade applicable at the place of delivery; or
(iii) the handing over of the Goods to an authority or other third party to whom, pursuant to the law or regulations applicable at the place oil delivery, the Goods must be handed over.
"Special Drawing Rights" (SDR) means the unit of account as defined by the International Monetary Fund.
"Goods" means any property including live animals as well as containers, pallets or similar articles of transport or packaging not supplied by the MTO, irrespective of whether such property is to be or is carried on or under deck.

3. MTO's Tariff
The terms of the MTO's applicable tariff at the date of shipment are incorporated herein. Copies of the relevant provisions of the applicable tariff are available from the MTO upon request. In the case of inconsistency between this MT Waybill and the applicable tariff, this MT Waybill shall prevail.

4. Time Bar
The MTO shall, unless otherwise expressly agreed, be discharged of all liability under this MT Waybill unless suit is brought within nine months after:
(i) the Delivery of the Goods; or
(ii) the date when the Goods should have been delivered; or
(iii) the date when, in accordance with sub-clause 10 (e) failure to deliver the Goods would give the Consignee the right to treat the Goods as lost.

5. Law and Jurisdiction
Disputes arising under this MT Waybill shall be determined by the courts and in accordance with the law at the place where the MTO has his principal place of business.

II. PERFORMANCE OF THE CONTRACT

6. Methods and Routes of Transportation
(a) The MTO is entitled to perform the transport in any reasonable manner and by any reasonable means, methods and routes.
(b) In accordance herewith, for instance, in the event of carriage by sea, vessels may sail with or without pilots, undergo repairs, adjust equipment, drydock and tow vessels in all situations.

7. Optional Stowage
(a) Goods may be stowed by the MTO by means of containers, trailers, transportable tanks, flats, pallets, or similar articles of transport used to consolidate Goods.
(b) Containers trailers, transportable tanks and covered flats, whether stowed by the MTO or received by him in a stowed condition, may be carried on or under deck without notice to the Merchant.

8. Delivery of the Goods to the Consignee
The MTO undertakes to perform or to procure the performance of all acts necessary to ensure Delivery of the Goods, upon proof of his identity, to the person named as Consignee in the document or a person as instructed by the Consignor or by a person who has acquired the Consignor's or the Consignee's rights under the Multimodal Transport Contract to give such instructions.

9. Hindrances, etc. Affecting Performance
(a) The MTO shall use reasonable endeavours to complete the transport and to deliver the Goods at the place designated for Delivery.
(b) If at any time the performance of the Contract as evidenced by this MT Waybill is or will be affected by any hindrance, risk, delay, difficulty or disadvantage of whatsoever kind, and if by virtue of sub-clause 9 (a) the MTO has no duty to complete the performance of the Contract, the MTO (whether or not the transport is commenced) may elect to
(i) treat the performance of this Contract as terminated and place the Goods at the Merchant's disposal at any place which the MTO shall deem safe and convenient; or
(ii) deliver the Goods at the place designated for Delivery.
(c) If the Goods are not taken Delivery of by the Merchant within a reasonable time after the MTO has called upon him to take Delivery, the MTO shall be at liberty to put the Goods in safe custody on behalf of the Merchant at the latter's risk and expense.
(d) In any event the MTO shall be entitled to full freight for Goods received for transportation and additional compensation for extra costs resulting from the circumstances referred to above.

III. LIABILITY OF THE MTO

10. Basis of Liability
(a) The responsibility of the MTO for the Goods under this Contract covers the period from the time the MTO has taken the Goods into his charge to the time of their Delivery.
(b) Subject to the defences set forth in Clauses 11 and 12, the MTO shall be liable for loss of or damage to the Goods, as well as for delay in Delivery, if the occurrence which caused the loss, damage or delay in Delivery took place while the Goods were in his charge as defined in sub-clause 10 (a) unless the MTO proves that no fault or neglect of his own his servants or agents or any other person referred to in sub-clause 10 (c) has caused or contributed to the loss, damage or delay in Delivery.
However, the MTO shall only be liable for loss following from delay in Delivery if the Consignor has made a written declaration of interest in timely Delivery which has been accepted in writing by the MTO.
(c) The MTO shall be responsible for the acts and omissions of his servants or agents, when any such servant or agent is acting within the scope of his employment, or of any other person of whose services he makes use for the performance of the Contract, as if such acts and omissions were his own.
(d) Delay in Delivery occurs when the Goods have not been delivered within the time expressly agreed upon or, in the absence of such agreement, within the time which it would be reasonable to require of a diligent MTO, having regard to the circumstances of the case.
(e) If the Goods have not been delivered within ninety (90) consecutive days following the date of Delivery determined according to Clause 10 (d) above, the claimant may, in the absence of evidence to the contrary, treat the Goods as lost.

11. Defences for Carriage by Sea or Inland Waterways
Notwithstanding the provisions of Clause 10 (b), the MTO shall not be responsible for loss, damage or delay in Delivery with respect to Goods carried by sea or inland waterways when such loss, damage or delay during such carriage results from:
(i) act, neglect or default of the master, mariner, pilot or the servants of the Carrier in the navigation or in the management of the vessel;
(ii) fire, unless caused by the actual fault or privity of the Carrier;
(iii) the causes listed in the Hague-Visby Rules article 4.2 (c) to (p);
however, always provided that whenever loss or damage has resulted from unseaworthiness of the vessel, the MTO can prove that due diligence has been exercised to make the vessel seaworthy at the commencement of the voyage.

12. Limitation of Liability
(a) Unless the nature and value of the Goods have been declared by the Consignor before the Goods have been taken in charge by the MTO and inserted in the MT Waybill, the MTO shall in no event be or become liable for any loss of or damage to the Goods in an amount exceeding:
(i) when the Carriage of Goods by Sea Act of the United States of America, 1936 (US COGSA) applies USD 500 per package or customary freight unit; or
(ii) when any other law applies, the equivalent of 666.67 SDR per package or unit or two SDR per kilogramme of gross weight of the Goods lost or damaged, whichever is the higher.
(b) Where a container, pallet, or similar article of transport is loaded with more than one package or unit, the packages or other shipping units enumerated in the MT Waybill as packed in such article of transport are deemed packages or shipping units. Except as aforesaid, such article of transport shall be considered the package or unit.
(c) Notwithstanding the above-mentioned provisions, if the Multimodal Transport does not, according to the Contract, include carriage of Goods by sea or by inland waterways, the liability of the MTO shall be limited to an amount not exceeding 8.33 SDR per kilogramme of gross weight of the Goods lost or damaged.
(d) In any case, when the loss of or damage to the Goods occurred during one particular stage of the Multimodal Transport, in respect of which an applicable international convention or mandatory national law would have provided another limit of liability if a separate contract of carriage had been made for that particular stage of transport, then the limit of the MTO's liability for such loss or damage shall be determined by reference to the provisions of such convention or mandatory national law.
(e) If the MTO is liable in respect of loss following from delay in Delivery, or consequential loss or damage other than loss of or damage to the Goods, the liability of the MTO shall be limited to an amount not exceeding the equivalent of the freight under the Multimodal Transport Contract for the Multimodal Transport.
(f) The aggregate liability of the MTO shall not exceed the limits of liability for total loss of the Goods.
(g) The MTO is not entitled to the benefit of the limitation of liability if it is proved that the loss, damage or delay in Delivery resulted from a personal act or omission of the MTO done with the intent to cause such loss, damage or delay, or recklessly and with knowledge that such loss, damage or delay would probably result.

13. Assessment of Compensation
(a) Assessment of compensation for loss of or damage to the Goods shall be made by reference to the value of such Goods at the place and time they are delivered to the Consignee or at the place and time when, in accordance with the Multimodal Transport Contract they should have been so delivered.
(b) The value of the Goods shall be determined according to the current commodity exchange price or, if there is no such price, according to the current market price or, if there is no commodity exchange price or current market price, by reference to the normal value of Goods of the same kind and quality.

14. Notice of Loss of or Damage to the Goods
(a) Unless notice of loss of or damage to the Goods, specifying the general nature of such loss or damage, is given in writing by the Consignee to the MTO when the Goods are handed over to the Consignee, such handing over is prima facie evidence of the Delivery by the MTO of the Goods as described in the MT Waybill.
(b) Where the loss or damage is not apparent, the same prima facie effect shall apply if notice in writing is not given within six consecutive days after the day when the Goods were handed over to the Consignee.

15. Defences and Limits for the MTO, Servants, etc.
(a) The provisions of this Contract apply to all claims against the MTO relating to the performance of the Multimodal Transport Contract, whether the claim be founded in contract or in tort.
(b) The Merchant undertakes that no claim shall be made against any servant. agent or other persons whose services the MTO has used in order to perform the Multimodal Transport Contract and if any claim should nevertheless be made, to indemnify the MTO against all consequences thereof.
(c) However, the provisions of this Contract apply whenever claims relating to the performance of the Multimodal Transport Contract are made against any servant, agent or other person whose services the MTO has used in order to perform the Multimodal Transport Contract, whether such claims are founded in contract or in tort. In entering into this Contract, the MTO, to the extent of such provisions, does so not only on his own behalf but also as agent or trustee for such persons. The aggregate liability of the MTO and such persons shall not exceed the limits in Clause 12.

IV. DESCRIPTION OF GOODS

16. MTO's Responsibility
The information in the MT Waybill shall be prima facie evidence of the taking in charge by the MTO of the Goods as described by such information unless a contrary indication, such as "shipper's weight, load and count", "shipper-packed container" or similar expressions, have been made in the printed text or superimposed on the document. As between the Carrier and the Consignee the information in the MT Waybill shall be conclusive evidence of receipt of the Goods as so stated and proof to the contrary shall not be permitted provided always that the Consignee has acted in good faith.

17. Consignor's Responsibility
(a) The Consignor shall be deemed to have guaranteed to the MTO the accuracy, at the time the Goods were taken in charge by the MTO, of all particulars relating to the general nature of the Goods, their marks, number, weight, volume and quantity and, if applicable, to the dangerous character of the Goods as furnished by him or on his behalf for insertion in the MT Waybill.
(b) The Consignor shall indemnify the MTO for any loss or expense caused by inaccuracies in or inadequacies of the particulars referred to above.
(c) The right of the MTO to such indemnity shall in no way limit his liability under the Multimodal Transport Contract to any person other than the Consignor.
(d) The Consignor shall remain liable even if the Goods have been delivered.

18. Return of Containers
(a) Containers pallets or similar articles of transport supplied by or on behalf of the MTO shall be returned to the MTO in the same order and condition as handed over to the Merchant, normal wear and tear excepted, with interiors clean and within the time prescribed in the MTO's tariff or elsewhere.
(b) (i) The Consignor shall be liable for any loss of, damage to, or delay, including demurrage, of such articles, incurred during the period between handing over to the Consignor and return to the MTO for carriage.

(ii) The Consignor and the Consignee shall be jointly and severally liable for any loss of, damage to, or delay, including demurrage, of such articles, incurred during the period between handing over to the Consignee and return to the MTO.

19. Dangerous Goods
(a) The Consignor shall comply with all internationally recognised requirements and all rules which apply according to national law or by reason of international convention, relating to the carriage of Goods of a dangerous nature, and shall in any event inform the MTO in writing of the exact nature of the danger before Goods of a dangerous nature are taken in charge by the MTO and indicate to him, if need be, the precautions to be taken.
(b) If the Consignor fails to provide such information and the MTO is unaware of the dangerous nature of the Goods and the necessary precautions to be taken and if, at any time, they are deemed to be a hazard to life or property, they may at any place be unloaded, destroyed or rendered harmless, as circumstances may require, without compensation and the Consignor shall be liable for all loss, damage, delay or expenses arising out of their being taken in charge, or their carriage, or of any service incidental thereto.
The burden of proving that the MTO knew the exact nature of the danger constituted by the carriage of the said Goods shall rest upon the Claimant.
(c) If any Goods shipped with the knowledge of the MTO as to their dangerous nature shall become a danger to the vessel or cargo, they may in like manner be landed at any place or destroyed or rendered innocuous by the MTO without liability on the part of the MTO except to General Average, if any.

20. Consignor-packed Containers, etc.
(a) If a container has not been filled, packed or stowed by the MTO, the MTO shall not be liable for any loss of or damage to its contents and the Consignor shall indemnify any loss or expense incurred by the MTO if such loss, damage or expense has been caused by:
(i) negligent filling, packing or stowing of the container;
(ii) the contents being unsuitable for carriage in container; or
(iii) the unsuitability or defective condition of the container unless the container has been supplied by the MTO and the unsuitability or defective condition would not have been apparent upon reasonable inspection at or prior to the time when the container was filled, packed or stowed.
(b) The provisions of sub-clause (a) of this Clause also apply with respect to trailers, transportable tanks, flats and pallets which have not been filled, packed or stowed by the MTO.
(c) The MTO does not accept liability for damage due to the unsuitability or defective condition of reefer equipment or trailers supplied by the Merchant.

V. FREIGHT AND LIEN

21. Freight
(a) Freight shall be deemed earned when the Goods have been taken into charge by the MTO and shall be paid in any event.
(b) The Merchant's attention is drawn to the stipulations concerning currency in which the freight and charges are to be paid, rate of exchange, devaluation and other contingencies relative to freight and charges in the relevant tariff conditions. If no such stipulation as to devaluation exists or is applicable the following provision shall apply:
If the currency in which freight and charges are quoted is devalued or revalued between the date of the freight agreement and the date when the freight and charges are paid, then all freight and charges shall be automatically and immediately changed in proportion to the extent of the devaluation or revaluation of the said currency. When the MTO has consented to payment in other currency than the above mentioned currency, then all freight and charges shall - subject to the preceding paragraph - be paid at the highest selling rate of exchange for banker's sight draft current on the day when such freight and charges are paid. If the banks are closed on the day when the freight is paid the rate to be used will be the one in force on the last day the banks were open.
(c) For the purpose of verifying the freight basis, the MTO reserves the right to have the contents of containers, trailers or similar articles of transport inspected in order to ascertain the weight, measurement, value or nature of the Goods. If on such inspection it is found that the declaration is not correct, it is agreed that a sum equal either to five times the difference between the correct freight and the freight charges or to double the correct freight less the freight charges, whichever sum is the smaller, shall be payable as liquidated damages to the MTO notwithstanding any other sum having been stated on this MT Waybill as the freight payable.
(d) All dues, taxes and charges levied on the Goods and other expenses in connection therewith shall be paid by the Merchant.

22. Lien
The MTO shall have a lien on the Goods for any amount due under this Contract and for the costs of recovering the same, and may enforce such lien in any reasonable manner, including sale or disposal of the Goods.

VI. MISCELLANEOUS PROVISIONS

23. General Average
(a) General Average shall be adjusted at any port or place at the MTO's option and to be settled according to the York-Antwerp Rules 1994, or any modification thereof, this covering all Goods, whether carried on or under deck. The New Jason Clause as approved by BIMCO to be considered as incorporated herein.
(b) Such security including a cash deposit as the MTO may deem sufficient to cover the estimated contribution of the Goods and any salvage and special charges thereon shall, if required, be submitted to the MTO prior to Delivery of the Goods.

24. Both-to-Btame Collision Clause
The Both-to-Blame Collision Clause as adopted by BIMCO shall be considered incorporated herein.

25. U.S. Trade
In case the Contract evidenced by this MT Waybill is subject to U.S. COGSA, then the provisions stated in said Act shall govern before loading and after discharge and throughout the entire time the Goods are in the Carrier's custody.

Draft Copy

This computer generated form is printed by authority of BIMCO. Any insertion or deletion to the form must be clearly visible. In event of any modification being made to the preprinted text of this document, which is not clearly visible, the original BIMCO approved document shall apply. BIMCO assume no responsibility for any loss or damage caused as a result of discrepancies between the original BIMCO document and this document.

Page 1

Agents (full style and address)	**BIMCO LINER BOOKING NOTE** **CODE NAME: "CONLINEBOOKING 2000"**	
	Place and date	
	Vessel	
Carrier (full style and address)	Time for shipment (about)	
	Port of loading**	
	Port of discharge	
Merchant* (full style and address)	Merchant's representatives at loading port (full style and address)	

Container No./Seal No./Marks and Numbers (if available)	Number and kind of packages; description of cargo	Gross weight, kg (if available)	Measurement, m³ (if available)
	Draft Copy		

Freight details and charges	Special terms, if agreed
Freight (state prepayable or payable at destination)	

It is hereby agreed that this Contract shall be performed subject to the terms contained on Page 1 and 2 hereof which shall prevail over any previous arrangements and which shall in turn be superseded (except as to deadfreight) by the terms of the Bill of Lading.

Signature (Merchant)	Signature (Carrier)

*As defined hereinafter (Cl. 1)
**(or so near thereunto as the Vessel may safely get and lie always afloat)

Printed and sold by Fr. G. Knudtzons Bogtrykkeri A/S, Vallensbaekvej 61, DK-2625 Vallensbaek, Fax: +45 4366 0701
by authority of The Baltic and International Maritime Council (BIMCO), Copenhagen

FULL TERMS OF THE CARRIER'S BILL OF LADING FORM*

1. Definition.
"Merchant" includes the shipper, the receiver, the consignor, the consignee, the holder of the Bill of Lading, the owner of the cargo and any person entitled to possession of the cargo.

2. Notification.
Any mention in this Bill of Lading of parties to be notified of the arrival of the cargo is solely for the information of the Carrier and failure to give such notification shall not involve the Carrier in any liability nor relieve the Merchant of any obligation hereunder.

3. Liability for Carriage Between Port of Loading and Port of Discharge.
(a) The International Convention for the Unification of Certain Rules of Law relating to Bills of Lading signed at Brussels on 25 August 1924 ("the Hague Rules") as amended by the Protocol signed at Brussels on 23 February 1968 ("the Hague-Visby Rules") and as enacted in the country of shipment shall apply to this Contract. When the Hague-Visby Rules are not enacted in the country of shipment, the corresponding legislation of the country of destination shall apply, irrespective of whether such legislation may only regulate outbound shipments.
When there is no enactment of the Hague-Visby Rules in either the country of shipment or in the country of destination, the Hague-Visby Rules shall apply to this Contract save where the Hague Rules as enacted in the country of shipment or, if no such enactment is in place, the Hague Rules as enacted in the country of destination apply compulsorily to this Contract.
The Protocol signed at Brussels on 21 December 1979 ("the SDR Protocol 1979") shall apply where the Hague-Visby Rules apply, whether mandatorily or by this Contract.
The Carrier shall in no case be responsible for loss of or damage to cargo arising prior to loading, after discharging, or with respect to deck cargo and live animals.
(b) If the Carrier is held liable in respect of delay, consequential loss or damage other than loss of or damage to the cargo, the liability of the Carrier shall be limited to the freight for the carriage covered by this Bill of Lading, or to the limitation amount as determined in sub-clause 3(a), whichever is the lesser.
(c) The aggregate liability of the Carrier and/or any of his servants, agents or independent contractors under this Contract shall, in no circumstances, exceed the limits of liability for the total loss of the cargo under sub-clause 3(a) or, if applicable, the Additional Clause.

4. Law and Jurisdiction.
Disputes arising out of or in connection with this Bill of Lading shall be exclusively determined by the courts and in accordance with the law of the place where the Carrier has his principal place of business, as stated on Page 1, except as provided elsewhere herein.

5. The Scope of Carriage.
The intended carriage shall not be limited to the direct route but shall be deemed to include any proceeding or returning to or stopping or slowing down at or off any ports or places for any reasonable purpose connected with the carriage including bunkering, loading, discharging, or other cargo operations and maintenance of Vessel and crew.

6. Substitution of Vessel.
The Carrier shall be at liberty to carry the cargo or part thereof to the Port of discharge by the said or other vessel or vessels either belonging to the Carrier or others, or by other means of transport, proceeding either directly or indirectly to such port.

7. Transhipment.
The Carrier shall be at liberty to tranship, lighter, land and store the cargo either on shore or afloat and reship and forward the same to the Port of discharge.

8. Liability for Pre- and On-Carriage.
When the Carrier arranges pre-carriage of the cargo from a place other than the Vessel's Port of loading or on-carriage of the cargo to a place other than the Vessel's Port of discharge, the Carrier shall contract as the Merchant's Agent only and the Carrier shall not be liable for any loss or damage arising during any part of the carriage other than between the Port of loading and the Port of discharge even though the freight for the whole carriage has been collected by him.

9. Loading and Discharging.
(a) Loading and discharging of the cargo shall be arranged by the Carrier or his Agent.
(b) The Merchant shall, at his risk and expense, handle and/or store the cargo before loading and after discharging.
(c) Loading and discharging may commence without prior notice.
(d) The Merchant or his Agent shall tender the cargo when the Vessel is ready to load and as fast as the Vessel can receive including, if required by the Carrier, outside ordinary working hours notwithstanding any custom of the port. If the Merchant or his Agent fails to tender the cargo when the Vessel is ready to load or fails to load as fast as the Vessel can receive the cargo, the Carrier shall be relieved of any obligation to load such cargo, the Vessel shall be entitled to leave the port without further notice and the Merchant shall be liable to the Carrier for deadfreight and/or any overtime charges, losses, costs and expenses incurred by the Carrier.
(e) The Merchant or his Agent shall take delivery of the cargo as fast as the Vessel can discharge including, if required by the Carrier, outside ordinary working hours notwithstanding any custom of the port. If the Merchant or his Agent fails to take delivery of the cargo the Carrier's discharging of the cargo shall be deemed fulfilment of the contract of carriage. Should the cargo not be applied for within a reasonable time, the Carrier may sell the same privately or by auction. If the Merchant or his Agent fails to take delivery of the cargo as fast as the Vessel can discharge, the Merchant shall be liable to the Carrier for any overtime charges, losses, costs and expenses incurred by the Carrier.
(f) The Merchant shall accept his reasonable proportion of unidentified loose cargo.

10. Freight, Charges, Costs, Expenses, Duties, Taxes and Fines.
(a) Freight, whether paid or not, shall be considered as fully earned upon loading and non-returnable in any event. Unless otherwise specified, freight and/or charges under this Contract are payable by the Merchant to the Carrier on demand. Interest at Libor (or its successor) plus 2 per cent. shall run from fourteen days after the date when freight and charges are payable.
(b) The Merchant shall be liable for all costs and expenses of fumigation, gathering and sorting loose cargo and weighing onboard, repairing damage to and replacing packing due to excepted causes, and any extra handling of the cargo for any of the aforementioned reasons.
(c) The Merchant shall be liable for any dues, duties, taxes and charges which under any denomination may be levied, *inter alia*, on the basis of freight, weight of cargo or tonnage of the Vessel.
(d) The Merchant shall be liable for all fines, penalties, costs, expenses and losses which the Carrier, Vessel or cargo may incur through non-observance of Customs House and/or import or export regulations.
(e) The Carrier is entitled in case of incorrect declaration of contents, weights, measurements or value of the cargo to claim double the amount of freight which would have been due if such declaration had been correctly given. For the purpose of ascertaining the actual facts, the Carrier shall have the right to obtain from the Merchant the original invoice and to have the cargo inspected and its contents, weight, measurement or value verified.

11. Lien.
The Carrier shall have a lien on all cargo for any amount due under this contract and the costs of recovering the same and shall be entitled to sell the cargo privately or by auction to satisfy any such claims.

12. General Average and Salvage.
General Average shall be adjusted, stated and settled in London according to the York-Antwerp Rules 1994, or any modification thereof, in respect of all cargo, whether carried on or under deck. In the event of accident, danger, damage or disaster before or after commencement of the voyage resulting from any cause whatsoever, whether due to negligence or not, for which or for the consequence of which the Carrier is not responsible by statute, contract or otherwise, the Merchant shall contribute with the Carrier in General Average to the payment of any sacrifice, losses or expenses of a General Average nature that may be made or incurred, and shall pay salvage and special charges incurred in respect of the cargo. If a salving vessel is owned or operated by the Carrier, salvage shall be paid for as fully as if the salving vessel or vessels belonged to strangers.

13. Both-to-Blame Collision Clause.
If the Vessel comes into collision with another vessel as a result of the negligence of the other vessel and any act, negligence or default of the Master, Mariner, Pilot or the servants of the Carrier in the navigation or in the management of the Vessel, the Merchant will indemnify the Carrier against all loss or liability to the other or non-carrying vessel or her Owner in so far as such loss or liability represents loss of or damage to or any claim whatsoever of the owner of the cargo paid or payable by the other or non-carrying vessel or her Owner to the owner of the cargo and set-off, recouped or recovered by the other or non-carrying vessel or her Owner as part of his claim against the carrying vessel or Carrier. The foregoing provisions shall also apply where the Owner, operator or those in charge of any vessel or vessels or objects other than, or in addition to, the colliding vessels or objects are at fault in respect of a collision or contact.

14. Government directions, War, Epidemics, Ice, Strikes, etc.
(a) The Master and the Carrier shall have liberty to comply with any order or directions or recommendations in connection with the carriage under this Contract given by any Government or Authority, or anybody acting or purporting to act on behalf of such Government or Authority, or having under the terms of the insurance on the Vessel the right to give such orders or directions or recommendations.
(b) Should it appear that the performance of the carriage would expose the Vessel or any cargo onboard to risk of seizure, damage or delay, in consequence of war, warlike operations, blockade, riots, civil commotions or piracy, or any person onboard to risk of loss of life or freedom, or that any such risk has increased, the Master may discharge the cargo at the Port of loading or any other safe and convenient port.
(c) Should it appear that epidemics; quarantine; ice; labour troubles, labour obstructions, strikes, lockouts (whether onboard or on shore); difficulties in loading or discharging would prevent the Vessel from leaving the Port of loading or reaching or entering the Port of discharge or there discharging in the usual manner and departing therefrom, all of which safely and without unreasonable delay, the Master may discharge the cargo at the Port of loading or any other safe and convenient port.
(d) The discharge, under the provisions of this Clause, of any cargo shall be deemed due fulfilment of the contract of carriage.
(e) If in connection with the exercise of any liberty under this Clause any extra expenses are incurred they shall be paid by the Merchant in addition to the freight, together with return freight, if any, and a reasonable compensation for any extra services rendered to the cargo.

15. Defences and Limits of Liability for the Carrier, Servants and Agents.
(a) It is hereby expressly agreed that no servant or agent of the Carrier (which for the purpose of this Clause includes every independent contractor from time to time employed by the Carrier) shall in any circumstances whatsoever be under any liability whatsoever to the Merchant under this Contract of carriage for any loss, damage or delay of whatsoever kind arising or resulting directly or indirectly from any act, neglect or default on his part while acting in the course of or in connection with his employment.
(b) Without prejudice to the generality of the foregoing provisions in this Clause, every exemption from liability, limitation, condition and liberty herein contained and every right, defence and immunity of whatsoever nature applicable to the Carrier or to which the Carrier is entitled, shall also be available and shall extend to protect every such servant and agent of the Carrier acting as aforesaid.
(c) The Merchant undertakes that no claim shall be made against any servant or agent of the Carrier and, if any claim should nevertheless be made, to indemnify the Carrier against all consequences thereof.
(d) For the purpose of all the foregoing provisions of this Clause the Carrier is or shall be deemed to be acting as agent or trustee on behalf of and for the benefit of all persons who might be his servants or agents from time to time and all such persons shall to this extent be or be deemed to be parties to this Contract of carriage.

16. Stowage.
(a) The Carrier shall have the right to stow cargo by means of containers, trailers, transportable tanks, flats, pallets, or similar articles of transport used to consolidate goods.
(b) The Carrier shall have the right to carry containers, trailers, transportable tanks and covered flats, whether stowed by the Carrier or received by him in a stowed condition from the Merchant, on or under deck without notice to the Merchant.

17. Shipper-Packed Containers, trailers, transportable tanks, flats and pallets.
(a) If a container has not been filled, packed or stowed by the Carrier, the Carrier shall not be liable for any loss of or damage to its contents and the Merchant shall cover any loss or expense incurred by the Carrier, if such loss, damage or expense has been caused by:
(i) negligent filling, packing or stowing of the container;
(ii) the contents being unsuitable for carriage in container; or
(iii) the unsuitability or defective condition of the container unless the container has been supplied by the Carrier and the unsuitability or defective condition would not have been apparent upon reasonable inspection at or prior to the time when the container was filled, packed or stowed.
(b) The provisions of sub-clause (i) of this Clause also apply with respect to trailers, transportable tanks, flats and pallets which have not been filled, packed or stowed by the Carrier.
(c) The Carrier does not accept liability for damage due to the unsuitability or defective condition of reefer equipment or trailers supplied by the Merchant.

18. Return of Containers.
(a) Containers, pallets or similar articles of transport supplied by or on behalf of the Carrier shall be returned to the Carrier in the same order and condition as handed over to the Merchant, normal wear and tear excepted, with interiors clean and within the time prescribed in the Carrier's tariff or elsewhere.
(b) The Merchant shall be liable to the Carrier for any loss, damage to, or delay, including demurrage and detention incurred by or sustained to containers, pallets or similar articles of transport during the period between handing over to the Merchant and return to the Carrier.

ADDITIONAL CLAUSE

U.S. Trade. Period of Responsibility.
(i) In case the Contract evidenced by this Bill of Lading is subject to the Carriage of Goods by Sea Act of the United States of America, 1936 (U.S. COGSA), then the provisions stated in said Act shall govern before loading and after discharge and throughout the entire time the cargo is in the Carrier's custody and in which event freight shall be payable on the cargo coming into the Carrier's custody.
(ii) If the U.S. COGSA applies, and unless the nature and value of the cargo has been declared by the shipper before the cargo has been handed over to the Carrier and inserted in this Bill of Lading, the Carrier shall in no event be or become liable for any loss or damage to the cargo in an amount exceeding USD 500 per package or customary freight unit.

***BIMCO LINER BILL OF LADING**
Code Name: "Conlinebill 2000"
Amended January 1950; August 1952; January 1973; July 1974; August 1976; January 1978; November 2000

VOYAGE CHARTER PARTY LAYTIME INTERPRETATION RULES 1993

issued jointly by BIMCO, CMI, FONASBA and INTERCARGO.

E 1.10

Code Name: VOYLAYRULES 93

PREAMBLE

The interpretations of words and phrases used in a charter party, as set out below, and the

corresponding initials if customarily used, shall apply when expressly incorporated in the charter party, wholly or partly, save only to the extent that they are inconsistent with any express provision of it.

When the word "charter party" is used, it shall be understood to extend to any form of contract of carriage or affreightment including contracts evidenced by bills of lading.

LIST OF RULES

1. "PORT"

2. "BERTH"

3. "REACHABLE ON HER ARRIVAL" or "ALWAYS ACCESSIBLE"

4. "LAYTIME"

5. "PER HATCH PER DAY"

6. "PER WORKING HATCH PER DAY" (WHD) or "PER WORKABLE HATCH PER DAY (WHD)

7. "DAY"

8. "CLEAR DAYS"

9. "HOLIDAY"

10. "WORKING DAY" (WD)

11. "RUNNING DAYS" or "CONSECUTIVE DAYS"

12. "WEATHER WORKING DAY" (WWD) or "WEATHER WORKING DAY OF 24 HOURS" or "WEATHER WORKING DAY OF 24 CONSECUTIVE HOURS"

13. "WEATHER PERMITTING" (WP)

14. "EXCEPTED" or"EXCLUDED"

15. "UNLESS SOONER COMMENCED"

16. "UNLESS USED" (UU)

17. "TO AVERAGE LAYTIME"

18. "REVERSIBLE LAYTIME"

19. "NOTICE OF READINESS" (NOR)

20. "IN WRITING"

21. "TIME LOST WAITING FOR BERTH TO COUNT AS LOADING OR DISCHARGING TIME" or "AS LAYTIME"

22. "WHETHER IN BERTH OR NOT" (WIBON) or "BERTH OR NO BERTH"

23. "VESSEL BEING IN FREE PRATIQUE" and/or "HAVING BEEN ENTERED AT THE CUSTOM HOUSE"

24. "DEMURRAGE"

25. "DESPATCH MONEY" or "DESPATCH"

26. "DESPATCH ON (ALL) WORKING TIME SAVED" (WTS) or "ON (ALL) LAYTIME SAVED"

27. "DESPATCH ON ALL TIME SAVED" (ATS)

28. "STRIKE"

RULES

1. "PORT" shall mean an area, within which vessels load or discharge cargo whether at berths, anchorages, buoys, or the like, and shall also include the usual places where vessels wait for their turn or are ordered or obliged to wait for their turn no matter the distance from that area. If the word "PORT" is not used, but the port is (or is to be) identified by its name, this definition shall still apply.

2. "BERTH" shall mean the specific place within a port where the vessel is to load or discharge. If the word "BERTH" is not used, but the specific place is (or is to be) identified by its name, this definition shall still apply.

3. "REACHABLE ON HER ARRIVAL" or "ALWAYS ACCESSIBLE" shall mean that the charterer undertakes that an available loading or discharging berth be provided to the vessel on her arrival at the port which she can reach safely without delay in the absence of an abnormal occurrence.

4. "LAYTIME" shall mean the period of time agreed between the parties during which the owner will make and keep the vessel available for loading or discharging without payment additional to the freight.

5. "PER HATCH PER DAY" shall mean that the laytime is to be calculated by dividing (A), the quantity of cargo, by (B), the result of multiplying the agreed daily rate per hatch by the number of the vessel's hatches. Thus:

Quantity of cargo

$$\text{Laytime} = \frac{\text{Quantity of cargo}}{\text{Daily rate X Number of Hatches}} = \text{Days}$$

Daily rate X Number of Hatches

Each pair of parallel twin hatches shall count as one hatch. Nevertheless, a hatch that iscapable of being worked by two gangs simultaneously shall be counted as two hatches.

6. "PER WORKING HATCH PER DAY" (WHD) or "PER WORKABLE HATCH PER DAY" (WHD) shall mean that the laytime is to be calculated by dividing (A), the quantity of cargo in the hold with the largest quantity, by (B), the result of multiplying the agreed daily rate per working or workable hatch by the number of hatches serving that hold.

Thus:

Largest Quantity in one Hold

$$\text{Laytime} = \frac{\text{Largest Quantity in one Hold}}{\text{Daily Rate per Hatch X Number of}} = \text{Days}$$

Daily Rate per Hatch X Number of

Hatches serving that Hold.

Each pair of parallel twin hatches shall count as one hatch. Nevertheless, a hatch that is capable of being worked by two gangs simultaneously shall be counted as two hatches.

7. "DAY" shall mean a period of twenty-four consecutive hours running from 0000 hours to 2400 hours. Any part of a day shall be counted pro rata.

8. "CLEAR DAYS" shall mean consecutive days commencing at 0000 hours on the day following that on which a notice is given and ending at 2400 hours on the last of the number of days stipulated.

9. "HOLIDAY" shall mean a day other than the normal weekly day(s) of rest, or part thereof, when by local law or practice the relevant work during what would otherwise be ordinary working hours is not normally carried out.

10. "WORKING DAYS" (WD) shall mean days not expressly excluded from laytime.

11. "RUNNING DAYS" or "CONSECUTIVE DAYS" shall mean days which follow one immediately after the other.

12. "WEATHER WORKING DAY" (WWD) or "WEATHER WORKING DAY OF 24HOURS" or "WEATHER WORKING DAY OF 24 CONSECUTIVE HOURS" shall mean a working day of 24 consecutive hours except for any time when weather prevents the loading or discharging of the vessel or would have prevented it, had work been in progress.

13. "WEATHER PERMITTING" (WP) shall mean that any time when weather prevents the loading or discharging of the vessel shall not count as laytime.

14. "EXCEPTED" or "EXCLUDED" shall mean that the days specified do not count as laytime even if loading or discharging is carried out on them.

15. "UNLESS SOONER COMMENCED" shall mean that if laytime has not commenced but loading or discharging is carried out, time used shall count against laytime.

16. "UNLESS USED" (UU) shall mean that if laytime has commenced but loading or discharging is carried out during periods excepted from it, such time shall count.

17. "TO AVERAGE LAYTIME" shall mean that separate calculations are to be made for loading and discharging and that any time saved in one operation is to be set off against any excess time used in the other.

18. "REVERSIBLE LAYTIME" shall mean an option given to the charterer to add together the time allowed for loading and discharging. Where the option is exercised the effect is the same as a total time being specified to cover both operations.

19. "NOTICE OF READINESS" (NOR) shall mean the notice to charterer, shipper, receiver or other person as required by the charter party that the vessel has arrived at the port or berth, as the case may be, and is ready to load or discharge.

20. "IN WRITING" shall mean any visibly expressed form of reproducing words; the medium of transmission shall include electronic communications such as radio communications and telecommunications.

21. "TIME LOST WAITING FOR BERTH TO COUNT AS LOADING OR DISCHARGING TIME" or "AS LAYTIME" shall mean that if no loading or discharging berth is available and the vessel is unable to tender notice of readiness at the waiting-place then any time lost to the vessel shall count as if laytime were running, or as time on demurrage if laytime has expired. Such time shall cease to count once the berth becomes available. When the vessel reaches a place where she is able to tender notice of readiness laytime or time on demurrage shall resume after such tender and, in respect of laytime, on expiry of any notice time provided in the charter party.

22. "WHETHER IN BERTH OR NOT" (WIBON) or "BERTH OR NO BERTH" shall mean that if no loading or discharging berth is available on her arrival the vessel, on reaching any usual waiting-place at or off the port, shall be entitled to tender notice of readiness from it and laytime shall commence in accordance with the charter party. Laytime or time on demurrage shall cease to count once the berth becomes available and shall resume when the vessel is ready to load or discharge at the berth.

23. "VESSEL BEING IN FREE PRATIQUE" and/or "HAVING BEEN ENTERED AT THE CUSTOM HOUSE" shall mean that the completion of these formalities shall not be a condition precedent to tendering notice of readiness, but any time lost by reason of delay in the vessel's completion of either of these formalities shall not count as laytime or time on demurrage.

24. "DEMURRAGE" shall mean an agreed amount payable to the owner in respect of delay to the vessel beyond the laytime, for which the owner is not responsible. Demurrage shall not be subject to laytime exceptions.

25. "DESPATCH MONEY" or "DESPATCH" shall mean an agreed amount payable by the owner if the vessel completes loading or discharging before the laytime has expired.

26. "DESPATCH ON (ALL) WORKING TIME SAVED" (WTS) or "ON (ALL) LAYTIME SAVED" shall mean that despatch money shall be payable for the time from the completion of loading or discharging to the expiry of the laytime excluding any periods excepted from the laytime.

27. "DESPATCH ON ALL TIME SAVED" (ATS) shall mean that despatch money shall be payable for the time from the completion of loading or discharging to the expiry of the laytime including periods excepted from the laytime.

28. "STRIKE" shall mean a concerted industrial action by workmen causing a complete stoppage of their work which directly interferes with the working of the vessel. Refusal to work overtime, go-slow or working to rule and comparable actions not causing a complete stoppage shall not be considered a strike. A strike shall be understood to exclude its consequences when it has ended, such as congestion in the port or effects upon the means of transportation bringing or taking the cargo to or from the port.

Index